ORNAMENTAL
FOLIAGE PLANTS

ORNAMENTAL
FOLIAGE
PLANTS

DENISE GREIG

FIREFLY BOOKS

A FIREFLY BOOK

Published by Firefly Books Ltd. 2004

Copyright © 2004 New Holland Publishers (UK) Ltd. All rights reserved
First published in North America by Firefly Books Ltd.
Published in the United Kingdom by New Holland Publishers (UK) Ltd.

First printing

Publisher Cataloging-in-Publication Data (U.S.)
Greig, Denise.
    Ornamental foliage plants / Denise Greig. —1st ed.
[400] p. : col. photos. ;   cm.
Includes bibliographical references and index.
Summary: Comprehensive guide to 1,500 garden and indoor plants grown mainly for their exceptional foliage. Includes A–Z directory of ornamental foliage plants organized by botanical name.
ISBN 1-55407-017-1
1. Foliage plants. I. Title.
635.9/75 21   SB431.G74   2004

National Library of Canada Cataloguing in Publication
Greig, Denise
        Ornamental foliage plants / Denise Greig.
Includes bibliographical references and index.
ISBN 1-55407-017-1
        1. Foliage plants. I. Title.
SB431.G73 2004   635.9'75   C2004-902572-4

Published in the United States in 2004 by
Firefly Books (U.S.) Inc.
P.O. Box 1338, Ellicott Station
Buffalo, New York 14205

Published in Canada in 2004 by
Firefly Books Ltd.
66 Leek Crescent
Richmond Hill, Ontario L4B 1H1

Picture credits: T = top, B = bottom, L = left, R = right: Lorna Rose: p. 10 T, p. 32, p. 39, p. 40, p. 52 L, p. 63 B, p. 75; Leigh Clapp: p. 10 B, p. 29, p. 54; Ivy Hansen: p. 9, p. 18, p. 43, p. 51, p. 52 R, p. 62, p. 68 L, p. 70; NHIL: p. 57

Printed in China

Thanks to the many people who have encouraged and assisted me with the preparation of this book, particularly Louise Egerton and Yani Silvana of New Holland Publishers. Thanks also to the many people and organisations in various countries who have kindly allowed me to photograph their gardens. Special thanks to Leo Schofield, and to the staff of Royal Botanic Gardens, Sydney, Royal Botanic Gardens, Kew, Royal Horticultural Garden, Wisley and the Bali Hyatt, Bali. Finally, thanks to my kind friend and floral decorator extraordinaire Andrew Franklin, Wai and Roger Davidson at Windyridge and to botanical artist and teacher Leonie Norton.

To my daughter, Kate Fallows, with love

CONTENTS

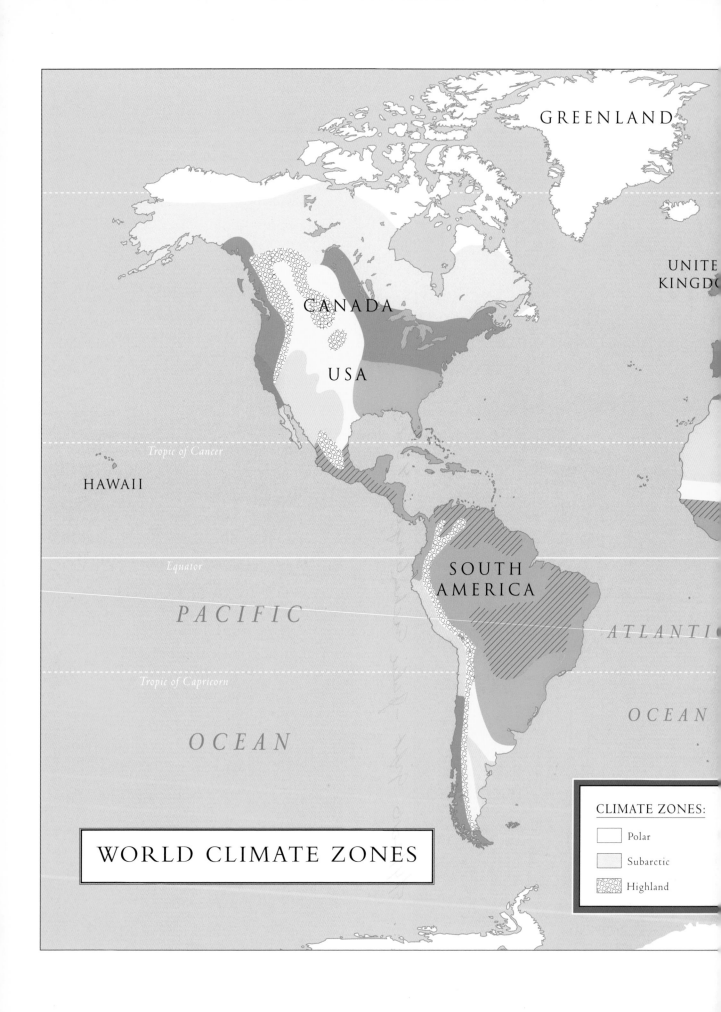

GREENLAND

CANADA

USA

HAWAII

Tropic of Cancer

SOUTH
AMERICA

Equator

Tropic of Capricorn

PACIFIC

OCEAN

ATLANTI

OCEAN

UNITE
KINGDO

CLIMATE ZONES:

Polar

Subarctic

Highland

WORLD CLIMATE ZONES

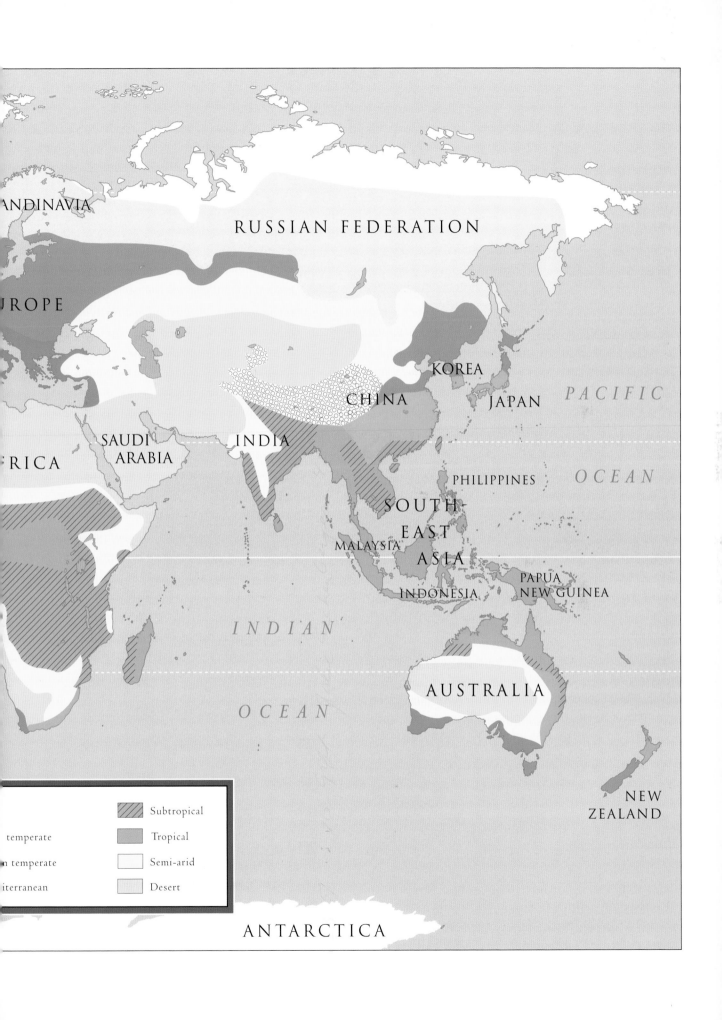

RUSSIAN FEDERATION

SCANDINAVIA

EUROPE

AFRICA

SAUDI
ARABIA

INDIA

CHINA

KOREA

JAPAN

PACIFIC

OCEAN

PHILIPPINES

SOUTH-
EAST
ASIA

MALAYSIA

INDONESIA

PAPUA
NEW GUINEA

INDIAN

OCEAN

AUSTRALIA

NEW
ZEALAND

Subtropical

temperate

Tropical

n temperate

Semi-arid

iterranean

Desert

ANTARCTICA

PREFACE

Most gardeners are mad about flowers but, as they say, 'flowers are fleeting'; it is the brilliant contrasts among leaf shape, texture and tone that will ensure a good year-round garden effect. Plants chosen for their well-defined foliage will unify the garden and give it an atmosphere of maturity without a great deal of expense or excessive upkeep. Some beautiful foliage plants can achieve dramatic effects while enhancing nearby plants and other garden features.

Whether a small city courtyard or a rambling country estate, the individual personality of each garden, its owner, its surroundings and particularly the prevailing conditions, combine to make a very special garden—one that relates to its environment and the spirit of the house. This book is about selecting good foliage plants—trees, shrubs, climbers, perennials and ferns—to give sculptural form and create a unique, interesting and beautiful garden that provides a welcome retreat that is enjoyable year-round.

Some of the best gardens are unified by a decisive theme or a particular period planting. Plants grown for their foliage effects will help you to easily achieve an enduring garden theme with a strong sense of identity. A private jungle oasis, a lush waterside planting, a dramatic exotic garden based on patterned or coloured foliage, a Mediterranean-style succulent feature garden, a minimalist grass and pebble garden, a tranquil shady woodland or an ordered, elegant town garden—all are possible with the creative use of good foliage plants.

HOW TO USE THIS BOOK

The book begins with a broad look at the world's **CLIMATE** patterns and a discussion of **FROST HARDINESS. ABOUT LEAVES** is a beautiful visual display of leaf structures, colours, forms and arrangements that illustrates some of the simple terms used in the book.

PART I, GARDEN THEMES AND SPECIAL FOLIAGE PLANTS, is about selecting and displaying foliage plants. It will help you to think about what foliage plants to use where and how to use them as a perennial backdrop to the seasonal display of flowers. Foliage plants may be hedges and topiaries, bamboos and grasses, conifers, ferns, groundcovers or climbing plants. Their selection may be dictated by climate, microclimate, difficult conditions, limited space or a desire for winter or autumn displays. All these areas are covered in this part of the book; refer to it when considering your garden design as a whole.

PART II, A–Z DIRECTORY OF PLANTS, represents the core of the book. Over 1500 plants from all over the world are listed alphabetically. Their country of origin, the climates for which they are suited and colour symbols indicating their outstanding features head up each entry. Descriptions follow. Common and useful cultivars and forms are picked out in bold for easy recognition. Most importantly, each entry provides invaluable information on cultivation, and advice on how the plant is best used in a garden landscape.

Where possible, I have avoided obscure botanical terminology, using instead a mixture of everyday and technical terms. A glossary at the back of the book explains these terms.

KEY TO SYMBOLS

	ARCHITECTURAL PLANTS		WINTER GARDENS
	AROMATIC PLANTS		CONIFERS
	AUTUMN COLOUR		GRASSES
	CLIMBERS AND CREEPERS		BAMBOO
	GREY, BLUE AND SILVER		FERNS
	GROUNDCOVERS		PALMS
	HEDGES AND TOPIARY		CYCADS
	SALT-TOLERANT PLANTS		SUCCULENTS
	VARIEGATED LEAVES		CONTAINER PLANTS
	WATERSIDE PLANTS		HOUSEPLANTS

CLIMATE

The climatic zones in which each species will grow are listed in the descriptions to help you choose the right plants for your garden. The seven major zones, abbreviated in the descriptions as in the table at right, are intended as a simple guide only; local differences are so numerous and diverse that a separate gardening book would be required for each region. The climate in your garden is unique— one suburb may, for example, suffer more frost than the next, and inland areas generally experience greater temperature extremes than neighbouring coastal zones. Observe which plants are flourishing in other gardens in your area and consult a good local nursery about plants best suited to your climate.

ABBREVIATIONS	
T	TROPICAL
ST	SUBTROPICAL
WT	WARM TEMPERATE
M	MEDITERRANEAN
CT	COOL TEMPERATE
H	HIGHLAND
SA	SEMI-ARID

TROPICAL

Tropical regions are divided into two main climatic types: equatorial and tropical monsoon climates. The hot, wet equatorial zone lies within about 5° latitude either side of the Equator with uninterrupted rainfall and high temperatures year round. It supports the equatorial rainforests of the Amazon basin, Borneo, Malaysia, parts of Indonesia and most of New Guinea—forests with a dense evergreen canopy, tall trees, many climbers and epiphytes and a large variety of plant species. This climate allows virtually year-round gardening and gives the freedom to create a truly luxurious effect using beautiful foliage plants in a dramatic supporting role to tall rainforest trees and palms.

Roughly between 5° and 15° latitude north and south of the Equator, the tropical monsoon climate revolves around periods of wet and dry which plants use to synchronise the phases of their life cycle. As a rule, tropical plants enter a dormant state during dry periods. In this type of tropical climate the gardener needs to select plants that will tolerate a long period of high humidity and heavy rainfall followed by a long dry period.

SUBTROPICAL

A subtropical climate is characterised by scattered rainfall in all seasons, with most falling during the summer, when temperatures are warm to hot. Rainfall is reliable, but not as heavy or concentrated as in tropical areas. Winters are generally dry and mild, and frosts are rare in coastal districts. This type of climate occurs roughly

Thriving in the warm moist air and shaded by palms these richly coloured crotons, cordylines and dracaenas provide a continuous display of leaf colour and texture in this tropical garden.

Decorative foliage plants, all of which thrive in subtropical areas, have been used to soften stark architectural lines and create a leafy retreat. At the lower level, bromeliads enjoy an ideal sheltered habitat with adequate moisture.

around the Tropic of Capricorn and the Tropic of Cancer: for example, parts of Florida and Central America, the West Indies, the Hawaiian Islands, southern China, the east coast of Australia from Brisbane north, and northeastern parts of South Africa.

A wide range of plants can be grown in the subtropical zone, including the more adaptable types from both tropical and temperate regions. It is an ideal climate for rainforest or jungle-style gardens. Palms can be used to great effect as they allow filtered light to penetrate to many different levels of foliage below. Plants from drier climates do not generally fare as well because of the high humidity in summer.

WARM TEMPERATE

In coastal warm temperate zones, between latitudes 30° and 35° north and south of the Equator, the climate is an extension of and similar to that in subtropical regions but subject to cooler winters; moderate frosts may occur away from the coast. Rainfall is spread throughout the year, though there is a tendency for a dry spring and heavy rain in late summer, when the combination of warmth and moisture can cause fungal problems in the garden.

In frost-free locations many tropical plants can be cultivated far from their homelands, but they may be slower growing because of the cooler winter. Gardeners in cooler areas can grow an assortment of borderline plants. Some

Well-spaced box domes and dry stone walls in this warm temperate garden provide the good air circulation and drainage needed to prevent fungal outbreaks in hot, humid weather. *Pyrus salicifolia* 'Pendula' brings rhythm and contrast to the planting.

plants from colder climates can be grown, but very few deciduous trees will take on really great autumn colour.

MEDITERRANEAN

This type of climate is named after the dry-summer areas around the Mediterranean Sea, where most rain

Trickling water and a canopy of mature evergreen trees and palms give respite from the heat in this Mediterranean garden.

falls in the winter months. Temperatures are generally warm to hot in summer and mild in winter. In coastal areas frosts are rare or unknown and temperatures do not fluctuate as much as they do in inland areas. Regions with a Mediterranean-type climate include coastal California, southwestern and southern parts of Australia, South Africa's southwestern Cape area and central Chile.

Plants which have adapted to dry summers, such as lavenders, bay, myrtle, eucalypts, shrubby euphorbias, agaves, aloes and many of the conifers, are typical of the Mediterranean garden. Some of the drought-adapted grey and silvery leaved plants, like artemesias, santolinas and sages, have hairy leaves and do best in this type of climate, away from excessive summer humidity.

COOL TEMPERATE

In the cool temperate zone, rain is plentiful throughout the year. While winters are relatively mild, some frosts are almost inevitable and there is sometimes snow. Summers may be cool, the weather erratic but rarely extreme, and skies cloudy. Spring and autumn are clearly marked. Coastal districts where maritime influences

In cool temperate areas deciduous trees such as the Common Beech (*Fagus sylvatica*) are invaluable in a woodland setting or edging a property for providing a lasting framework, contrast and seasonal colour.

Cold-tolerant conifers such as firs, pines and spruces establish to perfection in the deep, moist soils of highland regions. In this garden they give shelter to a weeping Japanese Maple, which thrives in cool, slightly shady conditions.

modify climatic extremes, resulting in the cool temperate climate type, include northwestern Europe and the British Isles, northwestern USA, Tasmania and the South Island of New Zealand. This type of climate is conducive to the cultivation of an exceptionally wide variety of plants. Many plants from similar zones grow happily far from their native regions—for example, some of the Tasmanian eucalypts thrive in England and on the Pacific coast of northwestern America.

In the continental interiors most rainfall occurs in summer, which is generally warm to hot. Winters are severe and long, with snowfalls being common. Areas with a cooler continental-type climate include Scandinavia, central Europe, Canada, much of the mid-West, New England and Rocky Mountains states of the USA, and northern China and North Korea. Many conifers and some outstanding deciduous trees found in cultivation come from the cold forest communities of North America—including the Sugar Maple (*Acer saccharum*), the Tulip Tree (*Liriodendron tulipifera*), the Sweet Gum (*Liquidambar styraciflua*), the White Ash (*Fraxinus americanus*) and the American Pin Oak (*Quercus palustris*).

HIGHLANDS

Gardens at higher altitudes have to cope not only with wetter conditions, but also with increasingly cold temperatures. Summers are generally mild, but winters are cold, with severe frosts and snowfalls. Rainfall is higher and distributed throughout the year, with winter or summer peaks, depending on latitude. Fogs may be frequent, so that at times atmospheric humidity is high.

Local species or those from other highland areas perform best in these cold areas. Coniferous trees such as fir, spruce, pine and larch are widely distributed in the mountainous regions of Europe, in Asia from the Himalayas northwards, Japan and North America. Notable for their combination of utility and beauty, these are among the most cold tolerant of trees and are highly suitable for highland areas. True alpine plants, which grow at high altitudes above the tree-line, are largely the domain of alpine plant specialists and are beyond the scope of this book.

SEMI-ARID

In some regions, usually between latitudes 20° and 30° north and south of the Equator, the climate can become extremely dry. Temperatures are mild to hot in winter and

Drought-hardy succulents such as *Agave*, *Kalanchoe* and *Senecio* are relatively low maintenance and are ideally suited to this semi-arid garden.

very hot in summer. Rainfall is occasional, erratic and unpredictable. Dryness is due not only to the lack of rain, but also to rapid evaporation of soil moisture. Heavy frosts are frequent during winter.

This is a difficult environment for plants, which have developed a number of strategies to survive long dry periods. Adaptations include succulent water-storing leaves; greyish or bluish foliage which reflects sunlight; thorns in place of leaves or to repulse grazing animals; reduced leaf surfaces which are often tough and leathery, to reduce loss of moisture by transpiration; and thick fleshy roots which conserve scarce water supplies. In semi-arid gardens the soil is usually poor in nutrients. To increase its fertility and water-holding capacity, work in generous amounts of organic matter such as compost, old straw, hay and well-rotted animal manures. Use a mulch to insulate roots from heat, retard evaporation and prevent erosion from the odd deluge of heavy rain. The mulch can be organic, but gravel, pebbles or stones are also suitable for hot, dry areas and can look good in a serious desert-style garden.

FROST HARDINESS

The term 'frost hardiness' refers to the ability of a plant to endure cold and frost. The hardiness rating allotted to each plant in this book is based on its ability to grow well outdoors without protection when exposed to the average minimum temperature. Hardiness ratings are guidelines only. Any district, city or town includes some locations where conditions vary from the general pattern.

HARDINESS RATINGS	AVERAGE MINIMUM TEMPERATURE	
	°F	°C
FULLY FROST HARDY	below freezing	
FROST HARDY	23°	−5°
MODERATELY FROST HARDY	32°	0°
FROST TENDER	41°	5°

In some species the rating is given as 'marginally frost hardy', which means that the plant is borderline and may become increasingly hardy as it matures or may perform reliably if given a favourable microclimate. Often you only have to keep a plant a few degrees warmer than it would otherwise be to endure a frosty spell. In colder regions, most borderline plants benefit from being grown against a warm sunny wall with overhanging eaves offering protection; the bricks give extra heat and ripen the wood in one season. The incidence of frost damage to small shrubs will be less if they are under the canopy of large trees. A herbaceous plant can be given a thick blanket of dry mulch to protect its crown from frost damage and excessive moisture in winter.

Plants that originate in a cold climate either develop strong woody cell walls or, as winter approaches, slow their growth and concentrate their sap so that its freezing point is as low as possible. Deciduous trees drop their leaves, while many ferns and perennials die back to their rootstocks, safely insulated below ground. Frost damage is more severe on soft new growth than on mature, hardened growth. Plants that have made rapid sappy growth in an unusually mild spring have soft immature tissues and are far more vulnerable to a late frost than those which have developed slowly. It is for this reason that fertiliser is held back until the danger of late frosts has passed. Similarly, plants should not be fed late in the season, since frost hardiness increases as growth slows in autumn.

Cold air, being heavier than warm air, accumulates in the lower areas of a garden. It flows along the ground and collects in low spots and ground hollows, where any frost-sensitive plant will suffer as a result. Frost also banks up behind closely planted hedges, solid walls and fences with the same effect. One way to reduce the risk of frost damage to sensitive species is to plant them in the higher parts of your garden. Still, clear nights, when the ground temperature falls rapidly until it is lower than the air temperature, are particularly dangerous. Clouds and overhanging trees help the soil to retain its heat, making it less likely that frost will form.

ABOUT LEAVES

STRUCTURE

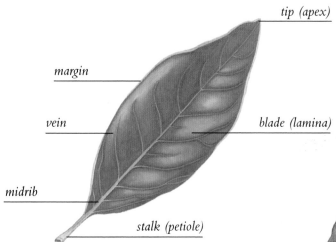

tip (apex)

margin

vein

blade (lamina)

midrib

stalk (petiole)

CHLOROPHYLL

The most important colour pigment in all plants is the green substance known as chlorophyll. This exists principally in leaves and is essential to the process called photosynthesis, the manufacture of plant foods. Oxygen, the by-product of photosynthesis, is essential to all life. Gold, bronze, purple and red foliage still contains chlorophyll, even though its green effect is masked by other more abundant colour pigments.

AUTUMN COLOUR

Deciduous trees and shrubs quickly lose their leaves in autumn, and in some cases the leaves change colour before falling. As nights get colder the chlorophyll breaks down and sugar builds up in the plant tissue, activating the colouring pigments and turning the leaves red and gold.

VARIEGATED LEAVES

Splashes of pale colour or variegations of other colours on a leaf indicate a lack of green cells. Many variegated plants are of interest to the foliage gardener, but they are often less vigorous than their plain green counterparts.

JUVENILE AND ADULT LEAVES

Some plants have different juvenile and adult stages in their foliage. This is most evident in some of the eucalypts with greyish or powdery (glaucous) leaves, which display a complete change of leaf shape and sometimes colour. The highly ornamental Argyle Apple (*Eucalyptus cinerea*) has almost circular or heart-shaped, opposite and stalkless leaves in its young stages, but mature leaves have alternate, slightly curved slender leaves on short stalks. Some eucalypts are cultivated specifically for their juvenile leaves for cut foliage; they are often known as 'silver dollar' eucalypts.

juvenile

adult

The shape and arrangement of leaves are often characteristic and necessary for botanical identification. This guide includes the most common shapes that will help home gardeners to describe and identify plants.

1. SHAPES

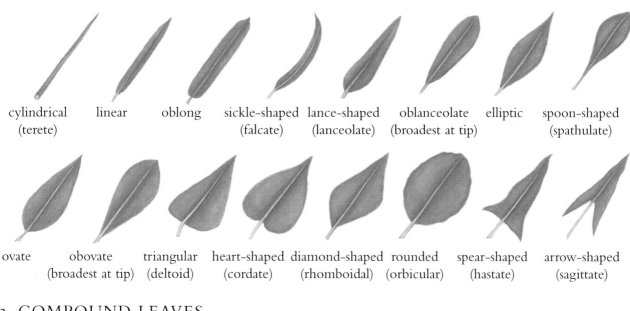

cylindrical (terete) linear oblong sickle-shaped (falcate) lance-shaped (lanceolate) oblanceolate (broadest at tip) elliptic spoon-shaped (spathulate)

ovate obovate (broadest at tip) triangular (deltoid) heart-shaped (cordate) diamond-shaped (rhomboidal) rounded (orbicular) spear-shaped (hastate) arrow-shaped (sagittate)

2. COMPOUND LEAVES

trifoliate pinnate bipinnate palmate

3. ARRANGEMENTS

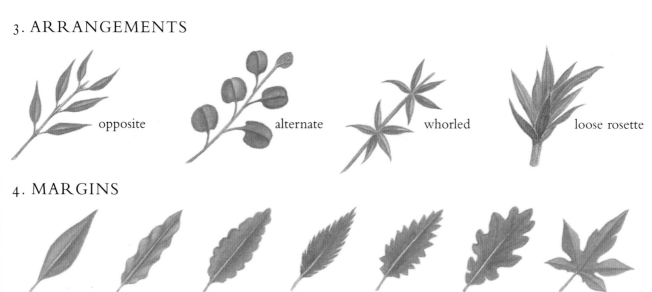

opposite alternate whorled loose rosette

4. MARGINS

entire wavy (undulate) scalloped (crenate) finely toothed (serrate) toothed (dentate) lobed palmately lobed

PART 1: GARDEN THEMES AND SPECIAL FOLIAGE PLANTS

ARCHITECTURAL PLANTS

An architectural plant is one that will bring form, texture or colour to the garden. There are two types of architectural plants: those that will stand out from their neighbours when set in isolation and those that are combined in a group to give definition to an area of planting, such as a minimalist carpet of fescue in a contemporary design, or clipped boxes and yew for a more formal style. When clipped to an emphatic topiary shape, the latter two can also be used as focal points.

All garden schemes benefit from an architectural element, and it makes no difference how large or small the available space is. Although it is important to focus on plants with the correct proportion and shape for your garden, occasionally a large-scale plant can have a dramatic effect in a small space. For example, a large urn of Crane Flower (*Strelitzia reginae*) or Gymea Lily (*Doryanthes excelsa*) is a simple way to make a real impact in a small inner courtyard.

A beautiful Chinese tradition is a planting of bananas in small courtyards, often framed by keyhole-shaped openings. The relatively short-stemmed *Musa ornata* is one of the best of the ornamental bananas, but in cool areas the Japanese Banana (*Musa basjoo*) will thrive in a warm, sheltered courtyard.

Few trees can match the palm for architectural interest and contrast to leaf shapes of other plants. Potted palms are among the most widely grown foliage plants in both temperate and tropical regions. The Golden Cane Palm (*Chrysalidocarpus lutescens*) has become one of the world's most user-friendly indoor plants, but when set in a warm, sheltered garden protected from direct exposure to hot sun it develops beautiful clumps of slender golden stems, making it an outstanding accent plant. For an instant tropical look in cool climates, the Chusan Palm (*Trachycarpus fortunei*) helps define an area and mixes beautifully with bamboos and broad-leaved plants such as hostas.

The luxuriantly leaved *Gunnera manicata* is best located with enough space to display its natural architectural form. Enjoying moist soil, it is perfect at the water's edge or in woodland areas. The shade it provides makes a good setting for hostas.

Magnolia grandiflora 'Little Gem' grown as a narrow formal group beside steps.

The foliage of bananas, palms, cordylines and phormiums all cast eye-catching shadow patterns, especially when reflected against a wall or water. Lit from ground level at night they cast striking silhouettes, or softly lit from above they evoke a theatrical moonlit mood.

Plants such as the silvery-leaved Cardoon and Globe Artichoke give real interest in herb or kitchen garden schemes. As a single plant or massed they provide a striking contrast to the green leaves of other edible plants. Angelica and lovage also have large architectural leaves and are especially useful as edible accent plants. An underplanting of Lemon Grass will give emphasis and foliage contrast at ground level.

Some plants take on architectural importance by the way in which they are grown—for instance, by introducing topiary or espalier into the garden or making ordinary plants into standards. Using topiary, close-knit evergreens such as Yew (*Taxus baccata*) and varieties of box (*Buxus*) can be trained and clipped into distinctive shapes. The Bay Laurel (*Laurus nobilis*) is one of the most adaptable plants for topiary and training as a standard, but even larger leaved evergreen plants such as *Magnolia grandiflora* can be lightly clipped to emphatic shapes. In cold climates this magnolia makes a handsome espalier against a warm wall.

New Zealand Flax (*Phormium tenax*), with its large tussocks of striking sword-shaped leaves, has great architectural value and can be used for dramatic effect beside water features and entrances, in rockeries or in contemporary gardens. Many brightly coloured varieties are now available, bordered or striped in combinations of bronze, red, pink or yellow. Also from New Zealand is one of the best-known architectural plants, the Cabbage Tree (*Cordyline australis*), which will provide an exotic vertical accent in both small and large gardens. Agaves and yuccas also have distinctive shapes, making them useful features for positions in full sun. These all need little water and present well throughout the year in areas with low or irregular rainfall.

With its striking spear-shaped leaves this small grouping of *Doryanthes excelsa* provides understated sculptural interest in this small garden beside an elaborately carved entrance.

The Traveller's Tree (*Ravenala madagascariensis*) makes a dramatic feature in tropical gardens.

The sculptural form and strong vertical accent of *Cordyline australis* make it a good architectural plant for any size garden.

GUIDE TO ARCHITECTURAL PLANTS

TREES AND SHRUBS

Beaucarnea recurvata
  (Bottle Palm, Ponytail Plant)
Buxus microphylla (Japanese Box)
  var. *japonica*
  var. *koreana*
Buxus sempervirens (European Box,
  Common Box)
  'Latifolia Maculata'
  'Marginata'
  'Suffruticosa'
  'Suffruticosa Variegata'
Cordyline australis
  (New Zealand Cabbage Tree)
  'Albertii'
  'Doucettii'
  'Purpurea'
Cordyline fruticosa (Ti Tree)
  'Amabilis'
  'Baby Ti'

  'Bicolor'
  'Firebrand'
  'Tricolor'
Cordyline indivisa (Toi, Blue Dracaena)
Cordyline stricta (Slender Palm Lily)
Cornus controversa
  'Variegata'
Cupressus cashmeriana (Bhutan
  Cypress, Kashmir Cypress)
Cupressus macrocarpa
  (Monterey Cypress)
  'Aurea Saligna'
  'Brunniana Aurea'
  'Goldcrest'
  'Greenstead Magnificent'
Cupressus sempervirens (Italian
  Cypress, Mediterranean Cypress)
  'Stricta'
  'Swane's Golden'
Dracaena draco (Dragon Tree)

Fatsia japonica
  (Japanese Aralia, Japanese Fatsia)
Hakea victoria (Royal Hakea)
Laurus nobilis (Bay Laurel)
Magnolia grandiflora (Southern
  Magnolia) **and cultivars**
Pandanus tectorius (Coastal Screw
  Pine, Pandang)
Pandanus veitchii (Veitch Screw Pine)
Pseudopanax crassifolius
  (Lancewood)
Pseudopanax lessonii (Houpara)
  and cultivars
Ravenala madagascariensis
  (Traveller's Tree)
Taxus baccata (Yew) **and cultivars**
Taxus cuspidata (Japanese Yew)
  and cultivars
Tetrapanax papyriferus
  (Rice-paper Plant)

PALMS AND CYCADS

Archontophoenix alexandrae
  (Alexandra Palm)
Archontophoenix cunninghamiana
  (Bangalow Palm)
Brahea armata (Big Blue Hesper Palm)
Chamaerops humilis (Dwarf Fan Palm,
  European Fan Palm)
Chrysalidocarpus lutescens
  (Golden Cane Palm, Butterfly Palm)
Cycas circinalis (Fern Palm,
  Queen Sago)
Cycas revoluta (Japanese Sago Palm)
Cyrtostachys renda (Lipstick Palm,
  Sealing Wax Palm)
Dioon edule (Mexican Fern Palm)
Dioon spinulosum
Encephalartos altensteinii
  (Prickly Cycad)
Encephalartos ferox
Encephalartos lebomboensis
  (Lebombo Cycad)
Encephalartos natalensis (Natal Cycad)
Lepidozamia hopei
Lepidozamia peroffskyana
Licuala grandis (Vanuatu Fan Palm,
  Palas Payung)
Licuala ramsayi (Australian Fan Palm)
Macrozamia communis (Burrawang)
Macrozamia miquelii
Macrozamia spiralis
Phoenix canariensis
  (Canary Island Date Palm)

Phormium tenax 'Purpureum' is a strong linear foliage plant.

Strelitzia reginae in a large jar makes an impressive centrepiece in a courtyard.

Phoenix dactylifera (Date Palm)
Phoenix roebelenii (Pygmy Date Palm)
Sabal mexicana (Texas Palmetto)
Sabal minor (Dwarf Palmetto)
Trachycarpus fortunei (Chusan Palm)

FERNS

Angiopteris evecta (King Fern,
  Giant Fern)
Cyathea australis (Rough Tree Fern)
Cyathea cooperi (Scaly Tree Fern)
Cyathea dealbata (Silver Fern)
Cyathea medullaris (Black Tree Fern)
Dicksonia antarctica (Soft Tree Fern)
Dicksonia fibrosa (Wheki-Ponga)
Dicksonia squarrosa (Wheki)

PERENNIALS

Acanthus mollis (Oyster Plant)
Acanthus spinosus
Alocasia macrorrhiza
  (Giant Taro, Cunjevoi)
Angelica archangelica (Angelica)
Crambe cordifolia (Colewort)
Crambe maritima (Sea Kale)
Cynara cardunculus (Cardoon)
Cynara scolymus (Globe Artichoke)
Dasylirion acrotrichum
Dasylirion longissimum
  (Mexican Grass Plant)
Doryanthes excelsa
  (Gymea Lily, Giant Lily)
Ensete ventricosum (Abyssinian Banana)

Gunnera manicata
Gunnera tinctoria
Musa acuminata (Banana)
  'Dwarf Cavendish'
Musa basjoo (Japanese Banana)
Musa ornata (Flowering Banana)
Musa velutina
Phormium cookianum (Mountain Flax)
  and cultivars
Phormium tenax (New Zealand Flax)
  and cultivars
Puya berteroniana
Sedum spectabile (Ice Plant)
Strelitzia nicolai (Wild Banana,
  Giant Bird of Paradise)
Strelitzia reginae (Crane Flower,
  Bird of Paradise)
Xanthorrhoea australis
  (Austral Grass Tree)
Xanthosoma violaceum (Blue Taro)

GRASS-LIKE PLANTS

Arundo donax (Giant Reed)
  'Versicolor'
Cymbopogon citratus (Lemon Grass)
Cyperus involucratus (Umbrella Sedge)
Cyperus papyrus (Egyptian Papyrus)

SUCCULENTS

Agave americana (Century Plant)
  'Marginata'
  'Mediopicta'
Agave angustifolia
  'Marginata'
Agave attenuata
Agave parryi
  var. *huachucensis*
Aloe arborescens (Candelabra Aloe)
Aloe dichotoma (Quiver Tree)
Aloe plicatilis (Fan Aloe)
Aloe pluridens
Furcraea foetida (Green Aloe)
  'Mediopicta'
Furcraea selloa var. *marginata*
Yucca aloifolia (Spanish Bayonet)
  and cultivars
Yucca elephantipes (Giant Yucca,
  Spineless Yucca)
  'Variegata'
Yucca filamentosa (Adam's Needle)
  'Bright Edge'
Yucca glauca (Dwarf Yucca, Soapweed)
Yucca gloriosa (Spanish Dagger)
  'Variegata'

AROMATIC PLANTS

One of the great pleasures of walking into the garden on a warm day is its scent. Leaf smells are sometimes given off freely by plants such as cypresses, eucalypts and Lemon Verbena, but most are stimulated by a gentle brushing or when splashed by a shower of rain.

Aromatic foliage plants are often native to countries with warm climates, like those surrounding the Mediterranean. Many of these, such as sage, rosemary, thyme, bay, oregano, lovage and fennel are well-known kitchen garden herbs—all with attractive foliage and useful for borders and along walkways where you can stroll among the plants and touch them regularly. Small carpeting plants such as creeping thymes can be allowed to grow on paths and between gaps in paving, providing fragrance and softness underfoot. Fennel adds a lacy accent and the tall stalks of lovage a casual architectural element. On the whole, herbs prefer the sunniest site, with protection from strong winds and heavy frosts.

Historically, herb gardens are associated with formal layouts. Often a small, enclosed area with sheltering walls will provide a charming, fragrant refuge in colder areas. Frost-tender herbs such as rosemary are better grown in containers so that they can be dug up and taken inside during the cold winter. The aromatic Bay Laurel (*Laurus nobilis*) is a particularly stylish container subject that can be clipped into a neat shape or trained as a standard and used as a decorative feature.

Scented-leaved pelargoniums make good informal hedges along a path or in island beds. The beautiful, textural Peppermint-scented Pelargonium (*Pelargonium tomentosum*), with its rich green velvety leaves, just begs to be touched. To create pleasing blocks of contrasting colour and texture use fragrant silvery plants such as artemisias, santolinas or the curry-scented *Helichrysum italicum*.

California, the Mediterranean regions and some parts of Australia have the best climates for releasing the scent of plants in the heat of the day. The eucalypts are undoubtedly the most important trees with aromatic foliage and a few provide essential oils. The Lemon-scented Gum (*Eucalyptus citriodora*) has strongly aromatic leaves whose scent on hot summer days permeates the air over a wide area. It also has a beautiful smooth white trunk. This species is grown commercially for its lemon-scented oil, which contains citronella. In the early days of Australian settlement the dried leaves were used to perfume linen. Other good lemony fragrances come from Lemon Verbena (*Aloysia triphylla*), Lemon Grass (*Cymbopogon citratus*), Lemon Balm (*Melissa officinalis*) and the Lemon-scented Pelargonium (*Pelargonium crispum*).

Some conifers have their own special fragrance in their leaves, bark and timber. On one particularly hot still day when I was photographing among a collection of

A long-term Yew hedge surrounding this enclosed garden shelters a charming fragrant walk lined with rosemary, lavender and purple sage.

well-established conifers, the air was heavy with the warm mysterious aroma of an Indian incense. I soon tracked the scent to a grand old Deodar (*Cedrus deodara*) nestled at the bottom of the group.

A classically trimmed Bay Laurel (*Laurus nobilis*) in a Versailles tub.

This mat-forming thyme, *Thymus caespititius*, tolerates occasional foot traffic and emits a spicy aroma when walked upon.

GUIDE TO AROMATIC PLANTS

TREES

Abies balsamea (Balsam Fir)
  'Hudsonia'
  'Nana'
Abies concolor '**Compacta**'
  (White Fir)
Cercidiphyllum japonicum
  (Katsura Tree)
  var. *magnificum*
  'Pendulum'
Cupressus cashmeriana (Bhutan
  Cypress, Kashmir Cypress)
Cupressus goveniana **var.** *pygmaea*
  (Gowan Cypress)
Cupressus macrocarpa
  (Monterey Cypress)
  'Aurea Saligna'
  'Brunniana Aurea'
  'Goldcrest'
Cupressus sempervirens (Italian
  Cypress, Mediterranean Cypress)

  'Stricta'
  'Swane's Golden'
Eucalyptus cinerea (Argyle Apple,
  Silver Dollar Tree)
Eucalyptus citriodora
  (Lemon-scented Gum)
Eucalyptus cordata
  (Heart-leaved Silver Gum)
Eucalyptus crenulata (Victorian Silver
  Gum, Buxton Gum)
Eucalyptus globulus
  (Tasmania Blue Gum)
  'Compacta'
Eucalyptus gunnii (Cider Gum)
Eucalyptus orbifolia
  (Round-leaved Mallee)
Eucalyptus perriniana (Spinning Gum)
Eucalyptus pulverulenta (Silver-leaved
  Mountain Gum, Powdered Gum)
Eucalyptus tetragona (Tallerack)
Juniperus chinensis (Chinese Juniper)

Juniperus communis (Common Juniper)
Juniperus scopulorum
  (Rocky Mountain Juniper)
Juniperus virginiana
  (Eastern Red Cedar, Pencil Cedar)
Laurus nobilis (Bay Laurel, Sweet Bay)
  'Aurea'
Thuja occidentalis (White Cedar)
  and cultivars
Thujopsis dolabrata (Hiba Arbor-vitae)
  and cultivars
Tsuga canadensis (Eastern Hemlock,
  Canadian Hemlock)

SHRUBS

Aloysia triphylla (Lemon Verbena)
Cupressus macrocarpa '**Greenstead
  Magnificent**'
Juniperus conferta (Shore Juniper)
Juniperus horizontalis (Creeping Juniper)
Juniperus x *pfitzeriana*

A massed planting of Peppermint-scented Pelargonium provides an aromatic, rich green contrast to the red-leafed cordyline in the background.

Juniperus procumbens (Creeping
  Juniper, Bonin Island Juniper)
Juniperus sabina (Savin)
Juniperus squamata
  (Himalayan Juniper)
Myrtus communis (Common Myrtle)
  'Variegata'
  subsp. *tarentina*
Pelargonium 'Atomic Snowflake'
Pelargonium capitatum
  (Rose-scented Pelargonium)
Pelargonium crispum
  (Lemon-scented Pelargonium)
  'Prince Rupert'
  'Variegatum'
Pelargonium 'Fragrans'
  (Nutmeg-scented Pelargonium)
  'Fragrans Variegatum'
Pelargonium graveolens
  'Lady Plymouth'
Pelargonium grossularioides
  (Coconut Pelargonium)
Pelargonium 'Mabel Grey'
Pelargonium odoratissimum
Pelargonium quercifolium
  (Oak-leaf Pelargonium)
Pelargonium radens
  (Rose-scented Pelargonium)
Pelargonium 'Rober's Lemon Rose'
Pelargonium tomentosum
  (Peppermint-scented Pelargonium)
Pinus aristata (Bristlecone Pine)
Rosmarinus officinalis
  (Rosemary)
  'Aureus'
  'Prostratus'

Santolina chamaecyparissus
  (Cotton Lavender)
  'Lemon Queen'
Santolina pinnata subsp. *neopolitana*
  'Edward Bowles'
Thymus caespititius
Thymus x *citriodorus* (Lemon-scented
  Thyme) **and cultivars**
Thymus herba-barona (Caraway Thyme)
Thymus pseudolanuginosus
  (Woolly Thyme)
Thymus serphyllum **and cultivars**
Thymus vulgaris (Garden Thyme)
  and cultivar 'Silver Posie'

PERENNIALS
Artemisia abrotanum (Lad's Love, Old
  Man, Southernwood)
Artemisia absinthium
  (Absinth, Wormwood)
  'Lambrook Silver'
Artemisia alba 'Canescens'
Artemisia arborescens
  (Silver Wormwood)
Artemisia ludoviciana
  (Western Mugwort,
  White Sage)
  var. *albula*
  'Valerie Finnis'
Artemisia schmidtiana
  'Nana'
Artemisia stelleriana
  (Beach Wormwood)
  'Broughton Silver'
Foeniculum vulgare (Fennel)
  'Purpureum'

Houttuynia cordata
  'Chameleon'
Levisticum officinale (Lovage)
Melissa officinalis (Lemon Balm,
  Bee Balm)
  'All Gold'
  'Aurea'
Mentha x *gracilis* 'Variegata'
  (Ginger Mint)
Mentha x *piperita* (Peppermint)
  f. *citrata* (Eau-de-cologne Mint)
Mentha pulegium (Pennyroyal)
Mentha requienii (Corsican Mint)
Mentha spicata (Spearmint)
  'Crispa'
Mentha suaveolens (Apple Mint)
  'Variegata'
Mentha x *villosa* f. *alopecuroides*
  (Bowles' Mint)
Origanum vulgare (Oregano,
  Wild Marjoram)
  'Aureum'
  'Country Cream'
  'Golden Tip'
Plectranthus madagascariensis (Mintleaf)
  'Variegated Mintleaf'
Salvia elegans (Pineapple Sage)
Salvia officinalis (Sage) **and cultivars**

GRASS-LIKE PLANTS
Acorus calamus (Sweet Flag)
  'Variegatus'
Acorus gramineus
  'Ogon'
Cymbopogon citratus (Lemon Grass)

Salvia officinalis 'Icterina' has pretty scented leaves.

AUTUMN COLOUR

As summer fades, some deciduous trees and shrubs start to take on brilliant autumn colours, the intensity and duration of the colour depending on species, soil and weather. In cold areas of highly acidic soils such as the east coast of America, autumn colours are startling, with fiery red and bright golden tones. In regions with early sharp frosts, leaves produce a more brilliant display of colour than in areas with a gradual decline in temperature. Autumn colour is one of the great bonuses of living in a cool climate. But even in relatively warm areas it is possible to produce quite a spectacular show if you choose plants which don't need too much cold weather and are capable of withstanding summer heat. Most popular is the Sweet Gum (*Liquidambar styraciflua*), but it can grow to 30m/100ft and is not for the small garden. The American Pin Oak (*Quercus palustris*) colours up well with only a hint of cold weather, and its leaves remain on the tree long after the colour has changed.

Carefully grouped deciduous plants chosen for their autumn tones can achieve different foliage effects against a background of strongly textured evergreens at a time where there is little else on show. Give them enough room to spread, in a position where they will highlight certain areas or can be viewed from a particular angle, especially against the light.

While the Tupelo (*Nyssa sylvatica*), the Chinese Pistachio (*Pistacia chinensis*) and some of the maples produce spectacular blazing red tones, the foliage of the European Beech (*Fagus sylvatica*), the Maidenhair Tree (*Ginkgo biloba*) and the Tulip Tree (*Liriodendron tulipifera*) turns beautiful shades of yellow and gold. The Common Ash (*Fraxinus excelsior*) is one of the prettiest of the golden-foliaged trees.

The Japanese Maple (*Acer palmatum*) and some of its shrubby cultivars are among the most admired deciduous plants for small gardens. Prized for their distinctive branching patterns, lacy foliage and good autumn colours, these

Japanese Maples come in a tremendous range of colours and vary enormously in their autumn showing—some plants can still be quite green while others have completed their display.

maples are easily grown in containers and can be used for handsome displays on terraces, courtyards or balcony gardens. Container-grown maples need humus-enriched soil kept moist but well drained.

Some deciduous climbers provide a striking display of autumn colour. One of the most popular is the Boston Ivy (*Parthenocissus tricuspidata*), which in cool climates produces colours from coppery pink to rich reds. It is a self-clinging climber and is excellent for rapidly covering stark walls where there is really no space to plant trees. The Crimson Glory Vine (*Vitis coignetiae*) gives impressive displays of a

The deeply cut leaves of *Fagus sylvatica* f. *lacinata* turn a rich orange–brown.

The Common Ash (*Fraxinus excelsior*) from Europe is an outstanding specimen tree with rich yellow autumn leaves.

blend of soft reds. It is ideal for arbours, trellises, verandas or any sitting area requiring summer shade and winter sun. *Vitus vinifera* 'Purpurea' has purple–red leaves that mature to a deeper shade in autumn and is beautiful for covering fences with a quieter display of colour.

Since leaf colour varies with each tree, especially those grown from seed, buy plants for their autumn tones in autumn, when the leaf colour will be indicative of future colouring. To be absolutely sure of good colour you can get specially selected grafted forms, but they do cost more.

GUIDE TO AUTUMN COLOUR

TREES

Acer buergerianum (Trident Maple) orange/red

Acer capillipes (Red Snakebark Maple) red

Acer carpinifolium (Hornbeam Maple) golden brown

Acer davidii (Father David's Maple, Snakebark Maple) yellow/orange

Acer griseum (Paperbark Maple) orange/red

Acer japonicum (Full-moon Maple) red

Acer negundo (Box Elder Maple) yellow

Acer palmatum **and cultivars** (Japanese Maple) yellow/orange/red

Acer saccharum (Sugar Maple) orange/red

Acer rubrum (Red Maple, Scarlet Maple) red

Aesculus hippocastanum (Horse Chestnut) gold/brown 'Baumannii' gold/brown

Aesculus pavia (Red Buckeye) gold/brown

Aralia elata (Japanese Angelica Tree) yellow/orange/purple

Betula nigra (River Birch) yellow
Betula papyrifera (Paper Birch,
   Canoe Birch) orange/yellow
Betula pendula (Silver Birch) yellow
   'Laciniata' yellow/orange
   'Tristis' yellow
   'Youngii' yellow
Betula utilis (Himalayan Birch) yellow
   var. *jacquemontii* yellow
Castanea sativa (Spanish Chestnut,
   Sweet Chestnut) gold/brown
Cercidiphyllum japonicum
   (Katsura Tree) yellow/orange/red
   var. *magnificum* yellow/orange/red
   'Pendulum' yellow/orange/red
Cercis canadensis (Eastern Redbud)
   crimson/purple/pink
   'Forest Pansy' purple/pink
Cercis controversa purple/red
   'Variegata' purple/red
Cercis florida (Flowering Dogwood)
   purple/red
   'Rubra' red
   'Welchii' rose red/purple
Cotinus obovatus (American
   Smoke Tree) orange/red/purple
Euptelea polyandra orange/red

Fagus sylvatica **and cultivars**
   (Common Beech, European Beech)
   gold/orange/brown
Fraxinus americana
   (White Ash) yellow
   'Autumn Purple' crimson
Fraxinus angustifolia
   (Narrow-leaved Ash) yellow/gold
   'Raywood' (Claret Ash) purple/red
Fraxinus excelsior
   (Common Ash) yellow
   'Aurea Pendula' (Weeping
   Golden Ash) yellow
   'Jaspidea' yellow
   'Pendula' (Weeping Ash) yellow
Fraxinus ornus (Manna Ash,
   Flowering Ash) purple/red
Fraxinus velutina (Arizona Ash,
   Velvet Ash) yellow
   'Fan Tex' yellow
   'Glabra' yellow
Ginkgo biloba (Maidenhair Tree)
   golden yellow
   'Autumn Gold' gold
   'Fastigiata' gold
   'Princeton Sentry' gold
   'Saratoga' gold

Gleditsia triacanthos (Honey Locust)
   and cultivars yellow
Larix decidua (European Larch) yellow
Larix kaempferi (Japanese Larch)
   yellow
Liquidambar orientalis (Oriental Sweet
   Gum) yellow/orange
Liquidambar styraciflua (Sweet Gum)
   orange/red/purple
   'Burgundy' red/purple
   'Golden Treasure' yellow
   'Lane Roberts' red
   'Worplesdon' orange/yellow/purple
Liriodendron tulipifera (Tulip Tree)
   golden yellow
   'Aureomarginata' golden yellow
Nothofagus fusca (Red Beech)
   red/brown
Nothofagus obliqua (Roble) orange/red
Nothofagus procera (Rauli)
   orange/brown
Nyssa sylvatica (Tupelo) red
Pistacia chinensis (Chinese Pistachio) red
Quercus alba (American White Oak)
   purple/red
Quercus cerris (Turkey Oak)
   yellow/brown

Acer palmatum 'Heptalobum Rubrum' never fails to produce
its spectacular red leaves in autumn.

The pretty crimson-coloured leaves of *Acer japonicum*
'Vitifolium'.

The glossy dark green leaves of the Tupelo (*Nyssa sylvatica*) turn brilliant red in autumn.

Acer palmatum var. *dissectum* 'Green Lace' is a small weeping tree with finely cut leaves that turn orange.

Quercus coccinea (Scarlet Oak) red
  'Splendens' red
Quercus palustris (Pin Oak) red
Quercus robur (English Oak) bronze
Quercus rubra (Red Oak) red/brown
Tilia cordata (Small-leaved Lime) yellow
Tilia x *europaea* (Common Lime) yellow
Tilia tomentosa (Silver Linden,
  Silver Lime) yellow
Ulmus americana (American Elm,
  White Elm) yellow
  'Delaware' yellow
Ulmus x *hollandica*
  (Dutch Elm) yellow
  'Jacqueline Hillier' yellow
Ulmus minor
  (European Field Elm) yellow
Ulmus parvifolia
  (Chinese Elm) yellow/red
  'Frosty' yellow
  'Hokkaido' yellow

SHRUBS

Berberis thunbergii (Japanese Barberry)
  orange/red
  'Atropurpurea' red
  'Atropurpurea Nana' red
  'Aurea' gold

  'Red Pillar' red
  'Rose Glow' red/purple
  'Silver Beauty' red
Cornus alba (Red-barked Dogwood)
  orange/red
Cornus stolonifera (Red Osier
  Dogwood) orange/red
Cotinus coggygria (Smoke Bush,
  Venetian Sumach) orange/red
  'Golden Spirit' orange/red
  'Purpureus' orange/red
  'Royal Purple' red
Disanthus cercidifolius
  orange/red/purple
Euonymus alatus (Winged Spindle
  Tree) red
  'Compactus' red
Euonymus europaeus (European
  Spindle Tree) red
  'Atropurpureus' red/purple
  'Red Cascade' red
Fothergilla major (Mountain Witch
  Hazel, Alabama Fothergilla)
  yellow/orange/red
Hamamelis x *intermedia* yellow
  'Arnold's Promise' yellow
  'Diane' yellow/orange/red
  'Hiltingbury' yellow

  'Jelena' orange/red
  'Pallida' yellow
  'Ruby Glow' orange/red
  'Westerstede' yellow
Hamamelis mollis
  (Chinese Witch Hazel) yellow
  'Brevipetala' yellow
  'Goldcrest' golden yellow
Hamamelis virginiana
  (Virginian Witch Hazel) yellow
Larix decidua 'Corley' yellow
Nandina domestica and cultivars
  (Sacred Bamboo, Heavenly Bamboo)
  yellow/orange/red

CLIMBERS

Parthenocissus quinquefolia
  (Virginia Creeper) red
Parthenocissus tricuspidata
  (Boston Ivy, Japanese Ivy)
  red/purple
Vitis coignetiae
  (Crimson Glory Vine) red
Vitis vinifera (Grape Vine) red
  'Alicante' red
  'Purpurea' (Claret Vine) purple

CLIMBERS AND CREEPERS

Most gardens will benefit from one or more climbing plants used for special effect, or just to provide a glorious vertical display of foliage. Some climbers can be used effectively to cover pergolas or arbours, providing shade, beauty and sometimes fine autumn colour; others can be used as privacy screens or windbreaks when grown on mesh fencing around a swimming pool or other outdoor living area. You can use them to convert a paling fence or a less-than-perfect wall into a decorative feature or to block out an unpleasant view.

When grown against a wall, climbers help to disguise its straight lines, at the same time blurring the boundaries of the garden. This is particularly valuable in small gardens, courtyards and narrow passageways, where a more spacious effect can be achieved without intruding too much on limited ground space.

Ivy provides a marvellous dark green background for other plants. Once established, most ivies can become quite rampant, however, and need to be clipped right back once a year in early spring to remain a decorative flat curtain of green. Ivy comes in different textures and leaf sizes, and in some highly attractive variegated versions. The larger leaved *Hedera canariensis* 'Gloire de Marengo' makes a decorative cover for low fences and walls.

Deciduous climbers such as Boston Ivy (*Parthenocissus tricuspidata*), and Crimson Glory Vine (*Vitis coignetiae*) make outstanding wall covers, but will also decoratively cover an arch enclosing a seat, making an efficient and attractive sun block in summer but allowing the sun to penetrate during the winter. Both these give impressive displays of crimson and scarlet in autumn. Claret Vine (*Vitis vinifera* 'Purpurea') is another attractive deciduous climber. In autumn its leaves

When clipped right back so that it is flush to the wall, this ivy retains its good looks even in winter. The well-grown evergreen magnolia on the right is trained against the wall, where it benefits from the extra protection and warmth.

A background curtain of Boston Ivy (*Parthenocissus tricuspidata*) is used to soften a courtyard wall behind a garden bench. It turns spectacular shades of red and purple in autumn.

Devil's Ivy is a robust climber that can quickly cover tree trunks in topical gardens.

mature to dark purple before falling, and in spring the pretty, purple-flushed new foliage provides shade.

The Creeping Fig (*Ficus pumila*) will effectively soften the look of a high masonry wall, where it will sit flush and send out pretty patterns of lacy growth. It is especially useful for a small garden, where it will grow admirably in partial light, but should be regularly checked to prevent it encroaching on guttering and eaves.

In warm climates, lush, large-leaved climbers such as species of *Epipremnum*, *Philodendron* and *Monstera* can be left to scramble across a moist rocky site or cliff face in a difficult shady area or be decoratively trained up trees as they do in their rainforest habitats.

ESTABLISHING CLIMBERS

Plants with aerial roots or adhesive pads such as ivy (*Parthenocissus* species) and Creeping Fig (*Ficus pumila*) do not need any special support, but may need to be held in place while they establish themselves. When planting climbers, do not restrict the growing area of their roots by putting them too close to a wall. Set climbing supports slightly away from the wall so that twiners and tendril climbers can wrap around them with ease. This will also allow air to circulate among the branches and help minimise possible damage from reflected heat. Don't forget that plants growing close to walls may also miss out on rain and need supplementary watering.

When covering a pergola or arch, set plants at both sides of the structure so that they will meet overhead. Tie young stems as necessary while they grow up the vertical support.

GUIDE TO CLIMBERS AND CREEPERS

Vitis vinifera 'Purpurea' has attractive purple-flushed spring leaves. It is good for screening fences and covering walls.

SCRAMBLERS

Aloe ciliaris (Climbing Aloe)
Epipremnum pictum
　'Argyraeum' (Silver Vine)
Epipremnum pinnatum
　'Aureum'
　'Marble Queen'
x *Fatshedera lizei* (Tree Ivy)
Monstera deliciosa (Fruit Salad Plant,
　Mexican Breadfruit)
　'Variegata'
Philodendron erubescens
　(Red-leaf Philodendron,
　Blushing Philodendron)
　'Burgundy'
Philodendron imbe
Philodendron scandens
　(Sweetheart Plant)

TWINERS

Actinidia kolomikta
Cissus antarctica (Kangaroo Vine)
Cissus discolor
Cissus hypoglauca (Water Vine)
Cissus rhombifolia (Grape Ivy)
　'Ellen Danica'
Cissus striata
　(Miniature Grape Ivy)
Piper novae-hollandiae
　(Giant Pepper Vine)
Piper ornatum
　(Celebes Pepper)
Senecio macroglossus
　(Cape Ivy, Natal Ivy)
Vitis coignetiae
　(Crimson Glory Vine)
Vitis vinifera (Grape Vine)
　'Alicante'
　'Purpurea' (Claret Vine)

WALL-HUGGERS

Ficus pumila (Creeping Fig)
Hedera canariensis (Canary Island Ivy,
　Algerian Ivy)
　'Gloire de Marengo'
　'Ravensholst'
Hedera colchica (Persian Ivy)
　'Dentata'
　'Dentata Variegata'
　'Sulphur Heart'
Hedera helix (Common Ivy,
　English Ivy) **and cultivars**
Hedera hibernica (Irish Ivy)
　'Deltoidea' (Sweetheart Ivy)
Parthenocissus quinquefolia
　(Virginia Creeper)
Parthenocissus tricuspidata
　(Boston Ivy, Japanese Ivy)
　'Lowii'
　'Veitchii'

Hedera helix 'Goldheart' retains its variegation best when grown as a wall cover.

PLANTS WITH GREY, BLUE OR SILVER FOLIAGE

Perennial plants with grey, blue and silver foliage add colour, contrast and bouncing light that might otherwise be found in a flower garden. As most retain their leaves throughout the winter they are labour saving compared with seasonal bedding plants.

Silver- and grey-leaved plants, such as the shrubby *Senecio cineraria*, many of the artemisias, helichrysums, lavenders and carpeting stachys, may be massed in formal patterns, freely grouped in open borders or used as accent plants in rockeries. They act as foils to the strong flower colours of neighbouring plants and provide a complementary backdrop to pale-coloured flowers, especially pink, mauve, blue and cream ones. They all show up well at night, making them ideal subjects for highlighting a walkway or entrance.

The architectural Cardoon (*Cynara cardunculus*) and Honey Flower (*Melianthus major*) make strong feature plants and provide fantastic accents to a flower border or vegetable garden. Blue Fescue (*Festuca glauca*) is an attractive low-growing grass ideal for edging and pebble gardens. 'Blaufuchs' and 'Elijah Blue' are among the best of the blue fescues. Full sun is essential for best colour.

The hardy Cotton Lavender (*Santolina chamaecyparissus*) has small fine foliage that can be trimmed to provide a good structured background to the more relaxed outlines of edging plants. It is a classic knot-garden plant used in parterres and formal gardens. From the western Mediterranean, *Teucrium fruticans* has grey–green leaves which are woolly white beneath. It is a densely branched shrub that responds well to pruning and makes a good formal hedge in mild climates.

Trees and shrubs with silvery grey or blue foliage add drama by subtly contrasting with a background of green foliage—and give interest to the winter garden. A cohesive grouping of greys is often more effective with the use of soft greens as gentle contrast. Good companions to the greys and silvers include blue–green hostas, some thymes, and other herbs such as Purple-leaved Sage (*Salvia officinalis*

The silvery grey glaucous leaves of *Senecio serpens*, grasses and succulents set off the regularly shaped hebe domes and lush green background jungle-like planting.

'Purpurascens'), spiky variegated grasses and *Ajuga reptans*. A beautiful groundcover combination is the grey–green succulent *Echeveria secunda*, set off by *Ajuga reptans* 'Burgundy Lace'.

Good trees with silvery grey foliage include some of the eucalypts, the Russian Olive (*Elaeagnus angustifolia* 'Quicksilver') and the deciduous Silver Pear (*Pyrus salicifolia* 'Pendula'). There are some excellent blue foliage types among the conifers. The larger ones, such as *Cedrus atlantica* 'Glauca', the Kashmir Cypress (*Cupressus cashmeriana*) and the Colorado Blue Spruce (*Picea pungens* 'Glauca'), make outstanding specimen trees. There are also some beautiful smaller growing blue-leaved forms, such as the dwarf *Picea pungens* 'Montgomery' and 'Koster Prostrate', and the popular groundcovering *Juniperus squamata* 'Blue Carpet'. These plants all have good colour that shimmers against the darker foliage of evergreens and provides visual texture to mixed plantings.

Often the name of the plant will give a clue to its foliage colour. *Glauca* means covered with a bluish white bloom, or of that colour; *argentea*—silvery; *candicans*—glistening white; *cinerea/cineraria*—ash coloured; *pulverulenta*—dusted or covered with a fine powder; *caesia*—with a silvery grey frosted appearance.

An underplanting of *Festuca glauca* 'Elijah Blue' provides neat fountains of silvery blue foliage year round.

Artemisia arborescens adds a touch of silver to a foliage border of many different leaf shapes and hues.

A silvery grey mound of *Plectranthus argentatus*, complemented by *Phalaris arundinacea* var. *picta* behind.

GROWING CONDITIONS

Most of these plants need good drainage and full sun. Their silvery appearance is often derived from the short hairs that protect the leaves from the sun's blast, enabling the plants to survive long periods of summer drought in their natural habitat. This is why they often flourish best in Mediterranean-type climates and many are suited to coastal sites. Good air circulation is important in humid areas to prevent stems rotting. They seldom need heavy feeding. Their flowers may detract from the overall effect and are usually removed.

Senecio cineraria, a very ornamental and reliable plant, makes a good feature in formal bedding or colour schemes.

Silver Sage (*Salvia argentea*) is a biennial with woolly leaves.

GUIDE TO PLANTS WITH GREY, BLUE OR SILVER FOLIAGE

TREES AND SHRUBS

Abies concolor **'Compacta'**
  (White Fir)
Abies lasiocarpa **var.** *arizonica*
  'Compacta'
  'Roger Watson'
Abies pinsapo (Spanish Fir) **'Glauca'**
Atriplex nummularia
  (Old Man Saltbush)
Brahea armata (Big Blue Hesper Palm)
Cedrus atlantica **'Glauca'** (Atlas Cedar)
  'Glauca Pendula'
Chamaecyparis **lawsoniana**
  (Lawson Cypress)
  'Alumii'
  'Aurea Densa'
  'Blue Jacket'
  'Fletcheri'
  'Pembury Blue'
  'Silver Queen'
Chamaecyparis pisifera **'Boulevard'**
Cupressus arizonica **var.** *glabra*
  (Smooth Arizona Cypress)
Cupressus cashmeriana (Bhutan
  Cypress, Kashmir Cypress)

Cupressus lusitanica 'Glauca Pendula'
  (Cedar of Goa, Mexican Cypress)
Cupressus macrocarpa
  'Greenstead Magnificent'
Elaeagnus angustifolia 'Quicksilver'
  (Oleaster, Russian Olive)
Eucalyptus cinerea (Argyle Apple,
  Silver Dollar Tree)
Eucalyptus cordata (Heart-leaved
  Silver Gum)
Eucalyptus crenulata (Victorian Silver
  Gum, Buxton Gum)
Eucalyptus globulus
  (Tasmania Blue Gum)
  'Compacta'
Eucalyptus gunnii (Cider Gum)
Eucalyptus orbifolia
  (Round-leaved Mallee)
Eucalyptus pauciflora (Snow Gum)
  subsp. *niphophila*
Eucalyptus perriniana (Spinning Gum)
Eucalyptus pulverulenta (Silver-leaved
  Mountain Gum, Powdered Gum)
Eucalyptus tetragona (Tallerack)
Helichrysum italicum (Curry Plant)

Helichrysum petiolare
Juniperus chinensis (Chinese Juniper)
  'Blaauw'
  'Blue Alps'
  'Obelisk'
  'Pyramidalis'
  'San Jose'
Juniperus communis (Common Juniper)
  'Compressa'
Juniperus conferta (Shore Juniper)
  'Blue Pacific'
Juniperus horizontalis
  (Creeping Juniper)
  'Bar Harbor'
  'Blue Chip'
  'Douglasii'
  'Glauca'
  'Grey Pearl'
  'Hughes'
  'Plumosa'
  'Wiltonii'
Juniperus x *pfitzeriana* 'Glauca'
Juniperus procumbens (Creeping Juniper,
  Bonin Island Juniper)
Juniperus sabina **'Blaue Donau'** (Savin)

Juniperus scopulorum
  (Rocky Mountain Juniper)
  'Blue Heaven'
  'Grey Gleam'
  'Sky Rocket'
Juniperus squamata (Himalayan Juniper)
  'Blue Carpet'
  'Blue Star'
  'Meyeri'
Juniperus virginiana (Eastern Red
  Cedar, Pencil Cedar)
  'Hetzii'
Leucophyta brownii (Cushion Bush)
Melianthus major (Honey Flower,
  Touch-me-not Plant, Honey Bush)
Picea pungens (Colorado Spruce)
  'Glauca'
  'Globosa'
  'Koster'
  'Koster Prostrate'
  'Montgomery'
Pinus sylvestris **'Beuvronensis'**
Pseudotsuga menziesii
  (Douglas Fir)
  var. *glauca* (Blue Douglas Fir)
Pyrus salicifolia
  (Willow-leaved Pear, Silver Pear)
  'Pendula'
Santolina chamaecyparissus
  (Cotton Lavender)
  'Lemon Queen'
Santolina pinnata **subsp.** *neopolitana*
  'Edward Bowles'
Sequoia sempervirens (California
  Redwood, Coast Redwood)
  'Pendula'
  'Prostrata'

Teucrium fruticans (Shrubby Germander)
Teucrium marum (Cat Thyme)
Teucrium subspinosum

PERENNIALS

Artemisia abrotanum (Lad's Love,
  Old Man, Southernwood)
Artemisia absinthium (Absinthe,
  Wormwood)
  'Lambrook Silver'
Artemisia alba **'Canescens'**
Artemisia arborescens
  (Silver Wormwood)
Artemisia ludoviciana
  (Western Mugwort, White Sage)
  var. *albula*
  'Valerie Finnis'
Artemisia schmidtiana **'Nana'**
Artemisia stelleriana
  (Beach Wormwood)
  'Broughton Silver'
Crambe maritima (Sea Kale)
Cynara cardunculus (Cardoon)
Cynara scolymus (Globe Artichoke)
Eryngium bourgatii
  'Oxford Blue'
Eryngium giganteum
  (Miss Willmott's Ghost)
Euphorbia characias
  subsp. *wulfenii*
Festuca glauca
  (Blue Fescue, Grey Fescue)
  'Blaufuchs'
  'Elijah Blue'
Hosta 'Halcyon'
Hosta sieboldiana
  var. *elegans*

Plectranthus argentatus
  (Silver Plectranthus)
Raoulia australis (Golden Scabweed)
Ruta graveolens
  (Common Rue, Herb of Grace)
  'Jackman's Blue'
Salvia argentea (Silver Sage)
Salvia officinalis (Sage)
Senecio cineraria (Dusty Miller)
  'Silver Dust'
Senecio viravira (Dusty Miller)
Stachys byzantina (Lambs' Ears,
  Lambs' Tails, Lambs' Tongues)
  'Big Ears'
  'Silver Carpet'
Tanacetum argenteum
Tanacetum haradjanii
Tanacetum ptarmiciflorum
  (Dusty Miller, Silver Lace)
Tradescantia sillamontana
  (White Velvet)
Verbascum bombyciferum

SUCCULENTS

Agave parryi
Aloe arborescens (Candelabra Aloe)
Aloe striata (Coral Aloe)
Cotyledon orbiculata
  var. *oblonga*
Crassula arborescens
  (Silver Jade Plant, Silver Dollar)
Crassula perfoliata **var.** *minor*
  (Propeller Plant)
Dudleya brittonii (Chalk Dudleya)
Dudleya pulverulenta (Chalk Lettuce)
Echeveria elegans (Pearl Echeveria,
  Hen and Chicks)
Echeveria pulvinata **'Frosty'** (Plush Plant)
Echeveria secunda (Blue Echeveria,
  Hen and Chicks)
Euphorbia mysinites
Graptopetalum bellum
Graptopetalum paraguayense
  (Ghost Plant, Mother of Pearl Plant)
  'Seeigel'
Sedum morganianum
  (Donkey's Tail, Burro Tail)
Sedum spathulifolium
  'Cape Blanco'
Sedum spectabile
Senecio serpens (Blue Chalksticks)
Tillandsia usneoides (Spanish Moss)
Yucca glauca
  (Dwarf Yucca, Soapweed)

The compact *Stachys byzantina* 'Silver Carpet' is non-flowering and is often selected
for formal displays.

GROUNDCOVERS

Groundcovers clothe bare soil, soften rocky slopes and rough banks, spill down steep walls and fill strips between driveway tracks. Broadly speaking, any plant that clings closely to the ground and is wider than its height can be called a groundcover or carpeting plant. They are useful substitutes for grass where mowing isn't an option and where low maintenance is required; they conserve moisture, control ground temperature and erosion and are highly decorative. But one of the best uses for groundcovers is as a natural way of controlling weeds while at the same time giving a garden an atmosphere of maturity.

Many groundcovering plants are beautiful in their own right. Lush plantings of Lady's Mantle (*Alchemilla mollis*), Lamb's Ears (*Stachys byzantina*) and varieties of *Ajuga reptans* will soften the line of a path and eliminate the chore of edging. Carpeting plants such as Baby's Tears (*Soleirolia soleirolii*) make a unifying groundcover in a rock garden, while creeping thymes set along paths can be a pleasure to walk on. Leathery-leaved bergenias and groups of one kind of hosta make an excellent feature for edging a winding pathway.

Selected forms of *Helichrysum petiolare* or *Tradescantia pallida* 'Purpurea' make stunning colourful carpets or drifts.

Choose a groundcover suitable for your soil and aspect, which will cover the ground quickly and well. Coloured-leaf, sun-loving forms of *Salvia officinalis* and *Origanum vulgare* have good-looking aromatic leaves. Low-growing mints *Ajuga* and *Lamium,* and *Persicaria virginiana* 'Painter's Palette', with its pretty variegated leaves, prefer less sun, and as they are relatively shallow rooted, can be planted beneath trees. Mass-plant *Hosta* and *Pulmonaria* in deep shade; these need a cool climate and rich, well-composted soil with plenty of water in summer. Prostrate junipers such as *Juniperus conferta* and *J. horizontalis* 'Bar Harbor', with attractive textured foliage, thrive on dry rocky banks, even at the seashore. On a large scale, ivies, with their wide spreading branches, will cover the ground in deep shade.

PLANTING GROUNDCOVERS

When selecting groundcovers, try to establish first how the mature plants will appear. They look best when

An edging of Black Mondo Grass and a bed of prostrate conifer provide contrasting textures and set off a huge urn.

several plants of a single species are massed as a group, with leaves all the same height and blending into a textured carpet. The area intended for planting should be as weed free as possible. This prevents competitive growth and saves the frustrating and tedious chore of weeding by hand while the groundcovers are establishing. After planting, cover the area between the plants with a generous layer of compost or mulch: this will reduce drying out and minimise weeding until the plants establish themselves and can take over the weed-suppressing role.

A neat circle of shade-loving *Ajuga reptans* 'Atropurpurea' beneath a tree.

GUIDE TO GROUNDCOVERS

FERNS

Adiantum aethiopicum
   (Common Maidenhair)
Asplenium flabellifolium
   (Necklace Fern)
Blechnum chilense
Blechnum penna-marina
   (Alpine Water Fern)
Dennstaedtia davallioides
   (Lady Ground Fern)
Nephrolepis cordifolia (Fishbone Fern,
   Southern Sword Fern)
   'Plumosa'
Pellaea falcata (Sickle Fern)
Pellaea rotundifolia (Button Fern)

MOUNDING

Ajuga pyramidalis (Pyramidal Bugle)
Alchemilla erythropoda
Alchemilla mollis (Lady's Mantle)
Bergenia ciliata
Bergenia cordifolia
Bergenia x *schmidtii*
Bergenia stracheyi
Callisia fragrans (Chain Plant)
   'Melnickoff'
Chlorophytum comosum (Spider Plant)
   'Mandaianum'
   'Picturatum'
   'Variegatum'
   'Vittatum'
Coprosma x *kirkii*
   'Variegata'
Epimedium diphyllum
Epimedium grandiflorum
   'Flavescens'
   'Rose Queen'

Graptopetalum paraguayense
   (Ghost Plant, Mother of Pearl Plant)
Hebe pinguifolia
Helichrysum petiolare
   'Limelight'
   'Variegatum'
Heuchera x *brizoides*
   'Coral Cloud'
   'Pearl Drops'
Heuchera micrantha
   var. *diversifolia* 'Purple Palace'
   'Pewter Moon'
Hosta **species** (Plantain Lily)
Houttuynia cordata 'Chameleon'
Lamium galeobdolon (Yellow Archangel)
   'Hermann's Pride'
   'Silver Carpet'
Lamium maculatum
   (Spotted Deadnettle)
   'Aureum'
   'Beacon Silver'
   'White Nancy'
Mentha x *piperita* (Peppermint)
   f. *citrata* (Eau-de-cologne Mint)
Mentha spicata (Spearmint) 'Crispa'
Mentha suaveolens (Apple Mint)
   'Variegata'
Mentha x *villosa* f. *alopecuroides*
   (Bowles' Mint)
Ophiopogon jaburan (White Lilyturf)
   'Vittatus'
Ophiopogon japonicus (Mondo Grass)
   'Kyoto Dwarf'
Ophiopogon planiscapus
   'Nigrescens'
Origanum vulgare **and cultivars**
   (Oregano, Wild Marjoram)

Pelargonium grossularioides
   (Coconut Pelargonium)
Pelargonium odoratissimum
Peperomia scandens 'Variegata'
Pilea cadierei (Aluminium Plant,
   Watermelon Pilea)
   'Minima'
Pilea involucrata (Friendship Plant)
   'Moon Valley'
Pilea microphylla (Artillery Plant)
Plectranthus madagascariensis
   (Mintleaf)
   'Variegated Mintleaf'
Pulmonaria **species** (Lungwort)
Rosmarinus officinalis 'Prostratus'
   (Prostrate Rosemary)
Salvia officinalis (Sage) **and cultivars**
Santolina chamaecyparissus
   (Cotton Lavender)
   'Lemon Queen'
Santolina pinnata
   subsp. *neopolitana*
   'Edward Bowles'
Saxifraga stolonifera (Mother of
   Thousands, Strawberry Begonia)
   'Tricolor'
Sedum sieboldii
   'Mediovariegatum'
Stachys byzantina (Lambs' Ears,
   Lambs' Tails, Lambs' Tongues)
   'Big Ears'
Syngonium podophyllum
   (Arrowhead Vine, Goosefoot)
   'Emerald Gem'
   'White Butterfly'
Tanacetum argenteum
Tanacetum haradjanii

A pretty combination of *Echeveria* and *Ajuga reptans* in a small rockery pocket.

Tanacetum ptarmiciflorum
  (Dusty Miller, Silver Lace)
Teucrium marum (Cat Thyme)
Teucrium subspinosum
Thymus x *citriodorus*
  (Lemon-scented Thyme)
  'Aureus'
  'Bertram Anderson'
  'Doone Valley'
  'Silver Queen'
Thymus vulgaris 'Silver Posie'
Tradescantia fluminensis
  (Wandering Jew)
  'Albovittata'
  'Quicksilver'
Tradescantia pallida 'Purpurea'
Tradescantia sillamontana (White Velvet)
Tradescantia spathacea
  (Boat Lily, Moses-in-the-cradle)
Tradescantia zanonia 'Mexican Flag'
Tradescantia zebrina (Silver Inch Plant)
  'Purpusii'
  'Quadcolor'

GROUND-HUGGERS
Ajuga reptans (Common Bugle)
  and cultivars
Alchemilla alpina (Alpine Lady's Mantle)
Alchemilla conjuncta
Alternanthera ficoidea (Parrot Leaf)
Artemisia schmidtiana
Artemisia stelleriana 'Broughton
  Silver' (Beach Wormwood)
Asarum europaeum (Asarabacca)
Begonia pustulata

Callisia elegans (Striped Inch Plant)
Callisia navicularis (Chain Plant)
Episcia cupreata (Flame Violet)
  'Metallica'
  'Mosaica'
Episcia lilacina
Ficus pumila (Creeping Fig)
Fittonia verschaffeltii
  var. *argyroneura* (Silver Net-leaf)
  'Nana'
Hebe chathamica
Hedera helix (Common Ivy, English Ivy)
  and cultivars
Lysimachia nummularia (Creeping Jenny,
  Moneywort)
  'Aurea'
Mentha pulegium (Pennyroyal)
Mentha requienii (Corsican Mint)
Raoulia australis (Golden Scabweed)
Saxifraga exarata subsp. *moschata*
  'Cloth of Gold'
Saxifraga x *urbium* (London Pride)
  'Miss Chambers'
Sedum ewersii
Sedum kamtschaticum
Sedum spathulifolium 'Cape Blanco'
Selaginella martensii
Selaginella pallescens
Sempervivum arachnoideum
  (Cobweb Houseleek)
Sempervivum ciliosum
Sempervivum tectorum
  (Common Houseleek)
Soleirolia soleirolii (Baby's Tears,
  Mind-your-own-business)

Thymus caespititius
Thymus herba-barona (Caraway Thyme)
Thymus pseudolanuginosus
  (Woolly Thyme)
Thymus serphyllum
  'Annie Hall'
  'Elfin'
  'Snowdrift'

VIGOROUS
Cissus antarctica (Kangaroo Vine)
Cissus hypoglauca (Water Vine)
Cissus rhombifolia (Grape Ivy)
  'Ellen Danica'
Epipremnum pinnatum
  'Aureum'
  'Marble Queen'
Euonymus fortunei (Wintercreeper
  Euonymus) **cultivars**
Hedera canariensis (Canary Island Ivy,
  Algerian Ivy)
  'Gloire de Marengo'
  'Ravensholst'
Hedera colchica (Persian Ivy)
  'Dentata'
  'Dentata Variegata'
  'Sulphur Heart'
Hedera hibernica (Irish Ivy)
  'Deltoidea' (Sweetheart Ivy)
Juniperus chinensis 'San Jose'
  (Chinese Juniper)
Juniperus communis 'Repanda'
  (Common Juniper)
Juniperus conferta (Shore Juniper)
  'Blue Pacific'
  'Emerald Sea'
Juniperus horizontalis (Creeping Juniper)
  and cultivars
Juniperus x *pfitzeriana*
  'Aurea'
  'Glauca'
  'Pfitzeriana'
Juniperus procumbens (Creeping Juniper,
  Bonin Island Juniper)
  'Nana'
Juniperus sabina 'Blaue Donau' (Savin)
Juniperus squamata (Himalayan Juniper)
  'Blue Carpet'
  'Blue Star'
Microbiota decussata
  (Russian Arbor-vitae)
Pelargonium tomentosum (Peppermint-
  scented Pelargonium)
Podocarpus nivalis (Mountain Totara)

HEDGES AND TOPIARY

Precisely clipped hedges are vital ingredients in the pattern-making of formal gardens and for dividing these gardens into sections. As they contribute towards a permanent framework throughout the year, it is important that hedges be designed and placed so that they are in scale with the rest of the garden.

Tall hedges make good living boundaries or give the feeling of an outdoor room. Miniature hedges can be planted along a path or to line the way to a particular feature. Beautifully manicured box hedges shaped to fit a small space are particularly well suited to the formality of many town gardens. The traditional sixteenth-century knot garden is made from clipped boxes and contrasting herbs, such as santolina, rosemary or thyme, to form charming geometric beds. Any part of such a garden can be adapted today to even the smallest space.

European Box (*Buxus sempervirens*) is the most popular for medium-sized hedging and topiary work. *B. sempervirens* 'Suffruticosa' is used for low edgings and container topiary, and is indispensable in a formal setting and for marking out parterres. It is a slow-grower, however, and sometimes Box Honeysuckle (*Lonicera nitida*), with its neat small leaves and vigorous growth, is preferred. It can be clipped as small as desired, but does need more frequent trimming to retain a sharp outline.

In spacious country gardens, lofty hedges of Leyland Cypress (x *Cupressocyparis leylandii*), and the strong-growing English Holly (*Ilex aquifolium*) are decorative and can serve as windbreaks. The Monterey Cypress (*Cupressus macrocarpa*) is also used and can be kept to 3m/10ft by pruning. The slow-growing Yew (*Taxus baccata*), with its dense tight growth, makes an excellent solid hedge for cool temperate climates. It lends stability and weight to a garden and can be used effectively to make permanent garden compartments or boundaries. It is also good for topiary.

Photinia glabra 'Rubens' has proved immensely popular for clipped hedges. It is pleasing in every stage of growth, but its most noteworthy feature is the brilliant red new foliage that follows each cutting. Other sturdy, adaptable plants suitable for clipped hedges include Orange Jessamine (*Murraya paniculata*), suitable for warm temperate areas, and *Coprosma repens*, excellent for seaside use.

DECIDUOUS AND PLEACHED HEDGES

In cold climates, evergreen hedges may create significant regions of dense shade which could have an adverse effect

This attractive textural planting of shapely conifers and clipped shrubs presents well for most of the year. The topiary theme is continued with some cone-shaped *Picea glauca* var. *albertiana* 'Conica' while the rich golden colour in the foreground is balanced with a well-grown *Cupressus macrocarpa* 'Brunniana Aurea' on the right.

Regular pruning of this neat hedge of *Photinia glabra* 'Rubens' keeps it compact and stimulates the production of brilliant red new foliage.

Organic matter in the form of animal manure, leaf mould or compost should be incorporated into the soil to improve structure. Add slow-release fertiliser in the backfill.

Spacing will depend on the tree that you use. After planting, water the hedge thoroughly and trim the plants so they are equally bushy and will be encouraged to grow uniformly. Feed in the growing season, especially after the hedge has been clipped, and water well in dry periods until established.

HEDGE TRIMMING

Most hedges need to be cut back several times during the first two or three years to encourage dense growth at the base. When clipping a hedge, make sure it is a little broader at the base and tapers towards the top. This shape is easier to clip and allows the

during the colder months. A narrow deciduous hedge will allow a certain amount of light to filter through during winter. Beech (*Fagus sylvatica*) and Hornbeam (*Carpinus betulus*) are traditional plants for this type of hedging. They retain their coppery-coloured leaves for a long time in winter, but when they eventually fall, a thick tracery of branches remains.

A pleached hedge is one where the lower branches of trees such as Lime (*Tilia* x *europaea*) or Hornbeam are stripped away and the upper branches are interlaced or pruned, leaving a kind of hedge on stilts. Pleaching provides a way of dividing a garden without placing a solid barrier between areas or obscuring the view through to the area beyond.

INFORMAL HEDGES

Screens, sometimes called informal hedges, are left unclipped. They can be made of one plant, but in small gardens they are often made up of a variety of evergreen plants that will slow the breeze and give year-round privacy. They give shelter without the worry of precise clipping. Bamboos and conifers make fine informal hedges, offering relatively dense screens where wind filters are needed. Fijian Fire Plant (*Acalypha wilkesiana*) makes a colourful informal screen for tropical and warm temperate gardens.

HEDGE PLANTING

Bear in mind that a hedge will occupy the ground for many years to come. Spend time planning, improving the soil and planting. Clipped hedges are usually, though not always, made of one plant. Choose plants from the nursery which are reasonably uniform in size and bushy at the base. The smaller and younger your hedging plants are to begin with, the stronger the hedge will eventually become.

An eye-catching small front garden, with a tight group of a shapely conifer, box topiary and ivy set off with red impatiens.

Parterre garden with boundary of *Thuja occidentalis* 'Smaragd' and a curved inner box hedge providing a perfect frame for contrasting Iceberg roses and *Lavandula angustifolia*.

Topiary is relatively easy to do, but it is time consuming and requires a great deal of patience as you wait for the trees to grow into their desired shapes. Even simple topiary requires regular clipping to develop and maintain its shape. Yew, Box and Bay are the traditional plants, but *Lonicera nitida*, *Teucrium*, myrtles, lavenders and rosemary also make good shapes. Freer, simpler shapes can be made with citrus, hollies and species of *Thuja*.

Buy a good strong plant about 1m/3ft high and plant it firmly. As the plant becomes established, decide what shape you want to create. The leading growth is the most important, because its strength and direction will help to produce the desired shape. Some support in the early stages will be useful. For a simple shape like an obelisk, a single stake will be enough. For a more intricate shape, use a temporary wire frame to train the plant. Once the shape and form are set, the wire framework can be removed.

To create a spiral design, start at the bottom with a piece of string wound evenly around the tree to get the right line, and then slowly clip a small indentation along the line of the string until the desired shape is achieved. Then extend the cut through to the trunk. Use razor-sharp clipping tools to ensure that you cut as evenly as possible without bruising the plant.

STANDARDS

A standard or 'mophead' is a tree or shrub trained on a single bare stem over several years to produce a small tree-like form with a (usually) rounded head. Clipped standards tend to look best when used symmetrically in pairs or groups, either confined to a tub or planted in a bed or border. Any evergreen small-leaved plant, including bay trees, figs, citrus, hollies and boxes, can be trained into a standard. Young container-grown plants will take some years to reach a good size, but it is reasonably easy to train your own.

Select a young plant with a strong, straight shoot up the centre. Start the training process by snipping off the lower branches on the main stem cleanly at their base. Be sure to leave at least the top third of the foliage. Continue to remove side-branches until the plant has grown to the desired height. If necessary, re-pot into a larger container and drive in a sturdy straight stake close to the trunk. Tie the trunk to the stake at intervals. When the plant has reached the height you want, pinch out the growing tip and side-branches to encourage further branching. Remove any shoots that appear on the trunk and shear the plants lightly to maintain the rounded head.

maximum sunlight to all parts of the plant. Conifers retain the leader until they have attained their intended height, and generally only the laterals are pruned during the early years.

Established hedges are generally clipped after the main spring growth and again in early autumn. Some hedges will need more frequent clipping to keep a tidy appearance.

TOPIARY

Topiary is the art of clipping trees or shrubs into any desired shape. Although fantastic bird shapes or ballerinas and the like will give a light-hearted touch to the garden, a pair of formal low box domes or obelisks can effectively frame a gate or doorway or punctuate a small knot garden.

GUIDE TO HEDGE AND TOPIARY PLANTS

TALL

Coprosma repens (Mirror Plant,
  Looking-glass Plant)
  'Green and Gold'
  'Marble Queen'
  'Picturata'
  'Pink Splendour'
x *Cupressocyparis leylandii*
  (Leyland Cypress)
  'Castlewellan'
  'Haggerston Grey'
  'Leighton Green'
  'Naylor's Blue'
Cupressus macrocarpa (Monterey Cypress)
  'Brunniana Aurea'
Euonymus japonicus (Japanese Spindle
  Tree) **and cultivars**
Fagus sylvatica (Common Beech,
  European Beech)
  and cultivars
Ilex x *altaclerensis* (Highclere Holly)
  and cultivars
Ilex aquifolium (English Holly)
  and cultivars
Ilex x *meserveae* (Blue Holly)
  and cultivars
Juniperus chinensis (Chinese Juniper)
  and cultivars
Juniperus virginiana
  (Eastern Red Cedar)
Nothofagus cunninghamii
  (Tasmanian Beech, Myrtle Beech)
Photinia x *fraseri*
  'Red Robin'
  'Robusta'
Photinia glabra 'Rubens'
Taxus baccata (Yew)
  'Aurea'
  'Fastigiata'
  'Fastigiata Aurea'
  'Fastigiata Aureomarginata'
Taxus cuspidata (Japanese Yew)
Thuja occidentalis (White Cedar)
  and cultivar
  'Filiformis'
Tilia x *europaea* (Common Lime)

MEDIUM

Acalypha wilkesiania
  (Fijian Fire Plant)
Berberis thunbergii (Japanese Barberry)
  'Atropurpurea'

'Atropurpurea Nana'
'Aurea'
'Bagatelle'
'Golden Ring'
'Red Pillar'
'Rose Glow'
'Silver Beauty'
Buxus sempervirens
  (European Box, Common Box)
  'Latifolia Maculata'
  'Marginata'
  'Suffruticosa'
  'Suffruticosa Variegata'
Ficus microcarpa var. *hillii*
  (Hill's Weeping Fig)
Ilex cornuta (Chinese Holly,
  Horned Holly)
Ilex crenata (Japanese Holly)
  and cultivars
Laurus nobilis
  (Bay Laurel, Sweet Bay)
Murraya paniculata
  (Orange Jessamine,
  Mock Orange)
Myrtus communis
  (Common Myrtle)
  'Variegata'
  subsp. *tarentina*
Taxus baccata (Yew)
  'Dovastonii Aurea'
  'Repens Aurea'
  'Semperaurea'
  'Standishii'
Taxus cuspidata 'Nana'
  (Japanese Yew)
Thuja occidentalis
  (White Cedar)
  cultivars
  'Globosa'
  'Holmstrup'
  'Rheingold'
  'Smaragd'

LOW

Alternanthera dentata
  'Rubiginosa'
Buxus microphylla
  (Japanese Box)
  var. *japonica*
  var. *koreana*
Lonicera nitida
  (Box Honeysuckle)

'Aurea'
'Baggesen's Gold'
Rosmarinus officinalis (Rosemary)
Santolina chamaecyparissus
  (Cotton Lavender)
  'Lemon Queen'
Santolina pinnata
  subsp. *neopolitana*
  'Edward Bowles'
Serissa foetida
  'Variegata'
Taxus baccata (Yew) **cultivars**
  'Repandens'
  'Repens Aurea'
Taxus cuspidata 'Densa'
  (Japanese Yew)
Teucrium fruticans
  (Shrubby Germander)
Thuja occidentalis (White Cedar)
  cultivars
  'Danica'
  'Golden Globe'
  'Hetz Midget'

Potted plants of box topiary and ivy make a stylish
arrangement to mark an entrance and balcony.

SALT-TOLERANT PLANTS FOR SEASIDE GARDENS

Beautiful gardens will thrive close to the sea as long as you select plants to suit the harsh environment. Seaside houses are almost always positioned to take advantage of a spectacular view, but this usually means gardens that open directly onto the beach are continually swept by salt-laden winds. The advantage of gardening near the coast is that temperatures are less extreme and there is usually little or no frost. Weeds are usually not so much of a problem as they tend to dislike salty air.

Where there is room you need to create a natural protective barrier of salt- and wind-resistant plants behind which less tolerant plants can find shelter from the harsh conditions.

Choose initially the toughest plants for windbreaks and shelter. Retain as much natural vegetation as possible—these plants may not necessarily be beautiful, but they are appropriate to the environment, often have their own special windswept character, and will provide valuable protection for more appealing and attractive specimens that are not so durable. Landscapers in tropical climates make good use of naturally occurring pandanus and palms as front-line plants. Native dune grasses and low-growing plants will help stabilise the sand and protect your property against erosion. They will also help trap abrasive wind-borne sand. Note which plants thrive in other gardens in your area with similar coastal exposure. A good local nursery will help you with selection.

Soils close to the sea are usually of a sandy nature, often poor in nutrients and water-holding capacity. Add as much organic matter as you can before you plant your

Clumps of salt-resistant shrubs such as *Senecio*, *Juniperus*, *Euonymus* and *Phormium* are untroubled by exposure to salty breezes. Silver-leaved plants protected by a waxy or hairy coating are especially suited to this harsh environment.

Happy in wind, salt and sun, *Yucca gloriosa* thrives at a beach house.

trees. A semi-permeable windbreak with a combination of open and solid material to break the wind's force is much more effective than a solid windbreak, which will create wind turbulence with the additional problem of soil erosion. Effective barriers can be made of a fence of open slatted timber, or a screen of burlap, lattice, wire or plastic mesh interlaced with flexible branches.

Trees and shrubs should be given a thorough soaking at well-spaced intervals to encourage deep penetration of roots. After heavy storms, hosing down the plants will prevent foliage being scorched by salt deposits.

Consider succulents for tub plants around the house. Agaves and aloes will live for years in tubs, even with a weekly watering. *Yucca filamentosa*

barrier—it will save trouble in the long run. Decomposed grass clippings and mushroom compost are useful for makes a good architectural plant, especially against a wall where its silhouette is accentuated.

building up the soil. A mulch layer at least 10cm/4in thick of compost mixed with well-rotted animal manure will help to conserve moisture and keep the weeds down and, as the organic material breaks down, will greatly improve the soil. Seaweed gathered from the beach is an excellent, easily obtained mulch for a seaside garden. It is a good soil conditioner and does not introduce any weeds. It usually breaks down in a few months.

It is best to plant trees and shrubs when they are still very small. Even though growth will be slower at first, they will form a stronger root system. In very harsh conditions, protection in the form of an artificial barrier helps to establish newly planted shrubs and

The striking Dragon Tree (*Dracaena draco*, centre) survives on almost total neglect. The elegant box hedge is set further back and protected in this windswept garden.

GUIDE TO SALT-TOLERANT PLANTS

VERY EXPOSED GARDENS
Agave americana (Century Plant)
 'Marginata'
 'Mediopicta'
Atriplex nummularia
 (Old Man Saltbush)
Carpentaria acuminata
 (Carpentaria Palm)

Coprosma repens (Mirror Plant, Looking-glass Plant)
 'Green and Gold'
 'Marble Queen'
 'Picturata'
 'Pink Splendour'
Crambe maritima
 (Sea Kale)

Cupressus macrocarpa
 (Monterey Cypress)
 'Aurea Saligna'
 'Brunniana Aurea'
 'Goldcrest'
 'Greenstead Magnificent'
Elaeagnus pungens
 (Silverberry, Thorny Elaeagnus)

Easy to grow and with very glossy leaves, *Coprosma repens* is very well suited to life by the sea as a hedge or windbreak.

Griselinia littoralis 'Variegata' withstands wind and rough coastal conditions.

Ficus rubiginosa
(Port Jackson Fig)
'Variegata'
Fraxinus angustifolia
(Narrow-leaved Ash)
Gleditsia triacanthos
(Honey Locust)
Hebe chathamica
Myosotidium hortensia (Chatham
Island Forget-me-not)
'Alba'
Phoenix canariensis (Canary
Island Date Palm)
Phoenix dactylifera (Date Palm)
Phormium cookianum
(Mountain Flax) **and
cultivars**
Phormium tenax (New Zealand
Flax) **and cultivars**
Pinus nigra (Austrian Pine,
Black Pine)
subsp. *laricio*
Pinus sylvestris
'Beuvronensis'
Pinus thunbergii
(Japanese Black Pine)
'Sayonara'
Pisonia umbellifera
(Bird-catcher Tree)
'Variegata'
Pseudopanax crassifolius (Lancewood)
Pseudopanax lessonii (Houpara)
Rosmarinus officinalis (Rosemary)
Sedum 'Herbstfreude'
Senecio cineraria (Dusty Miller)
'Silver Dust'
Tetrapanax papyriferus
(Rice-paper Plant)
Teucrium fruticans
(Shrubby Germander)

SHELTERED GARDENS
Hebe speciosa (Showy Hebe)
'Tricolor'
Howea belmoreana (Curly Palm)
Howea forsteriana (Kentia Palm,
Thatch Palm)
Miscanthus sinensis (Eulalia)
Strelitzia reginae (Crane Flower)
Taxus cuspidata (Japanese Yew)
'Densa'
'Nana'
Thuja occidentalis
(White Cedar)

'Dicksonii'
'Frederici'
'Maculata'
'Variegata'
Euonymus japonicus (Japanese
Spindle Tree)
Griselinia littoralis (Kapuka)
'Dixon's Cream'
'Green Jewel'
'Variegata'
Griselinia lucida (Puka)
Juniperus conferta (Shore Juniper)
Juniperus horizontalis (Creeping
Juniper) **and cultivars**
Juniperus procumbens (Creeping
Juniper, Bonin Island Juniper)
'Nana'
Leucophyta brownii (Cushion Bush)
Pandanus tectorius (Coastal Screw
Pine, Pandang)
Pandanus veitchii (Veitch Screw Pine)
Pinus halepensis (Aleppo Pine)
Pisonia grandis (Bird-lime Tree)
Yucca filamentosa (Adam's Needle)

LESS EXPOSED GARDENS
Acer pseudoplatanus (Sycamore Maple)
Agave angustifolia 'Marginata'

Agave attenuata
Agave filifera (Thread Agave)
Aloe arborescens (Candelabra Aloe)
Artemisia arborescens (Silver
Wormwood)
Artemisia schmidtiana
Chamaerops humilis (Dwarf Fan
Palm, European Fan Palm)
Codiaeum variegatum **var.** *pictum*
(Croton)
Coprosma **x** *kirkii*
'Variegata'
Cordyline australis (New Zealand
Cabbage Tree)
Crambe cordifolia (Colewort)
Dracaena draco (Dragon Tree)
Elaeagnus angustifolia
(Oleaster, Russian Olive)
'Quicksilver'
Elaeagnus **x** *ebbingei* **cultivars**
'Gilt Edge'
'Limelight'
Encephalartos ferox
Eucalyptus crenulata
(Victorian Silver Gum)
Eucalyptus tetragona (Tallerack)
x *Fatshedera lizei* (Tree Ivy)
Ficus macrophylla (Moreton Bay Fig)

VARIEGATED AND PATTERNED LEAVES

Variegated and patterned foliages give artistic splash and vitality to any planting. They have a lightening effect on heavily shaded places and, as they show up well at night, look good near driveways, paths and doorways.

In technical terms, 'variegation' means a naturally occurring or virally induced mutation that appears as lighter or coloured patches on the leaves of a normally green plant. Because these areas contain very little, or none, of the chlorophyll essential for photosynthesis, plants with variegated leaves are rarely as vigorous as their fully green counterparts. They are apt to be scorched by full sun and are more likely to suffer from drought and disease. Nonetheless, they are often highly prized for their attractive markings. Some need to be kept in shade if the leaves are to stay strongly marked. Conversely, indoor plants with variegated leaves generally need more light than plain green ones. In all variegated plants, cut out any full-green reversions immediately you notice them.

Although variegated plants are apt to clash with one another and thus should be used with discretion, a colour theme can be enhanced by using matching colours in variegations. For example, in a white garden scheme, shrubs and groundcovers with white and green variegations, and pulmonarias with silvery spotted leaves, can be used as a constant link in the planting. Yellow-edged hostas and cream-variegated plants will enhance and anchor a yellow border. Patterned foliage plants such as crotons and the Fijian Fire Plant (*Alcalypha wilkesiana*) add drama and colour to an exotic tropical garden. Heavily patterned and brightly coloured coleus, treated as temporary foliage plants, can be tucked in among plants with complementary hues.

Two variegated plants, *Furcraea selloa* var. *marginata* (succulent) and *Miscanthus sinensis* 'Variegatus' (grass), provide a lightening effect and year-round interest in this border with *Phormium tenax* 'Purpureum' (left) and neat box domes.

In the herb garden, variegated mints and coloured-leaved sages add colour to edging, for very few herbs can be described as outstanding in flower. Some species of *Tradescantia* have attractive variegation and often rich, colourful patterns to their leaves. As they thrive in partial shade they make excellent groundcovers beneath trees, at the front of the border or planted at the base of an urn or collection of pots.

Don't overlook the variegated sculptural plants, such as species of *Phormium* and *Agave*, for a touch of drama and accent among evergreen shrubs. Variegated grasses can provide an interesting airy effect on a textured walkway.

GUIDE TO VARIEGATED AND PATTERNED LEAVES

MULTI-COLOURED LEAVES

Acalypha wilkesiana
  (Fijian Fire Plant, Copperleaf)
Begonia rex cultivars
  (King Begonia, Painted Leaf Begonia)
Codiaeum variegatum var. *pictum*
  (Croton) and cultivars
Cordyline fruticosa 'Tricolor'
Ctenanthe oppenheimiana 'Tricolor'
Episcia cupreata (Flame Violet)
  'Metallica'
  'Mosaica'
Ficus elastica 'Tricolor'
Graptophyllum pictum 'Tricolor'
Hakea victoria (Royal Hakea)
Hedera helix (Common Ivy, English Ivy)
  and various cultivars
Heuchera micrantha 'Pewter Moon'
Houttuynia cordata 'Chameleon'
Maranta leuconeura (Prayer Plant,
  Ten Commandments) and cultivars
Neoregelia carolinae 'Tricolor'
  (Blushing Bromeliad)
Phormium cookianum subsp. *hookeri*
  'Tricolor'
Piper ornatum (Celebes Pepper)
Pseudowintera colorata
  (Pepper Tree, Horopito)
Salvia officinalis 'Tricolor'
Solenostemon scutellarioides
  (Coleus, Flame Nettle, Painted Nettle)
Tradescantia zebrina 'Quadcolor'

CREAM AND YELLOW LEAVES

Acer negundo 'Elegans'
  (Box Elder Maple)
Acorus calamus 'Variegatus'
  (Sweet Flag)
Acorus gramineus 'Ogon'
  (Japanese Rush)
Agave americana 'Marginata'
  (Century Plant)
Aralia elata 'Aureovariegata'
  (Japanese Angelica Tree)

Aucuba japonica
  (Japanese Laurel, Spotted Laurel)
  'Crotonifolia'
  'Gold Dust'
  'Variegata'
Berberis thunbergii (Japanese Barberry)
  cultivars
  'Aurea'
  'Golden Ring'
Caladium lindenii 'Magnificum'
Callisia fragrans 'Melnickoff'
  (Chain Plant)
Callisia x *generalis* 'Striata'
Carex morrowii 'Fisher' (Japanese Sedge)
Chlorophytum comosum (Spider Plant)
  'Mandaianum'
  'Picturatum'
Coprosma repens (Mirror Plant,
  Looking-glass Plant) cultivars
  'Green and Gold'
  'Picturata'
Cordyline australis 'Albertii'
  (New Zealand Cabbage Tree)
Cornus alba 'Spaethii'
  (Red-barked Dogwood)
Ctenanthe lubbersiana
  (Bamburanta)
Dieffenbachia seguine and
  cultivars
  'Rudolph Roehrs'
  'Tropic Snow'
Dracaena fragrans
  (Corn Plant, Happy Plant)
  cultivars
  'Massangeana'
  'Victoria'
Dracaena reflexa
  'Song of India'
Elaeagnus x *ebbingei* cultivars
  'Gilt Edge'
  'Limelight'
Elaeagnus pungens
  (Silverberry, Thorny
  Elaeagnus) cultivars

  'Dicksonii'
  'Frederici'
  'Maculata'
  'Variegata'
Epipremnum pinnatum 'Aureum'
Euonymus fortunei (Wintercreeper
  Euonymus) cultivars
  'Emerald 'n' Gold'
  'Golden Prince'
  'Sunspot'
Euonymus japonicus (Japanese
  Spindle Tree) cultivars
  'Aureomarginatus'
  'Aureus'
  'Microphyllus Aureovariegatus'
  'Ovatus Aureus'
Farfugium japonicum
  'Aureomaculatum'
Fatsia japonica (Japanese Aralia,
  Japanese Fatsia) cultivars
  'Aurea'
  'Moseri'

The highly coloured *Codiaeum variegata* var. *pictum* grows best in a warm frost-free garden.

The colourful coleus, such as *Solenostemon* 'Black Dragon', is most often grown as a temporary bedding plant during the warmer months.

Ficus benjamina **'Golden Princess'**
  (Weeping Fig)
Ficus elastica (Rubber Plant) **cultivars**
  'Aurea-marginata'
  'Variegata'
Furcraea selloa var. *marginata*
Griselinia littoralis (Kapuka) **cultivars**
  'Dixon's Cream'
  'Green Jewel'
Hakonechloa macra **'Aureola'**
  (Golden Variegated Hakonechloa)
Hedera canariensis **'Gloire de Marengo'**
  (Canary Island Ivy, Algerian Ivy)
Hedera colchica **'Sulphur Heart'**
  (Persian Ivy)
Hosta fortunei **cultivars**
  'Albopicta'
  'Aureomarginata'
Hosta **'Frances Williams'**
Hosta **'Gold Standard'**
Hosta tokudama **'Flavocircinalis'**
Ilex x *altaclerensis* **cultivars**
  'Golden King'
  'Lawsoniana'
Ilex aquifolium (English Holly)
  cultivars
  'Aurea Marginata'
  'Golden Milkboy'
Iresine herbstii **'Aureoreticulata'**
  (Beefsteak Plant)
Lamium maculatum **'Aureum'**
  (Spotted Deadnettle)
Liriodendron tulipifera **'Aureomarginata'**
  (Tulip Tree)

Melissa officinalis **'Aurea'**
  (Lemon Balm, Bee Balm)
Mentha x *gracilis* **'Variegata'**
  (Ginger Mint)
Miscanthus sinensis **'Zebrinus'**
Molinia caerulea subsp. *caerulea*
  'Variegata' (Purple Moor Grass)
Origanum vulgare **'Country Cream'**
  (Oregano, Wild Marjoram)
Pelargonium **'Atomic Snowflake'**
Pelargonium crispum **'Variegatum'**
  (Lemon-scented Pelargonium)
Peperomia obtusifolia (Pepper Face)
  cultivars
  'Green and Gold'
  'Variegata'
Peperomia scandens **'Variegata'**
Phalaris arundinacea var. *picta*
  'Luteopicta' (Gardeners' Garters)
Phormium cookianum subsp. *hookeri*
  'Cream Delight' (Mountain Flax)
Phormium tenax **'Variegatum'**
  (New Zealand Flax)
Phragmites australis **'Variegatus'**
  (Common Reed)
Pisonia umbellifera **'Variegata'**
  (Bird-catcher Tree)
Pseudopanax lessonii **'Gold Splash'**
  (Houpara)
Rhapis excelsa **'Zuikonishiki'**
  (Lady Palm, Bamboo Palm)
Salvia officinalis **'Icterina'** (Sage)
Sansevieria trifasciata (Mother-in-law's
  Tongue) **cultivars**

  'Laurentii'
  'Golden Hahnii'
Senecio macroglossus **'Variegatus'**
  (Cape Ivy, Natal Ivy)
Stenotaphrum secundatum
  'Variegatum' (Buffalo Grass)
Taxus baccata (Yew) **cultivars**
  'Dovastonii Aurea'
  'Fastigiata Aurea'
  'Fastigiata Aureomarginata'
  'Repens Aurea'
Thymus x *citriodorus* **'Doone Valley'**
  (Lemon-scented Thyme)
Yucca aloifolia (Spanish Bayonet) **cultivars**
  'Marginata'
  'Tricolor'
Yucca filamentosa **'Bright Edge'**
  (Adam's Needle)
Yucca gloriosa 'Variegata'
  (Spanish Dagger)

WHITE AND SILVER LEAVES
Acer negundo **'Variegatum'**
  (Box Elder Maple)
Acer palmatum **'Butterfly'**
  (Japanese Maple)
Acer platanoides **'Drummondii'**
  (Norway Maple)
Acer pseudoplatanus **'Variegatum'**
  (Sycamore Maple)
Agave americana **'Mediopicta'**
  (Century Plant)
Agave angustifolia **'Marginata'**
Agave victoria-reginae (Royal Agave)
Alocasia macrorrhiza **'Variegata'**
  (Giant Taro)
Alocasia sanderiana (Kris Plant)
Aloe aristata (Torch Plant, Lace Aloe)
Aloe saponaria (Soap Aloe)
Aloe striata (Coral Aloe)
Aloe variegata (Partridge-breasted Aloe)
Anthurium crystallinum
  (Crystal Anthurium)
Aralia elata 'Variegata'
  (Japanese Angelica Tree)
Arundo donax **'Versicolor'** (Giant Reed)
Aspidistra elatior **'Variegata'**
  (Aspidistra, Cast-iron Plant)
Begonia olsoniae
Begonia pustulata **'Argentea'**
Berberis thunbergii **'Silver Beauty'**
  (Japanese Barberry)
Caladium bicolor **'Candidum'** (Angel
  Wings, Elephant's Ears, Heart of Jesus)

Calathea picturata 'Argentea'

Callisia elegans (Striped Inch Plant)

Castanea sativa 'Albomarginata'
 (Spanish Chestnut)

Chlorophytum comosum (Spider Plant)
 cultivars
 'Variegatum'
 'Vittatum'

Coprosma x *kirkii* 'Variegata'

Coprosma repens 'Marble Queen'
 (Mirror Plant, Looking-glass Plant)

Cornus alba 'Elegantissima'
 (Red-barked Dogwood)

Cornus controversa 'Variegata'

Cryptanthus bivittatus

Cryptanthus zonatus 'Zebrinus'
 (Zebra Plant)

Ctenanthe oppenheimiana

Dieffenbachia seguine (Spotted
 Dumb Cane)
 'Amoena'
 'Exotica'
 'Maculata'

Dracaena deremensis **cultivars**
 'Longii'
 'Warneckei'

Dracaena fragrans 'Lindenii'
 (Corn Plant, Happy Plant)

Dracaena surculosa (Gold-dust
 Dracaena, Spotted Dracaena)
 and cultivar
 'Florida Beauty'

Epipremnum pictum 'Argyraeum'
 (Silver Vine)

Epipremnum pinnatum 'Marble Queen'

Euonymus fortunei (Wintercreeper
 Euonymus) **cultivars**
 'Emerald Gaiety'
 'Silver Queen'
 'Variegatus'

Euonymus japonicus 'Albomarginatus'
 (Japanese Spindle Tree)

Euphorbia marginata
 (Snow-on-the-mountains)

Farfugium japonicum 'Argenteum'

x *Fatshedera lizei* 'Variegata'
 (Tree Ivy)

Fatsia japonica (Japanese Aralia,
 Japanese Fatsia) **cultivars**
 'Marginata'
 'Variegata'

Ficus benjamina 'Variegata'
 (Weeping Fig)

Ficus pumila 'Variegata' (Creeping Fig)

Fittonia verschaffeltii var. *argyroneura*
 (Silver Net-leaf)
 'Nana'

Furcraea foetida 'Mediopicta'
 (Green Aloe)

Glyceria maxima 'Variegata'
 (Reed Sweet Grass)

Griselinia littoralis 'Variegata' (Kapuka)

Haworthia attenuata (Zebra Plant)

Hedera colchica 'Dentata Variegata'
 (Persian Ivy)

Helichrysum petiolare 'Variegatum'

Hosta crispula

Hosta fortunei 'Albomarginata'

Hosta undulata var. *undulata* (Wavy-
 leaved Plantain Lily) **and cultivar**

'Albomarginata'
 var. *univittata*

Ilex aquifolium (English Holly)
 cultivars
 'Argentea Marginata'
 'Argentea Marginata Pendula'
 'Ferox Argentea'
 'Handsworth New Silver'
 'Silver Milkmaid'
 'Silver Queen'

Lamium galeobdolon (Yellow Archangel)
 and cultivars
 'Hermann's Pride'
 'Silver Carpet'

Lamium maculatum (Spotted
 Deadnettle)
 'Beacon Silver'
 'White Nancy'

Mentha suaveolens 'Variegata'
 (Apple Mint)

Miscanthus sinensis 'Variegatus'
 (Eulalia)

Monstera deliciosa 'Variegata' (Fruit
 Salad Plant, Mexican Breadfruit)

Myrtus communis 'Variegata'
 (Common Myrtle)

Ophiopogon jaburan 'Vittatus'
 (White Lilyturf)

Oplismenus africanus 'Variegatus'
 (Basket Grass)

Pelargonium 'Fragrans Variegatum'
 (Nutmeg-scented Pelargonium)

Pelargonium graveolens 'Lady Plymouth'

Phalaris arundinacea var. *picta* 'Feesey'
 (Gardeners' Garters)

Pilea cadierei (Aluminium Plant,
 Watermelon Pilea)
 'Minima'

Plectranthus madagascariensis
 'Variegated Mintleaf' (Mintleaf)

Pleioblastus variegatus

Polygonatum multiflorum 'Striatum'

Polygonatum ornatum 'Variegatum'

Pteris cretica 'Albolineata'
 (Cretan Brake Fern)

Pteris ensiformis (Slender Brake
 Fern) **cultivars**
 'Arguta'
 'Victoriae'

Pulmonaria officinalis (Jerusalem
 Cowslip, Common Lungwort)
 and cultivars

Pulmonaria saccharata (Jerusalem Sage)
 and cultivars

Ideal as a lawn specimen for medium-sized gardens, *Acer pseudoplatanus* 'Variegatum' has particularly attractive fresh spring leaves blotched with white and cream.

Quercus cerris 'Argenteovariegata'
  (Turkey Oak)
Rhapis excelsa 'Ayanishiki'
  (Lady Palm, Bamboo Palm)
Sansevieria trifasciata 'Silver Hahnii'
  (Mother-in-law's Tongue)
Serissa foetida 'Variegata'
Thujopsis dolabrata 'Variegata'
  (Hiba Arbor-vitae)
Thymus x citriodorus 'Silver Queen'
  (Lemon-scented Thyme)
Thymus vulgaris 'Silver Posie'
Tradescantia fluminensis
  (Wandering Jew) cultivars
  'Albovittata'
  'Quicksilver'
Tradescantia zanonia 'Mexican Flag'
Ulmus parvifolia 'Frosty' (Chinese Elm)
Yucca aloifolia 'Variegata'
  (Spanish Bayonet)
Yucca elephantipes 'Variegata'
  (Giant Yucca, Spineless Yucca)
Zantedeschia elliottiana
  (Golden Arum Lily)

PINK LEAVES

Acer negundo 'Flamingo'
  (Box Elder Maple)
Acer palmatum (Japanese Maple)
  cultivars
  'Higasayama'
  'Kagiri-nishiki'
Acer pseudoplatanus 'Leopoldii'
  (Sycamore Maple)
Actinidia kolomikta
Berberis thunbergii 'Rose Glow'
  (Japanese Barberry)
Caladium bicolour 'Pink Beauty'
  (Angel Wings, Elephant's Ears,
  Heart of Jesus)
Calathea sanderiana
Cissus discolor
Coprosma repens 'Pink Splendour'
  (Mirror Plant, Looking-glass Plant)
Cordyline australis 'Doucettii'
  (New Zealand Cabbage Tree)
Cordyline fruticosa (Ti Tree) cultivars
  'Amabilis'
  'Baby Ti'
Cornus florida 'Welchii'
  (Flowering Dogwood)
Cryptanthus bivittatus 'Pink Starlight'
Cryptanthus bromelioides 'Tricolor'
  (Rainbow Star)

Dracaena marginata 'Tricolor'
Ficus elastica 'Schryveriana'
  (Rubber Plant)
Heuchera cultivars
  'Rachel'
  'Velvet Night'
Hypoestes phyllostachya (Polka-dot
  Plant, Freckle Face) and cultivar
  'Splash'
Phormium cookianum 'Maori Maiden'
  (Mountain Flax)

ORANGE, RED, PURPLE AND BRONZE LEAVES

Ajuga reptans (Common Bugle)
  and some cultivars
Alocasia cuprea (Giant Caladium)
Begonia 'Cleopatra'
Begonia masoniana
  (Iron Cross Begonia)
Begonia metallica (Metal-leaf Begonia)
Callisia x generalis 'Phasion'
Cordyline fruticosa (Ti Tree) cultivars
  'Bicolor'
  'Firebrand'
Cryptanthus fosterianus
Fittonia verschaffeltii
Graptophyllum pictum 'Purpureum
  Variegata' (Caricature Plant)
Hebe speciosa 'Tricolor'
  (Showy Hebe)
Heuchera micrantha var. *diversifolia*
  'Purple Palace'
Iresine herbstii 'Brilliantissima'
  (Beefsteak Plant)
Oxalis tetraphylla 'Iron Cross'
  (Good Luck Plant, Lucky Clover)
Persicaria virginiana 'Painter's Palette'
Phormium tenax (New Zealand Flax)
  cultivars
  'Bronze Baby'
  'Dazzler'
  'Purpureum'
  'Rainbow'
Pilea involucrata 'Moon Valley'
  (Friendship Plant)
Salvia officinalis 'Purpurascens'
  (Purple-leaved Sage)
Tradescantia zebrina 'Purpusii'
  (Silver Inch Plant)

SHADES OF GREEN

Arum italicum 'Marmoratum'
  (Italian Arum)

When closely massed, *Iresine herbstii* 'Brilliantissima' makes a good edging to taller growing cannas.

Calathea burle-marxii
Calathea lancifolia (Rattlesnake Plant)
Calathea makoyana (Cathedral
  Windows, Peacock Plant)
Calathea veitchiana (Peacock Plant)
Cornus stolonifera 'Sunrise'
  (Red Osier Dogwood)
Ctenanthe burle-marxii
Episcia lilacina
Euonymus fortunei 'Kewensis'
  (Wintercreeper Euonymus)
Ficus aspera 'Parcellii'
Ficus elastica 'Doescheri' (Rubber Plant)
Haworthia cymbiformis
Haworthia reinwardtii
Hosta 'Sum and Substance'
Hosta tokudama 'Aureonebulosa'
Peperomia argyreia (Watermelon
  Peperomia)
Peperomia caperata (Emerald Ripple)
  and cultivars
Stromanthe sanguinea
Syngonium podophyllum (Arrowhead
  Vine, Goosefoot) cultivars
  'Emerald Gem'
  'White Butterfly'
Vriesea hieroglyphica
  (King of Bromeliads)
Vriesea splendens
  (Flaming Sword)

WATERSIDE PLANTS

Whether a formal or natural design, water features bring interest and vitality to the garden. Still pools are peaceful and tranquil, while the sight and sound of water in a stream or fountain is always refreshing. A water feature gives the garden a focus around which to arrange a planting. As many moisture-loving plants are architecturally leafy, waterside plantings are among the most beautiful and interesting for foliage effects. An open sunny position provides the best conditions. Avoid overhead trees and shrubs that may create dark shadows and pollute the water with their leaves.

Plants suitable for edging a water garden range from marginal plants that live in shallow water or boggy soil to those that, while inhabiting permanently moist or wet conditions, do not like their roots submerged. True aquatic plants, such as water lilies, grow in water, either submerged, partially submerged or floating, with roots anchored in soil beneath the water. Except for the nardoos (*Marsilea* species), the Water Lettuce (*Pistia stratiotes*) and the fabulous *Victoria amazonica*, which are all aquatic, the plants listed in the Guide to Waterside Plants are either marginal or moisture loving. Details of their growing preferences can be found under the species entry in the A–Z Directory of Plants.

MARGINAL PLANTS

Plants that will grow in the shallow waters and water-logged conditions around the edge of the water garden are commonly called marginal plants or bog plants. They can add texture and soften the pond edges, and include *Acorus calamus*, *Colocasia esculenta*, Pickerel Weed (*Pontederia cordata*) and various sedges and rushes which actually grow in shallow water. Umbrella Grass (*Cyperus involucratus*) and Arum Lily (*Zantedeschia aethiopica*) seem to grow more happily in water than they do on land. These plants can all be planted in tubs submerged in the water. *Houttuynia cordata*, a pretty but rather invasive groundcover at the water's edge, is best grown in a container where its widely spreading rhizomes can be kept in check.

Gunnera manicata, from Brazil, can withstand occasional flooding and is a magnificent waterside plant whose giant leaves will reflect beautifully in a large pool or lake.

A timber walkway complements this natural wetland that provides the right conditions for a collection of hostas and contrasting linear-foliaged plants such as moisture-loving *Iris* and *Miscanthus*. Set further back are two key waterside plants: *Gunnera manicata* and *Ligularia dentata*. Colour is provided by *Iris*, red primula and a purple-leaved *Alternanthera*.

Carefully groomed pines and shrubs, natural rock, stepping stones and a stone lantern provide the important elements in this Japanese-style water garden.

roots. Hostas also do well in these conditions, and with their impressive range of leaf colour and variegation will provide valuable focal points in dappled shade.

While a number of plants are well adapted to moist conditions, excess water and lack of air mean that the great majority of plants just won't grow. Raising the soil above the water level will allow a wider variety of plants to grow without diminishing the visual contribution of the water's edge and the water itself. Often a small body of water lends itself particularly well to rock gardening, where well-drained pockets of soil can allow for decorative shrubs such as dwarf Japanese maples and the eye-catching phormiums to provide contrasting associations of colour and form.

For a natural look, leave part of the bank clear and encourage drifts of marginal plants such as Umbrella Grass (*Cyperus involucratus*) and *Iris laevigata* 'Variegata' to colonise the water's edge.

This narrow rectangular pool gives a sense of space by reflecting the sky and surrounding plants.

MOISTURE-LOVING PLANTS
Further back from the water's edge, ligularias, rodgersias, darmeras and some ferns flourish in damp soils that contain extra moisture without having water around their

GUIDE TO WATERSIDE PLANTS

MARGINAL PLANTS

Acorus calamus (Sweet Flag)
 'Variegatus'
Acorus gramineus (Japanese Rush)
 'Ogon'
Cyperus albostriatus 'Variegatus'
Cyperus involucratus (Umbrella Sedge)
Cyperus papyrus (Egyptian Papyrus)
Darmera peltata (Umbrella Plant,
 Indian Rhubarb)
Glyceria maxima (Reed Sweet Grass)
 'Variegata'
Gunnera magellanica
Gunnera manicata
Gunnera tinctoria
Houttuynia cordata 'Chameleon'

Lysichiton americanus
 (Yellow Skunk Cabbage)
Lysichiton camtschatcensis
 (White Skunk Cabbage)
Marsilea drummondii
 (Common Nardoo)
Marsilea mutica
Phragmites australis
 (Common Reed)
 'Variegatus'
Pistia stratiotes (Water Lettuce)
Pontederia cordata (Pickerel Weed)
Zantedeschia aethiopica (Arum Lily)
 'Apple Court Babe'
 'Crowborough'
 'Green Goddess'

MOISTURE-LOVING PLANTS

Ajuga pyramidalis (Pyramidal Bugle)
Ajuga reptans (Common Bugle)
 and cultivars
Alocasia brisbanensis
 (Cunjevoi, Spoon Lily)
Alocasia macrorrhiza (Giant Taro)
 'Variegata'
Angelica archangelica (Angelica)
Angiopteris evecta
 (King Fern, Giant Fern)
Arundo donax (Giant Reed)
 'Versicolor'
Blechnum brasiliense
 (Brazilian Tree Fern)
Blechnum cartilagineum (Gristle Fern)

Blechnum chilense

Blechnum gibbum (Dwarf Tree Fern)
  'Silver Lady'

Blechnum nudum (Fishbone Water Fern)

Blechnum penna-marina
  (Alpine Water Fern)

Blechnum spicant
  (Deer Fern, Hard Fern)

Carex elata (Tufted Sedge) **'Aurea'**

Carex hachijoensis **'Evergold'**

Carex morrowii (Japanese Sedge)
  'Fisher'

Carex muskingumensis (Palm Sedge)

Carex siderosticha **'Variegata'**

Colocasia esculenta
  (Taro, Dasheen, Elephant's Ears)
  'Black Magic'
  'Fontanesii'

Cornus stolonifera (Red Osier
  Dogwood) **and cultivars**

Dennstaedtia davallioides
  (Lady Ground Fern)

Doodia aspera (Rasp Fern)

Doodia media (Common Rasp Fern)

Dryopteris affinis (Golden Male Fern,
  Golden Shield Fern)
  'Cristata'

Dryopteris carthusiana
  (Narrow Buckler Fern)

Dryopteris erythrosora
  (Autumn Fern, Japanese Shield Fern)

Dryopteris filix-mas (Male Fern)
  'Grandiceps Wills'

Dryopteris wallichiana
  (Wallich's Wood Fern)

Hosta **species** (most plantain lilies)

Ligularia dentata **'Desdemona'**

Ligularia hodgsonii

Ligularia x *palmatiloba*

Lysimachia nummularia
  (Creeping Jenny, Moneywort)
  'Aurea'

Matteuccia struthiopteris
  (Ostrich Fern, Shuttlecock Fern)

Molineria capitulata (Weevil Lily)

Molinia caerulea subsp. *caerulea*
  (Purple Moor Grass) **and cultivars**

Osmunda regalis (Royal Fern)
  'Cristata'
  'Purpurascens'

Persicaria virginiana
  'Painter's Palette'

Phalaris arundinacea var.
  picta (Gardeners' Garters)
  'Feesey'
  'Luteopicta'

Phormium cookianum
  (Mountain Flax)
  and cultivars

Phormium tenax
  (New Zealand Flax)
  and cultivars

Restio tetraphyllus
  (Tassel Cord Rush)

Rheum palmatum
  (Chinese Rhubarb)
  and cultivars

Rheum officinale

Rodgersia aesculifolia

Rodgersia pinnata 'Superba'

Rodgersia podophylla

Rodgersia sambucifolia

Selaginella martensii

Selaginella pallescens

Zantedeschia elliottiana
  (Golden Arum Lily)

Rodgersia (centre) and *Darmera peltata* (behind)
flourish in damp soils.

PLANTS THAT LIKE A MOIST, WELL-DRAINED SITE

Cyathea australis
  (Rough Tree Fern)

Cyathea cooperi
  (Scaly Tree Fern)

Cyathea dealbata (Silver Fern)

Cyathea medullaris
  (Black Tree Fern)

Cycas circinalis
  (Fern Palm, Queen Sago)

Cycas revoluta (Japanese Sago Palm)

Dicksonia antarctica (Soft Tree Fern)

Ensete ventricosum
  (Abyssinian Banana)

Farfugium japonicum
  'Argenteum'
  'Aureomaculatum'

Lomandra hystrix

Lomandra longifolia
  (Spiny-headed Mat Rush)

Melianthus major (Honey Flower,
  Touch-me-not Plant, Honey Bush)

Miscanthus sinensis (Eulalia)
  and cultivars

Monstera deliciosa (Fruit Salad Plant,
  Mexican Breadfruit)
  'Variegata'

Nephrolepis cordifolia (Fishbone Fern,
  Southern Sword Fern)
  'Plumosa'

Nephrolepis exaltata (Sword Fern)
  'Bostoniensis'
  'Hillii'
  'Rooseveltii'

Phyllostachys nigra (Black Bamboo)
  var. *henonis*

Phyllostachys viridiglaucescens

Pleioblastus auricomus (Kamuro-zasu)

Pleioblastus pygmaeus (Pygmy Bamboo)
  var. *distichus*

Spathiphyllum 'Mauna Loa' (Peace Lily)

Spathiphyllum 'Sensation'

Spathiphyllum wallisii

Xanthosoma violaceum (Blue Taro)

WINTER GARDENS

In the cold of mid-winter deciduous trees and shrubs will have no leaves, just their older stems and roots clothed in bark. Conifers and evergreens will still be leafy, but bulbs and corms will have retreated underground. Only a few species will be in flower. This all sounds rather dull, but while plants are resting and renewing their strength the season has its own special charm.

When their skeletal framework is entirely revealed, deciduous trees vary the skyline and are a great source of interest during these months. Conifers become central features. Sculptural elements such as hedges, clipped hollies and pyramids or domes of box take on increased importance. Evergreen shrubs accentuate points in the design and hold the fort in beds and borders while the perennials have retired. Some shrubs, such as the dogwoods (*Cornus* species), display brightly coloured winter stems. In the case of *Cornus alba* 'Sibirica', the stems can be blazing red, while those of *C. stolonifera* 'Flaviramea' are bright lemon green. To encourage the growth of new stems, which have the best colour, cut the older stems back to the base of the plant in early spring.

Mist, frost and snow can actually accentuate the sculptural element of a garden. Without flowers to consider, plants chosen for their foliage and form are especially important for winter effects. If you don't want to be outdoors during winter, locate your special winter-interest garden where it can be seen most comfortably from inside the house.

The intricate patterns of bare branches and trunks in this glade of Silver Birch (*Betula pendula*) glow in the winter light and form attractive tracery against the sky.

Cornus alba 'Sibirica' has glistening bright red winter shoots.

A clipped English Holly provides strong sculptural form throughout the year.

GUIDE TO PLANTS FOR WINTER GARDENS

EVERGREEN
Abies **species** (Firs)
Buxus microphylla (Japanese Box)
  and cultivars
Buxus sempervirens
  (European Box, Common Box)
  and cultivars
Cedrus atlantica (Atlas Cedar)
Cedrus deodara (Deodar Cedar)
  and cultivars
Cedrus libani (Cedar of Lebanon)
Chamaecyparis lawsoniana
  (Lawson Cypress) **and cultivars**
Chamaecyparis obtusa
  (Hinoki Cypress) **and cultivars**
Chamaecyparis pisifera
  (Sawara Cypress) **and cultivars**
Cryptomeria japonica (Japanese Cedar)
  and cultivars
x *Cupressocyparis leylandii*
  (Leyland Cypress) **and cultivars**
Cupressus arizonica var. *glabra*
  (Smooth Arizona Cypress)

Cupressus cashmeriana
  (Bhutan Cypress, Kashmir Cypress)
Cupressus goveniana var. *pygmaea*
  (Gowan Cypress)
Cupressus lusitanica
  (Cedar of Goa, Mexican Cypress)
  'Glauca Pendula'
Cupressus macrocarpa (Monterey
  Cypress) **and cultivars**
Cupressus sempervirens (Italian
  Cypress, Mediterranean Cypress)
  and cultivars
Ilex x *altaclerensis* **and cultivars**
Ilex aquifolium (English Holly)
  and cultivars
Ilex cornuta (Chinese Holly,
  Horned Holly)
Ilex crenata (Japanese Holly)
  and cultivars
Ilex x *meserveae* (Blue Holly)
  and cultivars
Juniperus chinensis (Chinese Juniper)
  and cultivars

Juniperus communis (Common
  Juniper) **and cultivars**
Juniperus scopulorum
  (Rocky Mountain Juniper)
Juniperus squamata
  (Himalayan Juniper)
Juniperus virginiana
  (Eastern Red Cedar, Pencil cedar)
Myrtus communis (Common Myrtle)
Picea abies (Norway Spruce,
  Common Spruce) **and cultivars**
Picea breweriana
  (Brewer's Weeping Spruce)
Picea glauca (White Spruce)
  var. *albertiana* 'Conica'
Picea omorika (Serbian Spruce)
Picea pungens (Colorado Spruce)
  and cultivars
Picea smithiana (Morinda Spruce,
  West Himalayan Spruce)
Pinus aristata (Bristlecone Pine)
Pinus cembra (Arolla Pine, Swiss Pine)
Pinus densiflora (Japanese Red Pine)

Ilex aquifolium 'Aurea Marginata' has the bonus of winter berries.

The colourful bark of the Snow Gum (*Eucalyptus pauciflora* subsp. *niphophila*).

Pinus halepensis (Aleppo Pine)
Pinus mugo (Swiss Mountain Pine)
  and cultivars
Pinus nigra (Austrian Pine, Black Pine)
  subsp. *laricio*
Pinus parviflora (Japanese White Pine)
  and cultivars
Pinus patula (Mexican Weeping Pine)
Pinus strobus (Eastern White Pine,
  Weymouth Pine)
  'Fastigiata'
  'Radiata'
Pinus sylvestris **'Beuvronensis'**
Pinus thunbergii (Japanese Black Pine)
Pinus wallichiana (Bhutan Pine,
  Blue Pine)
Sequoia sempervirens (California
  Redwood, Coast Redwood)
  and cultivars
Taxus baccata (Yew) **and cultivars**
Taxus cuspidata (Japanese Yew)
  and cultivars
Thuja occidentalis (White Cedar)
  and cultivars
Thujopsis dolabrata (Hiba Arbor-vitae)
Tsuga canadensis (Eastern Hemlock,
  Canadian Hemlock)
  'Bennett'
  'Jeddeloh'
  'Pendula'
Tsuga heterophylla (Western Hemlock)

DECIDUOUS

Betula nigra (River Birch)

Betula papyrifera (Paper
  Birch, Canoe Birch)
Betula pendula (Silver
  Birch) **and cultivars**
Betula utilis (Himalayan
  Birch) var. *jacquemontii*
Cornus alba (Red-barked
  Dogwood) **and cultivars**
Cornus stolonifera (Red Osier
  Dogwood) **and cultivars**
Fagus sylvatica (Common Beech,
  European Beech) **and cultivars**
Hamamelis x *intermedia*
  and cultivars
Hamamelis mollis (Chinese
  Witch Hazel) **and cultivars**
Hamamelis virginiana
  (Virginian Witch Hazel)
Quercus alba (American White Oak)
Quercus cerris (Turkey Oak)
Quercus coccinea (Scarlet Oak)
Quercus palustris (Pin Oak)
Quercus robur (English Oak)
Quercus rubra (Red Oak)
Tilia cordata (Small-leaved Lime)
Tilia x *europaea* (Common Lime)
Tilia tomentosa (Silver Linden,
  Silver Lime)
Ulmus americana (American Elm,
  White Elm) **'Delaware'**
Ulmus x *hollandica* (Dutch Elm)
  'Jacqueline Hillier'
Ulmus minor (European Field Elm)
Ulmus parvifolia (Chinese Elm)

ADDITIONAL WINTER FEATURES

Acer griseum (Paperbark Maple)
  Peeling orange–brown bark
Acer palmatum var. *dissectum*
  Mound-forming with fine tracery
  of weeping branches
Cornus alba 'Sibirica' Bright red
  winter shoots
Cornus controversa Bare branches
  in horizontal tiered pattern
Cornus stolonifera 'Flaviramea'
  Bright yellow-green winter shoots
Eucalyptus pauciflora subsp. *niphophila*
  Striking orange, red, white and olive
  green bark
Hamamelis species (Witch Hazel)
  Fragrant spider-shaped flowers
  on bare branches
Ilex species (Holly) Colourful
  winter berries
Picea abies (Norway Spruce)
  Traditional Christmas-tree
  appearance
Picea glauca var. *albertiana* 'Conica'
  One of the best dwarf conifers,
  with a perfect natural cone-shape
Taxus baccata (Yew) Long lived;
  excellent for formal planting and
  often used for topiary

CONIFERS

Conifers are an ancient group of cone-bearing plants which have existed on earth for over 300 million years—they evolved long before the flowering plants. They still grow in most parts of the world, particularly in cold northern regions. Often referred to as softwoods, they supply the bulk of the world's timber.

They vary in size and shape from small prostrate shrubs suitable for tubs, rock gardens or small courtyards to magnificent specimens 30m/100ft or more tall. While varying widely in leaf colour, most are evergreen, long lived, grow to a definite shape and almost never need pruning. Many are widely used for large hedges and windbreaks, as ornamental specimens and along avenues. In Japanese garden design, conifers are often chosen where minimal change is desirable. They are ideal for creating bonsai.

SELECTING PLANTS

The individuality of form, texture and colour of the conifers chosen can determine the essential character of the garden. Take care to select plants which will be of suitable shape and size when fully mature. Consider the permanent dense shade they may create. A large, bulky shrub or tree could cast gloomy shadows in a small garden.

Cedars are beautiful trees for big gardens. With their graceful spreading branches and long lives, they are aristocrats among the larger conifers and add a special touch of grandeur to any landscape. They should only be planted in places where they will not be crowded and can fully display their individuality—as lawn specimens or street trees, in parks or reserves. Golden Deodar, *Cedrus deodara* 'Aurea', which is very slow growing to 5m/17ft and has

Most conifers are very hardy and long lived. Here they provide colour throughout the year and with their handsome and varied shapes create a strong impact and permanence in this spacious cool climate garden.

Cupressus macrocarpa 'Aurea saligna' is superb for a large garden.

When choosing a conifer for a small space or a particular purpose, check the label to make sure that you are getting the right cultivar, one that will not outgrow its allotted space. For example, the slow-growing White Spruce (*Picea glauca*) grows to 24m/80ft and makes a beautiful feature in a large garden, while *P. glauca* var. *albertiana* 'Conica' remains a compact dark green pyramid 1m/3ft high for many years, eventually reaching 3m/10ft with great age, and is best suited to small gardens. Other delightful spruces for small areas or rock gardens include *P. pungens* 'Montgomery', to 1.5m/5ft tall with outstanding glaucous grey–blue foliage, and *P. abies* 'Maxwellii', which develops a broad cone shape to about 1m/3ft high and 1.5m/5ft across.

Spreading conifers, such as *Juniperus conferta* and its cultivars, with their attractive blue–green foliage and prostrate creeping habit, are good spillover plants for rockeries and banks and make first-rate groundcovers in coastal gardens. The tough, spreading *Juniperus horizontalis* and its cultivars also make excellent groundcover plants, eventually forming carpets to 2m/7ft across, making it impossible for weeds to grow.

Juniperus x *pfitzeriana* forms a wide-spreading flat-topped bush to 1.2m/4ft high and to 3m/10ft across and has beautiful grey–green tiered foliage with feathery drooping tips, making a highly decorative large-scale groundcover or low screen.

CULTIVATION

As a group, conifers are slow-growers but respond to attention with watering, mulching and fertilising. As with most other trees and shrubs, slow-release fertilisers are most suitable. As a group they are best suited to temperate and cold climates, where they are valuable for winter effect. Most conifers dislike heavy soil and exposure to drying winds. Deeply dug, free-draining soil and a mulch

pendent branches tipped with gold, is good for home gardens.

Other eye-catching specimens at their best in large gardens include some cypresses, particularly the Weeping Golden Cypress (*Cupressus macrocarpa* 'Aurea Saligna'), and the tall and elegant Italian Cypress (*Cupressus sempervirens*), a feature of Mediterranean gardens. The hybrid x *Cupressocyparis leylandii* and its cultivars are popular, fast-growing, tapering trees often used as tall windbreaks and screens.

The closely related *Chamaecyparis* is a small genus of mostly medium-sized conifers with variously coloured foliage useful as specimen trees and for hedging. They have given rise to a large number of cultivars, including a fantastic selection of highly decorative dwarf conifers particularly suited to the small garden, courtyard or containers. Colours range from rich gold through brilliant greens to pale blues and silvers, and shapes include buns, cushions, spires, domes, pyramids and columns.

The unusual form of the grafted *Cupressus macrocarpa* 'Greenstead Magnificent' used as a low lawn specimen.

of peat moss or other organic matter to keep the roots cool through hot periods and protected in winter will keep them happy.

Natural branch formation is preferable to a trimmed appearance. Pruning is not usually necessary apart from obvious shaping or the removal of dead wood. If necessary, trim just before new growth begins in early spring. Prune restricted shapes for hedges or topiary work in the growing season. Careful tip pruning of some dwarf cultivars while they are young will keep them dense and compact.

GUIDE TO CONIFERS

TREES

Abies balsamea (Balsam Fir)
Abies concolor (White Fir) **'Argentea'**
Abies grandis (Giant Fir)
Abies lasiocarpa var. *arizonica* (Corkbark Fir) **'Compacta'**
Abies pinsapo (Spanish Fir) **'Glauca'**
Cedrus atlantica (Atlas Cedar)
 'Aurea'
 'Glauca'
 'Glauca Pendula'
Cedrus deodara (Deodar Cedar) **'Aurea'**
Cedrus libani (Cedar of Lebanon)
 subsp. *stenocoma*
Chamaecyparis lawsoniana (Lawson Cypress)
 'Alumii'
 'Erecta'
 'Fletcheri'
 'Lane'
 'Lutea'
 'Pembury Blue'
 'Silver Queen'
 'Winston Churchill'
 'Wisselii'
Chamaecyparis obtusa (Hinoki Cypress)
 'Albospica'
 'Crippsii'
 'Tetragona Aurea'
Chamaecyparis pisifera (Sawara Cypress)
 'Boulevard'
 'Filifera'
 'Filifera Aurea'
 'Squarrosa'
Cryptomeria japonica (Japanese Cedar)
 'Elegans'
x *Cupressocyparis leylandii* (Leyland Cypress)
 'Castlewellan'
 'Haggerston Grey'
 'Leighton Green'
 'Naylor's Blue'

Cupressus arizonica var. *glabra* (Smooth Arizona Cypress)
Cupressus cashmeriana (Bhutan Cypress, Kashmir Cypress)
Cupressus goveniana var. *pygmaea* (Gowan Cypress)
Cupressus lusitanica (Cedar of Goa, Mexican Cypress)
 'Glauca Pendula'
Cupressus macrocarpa (Monterey Cypress)
 'Aurea Saligna'
 'Brunniana Aurea'
Cupressus sempervirens (Italian Cypress, Mediterranean Cypress)
 'Stricta'
 'Swane's Golden'
Dacrydium cupressinum (Rimu)
Juniperus chinensis (Chinese Juniper)
 'Aurea'
 'Spartan'
Juniperus communis (Common Juniper)
 'Suecica'
Juniperus scopulorum (Rocky Mountain Juniper)
 'Blue Heaven'
 'Sky Rocket'
Juniperus squamata (Himalayan Juniper)
Juniperus virginiana (Eastern Red Cedar, Pencil Cedar)
Larix decidua (European Larch)
Larix kaempferi (Japanese Larch)
Picea abies (Norway Spruce, Common Spruce)
Picea breweriana (Brewer's Weeping Spruce)
Picea glauca (White Spruce)
Picea omorika (Serbian Spruce)
Picea pungens (Colorado Spruce)
 and cultivar 'Glauca'
Picea smithiana (Morinda Spruce, West Himalayan Spruce)
Pinus aristata (Bristlecone Pine)
Pinus cembra (Arolla Pine, Swiss Pine)

Pinus densiflora (Japanese Red Pine)
Pinus halepensis (Aleppo Pine)
Pinus nigra (Austrian Pine, Black Pine)
 subsp. *laricio*
Pinus parviflora (Japanese White Pine)
Pinus patula (Mexican Weeping Pine)
Pinus strobus (Eastern White Pine, Weymouth Pine)
 'Fastigiata'
Pinus sylvestris
Pinus thunbergii (Japanese Black Pine)
Pinus wallichiana (Bhutan Pine, Blue Pine)
Pseudolarix amabilis (Golden Larch)
Pseudotsuga menziesii (Douglas Fir) var. *glauca* (Blue Douglas Fir)
Sequoia sempervirens (California Redwood, Coast Redwood)
Taxodium distichum (Swamp Cypress) var. *imbricarium* 'Nutans'
Taxus baccata (Yew)
 'Dovastonii Aurea'
 'Fastigiata'
 'Fastigiata Aurea'
 'Fastigiata Aureomarginata'
Taxus cuspidata (Japanese Yew)
Thuja occidentalis (White Cedar)
 and cultivar
 'Filiformis'
Thujopsis dolabrata (Hiba Arbor-vitae)
 'Variegata'
Tsuga canadensis (Eastern Hemlock, Canadian Hemlock)
Tsuga heterophylla (Western Hemlock)

SHRUBS

Cedrus libani 'Sargentii' (Cedar of Lebanon)
Chamaecyparis lawsoniana (Lawson Cypress) **cultivars**
 'Aurea Densa'
 'Ellwoodii'
 'Erecta Aurea'
 'Stewartii'

Chamaecyparis obtusa (Hinoki Cypress) **cultivars**
'Fernspray Gold'
'Kosteri'
'Templehof'
Chamaecyparis pisifera (Sawara Cypress) **cultivars**
'Plumosa'
'Plumosa Aurea'
Cryptomeria japonica (Japanese Cedar) **cultivars**
'Bandai-sugi'
'Cristata'
'Globosa Nana'
'Spiralis'
Cupressus macrocarpa (Monterey Cypress)
'Goldcrest'
Juniperus chinensis (Chinese Juniper) **cultivars**
'Blaauw'
'Blue Alps'
'Kaizuka'
'Kuriwao Gold'
'Obelisk'
'Pyramidalis'
'Variegata'
Juniperus communis (Common Juniper) **cultivars**
'Gold Cone'
'Hibernica'
Juniperus sabina (Savin)
var. *tamariscifolia*
Juniperus scopulorum (Rocky Mountain Juniper) **cultivars**
'Blue Heaven'
'Grey Gleam'
Juniperus squamata **'Meyeri'** (Himalayan Juniper)
Juniperus virginiana (Eastern Red Cedar, Pencil Cedar) **cultivars**
'Hetzii'
'Sulphur Spray'
Picea abies (Norway Spruce, Common Spruce) **cultivars**
'Acrocona'
'Clanbrassiliana'
'Nidiformis'
Picea glauca var. *albertiana* **'Conica'** (White Spruce)
Pinus mugo **'Gnom'** (Swiss Mountain Pine)
Pinus sylvestris
'Beuvronensis'

Sequoia sempervirens 'Pendula' (California Redwood, Coast Redwood)
Taxus baccata (Yew) **cultivars**
'Aurea'
'Semperaurea'
'Standishii'
Taxus cuspidata (Japanese Yew) **cultivars**
'Densa'
'Nana'
Thuja occidentalis (White Cedar) **cultivars**
'Danica'
'Globosa'
'Holmstrup'
'Rheingold'
'Smaragd'
Tsuga canadensis (Eastern Hemlock, Canadian Hemlock) **cultivars**
'Jeddeloh'
'Pendula'

DWARF FORMS

Abies balsamea (Balsam Fir) **cultivars**
'Hudsonia'
'Nana'
Abies concolor **'Compacta'** (White Fir)
Abies lasiocarpa var. *arizonica* **'Roger Watson'** (Corkbark Fir)
Cedrus libani **'Nana'** (Cedar of Lebanon)
Chamaecyparis lawsoniana (Lawson Cypress) **cultivars**
'Blue Jacket'
'Green Globe'
'Minima Aurea'
Chamaecyparis obtusa (Hinoki Cypress) **cultivars**
'Flabelliformis'
'Minima'
'Nana'
'Nana Aurea'
'Nana Gracilis'
'Sanderi'
'Templehof'
Chamaecyparis pisifera (Sawara Cypress) **cultivars**
'Plumosa Compressa'
'Snow'

Cryptomeria japonica **'Pygmaea'** (Japanese Cedar)
Juniperus communis (Common Juniper) **cultivars**
'Compressa'
'Depressa Aurea'
Larix decidua **'Corley'** (European Larch)
Picea abies (Norway Spruce, Common Spruce) **cultivars**
'Gregoryana'
'Little Gem'
'Maxwellii'
Picea pungens (Colorado Spruce) **cultivars**
'Globosa'
'Montgomery'
Pinus densiflora **'Alice Verkade'** (Japanese Red Pine)
Pinus mugo (Swiss Mountain Pine) **cultivars**
'Amber Gold'
'Mops'
var. *pumilo*
Pinus parviflora **'Adcock's Dwarf'** (Japanese White Pine)
Pinus strobus **'Radiata'** (Eastern White Pine, Weymouth Pine)

A pair of sentinel-like *Cupressus sempervirens* 'Stricta' clearly define this front entrance.

Two majestic lawn specimens, *Cedrus deodara* (left) and *Picea pungens* 'Glauca'.

Juniperus conferta spreads its prickly bluish green foliage over rocks.

Pinus thunbergii **'Sayonara'** (Japanese Black Pine)

Sequoia sempervirens **'Adpressa'** (California Redwood, Coast Redwood)

Thuja occidentalis (White Cedar) **cultivars**
  'Golden Globe'
  'Hetz Midget'

Thujopsis dolabrata **'Nana'** (Hiba Arbor-vitae)

Tsuga canadensis **'Bennett'** (Eastern Hemlock, Canadian Hemlock)

GROUNDCOVERS

Cupressus macrocarpa **'Greenstead Magnificent'** (Monterey Cypress)

Juniperus chinensis (Chinese Juniper) **cultivars**
  'Expansa Aureospicata'
  'Expansa Variegata'
  'San Jose'

Juniperus communis (Common Juniper) **cultivars**
  'Hornibrookii'
  'Repanda'

Juniperus conferta (Shore Juniper)
  'Blue Pacific'
  'Emerald Sea'

Juniperus horizontalis (Creeping Juniper)
  'Bar Harbor'
  'Blue Chip'
  'Douglasii'
  'Emerald Spreader'
  'Glauca'
  'Grey Pearl'
  'Hughes'
  'Plumosa'
  'Wiltonii'

Juniperus x *pfitzeriana*
  'Armstrongii'
  'Aurea'
  'Glauca'

  'Pfitzeriana'

Juniperus procumbens (Creeping Juniper, Bonin Island Juniper)
  'Nana'

Juniperus sabina **'Blaue Donau'** (Savin)

Juniperus squamata (Himalayan Juniper)
  'Blue Carpet'
  'Blue Star'

Microbiota decussata (Russian Arbor-vitae)

Picea abies **'Reflexa'** (Norway Spruce, Common Spruce)

Picea pungens **'Koster Prostrate'** (Colorado Spruce)

Sequoia sempervirens **'Prostrata'** (California Redwood, Coast Redwood)

Taxus baccata (Yew) **cultivars**
  'Repandens'
  'Repens Aurea'

GRASSES AND THEIR RELATIVES

GRASSES AND GRASS-LIKE PLANTS

Natural-looking, but rather glamorous in their own way, ornamental grasses belong to the same family as lawn and pasture and cereal grasses, but in most cases they form graceful clumps of relatively long, finely textured leaves. Some are used as specimens for highlighting or creating accent points near pools, on patios and in courtyards. Others, such as the smaller tufted grasses, are planted in sparse, stylised gardens with pebbles and rocks. When used to edge a walk these provide an interesting low-maintenance groundcover.

Eulalia (*Miscanthus sinensis*) and its cultivars are among the most spectacular and best known of the taller grasses. They are all striking plants with long, narrow, arching leaves forming large solid clumps and bearing tall feathery flowers in late summer. As autumn arrives the leaves take on a honey brown glow. 'Variegatus' has creamy white longitudinal stripes and 'Zebrinus' has bright green leaves, striped horizontally in yellow—both are outstanding for waterside planting and for impact in a mixed border. Cut back these cold-hardy grasses in late winter or early spring to make way for attractive new growth. In warm frost-free locations the gracefully arching Lemon Grass (*Cymbopogon citratus*) remains handsome all year and is there for the picking. You can finely chop the fleshy white bases for use in Southeast Asian recipes, and the green leaves for tea.

Many larger feather grasses (*Stipa* species) form neat tussocks and mix perfectly with other grasses. Mexican Feather Grass (*S. tenuissima*) has very slender leaves and

Large pavers interspersed with dwarf Mondo Grass form a defining, low-maintenance groundcover. The same variety is repeated inside the central circular design of neatly clipped box domes. Larger clumps of Mondo Grass are used to edge the outer curved garden.

Collection of grasses with a graceful clump of Black Bamboo (*Phyllostachys nigra*) in the background.

BAMBOOS

With their graceful habit, smooth elegant culms (stems), airy delicate foliage and, not least, the restful rustling sounds they make, bamboos add a touch of style to any garden. They are superb accent plants and cast striking shadows and reflections when sited beside walls and pools.

Bamboos have earned themselves a bad reputation because the few truly invasive species which were commonly used for many years can cause havoc to gardens and paths if left unchecked. The most important consideration when choosing a bamboo is whether it has clump-forming or spreading rhizomes, for it is from the rhizomes that the shoots arise. The spread of most species, however, is relatively easily controlled by cutting unwanted new shoots at or below ground level as they emerge, which is usually for just a few weeks in spring. The rampant, spreading bamboos can be contained by a substantial barrier, such as a sheet of metal, buried around the plant to reduce the root-run. Often a deeper than normal concrete or paved edging will work for all but the most invasive. Some of the spreading species stay in clumps for a few years when grown in cold climates or under unfavourable conditions.

Attractive clumps of a small variegated bamboo *Pleioblastus auricomus* enjoy the moist conditions and shelter of this natural rock feature.

bears shimmering masses of soft silky flowerheads that sway in the lightest breeze. It looks good featured in groups in a large rockery or in a late flower border.

The lower tufted or mounded grasses such as Blue Fescue (*Festuca glauca*) make outstanding edging or rockery plants. Ideal for Japanese or pebble gardens, this grass and its cultivars provide refreshing contrast in texture and colour. It remains neatly in place, so that clumps can be grown in a geometrical pattern for a formal garden design.

Despite the name, Mondo Grass (*Ophiopogon japonicus*) is not a grass at all, but belongs to the same family as Lily-of-the-valley. Neat, compact and extremely adaptable, it is a first-class tuberous-rooted perennial with curved dark green leaves. It makes a valuable contribution to Japanese gardens, as an edging or border definer, and as a groundcover in shady areas where few other grassy plants will grow.

For colour contrast in cool climate gardens, borders and courtyards, use the bright yellow *Hakonechloa macra* 'Aureola' for lightening a semi-shaded spot. Some New Zealand sedges, such as *Carex buchananii* and *C. comans*, have beautiful rusty gold and reddish brown grass-like leaves that retain their warm autumn shades all year.

Some ornamental grasses are self-seeding and have considerable weed potential, so pick mature seed heads to confine plants.

Bamboos are available in every size and there are species to suit all gardens. Tall bamboos make effective screens and provide shelter for more tender plants such as ferns and palms. One of the most widely used taller bamboos is the Golden Bamboo (*Phyllostachys aurea*). This giant grass has sturdy vertical canes and can reach 5m/17ft in temperate gardens, much more in the tropics. It is extremely cold tolerant; so too is the stunning Black Bamboo (*P. nigra*), which grows to 4m/13ft. Its stems are green at first, become speckled, then turn black. When planted in groves, both create an oriental atmosphere and look particularly good associated with water. Protect young plants from strong winds. They do run, so curtail their spread outside their designated area.

Bambusa species don't run, but form attractive low-maintenance clumps. In frost-free climates *B. multiplex* is useful as a hedge or windbreak; its cultivar 'Alphonse Karr' has golden culms striped with green and is an outstanding specimen that suits many garden styles. One of the more cold-tolerant *Bambusa* species, the Buddha's Belly Bamboo, *B. ventricosa*, is grown for its interesting swollen internodes. The bulges are more noticeable when the plant is kept on the dry side in poor soil; to help achieve this, it is often confined to pots.

Smaller bamboos less than 75cm/30in tall and suitable as groundcovers and low hedges, or for small gardens and containers, include the leafy green *Pleioblastus pygmaeus* var. *distichus* and *P. variegates*, with attractive white-striped leaves. They are both frost hardy and enjoy moist conditions, making them particularly useful for preventing soil erosion along stream banks. They can become moderately invasive and in smaller areas are best restrained.

GUIDE TO GRASSES AND THEIR RELATIVES

Acorus calamus (Sweet Flag)
 'Variegatus'
Acorus gramineus (Japanese Rush)
 'Ogon'
Arundo donax (Giant Reed)
 'Versicolor'
Carex albula
Carex buchananii (Leatherleaf Sedge)
Carex comans
 (New Zealand Hair Sedge)
Carex elata (Tufted Sedge) 'Aurea'
Carex flagellifera (Weeping Brown
 New Zealand Sedge)
Carex hachijoensis 'Evergold'
Carex morrowii (Japanese Sedge)
 'Fisher'
Carex muskingumensis (Palm Sedge)
Carex siderosticha 'Variegata'
Cymbopogon citratus (Lemon Grass)
Cyperus albostriatus
 'Variegatus'
Cyperus involucratus (Umbrella Sedge)
Cyperus papyrus (Egyptian Papyrus)
Festuca amethystina
 (Large Blue Fescue, Tufted Fescue)
 'Bronzeglanz'
Festuca eskia (Beargrass, Bearskin Grass)
Festuca glauca (Blue Fescue,
 Grey Fescue) **and cultivars**
Glyceria maxima (Reed Sweet Grass)
 'Variegata'
Hakonechloa macra 'Aureola'
 (Golden Variegated Hakonechloa)

Imperata cylindrica 'Rubra'
 (Japanese Blood Grass)
Lomandra hystrix
Lomandra longifolia
 (Spiny-headed Mat Rush)
Miscanthus sinensis (Eulalia)
 and cultivars
Molinia caerulea **subsp.** *caerulea*
 (Purple Moor Grass) **and cultivars**
Ophiopogon jaburan (White Lilyturf)
 'Vittatus'
Ophiopogon japonicus (Mondo Grass)
 'Kyoto Dwarf'
Ophiopogon planiscapus
 'Nigrescens'
Oplismenus africanus (Basket Grass)
 'Variegatus'
Phalaris arundinacea **var.** *picta*
 (Gardeners' Garters)
 'Feesey'
 'Luteopicta'
Phragmites australis (Common Reed)
 'Variegatus'
Poa labillardieri
 (Common Tussock Grass)
Restio tetraphyllus (Tassel Cord Rush)
Stenotaphrum secundatum (Buffalo Grass)
 'Variegatum'
Stipa arundinacea
 (Pheasant's Tail Grass)
Stipa gigantea (Giant Feather Grass)
Stipa tenuissima
 (Mexican Feather Grass)

GUIDE TO BAMBOOS

Bambusa multiplex (Hedge Bamboo)
 'Alphonse Karr'
 'Riviereorum'
Bambusa ventricosa
 (Buddha's Belly Bamboo)
Bambusa vulgaris
 (Common Bamboo)
 'Vittata'
 'Wamin'
Chusquea culeou
Fargesia murieliae (Umbrella Bamboo)
Fargesia nitida (Fountain Bamboo)
Phyllostachys aurea (Fishbone
 Bamboo, Golden Bamboo)
 'Flavescens Inversa'
Phyllostachys aureosulcata
 (Yellow-groove Bamboo)
 var. *aureocaulis*
Phyllostachys bambusoides
 (Madake, Giant Timber Bamboo)
 'Allgold'
 'Castillonis'
Phyllostachys nigra
 (Black Bamboo)
 var. *henonis*
Phyllostachys viridiglaucescens
Pleioblastus auricomus
 (Kamuro-zasu)
Pleioblastus pygmaeus
 (Pygmy Bamboo)
 var. *distichus*
Pleioblastus variegatus
Pseudosasa japonica (Arrow Bamboo)

FERNS

With their beautiful lacy fronds in many shades of green, ferns add new shape, foliage contrast and texture to the garden. Whether grown in containers in a small court-yard, used to edge a woodland area or steps, or massed beside a water feature, they are among the best foliage plants for softening the lines of hard landscaping, creating a cool atmosphere or enhancing a tropical effect.

Varying in size from robust varieties of tree fern to tiny moss-like specimens, ferns are found throughout temperate and tropical areas of the world at all altitudes. Some inhabit sunny and exposed places, but the majority grow in moist and lightly shaded environments. They are perennials, almost always with some kind of rootstock or rhizome, and have relatively large, usually compound leaves frequently called fronds. Ferns do not produce seeds; instead they bear spores in brownish spore pads called sori which form on the undersides of the mature fertile fronds.

Although ferns are often grown in ferneries and as indoor plants, many species will grow in the open garden under the right conditions. Most ferns dislike deep shade and do best in filtered sun. Morning sun is often quite acceptable. Lightly canopied overhead trees, the protection of a gully, cool house walls, fences and the foliage of other plants all assist in the growing of ferns outdoors. The edge of a water garden with effective cover can provide an excellent environment. They can also be used in a partially shaded border as a foliage contrast for other moisture-loving plants, such as hostas. Hardy ferns, such as species of *Matteuccia* and *Dryopteris*, are especially effective in the cool dappled shade of a woodland edge. A bed of ferns of varying heights and complementary foliage patterns could transform a narrow passage down the side of a house.

Tree ferns provide beautiful lacy umbrellas that can be both softening and dramatic. They make excellent architectural subjects and can be used singly as a feature in a small garden or courtyard. Massed ferns give the garden a shady forest look and provide an ideal canopy under which smaller ferns will flourish. Most tree ferns, however, need some overhead protection and shelter from drying winds.

Bird's Nest Fern (*Asplenium australasicum*), with its broad undivided fronds emerging from a central point, can also be

A colony of Bird's Nest Ferns and a bromeliad, *Vriesea hieroglyphica*, featured in a classical urn, all thrive beneath shady trees.

Graceful tree ferns and a Bird's Nest Fern in a raised bed.

should not be exposed to direct sunlight or draught, so position them away from windows and doors.

MAINTENANCE

Mulch outdoor fern gardens well with compost or leaf mould. Few ferns thrive in poorly drained soil, although some do adapt. A gritty soil reinforced with leaf compost suits most.

Ferns require a minimum of fertiliser; in fact, overfeeding can kill them. Feed with a one-third strength liquid fertiliser about once a month during times of active growth.

Nephrolepis exaltata 'Bostoniensis' in hanging baskets.

used as a feature. It looks particularly impressive in groups of varying heights, as a groundcover or set among rocks.

Ferns make excellent pot or basket plants. It is possible to have a container fernery on a protected patio or in a garden room if shade and regular water are provided, especially in summer. Keep the soil damp, but not overwet—they may need more frequent watering than most plants. Good basket ferns include the giant Boston Fern (*Nephrolepis exaltata* 'Bostoniensis'), the maidenhairs and the hare's foot ferns (*Davallia* species). Indoors, they

GUIDE TO FERNS

TALL

Angiopteris evecta
  (King Fern, Giant Fern)
Cyathea australis (Rough Tree Fern)
Cyathea cooperi (Scaly Tree Fern)
Cyathea dealbata (Silver Fern)
Cyathea medullaris (Black Tree Fern)

Dicksonia antarctica (Soft Tree Fern)
Dicksonia fibrosa (Wheki-Ponga)
Dicksonia squarrosa (Wheki)

SMALL TO MEDIUM
Adiantum aleuticum
  (Aleutian Maidenhair)

Adiantum capillus-veneris
  (Venus-hair Fern)
Adiantum formosum
  (Giant Maidenhair)
Adiantum pedatum
  (American Maidenhair)
  'Imbricatum'

Adiantum venustum
  (Himalayan Maidenhair Fern)
Asplenium australasicum
  (Bird's Nest Fern)
Asplenium flabellifolium
  (Necklace Fern)
Asplenium scolopendrium subsp.
  scolopendrium (Hart's Tongue Fern)
  'Crispum'
  'Ramocristatum'
Asplenium trichomanes
  (Maidenhair Spleenwort)
Athyrium felix-femina (Lady Fern)
  'Frizelliae'
  'Minutissimum'
Athyrium niponicum
  (Japanese Painted Fern)
  'Pictum'
Blechnum brasiliense
  (Brazilian Tree Fern)
Blechnum cartilagineum (Gristle Fern)
Blechnum chilense
Blechnum gibbum (Dwarf Tree Fern)
  'Silver Lady'
Blechnum nudum (Fishbone Water Fern)
Blechnum penna-marina
  (Alpine Water Fern)
Blechnum spicant (Deer Fern, Hard Fern)
Cyrtomium falcatum (Holly Fern)
  'Rochfordianum'

Dennstaedtia davallioides
  (Lady Ground Fern)
Doodia aspera (Rasp Fern)
Doodia media (Common Rasp Fern)
Dryopteris affinis (Golden Male Fern,
  Golden Shield Fern)
  'Cristata'
Dryopteris carthusiana
  (Narrow Buckler Fern)
Dryopteris erythrosora (Autumn Fern,
  Japanese Shield Fern)
Dryopteris filix-mas (Male Fern)
  'Grandiceps Wills'
Dryopteris wallichiana
  (Wallich's Wood Fern)
Marsilea drummondii (Common
  Nardoo)
Marsilea mutica
Matteuccia struthiopteris (Ostrich Fern,
  Shuttlecock Fern)
Nephrolepis cordifolia (Fishbone Fern,
  Southern Sword Fern)
  'Plumosa'
Osmunda regalis (Royal Fern)
  'Cristata'
  'Purpurascens'
Pellaea falcata (Sickle Fern)
Pellaea rotundifolia (Button Fern)
Platycerium bifurcatum (Elkhorn Fern)
Platycerium superbum (Staghorn)

Polypodium cambricum
  (Southern Polypod)
Polypodium vulgare
  (Common Polypod)
Polystichum acrostichoides
  (Christmas Fern)
Polystichum setiferum (Soft Shield
  Fern) Divisilobum Group
  'Plumosum Bevis'
Pteris cretica (Cretan Brake Fern)
  'Albolineata'
  'Distinction'
  'Wimsettii'
Pteris ensiformis (Slender Brake Fern)
  'Arguta'
  'Victoriae'
Pteris umbrosa (Jungle Brake)

SUITABLE FOR HANGING BASKETS
Adiantum aethiopicum
  (Common Maidenhair)
Adiantum raddianum
  (Delta Maidenhair Fern)
  'Fragrantissimum'
  'Fritz Luth'
  'Gracillimum'
Adiantum tenerum
  (Brittle Maidenhair Fern)
  'Farleyense'
  'Lady Moxham'
Asplenium bulbiferum
  (Hen and Chicken Fern,
  Mother Spleenwort)
Davallia canariensis
  (Canary Island Hare's Foot Fern)
Davallia fejeensis
  (Rabbit's Foot Fern)
  'Major'
Davallia pyxidata
  (Hare's Foot Fern)
Davallia trichomanoides
  (Squirrel's Foot Fern)
Microsorum punctatum
  'Cristatum'
Nephrolepis exaltata (Sword Fern)
  'Bostoniensis' (Boston Fern)
  'Hillii'
  'Rooseveltii'
Phlebodium aureum (Hare's Foot Fern,
  Rabbit's Foot Fern)
  'Mandaianum'

Tree ferns, among the best for casting pretty reflections, are ideal for edging a water garden.

PALMS

Palms are a much-admired group of plants which over the centuries have endeared themselves to gardeners everywhere. During the Victorian era, they became the most treasured of plants for decorating households, hotels and theatres, and today are recognised as among the most stately and elegant of subjects for almost every design occasion, both indoors and out.

They are a natural choice for swimming pool settings, not only for their touch of tropical glamour, but also because they give shade with a minimum of leaf drop. Occasional shed fronds are easily removed and do not create problems in the pool filter. Their overall size and shape is predictable and, as their roots do not thicken unduly, they are not likely to cause cracks in paving.

Tall palms such as kentias and the Bangalow Palm (*Archontophoenix cunninghamiania*) are good for feature gardens or private courtyards, and when mixed with cycads, bamboos, ferns and coloured foliage plants provide a beautiful tropical garden composition. Many have a single stem contributing to their graceful form and look appealing grouped close together to create a natural grove. A cluster-stemmed variety such as the Golden Cane Palm (*Chrysalidocarpus lutescens*) develops handsome clumps of slender stems when set in a warm sheltered garden.

Ideal as container subjects, certain varieties of palm are suitable for entrance halls, large rooms, porches or patios or as poolside decoration. Beware of moving any palm that has been growing indoors, or in shade, out into full sun. Unless it is conditioned gradually to the move, the leaves will be badly scorched by the sudden exposure.

One of the main reasons indoor palms fail is either too little or, more usually, too much water. Always wait until the soil surface feels dry before watering again.

DON'T CUT BACK

As old palm leaves wither and die they are replaced by new ones, which develop at the crown. Growth is from

The palms in this jungle-like setting provide graceful arching fronds that catch the morning light. The lower level is populated by a mixture of cannas, cycads, crotons and cordylines.

The Dwarf Date Palm (*Phoenix roebelenii*) provides a beautiful accent to a small garden.

Kentia and *Livistona* palms are used as sculptural features beside a pool, with *Cordyline* and *Dracaena* as compatible companions.

the terminal bud, hidden inside the leaf cluster at the crown of the palm. If this is destroyed the palm has no capacity to form a new growing point and will die. For this reason palms cannot be cut back or limited in height by topping. If your indoor palm reaches ceiling height, it will have to be moved outside or placed in a more spacious setting. The plant will, however, suffer no ill effects if damaged leaves are cut from the trunk at their bases.

GUIDE TO PALMS

Archontophoenix alexandrae
  (Alexandra Palm)
Archontophoenix cunninghamiana
  (Bangalow Palm)
Areca catechu
  (Betel Nut Palm, Pinang)
Brahea armata
  (Big Blue Hesper Palm)
Carpentaria acuminata
  (Carpentaria Palm)
Caryota mitis
  (Clustered Fishtail Palm)
Caryota urens
  (Toddy Palm, Wine Palm)
Chamaedorea costaricana
Chamaedorea elegans (Parlour Palm)
  'Bella'
Chamaedorea metallica
  (Miniature Fishtail Palm)

Chamaedorea microspadix
  (Mexican Bamboo Palm)
Chamaerops humilis
  (Dwarf Fan Palm, European Fan Palm)
Chrysalidocarpus lutescens
  (Golden Cane Palm, Butterfly Palm)
Cyrtostachys renda
  (Lipstick Palm, Sealing Wax Palm)
Howea belmoreana (Curly Palm)
Howea forsteriana
  (Kentia Palm, Thatch Palm)
Licuala grandis
  (Vanuatu Fan Palm, Palas Payung)
Licuala ramsayi
  (Australian Fan Palm)
Linospadix monostachya
  (Walking Stick Palm)
Livistona australis (Australian Fan
  Palm, Cabbage-tree Palm)

Livistona chinensis
  (Chinese Fan Palm)
Livistona decipiens (Ribbon Fan Palm,
  Weeping Cabbage Palm)
Livistona saribus
Phoenix canariensis
  (Canary Island Date Palm)
Phoenix dactylifera (Date Palm)
Phoenix roebelenii (Pygmy Date Palm)
Rhapis excelsa
  (Lady Palm, Bamboo Palm)
  'Ayanishiki'
  'Koban'
  'Zuikonishiki'
Rhapis humilis (Slender Lady Palm)
Sabal mexicana (Texas Palmetto)
Sabal minor (Dwarf Palmetto)
Trachycarpus fortunei (Chusan Palm,
  Chinese Windmill Palm)

CYCADS

Although cycads resemble palms, they are a distinct and unrelated group of plants. Cycads do not flower and their seed is generally produced in cones. Male and female cones are usually quite different in shape and size and are generally produced on separate plants. In many species the ripe cones are highly decorative.

The ornamental palm-like leaves form a radiating crown at ground level or at the top of a short trunk. They are tough and leathery, often with prickly leaflets which can be quite nasty. Bear this in mind when handling them and choosing their site, preferably a safe distance from paths.

In the garden they make attractive feature plants and look appealing in groups. They can be used as accents among shrubs, mingle well with ferns and palms and thrive under large spreading trees. Cycads have a predictable growth habit, but do resent crowded conditions and need sufficient space to ensure adequate air movement. Cut foliage is used for indoor decoration.

Most cycads are sun-loving, but some may need a position protected from hot sun, especially when young. They are widely distributed in tropical and warm temperate regions of the world and most like warm growing conditions, although a few species, such as the Japanese Sago Palm (*Cycas revoluta*), will tolerate light frosts if given some protection. Large specimens are expensive, but when provided with optimum growing conditions, such as well-drained soil rich in organic matter, regular water and feeding, smaller specimens grow at a reasonable rate.

Cycads make excellent long-term container specimens for verandas, patios and indoors where there is sufficient natural light. The two *Lepidozamia* species and *Cycas revoluta* will tolerate average room temperature, lower light levels, and a reasonable amount of neglect. Apply fertilisers only when the plant is in active growth.

Palms of different heights and forms are underplanted with a handsome collection of well-spaced cycads. With their perfect symmetry, cycads provide an interesting and balanced design to this luxurious garden.

Cycas revoluta makes an excellent long-term container specimen.

The young leaves of *Encephalartos lebomboensis* are light green, covered with light golden hairs.

A relatively carefree planting of *Cycas revoluta* surrounding a rustic bush seat.

GUIDE TO CYCADS

Cycas circinalis (Fern Palm, Queen Sago)
Cycas revoluta (Japanese Sago Palm)
Dioon edule (Mexican Fern Palm)
Dioon spinulosum
Encephalartos altensteinii (Prickly Cycad)
Encephalartos ferox
Encephalartos lebomboensis (Lebombo Cycad)
Encephalartos natalensis (Natal Cycad)
Lepidozamia hopei
Lepidozamia peroffskyana
Macrozamia communis (Burrawang)
Macrozamia miquelii
Macrozamia spiralis
Zamia furfuracea (Cardboard Palm)

SUCCULENTS

For sculptural form, strong leaf shapes, good looks and drought tolerance, few plant groups rival the succulents. They are interesting, very collectible and can be easily grown in the garden, in pots, indoors and in window boxes. Provided the climate is appropriate, larger species provide a very effective garden display, while dainty ones can be strategically placed in the protected environment of a rock garden. In fact a whole rock garden could be devoted to a stunning collection of succulents—here they will receive the seriously good drainage they like best.

Although succulents occur throughout the world, most of the popular garden varieties come from semi-arid regions of Africa and the Americas. A number of the smaller rosette-forming succulents, such as species of *Sempervivum* and *Sedum*, occur in Europe and are among the hardiest. The shelter of a warm, sunny wall will provide additional protection from frost.

Most succulents have evolved adaptations, such as fleshy or thickened tissues in the stems, leaves and roots, to withstand the long dry periods of their natural habitats. Some have a protective outer waxy, glaucous or felted layer that helps retain moisture. Some, such as *Cyphostemma juttae* and some species of *Euphorbia*, have a swollen rootstock (or caudex) that may gradually emerge to form a thickened above-ground stem. Such caudiciform succulents are grown for this interesting effect.

Although succulents are great plants for areas that receive low or erratic rainfall, they do respond to additional watering during dry periods, especially when in active growth. Few, however, tolerate excess moisture. Where rainfall is likely to be excessive, grow plants on a steep slope or in raised beds. The areas beneath the eaves of a house can also be used to advantage.

CONTAINERS

Most succulents have compact root systems and respond well to container cultivation. For best effects, and to provide optimum growing conditions, choose containers that suit

Agave attenuata requires little water and looks impressive as a relaxed, informal border.

Like a living sculpture, *Agave angustifolia* 'Marginata' is used here to create space, atmosphere and shape.

requirements can be grown in troughs and window-box planters. Whatever container you choose, it should be only as large as necessary and have excellent drainage.

INDOORS

Because you have a certain amount of control over the environment, a large range of succulents can be grown indoors. In some cases they are better suited to the warm dry atmosphere of heated rooms than many of the leafy, non-succulent houseplants, which often need humidity and frequent watering to look their best. Most succulents need plenty of bright light with protection from hot sun. Allow the soil to dry out somewhat between waterings, especially in winter. For busy indoor areas it is important to position plants with spiny tips and margins out of harm's way.

the habit of the plant. Give rosette-forming plants such as the echeverias a shallow bowl and enough space to attractively spread and multiply across the soil. Those with large symmetrical rosettes, such as the agaves and aloes, are ideal specimens for large upright pots or urns. Narrow, tall-growing succulents like *Sansevieria trifasciata* and some yuccas make good accents in traditional terracotta pots. A collection of different species with similar watering and light

SOIL

Whether grown outside or indoors, the potting mix should be nutritious, porous, free draining and fairly acid. A potting medium consisting of two parts of a fairly rich loam-based potting mix and one part of sharp sand or grit, with the addition of a small amount of balanced, slow-release fertiliser, will provide sufficient plant food in the correct proportions for 12 months.

GUIDE TO SUCCULENTS

LARGE
Agave americana (Century Plant)
  'Marginata'
  'Mediopicta'
Agave angustifolia **'Marginata'**
Aloe arborescens (Candelabra Aloe)
Aloe ciliaris (Climbing Aloe)
Aloe dichotoma (Quiver Tree)
Aloe plicatilis (Fan Aloe)
Aloe pluridens
Crassula arborescens (Silver Jade Plant,
  Silver Dollar)
Crassula ovata (Jade Plant, Jade Tree)
Cyphostemma juttae
Dasylirion acrotrichum
Dasylirion longissimum
  (Mexican Grass Plant)

Furcraea foetida (Green Aloe)
  'Mediopicta'
Furcraea selloa var. *marginata*
Kalanchoe beharensis
  (Velvet Elephant Ear)
Yucca aloifolia (Spanish Bayonet)
  'Marginata'
  'Tricolor'
  'Variegata'
Yucca elephantipes (Giant Yucca,
  Spineless Yucca) 'Variegata'
Yucca gloriosa (Spanish Dagger)
  'Variegata'

MEDIUM
Aeonium arboreum 'Atropurpureum'
  'Zwartkop'

Aeonium canariense
Aeonium haworthii
Agave attenuata
Agave filifera (Thread Agave)
Agave parryi var. *huachucensis*
Agave victoria-reginae
  (Royal Agave)
Aloe comptonii
Aloe harlana
Aloe pratensis
Aloe saponaria (Soap Aloe)
Aloe striata (Coral Aloe)
Aloe vera (Medicinal Aloe,
  Medicine Plant)
Cotyledon orbiculata var. *oblonga*
Crassula perfoliata var. *minor*
  (Propeller Plant)

A steep slope edging steps provides excellent drainage for these predominantly grey-leaved succulents.

Agave angustifolia 'Marginata' provides a dramatic focal point.

Pretty rosettes of *Echeveria elegans* in an urn.

Euphorbia caput-medusae
  (Medusa's Head)
Kalanchoe thyrsiflora **'Flapjacks'**
Kalanchoe tomentosa
  (Panda Plant, Pussy Ears)
Sansevieria trifasciata
  (Mother-in-law's Tongue)
Sedum morganianum
  (Donkey's Tail, Burro Tail)
Sedum spectabile
  'Brilliant'
  'Iceberg'
  'Stardust'
Senecio articulatus (Candle Plant)
  'Variegatus'
Senecio macroglossus
  (Cape Ivy, Natal Ivy)
Yucca filamentosa (Adam's Needle)
  'Bright Edge'
Yucca glauca (Dwarf Yucca, Soapweed)

SMALL
Aloe aristata (Torch Plant, Lace Aloe)
Aloe variegata
  (Partridge-breasted Aloe)
Dudleya brittonii (Chalk Dudleya)
Dudleya pulverulenta
  (Chalk Lettuce)
Echeveria agavoides
Echeveria pulvinata (Plush Plant)
  'Frosty'
Graptopetalum bellum
Haworthia attenuata (Zebra Plant)
Haworthia cymbiformis
Haworthia reinwardtii
Sansevieria trifasciata (Mother-in-law's
  Tongue) **cultivars**
  'Golden Hahnii'
  'Silver Hahnii'
Sedum sieboldii
  'Mediovariegatum'

GROUND-HUGGING
Echeveria elegans
  (Pearl Echeveria, Hen and Chicks)
Echeveria secunda
  (Blue Echeveria, Hen and Chicks)
Echeveria setosa
  (Mexican Firecracker)
Euphorbia mysinites
Graptopetalum paraguayense
  (Ghost Plant, Mother of Pearl Plant)
Sedum ewersii
Sedum kamtschaticum
Sedum spathulifolium
  'Cape Blanco'
  'Purpureum'
Sempervivum arachnoideum
  (Cobweb Houseleek)
Sempervivum ciliosum
Sempervivum tectorum
  (Common Houseleek)

CONTAINER PLANTS

Handsome potted foliage plants provide unlimited possibilities for garden design, especially in small areas that have no soil at all, such as balconies, rooftops and basements. In fact an entire potted garden can be rearranged to create different groupings according to the season or as part of a special planting theme. Palms, bamboos, dracaenas, vines and ferns create a mini jungle effect, or use a selection of different grasses in a contemporary courtyard setting. Potted plants with variegated foliage will lighten the atmosphere in dreary corners. They can be used as stylised balanced arrangements or clustered together in an informal grouping. In a long narrow courtyard, group them as in a border, graded by height and organised by habit and texture.

Move less hardy tropical foliage plants indoors when they need it. Architectural plants such as agaves, yuccas and phormiums further diversify the overall garden picture. For a terminal focal point, set a large special container on a handsome plinth at the end of a garden.

Pots of conifers, hollies and box clipped into topiary shapes are particularly effective for year-round decoration, perhaps repeated on both sides of a path or entrance or set in neat groups of varying heights. Clipped bay trees set in Versailles containers make outstanding corner plants for formal gardens and still look beautiful in winter.

POTTED ARRANGEMENTS

One of the beauties of using pots is that it is possible to provide specialised growing conditions for a group of plants that would not thrive if planted together in the same soil. Conversely, for a stunning effect plant a large container with an overflowing composition of different plants that all enjoy the same growing conditions. You can have fun using different foliage effects such as coloured or striped canna lilies, spiky-leaved cordylines or phormiums for accent, green or variegated trailing ivy, silver or grey perennials to give pattern, and scented pelargoniums for form and fragrance. These plants all like a well-drained sunny position. In a shadier site a showy arrangement of hostas, plectranthus, ferns, begonias or ivies will thrive in pots containing richer soil and plenty of water in summer. Summer annuals such as coleus can be tucked in for an exotic splash of colour.

POTTING AND MAINTENANCE

Most plants will eventually need to be re-potted into progressively larger

Mature clusters of rosette-forming echeverias cascading from containers provide sculptural interest and become the focal point of this courtyard garden.

pots. Choose a pot to suit the plant it will contain. Match the size, depth and drainage to the needs of the plant. If the drainage holes are large, cover them with a piece of mesh to stop soil running out and prevent the entry of insect pests. Use a premium-quality potting mix that provides good drainage and aeration while holding moisture and nutrients. Make sure that the potting mix does not come right up to the rim—leave a space of at least 2.5cm/1in to allow room for watering. Water the plant immediately after potting.

Avoid feeding a newly potted plant for the first few weeks while it gets established. Then supplement the soil regularly with slow-release fertiliser during the growing period. Water the plant immediately before and after applying fertiliser.

WATERING

Potted plants dry out more quickly than those in the ground. As a general rule, wait until the top 2.5cm/1in of container mix feels dry to the touch. Then water gently but thoroughly near the stem of the plant until the water drips freely from the drainage holes. Very small pots, unglazed terracotta and hanging baskets dry out especially quickly, and in dry windy weather you may have to water these as often as twice a day. A layer of mulch such as leaf mould or compost will help to conserve moisture and protect the roots from summer heat.

White marble urns planted with spiky *Dracaena marginata* 'Tricolor' surrounded by *Echeveria agavoides* 'Black Magic'.

GUIDE TO CONTAINER PLANTS

CONIFERS
Abies balsamea (Balsam Fir)
  'Hudsonia'
  'Nana'
Chamaecyparis lawsoniana
  (Lawson Cypress) **dwarf forms**
Chamaecyparis obtusa
  (Hinoki Cypress) **dwarf forms**
Chamaecyparis pisifera
  (Sawara Cypress) **dwarf forms**
Cryptomeria japonica (Japanese Cedar)
  dwarf cultivars
Cupressus macrocarpa 'Goldcrest'
  (Monterey Cypress)
Cupressus sempervirens (Italian
  Cypress, Mediterranean Cypress)
  'Stricta'
  'Swane's Golden'
Picea abies (Norway Spruce,
  Common Spruce) **cultivars**
Picea glauca **var. albertiana** 'Conica'
  (White Spruce)
Picea omorika 'Nana' (Serbian Spruce)

Picea pungens (Colorado Spruce)
  cultivars
Pinus aristata (Bristlecone Pine)
Pinus cembra (Arolla Pine, Swiss Pine)
Pinus densiflora 'Alice Verkade'
  (Japanese Red Pine)
Pinus mugo (Swiss Mountain Pine)
  and cultivars
Pinus parviflora 'Adcock's Dwarf'
  (Japanese White Pine)
Pinus strobus 'Radiata' (Eastern White
  Pine, Weymouth Pine)
Pinus sylvestris 'Beuvronensis'
  (Scots Pine)
Pinus thunbergii 'Sayonara'
  (Japanese Black Pine)
Taxus baccata (Yew) **and cultivars**
Taxus cuspidata (Japanese Yew)
  and cultivars
Thuja occidentalis (White Cedar)
  cultivars
Thujopsis dolabrata 'Nana'
  (Hiba Arbor-vitae)

SHRUBS
Acalypha wilkesiana
  (Fijian Fire Plant, Copperleaf)
Acer palmatum (Japanese Maple)
  and cultivars
Aloysia triphylla (Lemon Verbena)
Aucuba japonica
  (Japanese Laurel, Spotted Laurel)
Buxus microphylla (Japanese Box)
Buxus sempervirens (European Box,
  Common Box)
Cordyline fruticosa (Ti Tree)
Cordyline stricta (Slender Palm Lily)
Dracaena deremensis **and cultivars**
Dracaena fragrans (Corn Plant,
  Happy Plant) **and cultivars**
Dracaena marginata **and cultivars**
Dracaena reflexa **and cultivars**
Dracaena surculosa (Gold-dust
  Dracaena, Spotted Dracaena)
  and cultivars
x *Fatshedera lizei* (Tree Ivy)
  'Variegata'

Fatsia japonica (Japanese Aralia,
  Japanese Fatsia) **and cultivars**
Ficus benjamina (Weeping Fig)
  and cultivars
Ficus carica (Common Fig)
Ficus deltoidea (Mistletoe Fig)
Ficus elastica (Rubber Plant)
  and cultivars
Ficus lyrata (Fiddleleaf Fig)
Graptophyllum pictum (Caricature Plant)
  and cultivars
  'Purpureum Variegata'
  'Tricolor'
Hebe **species**
Helichrysum ilalicum
Helichrysum petiolare
  'Limelight'
  'Variegatum'
Leucophyta brownii (Cushion Bush)
Lonicera nitida (Box Honeysuckle)
Murraya paniculata (Orange Jessamine,
  Mock Orange)
Myrtus communis (Common Myrtle)
  and cultivars
Nandina domestica (Sacred Bamboo,
  Heavenly Bamboo) **and cultivars**
Pisonia umbellifera '**Variegata**'
  (Bird-catcher Tree)
Podocarpus lawrencei (Mountain
  Plum Pine) **cultivars**
  'Alpine Lass'
  'Blue Gem'
Pseudopanax lessonii (Houpara)
  and cultivars
Rosmarinus officinalis (Rosemary)
  and cultivars
Sanchezia speciosa
Santolina chamaecyparissus
  (Cotton Lavender) **and cultivars**
Santolina pinnata **and cultivars**
Schefflera arboricola
  (Hawaiian Elf Schefflera)
Schefflera elegantissima (False Aralia)
Serissa foetida '**Variegata**'
Thymus **species** (Thyme)

GRASSES AND GRASS-LIKE PLANTS
Acorus gramineus '**Ogon**'
  (Japanese Rush)
Carex **species** (Sedges)
Chlorophytum comosum (Spider Plant)
Cymbopogon citratus (Lemon Grass)
Cyperus albostriatus '**Variegatus**'
Cyperus involucratus (Umbrella Sedge)

Cyperus papyrus (Egyptian Papyrus)
Hakonechloa macra '**Aureola**'
  (Golden Variegated Hakonechloa)
Lomandra hystrix
Lomandra longifolia
  (Spiny-headed Mat Rush)
Ophiopogon jaburan (White Lilyturf)
  'Vittatus'
Ophiopogon japonicus (Mondo Grass)
  'Kyoto Dwarf'
Ophiopogon planiscapus '**Nigrescens**'
Oplismenus africanus (Basket Grass)
  'Variegatus'
Phragmites australis (Common Reed)
  'Variegatus'
Restio tetraphyllus (Tassel Cord Rush)
Stenotaphrum secundatum
  '**Variegatum**' (Buffalo Grass)

BAMBOOS
Bambusa multiplex (Hedge Bamboo)
Bambusa ventricosa
  (Buddha's Belly Bamboo)
Phyllostachys aurea (Fishbone
  Bamboo, Golden Bamboo)
  'Flavescens Inversa'
Phyllostachys aureosulcata
  (Yellow-groove Bamboo)
  var. *aureocaulis*
Phyllostachys bambusoides
  (Madake, Giant Timber Bamboo)
  'Allgold'
  'Castillonis'
Phyllostachys nigra (Black Bamboo)
  var. *henonis*
Phyllostachys viridiglaucescens
Pleioblastus auricomus (Kamuro-zasu)
Pleioblastus pygmaeus (Pygmy Bamboo)
  var. *distichus*
Pleioblastus variegatus

FERNS
Asplenium **species** (Spleenworts)
Athyrium **species** (Lady Ferns)
Cyathea **species** (Tree Ferns)
Cyrtomium falcatum (Holly Fern)
  'Rochfordianum'
Davallia **species** (Hare's Foot Ferns)
Dicksonia antarctica (Soft Tree Fern)
Dicksonia fibrosa (Wheki-Ponga)
Dicksonia squarrosa (Wheki)
Doodia aspera (Rasp Fern)
Doodia media
  (Common Rasp Fern)

Lycopodium phlegmaria
  (Common Tassel Fern)
Lycopodium phlegmarioides
  (Layered Tassel Fern)
Microsorum punctatum **and cultivars**
Nephrolepis cordifolia (Fishbone Fern,
  Southern Sword Fern) **and cultivars**
Nephrolepis exaltata (Sword Fern)
  and cultivars
Osmunda regalis (Royal Fern)
Pellaea falcata (Sickle Fern)
Pellaea rotundifolia (Button Fern)
Phlebodium aureum (Hare's Foot Fern,
  Rabbit's Foot Fern)
  'Mandaianum'
Polypodium cambricum
  (Southern Polypod)
Polypodium vulgare
  (Common Polypod)
Polystichum acrostichoides
  (Christmas Fern)
Polystichum setiferum (Soft Shield
  Fern) Divisilobum Group
Pteris cretica (Cretan Brake Fern)
  and cultivars
Pteris ensiformis (Slender Brake Fern)
  and cultivars
Pteris umbrosa (Jungle Brake)

SUCCULENTS
Aeonium **species and cultivars**
Agave **species and cultivars**
Aloe aristata (Torch Plant, Lace Aloe)
Aloe comptonii
Aloe harlana
Aloe saponaria (Soap Aloe)
Aloe striata (Coral Aloe)
Aloe variegata (Partridge-breasted Aloe)
Aloe vera (Medicinal Aloe,
  Medicine Plant)
Cotyledon orbiculata var. *oblonga*
Crassula arborescens (Silver Jade Plant,
  Silver Dollar)
Crassula ovata (Jade Plant, Jade Tree)
Crassula perfoliata var. *minor*
  (Propeller Plant)
Cyphostemma juttae
Dudleya brittonii (Chalk Dudleya)
Dudleya pulverulenta (Chalk Lettuce)
Echeveria **species**
Euphorbia caput-medusae
  (Medusa's Head)
Furcraea foetida (Green Aloe)
  'Mediopicta'

Furcraea selloa var. *marginata*

Graptopetalum bellum

Graptopetalum paraguayense
(Ghost Plant, Mother of Pearl Plant)

Haworthia species

Kalanchoe beharensis
(Velvet Elephant Ear)

Kalanchoe thyrsiflora 'Flapjacks'

Kalanchoe tomentosa
(Panda Plant, Pussy Ears)

Sansevieria trifasciata (Mother-in-law's
Tongue) and cultivars

Sedum species (Stonecrop)

Sempervivum arachnoideum
(Cobweb Houseleek)

Sempervivum ciliosum

Sempervivum tectorum
(Common Houseleek)

Senecio articulatus (Candle Plant)
'Variegatus'

Senecio serpens (Blue Chalksticks)

Yucca aloifolia (Spanish Bayonet)
and cultivars

Yucca elephantipes (Giant Yucca,
Spineless Yucca) 'Variegata'

Yucca filamentosa (Adam's Needle)
'Bright Edge'

Yucca glauca (Dwarf Yucca, Soapweed)

PERENNIALS

Aglaonema commutatum

Aglaonema modestum
(Chinese Evergreen)

Ajuga species (Bugle)

Alocasia species (Elephant's Ear)

Amaranthus tricolor and cultivars
(Joseph's Coat)

Anthurium crystallinum
(Crystal Anthurium)

Aphelandra squarrosa (Zebra Plant)

Artemisia species (Wormwood)

Arum italicum (Italian Arum)
'Marmoratum'

Asarum europaeum (Asarabacca)

Asparagus densiflorus (Asparagus Fern)

Asparagus setaceus (Asparagus Fern)

Aspidistra elatior (Aspidistra,
Cast-iron Plant)

Begonia species and cultivars

Brassica oleracea var. *acephala*
(Ornamental Cabbage and Kale)
cultivars

Calathea species

Callisia elegans (Striped Inch Plant)

Callisia fragrans (Chain
Plant) 'Melnickoff'

Callisia navicularis
(Chain Plant)

Canna iridiflora
(Indian Shot Plant)

Canna x *generalis*

Carludovica palmata
(Panama Hat Palm)

Codiaeum variegatum
var. *pictum* (Croton)

Colocasia esculenta (Taro,
Dasheen, Elephant's Ears)

Ctenanthe burle-marxii

Ctenanthe lubbersiana
(Bamburanta)

Ctenanthe oppenheimiana
'Tricolor'

Dieffenbachia seguine (Spotted
Dumb Cane) and cultivars

Doryanthes excelsa
(Gymea Lily, Giant Lily)

Episcia cupreata (Flame Violet)
and cultivars

Episcia lilacina

Euphorbia amygdaloides (Wood Spurge)
'Purpurea'
var. *robbiae*

Euphorbia characias subsp. *wulfenii*

Farfugium japonicum and cultivars

Fittonia verschaffeltii var. *argyroneura*
(Silver Net-leaf)
'Nana'

Foeniculum vulgare (Fennel)
'Purpureum'

Hosta species (Plantain Lily)

Houttuynia cordata 'Chameleon'

Hypoestes phyllostachya
(Polka-dot Plant, Freckle Face)
'Splash'

Iresine herbstii (Beefsteak Plant)
and cultivars

Lysimachia nummularia
(Creeping Jenny, Moneywort)
'Aurea'

Maranta leuconeura (Prayer Plant,
Ten Commandments) and cultivars

Melissa officinalis (Lemon Balm,
Bee Balm)

Mentha species (Mint)

Molineria capitulata (Weevil Lily)

Musa species (Banana)

Origanum vulgare (Oregano, Wild
Marjoram) and cultivars

Acer palmatum 'Dissectum'.

Oxalis tetraphylla
(Good Luck Plant, Lucky Clover)
'Iron Cross'

Pelargonium species

Peperomia species

Philodendron 'Winterbourn'

Pilea cadierei (Aluminium Plant,
Watermelon Pilea)
'Minima'

Pilea involucrata (Friendship Plant)
'Moon Valley'

Pilea microphylla (Artillery Plant)

Pistia stratiotes (Water Lettuce)

Plectranthus argentatus
(Silver Plectranthus)

Plectranthus australis (Swedish Ivy)

Plectranthus madagascariensis
(Mintleaf)
'Variegated Mintleaf'

Plectranthus oertendahlii

Raoulia australis

Ruta graveolens (Common Rue,
Herb of Grace)
'Jackman's Blue'

Salvia elegans (Pineapple Sage)

Salvia officinalis (Sage) and
cultivars

Saxifraga stolonifera (Mother of
Thousands, Strawberry Begonia)
'Tricolor'

Selaginella martensii

Selaginella pallescens

Senecio cineraria (Dusty Miller)
'Silver Dust'

Senecio viravira (Dusty Miller)

Soleirolia soleirolii (Baby's Tears,
  Mind-your-own-business)

Solenostemon scutellarioides (Coleus,
  Flame Nettle, Painted Nettle) **cultivars**

Spathiphyllum **species** (Peace Lily)

Stachys byzantina (Lambs' Ears, Lambs'
  Tails, Lambs' Tongues) **and cultivars**

Strelitzia nicolai (Wild Banana,
  Giant Bird of Paradise)

Strelitzia reginae (Crane Flower,
  Bird of Paradise)

Stromanthe sanguinea

Tradescantia fluminensis (Wandering
  Jew) **and cultivars**

Tradescantia pallida 'Purpurea'

Tradescantia sillamontana (White Velvet)

Tradescantia spathacea (Boat Lily,
  Moses-in-the-cradle)

Tradescantia zanonia 'Mexican Flag'

Tradescantia zebrina (Silver Inch Plant)

Xanthosoma violaceum (Blue Taro)

PALMS AND CYCADS

Archontophoenix alexandrae
  (Alexandra Palm)

Archontophoenix cunninghamiana
  (Bangalow Palm)

Brahea armata (Big Blue Hesper Palm)

Carpentaria acuminata
  (Carpentaria Palm)

Caryota mitis (Clustered Fishtail Palm)

Caryota urens (Toddy Palm, Wine Palm)

Chamaedorea costaricana

Chamaedorea elegans (Parlour Palm)
  'Bella'

Chamaedorea metallica
  (Miniature Fishtail Palm)

Chamaedorea microspadix
  (Mexican Bamboo Palm)

Chamaerops humilis (Dwarf Fan Palm,
  European Fan Palm)

Chrysalidocarpus lutescens
  (Golden Cane Palm, Butterfly Palm)

Cycas circinalis (Fern Palm, Queen Sago)

Cycas revoluta (Japanese Sago Palm)

Cyrtostachys renda
  (Lipstick Palm, Sealing Wax Palm)

Dioon edule (Mexican Fern Palm)

Dioon spinulosum

Howea belmoreana (Curly Palm)

Howea forsteriana (Kentia Palm,
  Thatch Palm)

Lepidozamia hopei

Lepidozamia peroffskyana

Licuala grandis (Vanuatu Fan Palm,
  Palas Payung)

Licuala ramsayi (Australian Fan Palm)

Linospadix monostachya
  (Walking Stick Palm)

Livistona australis (Australian Fan
  Palm, Cabbage-tree Palm)

Livistona chinensis (Chinese Fan Palm)

Livistona decipiens (Ribbon Fan Palm,
  Weeping Cabbage Palm)

Macrozamia communis (Burrawang)

Macrozamia miquelii

Macrozamia spiralis

Phoenix canariensis (Canary Island
  Date Palm)

Phoenix dactylifera (Date Palm)

Phoenix roebelenii (Pygmy Date Palm)

Rhapis excelsa (Lady Palm, Bamboo
  Palm) **and cultivars**

Rhapis humilis (Slender Lady Palm)

Trachycarpus fortunei (Chusan Palm,
  Chinese Windmill Palm)

Zamia furfuracea (Cardboard Palm)
)

CLIMBERS AND CREEPERS

Cissus antarctica (Kangaroo Vine)

Cissus discolor

Cissus hypoglauca (Water Vine)

Cissus rhombifolia (Grape Ivy)
  'Ellen Danica'

Cissus striata (Miniature Grape Ivy)

Ficus pumila (Creeping Fig)

Hedera canariensis (Canary Island Ivy,
  Algerian Ivy) **and cultivars**

Hedera colchica (Persian Ivy)
  and cultivars

Hedera helix (Common Ivy,
  English Ivy) **and cultivars**

Monstera deliciosa (Fruit Salad Plant,
  Mexican Breadfruit) 'Variegata'

Philodendron bipinnatifidum
  (Tree Philodendron)

Philodendron erubescens (Red-leaf
  Philodendron, Blushing Philodendron)
  'Burgundy'

Philodendron imbe

Philodendron scandens
  (Sweetheart Plant)

Piper novae-hollandiae
  (Giant Pepper Vine)

Piper ornatum (Celebes Pepper)

Senecio macroglossus (Cape Ivy,
  Natal Ivy)

Syngonium podophyllum (Arrowhead
  Vine, Goosefoot) **and cultivars**

BROMELIADS

Cryptanthus (Earth Star, Starfish Plant)
  species and cultivars

Fascicularia bicolor

Fascicularia pitcairniifolia

Neoregelia carolinae (Blushing Bromeliad)

Neoregelia concentrica

Puya berteroniana

Tillandsia usneoides (Spanish Moss)

Vriesea hieroglyphica
  (King of Bromeliads)

Vriesea splendens (Flaming Sword)

TREES

Beaucarnea recurvata (Bottle Palm,
  Ponytail Plant)

Cedrus atlantica (Atlas Cedar)
  'Glauca'
  'Glauca Pendula'

Cedrus deodara 'Aurea' (Deodar Cedar)

Cedrus libani (Cedar of Lebanon)
  'Nana'
  'Sargentii'

Cordyline australis (New Zealand
  Cabbage Tree)

Dracaena draco (Dragon Tree)

Eriobotrya japonica (Loquat)

Ficus aspera (Mosaic Fig, Clown Fig)

Ficus auriculata (Roxburgh Fig)

Ficus dammaropsis (Dinner Plate Fig)

Ficus microcarpa **var.** *hillii* (Hill's
  Weeping Fig) 'Hawaii'

Ficus rubiginosa (Port Jackson Fig)

Laurus nobilis (Bay Laurel, Sweet Bay)
  'Aurea'

Magnolia grandiflora 'Little Gem'

Omalanthus populifolius (Bleeding
  Heart Tree)

Pandanus tectorius (Coastal Screw
  Pine, Pandang)

Pandanus veitchii (Veitch Screw Pine)

Podocarpus elatus (Brown Pine,
  Plum Pine)

Podocarpus macrophyllus 'Maki'
  (Kasamaki, Buddhist Pine)

Ravenala madagascariensis
  (Traveller's Tree)

Schefflera actinophylla (Queensland
  Umbrella Tree)

Xanthorrhoea australis
  (Austral Grass Tree)

HOUSEPLANTS

The term 'houseplant' as used in this book includes those plants that will grow successfully in conservatories, atriums and greenhouses. Indoor gardeners want healthy thriving houseplants to accent various spots around their homes and bring an element of life, nature and freshness to their surroundings. Those in less temperate climates and with conservatories want to grow all those marvellous tropical species and frost-tender plants that would perish if grown outside in their garden—and they get to 'potter in the garden' in all weather.

Houseplants today are not restricted to houses. Many workplaces, hotels, public buildings and even factories are introducing natural greenery to counteract the harsh lines of modern architecture and help create a less stressful atmosphere. Acting as screens and pleasant dividers for open-plan areas, indoor plants also help to deaden the noise and purify the air in the working environment.

Conditions vary from house to house, even from room to room, but to make your houseplants feel at home you need to provide adequate light and water, steady warmth, sufficient humidity and freedom from draughts.

TEMPERATURE AND LOCATION

Some plants need more warmth than others; most will wilt and shed their leaves if exposed to cold conditions and draughts. Buy houseplants that suit the conditions of your home. Basically, a room temperature of around 18–21°C (60–70°F) keeps most plants happy, but always check their individual care instructions. Avoid placing plants in the stream of air ascending from heating systems.

Fortunately, many of the most desirable foliage plants grow with comparative ease in well-lighted rooms. Many exotic plants with large, often shiny, dark green leaves grow in their native habitat beneath a heavy canopy of dense rainforest and are accustomed to medium to low light intensity. These include many figs, philodendrons and spathiphyllums, the Umbrella Tree (*Schefflera actinophylla*), Devil's Ivy (*Epipremnum pinnatum*) and of course aspidistras.

Plants with variegated leaves need more light than those with plain green leaves, but over-strong sunlight will damage the foliage. In fact few houseplants can withstand direct sunlight all the time; most like bright indirect light and only a few hours of early morning sun each day.

Collection of indoor plants on Victorian wire plant stand.

A well-lit sunroom provides a wonderful setting for indoor plants such as begonias dracaenas, ferns and bromeliads.

HUMIDITY CONTROL

Many tropical plants make highly desirable houseplants, but most require a considerable amount of humidity, which is often lacking in the home atmosphere, particularly when rooms are heated. This problem can be partially relieved by spraying the foliage every few days with a fine mist spray. Another method of increasing humidity is to stand a group of plants in a water-filled tray on a bed of gravel or pebbles which keeps the pots out of the water. The evaporation of moisture increases as the temperature rises and helps to keep the air around the plants humid.

WATERING AND FEEDING

How often watering is needed depends on temperature and to some extent on the amount of light the plant receives. Plants in bright light and reasonably warm rooms will use up to two or three times as much water as those in darker situations. A general rule is to give a good watering when the soil about 2.5cm/1in below the surface feels dry to the touch. Ferns, especially maidenhairs, need a little more water than other plants. Plants in plastic pots need less water than those in porous clay pots. All plants will need less water during the winter dormancy period.

Long-lasting, slow-release fertilisers are convenient and safe to use on ferns, palms and other foliage plants. Houseplants can be severely damaged or killed if given too much plant food. Give small quantities every two to four weeks and only while the plants are in active growth during the warmer months. Don't fertilise dry plants. Feed only after watering, when the soil is evenly moist.

RE-POTTING INDOOR PLANTS

Re-pot indoor plants that have outgrown their containers in early spring so that they have plenty of space to grow over the warmer months. Before you remove the plant from the pot, water thoroughly and prune off any dead or diseased growth. Choose a pot one or two sizes larger than the old one. Make sure the plant is re-potted at the original soil level, which should be about 2.5cm/1in below the rim of the pot. Water the plant thoroughly to remove any air pockets left in the soil

GUIDE TO HOUSEPLANTS

HIGH LIGHT
Plants can tolerate some sun. Provide the brightest possible light at all times.

Callisia species
Canna iridiflora
Canna x *generalis*
Codiaeum variegatum var. *pictum* (Croton) **cultivars**
Cordyline australis (New Zealand Cabbage Tree) **and cultivars**
Cyperus albostriatus 'Variegatus'
Cyperus involucratus (Umbrella Sedge)
Cyperus papyrus (Egyptian Papyrus)
Eriobotrya japonica (Loquat)
Euphorbia caput-medusae (Medusa's Head)
Laurus nobilis (Bay Laurel, Sweet Bay)
Musa species (Banana)
Oplismenus africanus (Basket Grass) 'Variegatus'
Pandanus tectorius (Coastal Screw Pine, Pandang)
Pandanus veitchii (Veitch Screw Pine)
Pelargonium species
Pisonia umbellifera 'Variegata' (Bird-catcher Tree)
Plectranthus australis (Swedish Ivy)
Plectranthus madagascariensis (Mintleaf) 'Variegated Mintleaf'
Plectranthus oertendahlii
Ravenala madagascariensis (Traveller's Tree)
Strelitzia reginae (Crane Flower, Bird of Paradise)

BRIGHT LIGHT
Give these plants bright, filtered light without direct sunlight.

Acorus gramineus 'Ogon' (Japanese Rush)
Aphelandra squarrosa (Zebra Plant)
Asparagus densiflorus (Asparagus Fern)
Asparagus setaceus (Asparagus Fern)
Aucuba japonica (Japanese Laurel, Spotted Laurel) **and cultivars**
Bambusa multiplex 'Riviereorum' (Hedge Bamboo)
Begonia species and cultivars
Caladium species (Elephant's Ears)
Carex hachijoensis 'Evergold'
Carludovica palmata (Panama Hat Palm)
Chlorophytum comosum (Spider Plant) and cultivars
Cissus species
Colocasia esculenta (Taro, Dasheen, Elephant's Ears) 'Black Magic' 'Fontanesii'
Cordyline fruticosa (Ti Tree) **and cultivars**
Cordyline stricta (Slender Palm Lily)
Ctenanthe species and cultivars
Dieffenbachia seguine (Spotted Dumb Cane) **cultivars**
Dracaena species
Epipremnum species (Devil's Ivy)
Episcia species (Flame Violet)
Fatsia japonica (Japanese Aralia, Japanese Fatsia) **and cultivars**
Ficus species (Fig)
Graptophyllum pictum (Caricature Plant)
Hedera helix (Common Ivy, English Ivy) **and cultivars**
Hypoestes phyllostachya (Polka-dot Plant, Freckle Face)
Monstera deliciosa (Fruit Salad Plant, Mexican Breadfruit) 'Variegata'
Peperomia species
Philodendron bipinnatifidum (Tree Philodendron)

Philodendron erubescens (Red-leaf
Philodendron, Blushing Philodendron)
'Burgundy'
Philodendron imbe
Philodendron scandens (Sweetheart Plant)
Philodendron 'Winterbourn'
Piper novae-hollandiae
(Giant Pepper Vine)
Piper ornatum (Celebes Pepper)
Pseudopanax crassifolius (Lancewood)
Pseudopanax lessonii (Houpara)
and cultivars
Raoulia australis
Sanchezia speciosa
Saxifraga stolonifera (Mother of
Thousands, Strawberry Begonia)
'Tricolor'
Schefflera actinophylla (Queensland
Umbrella Tree)
Schefflera arboricola (Hawaiian Elf
Schefflera)
Schefflera elegantissima (False Aralia)
Soleirolia soleirolii (Baby's Tears,
Mind-your-own-business)
Solenostemon scutellarioides (Coleus,
Flame Nettle, Painted Nettle)
cultivars
Syngonium podophyllum (Arrowhead
Vine, Goosefoot)
'Emerald Gem'
'White Butterfly'
Tradescantia species (Wandering Jew)

MEDIUM LIGHT
Site these plants away from windows.

Aglaonema commutatum
Aglaonema modestum
(Chinese Evergreen)
Alocasia brisbanensis
(Cunjevoi, Spoon Lily)
Alocasia cuprea (Giant Caladium)
Alocasia macrorrhiza
(Giant Taro, Cunjevoi)
Alocasia sanderiana (Kris Plant)
Alocasia veitchii
Anthurium crystallinum
(Crystal Anthurium)
Aspidistra elatior
(Aspidistra, Cast-iron Plant)
Calathea species
x *Fatshedera lizei* (Tree Ivy)
'Variegata'
Fittonia verschaffeltii

Maranta leuconeura (Prayer Plant,
Ten Commandments)
and cultivars
Pilea species
Spathiphyllum 'Mauna Loa'
(Peace Lily)
Spathiphyllum 'Sensation'
Spathiphyllum wallisii
Stromanthe sanguinea
Xanthosoma violaceum (Blue Taro)

Princess of Wales Conservatory at Kew
with *Victoria amazonica* (foreground).

SUCCULENTS
Most succulents in interior settings
need maximum light with some direct
sunlight. Inadequate light causes
elongated or distorted growth.
Haworthias require bright, indirect
light. Turn plants regularly to prevent
lop-sided growth. Allow to dry
somewhat between waterings,
especially in winter.

Aeonium arboreum
'Atropurpureum'
'Zwartkop'
Aeonium canariense
Aeonium haworthii
Agave attenuata
Agave filifera (Thread Agave)
Agave victoria-reginae (Royal Agave)
Aloe harlana
Aloe striata (Coral Aloe)
Aloe variegata
(Partridge-breasted Aloe)

Aloe vera (Medicinal Aloe,
Medicine Plant)
Cotyledon orbiculata
var. *oblonga*
Crassula arborescens (Silver Jade Plant,
Silver Dollar)
Crassula ovata (Jade Plant, Jade Tree)
Crassula perfoliata var. *minor*
(Propeller Plant)
Cyphostemma juttae
Dudleya brittonii (Chalk Dudleya)
Dudleya pulverulenta (Chalk Lettuce)
Echeveria species
Furcraea foetida (Green Aloe)
'Mediopicta'
Furcraea selloa var. *marginata*
Graptopetalum bellum
Graptopetalum paraguayense (Ghost
Plant, Mother of Pearl Plant)
Haworthia species (Zebra Plant)
Kalanchoe beharensis
(Velvet Elephant Ear)
Kalanchoe thyrsiflora 'Flapjacks'
Kalanchoe tomentosa (Panda Plant,
Pussy Ears)
Sansevieria trifasciata
(Mother-in-law's Tongue)
Sedum morganianum
(Donkey's Tail, Burro Tail)
Senecio articulatus (Candle Plant)
'Variegatus'
Yucca species

PALMS
Most palms do best in bright, indirect
light. Keep them out of direct midday
sun which may scorch the leaves. Wash
foliage frequently with a hose or under
a tepid indoor shower. Allow the soil
surface to almost dry out between
waterings. Don't let pots stand in water.

Archontophoenix alexandrae
(Alexandra Palm)
Archontophoenix cunninghamiana
(Bangalow Palm)
Brahea armata (Big Blue Hesper Palm)
Carpentaria acuminata
(Carpentaria Palm)
Caryota mitis (Clustered Fishtail Palm)
Caryota urens (Toddy Palm,
Wine Palm)
Chamaedorea costaricana
Chamaedorea elegans (Parlour Palm)

Begonia 'Cleopatra'.

Chamaedorea metallica
  (Miniature Fishtail Palm)
Chamaedorea microspadix
  (Mexican Bamboo Palm)
Chamaerops humilis (Dwarf Fan Palm,
  European Fan Palm)
Chrysalidocarpus lutescens
  (Golden Cane Palm, Butterfly Palm)
Cyrtostachys renda (Lipstick Palm,
  Sealing Wax Palm)
Howea belmoreana (Curly Palm)
Howea forsteriana (Kentia Palm,
  Thatch Palm)
Licuala grandis (Vanuatu Fan Palm,
  Palas Payung)
Licuala ramsayi (Australian Fan Palm)
Linospadix monostachya
  (Walking Stick Palm)
Livistona australis (Australian Fan
  Palm, Cabbage-tree Palm)
Livistona chinensis (Chinese Fan Palm)
Livistona decipiens (Ribbon Fan Palm,
  Weeping Cabbage Palm)
Livistona saribus
Phoenix canariensis
  (Canary Island Date Palm)
Phoenix dactylifera (Date Palm)
Phoenix roebelenii (Pygmy Date Palm)
Rhapis excelsa (Lady Palm,
  Bamboo Palm) **and cultivars**
Rhapis humilis (Slender Lady Palm)
Trachycarpus fortunei (Chusan Palm,
  Chinese Windmill Palm)

CYCADS

Generally cycads need bright light with some exposure to direct sun, preferably early in the morning. *Lepidozamia* species will tolerate darker conditions. Do not overwater plants. All cycads benefit from a spell outdoors in a shady spot in the garden.

Cycas circinalis (Fern Palm,
  Queen Sago)
Cycas revoluta (Japanese Sago Palm)
Dioon edule (Mexican Fern Palm)
Dioon spinulosum
Lepidozamia hopei
Lepidozamia peroffskyana
Macrozamia communis (Burrawang)
Macrozamia miquelii
Macrozamia spiralis
Zamia furfuracea (Cardboard Palm)

BROMELIADS

Most bromeliads prefer full light with some direct sun; protect from midday sun. A position at a sunny window will bring out the colour of the leaves. Keep the centre cups of vase-shaped types filled with water. Allow other types to dry out between waterings.

Cryptanthus **species** (Earth Star,
  Starfish Plant) **and cultivars**
Fascicularia bicolor
Fascicularia pitcairniifolia
Neoregelia carolinae
  (Blushing Bromeliad)
Neoregelia concentrica
Puya berteroniana
Tillandsia usneoides
  (Spanish Moss)
Vriesea hieroglyphica
  (King of Bromeliads)
Vriesea splendens
  (Flaming Sword)

FERNS

Most ferns require medium to bright filtered light, but not direct sun. Turn plants often to ensure that they grow evenly. Keep uniformly moist.

Adiantum **species**
  (Maidenhair Ferns)

Blechnum **species** (Water Ferns)
  and cultivars
Cyathea australis (Rough Tree Fern)
Cyathea cooperi (Scaly Tree Fern)
Cyathea dealbata (Silver Fern)
Cyathea medullaris (Black Tree Fern)
Cyrtomium falcatum (Holly Fern)
  'Rochfordianum'
Davallia **species** (Hare's Foot Fern)
Dicksonia antarctica (Soft Tree Fern)
Dicksonia fibrosa (Wheki-Ponga)
Dicksonia squarrosa (Wheki)
Doodia aspera (Rasp Fern)
Doodia media (Common Rasp Fern)
Lycopodium phlegmaria
  (Common Tassel Fern)
Lycopodium phlegmarioides
  (Layered Tassel Fern)
Microsorum punctatum 'Cristatum'
Nephrolepis cordifolia (Fishbone Fern,
  Southern Sword Fern)
  'Plumosa'
Nephrolepis exaltata (Sword Fern)
  and cultivars
Pellaea falcata (Sickle Fern)
Pellaea rotundifolia (Button Fern)
Phlebodium aureum (Hare's Foot Fern,
  Rabbit's Foot Fern)
  'Mandaianum'
Pteris **species** (Brake)

Fernery with tree ferns, ginger plant and
Colocasia esculenta 'Black Magic'.

PART II: A–Z DIRECTORY OF PLANTS

ABIES

FIRS

FAMILY PINACEAE

From cool mountainous regions of the Northern Hemisphere, this genus consists of about 50 species of stately resinous conifers. With central erect trunks and tiered whorled branches, they are mostly tall and conical in habit, often grown for their traditional Christmas-tree appearance as lawn specimens in large spacious gardens. A number of handsome dwarf varieties will give year-round interest in the average-sized home garden. The needle-like flattened leaves are spirally arranged and often have silvery white bands on the undersides. Erect cylindrical female cones are frequently attractively coloured in shades of green to purplish blue. All are frost hardy, although severe frost may damage new growth. Propagate by seed. Most cultivars are propagated by grafting in winter.

Abies balsamea
Balsam Fir

ORIGIN Canada, USA

CLIMATE M, CT, H

Reaching to 15m/50ft, this conifer has a straight trunk and closely set branches forming a narrowing, spire-shaped crown. The aromatic leaves are short, stiff and slightly twisted upward, about 2.5cm/1in long, shiny dark green above with 2 white bands beneath. The cones are 8–10cm/3–4in long. **'Hudsonia'** is a good dwarf cultivar, forming a spreading, flat-topped mound about 60cm/24in high and 90cm/3ft across. It has semi-spirally arranged, spicy-scented, dark green leaves about 1.5cm/½ in long. No cones are produced. **'Nana'**, another attractive dwarf form, makes a neat mound of similar size.

USE & CULTIVATION The Balsam Fir is a useful lawn or garden specimen. Dwarf forms are suitable for rock and small feature gardens, courtyards, ornamental containers and for softening the edges of hard landscaping. They withstand a reasonable amount of shade and like moist but well-drained (preferably acid) soil. Fully frost hardy.

Abies concolor
Colorado White Fir

ORIGIN USA

CLIMATE M, CT, H

This extremely attractive fir to about 20–30m/70–100ft, usually less in cultivation, forms a neat slender pyramid. The fleshy, waxy blue leaves give off a citrus smell when crushed. The cones, to 10cm/4in long, range in colour from purplish brown to green. **'Argentea'** (syn. 'Candicans'), with extremely pale blue foliage, becomes somewhat columnar with maturity. **'Compacta'**, a slow-growing dwarf form rarely more than 2m/7ft high, has a graceful spreading habit and scented, widely spreading, bluish grey, waxy foliage.

Abies grandis

Abies pinsapo 'Glauca'

USE & CULTIVATION Choice lawn specimens. 'Compacta' is ideal for small gardens without extremes of heat. Plant individually as a feature or collectively to create a band of colour, in well-drained, moisture-retentive soil in sun or partial shade. Fully frost hardy.

Abies grandis
Giant Fir

ORIGIN Western North America
CLIMATE M, CT, H

This large, shapely tree, often reaching 90m/300ft in its native forests, in cultivation forms a slender conical tree 30–60m/100–200ft tall with spreading horizontal branches. The soft, dark green, linear leaves to 5cm/2in long have whitish bands beneath and emit a strong orange scent when crushed. Female cones to 10cm/4in long are greenish brown.

USE & CULTIVATION An outstanding specimen tree providing good shelter and screening in large gardens. Best in a cool, moist climate. Grow in deep, moist, fertile soil in full sun with protection from strong drying winds when young. Fully frost hardy.

Abies lasiocarpa var. arizonica
Corkbark Fir

ORIGIN USA (Arizona, New Mexico)
CLIMATE M, CT, H

This small narrow tree to 9m/30ft tall has thick corky bark, silvery grey leaves to 3.5cm/1½in long, and dark purplish cones to 8cm/3in long. The cultivar **'Compacta'**, a slow-growing conical tree to 5m/17ft tall with corky bark and blue–grey leaves, is most usually grown. The extremely slow-growing miniature **'Roger Watson'** takes about 10 years to reach its mature height of about 1m/3ft. It has silvery grey foliage.

USE & CULTIVATION Especially suited as specimen plants for small gardens or courtyards, requiring moisture-retentive, well-drained soil in sun. Fully frost hardy. The cultivars are propagated by grafting.

Abies lasiocarpa var. *arizonica* 'Compacta'

Abies pinsapo
Spanish Fir

ORIGIN Southern Spain
CLIMATE WT, M, CT

An erect tree to 24m/80ft tall with a pleasing conical shape; the horizontal to slightly drooping branches are densely packed with short, thick, dark grey–green or blue leaves with fine whitish bands on both surfaces. Cones to 15cm/6in long have a short pointed tip. It is largely known by **'Glauca'**, selected forms with bright glaucous blue foliage.

USE & CULTIVATION This beautiful, symmetrical species and its popular blue-foliaged forms make impressive lawn specimens. Very slow growing, but long-lived, they prefer a cool moist climate with fertile, moist well-drained soil. Fully frost hardy.

Acalypha wilkesiana 'Macafeeana'

Acalypha wilkesiana 'Marginata'

ACALYPHA

FAMILY EUPHORBIACEAE

Only a small number of species in this large genus of evergreen shrubs and perennials are cultivated. Some are grown for their brightly coloured catkin-like flowers, others are prized for their highly coloured, variegated foliage. Keep a watchful eye for red spider mite. Propagate from cuttings in summer.

Acalypha wilkesiana
Fijian Fire Plant, Copperleaf

ORIGIN Pacific islands
CLIMATE T, ST, WT

This very colourful, evergreen, bushy shrub 1–2m/3–7ft high has serrated oval leaves 10–20cm/4–8in long, bronze in colour with a wide pink border. Inconspicuous catkin-like flowers appear in summer and autumn. **'Macafeeana'** has bronze and coppery red leaves; **'Marginata'** has bronze foliage flushed with red and marked with cream near the margins.

USE & CULTIVATION In warm climates use for hedging, as colourful highlights and as feature foliage plants. Grow in humus-enriched soil in a warm, sheltered position in sun or semi-shade. Apply complete plant food in summer and water well during growing season. Remove 10cm/4in of growth in late winter to promote new foliage. Regular tip-pruning will encourage branching and maintain shape. Frost tender.

ACANTHUS

BEAR'S BREECHES
FAMILY ACANTHACEAE

From southern Europe, the Mediterranean region and parts of tropical Africa and Asia, this genus consists of about 30 species, mostly perennials, grown for their distinctive, handsome foliage and erect flower spikes. The deeply lobed and toothed leaves of *Acanthus mollis* and *A. spinosus* have since classical Greek times been the

A

inspiration for decorative motifs and architectural ornament. Cut foliage can be used for indoor decoration. Watch out for snails and caterpillars, which can damage new leaves. Propagate from seed, root cuttings or by division.

Acanthus mollis
Oyster Plant

ORIGIN Southern Europe, northern Africa

CLIMATE WT, M, CT, H

An attractive clump-forming plant with dark green, deeply indented, broadly toothed leaves to 1m/3ft long radiating from a central point at ground level. White flowers with purple bracts are closely packed on a tall spike held 1m/3ft or more above the leaves in summer. Varieties from the **Latifolius Group** have particularly handsome shiny rich green leaves to 1.2m/4ft long, but flowers are not so freely produced.

USE & CULTIVATION Use the bold architectural foliage as a dramatic focal point or to soften hard landscaping features. Plants tolerate some shade and are useful at the edge of a woodland setting under lightly canopied trees. Grow in deep, humus-enriched, well-drained soil. Ample water, especially in summer in hot climates, is essential. Remove spent foliage and flower stems. Fully frost hardy.

Acanthus spinosus

ORIGIN Eastern Mediterranean region

CLIMATE WT, M, CT

This clump-forming perennial produces deeply cut, dark green leaves 60–90cm/24–36in long with spiny margins. The mid-summer white flowers with purplish mauve bracts are freely produced, borne in spikes to about 1.2m/4ft high. Those in the **Spinosissimus Group** have even more finely cut and prickly leaves, some with white spiny margins.

USE & CULTIVATION As for *A. mollis*. Wear gloves when cutting flowers and foliage for indoors. Frost hardy.

Acanthus mollis

Acanthus spinosus

ACER

MAPLE TREES

FAMILY ACERACEAE

The maples are unequalled for their diversity of form, their astonishingly varied and intricate foliage shapes, brilliant autumn foliage colour and often year-round colour; some also have highly decorative bark or stems. The small, often greenish yellow flowers are followed by winged fruit (samaras), which in some species are quite showy. About 150 species of mainly deciduous trees and shrubs are grown as specimen and shade trees, in large containers or as bonsai subjects. Mulching aids growth of young maples, especially in dry times and when planted in containers. Most prefer a cool, moist climate and produce their best autumn colour on neutral to acid soil. The fresh soft green leaves are very tender when they first appear, so try to position maples away from drying winds. Fertilise annually in spring or summer with a balanced plant food. Most maples resent pruning. Propagate by seed for species and by grafting and layering for cultivars.

Acer buergerianum
Trident Maple

ORIGIN China, Korea, Japan
CLIMATE WT, M, CT, H

This relatively fast-growing tree forms a rounded crown of low, spreading branches to 9m/30ft in height and 8m/25ft across. It has 3-lobed glossy leaves to 9cm/3½in long. Autumn foliage colour varies from brilliant crimson to orange or yellow.

USE & CULTIVATION Ideal for the relatively small garden, patio or large containers, and frequently used in bonsai. It thrives in any well-drained soil and withstands air pollution and pruning. Fully frost hardy.

Acer capillipes
Red Snakebark Maple

ORIGIN Japan
CLIMATE WT, M, CT

A spreading medium-sized tree, 10–12m/30–40ft high, with red young shoots and dark green bark with longitudinal grey stripes. The irregularly toothed 3-lobed leaves to 12cm/5in long have prominent red stalks and turn yellow, orange and crimson in autumn. Yellow flowers are borne in pendent racemes in summer.

USE & CULTIVATION This charming quick-grower is good for fast screening or shade. Grow in a sheltered sunny position in deep cool soil with adequate summer moisture. It can be propagated from cuttings. Fully frost hardy.

Acer carpinifolium
Hornbeam Maple

ORIGIN Japan
CLIMATE WT, M, CT, H

A bushy tree to 6m/20ft or more with prominently veined leaves to 12cm/5in long, unlobed but sharply serrated. They turn rich golden shades in autumn. Green flowers are borne in short sprays.

USE & CULTIVATION For visual impact, grow as a lawn specimen where the golden autumn leaves will catch the light and can be viewed from all angles. It is slow maturing and at its best in humus-enriched soil in a cool winter climate. Fully frost hardy.

Acer buergerianum

Acer capillipes

A

Acer davidii

Acer japonicum 'Vitifolium'

Acer japonicum 'Aconitifolium'

Acer davidii
Father David's Maple, Snakebark Maple

ORIGIN Northern China
CLIMATE WT, M, CT, H

This distinctive deciduous tree to 15m/50ft has arching branches and shiny olive green bark striped silvery white. Glossy green ovate leaves to 15cm/6in long have long points and red stems. New foliage is bronze tinted, turning bright yellow and orange in autumn. It has showy pendent clusters of pale yellow flowers in early summer. The 12cm/5in leaves of **A. d. subsp. grosseri**, usually with 3 small lobes, turn yellow to orange or red in autumn. **'Ernest Wilson'** makes a small spreading tree to 8m/25ft high with bright orange autumn colour. **'George Forest'** is a popular form with dark red stems and sometimes shallowly lobed leaves, but poor autumn colour.

USE & CULTIVATION All forms make graceful specimens in larger gardens and look good planted in a group. Provide deep cool soil and adequate summer moisture. Good for bonsai. Fully frost hardy.

Acer griseum

Acer griseum
Paperbark Maple

ORIGIN China
CLIMATE M, CT, H

Widely planted for its attractive cinnamon brown peeling bark and colourful autumn foliage, this rather slow-growing deciduous tree to 9m/30ft high is erect then spreading in habit. Its dark green lobed leaves to 10cm/4in long turn bright orange and red in autumn.

USE & CULTIVATION With its neat appearance, this maple forms a fine specimen suited to medium-sized gardens. Grow in fertile, moist well-drained soil sheltered from cold winds. Fully frost hardy.

Acer japonicum
Full-moon Maple

ORIGIN Japan
CLIMATE M, CT, H

A small compact tree with a domed crown, growing to 9m/30ft tall with a short stocky trunk. Its almost rounded, toothed leaves to 20cm/8in across, with 7–11 lobes cut less than halfway to the base, are soft pale green in spring, midgreen in summer and turn beautiful shades of red in autumn. Reddish flowers appear in clusters with the young foliage. **'Aconitifolium'** reaches 5m/17ft and has large, deeply lobed leaves turning crimson in autumn. **'Vitifolium'** has large, shallowly lobed leaves that turn rich crimson in autumn and hold on well into winter.

USE & CULTIVATION All forms make outstanding specimen trees for gardens of all sizes. Grow in moist well-drained soil in full sun or partial shade, with some shelter from drying winds. Fully frost hardy.

Acer negundo 'Flamingo'

Acer negundo
Box Elder Maple

ORIGIN North America
CLIMATE WT, M, CT, H

Reaching 15m/50ft, this fast-growing deciduous tree has distinctive bright green compound leaves to 20cm/8in long, with 3–7 leaflets, turning gold in autumn. Pendent silky sprays of yellowish green flowers are followed by drooping clusters of winged fruits. It is mostly grown for its colourful cultivars, which have a less vigorous root system and usually reach no more than half its size. **'Elegans'** has leaflets edged yellow; **'Flamingo'** has attractive pink shoots in spring, gradually turning to white and green flushed soft pink; **'Variegatum'** (syn. 'Argenteo-variegatum') has handsome green leaves broadly edged with silvery cream; **'Violaceum'** has purplish young shoots covered with a whitish bloom, and hanging tassels of tiny pale purple flowers.

USE & CULTIVATION The green-leaved type, valued for its rapid development, is suitable for parks, streets and large gardens. It tolerates poor conditions, but prefers humus-enriched soil in full sun or light shade. The smaller growing coloured forms are often preferred as lawn specimens. Very hot sun will scorch the leaves so they are best placed in less exposed positions. Ample water in dry times is needed. Fully frost hardy.

Acer palmatum
Japanese Maple

ORIGIN China, Korea, Japan
CLIMATE WT, M, CT, H

Branching low, with a dense rounded crown and reaching no more than 4.5m/15ft high, the Japanese Maple is one of the most admired deciduous trees for small gardens. The slender pointed leaves with 5 lobes are a fresh light green in spring, darkening in summer and colouring brilliant shades of red and russet in autumn before falling to reveal the slender branches in winter. Grown in Japan for centuries, there are now more than 300 cultivars giving a great range of leaf shape and colour. As a bonus, some varieties have beautiful silvery trunks or brightly coloured stems; others take on appealing contorted shapes as they mature, rather like large bonsai. These forms are generally smaller than the species, many growing only to the size of large shrubs. **'Atropurpureum'** has dark purplish leaves from the time they unfurl in spring, turning deep scarlet tones in autumn. **'Bloodgood'**, a strong grower to 5m/17ft, has deeply cut dark red leaves turning bright red in autumn, and red fruit. **'Burgundy Lace'** is a small spreading form to 3.5m/12ft high with deeply cut and fringed leaves in deep burgundy wine tonings. **'Butterfly'** is upright to 3m/10ft, with small, shallowly 5-lobed, grey–green leaves with creamy white margins and a distinct twist. It does not colour well. **'Chitoseyama'** grows to around 2m/7ft with finely cut, 7-lobed, reddish green leaves through summer turning rich purple–red in autumn. **'Deshojo'** is a popular bonsai subject with bright pinkish red foliage that turns vivid shades of red and orange. Plants in the **Dissectum Group** are usually mound-forming shrubs with branches that are at first horizontal, then weep gracefully to the ground; slow growing, they eventually develop attractive gnarled trunks and interesting curves. The leaves are deeply and finely cut into narrow lobes. *A. p.* **var.** *dissectum* (syn. A. 'Dissectum') has finely cut rich green leaves that turn gold in autumn. **'Dissectum Atropurpureum'** has a low, spreading, dome-shaped habit and finely cut leaves changing from shades of rich purple to bright orange in autumn.

Acer palmatum

Acer palmatum 'Garnet'

Acer palmatum var. *dissectum* 'Green Lace'

'Dissectum Nigrum' is mound forming, with dark red, deeply cut foliage turning bright red in autumn. **'Filigree'** is mound forming to 2m/7ft with finely cut pastel green leaves mottled with cream specks, colouring rich gold in autumn. **'Garnet'** has a dome-shaped habit to 2m/7ft with finely cut, deep red leaves from spring through to autumn. **'Green Lace'** has a cascading habit and finely cut rich green leaves that turn shades of gold and orange in autumn. **'Heptalobum Rubrum'** is a small upright tree to 5m/17ft with dark purple, broadly lobed leaves that turn fiery red in autumn. **'Higasayama'** has small intricate leaves edged creamy white and pink, turning yellow, orange and red in autumn; a good bonsai subject. **'Kagiri-nishiki'** (syn. 'Roseomarg-

inatum') has a dense upright habit to 3m/10ft with small, deeply cut, 7-lobed green and white leaves delicately margined in rose pink and colouring pink and red in autumn. **'Osakazuki'** is a tall, vase-shaped shrub to 6m/20ft with bright green young foliage colouring brilliant red in autumn. **'Sango-kaku'** (syn. 'Senkaki') has an upright growth habit and bright coral red, glossy stems, highly attractive in winter, and soft green spring foliage turning pale yellow in autumn. **'Ukon'** is an upright grower to around 2.5m/8ft with soft yellow spring foliage turning lime green in summer and golden tones in autumn; a favourite bonsai subject, it looks particularly good planted as a group.

USE & CULTIVATION The Japanese Maple and the cultivars mentioned are

slow growing and long-lived. They make outstanding specimens and with the wide selection from which to choose are perfect for gardens of any size. Different forms can be planted in a group to make the most of the widely varying shapes and hues of the foliage. Those from the **Dissectum Group** make picturesque feature plants beside a pool, in a courtyard or as part of a Japanese-style planting scheme. Japanese Maples are at their best in humus-enriched soil in a cool winter climate. In hot summer climates, position in partial shade. Keep mulched and well watered in dry times, especially when planted in containers. Avoid staking and efforts to straighten the stems as this destroys their natural shape. Perfect for containers and as bonsai subjects. Fully frost hardy.

Acer palmatum 'Osakazuki'

Acer palmatum 'Dissectum Nigrum'

Acer palmatum 'Butterfly'

Acer palmatum 'Deshojo'

Acer palmatum 'Dissectum Atropurpureum'

Acer palmatum 'Filigree'

Acer palmatum 'Higasayama'

Acer palmatum 'Kagiri-nishiki'

Acer palmatum 'Chitoseyama'

Acer platanoides
Norway Maple

ORIGIN Europe
CLIMATE M, CT, H

This strong-growing deciduous tree to 30m/100ft has a dense spreading crown and a rather short trunk with smooth or fissured greyish bark. The large leaves, 10–15cm/4–6in long, with 5–7 sparsely toothed lobes, are similar to those of the Plane Tree, *Platanus* species, and in autumn take on brilliant shades of golden yellow. **'Crimson King'** has dark reddish purple leaves with attractive large lobes. **'Drummondii'** grows to 9m/30ft and has leaves broadly margined with white. **'Laciniatum'** has smaller leaves with lobes reduced to claw-like points. The leaves of **'Schwedleri'** are copper red at first, turning dark bronzy green through summer and deep red in autumn.

USE & CULTIVATION Widely planted as a street or park tree, the Norway Maple makes a superb shade tree for large gardens. The cultivars are smaller in stature, but still require adequate space to display their individuality. They thrive in cool temperate climates in a wide range of soils and conditions. Fully frost hardy.

Acer pseudoplatanus
Sycamore Maple

ORIGIN Europe, western Asia
CLIMATE M, CT, H

This fast-growing, spreading, deciduous tree to 30m/100ft has broad, 5-lobed, dark green leaves to 15cm/6in wide, coarsely toothed and turning brownish yellow in autumn. Conspicuous panicles of yellowish spring flowers are followed by numerous winged fruits. **'Atropurpureum'** has dark green leaves with deep plum undersides. **'Brilliantissimum'**, with a dense rounded crown to 6m/20ft, has salmon pink spring leaves changing to yellowish green in summer, then deep green before they fall. **'Leopoldii'** reaches 9m/30ft and has particularly attractive leaves, pink at first, later green and speckled with yellow and pink. **'Prince Handjery'** has leaves opening pinkish cream and tinted reddish purple on the undersides. **'Variegatum'** has mid-green leaves blotched and striped with white; they are reddish when young. **'Worlei'** has rich yellow leaves until mid-summer.

USE & CULTIVATION This species is rather large for the average home garden, but useful when rapid growth, shade and tolerance to salt-laden winds are desired. The cultivars are smaller and slower growing, making attractive lawn specimens or shade trees for medium-sized gardens. Grow in deep, well-drained soil and provide adequate summer moisture. Fully frost hardy.

Acer rubrum
Red Maple, Scarlet Maple

ORIGIN North America
CLIMATE WT, M, CT, H

This fast-growing deciduous tree to 20m/70ft develops a large rounded crown with maturity. It has reddish

Acer platanoides

Acer platanoides 'Crimson King'

Acer pseudoplatanus 'Variegatum'

stems and long-stalked leaves to 10cm/ 4in long with 3–5 triangular lobes. They are glossy dark green above with bluish white undersides, colouring to brilliant tones of red in autumn. The clusters of tiny red flowers are followed by red winged seeds. The numerous popular cultivars include: **'Columnare'**, a narrow columnar form to 8m/ 25ft with excellent autumn colour; **'October Glory'**, a particularly beautiful, broadly conical form with glossy foliage and brilliant red autumn colouring; and **'Scanlon'**, with a conical habit to 6m/20ft and orange– red autumn leaves.

USE & CULTIVATION This species and its shapely cultivars are fast-growing, beautiful specimen trees providing medium-density shade and a bold splash of autumn colour. Particularly suited to cool winter climates, they thrive in moisture-retentive acid soils with protection from strong winds. Fully frost hardy.

Acer pseudoplatanus 'Brilliantissimum'

Acer saccharum
Sugar Maple

ORIGIN Eastern North America
CLIMATE M, CT, H
This tall deciduous tree to 20m/70ft has a dense rounded crown. The large 3–5-lobed leaves to 15cm/6in across are mid-green above, pale beneath, and assume rich tones of yellow, orange and red in autumn. Its sap is the source of maple sugar. **'Temple's Upright'** is an attractive narrow up-right form to 20m/70ft.

USE & CULTIVATION Grow as out-standing feature trees in large spacious gardens. They are slower growing than other maples, but can withstand strong cold winds. Grow in moist well-drained soil. Fully frost hardy.

Acer saccharum

Acorus gramineus 'Ogon'

ACORUS

FAMILY ARACEAE

This is a small genus of only 2 species of grass-like marginal perennials found in marshes throughout temperate regions in the Northern Hemisphere. Tiny green flowers appear in mid-summer, but the plants are grown mainly for their attractive iris-like scented leaves. Cut back straggly foliage in autumn. Propagate by division of rhizomes.

Acorus calamus
Sweet Flag

ORIGIN Europe, Asia, North America
CLIMATE WT, M, CT, H
This perennial marginal water-plant has a knobbly aromatic rhizome and tough, green, scented leaves to 1m/3ft long. The dried rhizome and leaves have been used in herbal medicine, as food flavouring and as a strewing herb. **'Variegatus'** has 75cm/30in long mid-green leaves with cream variegations, flushed pink in spring.
USE & CULTIVATION It is well suited to a boggy spot edging a pond. Grow in full sun in shallow water (no deeper than 20cm/8in), in rich marshy soil. Fully frost hardy.

Acorus gramineus
Japanese Rush

ORIGIN Japan
CLIMATE WT, M, CT
This perennial marsh plant has soft, narrow, curved leaves to about 30cm/12in long. Insignificant greenish flower spikes are produced in summer. The popular **'Ogon'** reaches about 25cm/10in and has bright pale green leaves with cream variegation.
USE & CULTIVATION A pretty, very useful border plant for a boggy spot. It is often grown indoors and looks good in a display container with contrasting foliage plants that like the same conditions. The container must never be allowed to dry out. Frost hardy.

ACTINIDIA

FAMILY ACTINIDACEAE

This genus consists of over 90 species of woody twining climbers from eastern Asia. They are mainly deciduous and are grown mostly for their ornamental foliage, but in the case of the Chinese Gooseberry or Kiwi Fruit (*Actinidia deliciosa*) for its edible fruit. Cut back untidy stems in winter. Propagate from cuttings.

Actinidia kolomikta

ORIGIN China, Japan
CLIMATE M, CT, H
This deciduous woody-stemmed climber to 5m/17ft or more has ovate leaves to 10cm/4in long with the top half more or less variegated with white or pink. Small fragrant white flowers in summer are followed by yellowish fruit to 2.5cm/1in long.
USE & CULTIVATION Train over pergolas, trellis screens or against a wall or fence. Requires rich, well-drained soil in a protected sunny position with adequate summer moisture. Fully frost hardy.

ADIANTUM

MAIDENHAIR FERN
FAMILY ADIANTACEAE

A large genus of some 200 to 250 species of dainty terrestrial ferns found mostly in the tropical and temperate forested regions of both hemispheres. They have a short creeping or tufted rhizome, black or dark-coloured wiry stems and tiny flat leaflets. Often grown as indoor plants, they are among the most popular ferns in cultivation, some being favourite hanging basket subjects. Most maidenhair ferns resent direct sunlight and sudden changes to their environment. When moving a store-bought plant to a sheltered patio, fernery or shady position in your garden, ensure that a warm and humid atmosphere is maintained and that the soil does not dry out. Dead fronds on an untidy specimen can be cut down hard in spring; in a short time a crop of bright new foliage will unfurl. During the active growing period the regular application of a light solution of seaweed concentrate (the colour of weak tea) will maintain healthy growth. Propagate by division of the rhizomes or from spores.

A

Adiantum aethiopicum
Common Maidenhair

ORIGIN Asia, Africa, Australia, New Zealand
CLIMATE T, ST, WT
This, one of the best-known cultivated ferns, grows to about 45cm/18in high and has a thin creeping rhizome which suckers profusely and rapidly spreads into a dense clump. The lacy fronds to 35cm/14in long have shiny stems and pale green fan-shaped leaflets with shallow lobes.

USE & CULTIVATION In warm gardens, this vigorous creeping fern makes a beautiful groundcover or rockery plant. It resents total shade, doing best in a moist sheltered position where it gets some early morning sun. Excellent for hanging baskets or containers. Indoors, it requires humidity, warmth and light, but not direct sun. Keep slightly moist at all times. Frost tender.

Adiantum aethiopicum

Adiantum aleuticum
syn. *Adiantum pedatum* subsp. *aleuticum*
Aleutian Maidenhair

ORIGIN Alaska, western Canada
CLIMATE CT, H
This deciduous maidenhair has a short creeping or upright rhizome. Growing to 75cm/30in tall and wide, it has slightly arching fronds to 30cm/12in long held on purplish black stalks in a radiating fan-like arrangement. The pale green segments are more or less rectangular and finely frilled on the upper margin.

USE & CULTIVATION Although not widely cultivated, this species is very cold hardy and makes a good outdoor fern for cool rock gardens. Provide some shade and moist well-drained soil. Fully frost hardy.

Adiantum capillus-veneris
Venus-hair Fern

ORIGIN Widespread in warm temperate and subtropical regions
CLIMATE T, ST, WT, M
This maidenhair fern, to 30–60cm/12–24in in height, has short creeping rhizomes, black wiry stems and arching light green fronds with delicate-looking triangular to oval segments with lobed and finely cut outer margins.

USE & CULTIVATION In North America this species grows on moist limestone cliffs and rocks in the wild, and alkaline soils are often recommended in cultivation. Grow in partial shade in moist but well-drained soil. Indoors, provide bright indirect light, medium humidity and moderate water. Do not allow the root ball to dry out. Moderately frost hardy.

Adiantum aleuticum

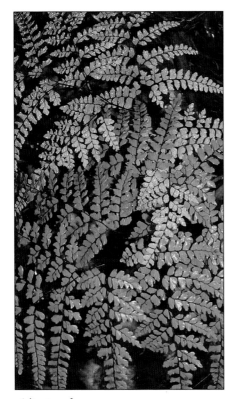

Adiantum formosum

Adiantum formosum
Giant Maidenhair

ORIGIN Australia, New Zealand
CLIMATE T, ST, WT
This tall vigorous fern to 1m/3ft
high has long creeping underground
rhizomes that spread to form large colonies in its rainforest habitat. The erect
dark green fronds, to 1.2m/4ft long, are
spaced quite far apart on shiny, black,
somewhat zigzagging stalks. The leaflets
are broadly triangular in shape with
regularly toothed upper margins.
USE & CULTIVATION A handsome fern
for a large pot, protected fernery or
warm shady spot in the garden with
moist humus-enriched soil. Indoors,
provide bright indirect light, medium
humidity and moderate water. Marginally frost hardy.

Adiantum pedatum
American Maidenhair

ORIGIN Eastern North America
CLIMATE M, CT, H
Growing to 50cm/20in tall and wide,
this deciduous fern has creeping

Adiantum pedatum 'Imbricatum'

rhizomes and erect mid-green fronds
borne on dark brown or black glossy
stalks arranged in radiating spikes, somewhat like a bird's foot in outline. The
wedge-shaped leaflets are arranged in
neat rows and are lobed or toothed on
their upper margins. **'Imbricatum'** has
shorter but broader overlapping leaflets.
USE & CULTIVATION The edge of a
woodland garden provides perfect
conditions for this fern's attractive leafy
clumps. It can also be grown in a semi-
shaded border, courtyard or indoors in
well-drained soil that does not dry out.
Fully frost hardy.

Adiantum raddianum
Delta Maidenhair

ORIGIN Tropics of North America,
South America, Africa
CLIMATE T, ST, WT
This maidenhair has short creeping
rhizomes and a height and spread of
around 60cm/24in. Dark green fronds
to 60cm/24in long, borne on purplish
black stalks, are divided into numerous
wedge-shaped pale green leaflets. Fresh
young foliage may be pale pink. There
are numerous selected varieties, varying
in overall frond size and fineness of the

Adiantum raddianum 'Fragrantissimum'

Adiantum tenerum 'Lady Moxham'

Adiantum raddianum 'Fritz Luth'

segments. **'Fragrantissimum'** has denser fronds with larger leaflets and a slight fragrance. The light green fronds of **'Fritz Luth'** are longer than in other varieties, with the segments dense and overlapping. **'Gracillimum'** has long, elegant, weeping, finely divided fronds with tiny fan-shaped segments.
USE & CULTIVATION All forms are popular houseplants; in a cool climate they must be grown indoors or in

a heated conservatory. In the garden, provide warm humid conditions and humus-enriched, moist well-drained soil in a shady situation. Frost tender.

Adiantum tenerum
Brittle Maidenhair

ORIGIN Central America, South America, West Indies
CLIMATE T, ST, WT
This tuft-forming fern has short creeping rhizomes and dark stalks bearing mid-green fronds to 75cm/30in or longer with ovate frilly segments. Several cultivars are grown, some with attractive rosy-tinted new growth. **'Farleyense'** has segments cut into lobes that are further divided, and young fronds tinged coppery pink. **'Lady Moxham'** has large pendent fronds to 80cm/32in with broad, deeply cut segments and wavy margins.

USE & CULTIVATION Grow in hanging baskets indoors or outside in a warm, protected, partly to fully shaded position. Indoors, provide bright indirect light, medium humidity and moderate water. Do not allow the root ball to dry out. Remove any dead fronds from the base. Frost tender.

Adiantum venustum
Himalayan Maidenhair Fern

ORIGIN China, Himalayas
CLIMATE WT, M, CT, H
This fern has arching mid-green fronds to 30cm/12in long. The fan-shaped segments have toothed outer margins and waxy blue undersides. Young foliage has bright pinkish bronze tints.
USE & CULTIVATION An attractive cold-hardy fern for the edge of a woodland. Grow in moist well-drained soil in partial shade. Fully frost hardy.

AEONIUM

FAMILY CRASSULACEAE

This genus contains about 30 species of woody-stemmed succulents from Madeira, the Canary Islands and adjacent northern Africa. The fleshy leaves may be produced in stemless rosettes or carried in rosettes at the end of thick stems. All rosettes constantly shed their lower leaves, leaving a characteristic scarred woody stem. Sprays of small, usually star-shaped flowers, mainly yellow, but also pink or white, are produced from the rosette centre of mature plants. In some species the stem dies once a rosette has flowered. Propagate from seed or stem or leaf cuttings.

Aeonium arboreum 'Atropurpureum'

Aeonium canariense

Aeonium arboreum

ORIGIN Morocco

CLIMATE T, ST, WT

An erect, branching succulent to around 1m/3ft high producing tightly packed rosettes of spoon-shaped, shiny, bright green leaves at the top of sturdy stems. In spring, clusters of bright yellow flowers are produced on 2- or 3-year-old stems which then die back. **'Atropurpureum'** has slightly smaller, deep plum-coloured leaves. **'Zwartkop'** has very dark purplish black leaves.

USE & CULTIVATION Popular rock-garden and border plants in warm climates. Where winters are cold, they are often used for summer bedding display. Grow in very well-drained soil in full sun or partial shade. They do well in containers and can be grown indoors; provide bright light and water when potting mix feels dry to the touch. Frost tender.

Aeonium arboreum

Aeonium canariense
syn. *Aeonium exsul*

ORIGIN Canary Islands

CLIMATE ST, WT

Growing only about 20cm/8in high, this short-stemmed succulent forms rosettes to 50cm/20in wide of spoon-shaped leaves 10–30cm/4–12in long with fine red edges. After 2 or 3 years a raceme of numerous pale yellow, star-shaped flowers appears in spring, after which the whole plant dies.

USE & CULTIVATION An excellent rock-garden plant for warm climates, it is also well suited to containers and cultivation indoors. Grow in light well-drained soil in full sun or partial shade. Indoors, provide very good light and water moderately. Frost tender.

Aeonium haworthii

ORIGIN Canary Islands

CLIMATE T, ST, WT

This shrubby succulent has shortly branched, erect stems to about 60cm/24in tall, each topped with a rosette about 15cm/6in across of thick, bluish green, pointed leaves with red margins. Pale pinkish white to creamy yellow

A

Aeonium haworthii

Aesculus hippocastanum

flowers are borne in loose panicles in spring and summer.

USE & CULTIVATION Well suited to a raised rock garden or containers in warm climates. A porous well-drained soil in partial shade is best. Frost tender.

Aesculus pavia

AESCULUS

HORSE CHESTNUT, BUCKEYE

FAMILY HIPPOCASTANACEAE

Found in northern temperate regions, this genus consists of 13 species of deciduous trees and shrubs. They have wide-spreading branches clothed with heavily veined palmate leaves composed of 5–7 leaflets radiating from a long stalk. These are bold-foliaged trees, some also producing outstanding displays of flowers. Propagate from seed or by grafting.

Aesculus hippocastanum
Horse Chestnut

ORIGIN Southeastern Europe
CLIMATE M, CT, H

This vigorous wide-spreading tree has a large rounded crown reaching 30m/ 100ft or more. The heavily veined, palmate leaves are divided into 5–7 oval, toothed, bright green leaflets, each 30cm/12 cm or more long. They turn yellow and brown in autumn. White flowers tinged with red are borne in erect conical spikes to 30cm/12in tall in late spring and early summer. The fruit, to 6cm/2½in across, has a thick spiny husk containing large brown seeds known as conkers. **'Baumannii'**, with double flowers, is sterile and does not bear fruit.

USE & CULTIVATION Often massive when mature, this is a magnificent shade tree for large gardens and rural properties in cool climates. Grow in moist well-drained soil. 'Baumannii', being less messy, is sometimes preferred as a lawn specimen. Fully frost hardy.

Aesculus pavia
Red Buckeye

ORIGIN Eastern USA
CLIMATE M, CT, H

An attractive, spreading, deciduous shrub or small tree to 5m/17ft tall. The palmate leaves, divided into 5–7 oblong leaflets to 12cm/5in long, and carried on red stalks, turn golden yellow with reddish tints in autumn. Red flowers borne in erect conical spikes to 15cm/ 6in tall in early summer are followed by smooth fruit to 6cm/2½in long containing shiny brown nuts.

USE & CULTIVATION Worthwhile specimen plant for a medium-sized garden. Grow in deep, fertile, moist soil with good drainage. Fully frost hardy.

AGAVE

FAMILY AGAVACEAE

A genus of around 200 species of large, sculptured succulents with rosettes of sword-shaped, often spiny leaves, native to the Americas but naturalised in other parts of the world. The powerful alcoholic drink of Mexico, tequila, is obtained from the sweet sap of *Agave tequilana*. Most species are slow growing and, after taking a number of years to reach the flowering stage, flower once and die. In most species, however, numerous offsets are produced to form new plants. They can be selected for a wide range of conditions and make excellent accent plants. In frost-prone areas small varieties or young plants can be grown in containers and brought indoors in cold weather. Flowers are not normally produced on plants grown indoors. Propagate from offsets or from seed.

Agave americana
Century Plant

ORIGIN Mexico
CLIMATE WT, M, SA

A large ornamental succulent forming huge clumps, with sharply toothed grey–green leaves to 2m/7ft long and flower spikes to 9m/30ft high. Although the common name suggests that these plants take 100 years to come into bloom, 10–15 years is nearer the mark. Because of its fierce spines, this species can become very difficult to remove. It tends to spread readily, and when neglected can become a weed. The variegated cultivars grow half or two-thirds the size of the normal form. **'Marginata'** has leaves edged with yellow; **'Mediopicta'** has broad white or yellow central bands bordered with green.

USE & CULTIVATION Suitable for large landscape designs; they make spectacular features in desert gardens. Provide full sun and well-drained soil, and water only during hot dry weather. Young plants can be grown in containers. Frost tender.

Agave americana 'Marginata'

Agave angustifolia 'Marginata'

Agave angustifolia

ORIGIN Tropical America
CLIMATE T, ST, WT

This perennial succulent eventually forms a thick stem to 90cm/36in high crowned by a compact rosette of pale green to grey–green spine-tipped leaves to 1m/3ft long. **'Marginata'** has white margins.

USE & CULTIVATION An excellent architectural plant for spacious frost-free gardens. Grow in well-drained soil in full sun. Frost tender.

Agave attenuata

ORIGIN Mexico
CLIMATE WT, M, SA

This popular succulent has a thick stem to approximately 1.5m/5ft high crowned by a tight cluster of tapering, sword-shaped, pale green leaves to 60cm/24in long, rather soft in texture and without spines. The densely packed, creamy green, bell-shaped flowers are carried on an arching spike 2–3m/7–10ft long.

USE & CULTIVATION Good as a dense border to taller shrubs or palms; it will grow in any well-drained soil in full

Agave attenuata

sun. Also ideal as rockery or container plant. Take care when handling as the leaves are easily damaged. Frost tender.

Agave filifera
Thread Agave

ORIGIN Mexico
CLIMATE WT, M, SA

This perennial succulent forms a basal rosette of slender dark green leaves to

Agave filifera

Agave parryi var. *huachucensis*

Agave victoria-reginae

25cm/10in long. Each leaf is spine-tipped and has long, white, thread-like fibres along the edges. It bears yellowish green flowers on erect stems to 2.5m/8ft tall.

USE & CULTIVATION Makes an ideal slow-growing rockery or container plant, thriving in any well-drained soil in full sun. Its small size enables it to be grown indoors, in the sunniest position possible. It offsets freely. Frost tender.

Agave parryi
syn. *Agave neomexicana*

ORIGIN USA (New Mexico)
CLIMATE WT, M, SA

This attractive succulent produces a dense basal rosette of broadly oblong, grey–blue leaves to 30cm/12in long, with prickly teeth along the margins and ending in a long spine. After several years the plant sends up a branched flowering stem to 4.5m/15ft tall, topped with dense clusters of creamy yellow flowers. *A. p.* **var.** *huachucensis* occurs only in the Huachuca Mountains of southeastern Arizona, and with its wide, densely overlapping leaves is considered highly desirable.

USE & CULTIVATION Both forms make outstanding landscape plants in a large rockery or desert garden in sharply drained soil in full sun. Frost tender.

Agave victoria-reginae
Royal Agave

ORIGIN Mexico
CLIMATE WT, M, SA

This very slow-growing succulent forms a tight dome-shaped rosette to 50cm/20in in diameter. It has white-edged dark green leaves with white surface lines. When mature, this is one of the most attractive of the agaves. Creamy green flowers are carried on a 3.5m/12ft tall spike.

USE & CULTIVATION Position this beautifully marked agave in the foreground of a sharply drained rockery where its charm can be fully appreciated. Indoors, provide bright light, and water moderately when in active growth. It bears a solitary rosette, and must be grown from seed after flowering. Frost tender.

AGLAONEMA

FAMILY ARACEAE

These tuft-forming perennials, mainly grown indoors for their neat habit and lightly feathered or subtly patterned leaves, have fleshy cane-like stems branching from the base and bear small flowering spathes similar to arum lilies although less showy. There are about 20 species originating in tropical Southeast Asia; being cold sensitive, they can be grown outdoors only in warm frost-free areas. They are sometimes prone to mealy bugs, particularly where the leaf stalks join the main stems. Propagate from cuttings or by division.

Aglaonema commutatum

ORIGIN Philippines, Indonesia
CLIMATE T, ST

This upright bushy perennial to around 60cm/24in high has broad, oblong leaves to 30cm/12in long. The standard form has dark green leaves with greyish white patches along the lateral veins; pale green spathes are produced on mature plants, mainly in summer. **'Malay Beauty'** (syn. 'Pewter') has dark

green oval leaves mottled with greenish white and cream splashes. **'Pseudo-bracteatum'** (syn. 'White Rajah') has very attractive narrow-oblong, dark glossy green leaves with white and pale green splashes along the lateral veins. **'Silver Queen'** has dark grey–green leaves liberally spotted with silver. **'Treubii'** has narrow dark green leaves marked with pale green or silver.

USE & CULTIVATION Grown for foliage contrast, these plants mingle particularly well with ferns in a moist, shady spot in tropical gardens. Easily grown indoors in humus-rich, well-drained soil with filtered light and high humidity. Plants must be kept moist at all times, but not saturated. Water sparingly in winter. Frost tender.

Aglaonema modestum
Chinese Evergreen

ORIGIN Southern China, Southeast Asia
CLIMATE T, ST, WT

This erect tufted perennial to around 60cm/24in in diameter has broad, medium green, waxy leaves to 20cm/8in long with elongated tips and

wavy margins. Pale green spathes are produced in summer. Although lacking the attractive foliage patterns of others in the group, this species is extremely tolerant of neglect indoors.

USE & CULTIVATION As for *A. commutatum*. Frost tender.

AILANTHUS

FAMILY SIMAROUBACEAE

A genus of 5 species of deciduous trees native to China and Southeast Asia with one species extending to Australia. They are generally fast-growing spreading trees with attractive large pinnate leaves and decorative winged fruits. Propagate by seed, suckers or cuttings.

Ailanthus altissima
syn. *Ailanthus glandulosa*
Tree of Heaven

ORIGIN China
CLIMATE ST, WT, M, CT

This deciduous tree to 24m/80ft forms a spreading dome-shaped crown to 15m/50ft across. Large pinnate leaves to 60cm/24in long have up to 30 coarsely toothed oval leaflets. The small whitish

Aglaonema commutatum 'Pseudobracteatum'

Aglaonema commutatum 'Silver Queen'

A

green summer flowers are not very showy but are followed by colourful reddish brown winged fruits on female trees in late summer and autumn.

USE & CULTIVATION Extremely tolerant of urban pollution and especially useful in cities. Grow in a spacious area as a lawn specimen in fertile well-drained soil in sun or partial shade. It produces many suckers and is often considered a weed. Fully frost hardy.

AJUGA

BUGLE

FAMILY LABIATAE/LAMIACEAE

This genus consists of around 50 species of low-growing annuals and perennials. The neat oval or spoon-shaped leaves forming leafy rosettes are normally green, but there are numerous cultivars with colourful leaves in shades of purple, cream and bronze, often with a metallic lustre. Whorls of mauve, purple or pink tubular flowers are carried on leafy spikes in spring and summer. They are frost hardy, mostly trouble free and mainly cultivated as ornamental groundcovers. Protect from snails and slugs. Propagate by division.

Ajuga pyramidalis
Pyramidal Bugle

ORIGIN Europe
CLIMATE WT, M, CT, H
This perennial plant to about 15cm/6in high spreads by short underground rhizomes to form an attractive carpet of soft, slightly toothed, dark green leaves to about 10cm/4in long. Pale blue flowers in spike-like whorls appear in spring and early summer. **'Metallica Crispa'** has crisp, crinkly, greenish purple leaves with a metallic lustre and dark blue flowers.

USE & CULTIVATION Perfect for rockeries, borders and containers, and particularly attractive for edging a partially shaded water garden. They thrive in any moist well-drained soil in partial shade sheltered from strong sun. Fully frost hardy.

Ajuga reptans
Common Bugle

ORIGIN Europe
CLIMATE WT, M, CT, H
This evergreen perennial spreads freely by surface runners, sometimes forming extensive low mats to 1m/3ft or more across. It has smooth leaves to 7cm/2½in long and short spikes of blue, sometimes white or pink flowers in spring to summer. Several attractive cultivars are widely available. **'Atropurpurea'** (syn. 'Purpurea') has glossy reddish purple to bronze leaves and small bright blue flowers. The silvery green leaves of **'Burgundy Glow'** have wine red tints. **'Burgundy Lace'** is a pretty variety with leaves marked with burgundy, cream and pink. **'Catlin's Giant'** has larger purple-tinted leaves to 15cm/6in long and spikes of deep blue flowers. **'Delight'** has leaves variegated silvery white and pink. **'Jungle Beauty'** has large, toothed or slightly lobed, dark green leaves tinged with purple. **'Multicolor'** (syn. 'Rainbow') has dark green and bronze

leaves mottled cream and flushed pink. **'Pink Elf'** is a neat compact form with deep pink flowers. **'Variegata'** has grey–green leaves splashed creamy white.

USE & CULTIVATION As for *A. pyramidalis*. Fully frost hardy.

Ajuga reptans

Ajuga reptans 'Burgundy Lace'

ALCHEMILLA

LADY'S MANTLE
FAMILY ROSACEAE

Only a small number of this genus of about 250 species of herbaceous perennials is in cultivation. Forming attractive soft clumps, they are grown for their palmate, rounded or deeply lobed grey–green leaves and small plumes of tiny flowers. Plants will produce fresh leaves if cut back as soon as flowering is over. Slugs and snails may damage new growth.

Propagate from seed or by division in spring or autumn.

Alchemilla alpina
Alpine Lady's Mantle

ORIGIN Northern Europe, Greenland
CLIMATE M, CT, H

This mat-forming perennial grows about to 15cm/6in high with a spread of about 45cm/18in. Attractive, deeply lobed, greyish green leaves to 3.5cm/1½in long are silvery on the reverse. Tiny greenish flowers appear in summer.

USE & CULTIVATION This and the following species look beautiful planted in masses to frame paving, steps and paths, or naturalised in wild gardens or rockeries. Also use in the foreground of shrubs and rose bushes, especially those with bare branches at the base. Grow in moist well-drained soil in sun or semi-shade. Fully frost hardy.

Alchemilla conjuncta

ORIGIN French and Swiss Alps
CLIMATE M, CT, H

This low clump-forming plant reaches a height and spread of about 40cm/16in. Delightful rounded leaves are deeply lobed and backed with silvery hairs, giving the toothed margins a pretty white edging. Tiny yellow–green flowers develop in summer.

USE & CULTIVATION As for *A. alpina*. Fully frost hardy.

Alchemilla erythropoda

ORIGIN Eastern Europe
CLIMATE M, CT, H

This low, spreading perennial no more than 30cm/12in high and wide has

Alchemilla conjuncta

Alchemilla erythropoda

Alchemilla mollis

Alocasia brisbanensis

conservatory plants for their large, long-stemmed, often attractively marked leaves. The arum-like flowers are insignificant, but some are beautifully perfumed. All parts are poisonous and contact with the sap may irritate skin. Propagate from fresh seed, stem cuttings or by division of rhizomes.

Alocasia brisbanensis
Cunjevoi, Spoon Lily

ORIGIN Eastern Australia
CLIMATE T, ST, WT
This fleshy perennial herb has stout rhizomes and mid-green heart-shaped leaves to 80cm/32in long held on long fleshy stalks. The creamy green, arum-like flowers have a soft perfume and appear in summer.
USE & CULTIVATION This rainforest species is easily grown outdoors in warm temperate gardens, where it looks good massed in drifts beneath trees. For a lush tropical effect, grow with tree ferns near a water feature, providing some shade and fertile moist soil. An excellent container subject inside the house or on a sheltered patio. Indoors, it needs filtered light, a warm humid atmosphere and moist humus-rich soil. Water less in winter. Frost tender.

Alocasia cuprea
Giant Caladium

ORIGIN Malaysia, Borneo
CLIMATE T, ST
This beautiful perennial has iridescent coppery green ovate leaves to 45cm/18in long with contrasting darkly marked veins and a purplish red lower surface, held on stems to 1m/3ft long. The summer flowers have a purplish tube and a green spathe about 15cm/6in long.
USE & CULTIVATION Strictly for growing outdoors in tropical climates only, this species is ideal for mingling with other fabulous foliage plants. Also a first-rate conservatory plant—provide filtered light, a warm humid atmosphere, rich moist soil and ample feeding. Frost tender.

rounded, softly hairy, bluish green leaves about 5cm/2in long, deeply lobed and regularly toothed. Tiny yellowish green flowers in small loose clusters appear from late spring to mid-summer.
USE & CULTIVATION As for *A. alpina*. Fully frost hardy.

Alchemilla mollis
Lady's Mantle

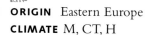

ORIGIN Eastern Europe
CLIMATE M, CT, H
A clump-forming plant with height and spread of 60cm/24in and soft blue–green, almost circular, shallowly lobed leaves to about 15cm/6in long. Loose clusters of tiny greenish flowers are produced throughout summer. The whole of the plant has medicinal properties.
USE & CULTIVATION As for *A. alpina*. Cut flowers and leaves are used in herbal posies. Fully frost hardy.

ALOCASIA

FAMILY ARACEAE
A genus of around 70 species of large-leaved, mainly rhizomatous perennials mostly from tropical Asia, with one, *Alocasia brisbanensis*, occurring in rainforests of eastern Australia. They are cultivated mainly as house and

Alocasia macrorrhiza

Alocasia sanderiana

Alocasia macrorrhiza
Giant Taro

ORIGIN Southeast Asia
CLIMATE T, ST, WT

This large perennial herb has stout fleshy rhizomes and large dark green leaves with heart-shaped bases to 1m/3ft or longer, held on fleshy stems to 1.5m/5ft long. Fragrant, greenish cream, arum-like flowers to 20cm/8in long appear in summer. **'Variegata'** has large dark green leaves with irregular splotches of white and grey–green.
USE & CULTIVATION The strong architectural leaf shape looks superb in a tropical garden setting or near a water feature with tree ferns. For a dramatic effect, plant in bold clumps. Grow in a moist, sheltered position. Indoors, provide filtered light, a warm humid atmosphere and moist humus-rich soil. Keep on the dry side during winter. Frost tender.

Alocasia sanderiana
Kris Plant

ORIGIN Philippines
CLIMATE T, ST, WT

Mainly grown as a houseplant, this striking perennial has thick-textured greenish black leaves to 40cm/16in long with a metallic sheen, silvery veins, wavy or lobed margins and a dark purplish underside. Creamy white flower spathes to 10cm/4in long appear in summer.
USE & CULTIVATION As for *A. cuprea*. Frost tender.

Alocasia veitchii
syn. *Alocasia picta*

ORIGIN Borneo
CLIMATE T, ST, WT

The narrow-triangular leaves of this species are very dark green with contrasting grey margins and veins and a red reverse, to 75cm/30in long and held on fleshy stems to 1.2m/4ft long. The yellowish green spathes are about 12cm/5in long.
USE & CULTIVATION As for *A. cuprea*. Frost tender.

ALOE

FAMILY ASPHODELACEAE/LILIACEAE
From Africa, Madagascar and the Arabian peninsula, this is a large genus of about 360 species of small to large shrubs or small trees. Leaves and habit vary greatly, but the most common growth form is a rosette of sword-shaped succulent leaves with or without a stem. They bear long-stemmed spikes of tubular or bell-shaped flowers. Aloes make excellent accent and landscape plants for rockeries and desert gardens. Some of the dwarf species are good pot plants for the smallest patio, courtyard or indoors. Infestation of mealy bugs can

Aloe arborescens

Aloe arborescens 'Variegata'

Aloe ciliaris

be troublesome on indoor plants. Propagation is from offsets or stem cuttings.

Aloe arborescens
Candelabra Aloe

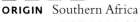

ORIGIN Southern Africa
CLIMATE ST, WT, M, SA
A variable many-branched succulent, usually seen as a dense shrubby bush to 3m/10ft tall with greyish blue sickle-shaped leaves to 60cm/24in long carried in both terminal and lateral rosettes. Individual leaves are partly concave above, with wavy, toothed margins. Each rosette produces branched spikes of red, yellow or orange cylindrical flowers in winter and early spring. **'Variegata'** has pale yellow stripes on the leaves.
USE & CULTIVATION Use as an architectural or feature plant in a large well-drained rockery or a desert garden. Withstanding intense sun, high temperatures, drought and salt-laden winds, it is useful for seaside plantings. Tolerates light frost without much damage. Frost tender.

Aloe aristata
Torch Plant, Lace Aloe

ORIGIN South Africa
CLIMATE ST, WT, M
This miniature clump-forming aloe forms a basal rosette to 12cm/5in tall of pointed, dark green leaves with white spots and soft-toothed white margins, and tipped by fine bristles. Loose spikes of orange–red flowers appear in spring.
USE & CULTIVATION Grow in a small rockery pocket or as a small pot plant for the patio. Provide well-drained fertile potting mix and position in full sun. As a houseplant it likes bright light, a fairly dry atmosphere and moderate watering. Water sparingly when dormant. Frost tender.

Aloe ciliaris
Climbing Aloe

ORIGIN South Africa
CLIMATE WT, M, SA
This relatively fast-growing, scrambling or climbing succulent will reach 3.5m/12ft with a suitable support. It has slender whitish stems crowned by rosettes of narrow fleshy green leaves 10–15cm/4–6in long with white marginal teeth. Bell-shaped scarlet flowers tipped with yellow and green are produced throughout the year.
USE & CULTIVATION This species does well in warm dry climates trained against a fence or trellis. It requires a sunny position with protection from hot afternoon sun. Frost tender.

Aloe comptonii

Aloe plicatilis

Aloe comptonii

ORIGIN South Africa
CLIMATE ST, WT, M
This stemless or short-stemmed succulent forms rosettes around 40cm/16in high. The broadly ovate, fleshy, bluish green leaves to 30cm/12in long are concave and have rather sharp teeth. Scarlet flowers are borne on branched spikes to 80cm/32in long in autumn.
USE & CULTIVATION Ideal for a desert garden, rockery pocket or container, this species likes reasonably good, well-drained soil and a sunny position. Indoors, provide bright light, a fairly dry atmosphere and moderate watering. Water sparingly when dormant. Frost tender.

Aloe dichotoma
Quiver Tree

ORIGIN Namibia, South Africa
CLIMATE WT, M, SA
This species is one of the largest members of the genus. In the wild, full-grown trees reach 9m/30ft, with a massive trunk and peeling bark. The African Bushmen made quivers for their arrows from its soft branches. It is very slow growing, and in cultivation will eventually form an attractive thick trunk that branches and bears individual rosettes of dull green leaves about 20cm/8in long at the tips. The pale yellow flowers are produced on 60cm/24in branched spikes in winter.

USE & CULTIVATION An outstanding feature plant for the desert garden, rockery or modern minimalist landscape. It likes warm dry climates, reasonably good, well-drained soil and a sunny position. Once established it will tolerate a few degrees of frost. Frost tender. It is grown from seed.

Aloe harlana

ORIGIN Ethiopia
CLIMATE WT, M, SA
This stemless aloe forms a neat rosette to about 60cm/24in in diameter with attractive olive green leaves to 20cm/8in long marked with light green splotches. In spring and summer it

produces multi-branched spikes to 1m/3ft of pale pink flowers.

USE & CULTIVATION Outdoors, grow in a well-drained, partially shaded rockery. Ideal as a houseplant, it likes bright indirect light and a warm dry atmosphere. Water sparingly when dormant. Frost tender.

Aloe plicatilis
Fan Aloe

ORIGIN South Africa
CLIMATE WT, M, SA

In cultivation this extremely attractive aloe grows to a height of 2.5m/8ft. Fan-like clusters of pale blue–green leaves are carried at the ends of the branched stems. Scarlet tubular flowers are borne in open spikes in spring.

USE & CULTIVATION A good feature plant for a well-drained rockery, desert garden or large container. Provide some shade in the heat of the day. Frost tender.

Aloe pluridens
syn. Aloe atherstonei

ORIGIN South Africa
CLIMATE WT, M, SA

A shrubby or tree-like succulent, 2–3m/7–10ft tall, with single or branching stems. Dense rosettes of rather narrow, strap-shaped, toothed leaves to about 60cm/24in long form at stem tips. Salmon pink tubular flowers are produced in conical spikes to 80cm/32in long in spring.

USE & CULTIVATION A good feature plant for the well-drained rockery, desert garden or large container. Grow in full sun or partial shade. Frost tender.

Aloe pratensis

ORIGIN South Africa
CLIMATE WT, M, SA

This stemless species forms rosettes to 60cm/24in in diameter, usually in clumps of up to 6. Fleshy, bluish green, ovate leaves to 15cm/6in long are edged with sharp reddish teeth. Green-tipped cylindrical flowers develop in a single rounded spike in spring and summer.

Aloe saponaria

USE & CULTIVATION In warm dry climates this prickly species likes a well-drained, partly shaded rockery or container. Frost tender.

Aloe saponaria
Soap Aloe

ORIGIN South Africa
CLIMATE WT, M, SA

This suckering succulent forms stemless rosettes of broad, pale to dark green leaves to 20cm/8in long flecked with oblong white marks and edged with short teeth. In summer orange cylindrical flowers appear on multi-branched upright stems to 60cm/24in high.

USE & CULTIVATION Easily grown in a well-drained rock garden, where it makes a good feature when massed in groups. It will tolerate high temperatures, periods without water and some brief frost. Grow in a sunny or partially shaded position. Frost tender.

Aloe striata
syn. *Aloe paniculata*
Coral Aloe

ORIGIN Southern Africa
CLIMATE WT, M, SA

This usually stemless succulent forms rosettes of broad, pale grey leaves to 45cm/18in long, often tinged pink and irregularly spotted and striped with green lines. Pendulous orange–red waxy flowers are borne on branched upright stems in spring.

USE & CULTIVATION Ideal for a rock or desert garden in a sunny well-drained position in relatively good soil; water regularly. Also suitable for a well-lit glasshouse or sunroom. Water sparingly when dormant. Frost tender.

Aloe variegata
syns *Aloe ausana, A. punctata*
Partridge-breasted Aloe

ORIGIN Namibia, South Africa
CLIMATE WT, M, SA

Reaching only about 20cm/8in, this highly attractive aloe forms rosettes of overlapping, fleshy, dark green leaves to about 12cm/5in long, boldly marked with white cross-bands and having small white marginal teeth. In spring, pink or red pendent tubular flowers are produced at the ends of slender stalks.

USE & CULTIVATION A popular ornamental pot plant. Grow in a light well-drained potting mix in full sun or light shade. Indoors, provide bright light and good ventilation. Water sparingly when dormant. Frost tender.

Aloe vera
syn. *Aloe barbadensis*
Medicinal Aloe, Medicine Plant

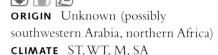

ORIGIN Unknown (possibly southwestern Arabia, northern Africa)
CLIMATE ST, WT, M, SA

Long used medicinally, this perennial succulent to 60cm/24in high forms stemless clumps of fleshy, tapering, green leaves mottled with pale green and often edged with small whitish teeth. Small yellow or orange trumpet-shaped flowers are produced on unbranched spikes about 1m/3ft high in early summer. The sap is widely used in cosmetics and skin care products and for the treatment of burns, including sunburn.

USE & CULTIVATION In a rock garden, herb garden or container, grow in a sunny position with protection from hot afternoon sun. Given bright light, good ventilation and relatively good potting mix, it is an excellent indoor plant. Water sparingly when dormant. Frost tender.

ALOYSIA

FAMILY VERBENACEAE

This small genus of around 37 species of deciduous or evergreen shrubs comes from the warmer parts of North and South America. It includes the well-known Lemon Verbena, *Aloysia triphylla*, commercially grown for the lemon-scented essential oil distilled from the leaves and used in perfumery and to flavour French liqueurs. Dried leaves retain their fresh lemon scent well and are an excellent ingredient for potpourri; they are also used in cooking and as a mildly sedative herbal tea. Propagate from cuttings.

Aloe vera

Aloysia triphylla Lemon Verbena

A

Aloysia triphylla

Alpinia zerumbet 'Variegata'

Aloysia triphylla
syns *Aloe citriodora, Lippia citriodora*
Lemon Verbena

ORIGIN   Chile, Argentina
CLIMATE   ST, WT, M, CT

This deciduous shrub reaches about 2.5m/8ft in height; its crinkly, narrow lance-shaped, lemon-scented leaves to 10cm/4in long are arranged in whorls of 3. Tiny purplish white flowers are carried on dainty spikes in late summer and autumn.

USE & CULTIVATION Grow near a path or gateway where the scent may be enjoyed by passers-by. Grow in a well-drained, light-textured poor soil in a sheltered, sunny position. Water well in the growing season. Although not fully frost hardy, strong, well-mulched plants against a sheltered wall should survive some frost. In colder districts, container-grown plants can be brought indoors over winter. Remove dead wood and prune well in late winter to encourage branching. It can be trained into formal shapes. Pick and dry the leaves in summer before flowering. Moderately frost hardy.

ALPINIA

GINGER LILY
FAMILY ZINGIBERACEAE

This is a large tropical genus of about 200 species of clump-forming perennials grown mainly for their striking waxy flowers. They are members of the ginger family; galangal, the aromatic rhizome of *Alpinia galangal*, is widely used for flavouring in Thai, Malay and Indonesian cooking. Many of the garden ginger lilies have attractive foliage and slender reed-like stems and look good in any tropical setting, even when not in flower. Indoors, they are also useful foliage plants for large containers. Propagate by division.

Alpinia zerumbet
syns *Alpinia nutans, A. speciosa*
Pink Porcelain Lily

ORIGIN   East Asia
CLIMATE   T, ST

This plant makes a dense clump of clustered leafy stems to 3m/10ft with a spread of about 2m/7ft. The stalkless, oblong, mid-green leaves to 60cm/24in long are thin-textured and form 2 rows. Fragrant, slightly hooded white flowers about 6cm/2¼in long, with red and yellow throats, appear in drooping racemes to 40cm/16in long mainly in spring. **'Variegata'** is a particularly attractive form with pale yellow stripes on the leaves.

USE & CULTIVATION Outstanding feature plant for the background of spacious borders or informal gardens in a lush tropical setting. Provide rich soil, semi-shade and ample water in the growing period. Frost tender.

ALTERNANTHERA

FAMILY AMARANTHACEAE

The cultivated species in this large genus of tropical and subtropical distribution are grown as neat annual or perennial groundcovers or edging plants. They often have attractively variegated foliage in shades of pink, yellow, green and purple. Propagate from cuttings or division to ensure consistency of colour.

Alternanthera dentata

ORIGIN West Indies
CLIMATE T, ST, WT

An erect perennial to 45cm/18in or more with dark green, obscurely toothed, ovate leaves to 10cm/4in long, often coloured red or purple. Its spikes of white or greenish white flowers are insignificant. **'Rubiginosa'** has deep red or purple leaves.

USE & CULTIVATION A good dark-coloured foliage plant that responds well to clipping and can be used as a border or for edging. Grow in full sun in moisture-retentive, well-drained soil. Frost tender.

Alternanthera ficoidea
Parrot Leaf

ORIGIN Mexico, South America
CLIMATE T, ST, WT

This spreading or erect perennial reaching no more than 20cm/8in high has weak stems and small elliptic leaves arranged in opposite pairs. They are mid-green and variously marked with combinations of red, orange, purple and yellow. Insignificant white flowers appear in small spikes. **'Bettzickiana'** has blotched and veined red, orange and purple leaves. ***A. f.* var. *amoena*** is a dwarf to 5cm/2in high with leaves having reddish brown, orange and green or purple markings.

USE & CULTIVATION Useful for neat borders and bedding or mass-planted as a colourful groundcover. Var. *amoena* is popular for low hedges, edges and formal floral work. Grow in good well-drained soil in full sun. Frost tender.

Alternanthera dentata 'Rubiginosa'

AMARANTHUS

FAMILY AMARANTHACEAE

This cosmopolitan genus of around 60 species of annuals or short-lived perennials includes a number of weeds, grain crops and a few species used as food plants in Asia. Garden amaranthus are grown for their brightly coloured leaves and to a lesser extent for their panicles of tiny flowers. They are popular bedding plants and can be grown in containers or hanging baskets. Protect from snails when young. Aphids may sometimes be troublesome. Propagate from seed sown in spring. They can be sown directly, but only when danger from frost has passed in cold areas.

Amaranthus tricolor **cultivars**
Joseph's Coat

ORIGIN Tropical Africa and Asia
CLIMATE T, ST, WT

A number of cultivars have been bred for their brilliantly coloured foliage. They are erect, bushy, warm-season summer annuals, reaching a height of about 1.2m/4ft, with oval to lance-shaped multi-coloured leaves 20cm/8in or more long. Insignificant green or red flowers appear in summer. **'Joseph's Coat'** is an outstanding cultivar with crimson leaves with bronze, gold and orange variegations. The leaves of **'Molten Fire'** are brilliant red with dark purplish red at the tips of the

Amaranthus tricolor 'Joseph's Coat'

Amaranthus tricolor cultivar

shoots. **'Splendens'** has dark red leaves with lighter, brilliant red tips.

USE & CULTIVATION Useful as background plants in a shrub or mixed border. Grow in moderately fertile, well-drained soil in full sun, with protection from strong winds. Water and feed regularly in summer. As short-lived houseplants, provide moist well-balanced potting compost and high humidity. Frost tender.

ANGELICA

FAMILY APIACEAE/UMBELLIFERAE

This Northern Hemisphere genus consists of about 50 species of herbaceous perennials and biennials. A few are cultivated for their bold, deeply divided foliage and yellowish green flowers, produced in somewhat globular umbels in summer. For centuries the commonly cultivated *Angelica archangelica* was valued as an important medicinal herb, used as a digestive tonic, and for migraine, flu and fatigue. The stems are candied for cake decoration and sweet dishes. Protect young plants from snails and slugs. Propagate from seed.

Angelica archangelica
Angelica

ORIGIN Northern Europe
CLIMATE WT, M, CT, H
Reaching to 2m/7ftin high, the statuesque Angelica has hollow jointed stems and deeply dissected, fresh green leaves to 60cm/24in long during its first season. In the following year, tall, distinguished yellowish green flowerheads are produced on thick ribbed stems in summer.

USE & CULTIVATION A good dramatic plant for part of a large border, beside a water feature or for giving architectural interest to kitchen or herb garden schemes. It likes some protection from strong winds and thrives in a woodland setting. Grow in rich moist soil in full sun or partial shade. Fully frost hardy.

Angelica archangelica

ANGIOPTERIS

FAMILY MARRATIACEAE

Some botanists have chosen to lump the previously recognised 100 or so species of this primitive fern genus into a single but variable species, *Angiopteris evecta*. It has a wide distribution in tropical and subtropical regions ranging from Madagascar to Asia, the Pacific islands and Australia. It is a magnificent, sometimes tree-like fern with huge fronds to 3m/10ft or more in length. Propagate from the fleshy offsets found at the base of each frond.

Angiopteris evecta
King Fern, Giant Fern

ORIGIN Madagascar, tropical Asia, Pacific islands, Australia
CLIMATE T, ST, WT

With age this fern develops a black trunk that can be up to 1m/3ft in diameter. The arching fronds to 3m/10ft long are twice divided and have semi-weeping, glossy, narrow segments to 90cm/36in long along the smooth green frond stalks.

USE & CULTIVATION An outstanding specimen and waterside fern that needs plenty of room to display its fronds. Grow in moist well-drained soil in a sheltered shady position. Frequent watering is necessary in dry periods. Frost tender.

ANTHURIUM

FLAMINGO FLOWER
FAMILY ARACEAE

This large genus contains more than 600 species of evergreen perennials, often epiphytic, native to subtropical and tropical America and cultivated mainly as greenhouse and indoor plants. In tropical gardens they are sometimes used as luxurious bedding plants. Although grown mainly for their elegant glossy red flower spathes, some species also have highly decorative leaves. Potted plants need dividing and re-potting about every 2 years. Propagate from fresh seed, stem cuttings or division of rhizomes.

Anthurium crystallinum
Crystal Anthurium

ORIGIN Colombia
CLIMATE T, ST

This highly ornamental epiphytic perennial grows to about 60cm/24in high and has large, broadly ovate, velvety leaves to about 45cm/18in long with prominent white veins. Long-lasting green spathes appear sporadically throughout the year.

USE & CULTIVATION Intolerant of cold, it can only be grown outdoors in a tropical climate, making a beautiful contrasting feature plant. Keep moist and sheltered from direct sunlight and wind. It is often container-grown in a warm greenhouse or indoors, where it prefers bright indirect light, a rich fibrous potting mix, high humidity and

Angiopteris evecta

Anthurium crystallinum

Aphelandra squarrosa

constant moisture during the growing season. Water sparingly in winter. Frost tender.

APHELANDRA

FAMILY ACANTHACEAE
A genus of about 170 species of evergreen perennials and shrubs from tropical America. A small number of species are cultivated for their handsome glossy leaves and sculptured flowering spikes in red, yellow and orange. After flowering, cut plants back to the main stem to encourage thicker growth. Propagate from seed or cuttings.

Aphelandra squarrosa
Zebra Plant

ORIGIN Brazil
CLIMATE T, ST
Reaching about 1m/3ft, this small compact shrub has opposite pairs of dark green leaves about 30cm/12in long, broadly veined in white. Four-sided bright yellow flower spikes to 15cm/6in long are borne above the

leaves in summer. **'Dana'** has oval, glossy dark green leaves to 30cm/12in long with prominent white veins and midribs. **'Louisae'** is the best-known cultivar, with prominent white veins and 10cm/4in spikes of golden yellow summer flowers lasting over a long period.
USE & CULTIVATION Most often used as decorative indoor and conservatory plants. In the warm tropics they thrive outdoors in fertile well-drained soil in partial shade. Indoors, provide strong indirect light and a humid atmosphere. Keep soil moist but not waterlogged. Frost tender.

ARALIA

FAMILY ARALIACEAE
This genus of about 40 species of trees, shrubs and herbaceous perennials hails from the Americas, eastern Asia and Malaysia. They are grown for their large pinnate or bipinnate leaves and small, 5-petalled, creamy white flowers borne in large terminal panicles. Propagate from fresh seed, basal suckers or root cuttings. Variegated cultivars are grafted.

Aralia elata
syn. *Aralia chinensis* of gardens
Japanese Angelica Tree

ORIGIN Northeast Asia
CLIMATE WT, CT, H
This, the most widely grown species, is a sparsely branched, suckering, deciduous shrub or small tree to 3.5m/12ft or more with an umbrella-shaped crown. Large bipinnate leaves to 1.2m/4ft long with numerous oval leaflets are crowded towards the stout, spiny stem tips. They turn yellow, orange or purple in autumn. The tiny white flowers form large panicles to 60cm/24in long in late summer and autumn. **'Aureovariegata'** has leaflets broadly edged with yellow, ageing to silvery white; **'Variegata'** (syn. 'Albomarginata') has irregular white-margined leaflets.
USE & CULTIVATION Grow as part of a mixed evergreen/deciduous planting, in a woodland setting or in a partially shaded corner with shelter from strong drying winds. Provide well-drained, humus-enriched soil in partial shade or sun. In warm climates, avoid hot midday sun. Fully frost hardy.

Archontophoenix alexandrae

Archontophoenix cunninghamiana

ARCHONTOPHOENIX

FAMILY ARECACEAE/PALMAE

Native to the rainforests of eastern Australia, this is a small genus of 6 species of single-stemmed palms. They have a slender straight trunk and a neat crown of gracefully arching fronds. Older leaves are shed cleanly from the trunk, leaving smooth ringed scars. Drooping sprays of white or pale mauve flowers emerge from the base of the crownshaft and are followed by rounded red or orange fruit. The large interlocking bracts that enclose the unopened flowers were used by indigenous Australians as water containers. The arching flowering panicles are used by contemporary florists for sculptural indoor decoration. Young plants make particularly good container subjects. Propagate from fresh seed.

Archontophoenix alexandrae
Alexandra Palm

ORIGIN Australia
CLIMATE T, ST, WT

This elegant palm to about 15m/50ft tall has a slender straight trunk that is noticeably enlarged at the base. The slightly arching pinnate leaves to 3m/10ft long have a large sheathing base encircling the trunk. They are dark green above and silvery grey below, which readily distinguishes this species from the similar Bangalow Palm (*A. cunninghamiana*). Large panicles, to 40cm/16in long, of small creamy white flowers appear mostly in summer and autumn.

USE & CULTIVATION Commonly grown in tropical gardens and parks, it adapts well to frost-free warm temperate climates if given plenty of organic

mulch and fertiliser and adequate water during dry periods. Indoor plants decline rapidly in dry conditions, preferring good light and ample moisture. Low temperatures should be avoided. Frost tender.

Archontophoenix cunninghamiana
Bangalow Palm

ORIGIN Australia
CLIMATE ST, WT

This tall erect palm to 18m/60ft or more has a very slender trunk with only a slight enlargement at the base. The arching pinnate leaves about 3–4m/ 10–12ft long have large sheathing leaf bases and numerous linear leaflets with long elongated tips. They are dark glossy green on both surfaces. Small pale purple flowers are carried on branched drooping panicles up to 40cm/16in long in summer to early autumn.

USE & CULTIVATION Grow in groves of varying heights to achieve a tropical effect in warm temperate gardens. It grows rapidly if provided with ample water, and tolerates cooler conditions than *A. alexandrae*, but is frost tender while young. Excellent container plant for sheltered courtyards, patios or verandas. Frost tender.

ARECA

FAMILY ARECACEAE/PALMAE

This palm genus of around 60 species is well known for the betel nut, obtained from *Areca catechu*, chewed as a mild narcotic by many people in India, Southeast Asia and the Pacific. The nuts are crushed with lime and wrapped in a betel leaf, which comes from the plant

Piper betel. They are mostly single-stemmed palms with rather stiff pinnate leaves held above a well-developed crownshaft, just beneath which panicles of cup-shaped flowers emerge. The showy, brightly coloured, one-seeded oval fruit is red, orange or yellow. All species are frost tender and thrive outside only in the wet tropics. Propagate from fresh seed.

Areca catechu
Betel Nut Palm, Pinang

ORIGIN Malay Archipelago
CLIMATE T, ST

A single-stemmed palm to 18m/60ft high, with a swollen green crownshaft and arching mid-green pinnate leaves about 1.5m/6ft long. Panicles of pale yellow flowers encircle the trunk in summer, followed by orange to red fruit containing betel nuts.

Areca catechu

USE & CULTIVATION In tropical areas, grow as a specimen plant in a permanently moist but well-drained soil in a sheltered position. In cooler climates it requires a heated conservatory or greenhouse where high humidity is maintained. Frost tender.

ARTEMISIA

WORMWOOD
FAMILY ASTERACEAE/COMPOSITAE

There are about 350 species of herbs and shrubs in this genus, named in honour of the Greek goddess of childbirth and hunting, Artemis, twin sister of Apollo. They are native to semi-arid and temperate regions of the Northern Hemisphere and are grown mainly for their decorative, deeply dissected silvery foliage, which adds stunning texture and colour to the garden. Many are aromatic and several are used as culinary or medicinal herbs. The leaves of some species are used as an insect repellent. A tendency to become leggy can easily be overcome by judicious pruning in spring. Propagate from seed, semi-hardwood cuttings in late summer or by division.

Artemisia abrotanum
Lad's Love, Old Man, Southernwood

ORIGIN Southern Europe
CLIMATE WT, M, CT, H

This erect, deciduous or semi-evergreen shrub to 1m/3ft tall has sweet-smelling, finely dissected, grey–green leaves to 5cm/2in long with slender thread-like lobes. Clusters of small yellow flowers appear in summer.

USE & CULTIVATION This and the following species make beautiful neat hedges and good accent plants in a herb or cottage garden or mixed border. The decorative silvery forms are good for picking and arrangement in bouquets, wreaths and herbal posies. Grow in light well-drained soil in an open sunny position. Prune lightly in spring. Fully frost hardy.

Artemisia absinthium

Artemisia absinthium 'Lambrook Silver'

Artemisia absinthium
Absinthe, Wormwood

ORIGIN Europe, temperate Asia
CLIMATE WT, M, CT, H
One of the bitter herbs, this shrubby perennial to just over 1m/3ft tall has aromatic, deeply indented, grey–green leaves to 10cm/4in long covered in fine silky hairs. Small rounded heads of greyish yellow flowers appear in late summer. It has been used commercially for making absinthe and is also renowned for its medicinal properties and as a pest control. **'Lambrook Silver'** has bright silvery grey leaves and a neat habit to 75cm/30in tall.
USE & CULTIVATION As for *A. abrotanum*. A handsome foliage plant for herbaceous borders. Fully frost hardy.

Artemisia alba 'Canescens'
syns *Artemisia canescens,*
A. splendens, A. vulgaris 'Canescens'

ORIGIN Europe
CLIMATE WT, M, CT, H
This semi-evergreen perennial forms a soft mound to 45cm/18in of delicate,

Artemisia arborescens

finely cut, silvery leaves with curling lobes and a fairly weak scent. Insignificant brownish yellow, rather knobbly flowers appear in mid-summer. Cut foliage is suitable for floral decoration.
USE & CULTIVATION As for *A. abrotanum*. Fully frost hardy.

Artemisia arborescens
Silver Wormwood

ORIGIN Mediterranean region
CLIMATE WT, M, CT
This rounded shrubby perennial to 1–2m/3–7ft tall has aromatic, deeply dissected, grey–green leaves covered with fine silky hairs on both surfaces, giving the whole plant a silvery sheen. The insignificant yellow flowers have no appeal and are best removed if the foliage is to be kept fresh.
USE & CULTIVATION As for *A. abrotanum*. This versatile shrub will tolerate salt-laden winds, sandy and salty soils and some shade. Frost hardy.

Artemisia ludoviciana
syns *Artemisia palmeri, A. purshiana*
Western Mugwort, White Sage

ORIGIN North America
CLIMATE WT, M, CT, H
A variable, aromatic, clump-forming perennial reaching about 1m/3ft, with narrow, lance-shaped, greyish green leaves to 12cm/5in long, entire or coarsely lobed and white below.

Slender plumes of tiny greyish flowers are produced on velvety stems from mid-summer to autumn. It has an invasive root system. *A. l.* **var. albula** has entire white-woolly leaves to only 4cm/1½in long. **'Valerie Finnis'** has silvery grey leaves with jagged margins.

USE & CULTIVATION As for *A. abrotanum*. Frost hardy.

Artemisia pontica
Roman Wormwood

ORIGIN Central Europe
CLIMATE WT, M, CT, H
This rhizomatous herb forms a neat upright plant to about 80cm/32in, with attractive feathery greyish green leaves to 4cm/1½in long. Panicles of creamy yellow flowers appear in summer.

USE & CULTIVATION As for *A. abrotanum*. Its rather invasive habit can be used to advantage in poor soils where other plants might fail. Frost hardy.

Artemisia schmidtiana

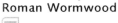

ORIGIN Japan
CLIMATE WT, M, CT, H
This low-growing creeping herb to about 30cm/12in has fern-like, deeply cut, fragrant silver leaves to 5cm/2in long. In late spring and summer, short racemes of small, rounded, pale yellow flowerheads are carried above the bush. The cushion-forming cultivar **'Nana'** rarely gets above 10cm/4in tall and 30cm/12in across and is a popular edging plant.

USE & CULTIVATION As for *A. abrotanum*. Excellent groundcover for seaside gardens. Fully frost hardy.

Artemisia stelleriana
Beach Wormwood

ORIGIN Northeast Asia
CLIMATE WT, M, M, H
An evergreen rounded perennial with a woody base, growing 30–60cm/12–24in high and spreading to 1m/3ft across. It has deeply lobed, white-haired, silver leaves to 7cm/2½in long and bears

Artemisia pontica

Artemisia stelleriana 'Broughton Silver'

slender sprays of small creamy flowers in summer. The compact, almost prostrate form **'Broughton Silver'** (syns 'Mori, 'Silver Brocade') is most often seen in cultivation and makes an excellent groundcover for seaside gardens.

USE & CULTIVATION As for *A. abrotanum*. Fully frost hardy.

Arum italicum

Arundo donax

ARUM

FAMILY ARACEAE

Grown for its attractively marked arrow- or heart-shaped leaves and conspicuous sail-like spathes, this small genus of around 25 species of tuberous perennials is native to Europe and Asia. The well-known florist's arum lilies, however, belong to the genus *Zantedeschia*. Propagate from seed or by division of tubers after flowering.

Arum italicum
Italian Arum

ORIGIN Europe, Turkey, north Africa
CLIMATE ST, WT, M, CT
Growing to 30cm/12in, this tuberous-rooted perennial bears its semi-erect, arrow-shaped, white-veined leaves to 35cm/14in long from winter to late spring. Pale green or creamy yellow spathes to 40cm/16in long appear in spring and early summer, followed by orange berries. **'Marmoratum'** (syn. 'Pictum') has highly ornamental deep green leaves with bold cream or pale green veins. The cut leaves are good in flower arrangements.

USE & CULTIVATION A good foliage plant easily grown in partial shade among shrubs. It prefers moist but well-drained, humus-enriched soil. In very cold areas it should be grown in containers and over-wintered in a greeenhouse. Frost hardy.

ARUNDO

FAMILY GRAMINEAE/POACEAE

A small genus containing 3 species of tall perennial grasses native to the subtropics and warm temperate regions of the Northern Hemisphere. They form large leafy clumps rather like well-behaved bamboos and make striking accent plants for large gardens. They are best cut back to the ground in winter to encourage fresh new spring growth. Propagate from seed or by division.

Arundo donax
Giant Reed

ORIGIN Mediterranean region
CLIMATE T, ST, WT, M, CT
This striking clump-forming grass has stout stems to 3m/10ft or more. Arching, grey–green, strap-like leaves 40–60cm/16–24in long arising from the nodes are arranged in alternate ranks. Showy plume-like flowerheads to 60cm/24in long are produced in autumn. The less hardy **'Versicolor'** (syn. 'Variegata') is smaller, growing to 1.8m/6ft, with white-striped leaves.

USE & CULTIVATION An outstanding feature plant for many landscaping styles, from the lush tropical to the minimalist pebble courtyard. It thrives in moist conditions and serves as an excellent waterside plant. Grow in a sheltered sunny position. Where spring frosts are severe, the variegated form can be over-wintered in a cool conservatory or greenhouse. Fully frost hardy.

ASARUM

WILD GINGER
FAMILY ARISTOLOCHIACEAE

A genus of 70 species of evergreen or deciduous rhizomatous perennials from temperate regions of the Northern Hemisphere. They are low, tufted or carpeting plants with mainly heart- or kidney-shaped, long-stalked leaves, sometimes flecked or marbled in grey or white. Small pitcher-shaped flowers appear at ground level and are often concealed by the foliage. Plants are prone to attack from slugs and snails. Propagate from ripe seed or by division.

Asarum europaeum
Asarabacca

ORIGIN Western Europe
CLIMATE WT, M, CT, H
This vigorous prostrate perennial forms low carpets to 30cm/12in wide

of lustrous dark green kidney-shaped leaves to 8cm/3in long. Insignificant greenish brown tubular flowers with triangular lobes appear beneath the leaves in late spring and summer.
USE & CULTIVATION A leafy ground-cover ideal for a shady woodland garden. It also looks good in medium-sized shallow containers. Grow in moisture-retentive but well-drained fertile soil in part or full shade. Fully frost hardy.

ASPARAGUS

FAMILY ASPARAGACEAE/LILIACEAE
Best known for the delicious edible *Asparagus officinalis*, this is a genus of around 140 species of evergreen and deciduous cool temperate perennials native to Europe, Africa and Asia. A number of species, sometimes referred to as asparagus ferns, are grown in pots or hanging baskets for their attractive, arching, feathery foliage. The white or pink flowers are insignificant but are often followed by colourful red, orange or purple berries. Propagate from seed or by division of tubers.

Asparagus densiflorus
Asparagus Fern

ORIGIN South Africa
CLIMATE WT, M
This small woody evergreen perennial to about 90cm/36in high has 3 or more linear and flattened, leaf-like, light green stems forming at the nodes, giving the plant a compact appearance. Small white summer flowers are followed by showy red berries. **'Myersii'** (syn. *A. meyeri*), known as the Foxtail Fern, is an erect form with dense pale green fronds to 45cm/18in long. **'Sprengeri'** has graceful cascading stems to 1m/3ft long covered in fine, needle-like, leaf-like stems.
USE & CULTIVATION These plants add a leafy luxuriance to rockeries and bordering steps and are popular in hanging baskets for decorating a patio or veranda. Grow in humus-enriched, moist well-drained soil in full sun or partial shade. Indoors, provide bright filtered light and a rich potting mix, and water well during the growing season. Less water is required in winter. Frost tender.

Asarum europaeum

Asparagus officinalis

Asparagus densiflorus 'Sprengeri'

Aspidistra elatior 'Variegata'

Asparagus officinalis
Asparagus

ORIGIN Mediterranean region, western Asia

CLIMATE WT, M, CT

This long-lived erect perennial grows to 1m/3ft or so high with a spread of about 50cm/20in. Its dainty thread-like foliage is carried on drooping branched stems. Female plants produce many small red berries.

USE & CULTIVATION Asparagus is traditionally grown by planting one-year-old bought plants or crowns in spring. The emerging edible spears are harvested in the second or third season, depending on the age of the crowns. Allowed to grow uncut, it forms an elegant, soft, leafy plant—a charming addition among shrubs. Grow in full sun in moderately fertile soil with good drainage. Frost hardy.

Asparagus setaceus
syn. *Asparagus plumosus*
Asparagus Fern

ORIGIN South Africa

CLIMATE WT, M

This climbing species has wiry stems and flattened feathery sprays consisting of delicate, hair-like, bright green branchlets. It sometimes produces small white flowers, followed by black berries. The foliage is used by florists for buttonholes and other small floral arrangements.

USE & CULTIVATION Grow this easy-going houseplant in rich potting mix in bright indirect light. Water well during the growing season and less in winter. Frost tender.

ASPIDISTRA

FAMILY CONVALLARIACEAE/ LILIACEAE

Although there are about 8 species in this genus of evergreen, rhizomatous perennials from the Himalayas, China and Japan, only *Aspidistra elatior* is commonly grown as an indoor, shadehouse or patio plant. Its ability to thrive in poorly lit situations has made it one of the most successful indoor plants. Propagate by division in early spring.

Aspidistra elatior
Aspidistra, Cast-iron Plant

ORIGIN China

CLIMATE ST, WT, M, CT

The Aspidistra is a rhizomatous perennial with long-stalked, broad, dark green leaves to about 60cm/24in long which grow straight out of the soil and arch gracefully. Small purplish flowers are produced close to the ground and are hard to see. **'Variegata'** has green and cream striped leaves.

USE & CULTIVATION Mingles well with ferns, tree ferns, palms and other broad-leaved foliage plants in a sheltered shady position in moist well-drained soil. Indoors, provide medium light, evenly moist conditions and an occasional feed. Avoid using unsuitable household chemicals to clean the leaves. It does best when slightly pot-bound. Moderately frost hardy.

ASPLENIUM
SPLEENWORT
FAMILY ASPLENIACEAE

Widely distributed throughout the world, this is a large genus of around 700 species of mainly evergreen epiphytic or terrestrial ferns. In general, they have creeping or short rhizomes giving rise to tufts of entire, pinnate or bipinnate fronds. A number of species have become popular in cultivation and are grown in pots and baskets, or on rocks and trees. These ferns can be seriously attacked by slugs and snails. Propagate from spores, by division of the rhizome or from the small plantlets that may form in the upper part of the fronds in some species.

Asplenium australasicum
Bird's Nest Fern

ORIGIN Australia, South Pacific islands
CLIMATE T, ST, WT
Growing naturally on rocks and in the branches of rainforest trees, this handsome fern forms a large rosette of undivided leathery fronds to 1m/3ft or more long and to 20cm/8in wide, with a ridged dark brown midrib. The rich green leaves radiate from an open centre that collects debris as a source of nutrients. It is sometimes confused with *A. nidus*, a closely related and widespread tropical species with a less prominent, almost black, rounded midrib.
USE & CULTIVATION Makes a very attractive understorey to palms and tree ferns, where it thrives in filtered sunlight and humus-enriched soil with good drainage. Because of its relatively small root system, it is highly recommended for growing in containers. It needs a potting mix with a high humus content. Indoors, provide good light, warmth and moderate humidity. Frost tender.

Asplenium bulbiferum
Hen and Chicken Fern, Mother Spleenwort

ORIGIN Australia, New Zealand
CLIMATE T, ST, WT
This erect clumping fern has finely divided semi-weeping fronds to 1m/3ft long and 30cm/12in wide. Tiny reproductive plantlets form on the outer parts of the mature fronds. These eventually take root and may be detached and transplanted when they are a reasonable size.
USE & CULTIVATION For a rich ferny glade, grow in groups beneath palms or among shrubs in a partially shaded, protected position. It likes moist humus-rich, well-drained soil. In a pot or hanging basket, grow on a patio or as a houseplant if conditions are not too dry. Provide a humus-rich potting mix and bright filtered light. Feed container-grown specimens with a slow-release fertiliser annually in spring or summer. Keep the soil evenly moist; less water is needed during the winter rest period. Moderately frost hardy.

Asplenium australasicum

Asplenium bulbiferum

Asplenium flabellifolium

Asplenium flabellifolium
Necklace Fern

ORIGIN Australia
CLIMATE WT, M, CT
This small trailing fern forming mini-ature spreading colonies has slender light green fronds to about 20cm/8in long with small fan-shaped leaflets. These prostrate fronds extend into a slender tail which may take root at the tip and form a new plantlet.
USE & CULTIVATION A dainty, lacy fern for a small rockery pocket or for use as a tiny groundcover in a protected, partially shaded position with good drainage. Also grow as a basket plant or indoor pot plant. Frost hardy.

Asplenium scolopendrium subsp. scolopendrium
syn. *Phyllitis scolopendrium*
Hart's Tongue Fern

ORIGIN Europe, western Asia
CLIMATE WT, M, CT
This evergreen fern with an erect or short creeping rhizome forms a crown of entire, rich green, strap-shaped fronds to 60cm/24in long with wavy margins and heart-shaped bases. Several cultivated forms have variously cut or ruffled fronds. **'Crispum'** has strongly wavy, almost ruffled fronds. **'Ramocr-istatum'** has crested fronds to 30cm/12in long that branch from the base.

USE & CULTIVATION The partial shade and moist humus-enriched soil of a woodland edge provide ideal growing conditions for this decorative fern. Container-grown plants need fertile soil with peat moss and sand added. Indoors, provide good light and mod-erate humidity. Fully frost hardy.

Asplenium trichomanes
Maidenhair Spleenwort

ORIGIN Temperate regions
CLIMATE WT, M, CT, H
This small terrestrial fern forms upright clumps of narrow, dark green, lacy

Athyrium felix-femina

fronds to about 20cm/8in long with small oblong leaflets with rounded tips. The stems are stiff, black and shiny.
USE & CULTIVATION Grow in a cool, moist partially shaded rockery pocket or as a basket or pot plant. It occurs naturally on limestone outcrops and may need lime added to the soil for successful growth. Fully frost hardy.

ATHYRIUM

LADY FERN
FAMILY ATHYRIACEAE
A cosmopolitan genus of around 180 species of tufted or clump-forming evergreen or deciduous ferns that are found mainly in moist woodlands and swampy places. Propagate from spores or by division.

Athyrium felix-femina
Lady Fern

ORIGIN Temperate regions of Northern Hemisphere
CLIMATE WT, M, CT
This deciduous clump-forming fern has arching, light green, lacy fronds to 1m/3ft long. Popular since Victorian times, several forms or cultivars are grown, varying in size and shape of fronds and leaflets, in some cases with

Athyrium felix-femina 'Minutissimum'

ornamental crested or tasselled edges.
'Frizelliae' has fronds to 20cm/8in
long with tiny rounded leaflets. **'Minutissimum'** forms smaller clumps to
30cm/12in high and wide.
USE & CULTIVATION Ideal for a woodland setting. Grow in humus-enriched
moist soil in dappled shade. Remove
fading fronds regularly. In the fernery
or greenhouse, provide bright light and
a humid atmosphere. Do not allow the
plants to dry out. Fully frost hardy.

Athyrium niponicum 'Pictum'

Athyrium niponicum
syn. *Athyrium goeringianum*
Japanese Painted Fern

ORIGIN Japan
CLIMATE WT, M, CT, H
This deciduous fern has scaly, creeping,
reddish brown rhizomes and tufted,
triangular, purple-tinged, greyish green
fronds to 35cm/14in long. They are
irregularly lobed with notched or
lobed margins. The new fronds of
'Pictum' are silvery grey with reddish
blue tinges.
USE & CULTIVATION As for *A. felix-
femina*. Fully frost hardy.

ATRIPLEX

SALT BUSH
FAMILY CHENOPODIACEAE
A genus of around 100 species of
annuals, perennials and shrubs with a
worldwide distribution, found on sea
coasts and in drier inland saline habitats.
They have obovate to triangular silvery
green leaves and tiny petalless flowers.
Eye-catching foliage, soil-binding ability
and resistance to salt spray, drought and
fire are all good reasons for growing
these decorative plants. The Red
Mountain Spinach or Orach (*Atriplex
hortensis*), found throughout Europe
and around the Mediterranean coast, is
cooked as a green vegetable like
spinach or used in salads. Propagate
from seed, cuttings or by division.

Atriplex nummularia
Old Man Saltbush

ORIGIN Australia
CLIMATE WT, M, SA
This dense rounded shrub growing to a
height and spread of 3m/10ft has oval,
silvery grey leaves about 4cm/1½in
long covered with a fine coating of
white scales. Separate clusters of male

and female flowers appear throughout
the year.
USE & CULTIVATION A tough grey-
leaved shrub for an informal hedge and
windbreak in both coastal and dry
inland areas. It tolerates most soils, but
does best in a sunny well-drained position. Marginally frost hardy.

Atriplex nummularia

Atriplex nummularia

Aucuba japonica 'Crotonifolia'

Aucuba japonica 'Variegata'

AUCUBA

FAMILY CORNACEAE
This is a small genus of 3 or 4 species of evergreen shrubs grown mainly for their bold leaves and fruits. They are useful for growing in heavy shade under large trees. To shape and restrict growth, cut shrubs back hard in spring. Propagate from seed or cuttings.

Aucuba japonica
Japanese Laurel, Spotted Laurel

ORIGIN Japan
CLIMATE ST, WT, M, CT, H
This evergreen, bushy shrub to around 1.8m/6ft high has stout green shoots and oval glossy green leaves to 20cm/ 8in long. It bears small reddish star-shaped flowers in spring and drooping clusters of bright red berries on female plants in early autumn. The popular cultivar **'Crotonifolia'** is female, with dark green leaves heavily mottled yellow. **'Gold Dust'** is female, with gold-speckled dark green leaves. The leaves of **'Variegata'** are heavily splashed with yellow.
USE & CULTIVATION All these plants will tolerate shade and are good mixers among other shrubs, particularly the variegated forms, which give a splash of colour to a dark corner. Grow in fertile, moist well-drained soil in full or partial shade. They make neat large container subjects and can be grown indoors. Water freely while the plants are in active growth and less in winter. Fully frost hardy.

BAMBUSA

FAMILY GRAMINEAE/POACEAE
There are 100 or so species in this genus of tropical and subtropical bamboos from southern Asia. They form tight clumps of slender hollow canes (or culms) with masses of linear leaves arising from each node. Their light airy gracefulness can bring a real presence to the garden, particularly in modern styles of planting. Because their short rhizomes are non-invasive, controlling their spread is no more difficult than pruning a shrub annually. In very small gardens you can curtail their spread by sinking barriers around the planting. Regularly thin out older, dead and weak culms. Propagate by division.

Bambusa multiplex
syn. *Bambusa glaucescens*
Hedge Bamboo

ORIGIN Southern China
CLIMATE T, ST, WT
This clump-producing species develops slender culms 3–9m/10–30ft tall with numerous branchlets arising from the nodes. Narrow deep green leaves to 9cm/3½in long with a silvery reverse are borne in pairs on slender branchlets at each node. **'Alphonse Karr'** has yellow culms with green stripes of varying widths. **'Riviereorum'** is a dwarf form to 3m/10ft tall with small fern-like leaves on thin arching branchlets.
USE & CULTIVATION Both the species and 'Alphonse Karr' are widely grown for hedging and ideal for use as a windbreak or privacy screen. Grow in moist humus-rich soil and water well during dry periods. Use 'Riviereorum' as a low space-divider within the garden or for small-scale plantings. One of the best bamboos for pot culture, it makes an attractive indoor plant if given bright indirect light and humid conditions. Moderately frost hardy.

Bambusa multiplex

A
B

Bambusa multiplex 'Alphonse Karr'

Bambusa vulgaris 'Vittata'

Bambusa ventricosa
Buddha's Belly Bamboo

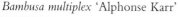

ORIGIN Southern China

CLIMATE ST, WT

Grown in the ground, this vigorous clumping species reaches a height of 6–7m/20–22ft, but often no more than 2.5m/8ft in pots. Its short swollen internodes are more evident when it is grown as a pot plant or under poor conditions. The dark green linear leaves are up to 18cm/7in long.

USE & CULTIVATION To encourage the unusual shape of the culms, grow in containers, with relatively poor soil and moderate water. Frost tender.

Bambusa vulgaris
Common Bamboo

ORIGIN Uncertain; widely cultivated and naturalised in the tropics

CLIMATE ST, WT

This vigorous bamboo sends up vertical shoots forming a neat tight grove around 18–24m/60–80ft high. It has thick culms, and wiry branches bearing

Bambusa multiplex 'Riviereorum'

Bambusa ventricosa

linear, grass-like leaves arise from the nodes. It is more often seen in the somewhat smaller growing ornamental forms **'Vittata'**, with golden culms irregularly striped dark green, and the popular **'Wamin'**, to 5m/17ft tall with shiny green culms with short and slightly swollen internodes.

USE & CULTIVATION Use in oriental-style gardens or to create a jungle effect in a tropical planting scheme. Grow in a moist but well-drained soil. 'Wamin' can be grown as a container plant and used as a feature in small gardens. If using a deep pot, put some rocks in the bottom to add stability. Frost tender.

Beaucarnea recurvata

many metres in the open. Small plants produce neat firm bulbs at the base of the plant, changing into wide-spreading and grotesque shapes as the plant ages. For this reason, and because of the wrinkled texture of the greyish brown bark, it is sometimes called the Elephant-foot Tree. Each stem is topped with dense pendulous tufts of narrow recurved leaves to 1.8m/6ft long. Numerous small creamy flowers are produced in feathery panicles to 1m/3ft long in summer.

USE & CULTIVATION Because of its unusual overall appearance, the Ponytail Plant is ideally grown as a specimen in a desert garden. Grow in a sunny position with excellent drainage. Indoors, provide bright light and a warm dry atmosphere. Do not allow the soil to remain permanently saturated; less water is required in winter. It will tolerate air-conditioning. Flowers are unlikely to appear on indoor plants. Frost tender.

BEGONIA

FAMILY BEGONIACEAE

This very large genus of around 900 species has given rise to over 10 000 hybrids and cultivars, ranging in size from small fleshy herbs to large shrubs, climbers and tree-like plants. They are grown for their colourful flowers and in many cases for their highly ornamental leaves, which come in a wonderful variety of shapes and colours. The leaves are usually asymmetric, some with a velvety or glossy surface, with intricate patterns or variegations. There are many types; the **tuberous group** and **fibrous-rooted begonias** are mostly grown for their large double flowers. Also tuberous by nature are some of the attractive shrub-like begonias, such as the Metal-leaf Begonia, *B. metallica*, and the Palm-leaf Begonia, *B. luxurians*, which have a bushy habit and beautiful leaves. The **rhizomatous begonias**, which include the decorative **Rex begonias**, have magnificently coloured and variegated shield-like or spiralled leaves

BEAUCARNEA

FAMILY AGAVACEAE/
DRACAENACEAE

Native to semi-arid regions of southern USA and Mexico, this genus consists of about 24 species of evergreen shrubs and trees. Most have a sparsely branched stem that develops an unusually swollen bottle-like base that becomes larger as the plant ages. The stems are topped with tufts of long, thin, strap-like leaves. Mature plants bear small creamy white flowers

in large terminal panicles. Propagate from seed or from the small suckers that develop around the base of the plant.

Beaucarnea recurvata
syn. *Nolina recurvata*
Bottle Palm, Ponytail Plant

ORIGIN Mexico
CLIMATE ST, WT, SA
This slow-growing yucca-like plant will eventually grow to a height of

B

Begonia acetosa

Begonia 'Cleopatra'

Begonia 'Cathedral'

shaped leaves, maroon below. The veins and leaf stalks are covered with soft pinkish hairs. Masses of white flowers are produced in late spring.

USE & CULTIVATION An attractive edging plant for a shady sheltered position with well-drained, humus-enriched soil. Grow potted plants in a free-draining standard potting mix with some grit added. Indoors, provide good light but not direct sun. Water thoroughly, but only when the compost has almost dried out. Frost tender.

Begonia 'Cathedral'
Cathedral Windows

ORIGIN Gardens
CLIMATE ST, WT
This small rhizomatous begonia grows to a height of about 35cm/14in with a spread of 40cm/16in or more. It has short green stems with fleshy, ear-like, shiny green leaves that are ruffled and puckered with a deep purplish red underside. Tall spikes of pink flowers appear in early spring.
USE & CULTIVATION As for *B. acetosa*. Frost tender.

Begonia 'Cleopatra'

ORIGIN Gardens
CLIMATE T, ST, WT
Growing to less than 20cm/8in, this begonia has shortly creeping rhizomes that spread over the surface of the soil. The yellowish green star-shaped leaves are red beneath, edged with white bristly hairs and have a large area covered with reddish brown markings. Sprays of pink perfumed flowers appear in early spring.
USE & CULTIVATION This easy-to-grow begonia looks best when planted in large clumps in a shaded rock garden or near a water feature. Also well suited to shallow containers or hanging baskets in a free-draining standard potting mix with some grit added. Indoors, provide good light but not direct sun. Water thoroughly, but only when the compost has almost dried out. Frost tender.

which may have a smooth, hairy or warty surface and often have a lustrous metallic sheen. Flowers are always small. The **cane-stemmed begonias** are erect growers with fibrous roots and swollen bamboo-like stems. Many of these are known as 'Angel-wings', often bearing pairs of beautifully marked leaves with elongated tips that resemble extended wings; *B. stipulacea* is an excellent example. Tip-prune shrubby types to encourage compact growth. Begonias are susceptible to fungal diseases such as grey mould (*Botrytis*), powdery mildew and stem or rhizome rot if conditions are too damp. Outdoors, protect them from slugs and snails. Propagate from seed, tip cuttings or by division of tubers or rhizomes. Leaf cuttings can be placed underside down on damp peat with a few pebbles on top to keep the leaf in contact with the soil.

Begonia acetosa

ORIGIN Brazil
CLIMATE ST, WT
A small-growing, fibrous-rooted variety with erect stems and deep green heart-

Begonia coccinea
Angel-wing Begonia

ORIGIN Brazil

CLIMATE T, ST, WT

This slender cane-stemmed begonia, 1–2m/3–7ft tall, has succulent, deep green, ovate leaves to 10–15cm/4–6in long with red margins and a darker red underside. Drooping clusters of rose red waxy flowers are produced from spring to autumn.

USE & CULTIVATION Mingles very well with ferns and can be positioned beneath a light canopy of palms. Grow in a partially shaded position with some morning sun. Remove old woody stems at ground level. A very good house or conservatory plant, it needs bright filtered light, good ventilation and moderate water. Frost tender.

Begonia grandis subsp. evansiana
Hardy Begonia

ORIGIN Japan, China, Malaysia

CLIMATE ST, WT, M

This tuberous begonia has branched, erect, fleshy stems to about 50cm/20in. The glistening, waxy, olive green leaves to 10cm/4in long are pinkish red-tinged around the veins on the underside. Fragrant pink or white single flowers appear in drooping clusters in summer. It reproduces by small bulbils in late summer. All the top growth dies down in early winter.

USE & CULTIVATION The only begonia that can be grown outdoors in temperate regions, and well suited to a woodland setting. Grow in a warm position, dappled shade and well-drained, humus-enriched soil. Container-grown plants require free-draining peaty soil. Indoors, provide bright filtered light, good ventilation and moderate water. Marginally frost hardy.

Begonia luxurians
Palm-leaf Begonia

ORIGIN Brazil

CLIMATE T, ST, WT

This shrub-like begonia with an upright habit and slightly hairy red stems can reach 1.5m/5ft in height. The dark green or bronze green palm-like leaves have finely toothed margins and radiate from the centre. Small creamy white flowers, to 1cm/^{1}/3in wide are produced from spring to summer.

USE & CULTIVATION As for *B. coccinea*. Frost tender.

Begonia masoniana
Iron Cross Begonia

ORIGIN New Guinea

CLIMATE T, ST

A rhizomatous begonia growing to a height of 60cm/24in, with oval mid-green leaves to 20cm/8in long with a distinctive dark brown cross-shaped pattern radiating from the centre. The leaf surfaces are puckered and covered with fine red hairs. The small green or pinkish white flowers produced in summer seldom appear on indoor plants.

Begonia luxurians

Begonia masoniana

B

Begonia metallica

USE & CULTIVATION Outdoors in tropical gardens, it makes a good edging plant if protected from direct sun and slug and snail attack. Indoors, position in a warm well-ventilated room with bright indirect light, in moist, well-drained soil, with regular weak liquid fertiliser during the growing season. Less water is required in winter. Frost tender.

Begonia metallica
Metal-leaf Begonia

ORIGIN Brazil
CLIMATE T, ST, WT
This shrubby begonia reaches about 1m/3ft in height. It has slightly hairy, bronze green leaves to 18cm/7in long with a glossy sheen and deep-set purplish veins. Pinkish white flowers are produced on hairy stalks in summer and autumn.
USE & CULTIVATION As for *B. coccinea*. Frost tender.

Begonia olsoniae

ORIGIN Brazil
CLIMATE ST, WT
This small shrub-like begonia reaching only 20cm/8in high has rounded, satiny, bronze green leaves 12–20cm/5–8in long with contrasting ivory veins. Single pale pinkish white flowers appear year-round on reddish arching stems held well above the foliage.
USE & CULTIVATION As for *B. coccinea*. Frost tender.

Begonia pustulata

ORIGIN Mexico, Guatemala
CLIMATE ST, WT
This rhizomatous plant grows to 15–20cm/6–8in with a similar spread.

Its thick-textured oval leaves to 15cm/6in long have a warty and slightly hairy surface. Small rose pink flowers are borne in early summer. **'Argentea'** (syn. 'Silver') has silver-splashed leaves and greenish white flowers.
USE & CULTIVATION In warm climates 'Argentea' makes a beautiful ground-cover beneath taller growing ferns and will gently follow the contour of low rounded rocks. Also suitable for hanging baskets. Grow in soil enriched with organic matter in a partially shaded position with some gentle morning sun. In the garden, plants are vulnerable to caterpillars and fungal disease during the warmer months if conditions are too damp. Indoors, provide bright filtered light, good ventilation and moderate water. Frost tender.

Begonia pustulata 'Argentea'

Begonia rex
King Begonia, Painted-leaf Begonia

ORIGIN Northern India (Himalayas)
CLIMATE ST, WT

This creeping, rhizomatous begonia 30–40cm/12–16in tall has obliquely heart-shaped deep green leaves with a lustrous metallic sheen and silvery white edges arising vertically on red hairy stalks from the rhizome. It produces sparse and relatively inconspicuous pale pink flowers in late winter. The true *Begonia rex* is probably no longer in cultivation, but is the parent of many beautiful cultivars grown for their extremely decorative foliage and known collectively as the Rex-cultorum begonias. **'American Beauty'** has silvery, metallic, deep red leaves with a blackish centre and edges. **'Emerald Giant'** has ovate, vibrant green leaves with silvery green zones, an emerald green outer zone and red edging. **'Lospe-tu'** is a spiral-leaved variety with fresh green leaves edged with purple and covered in white hairs. The popular **'Merry Christmas'** (syn. 'Ruhrtal') has satiny red leaves with a broad outer band of emerald green and a darker red centre and edging. The large spiralled ovate leaves of **'Princess of Hanover'** have a broad band of silvery white spots and are edged with deep purple. **'Salamander'** bears sharply lobed, silvery leaves faintly threaded with forest green. **'Silver Queen'** has silvery grey leaves with dark green centre veining and edging.

USE & CULTIVATION Among the showiest of all foliage plants, these begonias are most often grown in containers and used for indoor display, for garden rooms and on warm sheltered verandas. Indoors, provide bright filtered light, good ventilation, moderate water and slightly acidic soil. Less water is required in winter. Do not allow water to remain on the leaves otherwise they become susceptible to grey mould (*Botrytis*). Plants that have filled their existing pots can be potted on into slightly larger containers at any time during spring using a peaty potting mix. Frost tender.

Begonia rex 'Lospe-tu'

Begonia rex silver-leaved hybrid

Begonia stipulacea

Begonia stipulacea
syn. *Begonia angularis*

ORIGIN Brazil

CLIMATE ST, WT

This extremely attractive cane-stemmed begonia has slender reddish stems to 60cm/24in high. The elongated, slightly scalloped pointed leaves to 15cm/6in long have silvery veins and a red underside. White bearded flowers are produced throughout the year.

USE & CULTIVATION As for *B. coccinea*. It may need some support to stay upright. Frost tender.

BERBERIS

BARBERRY
FAMILY BERBERIDACEAE

A genus of about 450 species of evergreen and deciduous shrubs from many parts of the world, but mostly centred around temperate parts of Asia. Characteristic of this genus are long cane-like shoots bearing 3-pronged spines. Within the axils of these spines are short shoots bearing groups of 1 to several leaves. Barberries are grown for their fiery autumn colours and colourful fruits. They withstand hard pruning and are useful for hedging. Some species are used for bonsai. Propagate from seed or cuttings.

Berberis thunbergii
Japanese Barberry

ORIGIN Japan

CLIMATE WT, M, CT, H

This striking, low-growing deciduous shrub to about 1.5m/5ft high has obovate leaves to 3cm/1¼in long; bright green above and greyish beneath, they turn bright red in autumn. Pale yellow flowers with dull red sepals in summer are followed by shiny red bead-like berries. **'Atropurpurea'** has dark reddish purple leaves, turning crimson in autumn. **'Atropurpurea Nana'** (syns 'Crimson Pygmy', 'Little Favourite'), a compact miniature version, makes an ideal rockery plant. **'Aurea'** is a low

Berberis thunbergii 'Rose Glow'

compact form with yellow young leaves, maturing pale green and turning golden in autumn. **'Bagatelle'** grows only about 30cm/12in high and has compact deep red–purple foliage. **'Golden Ring'** has particularly attractive purple leaves with a narrow golden yellow margin. **'Red Pillar'** has a narrow erect habit to 90cm/36in; its reddish purple leaves turn scarlet in autumn. **'Rose Glow'** is a small bushy shrub with young purple leaves mottled white and flushed soft pink or bright pink, maturing purple through-

out. **'Silver Beauty'** is a rounded compact form to 60cm/24in with leaves mottled and splashed creamy white, turning brilliant red in autumn.

USE & CULTIVATION Well suited to the edge of a woodland garden where their attractive range of tints provide a pleasing contrast against darker foliage shrubs. Also, valuable specimen shrubs for small gardens or courtyards. They respond to heavy pruning in winter and can be shaped or used as a hedge. Grow in well-drained soil in sun or light shade. Fully frost hardy.

BERGENIA

FAMILY SAXIFRAGACEAE

A genus of 6 to 8 species of evergreen perennials native to temperate Asia. They have stout fleshy rhizomes and form low carpeting clumps of large, paddle-shaped, leathery leaves, making them excellent groundcover plants. Spikes of pink or white bell-shaped flowers appear in winter and spring. Guard against slugs and snails. Propagate from seed or by division.

Bergenia ciliata

ORIGIN Northern India (Assam)
CLIMATE WT, M, CT

This clump-forming perennial forms an attractive mound about 40cm/16in tall and wide of broadly ovate or rounded mid-green leaves to 25cm/10in or more across. They are hairy on both sides. The white or pinkish flowers appear on 30cm/12in tall stems in spring.
USE & CULTIVATION These make first-rate borders and edging plants, especially for highlighting the contour of paths. Their handsome large clumps can increase visual interest beneath trees. Often bergenias can be used where hostas will not flourish, such as

Bergenia ciliata

in poorish dry soils. For best results, grow in humus-rich, well-drained soil in partial shade. Frost hardy.

Bergenia cordifolia

ORIGIN Russia
CLIMATE M, CT, H

This species forms a low clump to 60cm/24in tall of round leathery leaves to 30cm/12in long, deep green and edged with crimson. Panicles of deep pink or red flowers are borne on red stems in late winter and spring. **'Purpurea'** has thicker reddish leaves that take on purplish tints in winter. Magenta flowers are carried on stems to 60cm/24in tall.
USE & CULTIVATION As for *B. ciliata*. In poor soils and dry conditions plants

will take on stronger winter leaf colour, making them very useful for difficult areas. Frost hardy.

Bergenia x schmidtii

ORIGIN Gardens
CLIMATE WT, M, CT, H

A hybrid between *Begonia ciliata* and *B. crassifolia*, this vigorous perennial makes a substantial groundcover to 30cm/12in high and 60cm/24in wide. It has fleshy, dull green, obovate leaves to 25cm/10in long with finely toothed margins. Sprays of clear pink flowers are borne on short stout stems in late winter and early spring.
USE & CULTIVATION As for *B. ciliata*. Frost hardy.

Bergenia x *schmidtii*

Bergenia stracheyi

Bergenia stracheyi
syn. *Bergenia milesii*

ORIGIN Himalayas

CLIMATE WT, M, CT

This clumping species produces erect, prominently veined, obovate leaves to 20cm/8in long, wedge-shaped at the base. Fragrant deep pink or white nodding flowers are produced in early spring. **USE & CULTIVATION** As for *B. ciliata*. Frost hardy.

BETULA

BIRCH

FAMILY BETULACEAE

Grown for their often sparkling white bark and luxurious bright green spring foliage that turns shades of gold in autumn, this genus of about 60 species of deciduous trees and shrubs is found throughout the Northern Hemisphere. Male and female catkins are produced on the same tree. Birches are shallow rooted and will need watering during dry periods. Many species are suited to small gardens, but need a fairly cool climate to be grown successfully. Propagate from seed or softwood cuttings taken in early summer, or by grafting in late winter.

Betula papyrifera

Betula nigra
River Birch

ORIGIN Eastern USA

CLIMATE M, CT, H

Reaching 9m/30ft in height, this open cone-shaped tree has a trunk that is inclined to fork into 2 or 3 stems near the ground. The shiny pinkish bark, peeling in layers when young, becomes distinctly dark and furrowed on older trees. The glossy diamond-shaped leaves to 7cm/2½ in long have toothed edges and a silvery reverse. Yellowish male catkins to 8cm/3in long appear in early spring.

USE & CULTIVATION In nature this species inhabits wet ground on riverbanks and is among the best ornamental trees for planting in damp areas. It will also do well in well-drained soil, but needs plenty of water during dry spells. Fully frost hardy.

Betula papyrifera
Paper Birch, Canoe Birch

ORIGIN North America

CLIMATE M, CT, H

The distinctive white papery bark of this decorative tree to 15m/50ft was used by Native Americans to make canoes. The branches are strongly ascending within a sparse conical crown. The leaves are oval, with long pointed tips, and to 10cm/4in long. They colour yellow in autumn. Male catkins to 10cm/4in long occur in clusters in early spring.

USE & CULTIVATION With its ghostly white bark and luxuriant spring foliage, this medium-sized tree is a charming

Betula nigra

addition to any garden, used as a specimen or in small groups. Thrives in intense winter cold. Grow in deep, well-drained soil in full sun or dappled shade. Fully frost hardy.

Betula pendula

Betula pendula 'Tristis'

Betula utilis var. *jacquemontii*

Betula pendula
Silver Birch

ORIGIN Northern Europe
CLIMATE WT, M, CT, H
This elegant and extremely popular tree has slender arching branches to 15m/50ft or more high. Its silvery white bark becomes dark and fissured at the base of the trunk in older specimens. The diamond-shaped bright green leaves to 6cm/2¼ in long have toothed margins and turn golden yellow in autumn. Clusters of 2–4 yellowish green male catkins appear in spring. **'Laciniata'** (syn. 'Dalecarlica') has deeply cut leaves with serrated lobes and provides excellent golden colour in autumn. **'Tristis'** has slender weeping branches and a sparkling, silvery white trunk that remains white at the base. **'Youngii'** is dome-shaped to 8m/25ft with a very pronounced weeping habit.
USE & CULTIVATION Widely grown for ornament, these trees make charming lawn specimens and look beautiful in small irregular groups, casting a dappled shade in spring and summer; their handsome trunks are a winter feature. Their relatively small root system enables them to be sited quite close to buildings. Grow in a sunny position in deep, well-drained soil. Popular for bonsai. Fully frost hardy.

Betula utilis
Himalayan Birch

ORIGIN China, Himalayas
CLIMATE WT, M, CT, H
This species reaches about 18m/60ft in cultivation, but may be taller in nature. It has pinkish bark with grey patches, or peeling orange–brown bark. The glossy ovate leaves to 12cm/5in long have downy stems and turn yellow in autumn. Yellowish brown male catkins to 12cm/5in long are produced in spring. The variety most often seen in gardens is **B. u. var. *jacquemontii***, with distinctive white bark that peels in horizontal bands and very glossy leaves.
USE & CULTIVATION As for *B. pendula*. Fully frost hardy.

BLECHNUM

WATER FERN, HARD FERN

FAMILY BLECHNACEAE

This genus contains about 200 species widely distributed throughout the world. Most are ground-dwellers (or occasionally epiphytic), with short or creeping rhizomes often densely covered with black scales. Some species form a short scaly trunk. Mature plants have erect, often leathery fronds deeply divided into numerous leaflets and forming neat rosettes. Usually found in wet places, they are commonly called water ferns. Many are popular as pot plants for indoor decoration and are more tolerant of a certain amount of dry air than most other ferns. Remove fading fronds regularly. Propagate from spores or by division of rhizome.

Blechnum brasiliense
Brazilian Tree Fern

ORIGIN Peru, Brazil

CLIMATE ST, WT, M

This fern eventually forms a trunk to 30cm/12in tall, topped by a loose rosette of fronds, making a total height to 1.5m/5ft. The tough fronds to 1m/3ft long and nearly 40cm/16in wide are pink at first, becoming pale green. The closely spaced segments reduce in size towards the base of the frond.

USE & CULTIVATION Enjoying moist humus-rich soil, this fern is ideal for edging a water feature or pool. It requires shelter and warmth in a shady situation. Potted plants can be moved indoors in cold weather. Provide bright filtered light, plenty of water during the growing season, fairly humid conditions and good ventilation. Frost tender.

Blechnum cartilagineum
Gristle Fern

ORIGIN Australia

CLIMATE ST, WT, M

This erect or semi-erect fern to 1.5m/5ft tall has broad pinnate fronds forming a loose rosette from a central clump. The new fronds are pink, changing to pale green as they mature, sometimes darker in shady locations.

USE & CULTIVATION An attractive fern creating a striking tropical effect near water or next to a shady patio. It prefers moist shaded positions, but stands periods of dryness. Also good in containers and can be cared for indoors in the same way as *B. brasiliense*. Frost tender.

Blechnum chilense

ORIGIN Chile, Argentina

CLIMATE M, CT, H

This vigorous fern extends itself by creeping rhizomes, which may become erect and trunk-like, spreading to produce extensive colonies. The dark green pinnate fronds to 1m/3ft long have oblong toothed segments and brown scaly stalks.

USE & CULTIVATION Ideal for forming large luxurious colonies in a cool woodland setting or beside a water feature. Grow in moist, humus-rich soil in partial shade. Fully frost hardy.

Blechnum brasiliense

Blechnum cartilagineum

Blechnum chilense

Blechnum nudum

Blechnum penna-marina

Blechnum gibbum

Blechnum gibbum
syn. *Lomaria gibba*
Dwarf Tree Fern

ORIGIN Fiji
CLIMATE T, ST, WT

This is the most popular water fern, especially for indoor use. It forms a neat rosette of fronds and eventually develops a scaly black trunk which can reach a height of 90cm/36in. The bright green fronds to 90cm/36in long have erect, then spreading, narrow segments. The spore-bearing fronds are distinct, with narrower segments. There are several forms, distinguished by narrower, wider or more pointed leaflets. **'Silver Lady',** to 1.2m/4ft high, has broad emerald green fronds with slender wavy segments.

USE & CULTIVATION Ideal foliage plants for a shady spot in the garden and for creating a tropical atmosphere in small spaces. Grow in moist humus-rich soil in a shaded, protected position away from hot winds and harsh sun. Long-lived plants for spacious containers. Indoors, they can be cared for in the same way as *B. brasiliense*. Frost tender.

Blechnum nudum
Fishbone Water Fern

ORIGIN Australia
CLIMATE ST, WT, M

This fern often forms large colonies along moist creek banks in the wild, where it may develop a short trunk, the erect arching fronds forming a spreading rosette. They are fishbone-shaped, to

1m/3ft long, with narrow pointed segments; new fronds have a pinkish tinge.
USE & CULTIVATION An easy-to-grow fern that will tolerate cool conditions, thriving in winter-wet shady places where many plants won't grow. An excellent container plant; it can be brought indoors and positioned in bright indirect light. Keep the soil moist when in growth. Moderately frost hardy.

Blechnum penna-marina
syn. *Blechnum alpinum*
Alpine Water Fern

ORIGIN Australia
CLIMATE WT, M, CT, H

This small species has crowded, narrow, dark green fronds to 20cm/8in long with leathery stalks covered in minute reddish hairs. The narrow branching rhizome is wiry and creeping, forming a low groundcover. It grows quickly in the summer months and becomes dormant in winter.

USE & CULTIVATION Found at high altitudes, this fern will tolerate cold conditions, including frost and snow. It will thrive at the edge of a pool, in moist wall crevices and rockery pockets, or as a groundcover in a moist woodland setting. A decorative pot plant or basket specimen if assured of regular water during summer. Fully frost hardy.

Blechnum spicant
Deer Fern, Hard Fern

ORIGIN Europe, northern Asia, North America
CLIMATE WT, M, CT, H

This rosette-forming fern has short creeping rhizomes and somewhat arching, leathery green fronds about 20–50cm/8–20in long with oblong segments. Arising from the centre of the rosette are taller, erect, spore-bearing fronds 30–60cm/12–24in long with narrow linear segments.

USE & CULTIVATION In nature this fern inhabits wet woodlands and swamps, and is an ideal waterside plant in cool climates. Grow in full or partial shade in a constantly moist soil. A decorative pot plant requiring a moist potting mix. Fully frost hardy.

BRAHEA

HESPER PALM
FAMILY ARECACEAE/PALMAE

From dry regions of Central America, this is a small genus of about 16 species of fan-leafed palms. Most have tall single stems and are grown as specimen trees for their magnificent foliage and stately appearance. They are particularly useful for poor, dry soils. Propagate from seed.

Brahea armata
Big Blue Hesper Palm

ORIGIN Southern California, Mexico
CLIMATE ST, WT, SA

This slow-growing palm has a relatively stout trunk to 9m/30ft topped with a compact crown of striking, stiff, waxy, blue–green, fan-like leaves 1–2m/3–7ft across, borne on long spiny stalks. Small yellow flowers in long arching panicles to 4.5m/15ft, held well beyond the foliage, are followed by date-like fruits.

USE & CULTIVATION An outstanding feature plant for a desert garden, thriving in an open sunny position and well-drained soil. Once established, it withstands light frosts. In cooler areas young plants make excellent container plants; indoors, position in bright indirect light. Water frequently in summer, less in winter. Frost tender.

Brahea armata

BRASSICA

FAMILY BRASSICACEAE/CRUCIFERAE
This genus of around 35 species of annuals, biennials and perennials ranges from around the Mediterranean to temperate Asia. It is well known for the many edible vegetable species that have long been cultivated, including cabbage, cauliflower, broccoli, Brussels sprouts and kohlrabi. The ornamental kales, with their interesting coloured and variegated foliage, are used in exotic bedding schemes. Propagate from seed.

Brassica oleracea var. acephala cultivars
Ornamental Cabbage and Kale

ORIGIN Gardens
CLIMATE WT, M, CT
Popular in Victorian times for bedding displays and as table decorations, these are variously coloured, deeply lobed or curly-leafed cabbage cultivars that do not form a head. They are grown as annuals from seed mixtures or sold in pots by florists. They can be planted among flowers and herbs, as an attractive group on their own, or in tubs. Some cultivars are strikingly veined; the fast-growing **Osaka Series** has frilled leaves of mixed colours.
USE & CULTIVATION Most kinds develop their best colouring from late summer onwards. Grow in lime-rich, well-drained soil in a sheltered sunny spot. Frost hardy.

BUXUS

BOX

FAMILY BUXACEAE
This genus consists of around 50 species of evergreen shrubs and trees, the majority of which come from tropical and subtropical regions of Central America, the West Indies and southern Africa. The European and temperate Asian species are best known in cultivation, being grown for their small, glossy, leathery leaves, neat dense habit and ability to withstand clipping.

Buxus microphylla

Promote new growth by cutting back stems hard in late spring; trim hedges in summer. Bonsai subjects need protection from cold winds and daily watering during summer. Propagate from semi-ripe cuttings in summer.

Buxus microphylla
Japanese Box

ORIGIN Gardens
CLIMATE WT, M, CT
This slow-growing compact shrub 1–2m/3–7ft high has dark green, shiny, elliptic leaves to 2cm/³⁄₄in long which turn a soft orange in cold winters without falling. Small yellowish green flowers are produced in spring. **'Compacta'** is a popular low-growing form to 30cm/12in high with tiny obovate leaves to 5mm/¹⁄₄in long. **B. m. var. japonica** has slightly more rounded leaves, a dense, rounded, upright habit to 1.5m/5ft or more, and tolerates heat better than other boxes. **B. m. var. koreana** is very cold hardy, with a compact low-growing habit to about 60cm/24in.
USE & CULTIVATION Traditional garden use is as low formal hedges, edging or topiary. Left untrimmed, var. *japonica* is an effective low screen. Grow in a sunny or partially shaded position in any well-drained soil. Fully frost hardy.

Buxus microphylla var. *japonica*

Buxus sempervirens
European Box, Common Box

ORIGIN Europe and Mediterranean region
CLIMATE WT, M, CT, H
This bushy rounded shrub reaches a height of around 1.8m/6ft. The small oval leaves to about 3cm/1¹⁄₄in long are deep glossy green and notched at the tips. There are many forms named for their shape or variegated foliage. **'Latifolia Maculata'**, to 2.5m/8ft high, has bright yellow young foliage becoming green and yellow with age. **'Marginata'** (syn. 'Aureomarginata')

B

Buxus sempervirens

Buxus sempervirens 'Latifolia Maculata'

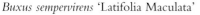

Buxus sempervirens 'Marginata'

has tiny dark green leaves splashed and margined with yellow. A very slow-grower, it can be trimmed to any shape. The compact **'Suffruticosa'** has a dense habit and is used extensively in Europe for dwarf edging, garden dividers and topiary. It eventually reaches about 1m/3ft, but can be maintained as a dwarf hedge of 30cm/12in or less. **'Suffruticosa Variegata'** has leaves edged creamy white.

USE & CULTIVATION Popular hedging and topiary subjects. They are very slow growing but long lasting, useful for formal effects, whether singly or in groups, in the garden or in containers. Grow in well-drained soil. Very tolerant of climatic extremes, but protection from hot sun and care in watering, feeding and mulching will result in better colour in hot dry areas. Fully frost hardy.

CALADIUM

FAMILY ARACEAE

A genus of around 7 species of tuberous-rooted perennials from tropical jungles of South America, related to the arum lilies. The large, heart-shaped or arrow-shaped leaves on long stalks arising directly from the tubers give rise to the common names of 'elephant's ears' and 'angel wings'. Extremely popular during the Victorian era, caladiums are now undergoing a revival, prized for the spectacular variations and colouring of their paper-thin leaves. Although all varieties intermittently produce small arum-type flowers, these plants are generally grown only for their beautiful foliage. The tubers go through a dormant stage after the leaves have died down. Given a lengthy rest period and minimal water, they will produce new growth the following year. Propagate from division of small tubers in spring.

Caladium bicolor
syn. *Caladium* x *hortulanum*
Angel Wings, Elephant's Ears,
Heart of Jesus

ORIGIN Gardens
CLIMATE T, ST

The caladiums in cultivation are hybrids of mixed origin, many known by varietal names, of which there are thousands. One of the parents is thought to be the South American *Caladium bicolor*, which produces slender stems to 60cm/24in long with peltate arrow-shaped leaves of similar length. The beautifully marked leaves can be spotted, veined, blotched or marbled red, pink or white on green. **'Candidum'** has almost translucent white leaves with heavy green veining; **'Pink Beauty'** has arrow-shaped, pink-mottled green leaves to 45cm/18in long with darker pink veins.

USE & CULTIVATION Grow outdoors in partially shaded tropical and subtropical gardens in moist humus-enriched soil. To remain looking good they need shelter from drying winds, so are ideally sited beneath trees or in protected courtyards. In cool climates, grow in a warm conservatory or greenhouse with constant high humidity during the growing season and a temperature of at least 18°–24°C/65°–75°F. Provide bright indirect light and a peat-based potting mix. Water freely during the growing season; less water is

Caladium bicolor 'Candidum'

Caladium bicolor 'Pink Beauty'

required as the leaves begin to die down. Frost tender.

Caladium lindenii

ORIGIN Tropical South America
CLIMATE T, ST

A clump-forming perennial to 80cm/ 32in high with striking, arrow-shaped, leathery leaves to 45cm/18in long, dark green above with the midrib and main veins broadly marked white or cream. It bears white arum-like flowers intermittently. **'Magnificum'** is broadly veined with cream and has a distinct cream line inside the margins.
USE & CULTIVATION As for *C. bicolor*.

CALATHEA

FAMILY MARANTACEAE

This is a large genus of around 300 species of mostly clump-forming tropical rhizomatous perennials native to Central and South America and the West Indies. They are valued for their decorative patterned and coloured long-stalked leaves. Their small tubular flowers are rarely showy and not often produced in cultivation. Calatheas should be fertilised regularly during the growing season. Take care when removing withered and dead leaves as new leaves arise from the stalks of older leaves. Scale and red spider mites can be a problem. Propagate by division in late spring.

Calathea burle-marxii

ORIGIN Brazil
CLIMATE T, ST

This beautiful species is named after Brazilian landscape architect Roberto Burle Marx, whose brightly coloured designs featured massed plantings of dramatic Brazilian foliage plants. It has upright bamboo-like stems to 1.5m/5ft high with slightly arching, bright green, ovate leaves to 60cm/24in long with a yellowish green midrib. The underside of the leaf is lightly shaded grey. Small purple flowers are grouped on spikes to 18cm/7in long.

USE & CULTIVATION This species thrives outdoors in tropical and subtropical gardens in moist humus-enriched soil. Grow as an attractive border under taller, bolder plants and in sheltered courtyards. To keep the leaves looking fresh, grow in partial shade and shelter from drying winds. In cool climates, it is best suited to a warm conservatory or well-heated greenhouse with constant high humidity and draught-free conditions. Provide medium light and a well-drained peat-based potting mix. Keep the potting mix moist during the growing season but never saturated, and fertilise established plants regularly. Frost tender.

Calathea lancifolia
syn. *Calathea insignis*
Rattlesnake Plant

ORIGIN Brazil
CLIMATE T, ST

This species has upright leaf stalks to 30cm/12in and linear to lance-shaped, wavy leaves to 45cm/18in long and 5cm/2in wide. The pale green upper surface is marked with alternate large and small patches of darker green on either side of the midrib. The underside is reddish purple. Yellow flowers are produced on short spikes in summer.
USE & CULTIVATION As for *C. burle-marxii*. Frost tender.

Caladium lindenii

Calathea makoyana

Calathea sanderiana

Calathea makoyana
syn. *Maranta makoyana*
Cathedral Windows, Peacock Plant

ORIGIN Brazil
CLIMATE T, ST

This outstanding foliage plant has paper-thin and almost transparent broadly oval leaves 25–30cm/10–12in long on 30cm/12in stalks. Both surfaces have oblong patches and fine feathery lines of dark green along the lateral veins; the undersides are reddish purple. Occasionally, short spikes of white flowers appear.
USE & CULTIVATION As for *C. burle-marxii*. Frost tender.

Calathea picturata

ORIGIN Brazil
CLIMATE T, ST

This neat compact species has oval, deep olive green leaves to 15–20cm/

6–8in long carried on short stalks closely grouped at soil level. The leaf margin is dark green and the centre has striking silvery grey lines; the reverse is maroon. Almost the entire leaf surface of **'Argentea'** is a metallic silvery grey, except around the edges, which are emerald green.
USE & CULTIVATION As for *C. burle-marxii*. Frost tender.

Calathea sanderiana
syns *Calathea majestica* 'Sanderiana',
C. ornata var. *sanderiana*,
C. 'Sanderiana'

ORIGIN Peru
CLIMATE T, ST

This frequently grown species forms clumps of broadly oval, glossy leaves to 60cm/24in long. They are rather leathery and attractively marked with fine pink to white lines on a dark green background; the reverse is purple.

USE & CULTIVATION As for *C. burle-marxii*. Frost tender.

Calathea veitchiana
Peacock Plant

ORIGIN Brazil
CLIMATE T, ST

This striking perennial forms clumps to about 1m/3ft high of ovate leaves to 30cm/12in long. They are dark green with feathery markings in different shades of green. The undersides are purple.
USE & CULTIVATION As for *C. burle-marxii*. Frost tender.

Calathea zebrina
Zebra Plant

ORIGIN Brazil
CLIMATE T, ST

This beautiful clump-forming species reaches a height of around 90cm/36in

Calathea zebrina

Callisia elegans

Calathea veitchiana

and has arching, deep velvety green leaves with prominent yellowish green stripes, midribs and margins; the undersides are reddish purple. It bears short dense spikes of white to dark purple flowers in spring.

USE & CULTIVATION Densely grouped, it makes an outstanding bedding plant beneath trees in tropical and subtropical gardens. Grow in moist humus-enriched soil. It survives slightly cooler conditions than most other calatheas and makes an outstanding feature plant in warm temperate ferneries. In cooler climates, indoor cultivation is the same as for *C. burle-marxii*. Frost tender.

CALLISIA

FAMILY COMMELINACEAE

This is a small tropical genus of around 20 species of prostrate evergreen perennials that are very similar to the closely related *Tradescantia* (Wandering Jew). They have a trailing habit and are mostly grown for their ornamental foliage as groundcovers or in hanging baskets. Insignificant white or pink flowers are occasionally produced. Because they are fast growing and can quickly lose their compact habit, old plants are periodically

replaced with new. Propagate from tip cuttings or by division.

Callisia elegans
syn. *Setcreasea striata*
Striped Inch Plant

ORIGIN Guatemala, Honduras
CLIMATE T, ST, WT

This rapidly spreading perennial has 60cm/24in long stems that are erect when young and then trail as they develop. It has olive green oval leaves, 2–5cm/1–2in long, liberally marked with longitudinal white lines; the undersides are purple. Small white flowers are produced from autumn to winter.

USE & CULTIVATION An excellent groundcover for edging a border or pathway; it is also good for hanging baskets. Grow in moist well-drained soil in partial shade. Indoors, it thrives in warm rooms with bright filtered or indirect light. During the growing period, apply a balanced liquid fertiliser monthly and keep the soil moist. Frost tender.

Callisia fragrans

Callisia fragrans
syn. *Spironema fragrans*
Chain Plant

ORIGIN Mexico
CLIMATE ST, WT

Spreading by long surface runners, this species forms extensive mats of narrow, succulent, pointed leaves to 25cm/10in long and 5cm/2in wide, carried on crowded fleshy stems to 90cm/36in long. The glossy green leaves tend to become dull purple in strong light. Very small, fragrant white flowers are borne on reddish stems from winter to spring. The upper leaf surfaces of **'Melnickoff'** have longitudinal yellowish stripes of differing widths.

USE & CULTIVATION Quickly forms an attractive dense groundcover in a moist shady position; also suited to hanging baskets in courtyards, ferneries or indoors. As a houseplant, provide medium to bright light and moist well-drained soil. Apply a balanced liquid fertiliser during summer. It may need re-potting every spring. Frost tender.

Callisia navicularis
syn. *Tradescantia navicularis*
Chain Plant

ORIGIN Mexico
CLIMATE T, ST

This low-growing perennial has creeping stems to 50cm/20in or longer with 2 rows of rather succulent, coppery green, oval leaves 2.5cm/1in long sheathing the stem. In strong light they tend to become dull red and spotted beneath with purple–grey. Small pinkish purple flowers are borne in the leaf axils from summer to autumn.

USE & CULTIVATION Good rockery or groundcover plant in a lightly shaded sheltered position in moist well-drained soil; also good in hanging baskets, either indoors or out. As a houseplant, provide medium to bright light, water moderately and apply a balanced liquid fertiliser during summer. Frost tender.

CANNA

INDIAN SHOT
FAMILY CANNACEAE

Native to tropical and South America, this is a genus of about 25 species of showy rhizomatous perennials grown for their striking, often gladioli-like flowers and ornamental foliage. Many of the hybrid cannas have huge banana-like green, bronze, purple or sometimes striped leaves. They are generally used for summer bedding displays, often for tropical-style effects. To evoke the lush growth of the jungle, plant in large clumps rather than regimented rows. In cool areas protect the roots with a thick mulch in winter, or lift the rhizomes in late autumn and store in a dry frost-free place until early spring. Cannas make outstanding plants for cool conservatories.

Canna x *generalis* 'Pandora'

Canna x *generalis* 'Striata'

colours. **'Black Knight'**, to 1.2m/4ft, has red flowers and bronze-coloured foliage. **'King Humbert'** (syn. 'Roi Humbert') is an old variety with bright red flowers and vivid purple leaves, reaching a height of 1.8m/6ft. **'Lucifer'**, with purple leaves and yellow-edged red flowers, is considerably shorter, to 60cm/24in. **'Pandora'** has purple leaves and bright red flowers on stalks to 1.2m/4ft. **'Phasion'** is a striking variety with broad orange and green variegated leaves and deep orange flowers; it grows to 1.5m/5ft. **'Striata'** (syn. *C. malawiensis* 'Variegata') has broad oval leaves boldly striped in green, and yellow and orange flowers. It is a popular bedding plant, reaching 1.5m/5ft. **'Wyoming'**, to 1.8m/6ft, has broad, rich purple leaves with darker veins and orange flowers.

USE & CULTIVATION Often used as summer bedding plants to create a tropical effect in areas where genuine tropical plants would be unsuitable. Grow in full sun and damp, humus-enriched soil. In frosty areas they are best lifted and stored under cover for winter. Marginally frost hardy.

Canna iridiflora

ORIGIN Peru
CLIMATE ST, WT, M
Growing to about 2.5m/8ft tall, this robust perennial has banana-like dark bluish green leaves to 1m/3ft long. From mid-summer it bears spikes of pendent, rose pink, funnel-shaped flowers, each 10–15cm/4–6in long, and with reflexed petals. The leaves of **'Ehemanii'** have red margins and the small flowers are bright rose pink.
USE & CULTIVATION One of the best cannas for creating a tropical effect in colder areas. Grow in humus-enriched moist soil in full sun and water freely in dry periods. Plants respond well to monthly feeding. Cut back to the ground after flowers finish. In warm gardens protect with thick mulch; lift the rhizomes for winter storage in cold areas. Marginally frost hardy.

Canna x generalis

ORIGIN Gardens
CLIMATE T, ST, WT
This name is given to a range of hybrid cultivars with varying flower and foliage

Canna x *generalis* 'Phasion'

Propagate from seed in winter or by division in spring.

Canna x *generalis* 'Wyoming'

CAREX

SEDGE

FAMILY CYPERACEAE

This large genus of sedges contains 1500 to 2000 species of deciduous and evergreen, often tussock-forming perennials. Most species occur naturally in swamps, damp localities or along stream banks, often in cool temperate areas; many are frost hardy. A few species are grown for their ornamental grass-like leaves, which contrast well with broader leaved plants. They look particularly good as part of a wild garden; some of the water-loving species are useful for edging ponds and water features. The popular New Zealand sedges are not fully frost hardy where temperatures fall below −7°C/20°F for long periods. Propagate from seed or by division of the rhizome.

Carex albula

Carex albula
syn. *Carex* 'Frosted Curls'

ORIGIN New Zealand
CLIMATE WT, CT, M
This evergreen tuft-forming sedge has silvery green grass-like leaves to 60cm/24in long forming arched tussocks to 30cm/12in high and 50cm/20in across. It has curled leaf tips. Hidden beneath the leaves in summer are inconspicuous green flower spikes.
USE & CULTIVATION Adds interest and foliage contrast to borders and rock gardens, thriving in any well-drained soil in sun or partial shade. Its soft arching habit is suited to a saucer-shaped container. Frost hardy.

Carex buchananii
Leatherleaf Sedge

ORIGIN New Zealand
CLIMATE WT, M, CT
Forming a loose open clump, this tuft-forming sedge has very narrow, copper-coloured, glossy leaves to 45cm/18in long, curled at the tips and turning red towards the base. Triangular stems to 50cm/20in long bear insignificant brown flower spikes in summer.
USE & CULTIVATION As for *C. albula*. Useful in mass plantings for special effects in a grass garden, for adding form to minimalist courtyard gardens or planted in a row of terracotta pots. Frost hardy.

Carex comans
New Zealand Hair Sedge

ORIGIN New Zealand
CLIMATE WT, M, CT
Forming a dense spreading mound 40cm/16in high and 70cm/28in wide, this sedge has very fine greenish yellow to copper-coloured foliage to 25cm/10in long that fades to a soft cinnamon brown in autumn. It bears insignificant

Carex buchananii

Carex comans

25cm/10in long; each leaf is broadly edged with creamy yellow. Insignificant flower spikes are borne on stems to 15cm/6in long in summer.

USE & CULTIVATION This moisture-loving sedge can be grown in partial shade at the edge of a water feature, provided it is not flooded for any length of time. One of the few species of *Carex* widely grown indoors, adapting well to bright filtered light and moderate watering. Contrasts well with broad-leaved plants enjoying similar conditions. Fully frost hardy.

Carex morrowii
Japanese Sedge

ORIGIN Japan
CLIMATE ST, WT, M, CT

This evergreen sedge has short rhizomes running just below the surface, forming stiff clumps of shiny, rich green leaves to 30cm/12in long. The small flowers are insignificant. In gardens it is better known by the cultivar **'Fisher'**, with broad yellowish green leaves conspicuously striped and edged with cream.

USE & CULTIVATION Makes a good waterside plant provided it is not flooded for any length of time. Grow in a moist but well-drained position in sun or partial shade. Moderately frost hardy.

brown flower spikes on stems to 25cm/10in high in summer.

USE & CULTIVATION As for *C. albula*. Frost hardy.

Carex elata
syn. *Carex stricta*
Tufted Sedge

ORIGIN Europe, northern Africa
CLIMATE WT, M, CT

A deciduous tuft-forming sedge with gently arching grass-like leaves about 45cm/18in long. In summer, erect stems to 80cm/32in high bear blackish brown flower spikes. In gardens it is best known by **'Aurea'** (Bowles' Golden Sedge), which develops a rich yellow colour on new spring growth.

USE & CULTIVATION Bowles' Golden Sedge is useful for adding tone, texture and highlights to moist places and beside ponds in full sun or partial shade. Potted specimens can be cut to ground level in winter to encourage bright new growth. Fully frost hardy.

Carex flagellifera
syn. *Carex lucida*
Weeping Brown New Zealand Sedge

ORIGIN New Zealand
CLIMATE WT, M, CT

This evergreen sedge has short rhizomes, forming spreading tufts of very narrow, dark copper-coloured to orange leaves to 70cm/28in long, curled at the tips and turning red towards the base. Stems bearing light brown flower spikes elongate with the fruit to over 1m/3ft in.

USE & CULTIVATION As for *C. albula*. Frost hardy.

Carex hachijoensis 'Evergold'
syn. *Carex oshimensis* 'Evergold'

ORIGIN Gardens
CLIMATE WT, M, CT, H

This very popular species is often sold as *C. morrowii* 'Variegata'. It forms a soft rounded mound to 30cm/12in high of relatively broad, dark green leaves to

Carex elata 'Aurea'

Carex muskingumensis
Palm Sedge

ORIGIN North America
CLIMATE WT, M, CT, H
This evergreen sedge slowly produces an increasing clump of upright, bright green leaves to 75cm/30in long. It bears golden brown seed heads on stems to 75cm/30in high in summer.
USE & CULTIVATION As for *C. morrowii*. Fully frost hardy.

Carex siderosticha 'Variegata'

ORIGIN Gardens
CLIMATE WT, M, CT, H
This perennial mound-forming sedge to 30cm/12in or more high has broad linear leaves to 25cm/10in long, clearly edged and narrowly striped in white. Insignificant brown flowers are held above the plant in late spring.

USE & CULTIVATION As for *C. morrowii*. Fully frost hardy.

CARLUDOVICA

FAMILY CYCLANTHACEAE
From tropical America, this is a small genus of 4 species of almost stemless, palm-like perennials. They provide a lush jungle-like effect in tropical gardens and make outstanding conservatory plants. Propagate by seed or division in spring.

Carludovica palmata
Panama Hat Palm

ORIGIN Central America to Bolivia
CLIMATE T, ST, WT
This palm-like perennial to about 3m/10ft high has very long-stalked, rich green, almost circular leaves to 80cm/

32in long, each deeply lobed into 3–5 segments with pendent tips. In summer it bears insignificant flower spathes that develop into showy red berries. The large young leaves are used to make panama hats.

USE & CULTIVATION An attractive species for providing a luxuriant tropical effect in any garden, particularly when planted beneath taller growing shrubs or palms. It can be grown successfully outside the tropics if protected from frost. Grow in well-drained humus-enriched soil in dappled shade to encourage vigorous, deeper green foliage. An excellent indoor container plant in bright filtered light. Keep the potting mix thoroughly moist, but never allow the plant to stand in water; less water is required in winter. Apply liquid fertiliser once a month from early spring to mid-autumn. Frost tender.

Carludovica palmata

Carpentaria acuminata

CARPENTARIA

FAMILY ARECACEAE/PALMAE

This is a genus of only one species, a single-stemmed palm endemic to northern Australia. Popular in tropical regions, it has a graceful crown of arching feathery fronds, showy flowers and decorative fruit. It is commonly cultivated in parks and street plantings around Darwin, Australia and in Florida, USA. Propagate from fresh seed in spring.

Carpentaria acuminata
Carpentaria Palm

ORIGIN Northern Australia
CLIMATE T, ST

A tall, smooth-stemmed palm to 15m/50ft with a slender grey trunk and a crown of curved, feathery, dark green fronds to 3.5m/12ft long. The narrow segments have truncated or lobed tips. Clusters of creamy white spring flowers are followed in summer by waxy, bright red fruit.

USE & CULTIVATION In tropical gardens use this fast-growing reliable palm as a specimen or in a group planting of varying sizes. Tolerant of salt-laden winds. Grow in well-drained, humus-enriched soil in a sunny or semi-shaded position. Young specimens make ideal houseplants, responding to bright filtered light, monthly fertiliser and plenty of water during the growing season. Frost tender.

CARYOTA

FISHTAIL PALM

FAMILY ARECACEAE/PALMAE

This is a small genus of 12 species of very unusual palms. They differ from other palms in having bipinnate fronds with the primary leaflet divided into fishtail-like segments with rather ragged edges. In mature trees the flowering panicles open successively down the trunk; when the lowest panicle sets fruit the whole stem dies. The fruit has irritant flesh and may produce burning sensations on the skin. Flowers and fruit

Caryota mitis

are never produced on indoor plants. In warm tropical climates they are grown as spectacular specimen trees. The decorative leaves are sometimes used for cut foliage. Propagate from fresh seed.

Caryota mitis
Clustered Fishtail Palm

ORIGIN Southeast Asia
CLIMATE T, ST

This medium-sized, clump-forming palm to 9m/30ft forms a dense crown of rather erect, twice-divided, rich green fronds to 2.5m/8ft long with widely spaced, irregularly toothed segments. Pendent clusters of creamy white summer flowers are produced from the leaf axils and followed by round, dark red fruit.

USE & CULTIVATION This unusual palm quickly forms an attractive thicket in warm tropical gardens. Grow in a well-drained, humus-enriched soil and protect from full sun. In frosty areas young specimens make neat bushy houseplants, rarely reaching more than 2.5m/8ft. Indoors, provide bright filtered light, warmth, monthly fertiliser

and plenty of water during the growing season. Frost tender.

Caryota urens
Toddy Palm, Wine Palm

ORIGIN India, Myanmar, Malaysia
CLIMATE T, ST

This handsome fast-growing palm has a single, grey, ringed trunk 12–20m/40–70ft high topped with a dense crown of bipinnate dark green leaves to 6m/20ft long, with wedge-shaped leaflets about 30cm/12in long. Flowering panicles, up to 3m/10ft long, hang close to the trunk in mature trees. In some tropical countries the sugary sap is made into sugar or distilled into the alcoholic drink toddy. In Myanmar it is used as a wild source of sago.

USE & CULTIVATION Grown as an ornamental specimen tree in tropical climates, where it thrives in well-drained, humus-enriched soil and with protection from full sun. In frosty areas, young specimens make ideal houseplants, producing a stem up to 2.5m/8ft tall. Indoors, provide the same growing conditions as for *C. mitis*. Frost tender.

CASTANEA

CHESTNUT
FAMILY FAGACEAE

This small genus contains 10 species of deciduous trees from temperate regions of the Northern Hemisphere; they are well known for their high-quality edible nuts. They have bold toothed leaves and make beautiful long-lived shade trees for large open spaces. Propagate from seed.

Castanea sativa 'Albomarginata'

Castanea sativa
Spanish Chestnut, Sweet Chestnut

ORIGIN Mediterranean region, southwestern Asia

CLIMATE M, CT, H

Widely planted for its edible nuts, this imposing tree eventually reaches a height of 30m/100ft, forming a broadly spreading crown and, with age, a massive trunk with dark grey fissured bark. Its oblong glossy leaves to 25cm/10in long with a pointed tip and sharply toothed margins take on russet brown tones in autumn. Small groups of female flowers develop into a prickly burr enclosing up to 3 edible, shiny brown

Cedrus atlantica 'Glauca'

nuts. **'Albomarginata'** has leaves with irregular creamy white margins.

USE & CULTIVATION This outstanding specimen tree thrives in deeply worked and fertile soil with good drainage in sun or partial shade. Fully frost hardy.

CEDRUS

CEDAR
FAMILY PINACEAE

This is a small genus of 4 species of most impressive evergreen conifers. Cedars are grown for their graceful spreading form, long life and the colour and texture of their foliage. They can reach 35m/120ft and are best placed in large open spaces to fully display their individuality. The short, needle-like foliage is arranged in dense clusters on short lateral shoots and varies in colour according to the original stock and, to some extent, the season. The erect seed cones are mostly barrel-shaped. A number of interesting cultivars make good features in their own right. Dwarf varieties can be grown in containers. They are all suited to bonsai. Propagate by seed. Most cultivars are propagated from cuttings, layering and grafting.

Cedrus atlantica
syn. *Cedrus libani* subsp. *atlantica*
Atlas Cedar

ORIGIN Atlas Mountains (north Africa)

CLIMATE WT, M, CT, H

This magnificent conifer with its green to glaucous blue foliage and dark grey bark comes from the Atlas Mountains of Algeria and Morocco. At maturity the limbs become almost horizontal, forming a broadly pyramidal tree eventually reaching 30m/100ft high and 9m/30ft across. **'Aurea'** is slow growing to 6m/20ft and has yellow-tipped foliage. The Blue Atlas Cedar, **'Glauca'**, varies from 8–15m/25–50ft according to climate. Widely planted as a specimen tree, it has bright silvery blue foliage and paler grey bark. **'Glauca Pendula'**, to 3m/10ft high,

Castanea sativa

C

Cedrus atlantica 'Glauca Pendula'

Cedrus deodara

Cedrus libani subsp. *stenocoma*

has sweeping pendulous branches to 6m/20ft across and blue–green foliage. **USE & CULTIVATION** Taller growing forms make beautiful specimen plants in spacious gardens. 'Glauca Pendula' may be trained over a support. They do best in moderately cool climates, needing full sun and well-drained soil. A thick mulch of well-rotted organic matter helps keep the roots cool. They are all slow growing and can be used as container subjects for many years. Fully frost hardy.

Cedrus libani 'Nana'

Cedrus deodara
Deodar Cedar

 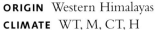

ORIGIN Western Himalayas
CLIMATE WT, M, CT, H
This charming, soft grey–green tree to 40m/130ft high is distinctly upright with a triangular crown and evenly spaced, downswept branches that are slightly pendulous towards the ends. The main trunk has a 'leader' (growing tip) which droops weakly and is usually without side-growth for 20cm/8in or more. The spirally arranged, short, needle-like leaves are mid-green to slightly greyish green. **'Aurea'**, to 5m/17ft, has golden-tipped spring foliage that becomes almost green at other times.

USE & CULTIVATION This long-lived, trouble-free tree is ideal as a lawn specimen where there is sufficient room for the base to spread. Grow in deep moist soil with good drainage. A large container can be used on patios. Fully frost hardy.

Cedrus libani
Cedar of Lebanon

ORIGIN Lebanon to Turkey
CLIMATE WT, M, CT, H
This majestic spreading conifer can reach 30m/100ft with a similar spread. Its massive arching branches carry flat layers of dark green to grey–green foliage. **'Nana'** is a slow-growing dwarf cultivar with yellowish green foliage, making a flattened rounded bush. **'Sargentii'** is also slow growing, with a height and spread of 1.5m/5ft and dense weeping branches clothed with mid-green foliage. **C. l. subsp. *stenocoma*,** from Turkey, becomes columnar and flat topped with age.

USE & CULTIVATION Best planted as a lawn specimen in large gardens, parks or reserves in areas with a cool climate and moderate rainfall. Dwarf forms are used in rock or feature gardens and are very well suited to containers. Provide deep moist soil with good drainage. Fully frost hardy.

CERCIDIPHYLLUM

FAMILY CERCIDIPHYLLACEAE
This genus contains a single species, a deciduous tree from China and Japan. It is grown mainly for its heart-shaped leaves, which take on beautiful smoky shades of orange, pink or red during autumn. Propagate from seed or cuttings.

Cercidiphyllum japonicum
Katsura Tree

ORIGIN China, Japan
CLIMATE M, CT, H
Reaching about 12m/40ft in cultivation, this tree has a rather conical crown and usually multiple main branches dividing low down but angled upwards. The opposite heart-shaped leaves, 8cm/3in wide, are purplish red on opening, then dark green, turning shades of yellow, orange and red in autumn. As they colour, the leaves give off a scent of toffee. Small dull red flowers appear before the leaves in spring. *C. j.* **var.** *magnificum* is smaller but its leaves are somewhat larger and more obviously heart-shaped and toothed. **'Pendulum'** has a dome-shaped crown and slender weeping branches.
USE & CULTIVATION Charming as a specimen tree or part of a woodland setting. Grow in fertile, moist but well-drained soil in a sunny or partially shaded position. Protect from hot sun and cold drying winds. Fully frost hardy.

CERCIS

**FAMILY LEGUMINOSAE/
PAPILIONACEAE**
The 7 species in this genus of deciduous shrubs and trees from the Northern Hemisphere have handsome heart-shaped leaves. They appear after a spectacular showing of pea-like flowers that are often borne directly on the larger stems and branches. Autumn leaf colour is good. Propagate from seed.

Cercis canadensis
Eastern Redbud

ORIGIN North America
CLIMATE M, CT, H
This small deciduous tree, growing to about 3.5m/12ft in cultivation, has a shapely bushy habit and broadly heart-shaped leaves to 10cm/4in long. They are pointed at the tips and turn yellow in autumn. It bears a mass of rosy pink flowers in spring before the leaves appear. The leaves of **'Forest Pansy'** are reddish purple.
USE & CULTIVATION An ornamental shade tree for small areas. It is best positioned when quite young, as it resents transplanting. Grow in rich well-drained soil in a sunny position. Fully frost hardy.

Cercis canadensis 'Forest Pansy'

Chamaecyparis lawsoniana 'Blue Jacket'

CHAMAECYPARIS

FALSE CYPRESS
FAMILY CUPRESSACEAE
This is a small genus of 8 species of evergreen conifers from the cool moist forests of North America and eastern Asia. Closely related to *Cupressus*, they differ mainly in their tiny, more flattened branchlets. They are pyramidal to columnar in outline, with a single, erect central trunk and many small branches, generally at right angles, and foliage arranged in small fan-like formations. Several species have given rise to a vast number of cultivars, and now virtually

CHAMAECYPARIS • 159

any size, shape, colour or texture can be obtained. Foliage colours include bluish green, gold, bronze, grey–green and dark green, and some variegated forms. Many of the smaller slow-growing varieties are popular hedge plants in formal courtyard gardens. Hedges are usually lightly pruned from late spring to early autumn. Propagate from seed, or from cuttings for cultivars.

Chamaecyparis lawsoniana
syn. *Cupressus lawsoniana*
Lawson Cypress

ORIGIN North America
CLIMATE WT, M, CT, H

This 35m/120ft tall conifer is conical in shape and has somewhat bluish green or rich green, tiny, scale-like leaves in flat sprays reaching to ground level. It is a very variable species and about 200 forms have been given cultivar names. **'Alumii'** is broadly columnar, 3–4m/10–12ft high, with spectacular waxy blue foliage in large sprays. **'Aurea Densa'** forms a small, dense, conical bush to 2m/7ft with golden yellow foliage. **'Blue Jacket'** is a dwarf form with spreading branches and bluish leaves with white markings. **'Ellwoodii'** is a slow-growing, dense, conical shrub eventually reaching several metres, with deep grey–green juvenile foliage that is bluish in winter. The foliage sprays of **'Ellwood's Gold'** are tipped light gold in early summer. **'Erecta'** forms a neat compact column when young and has rich bright green foliage. It can eventually reach 9m/30ft. **'Erecta Aurea'** is a symmetrical rounded form tapering to a point with upward sprays of bright yellow foliage. **'Fletcheri'** is a dense, broad columnar bush to 9m/30ft or more with bright bluish grey juvenile foliage. **'Green Globe'** is a neat, miniature, globe-shaped bush to 60cm/24in with fine, rich green foliage. Very slow growing, it is perfect for rock gardens. **'Lane'** forms a neat column to about 8m/25ft and is among the brightest of the yellow-foliaged cultivars. **'Lutea'** has a broad columnar habit

Chamaecyparis lawsoniana

and golden yellow foliage in large pendent sprays. It is slow growing at first, eventually reaching 15–20m/50–70ft. **'Minima Aurea'** is a slow-growing conical dwarf to 60cm/24in with tightly packed golden yellow foliage in vertical sprays. It fits the smallest garden. **'Pembury Blue'** forms a broad column to 9m/30ft with bright blue–green foliage held in open pendulous sprays. It does best in cool climates. **'Silver Queen'** has an upright conical habit to 3m/10ft and particularly attractive, silvery greenish white new growth. **'Stewartii'** is a conical, mostly upright shrub to 5–8m/17–25ft with golden yellow foliage sprays. **'Winston**

Churchill' has a pronounced conical habit and golden yellow foliage. **'Wisselii'** is fast growing, forming a distinctive slender column 20–25m/70–80ft high with dark bluish green foliage.

USE & CULTIVATION Taller growing varieties can be grown as lawn specimens, along driveways and boundaries, and as tall hedges or windbreaks. Dwarf forms are excellent in rock or feature gardens, and very well suited to ornamental containers and bonsai culture. They perform best in cooler climates. Grow in full sun and deep, moist, preferably slightly acid soil with good drainage. Mulch helps keep the roots cool over summer. Fully frost hardy.

Chamaecyparis obtusa
syn. *Cupressus obtusa*
Hinoki Cypress

ORIGIN Japan
CLIMATE WT, M, CT

This species is an important timber tree in Japan and is regarded as sacred in the Shinto faith. It reaches a height of 35m/120ft in the wild, but in cultivation grows to about 18m/60ft. It has rather dense spreading branches quite close to the ground. The blunt-tipped leaves are glossy green above and white-lined below. **'Albospica'** is an upright conical form with bright green foliage flecked with white. **'Crippsii'** usually reaches 3.5–5m/12–17ft with a base width of 2m/7ft. With rich golden yellow, frond-like sprays, it is regarded as one of the best golden-foliaged conifers and in full sun makes a first-class specimen tree. **'Fernspray Gold'**, to 2m/7ft, has bright yellow, fern-like foliage in summer, deepening to bronze in winter. The dwarf **'Flabelliformis'** is very slow growing, eventually reaching 25cm/10in in diameter, with deep green foliage in attractive whorled fans. **'Kosteri'**, to about 1m/3ft high, has tiered apple green foliage. **'Minima'** forms a miniature compact ball of tightly packed green foliage. **'Nana'** is a particularly slow-growing, dark green,

bun-shaped variety with moss-like twisted foliage, taking decades to reach 1m/3ft. **'Nana Aurea'** has golden-tipped foliage and forms a rounded bush to 1m/3ft high in 10 years. **'Nana Gracilis'** is pyramidal, quite loose in habit, with rich green foliage, and grows comparatively quickly to 1m/3ft. **'Sanderi'**, to 1m/3ft, has unusual soft blue–green foliage in summer, acquiring a rich purple toning in winter if subjected to low temperatures. **'Templehof'** is a compact rounded shrub to 2.5m/8ft, with greenish yellow foliage turning bronze in winter. **'Tetragona Aurea'** has a bushy upright habit to 5m/17ft or more with tightly crowded branchlets and rich golden yellow branch-tips.

USE & CULTIVATION With their well-groomed appearance, the taller growing forms can be used singly as a specimen or accent plant in a position with sufficient room for the base to spread. Among the shrubs, the golden-coloured cultivars provide colour and relief from too much greenery. Dwarf forms are particularly suited to small courtyards in beds or containers. Many are suitable for rock gardens or bonsai. Grow in full sun and moist but well-drained fertile soil. Most tend to lose their colour in shade and dislike exposure to drying winds. Fully frost hardy.

Chamaecyparis pisifera
syn. *Cupressus pisifera*
Sawara Cypress

ORIGIN Japan
CLIMATE WT, M, CT

This conical conifer grows to 30m/100ft or more in the wild, but less in gardens. It has ridged, peeling, red–brown bark and horizontal branches with tightly packed foliage. The scale-like, glossy green leaves have spreading spiny tips and are marked bluish white below. **'Boulevard'** forms a conical bush to 6m/20ft with silvery blue foliage that takes on purplish tints in cold locations. **'Filifera'**, to 5m/17ft, has slender thread-like branchlets and dark green foliage. **'Filifera Aurea'** has a broadly conical habit to 3m/10ft with pendulous thread-like branchlets and bright green and golden foliage. **'Nana'** forms a dense flat-topped hummock of dark blue–green foliage, eventually reaching 60cm/24in. **'Plumosa'** is a large bush or small conical tree to 3m/10ft tall with mid-green leaves. **'Plumosa Aurea'** is faster growing than most, to 2m/7ft, and has golden, mossy-textured foliage tinted bronze in winter. **'Plumosa Compressa'** is a dwarf, compact, bun-shaped bush to 45cm/18in with dense moss-like foliage. **'Snow'** is a dwarf form with rounded habit and rather soft blue–green

Chamaecyparis obtusa 'Albospica'

Chamaecyparis obtusa 'Kosteri'

C

Chamaecyparis pisifera

Chamaedorea costaricana

Chamaecyparis pisifera 'Snow'
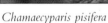

leaves with white tips. **'Squarrosa'** forms a wide-spreading tree to 20m/70ft with soft, feathery, glaucous foliage to ground level.

USE & CULTIVATION Smaller growing cultivars have a distinct oriental appearance and are ideal for Japanese-style gardens. When selecting for a small space, ensure that plants are correctly named and are true dwarf varieties. The taller growing forms are used singly as a specimen or accent in a position with sufficient room for the base to spread.

Grow in full sun in humus-rich, well-drained soil, and protect from drying winds. Fully frost hardy.

CHAMAEDOREA

FAMILY ARECACEAE/PALMAE

A genus of about 100 species of small palms from tropical America. A number are popular as indoor specimens, grown for their ornamental, somewhat arching, pinnate or undivided fishtail-like

fronds. Small orange–yellow flowers are borne on dainty sprays when plants are 3 or more years old, followed by small fruits. Indoors, they can tolerate dry air but flourish best in humid conditions. Mottled yellow leaves and thin webbing indicates red spider mites. Propagate from seed in spring.

Chamaedorea costaricana

ORIGIN Central America
CLIMATE T, ST, WT

This small clump-forming palm has flexible bamboo-like stems clustered from the base and reaching 2.5m/8ft in height. The arching pinnate fronds, to 1.8m/6ft long, are a rich dull green.

USE & CULTIVATION Forming large clumps with age, this species makes an attractive landscape feature in tropical and frost-free warm temperate gardens. It grows in full shade and is especially suitable for sheltered plantings around swimming pools. Grow in moist humus-rich soil and provide plenty of water during dry periods. Indoors, provide bright, filtered light and a free-draining potting mix. Water freely in summer; less water is required in winter. Frost tender.

Chamaedorea elegans

Chamaedorea metallica

Chamaedorea elegans
syns *Collinia elegans, Neanthe bella*
Parlour Palm

ORIGIN Mexico, Guatemala
CLIMATE T, ST, WT

This miniature single-stemmed species is one of the most popular indoor palms. It takes several years· to reach 1m/3ft; it has a short green trunk and very thin, medium green, slightly arched fronds, 45–60cm/18–24in long. Insignificant yellow flowers are borne in small erect panicles to 30cm/12in long, followed by small, pea-shaped, black fruit. **'Bella'** is the form most often seen in cultivation.
USE & CULTIVATION Elegant in appearance, it brings a tropical feel to the garden and is a good choice for shady narrow beds. Indoors, provide bright filtered light, relative warmth and a free-draining potting mix which is never allowed to dry out in summer. This palm enjoys cramped living space and a small group can be crowded in the same container. Re-pot only when the roots have completely filled the container. Frost tender.

Chamaedorea metallica
Miniature Fishtail Palm

ORIGIN Mexico
CLIMATE T, ST, WT

This slow-growing single-stemmed palm eventually reaches about 1m/3ft. It has a small crown of undivided, 2-lobed, deep bluish green leaves 30–50cm/12–20in long that take on a metallic sheen when wet. Female plants bear panicles of orange to red flowers, followed by greenish black fruit.
USE & CULTIVATION With bold puckered foliage, this is a highly ornamental small palm for partially shaded courtyards. Grow in humus-rich soil. Indoor plants need bright filtered light and a moist but free-draining potting mix. Water freely in summer, much less during the rest period. Frost tender.

Chamaedorea microspadix
Mexican Bamboo Palm

ORIGIN Mexico
CLIMATE T, ST, WT

This small palm forms a dense clump of slender bamboo-like stems clustered from the base and reaching 2–3m/ 7–10ft. The slightly arching, deep bluish green fronds to 40cm/16in long have well-spaced lance-shaped leaflets. Female flower stems become fleshy and bright orange as the scarlet fruits develop.
USE & CULTIVATION This attractive clump-forming palm is ideal for small sheltered courtyards as it can be planted quite close to buildings without causing damage to foundations. Indoors, provide bright filtered light and plenty of water during summer; less water is required in winter. Frost tender.

CHAMAEROPS

FAMILY ARECACEAE/PALMAE
The single species in this genus is the most widespread palm native to Europe, also occurring in northern Africa and Malta. Although a Mediterranean species, it is reasonably cold tolerant and will withstand short spells of temperatures as low as freezing point. Carefully cut off dead brown foliage close to the trunk. Propagate from fresh seed in spring or from suckers.

Chamaerops humilis
Dwarf Fan Palm, European Fan Palm

ORIGIN Mediterranean region
CLIMATE ST, WT, M,

This attractive palm may form a single trunk, but usually develops a suckering multi-stemmed clump to 3.5m/12ft high after many years. The green to bluish green fan-shaped foliage, 60cm/24in across, is carried on stiff, strong, spiny stalks. Creamy yellow flowers in panicles to 35cm/14in long are followed by orange–brown berries.

USE & CULTIVATION In milder temperate climates, this species can be used as an accent plant in many situations. It makes an attractive addition to poolsides and small tropical-style gardens. Grow in a warm sunny position in moist but well-drained soil. Provide indoor plants with 3–4 hours of direct sunlight every day, a standard potting mix and average house temperatures. Water freely in summer and less during the rest period. Moderately frost hardy.

CHLOROPHYTUM

FAMILY ANTHERICACEAE/LILIACEAE
This is a widespread genus of about 200 species of evergreen stemless perennials with short rhizomes and often large fleshy roots. Only the Spider Plant, *Chlorophytum comosum*, is widely cultivated; it is a familiar indoor plant, grown for its ribbon-like foliage. A number of variegated forms are available. Propagate from seed, by division or from the plantlets that form at the ends of the flower stems.

Chlorophytum comosum
Spider Plant

ORIGIN South Africa
CLIMATE ST, WT, M

A tufted, rosette-forming perennial to 30cm/12in high with soft, arching, very narrow leaves to 45cm/18in long. Racemes of small star-shaped white flowers are carried on thin pale yellow stems 60cm/24in or more long, at any time of year. Small rosettes of leaves may appear on flower stems, forming plantlets. **'Mandaianum'** has shorter leaves, 10–15cm/4–6in long, dark green with irregular pale yellow stripes. **'Picturatum'** has 30cm/12in long medium green leaves with a broad creamy yellow central stripe. **'Variegatum'** has leaves to 38cm/15in long, a fresh green edged with white. **'Vittatum'** has leaves 15–30cm/6–12in long, medium green with a wide white or pale cream central stripe.

USE & CULTIVATION These plants make good quick-spreading groundcovers or borders in partial shade, especially under trees. Among the most popular subjects for hanging baskets, they thrive in bright indirect light indoors. Their fleshy swollen roots require plenty of space for development, and fertile well-drained soil and applications of liquid fertiliser every few weeks will provide sufficient nourishment to keep plants looking healthy and attractive. Keep moist at all times, especially during summer. Frost tender.

Chamaerops humilis

Chlorophytum comosum 'Picturatum'

CHOISYA

FAMILY RUTACEAE

From southern USA and Mexico, this genus consists of about 8 species of evergreen shrubs. They are grown for their neat dense foliage and small white flowers with the fragrance of orange blossom. Propagate from cuttings.

Choisya ternata
Mexican Orange Blossom
ORIGIN Mexico
CLIMATE WT, M, CT, H

A neat compact shrub 1–2m/3–7ft high with deep green glossy leaves made up of 3 obovate leaflets each 4–8cm/ 1½–3in long. The late spring flowers are white, sweetly perfumed and resemble orange blossom. **'Goldfingers'** has bright yellow young foliage and narrower leaflets. **'Sundance'** is a popular variety with golden yellow young leaves.
USE & CULTIVATION Good as backgrounds, dividers or low screens. The yellow-foliaged forms offer interest, light and definition among green-leaved shrubs. Plants can be clipped as required and are useful for hedges. Grow in well-drained soil in a sunny site, preferably sheltered from cold winds. Fully frost hardy.

CHRYSALIDOCARPUS

FAMILY ARECACEAE/PALMAE

From Madagascar and nearby islands, this is a genus of around 20 species of feathery palms with solitary or clustered stems. Only one species is widely grown: *Chrysalidocarpus lutescens*, an elegant palm with attractive arching fronds arranged in terminal clusters. Propagate from seed in spring.

Chrysalidocarpus lutescens
syns *Areca lutescens,*
Dypsis lutescens
Golden Cane Palm, Butterfly Palm

ORIGIN Madagascar
CLIMATE T, ST, WT

This feathery palm forms clumps of slender golden stems eventually reaching 6–9m/20–30ft in height. The arching fronds to 1.5m/5ft long are divided into yellowish green or light green glossy segments arranged in almost opposite pairs on a prominent midrib. In summer it bears panicles to 60cm/24in long of small yellow flowers followed by small yellow fruit.
USE & CULTIVATION In tropical and warm temperate climates, this palm makes an attractive addition to pool

and tropical-style gardens, blending well with ferns and most broad-leaved evergreen plants. Grow in reasonably fertile, moist but well-drained soil in a protected, partially shaded position. In areas with quite cool winters it grows successfully in containers and is used to decorate patios, decks or verandas. Indoors, bright filtered light is best. Water freely in summer and less in winter. Frost tender.

Chrysalidocarpus lutescens

Choisya ternata 'Goldfingers'

Choisya ternata 'Sundance'

Chusquea culeou

Cissus antarctica

CHUSQUEA

FAMILY GRAMINEAE/POACEAE

There are about 100 species of clump-forming bamboos in this genus from Central and South America. They are a feature of the cloud forests of mountainous regions and can be grown in cool temperate areas like the UK. Propagate by division of clumps.

Chusquea culeou

ORIGIN Chile
CLIMATE M, CT, H
This erect bamboo forms dense clumps to 6m/20ft tall and 3m/10ft across. It has solid olive green glossy culms with contrasting papery white leaf sheaths in the first year. Arching side-branches arise from the nodes and bear deep green, grass-like leaves to 7cm/2½ in long.
USE & CULTIVATION Clumps look particularly effective in tropical-style plantings or to help create a shady woodland setting. Grow in sun or partial shade in moist but well-drained soil. It requires cool humid conditions, plenty of rainfall and shelter from cold drying winds. Fully frost hardy.

CISSUS

FAMILY VITACEAE

This mostly tropical genus contains about 350 species of evergreen shrubs and tendril-producing climbers. Closely related to the grape vine, they are grown for their decorative leaves and can be used in many ways; as climbers or trailers or in hanging baskets, for example. Some are popular houseplants. The alternate leaves may be entire, lobed or divided into leaflets. Insignificant greenish flowers are produced mainly in summer. Red spider mite can be a problem on indoor plants if the atmosphere is especially dry. Propagate from seed or stem cuttings in summer.

Cissus antarctica
Kangaroo Vine

ORIGIN Australia
CLIMATE T, ST, WT
From rainforests of eastern Australia, this vigorous woody climber scrambles to the tops of tall trees by means of clinging tendrils. It has toothed, bright shiny green, heart-shaped leaves to 12cm/5in long, with attractive, rust-coloured, hairy new growth, greenish flowers and round blackish fruit.
USE & CULTIVATION Ideal for covering a pergola or fence or scrambling over the ground on sloping banks. It grows well in shade in well-composted moist soil in a warm sheltered position. Prune back hard to prevent unwanted growth. In cooler climates, grow in containers. It makes an excellent indoor plant for garden rooms and conservatories, where it is best trained against a framework. Position in bright filtered light and water freely during summer. Frost tender.

Cissus discolor

ORIGIN Southeast Asia

CLIMATE T, ST

This beautifully coloured foliage plant has curly tendrils and slender red climbing stems to 3m/10ft and pointed heart-shaped leaves 10–20cm/4–8in long with silver and pink bands between the veins and a maroon underside. Reddish green flowers are followed by dark red fruit.

USE & CULTIVATION A highly decorative climber for training over trellis, fences and tree trunks in warm frost-free gardens. A popular indoor plant, climbing by means of tendrils if given some support. Provide bright indirect light, warmth, high humidity and moderate watering in summer. Less water is needed in winter. Frost tender.

Cissus hypoglauca

Water Vine

ORIGIN Eastern Australia

CLIMATE T, ST, WT

A vigorous climber with red stems and young shoots bearing rusty hairs. The palmate leaves are divided into 3 to 5 ovate to lance-shaped deep green leaflets with a glaucous underside. Yellowish green flowers in summer are followed by small black berries.

USE & CULTIVATION As for *C. antarctica*. Frost tender.

Cissus rhombifolia

syn. *Rhoicissus rhombifolia*

Grape Ivy

ORIGIN Tropical America

CLIMATE T, ST

This moderately vigorous tendril climber to 3m/10ft or more high has lustrous leaves divided into 3 coarsely toothed leaflets, roughly rhomboid (diamond-shaped) in outline. It bears insignificant greenish flowers. **'Ellen Danica'** has larger, almost circular leaflets with strongly lobed margins. It is more compact and bushy and is recommended for hanging baskets.

USE & CULTIVATION Outdoors in tropical and warm temperate climates it can be used similarly to *C. antarctica*. It can also be grown in containers and is a popular indoor plant. Train against a framework, if necessary tying vigorous stems to the support. Position in bright filtered light and water freely during summer. Pinch out growing tips to promote branching. Frost tender.

Cissus striata

syns *Ampelopsis sempervirens,*
Vitis striata

Miniature Grape Ivy

ORIGIN South America

CLIMATE T, ST, WT

A slender, moderately vigorous tendril climber with thin reddish shoots and palmate leaves to 8cm/3in across composed of 5 tiny, oval, serrated, glossy bronze green leaflets with pinkish undersides. The small greenish summer flowers are followed by purplish black, pea-like berries which ripen in autumn.

USE & CULTIVATION Use in much the same way as *C. antarctica*. It also looks good spilling over raised garden beds. Indoors, it is ideal for small hanging baskets and can also be trained on supports. Position in bright filtered light and water freely during summer. Marginally frost hardy.

CODIAEUM

CROTON

FAMILY EUPHORBIACEAE

These plants are among the most colourful of all foliage plants and have long been used for decoration. There are about 6 species, found in southern Asia, Malaysia and islands of the Pacific. The smooth, leathery, alternate leaves generally have short stalks, but can differ enormously in shape, size and colour. Some species have twisted leaves or wavy or variously lobed margins. Most are variegated, with colours appearing as spots, blotches and veining. Mature plants produce small, insignificant cream-coloured, star-shaped flowers in summer. Most crotons sold are forms of just one variety of a

Cissus hypoglauca

Cissus rhombifolia

Codiaeum variegatum var. *pictum*
'Emperor Alexander'

Codiaeum variegatum var. *pictum* 'Craigii'

Codiaeum variegatum var. *pictum* 'Bell'

single species, *Codiaeum variegatum* var. *pictum*. Check regularly for red spider mite and mealy bug on indoor plants. Propagate from cuttings.

Codiaeum variegatum var. pictum

ORIGIN Gardens
CLIMATE T, ST, WT
This upright bushy perennial, 1–2m/ 3–7ft high, with leathery, glossy leaves, has given rise to a large number of brilliant and highly colourful cultivars. **'Andreanum'** is compact and bushy; mature oval leaves to 20cm/8in long are copper green, veined and edged with reddish orange; juvenile leaves are fresh green, veined with yellow. **'Bell'** is a new variety with linear leaves variegated green, yellow, orange and red. Smaller bell-like leaves hang from the tips of many leaves. Leaf colours change according to the season and the amount of light received. **'Craigii'** has bright green lobed leaves, heavily veined in yellow, with some almost entirely yellow. **'Emperor Alexander'** has broad, deep green leaves with hot pink veins and margins. **'Imperiale'** has yellow elliptic leaves to 15cm/6in long with pink margins and green midribs. **'Interruptum'** has long, narrow, linear,

Codiaeum variegatum var. *pictum* 'Petra'

yellow leaves, sometimes twisted, with green margins and red midribs. **'Petra'** has green, red, orange and yellow leaves, with defined variegation following the veins and margins. **'Mrs Iceton'** (syn. 'Appleleaf') has blackish green elliptic leaves, heavily marked between the veins with yellow ageing to deep pink.
USE & CULTIVATION In warm humid gardens crotons make colourful hedging, border and accent plants. They

look best planted in considerable quantities of the same variety, to provide continuous colour and contrast. Grow in well-drained fertile garden beds in sun or partial shade. Also suitable for pots on verandas and patios. Indoors, provide a rich, well-drained potting mix in a well-lit position. Water and feed freely during the summer growing season. Re-pot large plants into pots one size larger in spring. Frost tender.

COLOCASIA

TARO

FAMILY ARACEAE

From tropical Asia, this genus consists of 8 species of evergreen tuberous perennials. They have large heart-shaped leaves and small, white, arum-like flowers. *Colocasia esculenta* is an important and ancient food crop grown in hot regions of the world for its edible brown tubers, leaves, leaf stalks and runners. In some parts it is a staple food. It is easy to grow in very warm and wet conditions and the bold leaves make a welcome addition to the edge of a pool. Propagate by division.

Colocasia esculenta
Taro, Dasheen, Elephant's Ears

ORIGIN Tropical Asia

CLIMATE T, ST, WT

This perennial marginal water-plant to 1.5m/5ft or more has long-stalked, lustrous, dark green, heart-shaped leaves to 60cm/24in long, which give the plant one of its names, Elephant's Ears. **'Black Magic'** has violet leaf stalks and purple young leaves that become greener with age. **'Fontanesii'** has bold, bronze-tinted dark green leaves with dark purple stalks and veins.

USE & CULTIVATION A beautiful garden plant thriving in wet soils and shallow water at the edge of a pool. It also grows well in moist, freely draining soil in a sheltered, sunny position. In a tub it responds vigorously to fertiliser and constant moisture during the growing season. Indoors, provide rich moist soil, bright filtered light and high humidity. Frost tender.

COPROSMA

FAMILY RUBIACEAE

A genus of about 90 species of evergreen shrubs and trees from New Zealand, other islands of the South Pacific and Australia, grown for their

Colocasia esculenta

Colocasia esculenta 'Fontanesii'

Colocasia esculenta 'Black Magic'

Coprosma x *kirkii* 'Variegata'

Coprosma repens 'Green and Gold'

foliage and fruits. Some species with highly polished leaves are sometimes known by the common name Mirror Plant. The female plants of some species are very decorative when in fruit, although separate male and female plants are needed for fertilisation. They respond to shaping or pruning once or twice a year, and as they will grow in poor, sandy soil, they are popular as coastal hedges and screens. Propagate from seed, cuttings or by division.

Coprosma x kirkii
syn. *Coprosma acerosa* x *C. repens*

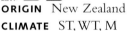

ORIGIN New Zealand
CLIMATE ST, WT, M
This densely branched prostrate shrub grows to about 40cm/16in high and to 2m/7ft across. The narrow oblong glossy olive green leaves to 4cm/1½ in long are opposite or in clusters. White berries ripen in autumn. The especially attractive **'Variegata'** is prostrate when young, later becoming semi-erect. It has small, elliptic, grey–green leaves edged creamy white.

USE & CULTIVATION Excellent fast-growing groundcovers for rock gardens and steep banks, especially on coastal sites, where they are particularly useful for erosion control. Grow in full sun in light well-drained soil. Marginally frost hardy.

Coprosma repens
syn. *Coprosma baueri*
Mirror Plant, Looking-glass Plant

ORIGIN New Zealand
CLIMATE ST, WT, M
This spreading then upright shrub forms a neat mound to 2m/7ft in diameter. It has highly polished, rich green leaves 4–8cm/1½–3in long. Insignificant flowers in late spring are followed on female plants by small orange–red fruit from late summer to autumn. **'Green and Gold'** has deep green leaves with broad, bright yellow margins. **'Marble Queen'** is a variegated form with creamy white and pale green foliage. **'Picturata'** is a rather more upright male plant with highly polished, rounded leaves with rich green margins and an irregular, creamy yellow central blotch. **'Pink Splendour'** has variegated leaves with a distinctive pink flush over the foliage, deepening with cooler temperatures.

USE & CULTIVATION With their good looks, easy maintenance and ability to withstand salt-laden winds, these plants make excellent hedges or screens in sandy well-drained soils in windswept coastal locations. They respond very well to pruning and can be trained or clipped to any desired shape. Marginally frost hardy.

Coprosma repens

Coprosma repens 'Marble Queen'

CORDYLINE

CABBAGE TREE
FAMILY AGAVACEAE

Mainly from the southwestern Pacific region, including New Zealand and Australia, there are about 15 species in this genus of palm-like, woody-stemmed perennials or small trees. Although grown mainly for their foliage, some bear attractive flowers and showy fruit. They usually have one short central stem with long strap-like leaves, but as the plants increase in height the lower leaves are eventually shed, leaving behind a clean trunk, so that they take on a palm-like appearance, rather like mature dracaenas. Some species are excellent for indoor decoration, tolerating darkish situations and neglect. Propagate from seed, cuttings or by division.

Cordyline australis 'Purpurea'

Cordyline australis
New Zealand Cabbage Tree

ORIGIN New Zealand
CLIMATE ST, WT, M

This erect palm-like tree has arching sword-like leaves to 90cm/36in long at ground level in juvenile plants. With age the plant develops a broad head and clean trunk to 6m/20ft in high. Large panicles of sweetly fragrant, creamy white flowers appear in late spring and early summer, followed by blue-tinted berries. **'Albertii'** is a magnificent variegated form with green leaves with red midribs and cream stripes. New growth is tinted salmon pink. It makes an outstanding container specimen. **'Doucettii'** has leaves with white stripes and pink margins. **'Purpurea'** has rich, bronzy purple leaf colouring.
USE & CULTIVATION These plants add a tropical atmosphere to sheltered warm gardens and are ideal for mingling with ferns and palms. Grow either singly as an accent or in a group. They are easily accommodated in courtyard gardens, on patios or in containers. 'Purpurea' is less vigorous and can be used as foliage contrast in window boxes. Provide fertile, moist well-drained soil in full sun or partial shade. Water potted plants regularly during summer, less in winter. Houseplants should be placed outdoors during summer and autumn. Remove the lower leaves as they wither to keep stems neat. Marginally frost hardy.

Cordyline fruticosa
syn. *Cordyline terminalis*
Ti Tree

ORIGIN Tropical Southeast Asia, South Pacific islands
CLIMATE T, ST, WT

This erect shrub to about 3m/10ft forms large clumps of thick woody stems bearing arching, dark green, thin-textured leaves to 75cm/30in long clustered at the top of the stem. In summer it bears white to purple flowers in slender loose panicles to 50cm/20in long, followed by round red berries. **'Amabilis'** has bronze leaves tinged with pink and edged with cream. **'Baby Ti'** has bronze red foliage with edges and stems suffused deep pink. **'Bicolor'** has broad green leaves edged and marked with deep pink or red. **'Firebrand'** has shiny purple–red leaves with bronze shading. **'Tricolor'** is a broad-leaved form with red, pink and cream colouring.

Cordyline fruticosa 'Baby Ti'

Cordyline stricta

USE & CULTIVATION Originating in cool mountainous forests in areas of high rainfall, it prefers a cool moist climate, humus-rich soil and light shade. Provide plenty of water during dry periods. An outstanding accent plant that can be grown in a tub for many years. Marginally frost hardy.

Cordyline stricta
Slender Palm Lily

ORIGIN Australia
CLIMATE T, ST, WT

This erect-growing shrub to 3m/10ft forms spreading clumps of slender cane-like stems bearing arching, narrow, dark green leaves to 60cm/24in long. Small purple flowers are borne on branched, drooping panicles to 60cm/24in long in summer and followed by black rounded berries.

USE & CULTIVATION An ornamental plant for the shady tropical section of the garden. It is ideal for narrow spaces near a driveway, entrance or courtyard. Grow in well-mulched soil with a plentiful supply of water and good drainage. An excellent container plant that does very well indoors. Frost tender.

Cordyline fruticosa 'Tricolor'

USE & CULTIVATION Commonly grown in the tropics, where the coloured-leaved forms provide year-round splashes of vivid colour. Of moderate size, they are excellent in courtyards and swimming pool landscapes, and can also be kept in pots for many years as indoor or patio plants. Grow in a sheltered well-drained position in partial shade. They respond to mulching and the application of fertiliser. Indoors, give them bright filtered light and plenty of water; less in winter. Frost tender.

Cordyline indivisa
Toi, Blue Dracaena

ORIGIN New Zealand
CLIMATE WT, M

This is an erect, usually unbranched thick-stemmed tree to 6m/20ft high with a tufted head of sword-shaped leaves to 1.5m/5ft long and 12cm/5in wide, often with a reddish or orange midrib and glaucous beneath. It bears tiny white flowers in dense pendulous clusters up to 1m/3ft long in summer followed by small blue berries.

CORNUS

DOGWOOD
FAMILY CORNACEAE

A genus of about 45 species of trees, shrubs and woody-stemmed perennials, mainly from the Northern Hemisphere. They are mostly deciduous, with their leaves taking on colourful autumn tints, and are grown for their ornamental foliage, flowers, fruits or brightly coloured winter stems. The small 4- or 5-petalled flowers are produced in umbels or flattened heads. In some species the flower clusters are surrounded by showy colourful bracts. Propagate from seed, cuttings, suckers or by division of perennials.

Cornus alba
Red-barked Dogwood

ORIGIN Siberia, China, Korea
CLIMATE M, CT, H

An upright, then spreading rounded shrub to about 3m/10ft tall and wide. It has dark green oval leaves to 10cm/4in long, often turning red or orange in autumn. Young shoots are bright red in winter. Creamy white flowers appear in flattened heads in late spring and early summer, followed by blue-tinted white fruits. **'Aurea'** has soft yellow leaves. **'Elegantissima'** has grey–green leaves with white margins. **'Kesselringii'** has dark green leaves becoming reddish purple in autumn, and dark purple winter shoots. **'Sibirica'** has bright red leaves in autumn and glistening red winter shoots. **'Spaethii'** has leaves margined bright yellow, and red winter shoots.
USE & CULTIVATION All these plants have attractive form, good autumn colour and colourful winter stems that can brighten even the bleakest of days. Good for massed plantings among other shrubs, in informal hedges, large rockeries and at the edge of a woodland garden. Grow in moist humus-rich, well-drained soil in sun or semi-shade. Cut back to the ground before new growth in each spring to encourage strong 1-year stems, which have the best colour. Fully frost hardy.

Cornus controversa 'Variegata'

Cornus controversa

ORIGIN China, Japan
CLIMATE M, CT, H

This is an elegant, slow-growing, deciduous tree to 15m/50ft tall with tiered branches of dark green elliptic leaves to 15cm/6in long that turn red and purple in autumn. White flowers appear in large flattened clusters in early summer. The tiny fruit is blue–black. **'Variegata'** grows to 8m/25ft and has smaller, bright green, lance-shaped leaves boldly variegated creamy white; they turn yellow in autumn. It is sometimes called the Wedding Cake Tree.
USE & CULTIVATION Both plants make outstanding specimens if given adequate space to display their natural architectural form. Best in a cool climate in fertile well-drained soil in full sun or partial shade. Fully frost hardy.

Cornus florida
Flowering Dogwood

ORIGIN North America
CLIMATE M, CT, H

This is a spreading deciduous shrub or small tree to 3–6m/10–20ft high in

Cornus alba 'Sibirica'

Cornus florida

Cornus florida 'Rubra'

Cornus stolonifera 'Sunrise'

Cornus florida 'Welchii'

cultivation. The oval, pointed dark green leaves, 7–15cm/2½–6in long, turn red and purple in autumn. The flowerheads, borne in late spring, consist of 4 white petal-like bracts around tiny white flowers. **'Rubra'** has young reddish leaves that turn brilliant red and orange in autumn. **'Welchii'** has grey–green leaves with creamy white, pink-tinged margins; they turn dark purple with bright pink margins in autumn. Most varieties bear red inedible berries.

USE & CULTIVATION Grow these charming small trees in lawns, court-yards or on patios, or as a front garden feature where their year-round beauty can be fully appreciated. They like cool conditions and rich moist soil in full sun or partial shade. Fully frost hardy.

Cornus stolonifera
syn. *Cornus sericea*
Red Osier Dogwood

ORIGIN North America
CLIMATE M, CT, H

A vigorous suckering shrub to 2m/7ft tall with dark green ovate leaves to 12cm/5in long that turn red or orange in autumn. The winter stems are bright red. Flattened loose clusters of white flowers are borne from late spring to mid-summer, followed by white berries. **'Flaviramea'** has bright greenish yellow winter twigs. **'Kelseyi'** is a dwarf form reaching only 60cm/24in. **'Sunrise'** has variegated mid-green leaves with lime green margins.

USE & CULTIVATION Use in informal hedges and screens or beside a pond. These plants reproduce by underground stolons, so site them where space is not limited. Provide moist conditions in sun or light shade. Fully frost hardy.

COTINUS

FAMILY ANACARDIACEAE

This is a genus of 3 deciduous shrubs and small trees found from southern Europe to China and southeastern USA. They are grown for their outstanding autumn colouring and large fluffy plumes of tiny flowers. Powdery mildew may affect purple-leaved forms in shaded or crowded positions. Propagate from seed or cuttings.

Cotinus coggygria

syn. *Rhus cotinus*

Smoke Bush, Venetian Sumach

ORIGIN Southern Europe to central China

CLIMATE M, CT, H

This bushy spreading shrub to 3m/10ft or so has oval mid-green leaves that turn yellow or orange–red in autumn. During summer, large plumes of very tiny, pinkish bronze flowers and masses of pale fawn, thread-like stalks give the bush a smoky effect. **'Golden Spirit'** has fresh yellowish green summer foliage that turns light red in autumn. **'Purpureus'** has rich purplish spring foliage,

becoming greener in summer before colouring to light red shades in autumn. **'Royal Purple'** has deep purplish red foliage with a fine crimson edge and brilliant scarlet colouring in autumn.

USE & CULTIVATION Ideal for adding colour accents to mixed shrub borders, as backgrounds or lawn specimens. Grow in an open sunny position in moderately fertile, well-drained soil.

Cotinus coggygria 'Purpureus'

Cotinus coggygria 'Royal Purple'

Better autumn colour is achieved in areas with cold winters. Trim back after flowering to encourage larger leaves and maintain shape. Fully frost hardy.

Cotinus obovatus
syns *Cotinus americanus, Rhus cotinoides*
American Smoke Tree

ORIGIN Southeastern USA
CLIMATE M, CT, H
In gardens this small tree reaches about 5m/17ft. It has obovate bronzy pink leaves to 12cm/5in or more long that change to glaucous green in summer and turn rich scarlet, orange and plum purple in autumn. The summer flowers are large but sparse, without the smoky haze effects, but this is a superb autumn foliage plant for cold climate gardens.
USE & CULTIVATION Use as a lawn or specimen tree. Grow in moderately fertile, well-drained soil in full sun. Fully frost hardy.

COTYLEDON

FAMILY CRASSULACEAE
A small genus of 9 species of small evergreen shrubs with succulent leaves and slightly thickened stems. Their geographical range is from southern and eastern Africa to the Arabian Peninsula. With their fleshy decorative leaves and spikes of aloe-like flowers they make good rockery plants in hot dry places. Propagate from seed, stem cuttings or leaf cuttings.

Cotyledon orbiculata

ORIGIN Southwest Africa
CLIMATE ST, WT, M
This highly variable species is usually a small shrub to 50cm/20in or more high. The swollen stems bear oval to almost rounded grey–green leaves to 14cm/5½in long, densely frosted with a mealy white bloom and finely edged with red. Pendent bell-shaped flowers in orange, pink or red are carried on branched spikes in late summer and autumn. **C. o. var. *oblonga*** (syn. *C. undulata*) has thick leaves with wavy edges and orange flowers.
USE & CULTIVATION This slow-growing succulent looks best planted in a group. It makes an attractive border in a desert or rock garden and is a good container plant for sunny patios or a hot corner by a swimming pool. Grow in very well-drained, humus-rich soil in full sun or partial shade. In frost-prone areas, grow indoors in bright light. Frost tender.

Cotyledon orbiculata

CRAMBE

**FAMILY BRASSICACEAE/
CRUCIFERAE**

A genus of about 20 species of annuals and perennials from Europe, central Asia and tropical Africa. Two species are grown for their handsome foliage and large billowing sprays of tiny white flowers. Propagate from seed or by division.

Crambe cordifolia
Colewort

ORIGIN Caucasus region
CLIMATE M, CT

This bold perennial has large, wavy-edged, toothed, dark green leaves to 35cm/14in or more across. In early summer it sends up strong stems bearing myriad tiny white scented flowers on many-branched panicles.

USE & CULTIVATION A dramatic accent plant in large herbaceous borders or massed in large-scale wild gardens. Grow in deep well-drained soil in a sunny open position. It will thrive in seaside gardens but needs shelter from strong winds. Trim off any damaged leaves as they appear in summer; the flowering stems are cut back when they turn yellow. Fully frost hardy.

Crambe maritima
Sea Kale

ORIGIN Europe
CLIMATE M, CT

This robust perennial makes a mound to 60cm/24in high with a similar spread of lobed, silvery grey, glaucous leaves to 30cm/12in long. Large heads of small fragrant white flowers are formed in branching sprays in early summer. The leafy shoots are eaten as a spring vegetable.

USE & CULTIVATION As for *C. cordifolia*. Fully frost hardy.

CRASSULA

FAMILY CRASSULACEAE

Most of the 200 species in this genus are from southern Africa. They include succulent plants of very different appearance, from tiny leafy perennials to tall tree-like shrubs. All have leaves arranged in pairs on opposite sides of the stem. Flowers are grouped in terminal clusters or panicles, and in a few species are quite showy. However, these plants are grown mainly for their thick fleshy leaves and their ability to withstand less than perfect conditions. Propagate from seed, or from stem or leaf cuttings.

Crassula arborescens
Silver Jade Plant, Silver Dollar

ORIGIN South Africa
CLIMATE WT, M, SA

This succulent perennial has thick, branched stems to 1m/3ft or more high, bearing obovate to almost circular greyish green leaves to 7cm/2½ in long, often with red edges and covered with tiny green dots. In autumn and winter it produces panicles of 5-petalled, pale pink, starry flowers.

USE & CULTIVATION A good garden and rockery plant, and also highly suitable as a potted house and patio plant. Provide sun, warm temperatures and light, very well-drained soil. Water moderately in spring and summer; less in winter. Frost tender.

Crassula ovata
syns *Crassula arborescens* of gardens, *C. portulacea*
Jade Plant, Jade Tree

ORIGIN South Africa
CLIMATE WT, M, SA

This species forms stout branching stems to about 1m/3ft or more high with fleshy, mid-green, spoon-shaped

Crambe maritima

C

Crassula arborescens

Crassula ovata

leaves to 4cm/1½ in long, set obliquely to the stem. They are sometimes edged with red. Clusters of tiny, star-shaped, white to pink flowers are produced in autumn and winter on mature plants.

USE & CULTIVATION A shapely potted specimen, with elderly specimens taking on fantastic gnarled forms giving the appearance of aged tree-like bonsai. A traditional glazed Chinese pot complements the stout trunks. Provide sun, warm temperatures and perfect drainage. Indoor plants require moderate amounts of water, less in winter. In cool climates plants can be summered outdoors. Frost tender.

Crassula perfoliata var. *minor*
syns *Crassula falcata, C. perfoliata* var. *falcata*
Propeller Plant

ORIGIN South Africa
CLIMATE WT, M, SA
This species has branching fleshy stems to about 1m/3ft or more high, with sickle-shaped pale grey–green leaves about 10cm/4in long with a slight

Crassula perfoliata var. *minor*

twist away from the stem. A dense cluster about 10cm/4in wide of scarlet or pink flowers appears in late summer.
USE & CULTIVATION A good highlight for a rockery or a special corner, it is also very suitable for containers.

Grow in a dry sunny spot in open, well-drained soil. Indoor plants should be watered moderately during spring and summer; less in winter. In cool climates plants can be summered outdoors. Frost tender.

CRYPTANTHUS

EARTH STAR, STARFISH PLANT

FAMILY BROMELIACEAE

This genus consists of about 20 species of small, star-shaped, rosette-forming bromeliads with distinctive flattish prickly-margined leaves. They are terrestrial and come mainly from Brazil, where they grow under widely varying conditions. They are mainly grown for the decorative leaves, which are handsomely marked, mottled and striped with many unusual colours. The name is derived from the Greek kryptos, *'hidden'*, and anthos, *'flower'*, as most have small white flowers that barely emerge from the centre of the rosettes. Their small size makes them good container plants for indoors. They should not be under-potted, as they develop a root system at least equal to the size of the plant. Use a balanced fertiliser in diluted form occasionally during the growing season. Propagate from seed or offsets.

Cryptanthus bivittatus

ORIGIN Brazil
CLIMATE T, ST, WT

A small clumping perennial to about 10cm/4in high and 25cm/10in across, forming loose rosettes of stiff, spiky lance-shaped olive green leaves with longitudinal stripes of white or salmon pink. Small clusters of white flowers are produced in summer. It produces many offsets. **'Pink Starlight'** forms a small tight rosette to 15cm/6in across of pink and green wavy-margined leaves.

USE & CULTIVATION Striking patterns and contrasting textures can be created by growing in masses as groundcovers along paths or as foreground plants to taller tropical plants such as richly coloured cordylines, cycads and palms. Grow in dappled shade in humus-enriched, well-drained soil. Indoor plants need bright diffused light and a high level of humidity. Potting mix should be loose and porous and should never be allowed to dry out totally. In winter, keep on the dry side. Frost tender.

Cryptanthus bromelioides
Rainbow Star

ORIGIN Brazil
CLIMATE T, ST, WT

This species forms an upright rosette to about 40cm/16in high. The centre of the plant tends to extend upwards with offshoots produced on upright stolons near the base of the parent plant. It has very finely toothed, mid-green to bronze leaves to 35cm/14in long with wavy margins and a silvery underside. The popular **'Tricolor'** has green and ivory striped leaves that take on a pink flush in bright light.

USE & CULTIVATION As for *C. bivittatus*. Frost tender.

Cryptanthus fosterianus

ORIGIN Brazil
CLIMATE T, ST, WT

A large, striking bromeliad forming a flat rosette to 12cm/5in high with a spread to 60cm/24in. The thick, reddish brown, strap-shaped leaves to 30cm/12in long have crinkled, wavy edges and zigzag cross-bands of contrasting grey. In summer white flowers are produced.

USE & CULTIVATION As for *C. bivittatus*. Frost tender.

Cryptanthus zonatus
Zebra Plant

ORIGIN Brazil
CLIMATE T, ST, WT

This species forms an attractive flat rosette about 40cm/16in across. It has wavy, strap-shaped, brownish green leaves to 20cm/8in long, heavily cross-banded with silvery grey markings above, and a white-scaly underside. In summer a small cluster of tubular white flowers is produced in the centre of each rosette. **'Zebrinus'** has similar colouring but stronger contrast.

USE & CULTIVATION As for *C. bivittatus*. Frost tender.

CRYPTOMERIA

FAMILY TAXODIACEAE

This genus contains the single species *Cryptomeria japonica*, an evergreen conifer cultivated in many highly ornamental forms and grown commercially in Japan for its high quality timber. Propagate from seed or cuttings.

Cryptomeria japonica 'Pygmaea'

Cryptomeria japonica 'Elegans'

Cryptomeria japonica 'Globosa Nana' (mature specimen)

Cryptomeria japonica
Japanese Cedar

ORIGIN China and Japan
CLIMATE WT, M, CT, H

This conifer forms a tall, stately conical tree to about 24m/80ft in cultivation. It has a tapering, slightly buttressed trunk with soft, thick, reddish bark. The whorled branches are slightly pendulous and clothed with bright green curved needles to 15cm/6in long and spirally arranged. Orange male cones are clustered at the tips of the shoots. Female cones, 3cm/1¼in long when ripe, are borne singly on stout sideshoots. **'Bandai-sugi'** is a slow-growing, rounded, dwarf form 1–2m/3–7ft high. **'Cristata'** (syn. 'Sekka-sugi') is a slow-growing narrow bush or small tree with an upright habit and contorted

fused shoots. The widely grown **'Elegans'**, to 9m/30ft high, has soft-textured foliage on dense drooping branches close to the ground. Juvenile leaves turn reddish bronze in winter. **'Globosa Nana'** is a popular dwarf dome-shaped bush to 1m/3ft high with short needles set close to the stem. **'Pygmaea'** is another dwarf form with twisted branches and foliage that turns coppery in winter. **'Spiralis'** forms a compact bush or small tree with leaves strongly twisted around the stem and light green to pale yellow new growth.
USE & CULTIVATION The species and 'Elegans' make beautiful specimen trees and are very suitable for tall screens, windbreaks and avenues. The dwarf cultivars are ideal for rock gardens, as elegant accent plants or grown in containers. Grow in humus-rich, well-

Cryptomeria japonica 'Globosa Nana'

drained soil that does not dry out in sheltered, sunny or partially shaded sites. Fully frost hardy.

CTENANTHE

FAMILY MARANTACEAE

There are about 15 species in this genus of evergreen rosette-forming perennials from tropical America, grown for their splendidly marked foliage. The leaves are produced on long or short stalks and have bars of contrasting or muted colourings along the main veins in herringbone fashion. Small irregularly shaped flowers in spikes are not showy. Propagate from basal offsets, stem cuttings or by division.

Ctenanthe burle-marxii

ORIGIN Brazil
CLIMATE T, ST, WT

A striking clump-forming perennial to about 60cm/24in high. Waxy, oblong to obovate leaves about 15cm/6in long are pale green above, feathered with dark green and maroon underneath. The leaves may be short-stalked along the stem or long-stalked and arise from the base. Intermittently, it bears inconspicuous 1-sided spikes of small white flowers.

USE & CULTIVATION In tropical and warm temperate gardens, mingle with ferns and palms in protected, moist, shaded places. Indoors, provide bright filtered light, a humid atmosphere, even temperatures and moist but well-drained soil that does not dry out completely during the growing period. Less water is required in winter. Feed with a slow-release fertiliser in spring. Frost tender.

Ctenanthe lubbersiana
Bamburanta

ORIGIN Brazil
CLIMATE T, ST, WT

One of the fastest growing and most popular ctenanthes, this species makes a bushy clump to about 75cm/30in high of long-stalked, lance-shaped or nearly oblong, slender-pointed leaves to 25cm/10in long. They are green above, handsomely marked and striped with pale yellowish green, and pale green below. Small white flowers are insignificant.

Ctenanthe burle-marxii

USE & CULTIVATION As for *C. burle-marxii*. Frost tender.

Ctenanthe oppenheimiana
syn. *Calathea oppenheimiana*

ORIGIN Brazil
CLIMATE T, ST, WT

A robust bushy perennial 1m/3ft or more high with lance-shaped leathery leaves 30cm/12in or more long. They are dark green above and dull red beneath, with pale green or silver bands along the veins on either side of the midrib. Spikes of small white flowers are produced intermittently. It is grown mainly in the variegated form **'Tricolor'**, the Never-never Plant, which has leaves splashed with large creamy white blotches and dark green markings. **USE & CULTIVATION** As for *C. burle-marxii*. Frost tender.

X CUPRESSOCYPARIS

FAMILY CUPRESSACEAE

These vigorous and fast-growing hybrid conifers are a cross between the genera *Chamaecyparis* and *Cupressus*. They have a dense columnar habit with ascending branches and deep green foliage in coarse, flattened, slightly drooping sprays. They respond very well to regular pruning and are widely planted for hedging. Unfortunately, they are

x *Cupressocyparis leylandii*

foliage hues. They have tiny, scale-like, closely overlapping leaves arranged in plume-like sprays. Their compact foliage and rapid growth makes them especially useful for ornament, shelter and windbreaks. Some are very susceptible to the disfiguring disease cypress canker, which affects the bark and eventually kills the tree. Propagate from seed, or cuttings for cultivars.

x *Cupressocyparis leylandii* 'Leighton Green'

susceptible to cypress canker and honey fungus. Propagate from cuttings.

x *Cupressocyparis leylandii*
syn. *Cupressus leylandii*
Leyland Cypress

ORIGIN Gardens
CLIMATE WT, M, CT

Arising from the original cross between the hardy *Cupressus macrocarpa* and *Chamaecyparis nootkatensis*, this dense tapering conifer can reach 20m/70ft or more in 20 years. It has flat sprays of dark green leaves with yellowish undersides. Female cones are globular, green when young, to 3cm/1¼in long, and brown and woody when ripe. **'Castlewellan'** (syn. 'Galway Gold') is a popular form with golden yellow-toned foliage. **'Haggerston Grey'** has slightly greyish foliage. **'Leighton Green'** makes a tall narrow column with fresh green foliage. **'Naylor's Blue'** is a narrow columnar

form with greyish green foliage that is noticeably glaucous during winter.
USE & CULTIVATION These fast-growing conifers can be pruned hard and are commonly grown as hedges, but if left untrimmed will rapidly make good shelter, boundary or specimen trees. Although tolerant of less than perfect growing conditions, including poorly drained clay soil, they do best in deep well-drained soil in full sun. They may grow too tall for average to small home gardens. Fully frost hardy.

CUPRESSUS

CYPRESS
FAMILY CUPRESSACEAE
There are about 20 species in this genus of handsome coniferous trees or shrubs from southern Europe, western China, the Himalayas, North and Central America. Most species are large, with bold symmetrical outlines and attractive

Cupressus arizonica var. *glabra*
syn. *Cupressus glabra*
Smooth Arizona Cypress

ORIGIN Southwestern North America
CLIMATE ST, WT, M, CT, SA
This fairly quick-growing conifer forms a regular conical or pyramidal outline to 15m/50ft. The smooth red bark peels off in thin sheets. It has upward spirally arranged sprays of glaucous blue–grey foliage that exudes white specks of resin. Prickly brown female cones are about 2.5cm/1in across. There are various forms in cultivation, some with attractively frosted blue foliage.
USE & CULTIVATION Occurring naturally at high altitudes in areas with low rainfall, this cypress withstands extremely dry conditions and is often used as a specimen tree and as a windbreak. Grow in full sun in deep well-drained soil with shelter from cold drying winds. Fully frost hardy.

Cupressus cashmeriana
Bhutan Cypress, Kashmir Cypress

ORIGIN Bhutan
CLIMATE WT, M

This beautiful conical conifer reaching about 9m/30ft has ascending branches and highly ornamental drooping branchlets draped with long flattened sprays of glaucous blue foliage. It bears small rounded cones that are waxy blue when young.
USE & CULTIVATION An outstanding specimen tree best suited to mild moist climates or cooler mountainous areas in subtropical regions. Grow in deep, well-drained, fertile soil in a position where its outstanding form can be appreciated. Marginally frost hardy.

Cupressus goveniana
var. pygmaea
Gowan Cypress

ORIGIN California
CLIMATE WT, M, CT

This conifer makes a small columnar tree to about 3m/10ft high with dense foliage to the ground. The mostly dark green, scale-like leaves carried in short sprays are citrus scented when crushed. The shiny brown small cones are less than 2cm/³/₄in across.
USE & CULTIVATION An attractive lawn specimen that can be lightly trimmed for formal landscape effects. Grow in well-drained fertile soil, preferably in full sun. Fully frost hardy.

Cupressus lusitanica
syn. Cupressus lindleyi
Cedar of Goa, Mexican Cypress

ORIGIN Mexico to Guatemala
CLIMATE ST, WT, M, CT

This broadly conical to dome-shaped tree can reach a height of 20m/70ft, with spreading branches, pendulous tips and spirally arranged sprays of dark grey–green or blue–green foliage. The rounded cones to 1.5cm/½in wide are glaucous when young, ripening to glossy brown. 'Glauca Pendula' is an attractive cultivar with glaucous blue foliage and conspicuous pendent branches and tips.

USE & CULTIVATION Widely cultivated as a hardy rapid-growing shelter tree, it withstands heavy trimming and is more resistant to cypress canker than other cypresses. Grow in full sun in deep well-drained soil with shelter from cold drying winds. Fully frost hardy.

Cupressus macrocarpa
Monterey Cypress

ORIGIN Californian coast, USA
CLIMATE WT, M, CT

This conifer to 35m/120ft or more has upswept branches with a narrow crown when young, but is broadly domed or flat-topped when mature. The dark to yellowish green foliage has a lemony aroma when crushed. Very variable in foliage, some specimens being softer and more feathery than others. The rounded female cones to 3cm/1¼in long are glossy brown and wrinkled. 'Aurea Saligna' is a graceful pyramidal form to 8m/25ft clothed in weeping, gold-tipped, thread-like foliage. 'Brunniana Aurea' makes a stately conical tree to 9m/30ft with soft foliage of a

Cupressus cashmeriana

Cupressus goveniana var. *pygmaea*

C

Cupressus macrocarpa 'Aurea Saligna'

Cupressus macrocarpa 'Greenstead Magnificent'

rich golden colour. **'Goldcrest'** is a small, narrow, conical form to 5m/17ft with rich golden yellow juvenile foliage. **'Greenstead Magnificent'** is a low, almost prostrate plant about 1m/3ft high spreading to 3m/10ft across with rich, glaucous, blue–green foliage on horizontal branches.

USE & CULTIVATION 'Aurea Saligna' is a top-rate specimen tree for special landscaping effects. Grow in a sheltered location to preserve colour and form. 'Brunniana Aurea' can be used as a screen or hedge, or as a colourful accent among green foliage. It responds well to trimming and can be used for topiary. 'Goldcrest' is good for accent and can be grown as a tub specimen. 'Greenstead Magnificent' is a beautiful groundcover or feature plant, but needs space for best development. These trees can be grown in seaside gardens and do best in areas with a long dry summer. Fully frost hardy.

Cupressus sempervirens
**Italian Cypress,
Mediterranean Cypress**

🌿 ⚶ ❄ ▲ ▽

ORIGIN Eastern Mediterranean region
CLIMATE ST, WT, M

This conifer is best known as a very narrow, spire-like tree to 20m/70ft high with upswept branches and aromatic grey–green or dark green foliage. The pale brown, rounded to ovoid cones to 4cm/1½ in diameter have 8–14 scales that meet edge to edge. It has long been cultivated in southern Europe, especially in Italy, and is frequently naturalised. The form usually cultivated is **'Stricta'**, a very narrow, pencil-like tree 9–12m/30–40ft high with ascending branches and dense, dark green foliage. Older trees are usually much broader. One of the most widely planted golden conifers is **'Swane's Golden'**, a highly successful Australian cultivar with a dependable narrow form to 6–8m/20–25ft; its golden yellow foliage maintains its colour throughout the year. It is slow growing but long-lived, retaining perfect form without trimming. Slightly frost tender.

USE & CULTIVATION Useful for architectural and large formal landscaping effects, these plants can also be clipped as a hedge. In cold gardens, they can be grown in large tubs and take well to topiary. Grow in deeply worked, well-drained soil in full sun. The term 'fall-out' is applied to seedlings that develop undesirable spreading side-branches. Cutting-grown plants are uniform in outline and preferable. Half hardy.

CYATHEA

TREE FERN

FAMILY CYATHEACEAE

Widely distributed throughout the world, this is a large genus of some 600 species of tree ferns found mainly in tropical and subtropical regions of the Southern Hemisphere. They have an erect trunk (or caudex) and large spreading fronds radiating from the crown. They make very beautiful garden subjects when protected from wind, heat and frost. Young plants are excellent in containers and can be used indoors in atriums, glasshouses and conservatories. When purchasing these tree ferns, ensure that the root system is intact, for unlike *Dicksonia* species they resent having their trunk severed. It is normal for their outer fronds to be removed. Transplant established plants with care. Propagate by spores.

Cyathea australis
Rough Tree Fern

ORIGIN Eastern Australia
CLIMATE ST, WT, M

A large-growing slender species to 3m/10ft tall with large, umbrella-like crown of finely divided dark green fronds to 3.5m/12ft long. The rough frond bases persisting towards the top of the narrow trunk give this tree fern its common name.

Cyathea australis

USE & CULTIVATION Grow as a specimen or in groves with other shade-lovers to give the garden a lush forest look. Provide a sheltered position and moist humus-enriched soil. A good mulch will keep the roots cool and moist. In frosty areas, grow indoors in a humid environment. Marginally frost hardy.

Cyathea cooperi
Scaly Tree Fern

ORIGIN Australia
CLIMATE T, ST, WT

This fast-growing tree fern 5–6m/17–20ft high has a slender trunk and large fronds to 3.5m/12ft long. The frond stalks are covered with reddish brown hair and have large straw-coloured scales at the base. The dead fronds are shed cleanly from the trunk, leaving a neat pattern of oval scars sometimes referred to as 'coin spots'.

USE & CULTIVATION An outstanding tree fern for planting beneath trees, either singly or in a group. Used to best advantage, the large crown of gracefully arching fronds will soften architectural lines and provide dappled shade, ideal for other, more delicate ferns. Grow in deep well-composted soil with plenty of moisture. It will tolerate a fair amount of sun provided the roots are in a damp, protected situation. An excellent container plant for courtyard gardens; in frosty areas will thrive in a humid atmosphere indoors. Frost tender.

Cyathea dealbata
Silver Fern

ORIGIN New Zealand
CLIMATE ST, WT, M

This beautiful tree fern occurs naturally in cool forests throughout the North and South Islands of New Zealand. It grows to a height of 3.5m/12ft and has a slender erect trunk topped with rather stiff fronds to 3m/10ft long. The fronds of mature plants have a distinctive silvery bloom on the undersides.

USE & CULTIVATION Grow singly or in a group in a shady or semi-shady

C

Cyathea cooperi

Cyathea medullaris

location with deeply worked, organically rich soil. It requires cool moist conditions and protection from hot sun and drying winds. Damp down the trunk regularly in hot weather. A good mulch will keep the roots cool and moist. In frosty areas, grow in a humid environment indoors with bright filtered light. Marginally frost hardy.

Cyathea medullaris
Black Tree Fern

ORIGIN New Zealand, other Pacific islands

CLIMATE T, ST, WT

This tall ornamental tree fern has a slender black trunk to 15m/50ft or more high and a large crown of gracefully arching fronds 3–6m/10–20ft long with black stalks covered in blackish hairy scales.

USE & CULTIVATION A dramatic garden feature which, once established, grows quite vigorously, producing a succession of soft lacy fronds. Partial shade and moist humus-enriched soil is best. Plants in full sun have a yellow appearance, but will provide filtered

sunlight and an ideal environment for smaller ferns and other shade-loving plants. An attractive indoor plant when young. Provide warm humid conditions and bright filtered light. Marginally frost hardy.

CYCAS

SAGO PALM
FAMILY CYCADACEAE

A genus of about 40 species of primitive palm-like plants with a trunk either below or above ground and clothed with persistent leaf bases. Native to Southeast Asia, eastern Africa, Madagascar, Australia and the Pacific islands, these plants are popular in cultivation, mainly for their highly decorative pinnate leaves and striking architectural appearance. Fruits are borne in cones, with rather dissimilar male and female cones produced on separate plants. Slow growing, they produce only a few new leaves each season, but over time become increasingly handsome and distinctive. When young they can be used for indoor

decoration. Annual feeding with a slow-release fertiliser is beneficial. Propagate from seed or suckers.

Cycas circinalis
Fern Palm, Queen Sago

ORIGIN India, southern Asia, South Pacific islands

CLIMATE T, ST

This cycad has an erect, above-ground, blackish trunk to 5m/17ft tall topped with a widely spreading crown of curved pinnate leaves to 1.5–3m/5–10ft long comprising hundreds of rich glossy green leaflets. Female cones produce spongy reddish yellow seeds which float when viable, enabling this species to become established in the coastal communities of many countries.

USE & CULTIVATION In tropical regions, this species is widely cultivated as a specimen plant. Grow in a sunny position in deep well-drained soil. Young plants can be grown in a temperate or warm greenhouse with moderate humidity. Adequate watering, especially in hot weather, is essential. Frost tender.

Cycas revoluta
Japanese Sago Palm

ORIGIN Japan
CLIMATE T, ST, WT, M

This attractive cycad may eventually develop a woody trunk 2–3m/7–10ft high. The glossy, dark green, pinnate leaves to 1.5m/5ft long are arranged in a widely spreading flat crown arising from a felted pineapple-like base. Plants are either male or female; both bear interesting brown furry cones, the female cones being larger and bearing bright orange to red seeds to 4cm/1½ in long.
USE & CULTIVATION Very slow growing but always attractive, even as a small plant. Well suited to oriental-style gardens and prized as a bonsai subject, especially in Japan. Grow in full sun in well-drained soil with plenty of water during dry periods. Place large pots at entrances, in courtyards, on patios and verandas. In frosty areas it can be brought indoors in winter. Frost tender.

CYMBOPOGON

FAMILY GRAMINEAE/POACEAE
There abut 56 species in this genus of densely tufted, aromatic, perennial grasses from tropical Asia and other warm climates, including Australia. The fleshy white lower part of Lemon Grass, *Cymbopogon citratus*, is a popular ingredient in Southeast Asian cooking. The leaves are used as a flavouring for tea. Propagate from seed or by division.

Cymbopogon citratus
Lemon Grass

ORIGIN Southern India, Sri Lanka
CLIMATE T, ST, WT

This moderately tall, tussock-forming grass can reach 1.5m/5ft. It has linear, strongly lemon-scented, blue–green leaves that arch over decoratively. It rarely flowers in cultivation.
USE & CULTIVATION Lemon Grass quickly forms a thick clump and provides an interesting foliage contrast in a roomy part of the herb garden. Once established it spreads rapidly as an informal border or rockery plant. Grow in a rich warm soil in full sun and give plenty of water. Frost tender.

Cymbopogon citratus

CYNARA

FAMILY ASTERACEAE
This genus contains about 8 species of clump-forming, thistle-like perennials from the Mediterranean region. They are cultivated for their striking, silvery grey, deeply divided leaves and large heads of thistle-like flowers. The immature swollen flower buds of the Globe Artichoke, *Cynara scolymus*, are eaten as a vegetable. Propagate from seed or offsets.

Cynara cardunculus
Cardoon

ORIGIN Southern Europe, Morocco
CLIMATE WT, M, CT
Towering to 1.8m/6ft, this striking perennial forms bold clumps of highly

Cycas revoluta

Cynara cardunculus

Cynara scolymus

ornamental, pointed, deeply lobed, grey–green leaves to 80cm/32in long. The large thistle-like purple flower-heads are borne singly on stout, grey-woolly stems in summer.
USE & CULTIVATION A highly decorative accent plant in a flower border or within the vegetable or herb garden. Position in full sun in well-drained fertile soil and shelter from strong winds. For good foliage display, remove the flowering stems as soon as they appear in summer. Winter mulch in cold areas. The blanched leaf stalks and midribs are edible. Frost hardy.

Cynara scolymus
Globe Artichoke

ORIGIN Unknown
CLIMATE WT, M, CT
This species makes a splendid clump, to 2m/7ft high and 1m/3ft across, of deeply lobed, grey–green leaves to 80cm/32in long with narrow, pointed

segments. The tall flowering stems appear in mid-summer; they can be cut down at once or allowed to grow, and the young swollen flower buds can be cut for cooking. If left to develop, the flowers form large purple thistle-like heads in autumn.
USE & CULTIVATION As for *C. cardunculus*. Frost hardy.

CYPERUS

FAMILY CYPERACEAE
Found in wet habitats throughout the warmer regions of the world, there are about 600 species in this large genus of annual or perennial sedges. They have triangular, rush-like, leafy stems topped with narrow, usually radiating, leaf-like bracts beneath branching umbels of flowers. A few ornamental species are popular in contemporary landscaping and are favoured waterside plants. Once established, they make few

demands, but a number have become serious weeds, including the highly invasive Nutgrass, *Cyperus rotundus*.

Cyperus albostriatus
syn. *Cyperus diffusus* of gardens

ORIGIN Southern Africa
CLIMATE T, ST, WT
This dense clump-forming perennial has stems 25–50cm/10–20in tall and broad, prominently veined, papery-looking mid-green foliage. Up to 8 leaf-like green bracts surround a well-branched umbel of pale brown spikelets from mid-summer to early autumn. **'Variegatus'** is smaller and has white-striped leaves and bracts.
USE & CULTIVATION Grow near ponds and water features in semi-shade, with its roots in constantly wet soil. Inclined to become invasive; if this should be a problem it is best contained. Indoor plants should be kept permanently moist. Marginally frost hardy.

Cyperus involucratus
syns *Cyperus alternifolius*,
C. flabelliformis
Umbrella Sedge

ORIGIN Madagascar
CLIMATE T, ST, WT

This dense tuft-forming perennial has ribbed, almost triangular stems to 1m/3ft or more with about 12 thin, slightly drooping, leaf-like bracts, radiating like umbrella ribs. Flowers are borne in dry, greenish brown spikelets in summer. A dwarf-growing form is also available.

USE & CULTIVATION In warm climates it is easily cultivated in wet soil, at the margins of a pool or in a rock garden. Locate in a sunny position. Established plants provide a tall, interesting feature for indoor water gardens in brightly lit, airy locations. Keep permanently moist. Frost tender.

Cyperus papyrus
Egyptian Papyrus

ORIGIN Egypt to tropical Africa
CLIMATE T, ST, WT

Since ancient Egyptian times the reeds or flower stems of the papyrus have been used as a source of parchment. It is thought to be the bulrush of the Bible. It is a tall-growing sedge to 2.5m/8ft with spreading underground rhizomes from which arise smooth triangular stems topped with a dense tuft of drooping thread-like bracts. Umbels of tiny brown flowers are produced in summer.

USE & CULTIVATION The stately papyrus is perfect alongside ponds or in boggy ground, used as a feature in small courtyards, and looks good as a background to stripy-leaved cannas. It grows in shallow water and prefers rich soil and a sunny position. Indoors, provide warm humid conditions and constantly wet soil. Brown tips develop if the atmosphere is too dry or the soil dries out. Frost tender.

CYPHOSTEMMA

FAMILY VITACEAE
This genus consists of about 150 species of mostly deciduous succulents from dry areas of Africa and Madagascar. They are found in a variety of forms, from climbing vines to small trees with thick trunk-like stems. The leaves are mostly divided into several leaflets, and small flowers are borne in long-stalked panicles. In late summer, small red or yellow grape-like fruit are produced. Propagate from seed.

Cyphostemma juttae
syn. *Cissus juttae*

ORIGIN Southern Namibia
CLIMATE ST, WT, M, SA

Probably the most common of the genus, it forms a thick swollen stem, usually to 2m/7ft, bearing a spreading crown of branches at the top. The yellowish green bark is paper thin and peels off as the plant grows in summer. The leaves are divided into 3 mid-green to grey–green toothed leaflets to 15cm/6in long that fold upwards from the sides. Yellowish green flowers produced in summer are followed by small bright red inedible fruit.

USE & CULTIVATION An unusual ornamental accent plant for a rockery or desert garden. Allow plenty of root room in very well-drained soil in full sun. When mature, it tolerates hot sun, but resents winter wet. Frost tender.

Cyperus involucratus

Cyphostemma juttae

C

Cyrtomium falcatum

Cyrtostachys renda

CYRTOMIUM

FAMILY DRYOPTERIDACEAE

A small genus of about 12 species of evergreen terrestrial woodland ferns from eastern and central Asia. They are clump-forming, with leathery pinnate fronds arising from a rhizome thickly covered with furry scales, which also cover most of the leaf stalks. The spore cases sprinkled densely on the undersides of the leaflets are green at first but gradually turn rich brown. Propagate from spores or by division of rhizomes.

Cyrtomium falcatum
syn. *Phanerophlebia falcata*
Holly Fern, House Holly

ORIGIN Japan
CLIMATE ST, WT
This decorative long-lasting fern forms a dense clump about 90cm/36in high. It has erect individual fronds to 60cm/24in long, divided into several pairs of 7cm/2½ in long, glossy, holly-like, dark green leaflets. The compact **'Rochford-ianum'** has shorter fronds to 30cm/12in, but larger, deeply cut leaflets.
USE & CULTIVATION In the garden, grow in semi-shade in organically rich moist well-drained soil. An extremely tolerant houseplant, but should be protected from direct sunlight and the soil should never be allowed to dry out. Marginally frost hardy.

CYRTOSTACHYS

FAMILY ARECACEAE/PALMAE
There are about 8 species in this palm genus, which ranges from Thailand to Indonesia, New Guinea, Borneo and the Solomon Islands. They are tall clumping plants with slender stems ringed with leaf scars, and terminal clusters of arching pinnate fronds. Branched panicles of small flowers emerge below the fronds. Propagate from fresh seed.

Cyrtostachys renda
syn. *Cyrtostachys lakka*
Lipstick Palm, Sealing Wax Palm

ORIGIN Southeast Asia
CLIMATE T
This outstanding clump-forming palm has slender erect stems with brilliant glossy red leaf bases and mid-green pinnate leaves to 1.5m/5ft long with scarlet stalks and midribs. It grows to about 6m/20ft tall. Greenish flowers are produced in summer.
USE & CULTIVATION One of the most ornamental of all palms, it is widely planted in the tropics, where it gets the constant heat needed for the red colour to develop properly. Grow in rich, constantly moist but well-drained soil in sun or partial shade. In cooler areas it needs a heated greenhouse with winter temperature no lower than about 16°C/60°F. Provide bright filtered light and moderate humidity. Frost tender.

DACRYDIUM

FAMILY PODOCARPACEAE

This genus of about 20 species of conifers extends from subtropical Southeast Asia to New Zealand. They are mostly large forest trees, a number of the New Zealand species yielding valuable timber. They have graceful arching branchlets and linear juvenile leaves grading into adult leaves that are closely pressed to the stem and spirally arranged. Male and female flowers occur on separate trees. The oblong male catkins are borne in the upper leaf axils, the female cones near the tips of the branches. Propagate from seed or cuttings.

Dacrydium cupressinum
Rimu

ORIGIN New Zealand
CLIMATE M, CT

This tall conical tree grows to 40m/130ft in nature but is much smaller in cultivation, usually about 6–9m/20–30ft. It has long pendulous branchlets with bright green linear young leaves. As the tree ages the leaves become much shorter and scale-like. Female cones each contain a small bluish seed.

USE & CULTIVATION A highly ornamental conifer eminently suited as a lawn specimen and feature plant. Rather slow growing, it thrives in mildly cool climates in higher rainfall areas. Grow in semi-shade and deep, moist, fertile soil and protect from strong drying winds. Moderately frost hardy.

DARMERA

FAMILY SAXIFRAGACEAE

This genus contains only the one species, a herbaceous perennial grown for the unusual large, scalloped leaves that follow the flowers in spring. It is native to northwestern California and southwestern Oregon, growing along streams in mountainous woodland, making it a first-rate specimen to grow at the water's edge. Propagate from seed or by division of rhizomes.

Darmera peltata
syn. *Peltiphyllum peltatum*
Umbrella Plant, Indian Rhubarb

ORIGIN USA
CLIMATE WT, M, CT, H

A spreading rhizomatous perennial 1–2m/3–7ft high with large, rounded, conspicuously veined leaves to 60cm/24in across, on thick stalks to 2m/7ft long. The leaves turn red in autumn. It bears clusters of white or pale pink flowers in spring, on white-haired 2m/7ft stems before the foliage appears. **'Nana'** is smaller, with purple-tinted leaves on stalks about 30cm/12in long.

USE & CULTIVATION A fine waterside plant; it will form a large colony in moist or boggy soil in sun or partial shade. Fully frost hardy.

DASYLIRION

FAMILY DRACAENACEAE/LILIACEAE

There are about 18 species in this genus of attractive yucca-like plants from southern USA and Mexico. They are stemless or tree-like and bear long thin leaves, often arranged as ball-shaped rosettes. Masses of small creamy white flowers are borne on a long towering spike; male and female flowers are on separate plants. Propagate from seed.

Dacrydium cupressinum

D

Darmera peltata

Dasylirion acrotrichum
syn. *Dasylirion gracile*

ORIGIN Mexico
CLIMATE ST, WT, SA
This yucca-like perennial has a rosette of linear, brush-tipped, spiny-margined leaves to 1m/3ft long. Older specimens form a trunk to 1.5m/5ft or more high. Masses of small star-shaped flowers are produced on stems to 5m/17ft in summer on mature plants.
USE & CULTIVATION A good accent plant for a desert garden or contemporary pebble courtyard. Grow in well-drained soil in a sunny position. Water well when in full growth, less at other times. Frost tender.

Dasylirion longissimum
Mexican Grass Plant

ORIGIN Mexico
CLIMATE ST, WT, SA
This tree-like succulent may develop a trunk to 3.5m/12ft tall. It has stiff, slightly succulent, dull green leaves to 1.5m/5ft or more long. In summer white bell-shaped flowers are borne on a tall flower spike to 4.5m/15ft high.
USE & CULTIVATION As for *D. acrotrichum*. Frost tender.

Dasylirion acrotrichum

DAVALLIA

FAMILY DAVALLIACEAE

There are 34 species in this widespread genus of mostly epiphytic ferns. Because the young parts of the above-ground creeping rhizome often have a furry appearance, they are sometimes given names such as Hare's Foot Fern or Rabbit's Foot Fern. The lacy, deeply dissected, arching fronds are borne in 2 rows arising from the rhizome. They are popular pot and hanging basket subjects for glasshouses or ferneries. Propagate from spores or by division of rhizomes.

Davallia canariensis
Canary Island Hare's Foot Fern

ORIGIN Southern Europe, northern Africa
CLIMATE ST, WT
This deciduous or semi-evergreen fern to about 50cm/20in high has broad mid-green fronds 20–50cm/8–20in long, with numerous finely dissected triangular segments, arising from a scaly brown rootstock.
USE & CULTIVATION It thrives in a protected warm garden, but is usually grown in hanging baskets in coarse, open, potting mix. In cooler climates it is a fine addition to a conservatory, fernery, atrium or sunroom with medium light and a moist environment. Keep plants moist when in active growth, drier in winter. Frost tender.

Davallia fejeensis
Rabbit's Foot Fern

ORIGIN Fiji
CLIMATE T, ST, WT
This evergreen fern to 1m/3ft high has thick, furry, brown rhizomes from which arise lacy, pale green fronds to 60cm/24in long with linear segments. **'Major'** has larger fronds, sometimes to 1.2m/4ft long.

USE & CULTIVATION It is very well suited to a hanging basket, which it will readily cover with its creeping rhizomes. Provide open, organically rich soil and keep moist during summer. Feed established plants weak liquid fertiliser during spring and summer. Indoors, provide bright indirect light and a humid atmosphere. Frost tender.

Davallia pyxidata
Hare's Foot Fern

ORIGIN Eastern Australia
CLIMATE ST, WT
This attractive epiphytic fern forms spreading clumps of thick woody rhizomes covered with brown papery scales. It has dark green, finely divided, glossy fronds to 1m/3ft long.
USE & CULTIVATION A beautiful fern for moist crevices among large rocks in a protected warm garden. Also an excellent basket subject, given an open, organically rich potting medium.

Davallia fejeensis

Davallia pyxidata

D

Davallia trichomanoides

Dennstaedtia davallioides

Indoors, provide filtered light and high humidity. Frost tender.

Davallia trichomanoides
Squirrel's Foot Fern

ORIGIN Southeast Asia
CLIMATE T, ST
A deciduous fern to about 35cm/14in high with long, thin, trailing rhizomes covered with yellowish brown scales with some silvery grey hairs. Its glossy green fronds to 38cm/15in long have narrowly triangular or linear segments. It dies back to the perennial rhizome for a short period during winter.
USE & CULTIVATION It grows readily as a garden plant in the tropics, doing best in a sheltered situation. In a container, it needs coarse, well-drained potting mix; it makes an excellent basket

subject. Indoors, provide filtered light and high humidity, although it will tolerate a drier atmosphere than most others in this genus. Frost tender.

DENNSTAEDTIA

FAMILY DENNSTAEDTIACEAE
This is a genus of about 70 species of deciduous or semi-evergreen terrestrial ferns, often with extensive underground rhizomes, and forming spreading patches of erect, roughly triangular, finely divided and lacy fronds. While often invasive, they are ideal for a moist neglected area that requires little care and attention. The fronds are frequently attacked by insects or snails, but damaged fronds can be simply removed and more will quickly grow.

Propagate from spores or by division of rhizomes.

Dennstaedtia davallioides
Lady Ground Fern

ORIGIN Australia
CLIMATE ST, WT
Sometimes forming large colonies, this terrestrial fern has a creeping rhizome covered with reddish brown hairs, and large, lacy, dark green fronds 1m/3ft or more long, soft, thin, broadly triangular and 3–4 times divided.
USE & CULTIVATION Growing naturally beside creeks in moist forests, it makes a good robust groundcover for bordering streams in the larger landscape. Provide moist humus-rich, acid soil in a sheltered, partially shaded position. Marginally frost hardy.

DICKSONIA

FAMILY DICKSONIACEAE

Native to tropical and temperate regions of Southeast Asia, Australia, New Zealand and South America, there are about 25 species in this genus of evergreen or semi-evergreen tree ferns. They are extremely attractive large ferns with trunks (caudices) either large or small, and handsome spreading fronds radiating from the crown. They are sold in a variety of heights, often with the trunk sawn off at the base. The trunk will grow new roots from the cut in several weeks and, new fronds will quickly unfurl in the warmer months. It is important to provide liberal water to the trunk and fronds while the plant establishes its roots, and during hot dry weather. Occasional removal of old fronds may be necessary. Propagate from spores.

Dicksonia antarctica
Soft Tree Fern

ORIGIN Southeastern Australia

CLIMATE ST, WT, M, CT

This magnificent plant is a feature of moist forests from southeastern Queensland to Tasmania. The thick woolly trunk covered in reddish brown hairs can grow to 9m/30ft tall, although in cultivation it rarely exceeds 3m/10ft. The soft, lacy, dark green fronds to 3m/10ft long uncurl rapidly in warm weather; many are produced in one season, providing a beautiful, arching, dense cover.

USE & CULTIVATION A slow-growing species that makes an outstanding feature plant in a rockery, near water or in a sheltered courtyard. Grow in well-drained, well-mulched soil, preferably in a semi-shaded, protected position. In dry weather apply plenty of water to crown and trunk. Use rotted leaf mould and peat at the base to keep roots moist. The fibrous trunk is an excellent host for epiphytic orchids and other ferns. As a potted plant, use on a veranda, in a courtyard or as a feature in a warm humid atrium. Marginally frost hardy.

Dicksonia fibrosa
Wheki-Ponga

ORIGIN New Zealand

CLIMATE ST, WT, M, CT

In average garden conditions this slow-growing tree fern will reach a height of around 2.5m/8ft. The stout trunk is covered with densely matted, brownish red, fibrous roots. The thick-textured dark green arching fronds to about 1.8m/6ft long are at first almost erect, then gradually spreading.

Dicksonia antarctica

Dieffenbachia seguine 'Maculata'

Dieffenbachia seguine 'Amoena'

Dieffenbachia seguine 'Exotica'

USE & CULTIVATION As for *D. antarctica*. Best in cool damp climates. Marginally frost hardy.

Dicksonia squarrosa
Wheki

ORIGIN New Zealand
CLIMATE ST, WT, M, CT

This species has a spreading, rhizomatous root system and may develop several slender brownish red stems to about 3.5m/12ft tall and sometimes more, clothed with the hardened remains of stalk bases. The harsh-textured deep green fronds are paler on the underside and up to 1.5m/5ft long.
USE & CULTIVATION As for *D. antarctica*. Marginally frost hardy.

DIEFFENBACHIA

DUMB CANE
FAMILY ARACEAE

A genus of about 30 species of stout tufted perennials from tropical America, grown for their highly decorative foliage, and among the more popular and successful indoor plants. Their thick cane-like stems carry rather soft, fleshy leaves on sturdy sheathed stalks. The oval leaves of most species and varieties are basically green, but some are heavily marked with yellow, pale cream or white. Mature plants may produce small white or cream arum-like flowers that are best removed as they appear. The common name Dumb Cane refers to the poisonous sap; if eaten it will swell the mouth and tongue, making speech impossible. Propagate from root or stem cuttings.

Dieffenbachia seguine
syns *Dieffenbachia maculata*,
D. picta
Spotted Dumb Cane

ORIGIN Brazil
CLIMATE T, ST

This tufted perennial grows to 1m/3ft or more. It has broadly lance-shaped, glossy dark green leaves to 45cm/18in long and spotted and blotched in cream along the lateral veins. This most popular species has many varieties. **'Amoena'** has bold, elliptic-oblong, dark green leaves to 45cm/18in long and splashed with creamy white between the main veins. **'Exotica'** grows to a maximum of 60cm/24in and has dark green oval leaves irregularly marked with white and very pale green. **'Maculata'** has mid-green leaves to 25cm/10in long, heavily veined and spotted creamy white. **'Rudolph Roehrs'**, to 1m/3ft, has chartreuse green, oval-elliptic leaves with green midribs and margins. **'Tropic Snow'** has large, striking, grey–green leaves with heavy cream markings.
USE & CULTIVATION In warm humid climates these plants make an attractive addition to shrub borders and look particularly good massed among ferns and palms in a swimming-pool landscape. Grow in fertile, moist well-drained soil in partial shade. Often grown indoors, they need bright filtered light and a reasonably good potting mix. Water moderately during the growing season, less in winter. Apply a balanced liquid fertiliser monthly. Frost tender.

DIOON

FAMILY ZAMIACEAE

This Mexican and Central American genus of cycads consists of 10 species. They are palm-like in appearance, with upright woody stems and pinnate leathery leaves with many slender leaflets. The ovoid female cones produced in the centre of the leaf rosette are often large and woolly. Cut fronds can be used for indoor decoration. Propagate from fresh seed.

Dioon edule
Mexican Fern Palm

ORIGIN Mexico
CLIMATE T, ST, WT

This very slow-growing cycad will eventually form a thick trunk to 3m/10ft high, but is usually less in cultivation. The upright, tough, feather-like leaves to 1.5m/5ft long have sharp-tipped, deep blue–green leaflets. The silvery grey female cones to 30cm/12in long contain edible seeds, which are cooked before consumption.

USE & CULTIVATION One of the more commonly cultivated members of the genus, this makes an outstanding land-scaping plant, especially when planted in a well-spaced group. Grow in full sun in an open, well-drained situation. In frost-prone areas, grow in a container and use for indoor decoration. Water freely during the growing season, less in winter. Frost tender.

Dioon spinulosum

ORIGIN Mexico
CLIMATE T, ST, WT

This medium-sized to large cycad has a slender trunk to 5–9m/17–30ft with a graceful, arching crown of pinnate leaves 1–2m/3–7ft long, with mid-green spiny-toothed leaflets, greyish blue and slightly hairy when young. The pendulous ovoid female cones, about 90cm/36in long to 35cm/14in wide, are coated with silvery white, silky hairs. They are among the largest cones of any cycad.

USE & CULTIVATION An outstanding specimen plant for tropical regions. Requiring warm humid conditions, it grows best in moist well-drained soil in partial shade. Water well during warmer months. Staking may be required for tall specimens. Young plants make good container plants for patios or a bright position indoors. Frost tender.

Dioon spinulosum

DISANTHUS

FAMILY HAMAMELIDACEAE

This is a genus of one species, a deciduous shrub from mountainous areas of China and Japan belonging to the witch-hazel family. It is grown for its overall appearance and spectacular autumn colour. Propagate by seed, cuttings or layering.

D

Doodia aspera

Doodia media

Disanthus cercidifolius

ORIGIN China, Japan
CLIMATE WT, M, CT
This is a slow-growing, deciduous, rounded shrub to about 6m/20ft high and 3m/10ft wide. The broadly oval to almost circular, smooth, bluish green leaves to 10cm/4in long turn to shades of red, purple or orange in autumn. It bears pairs of dark red spidery flowers in autumn as the leaves fall, or later.
USE & CULTIVATION A beautiful specimen for a woodland garden. Grow in a sheltered, partially shaded position in humus-rich, moisture-retentive neutral to acid soil. Frost hardy.

DOODIA

FAMILY BLECHNACEAE
Native to Australia, New Zealand and some Pacific islands, this genus comprises about 12 species of mostly low-growing terrestrial ferns. They have narrow feather-like fronds that are rather harsh to the touch. New fronds are flushed pink or red. Propagate by spores or division of clumps.

Doodia aspera
Rasp Fern

ORIGIN Australia
CLIMATE ST, WT
This tufted evergreen fern has a short creeping rhizome and grows to about 50cm/20in tall. The upright pinnate fronds to about 40cm/16in long widen at the base and have serrated segments with a slightly rough texture. Immature fronds have an attractive rosy pink tinge.
USE & CULTIVATION Its gentle creeping habit makes this a pretty fern for a garden edge or rockery pocket. Naturally from damp places, it likes moist well-drained soil in a sheltered, partially shaded position. It grows well in containers and is a good basket subject. Indoors, provide bright filtered light, moderate humidity and soil rich in organic matter. Marginally frost hardy.

Doodia media
Common Rasp Fern

ORIGIN Australia, New Zealand, some Pacific islands
CLIMATE ST, WT
This small tufted fern to about 30cm/12in tall has underground creeping rhizomes and can form small clumps to 60cm/24in across. It has erect, dark green, pinnate fronds about 30cm/12in long; new growth may be an attractive purplish pink.
USE & CULTIVATION Flourishing in a moist sheltered part of the garden, it is an ideal border plant in partial shade. Also a good container subject. Indoors, it likes the same conditions as *D. aspera*. Marginally frost hardy.

DORYANTHES

FAMILY DORYANTHACEAE

This is a genus of 2 species of large evergreen perennials from eastern Australia. They form large clumps of erect sword-shaped leaves and bear showy red flowers at the end of very tall stems. The flowers are spectacular, but take many years to appear; in the meantime the plants make outstanding architectural feature plants. Propagate from seed or by division.

Doryanthes excelsa
Gymea Lily, Giant Lily

ORIGIN Australia
CLIMATE ST, WT, M

This perennial forms a massive clump to 2.5m/8ft wide of large, stiff, sword-shaped leaves to 1.5m/5ft long. The flower stalk, to 5m/17ft tall, emerges from the centre of the rosette and carries a large terminal cluster of deep red flowers in spring.

USE & CULTIVATION Outstanding feature plant for large areas. Grow in a light-textured, well-drained soil in full sun or partial shade. Water well in dry periods. Young plants make striking accent plants in large deep containers. Established plants transplant successfully. Frost tender.

DRACAENA

FAMILY AGAVACEAE

This genus comprises 40 species of evergreen shrubs and trees highly regarded for their foliage and dramatic architectural appearance, and often grown as conservatory or indoor plants. They are generally single stemmed or branched shrubs with narrow, sword-like, arching leaves borne at the ends of tall cane-like stems. There is a loss of lower leaves as plants increase in height, so that they eventually take on a stately, palm-like appearance. With most species, removing the growing tip of the main stem when the plants are about 90cm/36in tall encourages

Doryanthes excelsa

branching. Flowers are rarely produced but are generally unimportant. A weak liquid fertiliser during the spring and summer months is beneficial. Propagate from seed or stem cuttings.

Dracaena deremensis

ORIGIN Tropical eastern Africa
CLIMATE ST, WT

This species, sometimes included in *Dracaena fragrans*, is a sparsely branched shrub to 2m/7ft or more high with bare cane-like stems and terminal rosettes of glossy deep green leaves to 70cm/28in long. Two variegated forms are popular indoor plants. The leaves of **'Longii'** have a broad clear white central stripe. **'Warneckei'** (syn. 'Souvenir de Schriever') has grey–green streaks with 2 white stripes and bright green edging.

USE & CULTIVATION The variegated forms look particularly good as a small group beneath trees in warm gardens. Leggy plants can be cut back to near ground level in spring. Alternatively,

Dracaena deremensis 'Warneckei'

Dracaena draco

pinch out the growing tip of the main stem when the plant is about 90cm/ 36in tall to encourage branching. Grow in moist well-drained soil in partial shade. Indoor plants require a standard potting mix, plenty of water during the growing season and bright diffused light. Frost tender.

Dracaena draco
Dragon Tree

ORIGIN Canary Islands

CLIMATE ST, WT

This picturesque, slow-growing, ever-green tree to 9m/30ft or more eventually forms a wide branching crown to 8m/25ft across. Mature plants develop several thick woody branches with contorted side-branchlets crowned with a rosette of stiff, strap-like, point-ed leaves. Young plants have smooth, thick, glaucous green leaves about 50cm/20in long with translucent edges and thin red margins. Large panicles of very small, greenish white flowers appear in summer, followed by large orange–red berries.

USE & CULTIVATION A mature plant makes a bold, dramatic statement in a large garden or park where there is

plenty of space to display its distinct individuality. In warm humid conditions it thrives in full sun and well-drained soil. Young plants can be grown in a container for many years, needing bright indirect light and moderate water if grown indoors. Mature plants are not suited to a confined space, but look fan-tastic in a large conservatory. Frost tender.

Dracaena fragrans
Corn Plant, Happy Plant

ORIGIN Africa

CLIMATE ST, WT

This is an erect shrub or small, sparsely branched tree to 6–15m/20–50ft high. It has erect to arching, glossy deep green leaves to 45cm/18in long. Mature plants occasionally bear large panicles of small, scented white flowers in sum-mer. Forms with variegated leaves are more popular than the original green-leaved species. **'Lindenii'** has leaves with broad, creamy white marginal stripes. **'Massangeana'** has leaves with a wide yellow central stripe, sometimes bordered by narrower yellow lines. **'Victoria'** has wide, arching, bright green leaves with a silvery central band and broad bright yellow margins.

USE & CULTIVATION Although used for bold accents in tropical gardens, in cooler areas they are mostly grown in containers to decorate courtyards, balconies, patios and poolsides, as well as indoors. Grow in standard potting mix in dappled shade. Water potted plants freely, but much less in low temperatures. Frost tender.

Dracaena fragrans 'Massangeana'

Dracaena marginata

Dracaena marginata 'Tricolor'

Dracaena marginata

ORIGIN Madagascar
CLIMATE ST, WT

This slow-growing shrub or small tree to 3m/10ft or more high usually has a straight, bare, upright stem topped with a cluster of arching sword-shaped leaves to 60cm/24in long, deep green with a thin reddish margin. The popular **'Tricolor'**, with leaves striped with pink, cream and green, is commonly grown as a houseplant.

USE & CULTIVATION In warm gardens it works well planted among shrubs and palms in a partially shaded pool-side setting. One of the easiest dracaenas to care for indoors, it tolerates poor light for short periods, but objects to excessive watering. Remove the growing tip when the plant is about 90cm/36in tall to encourage branching. Frost tender.

Dracaena reflexa

ORIGIN Tropical Africa
CLIMATE T, ST, WT

This is an erect shrub to about 2.5m/8ft tall with slender cane-liked stems clothed with spirally arranged, glossy green, lance-shaped leaves to 25cm/10in long. Panicles of scented creamy flowers are borne in spring. **D. r. var. linearifolia**, from Madagascar and Mauritius, has arching narrow dark green leaves. **'Song of India'** is a popular form with thin wavy stems and creamy yellow variegated leaves.

USE & CULTIVATION In warm gardens grow in a humus-rich, well-drained soil in a protected sunny position. 'Song of India' makes an outstanding feature plant in tropical gardens. Good indirect light is needed indoors. While new leaves are growing, water often to keep the potting mix moist, but don't

Dracaena reflexa 'Song of India'

allow the roots to stand in water; water less in winter. Frost tender.

Dracaena surculosa
syn. *Dracaena godseffiana*
Gold-dust Dracaena,
Spotted Dracaena

ORIGIN Tropical western Africa
CLIMATE T, ST

Unlike most dracaenas, this species has thin, wiry branching stems; to 3m/10ft high, it bears whorls of 2 or 3 dark green elliptic leaves to 8cm/3in long and 4cm/1¹/₂in wide with creamy white spots. **'Florida Beauty'** is slightly more shrubby, to about 90cm/36in tall, with heavier creamy white blotches that sometimes merge.

USE & CULTIVATION This spectacular plant is only grown outside in tropical gardens. Indoors, it requires high humidity, a moist well-drained potting mix and bright filtered light. Avoid cold and wet winter conditions. Frost tender.

DRYOPTERIS

WOOD FERN
FAMILY DRYOPTERIDACEAE

A large genus of about 200 species of deciduous and semi-evergreen terrestrial ferns found mostly in temperate regions of the Northern Hemisphere, often in shaded woodlands beside streams and lakes. They have erect or creeping rhizomes covered with papery scales and elongated, pinnately divided, lacy fronds, in many species forming shuttlecock-like crowns. Propagate from fresh spores in summer or by division of rhizomes.

Dryopteris affinis
syns *Dryopteris borreri*,
D. pseudomas
Golden Male Fern,
Golden Shield Fern

ORIGIN Europe to the Himalayas
CLIMATE M, CT, H
This mostly evergreen fern forms a neat tuft of finely divided fronds to 80cm/32in tall arising from an erect rhizome.

Dracaena surculosa

Dryopteris filix-mas

The new fronds are pale greenish gold as they unfurl in spring, ageing to dark green. **'Cristata'** (syn. 'Cristata The King') has arching fronds with fine segments with crested tips.

USE & CULTIVATION This and the following ferns grow easily in a cool, partially shady, moist position in the garden and look particularly attractive mass-planted beside a water feature or in a woodland setting. Protect from wind damage and regularly remove withered fronds to keep them looking their best. Fully frost hardy.

Dryopteris carthusiana
Narrow Buckler Fern

ORIGIN Europe
CLIMATE M, CT, H
This deciduous, creeping, rhizomatous fern to 60cm/24in high produces a tuft of lance-shaped, 2–3 times divided, pale green fronds with triangular to oval segments.
USE & CULTIVATION As for *D. affinis*. Fully frost hardy.

Dryopteris erythrosora
Autumn Fern, Japanese Shield Fern

ORIGIN China, Japan
CLIMATE M, CT
A deciduous fern reaching to 50cm/20in high and spreading to 30cm/12in across. Its broadly triangular fronds, 2–3 times divided into oval segments with rounded tips, are flushed coppery pink when young. As the fronds age they become glossy dark green; they persist until mid-winter.
USE & CULTIVATION As for *D. affinis*. Fully frost hardy.

Dryopteris filix-mas
Male Fern

ORIGIN Europe, North America
CLIMATE M, CT, H
This deciduous or semi-evergreen fern forms neat tufts to 1.2m/4ft high of broadly lance-shaped, arching, mid-green fronds arising from crowns of erect, brown-scaled rhizomes. **'Grandiceps Wills'** is an extremely attractive tasselled form with a crested top and finely crested leaflets.
USE & CULTIVATION As for *D. affinis*. Fully frost hardy.

Dryopteris wallichiana

Dudleya brittonii

Dryopteris wallichiana
Wallich's Wood Fern

ORIGIN Himalayas
CLIMATE M, CT

This fern has a large erect rhizome and makes a neat cluster of bipinnate, slightly arching fronds to 90cm/36in tall. The new fronds are yellowish green. As the fronds age they become soft textured and mid- to dark green.
USE & CULTIVATION As for *D. affinis*. Fully frost hardy.

DUDLEYA

FAMILY CRASSULACEAE

This genus of about 40 species of perennial succulents, closely related to *Echeveria*, comes mainly from southern USA and western Mexico. They are usually low growing, forming dense rosettes of ovate to strap-like glaucous leaves. Masses of star-shaped flowers in shades of white, yellow or red are borne in panicles from the leaf axils. Propagate by seed or division.

Dudleya brittonii
Chalk Dudleya

ORIGIN Mexico
CLIMATE ST, WT

Spreading to about 50cm/20in across, this species forms a dense rosette of broad, oblong, white-powdered, grey–green leaves to 25cm/10in long. Erect stems to 1m/3ft high carry branched panicles of pale yellow star-shaped flowers in spring and summer.
USE & CULTIVATION This and the following species make beautiful accent plants for a rock or desert garden, at the edge of a border with other succulents or mixed with broad-leaved perennials in courtyard gardens. Grow in full sun and well-drained soil. In containers, use a standard cactus potting mix and provide the brightest possible light if placed indoors. Normal room temperatures are suitable. Keep fairly dry in summer, when plants are semi-dormant. Frost tender.

Dudleya pulverulenta
Chalk Lettuce

ORIGIN USA, Mexico
CLIMATE ST, WT

This rosette-forming perennial reaches 1m/3ft high and has silvery grey strap-shaped, pointed leaves to about 30cm/12in long covered with a soft waxy bloom. It bears masses of red star-shaped flowers in panicles to 80cm/32in tall in summer.
USE & CULTIVATION As for *D. brittonii*. Frost tender.

ECHEVERIA

FAMILY CRASSULACEAE
These popular rosette-forming succulents or small bushy shrubs are native to semi-arid regions of the Americas, most occurring in Mexico. The fleshy, green or grey–green leaves are usually smooth and waxy, and sometimes marked with soft pastel shades or deeper colours that are particularly vivid during the colder months. Bell-shaped flowers form in clusters on long stalks from the leaf axils. They are used as compact bedding plants in warm climates and most are suitable for growing indoors. Propagate from seed, offsets or individual leaves.

Echeveria agavoides
syns *Echeveria obscura, E. yuccoides*

ORIGIN Mexico
CLIMATE ST, WT, SA

This slow-growing succulent forms stemless rosettes to 18cm/7in high and 30cm/12in across. The thick, tapering, pale apple green leaves to 10cm/4in long have pointed reddish tips and are edged with red. Yellow and red flowers are borne on a 1-sided spike up to 50cm/20in tall.
USE & CULTIVATION Forms attractive clumps in a sunny or partially shaded,

Echeveria pulvinata 'Frosty'

well-drained rockery pocket or desert garden. Not hardy, in areas of frost it is brought under cover for winter. In containers, use a porous cactus potting mix and provide the brightest possible light. Normal room temperatures are suitable, but they do require good ventilation. Water only when potting mix is completely dry to touch. Place outdoors during the warmer months. Frost tender.

Echeveria elegans
Pearl Echeveria, Hen and Chicks

ORIGIN Mexico
CLIMATE WT, M, SA

This mostly stemless succulent develops a tight symmetrical rosette to 5cm/2in high and spreads to about 45cm/18in across. The upturned spoon-shaped leaves to 5cm/2in long are frosted blue–green with red margins. Mature plants offshoot freely from below the lower leaves. Bell-shaped,

yellow-tipped, pinkish red flowers are produced on pink stalks up to 30cm/12in long from late winter to early summer.
USE & CULTIVATION As for *E. agavoides*. Frost tender.

Echeveria pulvinata
Plush Plant

ORIGIN Mexico
CLIMATE WT, WT, SA

This is a shrubby succulent with thick, light green, obovate leaves 5–8cm/2–3in long, covered with fine white hairs. The plant normally branches profusely, growing slowly to about 30cm/12in tall. In spring and summer it produces yellow or red urn-shaped flowers on short stems. The leaves of **'Frosty'** are paler and covered with dense white down.
USE & CULTIVATION As for *E. agavoides*. Frost tender..

Echeveria secunda
Blue Echeveria, Hen and Chicks

ORIGIN Mexico
CLIMATE WT, WT, SA

This succulent has a short stem bearing one or more rosettes in a cushion-like clump, with new rosettes constantly appearing from the leaf axils of the main plant. The pale green to grey, pointed, spoon-shaped leaves to 5cm/2in long develop red tips and margins as the plant matures. It bears red and yellow bell-shaped flowers in spring and summer.
USE & CULTIVATION As for *E. agavoides*. Frost tender.

Echeveria setosa
Mexican Firecracker

ORIGIN Mexico
CLIMATE WT, WT, SA

A stemless species usually forming a rounded rosette of thick, soft, densely packed 8cm/3in long, spoon-shaped leaves. Fine silvery hairs thickly coat the leaves and the short flower stems on which red and yellow flowers are produced in late spring and summer.
USE & CULTIVATION As for *E. agavoides*. Frost tender.

ELAEAGNUS

FAMILY ELAEGNACEAE

Most of the 45 species in this genus are scattered over many parts of the northern temperate regions, with one extending to Australia. They are evergreen and deciduous shrubs and trees, grown mostly for their ornamental foliage, silvery new growth and clusters of small, usually strongly fragrant flowers, followed by sometimes colourful berries. The evergreen species withstand trimming and make good bushy shrubs or hedges. Most grow well near the sea. Propagate by from seed. Cultivars can be raised from cuttings.

Elaeagnus angustifolia
Oleaster, Russian Olive

ORIGIN Southern Europe to China
CLIMATE WT, M, CT

This large, spiny, deciduous shrub or small tree to 9m/30ft high has young stems coated with silvery scales. The narrow willow-like leaves to 8cm/3in long are dark green above and have silvery scales beneath. The small, fragrant, bell-shaped flowers, pale yellow within, silvery on the outside, are borne in small

clusters in early summer. **'Quicksilver'** grows to about 3.5m/12ft high; its leaves are silvery on both surfaces.
USE & CULTIVATION A good lawn specimen and ornamental background for the shrub border. It grows fast and will provide an extra measure of wind protection in coastal gardens. 'Quicksilver' is useful for grey and silver foliage planting schemes. Plant in fertile well-drained soil in full sun. Fully frost hardy.

Elaeagnus x ebbingei
cultivars

ORIGIN Gardens
CLIMATE WT, M, CT

These rounded evergreen shrubs grow 3–3.5m/10–12ft high. They have oblong to oval, glossy dark green leaves to 10cm/4in long with a silvery underside. Sweetly scented, tiny, silvery white, bell-shaped flowers are borne in autumn. **'Gilt Edge'** has dark green leaves with golden yellow margins. The leaves of **'Limelight'** are silvery when young, later boldly splashed with green and gold.
USE & CULTIVATION These cultivars quickly form a good bushy screen or large hedge and make an excellent

Echeveria secunda

Echeveria setosa

shelter belt in seaside gardens. Cut back hard if a bushy shape is desired. Grow in well-drained soil in full sun or partial shade. Fully frost hardy.

Elaeagnus pungens
Silverberry, Thorny Elaeagnus

ORIGIN Japan
CLIMATE WT, M, CT, H

This is a wide-spreading, evergreen, spiny shrub to 3.5m/12ft or more high and 6m/20ft across, with brown-scaled young stems. It has lustrous, rich green, oval leaves to 8cm/3in long with wavy margins and white undersides speckled brown. Scented silvery white flowers are born in small clusters in late autumn. Some variegated forms are popular in cultivation. The leaves of **'Dicksonii'** have broad, deep yellow margins. **'Frederici'** has smaller and narrower pale yellow leaves to 3.5cm/1½ in long with a narrow dark green border. **'Maculata'** (syn. 'Aureovariegata') has oblong-pointed leaves to 10cm/4in with a broad yellow central splash. The leaves of **'Variegata'** (syn. 'Argenteovariegata') have narrow, irregular, creamy margins.

USE & CULTIVATION This vigorous fast-growing species makes a particularly hardy and useful shrub for hedging in difficult seaside gardens. The cultivars are highly ornamental and are good in cold areas. Lightly prune for size and shape. They thrive in most well-drained soils in full sun or partial shade. Fully frost hardy.

Encephalartos altensteinii

ENCEPHALARTOS

FAMILY ZAMIACEAE

There are about 50 to 60 species in this genus of slow-growing cycads from southern and tropical central Africa. Some have underground stems, but most eventually develop a stout trunk. The attractive, palm-like, pinnate fronds are spirally arranged in terminal crowns and have hard, often spiny-toothed leaflets. Male and female cones are borne within the leaf rosettes; the cylindrical male cones are usually smaller than the large ovoid female cones, which are often quite spectacular, borne either singly or in groups of up to 5, with colourful fleshy seeds. Propagate from seed or offsets.

Encephalartos altensteinii
Prickly Cycad

ORIGIN South Africa
CLIMATE ST, WT

This spectacular cycad has an erect trunk to 4.5m/15ft high, growing singly or in clumps with new basal suckers. It forms a widely spreading crown of arching leaves to 3.5m/12ft long, composed of numerous narrow, glossy bright green, sparsely toothed leaflets. Young leaves are pale green and erect at first. The large pineapple-like female cones are about 50cm/20in long with shiny red fruits.

USE & CULTIVATION Quite common in warmer regions; with its dramatic silhouette it is often grown as a lawn specimen in public and private gardens. Grow in fertile well-drained soil in full sun or partial shade with plenty of moisture. Frost tender.

Encephalartos ferox

ORIGIN Mozambique, Natal

CLIMATE ST, WT

This slow-growing cycad often has much of its stem below ground and rarely reaches 2m/7ft high. Its arching, dark green, pinnate leaves can be over 1m/3ft long, with glossy, spine-tipped leaflets. It produces spectacular pink, orange or red cones.

USE & CULTIVATION In warm climates, this highly ornamental species is ideal for creating tropical or exotic effects. Grow in fertile well-drained soil in filtered shade and water regularly in summer. Frost tender.

Encephalartos lebomboensis
Lebombo Cycad

ORIGIN Mozambique, Swaziland, South Africa

CLIMATE ST, WT

This slow-growing cycad eventually reaches 3.5m/12ft. Bright green, glossy leaves to 2m/7ft long are produced in an almost erect crown. They are composed of numerous linear leaflets that are sparsely toothed and spine tipped. Bright orange female cones are borne in clusters of up to 3.

USE & CULTIVATION An excellent feature plant that becomes increasingly

Encephalartos natalensis

handsome and distinctive as it develops. Grow in a sunny situation with excellent drainage. Water regularly in summer. Frost tender.

Encephalartos natalensis
Natal Cycad

ORIGIN South Africa

CLIMATE ST, WT

With time this cycad forms an erect trunk to 3.5–6m/12–20ft. It forms a rounded crown of bright glossy green leaves to 3m/10ft long with moderately crowded, lance-shaped, entire or sparsely spiny-toothed leaflets. Female cones are brown and woolly at first, maturing to deep apricot yellow. They appear mostly in summer.

USE & CULTIVATION Mature plants make highly decorative lawn specimens or accent plants where there is some shelter. Grow in full sun in humus-rich acid soil with excellent drainage. Water well during dry periods. Frost tender.

Encephalartos lebomboensis

Ensete ventricosum

Epimedium diphyllum

ENSETE

FAMILY MUSACEAE

This is a genus of 7 species of tropical evergreen perennials grown for their highly decorative, spreading, banana-like leaves. Cup-shaped flowers produced through the middle of the crown are followed by small banana-like fruits. After the fruits mature, the whole plant dies. Removing flowerheads as they appear may encourage longer life. Propagate from seed.

Ensete ventricosum
syns *Musa arnoldiana, M. ensete*
Abyssinian Banana

ORIGIN Tropical Africa
CLIMATE T, ST, WT
This large tropical-looking plant to 6m/20ft or more tall has a stout, erect, green stem and huge, spreading, bright green leaves to 3.5m/12ft long with a bright red midrib. It bears drooping dark red bracts concealing white flowers in spikes to 3m/10ft long, and eventually produces unpalatable banana-like fruits. It flowers once at between 5 and 7 years of age and then dies.
USE & CULTIVATION A very attractive plant for creating a bold tropical effect near pools or in jungle-style gardens with warm conditions and shelter from winds. Grow in full sun or partial shade in humus-rich, moist well-drained soil. Adequate watering is necessary, especially in summer. Frost tender.

EPIMEDIUM

FAMILY BERBERIDACEAE

This is a genus of about 20 species of perennials, some of which are evergreen. They are rhizomatous, forming clumps or colonies with long-stalked, roughly heart-shaped leaves that are particularly attractive in spring when tinted or flushed in shades of pink or bronze. Loose spikes of pendent short-spurred flowers are held above the foliage in spring. Propagate by division in spring or autumn.

Epimedium diphyllum

ORIGIN Japan
CLIMATE M, CT, H
This clump-forming perennial is almost evergreen. It grows to only about 25cm/10in high and bears leaves divided into 2 light green, irregular, heart-shaped leaflets to 5cm/2in long. Small white spurless flowers are borne in spring.
USE & CULTIVATION This and the following species make attractive weed-suppressing groundcovers in sun or shade. They prefer a cool position and humus-rich, moist well-drained soil, making them ideal for the edge of a woodland garden or bordering a path under trees. Cut back in late winter or early spring to reveal the fresh new foliage. Fully frost hardy.

Epimedium grandiflorum

ORIGIN China, Korea, Japan
CLIMATE M, CT, H

This deciduous carpeting perennial has a height and spread of about 30cm/ 12in. It has dense, light green, spiny-edged, heart-shaped leaves that are tinged copper when young. Prominently spurred flowers in shades of white, yellow, rose or violet appear in spring. **'Flavescens'** (syn. *E. koreanum*) has pale yellow flowers. **'Rose Queen'** has crimson–pink flowers with long white-tipped spurs held well above the leaves.

USE & CULTIVATION As for *E. diphyllum*. Fully frost hardy.

EPIPREMNUM

FAMILY ARACEAE
This is a genus of 8 species of vigorous evergreen climbers grown for their handsome, roughly heart-shaped, glossy leaves. They come from tropical areas in Southeast Asia and the western Pacific and scramble to great heights up forest trees by attaching their fleshy aerial roots to the bark. Most species are grown indoors and are either encouraged to climb on rough tree bark or a moss pole or to trail from hanging baskets. The spikes of tiny petalless flowers are usually not produced outside the tropics. Remove shoot tips to induce branching. Propagate from leaf or stem-tip cuttings or by layering.

Epipremnum pictum 'Argyraeum'
syn. *Scindapsus pictus* 'Argyraeus'
Silver Vine

ORIGIN Gardens
CLIMATE T, ST

This is the only form of this species commonly cultivated. It is slow growing and has woody stems 2–3m/7–10ft long. In its juvenile stage it has ovate, entire, dark olive green leaves to 10cm/ 4in long, heart-shaped at the base, with grey–green spots on the upper surface.

USE & CULTIVATION Both this and the following species make outstanding climbers in tropical gardens; elsewhere they are mostly cultivated as house-plants. Train to grow upright with the support of a moss pole, upright stakes or a wire frame, or allow to trail naturally from pots or hanging baskets. Both like a peaty potting mix and moist surroundings with humidity and bright filtered light. Frost tender.

Epipremnum pinnatum
syn. *Rhaphidophora pinnata*

ORIGIN Southeast Asia to tropical Australia
CLIMATE T, ST

This vigorous climbing plant reaches many metres high in tropical gardens. It has glossy, bright green, heart-shaped juvenile leaves to 30cm/12in long. Mature plants have deeply lobed or perforated leaves to 80cm/32in long. The form most commonly grown, and sold under a variety of different names, is the popular Devil's Ivy, **'Aureum'** (syns. *E. aureum*, *Pothos aureus*, *Rhaphidophora aurea*, *Scindapsus aureus*), with angular, yellowish green stems and bright green, heart-shaped leaves irregularly marked

Epimedium grandiflorum 'Flavescens'

Epipremnum pinnatum 'Aureum'

Episcia cupreata

Episcia cupreata 'Metallica'

with cream or yellow. Less robust is **'Marble Queen'**, with green and white stems and leaf stalks, and leaves that are mainly white, flecked with green, cream and grey–green markings. **USE & CULTIVATION** As for *E. pictum* 'Argyraeum'. In tropical gardens 'Aureum' is often trained as a groundcover. Frost tender.

EPISCIA

FAMILY GESNERIACEAE

There are 6 species in this genus of low-growing, creeping, evergreen perennials from tropical America and the West Indies. They form a spreading carpet by means of creeping stolons and have soft ornamental leaves with an embossed or puckered surface. The white or colourful 5-lobed flowers contrast well with the leaves, and they are attractive in hanging baskets. Propagate from stem cuttings, by division or by runners that have formed roots.

Episcia cupreata
Flame Violet

ORIGIN South America
CLIMATE T, ST

This is one of the best-known species. It grows to a height of 15cm/6in and forms a spreading mat of downy, wrinkled or nearly smooth leaves to 9cm/3^1/$_2$in long. The leaves vary in colour from deep coppery green to bright green, often with silvery or pale green markings around the main veins. Intermittently it bears tubular scarlet flowers to 6cm/2^1/$_4$in long with yellow centres. **'Metallica'** has olive green leaves with pale silvery stripes and red margins. **'Mosaica'** has dark coppery green leaves netted with silver.
USE & CULTIVATION In tropical gardens these plants look good trailing over a partially shaded, moist rocky ledge. They are, however, mostly grown as houseplants, and look good in a suspended shallow container or hanging basket. Use an African violet potting mix and provide bright filtered light, warm temperatures and high humidity. Keep the potting mix moist at all times, but do not let the containers stand in water. Frost tender.

Episcia lilacina

ORIGIN Costa Rica
CLIMATE T, ST

The red and green runners of this low-growing species bear oval, heavily embossed, copper green leaves to 10cm/4in long with bright green veins and midribs. Funnel-shaped white flowers tinged with mauve have a pale yellow throat and are produced in small clusters from spring to autumn.
USE & CULTIVATION As for *E. cupreata*. Frost tender.

ERIOBOTRYA

FAMILY ROSACEAE

A genus of about 30 species of ever-green trees and shrubs, of which the Loquat (*Eriobotrya japonica*) is the only one widely grown, for both its edible fruit and its handsome leaves. Cut branches can be used for indoor decor-ation. Propagate from seed or cuttings.

Eriobotrya japonica
Loquat

ORIGIN China, Japan
CLIMATE ST, WT, M

A large spreading shrub or small shapely tree to 9m/30ft high with bold, strongly veined, deep green leaves to 30cm/12in long, glossy above and rusty-hairy beneath. The fragrant white flowers usually produced in autumn in loose ter-minal clusters are followed by orange–yellow fruits which ripen in spring.

USE & CULTIVATION An interesting shade and specimen tree for small gar-dens. Grow in fertile well-drained soil in a sheltered sunny position. Adequate watering is necessary, especially as the fruits mature. Prune to shape. Young plants make highly decorative conserva-tory or houseplants. Use a good potting mix and provide bright light, warm temperatures and good ventilation. Keep the potting mix moist at all times, less in winter. Marginally frost hardy.

ERYNGIUM

FAMILY APIACEAE, UMBELLIFERAE

A genus of about 230 species of mainly tufted to clump-forming perennials from temperate to subtropical regions of the Mediterranean, China, Korea and South America. They have interesting deeply lobed and spiny-toothed basal leaves, often with silver or white veins. The handsome thistle-like flowerheads surrounded by ruffs of colourful spiny bracts are long lasting. Propagate from seed or by division.

Eryngium bourgatii

ORIGIN Spain (the Pyrenees)
CLIMATE M, CT, H

This clump-forming herbaceous peren-nial has leathery basal leaves to 8cm/3in long with spiny-toothed margins. They are grey–green, deeply cut, with distinct silvery veins and wavy margins.

Eryngium bourgatii

Eriobotrya japonica

Eriobotrya japonica

Eryngium giganteum

The branched, wiry flowering stems to 60cm/24in high support numerous oval heads of blue flowers surrounded by a collar of steel blue spiny bracts. **'Oxford Blue'** has deeper blue flowerheads with metallic blue bracts.

USE & CULTIVATION Highly decorative and interesting plants for a border or large rock garden. Plant in fertile well-drained soil in a sunny position. Fully frost hardy.

Eryngium giganteum
Miss Willmott's Ghost

ORIGIN Caucasus, Iran
CLIMATE M, CT

This clump-forming biennial or short-lived perennial dies after flowering. Its heart-shaped basal leaves, mid-green in spring, fade to almost translucent grey. The summer-flowering stems to 1m/3ft tall bear large domed heads of pale blue or pale green thistle-like flowers surrounded by broad, spiny, silvery bracts.

USE & CULTIVATION An outstanding accent plant for use in a silver planting theme, cottage or meadow garden. Plant in fertile well-drained soil in a hot sunny position. Fully frost hardy.

EUCALYPTUS

EUCALYPT
FAMILY MYRTACEAE

Most of the approximately 700 species of this large genus of evergreen trees and shrubs originate in Australia, where they dominate the landscape. Their ability to thrive in poor soils and harsh conditions has enabled them to adapt in many countries of the world, including northern Africa, Europe, the Middle East, India, South America and many parts of North America, particularly California. Some are grown for their artistic trunks or handsome form, others for the beauty of flower, foliage or capsules. Juvenile and adult foliage of most species is significantly different. The cut foliage sold by florists is usually the juvenile type, often with rounded, stalkless, waxy, bluish grey leaves. Adult leaves are generally narrow, stalked and greener. Almost all have a distinct fragrance, although some leaves need to be crushed before this is evident. Of the vast selection available, only a handful with ornamental foliage and some with irresistibly beautiful bark have been chosen for this book. In cold climates a small number are brought indoors, but only temporarily, since they are not long-lived as container plants and thrive much better in the open. Most of the eucalypts traditionally known as bloodwoods and ghost gums have been transferred to the newly named genus *Corymbia*. The popular Lemon-scented Gum, *Eucalyptus citriodora*, is one of these, but has been included here for the convenience of familiar reference. Pruning is not essential, but most species can be shaped or cut back heavily if desired, particularly if you want to encourage juvenile foliage. Propagate from seed.

Eucalyptus cinerea
Argyle Apple, Silver Dollar Tree

ORIGIN Southeastern Australia
CLIMATE WT, M, SA

This is a small to medium-sized tree with a fairly short trunk and a dense spreading crown reaching to around 12m/40ft. The rounded juvenile leaves, carried in pairs on slender graceful stems, are an attractive silvery grey and popular with florists. Some juvenile foliage is retained throughout the life of the tree. Adult leaves become elongated and pointed, and are also silvery grey and attractive. Small white blossoms are produced in spring or early summer.

USE & CULTIVATION Moderately fast growing, its low, branching habit makes it an ideal privacy or protection screen. With judicious pruning a very dense crown of foliage may be produced. It is suited to most well-drained soils and can be grown in areas with low rainfall. Marginally frost hardy.

Eucalyptus cinerea

Eucalyptus citriodora
syn. *Corymbia citriodora*
Lemon-scented Gum

ORIGIN Queensland, Australia
CLIMATE ST, WT, M
This tall stately gum has a slender straight trunk with smooth, powdery white to grey bark throughout that is shed during summer. It reaches a height of 15–30m/50–100ft and forms an open spreading crown of highly fragrant, narrow, lance-shaped leaves to 20cm/8in long that emit a sharp lemony scent during hot weather and when crushed. White flowers in umbels of 3 appear mostly in winter
USE & CULTIVATION Graceful, rather drooping foliage and a striking white trunk and branches make this an outstanding specimen tree for dramatic landscaping effects in large gardens. One of the most widely planted eucalypts in the world, it is valued for its timber and for the citronella oil distilled from its foliage. Also a popular avenue tree. Usually fast growing, in a variety of well-drained soils. Frost tender.

Eucalyptus cordata
Heart-leaved Silver Gum

ORIGIN Tasmania, Australia
CLIMATE WT, M, CT
This decorative tree, eventually reaching 20m/70ft or more, is popular for the attractive, silvery grey, heart-shaped juvenile leaves to 10cm/4in long that persist on most trees. The lance-shaped, grey–green to glaucous adult leaves are seen only on the top of tall mature trees. Profuse white to cream flowers are produced in late winter. The cut foliage is long lasting.
USE & CULTIVATION A handsome tree for larger areas, particularly in cold moist climates. Suitable for most soils, including slightly alkaline soils, but it must have good drainage. Moderately frost hardy.

Eucalyptus crenulata
Victorian Silver Gum, Buxton Gum

ORIGIN Victoria, Australia
CLIMATE WT, M, CT
This vigorous small tree grows to a height of 5–15m/17–50ft and usually forms a wide, dense crown. Young plants have delightful glaucous colourings on new growth, buds and leaves. The oval to heart-shaped, pointed mature leaves to 8cm/3in long are in opposite pairs and greyish green with shallow-toothed margins. Highly aromatic, both the smaller juvenile and the slightly larger adult leaves are used for cut foliage. Small white flowers are borne in showy clusters in spring.
USE & CULTIVATION A fast-growing tree suited to most well-drained soils. Regular hard pruning encourages the juvenile growth phase and keeps the plant in reasonable form. Moderately frost hardy.

Eucalyptus citriodora

Eucalyptus cordata

Eucalyptus gunnii

Eucalyptus orbifolia

Eucalyptus globulus
Tasmanian Blue Gum

ORIGIN Victoria and Tasmania, Australia

CLIMATE WT, M, CT, H

This large forest tree can grow to over 55m/180ft high. It has a tall straight trunk with dark grey bark shed in long ribbons. The attractive glaucous, blue–grey juvenile leaves are rounded and initially borne in opposite pairs. Adult leaves to 45cm/18in long are sickle-shaped, leathery and dark shiny green. Creamy white flowers to 4cm/1½ in across are borne singly in winter and spring. '**Compacta**' is a more manageable size than the species, usually about 9m/30ft. It retains its juvenile foliage for some years and is used in floral arrangements.

USE & CULTIVATION A fast-growing tree best suited to large parks and gardens. Allow adequate space for development. 'Compacta' can be used as a windbreak and is more suitable for home gardens. It likes deeply worked soil with adequate drainage and deep watering during summer. Moderately frost hardy.

Eucalyptus gunnii
Cider Gum

ORIGIN Tasmania, Australia

CLIMATE WT, M, CT, H

This is a tall straight tree to 20m/70ft, with deciduous, smooth, grey to pinkish bark and beautiful, frosted grey, almost circular juvenile foliage with silvery pink shoots; the adult leaves are grey–green, leathery and ovate. White flowers are produced freely in summer. It is a good source of foliage for floral decoration.

USE & CULTIVATION Tolerant of cold conditions and widely planted for ornamental purposes in cooler parts of Europe. Grow as a specimen in fertile well-drained soil in full sun with shelter from cold drying winds. Frost hardy.

Eucalyptus orbifolia
Round-leaved Mallee

ORIGIN Western Australia

CLIMATE WT, M, SA

This highly ornamental shrub to 6m/20ft high has slender multiple trunks with decorative reddish brown bark that sheds annually in curling longitudinal ribbons, revealing fresh green bark. The greyish green adult leaves to 4cm/1½ in long are rounded with a notched tip. Profuse pale yellow flowers in late winter are often produced when the plant is quite young.

USE & CULTIVATION Small enough for the suburban garden, it provides a good contrast in form and colour with other trees. Tolerates poor soils, dry periods, light frosts and responds well to hard pruning. One of the most suitable eucalypts for container cultivation, it is used for temporary indoor decoration in the UK. Provide free-draining, soil-based potting mix, full light and very good ventilation. Marginally frost hardy.

Eucalyptus pauciflora
Snow Gum

ORIGIN Southeastern Australia
CLIMATE M, CT, H

This beautiful cold-country species, usually less than 20m/70ft high, has a short trunk and deciduous bark shed in irregular patches, leaving a smooth, white, grey, yellow or greenish surface. Blue–green juvenile leaves are ovate

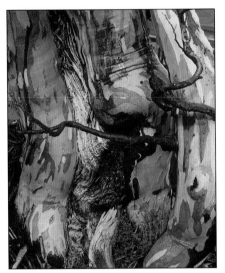

Eucalyptus pauciflora subsp. *niphophila*

and glaucous; the shiny adult leaves are narrowly lance-shaped to 18cm/7in long. Masses of small white flowers are borne in late spring and summer. The Alpine Snow Gum, ***E. p.* subsp. *niphophila*,** confined to high peaks in alpine areas, forms a smaller crooked tree with a smooth-barked trunk that takes on striking colours of gold, olive and red. Its buds, fruits and leaves are glaucous.

USE & CULTIVATION The Snow Gum is a handsome tree for larger areas, particular in cold moist climates. The Alpine Snow Gum is of a more manageable size and is one of the most cold-resistant species. Well-drained soil is essential. Fully frost hardy.

Eucalyptus perriniana
Spinning Gum

ORIGIN Southeastern Australia
CLIMATE WT, M, CT, H

This rather small, straggly tree to 9m/30ft branches from near the base or has multiple trunks with a attractive, smooth, whitish grey bark that is shed in summer. It has opposite, silvery grey, rounded juvenile leaves that are joined at the bases around the stem; adult leaves to 12cm/5in long are grey–green, pendulous, leathery and sickle shaped. Profuse creamy white flowers appear in summer.

USE & CULTIVATION It occurs naturally in alpine regions and is suitable for cold, windy areas. It requires well-drained, slightly acid soil and plenty of sunshine. Cut back hard each year to encourage juvenile growth and bushy shape. A good source of cut foliage. Frost hardy.

Eucalyptus pulverulenta
Silver-leaved Mountain Gum, Powdered Gum

ORIGIN New South Wales, Australia
CLIMATE WT, M, CT

This rather sprawling small tree to 9m/30ft branches from near the base or develops multiple trunks. Grey to white outer bark peels in long strips to reveal grey to bronze inner bark. Silvery grey, heart-shaped juvenile leaves to 5cm/2in long attach directly to the slender stems in close pairs. They appear to be dusted with a powdery bloom. The tree

Eucalyptus pauciflora subsp. *niphophila*

rarely produces adult leaves; they are usually found only at the top of the tree. Creamy white flowers are produced in the leaf axils in spring.

USE & CULTIVATION Small enough for the average suburban garden, it provides an attractive contrast in form and colour with other trees. Tolerates poor soils, dry periods and most frosts and responds well to hard pruning. Soils must be well drained. Moderately frost hardy.

Eucalyptus tetragona
Tallerack

ORIGIN Western Australia
CLIMATE M, SA

Distinctive and highly valued for its silvery white, glaucous appearance, this small straggly tree to 8m/25ft high has thickly stalked, mealy, grey–green, oval leaves to 15cm/6in long. The squarish stems, flower buds and 4-sided capsules are dusted with a white powdery bloom. Pale cream flowers appear in late spring and summer. Foliage, buds, flowers and fruit are highly valued for indoor decoration.

USE & CULTIVATION Suitable for small gardens, it can be used as a feature in a silver planting theme, in contrast with darker-leaved plants or as a decorative low screen. Prefers full sun, light-textured, well-drained soil and does well in dry conditions with low summer rainfall. Can be grown in coastal areas with some protection. Plants can be shaped or cut back heavily if desired. Frost tender.

EUONYMUS

FAMILY CELASTRACEAE
A genus with over 170 species of shrubs and trees distributed mainly across Asia, but also found in Europe, North and Central America, Madagascar and Australia. The evergreen species are chiefly oriental in origin and are highly valued for foliage, form and year-round colour; some cultivars have variegated foliage. The foliage and fruits of the deciduous species provide a

Eucalyptus tetragona

dazzling display of colour in autumn. Pruning is generally unnecessary, but the evergreen species stand clipping well. All parts of the plant may cause stomach upsets if eaten. Insect damage and powdery mildew can be a problem. Propagate from seed or cuttings.

Euonymus alatus
Winged Spindle Tree

ORIGIN China, Japan
CLIMATE WT, M, CT, H
This bushy deciduous shrub to about 2.5m/8ft has distinctive, corky, wing-like stems that are especially noticeable in winter. It is beautiful in autumn,

when its toothed, dark green, oval leaves to 7cm/2½ in long assume vivid tints of orange and red. The pale green summer flowers are followed on leafless branches by 4-lobed, reddish purple capsules that split to reveal orange–red seeds. **'Compactus'** (syn. 'Ciliodentatus') is a dwarf bushy form to about 1m/3ft in diameter with scarlet to purple foliage in autumn.

USE & CULTIVATION Extremely hardy anywhere, this fine autumn-colouring shrub makes an ideal specimen for well-drained alkaline soils. It likes full sun or light shade and does best in cool climates. A very attractive bonsai subject. Fully frost hardy.

Euonymus fortunei 'Variegatus'

Euonymus fortunei 'Emerald 'n' Gold'

Euonymus europaeus
European Spindle Tree

ORIGIN Europe

CLIMATE WT, M, CT, H

This slender, twiggy, deciduous shrub or small tree to about 3m/10ft high has narrowly oval leaves to 10cm/4in long, scalloped and slightly tapering towards the tip. They are deep green in summer, turning purplish red in autumn. After leaf fall, the plant is loaded with 4-lobed crimson fruit, which later split to display white seeds with orange arils. The inconspicuous greenish flowers are produced in late spring. The hard wood was once used in the making of spindles. **'Atropurpureus'** has dull purple leaves that turn bright red in autumn. **'Red Cascade'** has vivid red autumn colouring and rosy red fruit in abundance.

USE & CULTIVATION A highly ornamental plant used as a specimen or mixed with evergreen shrubs for a bold splash of autumn colour. Grow in any well-drained soil in sun or partial shade. Best colours are obtained under cool temperate conditions. Fully frost hardy.

Euonymus fortunei
Wintercreeper Euonymus

ORIGIN China, Japan, Korea

CLIMATE WT, M, CT, H

This evergreen species has stems climbing by aerial roots like ivy to 4.5m/15ft. If not supported, it forms a prostrate shrub to about 60cm/24in high with an indefinite spread. Like ivy, the climbing or trailing stems are juvenile. It has dark green, pointed, oval leaves to 6cm/2¼in long, inconspicuous greenish white flowers in summer and small white fruit with orange arils. Mostly compact bushy forms are seen in gardens. **'Coloratus'** has smaller oval leaves turning deep purple in winter. **'Emerald Gaiety'** forms a bushy shrub to 1m/3ft with deep green leaves margined white. **'Emerald 'n' Gold'** is trailing, providing either ground or wall cover. The bright green leaves are irregularly margined with gold and sometimes flushed pink in winter.

'**Golden Prince**' (syn. 'Gold Tip') has deep green leaves with gold tips. '**Kewensis**' forms a mat or low mound with small rounded leaves to 1cm/³⁄₈in or so long with pale veins. '**Minimus**' forms a low mat to 5cm/2in high with small oval leaves in pairs along slender stems, making it a dainty creeper for a rockery. '**Sheridan Gold**' has yellowish green young foliage. '**Silver Queen**' is a bushy shrub or climber to 2.5m/8ft high with dark green leaves broadly edged with white. '**Sunspot**' (syn. 'Gold Spot') is semi-prostrate, with large splashes of cream or yellow on the leaves. '**Variegatus**' has cream-edged leaves to 2.5cm/1in long and branches that tend to root or climb. '**Vegetus**' has almost round, dull green leaves to 5cm/2in long.

USE & CULTIVATION Most cultivars will climb if given some support and are useful for decoratively covering brickwork and fences. The smaller prostrate forms make delightful ground-covers and rockery specimens. They do best in cool districts. Grow in well-drained soil in sun or partial shade and protect from cold drying winds. Fully frost hardy.

Euonymus japonicus
Japanese Spindle

ORIGIN China, Japan, Korea
CLIMATE WT, M, CT

A dense evergreen shrub to about 3.5m/12ft high with shiny, deep green, oval leaves to 7cm/2½in long with toothed edges. Pale green summer flowers are followed by rounded pink fruits that open to reveal white seeds with orange arils. '**Albomarginatus**' is a bushy compact form to 1m/3ft in diameter with broadly oval or rounded leaves with a very narrow edge of white. '**Aureomarginatus**', to 2m/7ft high, has glossy, lightly serrated, oval leaves with yellow margins. It is easily clipped to any desired shape and makes an excellent hedge. '**Aureus**' (syns 'Aureopictus', 'Luna') has golden young stems and deep green leaves with a large patch of yellow in the middle,

with some leaves entirely yellow or green. '**Microphyllus Aureovariegatus**' has deep green leaves to 2.5cm/1in long with narrow yellow margins. The leaves of '**Ovatus Aureus**' (syn. 'Aureovariegatus'), a low-growing compact form to 1.5m/5ft, have bright yellow markings.

USE & CULTIVATION The species and many of its cultivars may be used for backgrounds or screens, hedges or clipped specimens. They thrive under various conditions, including somewhat exposed coastal sites. In full sun the cultivars will show their variegation better, but need slightly more moisture. Frost hardy.

EUPHORBIA

FAMILY EUPHORBIACEAE

This genus, which includes the plants commonly called spurges, comprises more than 2000 species of an astonishing variety of form, habit of growth and size, ranging from low-growing groundcovers to impressive tree-like succulents. Distribution is worldwide, but the bulk of the succulent species occur in South Africa and Madagascar. Some are grown for the colourful bracts that surround their insignificant flowers, like Poinsettia, *Euphorbia pulcherrima*, with its scarlet bracts, and some for their architectural cactus-like

form. Others are leafy perennials from cooler temperate regions which form attractive clumps and take on colourful tones in autumn. All euphorbias have a milky sap which can irritate sensitive skin and eyes, and in some species is quite toxic, so care should always be taken when handling these plants. Propagate from seed, basal cuttings or by division.

Euphorbia amygdaloides
Wood Spurge

ORIGIN Europe, Turkey, Caucasus
CLIMATE M, CT, H

An evergreen perennial with erect, seldom-branched, reddish stems to 80cm/32in high. It has dark green spoon-shaped leaves to 8cm/3in long and flowerheads with yellowish green cup-shaped bracts in spring and early summer. '**Purpurea**' has purplish leaves. **E. a. var. robbiae** (syn. *E. robbiae*), Mrs Robb's Bonnet, is a popular form with broader, dark green leaves closely set in spreading rosettes to 60cm/24in high, and open, rounded heads of lime green floral bracts.

USE & CULTIVATION Useful as a spreading rock garden specimen for moist shady sites. Mrs Robb's Bonnet is a traditional border perennial that thrives and spreads in dappled shade. Planted in a row, they make an attractive edging. Frost hardy.

Euonymus japonicus 'Albomarginatus'

Euphorbia caput-medusae
Medusa's Head

ORIGIN South Africa
CLIMATE WT, M

This spineless dwarf succulent has a short, rounded basal stem bearing fleshy grey–green branches which can grow to 30cm/12in high and 2.5cm/1in thick. A mature plant may spread to 1m/3ft or more across. Narrow leaves grow at branch ends. Interesting creamy green flowers appear in summer.

USE & CULTIVATION Suitable for a rock garden or border in a small courtyard, this charming plant requires well-drained light soil in full sun or partial shade. As a houseplant, it needs the brightest possible light all year long and good air movement. Water sparingly during the active growth period, less in winter. It is grown from seed. Frost tender.

Euphorbia characias

ORIGIN Portugal, Mediterranean region
CLIMATE WT, M, CT

A compact, rounded, evergreen shrub with numerous unbranched stems to 1m/3ft or more high, densely clothed with narrow, greyish green leaves to 12cm/5in long. It is topped in spring with showy dome-like heads of greenish yellow cup-shaped bracts, inside which sit tiny purplish brown nectar glands. *E. c.* **subsp.** *wulfenii* is a more robust type with lime green flower bracts and yellowish green nectar glands. The flowers can be picked for indoors.

USE & CULTIVATION A excellent easy-care foliage plant useful for accent in many landscape situations, from a traditional flower border to a minimalist courtyard garden. It thrives in light well-drained soil in full sun or partial shade. Dead-head and prune back after flowering. Moderately frost hardy.

Euphorbia cyparissias
Cypress Spurge

ORIGIN Europe
CLIMATE M, CT, H

This herbaceous perennial spreads by rhizomes and has slender branching stems to 40cm/16in tall. It has linear, feathery, grey–green leaves to 3.5cm/1½in long that turn yellow in autumn. The flowerheads of greenish yellow bracts in late spring and summer are not always freely produced. **'Orange Man'** has orange-tinted autumn leaves and orange floral bracts.

USE & CULTIVATION An attractive weed-suppressing groundcover thriving in well-drained light soil in full sun. It is rather invasive and can become a weed, especially on sandy soils. Fully frost hardy.

Euphorbia griffithii

ORIGIN Himalayas
CLIMATE M, CT, H

A bushy perennial with spreading rhizomes forming clumps or colonies to 1m/3ft high and wide. It has narrow, lance-shaped, mid-green leaves to 12cm/5in long with reddish midribs and orange tints. Terminal flowerheads surrounded by light red floral bracts appear in early summer and develop coppery tones with age. **'Dixter'**, with dark coppery coloured leaves and orange floral bracts, and **'Fireglow'**, with vivid brick red floral bracts, are both more compact, to 75cm/30in.

USE & CULTIVATION These bushes are decorative in a mixed border, particularly during autumn, preferring a moist well-drained soil in sun or partial shade. Fully frost hardy.

Euphorbia marginata
Snow-on-the-mountains, Ghost Weed

ORIGIN North America
CLIMATE M, CT, H

This bushy fast-growing annual to 1m/3ft tall and 30cm/12in across has pointed, broadly ovate, mid-green leaves to 8cm/3in long; the upper leaves are broadly margined in white. The flowerheads, surrounded by green and white variegated, petal-like floral bracts, appear in summer.

USE & CULTIVATION Grown for its pretty light-coloured leaves, it is a perfect foil for colourful flowers or darker foliaged plants. Grow in well-drained soil in sun or partial shade. Branches can be cut for indoor decoration. Fully frost hardy.

Euphorbia characias

Euphorbia mysinites

E

Euphorbia schillingii

Euphorbia mysinites

ORIGIN Southern Europe to central Asia

CLIMATE M, CT, H

This evergreen perennial has trailing stems to 30cm/12in long clothed in spirally arranged, succulent grey leaves to 10cm/4in long. Rounded heads of lime green flowering bracts are produced at the ends of the stems in spring.

USE & CULTIVATION Best allowed to sprawl in a rockery or over the low wall of a raised bed, with full sun and good drainage; it will tolerate dry conditions. Fully frost hardy.

Euphorbia schillingii
Schilling's Spurge

ORIGIN Eastern Nepal

CLIMATE M, CT, H

This striking clump-forming perennial to 1m/3ft tall has soft, dark green, lance-shaped leaves to 20cm/8in long with a conspicuous white midrib. By mid-summer it produces flat heads of lime green flowers which last into mid-autumn.

USE & CULTIVATION Makes an impressive feature in a sunny, sheltered garden. Grow in moist well-drained soil. Deadhead and prune back after flowering. Fully frost hardy.

EUPTELEA

FAMILY EUPTELEACEAE

From Japan, China and the eastern Himalayas, this is a small genus of 2 species of small deciduous trees grown mainly in temperate regions for their attractive, broadly oval, sharply toothed leaves that take on attractive autumn colours. Small petalless flowers appear just before the leaves emerge. Propagate from ripe seed.

Euptelea polyandra

ORIGIN Japan
CLIMATE M, CT, H
Seldom grows to more than 8m/25ft tall as a small tree, and sometimes suckers to form a large, spreading shrub. It has broadly ovate leaves to 15cm/6in long with a long tail-like tip and deeply toothed margins. They are tinted red when young and in autumn display yellow and reddish tones. Small reddish green flowers appear just before the leaves in globular clusters, followed by small winged fruits.
USE & CULTIVATION A useful small deciduous tree for a courtyard and other small spaces. Best suited to a cool moist climate, it will provide dappled shade at the edge of a woodland setting. Grow in a sunny, sheltered position in deep fertile soil. Remove basal suckers if necessary. Fully frost hardy.

F

FAGUS

BEECH
FAMILY FAGACEAE

This genus consists of 10 species of ornamental deciduous trees widely scattered throughout northern temperate regions, with many found in China and Japan. Most have a shapely crown of rich green foliage that turns golden brown before falling in autumn, leaving a picturesque framework in winter.

Fagus sylvatica

Insignificant male and female flowers appear with the leaves in spring; the bristly fruits ripen in autumn to release edible triangular nuts. The straight-grained timber is valued for turnery, furniture and kitchen utensils. Plants

Fagus sylvatica

Fagus sylvatica 'Dawyck Purple'

Fagus sylvatica 'Purpurea Pendula'

E

F

may be attacked by aphids and scale insects and are prone to powdery mildew. Propagate from seed; cultivars must be grafted.

Fagus sylvatica
Common Beech, European Beech

ORIGIN Europe to western Asia
CLIMATE WT, M, CT, H
This broad-crowned shapely tree to about 24m/80ft has a smooth slender trunk and often some lower branches sweeping to the ground. The soft, dark green, glossy leaves to 10cm/4in long have prominent veins and are fringed with silken hairs while young. They turn yellow to orange–brown in autumn and hang on well into winter. It has long thin winter buds, and flowers in spring. A large range of cultivars and forms is available. Some of the best-known include **'Dawyck'**, which develops a narrow columnar habit to 15m/50ft. **'Dawyck Gold'** usually grows to about 18m/60ft and has bright yellow young foliage turning to bright green through summer. **'Dawyck Purple'** reaches a height of 20m/70ft and has dark purple foliage. **F. s. var. *heterophylla*** has slender leaves variously cut or lobed. Variations of this form include the Fern-leaved Beech, **'Aspleniifolia'**, with deeply cut leaves, and **f. *lacinata***, with leaves cut into finger-like lobes. **F. s. f. *pendula***, the Weeping Beech, has slender weeping branches reaching to the ground. **'Purpurea Pendula'** is grafted onto a tall

stock and has weeping branches clothed in spring with rich purple foliage that turns a deep coppery-purple in autumn. **'Purpurea Tricolor'** (syns 'Roseomarginata', 'Tricolor') is a smaller tree to 7m/22ft with purple leaves edged and striped pink and cream. **'Riversii'** has purplish black leaves. **'Rohanii'** has reddish purple, deeply lobed leaves. **'Rotundifolia'** has strongly ascending branches and small rounded leaves to 5cm/2in long. **'Zlatia'** bears golden yellow leaves in autumn.

USE & CULTIVATION Suitable for backgrounds, silhouettes, features and hedges, these plants grow best in cool-climate gardens. They like sun or partial shade; purple-leaved forms prefer full sun and yellow-leaved ones a little shade. Grow in fertile, moisture-retentive, well-drained soil and shelter from strong winds. Trim hedges in summer. They are hugely rewarding, but very slow-growing bonsai subjects. Fully frost hardy.

Fagus sylvatica 'Dawyck Gold'

Fagus sylvatica var. *heterophylla*

Fagus sylvatica f. *pendula*

Fagus sylvatica f. *lacinata*

Farfugium japonicum 'Argenteum'

Farfugium japonicum 'Aureomaculatum'

FARFUGIUM

FAMILY ASTERACEAE/COMPOSITAE

There are 2 or 3 species in this small genus of evergreen perennials originating in temperate eastern Asia. They are grown mainly for their large leathery leaves, but also produce small yellow daisy-like flowerheads. Propagate from seed or by division of variegated cultivars.

Farfugium japonicum
syns *Farfugium tussilagineum,*
Ligularia tussilaginea

ORIGIN Japan
CLIMATE WT, M, CT

This is a clump-forming perennial to 60cm/24in high with shiny kidney-shaped leaves to 30cm/12in long on long stalks. Clusters of yellow daisy-like flowerheads are produced in autumn and winter. **'Argenteum'** (syns 'Albo-varietatum', 'Variegatum') is a popular variegated form with large, irregular, creamy white margins. **'Aureomaculatum'**, the Leopard Plant, has leaves variegated with irregular yellow blotches. **USE & CULTIVATION** The cool dappled shade at the edge of a woodland garden provides excellent growing conditions for these attractive plants. They need moist well-drained soil to perform well and can also be sited near a water feature or grown in a container in fertile moisture-retentive soil. Frost hardy.

Farfugium japonicum

FARGESIA

FAMILY GRAMINEAE/POACEAE
This small genus consists of 4 species of clumping bamboos from China and the northern Himalayas. They have slender arching culms that branch from quite low down and develop a bushy, weeping habit. These bamboos are extremely cold tolerant and although they look superb in oriental-style gardens suit many other garden styles. Propagate from cuttings of young rhizomes or by division.

Fargesia murieliae
syn. *Arundinaria murieliae*
Umbrella Bamboo

ORIGIN Central China
CLIMATE M, CT, H
This attractive clump-forming bamboo to about 3m/10ft has slender yellow culms that usually branch in the first year and are densely clothed with slender bright green leaves to 10cm/4in long, giving it a special weeping elegance. The culms have a white powdery bloom when young, later becoming yellow.
USE & CULTIVATION Its ability to tolerate a certain amount of wind makes it a good ornamental windbreak or boundary hedge. Grow in full sun and fertile, well-drained, moist soil. Fully frost hardy.

Fargesia nitida
syn. *Arundinaria nitida*
Fountain Bamboo

ORIGIN Central China
CLIMATE M, CT, H
This clumping bamboo reaches only 3.5m/12ft. Its rather slender culms are purplish and covered with white powder when young. The upper portions of the culms produce elegant weeping branchlets densely clothed with finely tapering, dark green leaves to 12cm/5in long.
USE & CULTIVATION This slow-growing bamboo is not as wind tolerant as *F. murieliae*, but will make a fine hedge or screen in a protected position. It does

Fargesia murieliae

best in light shade. Grow in fertile moist soil. Fully frost hardy.

FASCICULARIA

FAMILY BROMELIACEAE
A genus of 5 species of bromeliads from Chile in South America. They are rosette-forming perennials with spreading leaves that turn fiery red in the centre, and produce clusters of tubular blue flowers in summer and autumn. Propagate from seed or by division of offsets.

Fascicularia bicolor
syn. *Fascicularia andina*

ORIGIN Chile
CLIMATE T, ST, WT
This bromeliad forms dense rosettes of arching linear leaves, with serrated edges, to 50cm/20in long. They are dark grey–green and at flowering time

turn bright crimson–red at the centre. In summer a cluster of pale blue flowers is borne at the heart of each mature rosette. *F. pitcairniifolia* is similar, with mid-green leaves to 1m/3ft long.

USE & CULTIVATION Decorative plants for a rock garden, tropical border or container. They thrive in full sun in porous well-drained soil. Give indoor plants the brightest possible light to bring out the best leaf colour and to encourage flowering. Frost tender.

X FATSHEDERA

FAMILY ARALIACEAE

There is only one species in this hybrid genus that combines the genera *Fatsia* and *Hedera*. It is an evergreen shrubby vine grown mainly for its foliage and used as a conservatory or house plant in cool climates. Scale insects, mealy bugs, slugs and snails can be problems. Propagate from semi-ripe cuttings in summer.

Fatsia japonica

Fatshedera x lizei
Tree Ivy

ORIGIN Gardens
CLIMATE WT, M, CT
This loosely branched shrub sends up slender, trailing or climbing stems to 2m/7ft with long-stalked, usually 5-lobed, glossy dark green leaves to 10–25cm/4–10in across. Large trusses of small, greenish white, sterile flowers are produced in autumn. **'Variegata'** has deeply lobed leaves with irregular creamy white margins.

USE & CULTIVATION Plants can be trained as creepers against a solid or glass wall, a pillar or tree trunk, or allowed to spread as a groundcover. A reasonably bushy specimen can be encouraged if regularly pinched back when young. Tolerant of pollution and coastal exposure. Grow in fertile well-drained soil in full sun or partial shade. Indoor plants will need support and should be kept moist and well fed during the growing season. Provide medium to bright light

and keep on the dry side with little or no feeding in winter. Frost hardy.

FATSIA

FAMILY ARALIACEAE

This genus contains 2 or 3 species of evergreen shrubs or small trees from Japan, Korea and Taiwan. They are grown for their handsome, deeply lobed, tropical-looking leaves and striking architectural form. Rounded clusters of small white flowers appear in autumn and winter and are followed by small black berries. In very cold regions they are usually grown as houseplants. Propagate from seed or from cuttings in summer.

Fatsia japonica
syns *Aralia japonica, A. sieboldii*
Japanese Aralia, Japanese Fatsia

ORIGIN South Korea, Japan
CLIMATE WT, M, CT
A striking, sparsely branched plant to 3.5m/12ft high with large, palmately lobed, glossy leaves to 40cm/16in wide, supported on strong clean stems. Creamy white flower balls are produced in large compound umbels in autumn and are followed by black pea-like berries. **'Aurea'** has yellow variegations. **'Marginata'** has deeply lobed grey–green leaves with white margins. **'Moseri'** has a more compact habit, larger leaves and some yellowing on the veins. The leaves of **'Variegata'** are creamy white at the ends of the lobes.

USE & CULTIVATION Valued for its tropical appearance in mild areas and widely used in bold landscaping. Grow in well-drained, humus-enriched soil in a partially shady, sheltered spot. Variegated cultivars need more sun. In cold areas, shelter from strong drying winds or grow as indoor plants. Provide bright light and keep moist and well fed during the growing season, and on the dry side in winter. Rejuvenate by pruning by half in spring. Moderately frost hardy.

FESTUCA

FESCUE

FAMILY GRAMINEAE/POACEAE

Several of this large genus of 300 to 400 species of perennial grasses have become popular in contemporary garden design. Others are important constituents of fine lawns and bowling greens. They are tufted, sometimes rhizomatous, with often very narrow linear leaves that roll under in dry conditions. The spikelets are generally small and flattened, arranged in narrow erect panicles. Propagate from seed or by division.

Festuca amethystina
Large Blue Fescue, Tufted Fescue

ORIGIN Europe
CLIMATE WT, M, CT, H

A perennial grass growing in dense tufts to 45cm/18in high. It has slender, blue–green, rough-edged leaves to 25cm/10in long with rolled-under edges towards the base. Violet-tinged spikelets of flowers appear in late spring and early summer. **'Bronzeglanz'** has bronze-coloured leaves.

USE & CULTIVATION Suitable for edging or growing among rocks in full sun and well-drained soil. Fully frost hardy.

Festuca eskia
**syns *Festuca scoparia*,
F. varia var. *scoparia***
Beargrass, Bearskin Grass

ORIGIN Pyrenees (France/Spain)
CLIMATE WT, M, CT, H

This tuft-forming perennial grass to 15cm/6in high has spiky, very narrow, rich green leaves that blend to form a neat mound to 25cm/10in across. Narrow flowerheads are held above the foliage in summer.

USE & CULTIVATION Its neat, rich green appearance makes it suitable for edging, as a groundcover or in rock gardens. Grow in well-drained soil in full sun. Trim regularly to maintain density. Fully frost hardy.

Festuca glauca
syn. *Festuca ovina* var. *glauca*
Blue Fescue, Grey Fescue

ORIGIN Europe
CLIMATE WT, M, CT, H

This perennial species has very slender, blue–grey, hair-like leaves to 20cm/8in long in tufts to 30cm/12in high. The insignificant flower spikes that first appear in early summer are violet-tinged. **'Blaufuchs'** (syn. 'Blue Fox') is popular, with vivid blue leaves. **'Elijah Blue'** has highly ornamental, paler silvery blue leaves. **'Golden Toupee'** has bright green and yellow leaves. **'Seeigel'** (syn. 'Sea Urchin') forms a soft compact tuft of silver–blue leaves, to 15cm/6in across.

Festuca eskia

Festuca glauca 'Elijah Blue'

Festuca glauca

Ficus aspera 'Parcellii'

Ficus auriculata

F

USE & CULTIVATION Their ornamental colouring and neat appearance make these plants useful for geometric garden designs and for edging. Grow in a sunny open position in light well-drained soil. Divide every 2 or 3 years in spring to ensure fresh new foliage colour. Fully frost hardy.

FICUS

FIG
FAMILY MORACEAE
Figs are grown for their edible fruit, their outstanding foliage or as shade trees. This is a large genus of around 750 species of vigorous trees, shrubs and root-clinging vines found mostly in moist forests in warmer regions of the world. Most species are too large for the average garden, but make superb shade trees for parks, municipal gardens and large open areas. When young, many species make excellent leafy container plants and can tolerate low light levels when brought indoors. The small-leaved forms make good

bonsai subjects. Gardeners should not be tempted to plant overgrown house-plants in the average home garden: some species can grow into giants, with vigorous root systems that can damage underground pipes, paths and foundations. The seasonal pests, lerps and fig-leaf beetles, can cause defoliation. Red spider mites, which thrive in dry heat, may be troublesome on indoor plants. Propagate from seed, cuttings and aerial layers.

Ficus aspera
Mosaic Fig, Clown Fig

ORIGIN Southern Pacific islands
CLIMATE T, S, WT
This wide-spreading, non-strangling, evergreen fig reaches 9m/30ft in height. It has oblong to elliptic leaves to 25cm/10in long, roughened above but velvety beneath. It bears small, reddish brown, rounded figs. The cultivar **'Parcellii'** is most often seen in gardens and is of more manageable size, to about 5m/17ft. It is grown for its spectacular mottled leaves in shades of light

green, grey–green and dark green splotched with cream.
USE & CULTIVATION 'Parcellii' makes a rather open, spreading tree and can be used as a decorative low-shade tree in confined spaces. Grow in moist well-drained soil with a high organic content. Frost tender.

Ficus auriculata
Roxburgh Fig

ORIGIN Southern Asia
CLIMATE T, ST, WT
This small tree to about 8m/25ft is grown for its broad, extremely attractive leaves, about 30cm/12in across with conspicuous veining. The pear-shaped figs to about 8cm/3in across have a soft velvety covering, ripen to purplish brown and are freely produced in clusters on mature trees.
USE & CULTIVATION This highly ornamental fig makes a good shade tree in tropical gardens. Grow in full sun or partial shade in fertile, moist well-drained soil, and shelter from drying winds. Frost tender.

Ficus benjamina
Weeping Fig

ORIGIN Tropical Asia

CLIMATE T, S, WT

One of the most popular of the smaller-leaved figs and one of the world's most popular indoor foliage plants. In gardens it can reach as high as 20m/70ft with a pronounced weeping habit; its glossy ovate leaves 5–12cm/2–5in long have a slightly twisted, pointed tip. As a houseplant it averages about 2m/7ft. Small reddish rounded fruit are produced in pairs in the leaf axils, but are not always seen on potted specimens. The many named cultivars include **'Golden Princess'**, with mid-green leaves flushed with lemon yellow. **'Variegata'** has leaves with irregular creamy white markings. A form sold as *F. b.* **var.** *nuda* has non-drooping branches and slimmer, more elongated leaves.

USE & CULTIVATION The invasive root system makes this species generally unsuitable for small gardens. It is best used for street and park planting or in containers. Grow in humus-enriched soil with plenty of moisture and protect from harsh drying winds. Young trees will withstand quite harsh pruning and are often used for topiary or as a standard. Also a popular subject for plaiting of trunks when young. Indoors, plants will adapt to various light and temperature levels, although dramatic changes may cause some leaf drop. Keep the soil evenly moist during the growing season. Frost tender.

Ficus carica
Common Fig

ORIGIN Eastern Mediterranean to western Asia

CLIMATE WT, M, CT

This deciduous fruiting tree reaches about 9m/30ft in height. Mature trees have silvery grey trunks. The large, palmately lobed green leaves to 25cm/10in long are carried on long stalks. The pear-shaped fruits are green, turning deep purplish red, purplish brown or greenish yellow depending on the cultivar. They ripen in summer.

USE & CULTIVATION A decorative and dramatic rich green background for other plants. It can be wall-trained, trimmed to a mop-headed standard or allowed to form a more natural shape.

Ficus benjamina

Ficus carica

Ficus dammaropsis

Also makes an attractive small grove. Grow in well-drained soil in a sunny position. Do not overfeed; keep the soil consistently moist when the fruit is maturing. Frost hardy.

Ficus dammaropsis
Dinner Plate Fig

ORIGIN New Guinea
CLIMATE T, ST, WT

This is a highly ornamental, low-spreading tree to around 9m/30ft high. It has large, thick-textured, corrugated leaves to 60cm/24in or more in length, dark green above with a paler underside and often with reddish veins. Greenish fruit about 10cm/4in in diameter, produced freely in the leaf axils, are covered with fleshy overlapping scales.
USE & CULTIVATION Of manageable dimensions, it makes an interesting exotic addition to a tropical or warm temperate garden, where it will thrive in a sheltered spot. Grow in humus-rich, moist well-drained soil. Frost tender.

Ficus deltoidea
syn. *Ficus diversifolia*
Mistletoe Fig

ORIGIN Southeast Asia
CLIMATE T, ST WT

This is a slow-growing, evergreen, bushy shrub 2.5m/8ft high; its broad, bright green leaves to 8cm/3in long are roughly triangular and tinted reddish brown beneath. It bears small, greenish white fruits that mature to dull yellow.
USE & CULTIVATION It branches profusely and forms an attractive miniature tree in a container. Popular as a houseplant, it is one of the few figs to regularly bear fruit indoors. These cluster at the leaf axils and appear on quite young plants. To maintain plants in good condition, provide bright indirect light and keep evenly moist during the growing season. Frost tender.

Ficus elastica
Rubber Plant

ORIGIN Tropical Asia
CLIMATE T, ST, WT

Once the main source of natural rubber in the tropics, this evergreen species is well known throughout the world as an indoor and conservatory plant. In gardens it grows into a large tree to 30m/100ft tall and 60m/200ft across, forming massive aerial roots and buttresses with age. The glossy green oval leaves, 15–30cm/6–12in long, have a red protective sheath covering new growth as it emerges. There are many popular cultivars for indoors, including **'Aurea-marginata'**, with prominent golden margins on the leaves. **'Decora'**

Ficus elastica 'Doescheri'

has dark green to bronze-tinted oval leaves to 38cm/15in long and a bright red protective sheath. The leaves of **'Doescheri'** have grey–green and dark green patches with creamy white margins, and pink stalks and central midrib. **'Robusta'** has larger, more rounded leaves than the species. **'Schryveriana'** has cream, grey and pink variegated foliage. **'Tricolor'** has grey–green leaves with pink and cream patches. The deep green leaves of **'Variegata'** have a yellow border and yellow patches.
USE & CULTIVATION Although too large for home gardens, it forms a handsome shade tree where space permits. It has a voracious root system and should be sited with care away from drains, foundations and so on. Indoors, it thrives in a well-lit situation away from direct sunlight. Allow the root system to dry out a little between watering. Can be grown with a single stem or pruned to produce several branches. Frost tender.

F

Ficus lyrata

Ficus macrophylla

Ficus lyrata
Fiddleleaf Fig

ORIGIN Tropical central and western Africa

CLIMATE T, ST, WT

This evergreen tree 9–15m/30–50ft high has leathery, fiddle-shaped, lustrous leaves to 45cm/18in long, bright glossy green and heavily veined. It bears green figs about 2.5cm/1in across.

USE & CULTIVATION In tropical and warm temperate gardens this handsome species gives a bold exotic touch to poolside and courtyard landscaping. It can be encouraged to branch by having its growing tip removed. Grow in fertile, moist well-drained soil in a partially shaded, protected position. A beautiful indoor plant; provide medium light, keep evenly moist and well fed during the growing season, and on the dry side in winter. Frost tender.

Ficus macrophylla
Moreton Bay Fig

ORIGIN Eastern Australia

CLIMATE T, ST, WT

Eventually forming a massive, thick trunk with buttressed roots, this very wide-spreading tree may reach 30m/100ft high and 60m/200ft across. It has large, thick, glossy oval leaves up to 25cm/10in long and 10cm/4in wide and purple, white-dotted figs to 2.5cm/1in across.

USE & CULTIVATION In warm frost-free regions this outstanding shade tree is widely planted as an avenue or street tree, in botanical gardens and other municipal gardens. It survives extreme coastal conditions if protected when young. Grow in fertile well-drained soil in sun or partial shade. Young plants make splendid container specimens and adapt well to indoor conditions. Water potted plants moderately, less in winter. A successful bonsai subject. Frost tender.

Ficus microcarpa
syns Ficus nitida, F. retusa
Chinese Banyan

ORIGIN China, Japan, Malaysia, New Caledonia, Australia

CLIMATE T, ST, WT

A wide-spreading evergreen tree to 18m/60ft high with smooth, pale grey bark and leathery leaves 5–8cm/2–3in long. Copious aerial roots growing down from the branches may take root on touching the ground and develop into subsidiary trunks, as happens in many banyan-type trees. The small, pinkish red, rounded figs are about 1cm/³⁄₈in across. **F. m. var. hillii** (syn. *F. retusa*), Hill's Weeping Fig, is a popular compact variety with shiny green leaves. **'Hawaii'** has white patches on grey–green leaves.

USE & CULTIVATION Although too large for home gardens, it forms a handsome shade tree where space permits. Indoors, grow in humus-enriched potting mix and position in a well-lit situation away from direct sunlight. *F. m.* var. *hillii* adapts very well to clipping and is used outdoors as a standard and for topiary in large tubs. It makes a striking bonsai subject, with interesting sculptured trunks developing on elderly specimens. Frost tender.

Ficus pumila
Creeping Fig

ORIGIN China, Vietnam, Japan
CLIMATE T, ST, WT
This is a self-rooting evergreen climber with thin, heart-shaped juvenile leaves less than 2.5cm/1in long and slightly puckered. In warm regions, mature non-clinging branches grow out from the support, bearing leaves to 10cm/

4in long and occasionally purplish fruit to 7cm/2½in long. These mature branches and leaves are removed to retain the attractive juvenile foliage. **'Minima'** has slender stems and much smaller juvenile leaves. **'Variegata'** has tiny white or cream-coloured spots.

USE & CULTIVATION An attractive, well-behaved creeping plant that can be trained to cover masonry or timber walls or to cascade over rocks and boulders as a groundcover. Grow in moist well-drained soil in a sunny or shady position. Trim regularly and pinch out tips to encourage branching. This fig is also suitable for containers, trained up a totem, around a shaped support or trailing from a hanging basket. Keep indoor plants moist, as excessive drying out of the root system will result in the leaves dying off. Less water is required in winter. Frost tender.

Ficus religiosa
Bo Tree, Peepul, Sacred Fig

ORIGIN Southeast Asia, Himalayas
CLIMATE T, ST
This evergreen or briefly deciduous wide-spreading tree to 12m/40ft high and wide has thin, gracefully pendent,

heart-shaped leaves to 18cm/7in long, with a long, slender point and prominent light-coloured veins. Fruits are small, flat-topped, purple figs.

USE & CULTIVATION Sacred to Buddhism and often planted in the grounds of temples and monasteries. An outstanding feature shade tree, thriving in fertile well-drained soil in full sun or partial shade. It is normally deciduous in monsoon climates. Frost tender.

Ficus pumila

Ficus microcarpa

Ficus microcarpa var. *hillii*

Ficus pumila 'Variegata'

Ficus rubiginosa
Port Jackson Fig

ORIGIN Australia
CLIMATE T, ST, WT

This large, spreading, dome-shaped tree to 20m/70ft high develops hanging aerial roots and massive buttresses with age. It has dark green, leathery, oval leaves to 12cm/5in long, glossy above and rusty-hairy below. Pairs of warty, yellow to deep red, rounded fruit about 2.5cm/1in across are borne in the leaf axils; they ripen in autumn. **'Variegata'** has attractive cream, grey and green marbled leaves.

USE & CULTIVATION Although too large for average home gardens, it makes an outstanding shade tree for parks and larger gardens in warm frost-free climates. Grow in medium-rich soil with plenty of moisture but good drainage. May be planted in coastal areas. Juvenile plants in tubs are suitable for conservatories, patios and courtyards. It makes a particularly good bonsai subject. Frost tender.

FITTONIA

NERVE PLANT
FAMILY ACANTHACEAE

From tropical rainforests of South America, these 2 species of evergreen creeping perennials are grown for their attractive leaves with a fine network of colourful veins. They are extremely popular as conservatory and house plants and are sometimes grown in bottle gardens and terrariums, as well as in hanging baskets. Cut back straggly stems in spring. Propagate from tip cuttings or by layering stems.

Fittonia verschaffeltii

ORIGIN Peru
CLIMATE T, ST

This pretty prostrate plant reaching no more than 15cm/6in high is naturally shallow rooting and has an indefinite spread. It has reddish green leaves to 10cm/4in long netted with conspicuous red veins. Small yellow flowers rarely develop and are best removed if they do. **F. v. var. argyroneura** (syn. *F. argyroneura*), the Silver Net-leaf, has small, oval, white-veined leaves. The compact miniature form **'Nana'**, with leaves to 3.5cm/1½in long, is said to be much easier to grow indoors.

USE & CULTIVATION All forms make attractive groundcovers, establishing well in the shade of palms and trees. Grow indoor plants in rich peaty soil in shallow containers to suit their prostrate

Ficus rubiginosa

Fittonia verschaffeltii var. *argyroneura*

Foeniculum vulgare

F

Foeniculum vulgare 'Purpureum'

Fothergilla major

form. Protect from direct sunlight, provide warm draught-free conditions and keep evenly moist. Avoid cold and wet conditions. Frost tender.

FOENICULUM

FAMILY APIACEAE/UMBELLIFERAE

This genus contains only one species, a herbaceous perennial grown for its umbels of yellow flowers, and aromatic leaves used for flavouring; the seeds are also edible. It is decorative in borders. Florence Fennel, var. *azoricum*, is grown as a biennial for its edible bulbous stem bases. Propagate from seed.

Foeniculum vulgare
Fennel

ORIGIN Europe
CLIMATE ST, WT, M, CT
This erect branching perennial reaches 2m/7ft in height, with thick hollow stems and masses of strongly scented, feathery, thread-like leaves. Large flat umbels of small yellow flowers are produced in summer and are followed by small brown aromatic seeds which, like the foliage, are reminiscent of aniseed. **'Purpureum'** has a purplish tinge to the young feathery leaves; these become a soft bronze colour later in the season.

USE & CULTIVATION These tall foliage plants are useful where height, elegance and contrast are needed in a perennial border or herb garden. Grow in an open, sunny position in fertile well-drained soil. Remove flowerheads after fading to prevent self-seeding. Fully frost hardy.

FOTHERGILLA

FAMILY HAMAMELIDACEAE

A genus of 2 species of deciduous shrubs from southern USA. They are grown for their autumn colour and fragrant flowers, which are borne in short bottlebrush-like clusters. Propagate from cuttings.

Fothergilla major
syn. *Fothergilla monticola*
Mountain Witch Hazel,
Alabama Fothergilla

ORIGIN Southeastern USA
CLIMATE M, CT, H
This deciduous upright shrub grows to 2.5m/8ft tall; its glossy dark green leaves, slightly bluish white beneath, turn red, orange and yellow in autumn. Tufts of fragrant white flowers appear in spring and again in autumn.

USE & CULTIVATION Excellent in small gardens, at the edge of a woodland garden or among other shrubs. Grow in sun or semi-shade in moist, peaty, acid soil with good drainage. It flowers and colours best in full sun. Fully frost hardy.

Fraxinus excelsior

FRAXINUS

ASH

FAMILY OLEACEAE

This Northern Hemisphere genus comprises about 65 species of deciduous trees and shrubs. They are grown mainly for their attractive form and foliage, and good autumn colour. Most species have small insignificant flowers, although those known as the flowering ashes, and typified by *Fraxinus ornus*, bear prolific terminal panicles of creamy white flowers. All species have pinnate leaves in opposite pairs and narrow winged fruit called samaras. Propagate from seed, or by grafting cultivars onto stock of the original species.

Fraxinus americana
White Ash

ORIGIN North America
CLIMATE WT, M, CT, H

This fast-growing spreading tree, 15–24m/50–80ft tall, has a long straight trunk and a dome-shaped crown of well-spaced branches. The pinnate leaves to 35cm/14in or more long consist of 5–9 dark green oval leaflets that are whitish grey beneath and turn yellow or purple in autumn. Petalless flowers appear before the leaves. **'Autumn Purple'** has reddish purple autumn colour.

USE & CULTIVATION A shapely lawn specimen, shade or woodland tree. Grow in fertile, moist well-drained soil in a sunny position. Fully frost hardy.

Fraxinus angustifolia
syn. *Fraxinus oxycarpa*
Narrow-leaved Ash

ORIGIN Europe, northern Africa
CLIMATE WT, M, CT

This shapely, fast-growing, narrowly domed tree to 24m/80ft has pinnate glossy leaves to 15–25cm/6–10in long composed of up to 13 slender, dark green, toothed leaflets. They turn golden yellow in autumn. The vigorous and popular Claret Ash, **'Raywood'**, has bright green spring and summer leaves that turn to rich wine shades in autumn and hold on well into winter before falling.

USE & CULTIVATION Suitable for large or moderate-sized gardens as a lawn specimen or woodland planting. Grow in fertile, moist well-drained soil in full sun. It is tolerant of alkaline soils and hot conditions if water is available, but best colouring is in cooler districts. Fully frost hardy.

Fraxinus excelsior
Common Ash

ORIGIN Europe
CLIMATE WT, M, CT, H

Occasionally growing to 30m/100ft or more high, this vigorous tree has a broad rounded crown and smooth stems studded with characteristic black winter buds. The 30cm/12in dark green pinnate leaves are divided into toothed oval leaflets that are paler beneath and turn yellow in autumn. **'Aurea Pendula'**, the Weeping Golden Ash, has deep yellow twigs, golden pendulous branches and rich yellow foliage in both spring and autumn. The vigorous **'Jaspidea'** has golden yellow young shoots, yellowish older stems and pale yellowish green summer foliage that deepens in autumn. The Weeping Ash, **'Pendula'**, has branches weeping gracefully to the ground.

USE & CULTIVATION All forms are excellent specimen trees for large gardens and street planting. They are tolerant of a wide range of soils, but thrive in moist conditions. Fully frost hardy.

Fraxinus ornus
Manna Ash, Flowering Ash

ORIGIN Southern Europe, southwestern Asia
CLIMATE WT, M, CT

This shapely broad-crowned tree grows to a height and spread of 15m/50ft. It has smooth grey bark, grey or brown winter buds and pinnate leaves to 25cm/10in long with 5–9 irregular-toothed oval leaflets. The foliage takes on soft bronze or purplish red tones in autumn. Fragrant creamy white flowers are borne in large terminal clusters in late spring and early summer, and are followed by clusters of small narrow fruit. When damaged or attacked by insects, the bark exudes a sugary substance often referred to as manna.

USE & CULTIVATION This species is widely planted as a street tree in southern Europe. It is an ideal shade tree for large or moderate-sized gardens and will grow in either acid or alkaline soils. Fully frost hardy.

Fraxinus velutina
Arizona Ash, Velvet Ash

ORIGIN Arizona and New Mexico, USA
CLIMATE WT, M, CT, SA

This open spreading tree grows to 9m/30ft tall and wide. The young shoots and undersides of the leaves are densely coated with grey velvety down. The pinnate leaves comprise 3–7 narrow to oval, faintly toothed, grey–green leaflets that turn yellow in autumn. **'Glabra'** has thicker, smooth, mid-green leaves. **'Fan Tex'** is a particularly heat-tolerant non-fruiting variety.

USE & CULTIVATION Extremely useful shade trees for areas with hot and dry as well as cold conditions. Grow in any well-drained soil. All forms tolerate alkaline and saline soil conditions. Frost hardy.

FURCRAEA

FAMILY AGAVACEAE
This genus of about 20 species of perennial succulents is found in semi-arid regions of the West Indies, Central and South America. The thick fleshy leaves radiate from the centre of the plant in the form of a rosette. The plants resemble Agave but differ in having short-tubed flowers. Plantlets are often produced between the flowers. Propagate from seed in spring or by division.

Furcraea foetida
syn. Furcraea gigantea
Green Aloe

ORIGIN Northern South America
CLIMATE T, ST, WT

This large clump-forming species produces succulent sword-shaped leaves to 2.5m/8ft long bearing a few hooked spines on the margins near the base. In summer it bears a giant panicle to 9m/30ft long of strongly scented, bell-shaped, green flowers with white interiors. **'Mediopicta'** has mid-green leaves striped with creamy white longitudinal lines.

USE & CULTIVATION In hot dry desert gardens it can develop into a spectacular feature plant. Provide excellent drainage and full sun. Keep dry in winter. In frosty areas, grow indoors in a dry atmosphere with good light and reasonable space. Frost tender.

Furcraea selloa var. marginata

ORIGIN Central America
CLIMATE T, ST, WT

This rosette-forming succulent has sword-shaped leaves to 1m/3ft or more long with a sharp tip and pale yellow margins with widely spaced hooked teeth. Panicles to 6m/20ft high bear whitish bell-shaped flowers in spring and summer.

USE & CULTIVATION Suitable for a large rocky desert garden or contemporary courtyard; provide very good drainage and an open sunny position. Allow adequate space from walkways to avoid contact with the spiny leaves. Conservatory plants do best in a dry atmosphere with good air circulation and full light. Water moderately and keep fairly dry in winter. Frost tender.

Furcraea foetida

Furcraea selloa var. *marginata*

GINKGO

FAMILY GINKGOACEAE

The single species in this genus is the sole survivor of a family of deciduous trees, now known only in fossil form, which long ago formed an important part of the earth's forest flora. It originated in China, where it is today unknown in its natural state but widely cultivated. Magnificent ancient specimens can be seen in temple grounds. Pollinated female trees produce a plum-like fruit: the fleshy outer portion is smelly, but the nut-like kernel is edible and highly nutritious. Propagate from ripe seed or cuttings.

Ginkgo biloba
Maidenhair Tree

ORIGIN Southern China
CLIMATE WT, M, CT, H
This graceful deciduous tree to 24m/ 80ft tall is often erect and sparsely branched when young, but eventually develops a well-proportioned wide-spreading crown. The flat fan-like leaves to 12cm/5in across are usually lobed, and similar in shape to a maidenhair fern. The foliage colours golden yellow in autumn. The yellow male flowers are borne in pendulous catkins to 3cm/1¼in long; the round, solitary, female flowers produce fleshy yellow–green fruit to 3cm/1¼in long in late summer and autumn. **'Autumn Gold'**, a selected male form, has a symmetrical upright habit to 9m/30ft and bright golden yellow autumn foliage. **'Fastigiata'** is a slender columnar male form to 9m/30ft with semi-erect branches. **'Princeton Sentry'** is male, with a narrow upright habit. **'Saratoga'** is an upright rounded male form to about 7m/22ft with a graceful weeping appearance.
USE & CULTIVATION This highly attractive tree is resistant to air pollution,

Ginkgo biloba

making it well suited to both city parks and private gardens. Female trees can produce messy fruits, unpleasant as they decay, so male trees in grafted form are often preferred. The *Ginkgo* will reliably produce its beautiful autumn colour even in warm temperate climates where the temperature never drops below freezing. It prefers good rainfall and deep well-drained soil in full sun. Frost hardy.

GLEDITSIA

FAMILY CAESALPINACEAE/ LEGUMINOSAE

A genus of about 14 species of deciduous, generally spiny trees from North America, Asia and tropical Africa. The Honey Locust, *Gleditsia triacanthos*, is widely available and grown for its attractive habit and fresh green pinnate leaves that colour well in autumn. Propagate from heat-treated seed or budding of selected forms.

Gleditsia triacanthos
Honey Locust

ORIGIN Eastern and central USA
CLIMATE WT, M, CT, H
In the wild, this tree can reach 30m/ 100ft, but it is usually about 20m/70ft in cultivation. It forms a broad spreading crown with a dark purplish grey trunk armed with clusters of sharp spines. The fern-like, bipinnate, dark green leaves to 25cm/10in long with many small oblong leaflets turn deep yellow in autumn. Clusters of small greenish white summer flowers are followed in autumn by flattened, twisted seed pods to 45cm/18in or longer that remain on the tree through winter. The thornless **G. t. var. inermis** has given rise to a number of seedless cultivars, such as the shrubby, slow-growing **'Elegantissima'**, which reaches 5–8m/17–25ft. **'Rubylace'** forms a small round-headed tree to 8m/25ft with purplish red-tipped leaves in

Gleditsia triacanthos 'Sunburst'

Gleditsia triacanthos 'Sunburst'

spring turning bronzy red through summer and deepening in colour in autumn. **'Shademaster'** forms an attractive, broadly conical canopy to 9m/30ft with bright green spring and summer leaves and golden autumn colouring. **'Skyline'** is an upright then spreading form to 9m/30ft with deep green leaves that turn golden yellow in autumn. **'Sunburst'** is a popular small tree reaching 7–9m/22–30ft. The early spring foliage is a clear golden yellow which gradually turns a soft pale green through summer. It does not fruit.

USE & CULTIVATION Sometimes used for stock-proof hedging, the species is seldom planted as an ornamental tree. The cultivars are slower growing and, without the heavy seeding, are best for average-sized home gardens where they provide light dappled shade and make delightful lawn or patio specimens. The leaves drop in early autumn and disintegrate quickly. Grow in fertile moisture-retentive soil. They are prone to wind damage. Hard pruning will reduce height if necessary. Fully frost hardy.

GLYCERIA

FAMILY GRAMINEAE/POACEAE
A genus of about 16 species of perennial grasses from temperate regions throughout the world, the majority found in the Northern Hemisphere. They occur naturally in wetlands and are useful for decorating large ponds and stabilising swampy areas. Propagate from seed.

Glyceria maxima
syn. *Glyceria aquatica*
Reed Sweet Grass

ORIGIN Temperate Europe and Asia
CLIMATE WT, M, CT
This robust aquatic perennial grass has erect stems to 2m/7ft tall and flat, deep green leaf blades to 60cm/24in long. Green to purplish spikelets are borne in branched open panicles to 35cm/14in long in late summer. The less vigorous **'Variegata'** is more commonly grown, with green leaves boldly striped in cream or white.

Glyceria maxima 'Variegata'

USE & CULTIVATION The species can become a well-established weed; the variegated form is usually grown in boggy soil at the edge of a water feature or in shallow water to 15cm/6in deep. Grow in full sun and a container or basket to restrict its spread. Fully frost hardy.

GRAPTOPETALUM

FAMILY CRASSULACEAE

Native to Mexico and Arizona, USA, this genus consists of about 12 species of small, rosette-forming succulent plants grown for their interesting shapes and delicate flowers. They resemble some forms of the related genus *Echeveria*, with which they often hybridise. Mature plants freely produce basal offsets. Small star-shaped or tubular flowers are produced on branched stalks that arise from the leaf axils in spring and summer. Propagate from seed, cuttings or offsets.

Graptopetalum bellum

syn. *Tacitus bellus*

ORIGIN Mexico
CLIMATE ST, WT, M

This relatively newly discovered species forms a neat dome-shaped rosette to about 10cm/4in in diameter of fleshy, grey, triangular leaves to 3.5cm/1½in long. Bright pink starry flowers to 3cm/1¼in across are produced atop branched stalks for several weeks in early summer.

USE & CULTIVATION An attractive miniature plant for a small rockery pocket or container. Grow in sharply drained soil in full sun or light shade. Indoors, provide full light and a dry atmosphere with good air circulation. Frost tender.

Graptopetalum paraguayense

syn. *Sedum weinbergii*
Ghost Plant, Mother of Pearl Plant

ORIGIN Mexico
CLIMATE ST, WT, M

This clump-forming succulent will spread to 1m/3ft or more across. Dense rosettes of thick, silvery grey leaves to 8cm/3in long are produced on erect stems about 20cm/8in long, which tend to become prostrate with age. White star-shaped flowers appear in summer.

USE & CULTIVATION An attractive grey-foliaged groundcover for edging a desert garden, rockery or courtyard garden. Grow in very well-drained soil and full sun to maintain its characteristic growth and colouring. Houseplants need a dry atmosphere with good air circulation and full light. Frost tender.

GRAPTOPHYLLUM

FAMILY ACANTHACEAE

This tropical and subtropical genus comprises 10 species of evergreen shrubs from Australia and South Pacific islands. They are grown chiefly for their foliage, which is often patterned with various colours, although some Australian species have showy, rich red, tubular flowers. Propagate from fresh seed or cuttings.

Graptophyllum pictum

Graptophyllum pictum 'Tricolor'

G

Graptophyllum pictum
Caricature Plant

ORIGIN New Guinea
CLIMATE T, ST

This colourful shrub has a rather loose habit to about 1.5m/5ft high, with oval, pointed, green leaves to 15cm/6in long with yellow central blotches. Short terminal spikes of red tubular flowers appear mainly in spring and summer. **'Purpureum Variegata'** has reddish foliage with purple variegation. **'Tricolor'** has larger purplish green leaves with cream variegation, flushed pink when young.

USE & CULTIVATION These luxuriant understorey plants for tropical gardens thrive in a partially shaded, well-drained position. Houseplants need bright filtered light and plenty of water when in full growth, less in winter. Tip-prune after flowering to promote branching. Frost tender.

GRISELINIA

**FAMILY CORNACEAE/
GRISELINIACEAE**

This is a small genus of 6 species of evergreen shrubs and trees from New Zealand, Chile and Brazil. They are grown for their attractive, leathery, glossy leaves and overall neat, bushy habit. The tiny greenish flowers are insignificant. Black berries appear on female trees. They are tolerant of coastal conditions and are moderately frost hardy. Propagate from seed or cuttings.

Griselinia littoralis
Kapuka

ORIGIN New Zealand
CLIMATE ST, WT, M, CT

This densely branched shrub or small tree to 8m/25ft or more has lustrous, broadly ovate leaves to 10cm/4in long, rich deep green to yellowish green. **'Dixon's Cream'** has almost rounded leathery leaves splashed creamy yellow. **'Green Jewel'** has narrower deep

Griselinia littoralis 'Variegata'

green leaves with creamy yellow margins and grey–green central markings. The leaves of **'Variegata'** are irregularly splashed creamy white.

USE & CULTIVATION Ideal as a windbreak and screen in mild coastal areas, this reasonably fast-growing species thrives in a sunny or partially shaded well-drained position. Lightly trim in summer if used as a hedge. Frost hardy.

Griselinia lucida
Puka

ORIGIN New Zealand
CLIMATE ST, WT, M

Although often an epiphyte in the wild, this species will develop into a spreading shrub or small tree to 6m/20ft tall. The rich green, broadly ovate leaves, 10–18cm/4–7in long, are leathery, very glossy and have unequal sides at the base. Small yellowish flowers are produced in axillary panicles. Forms with variegated leaves are sometimes available, but they are rather frost tender.

USE & CULTIVATION In mild climates it provides luxuriant foliage effects as a screen, windbreak or hedge by the sea. Grow in well-drained soil in full sun to partial shade. Marginally frost hardy.

GUNNERA

FAMILY GUNNERACEAE

This genus consists of about 45 species of herbaceous perennials, native to moist temperate regions of the Southern Hemisphere and grown mainly for their highly ornamental foliage. Some species grow to gigantic proportions, forming clumps of enormous rhubarb-like leaves; the smaller kinds form decorative cushions or rosettes. Individual flowers are insignificant, but the larger species carry huge decorative flower spikes. Propagate from fresh seed or by division.

Gunnera magellanica

ORIGIN Southern South America
CLIMATE WT, M, CT

This mat-forming perennial to about 15cm/6in high has short creeping stems to 30cm/12in across. The rounded to kidney-shaped, scalloped leaves 5–9cm/2–3½in wide, carried on stalks to 15cm/6in long, are often bronze-tinged when young. Tiny green flowers are produced in summer.

USE & CULTIVATION This moisture-loving plant forms attractive colonies at the edges of ponds or streams. Grow in partial shade in permanently moist soil that is rich in organic matter. Moderately frost hardy.

Gunnera manicata
syn. *Gunnera brasiliensis*

ORIGIN Colombia to Brazil
CLIMATE WT, M, CT

This fantastic foliage plant forms massive clumps of long-stalked, deep green, palmately lobed leaves nearly 2.5m/8ft across. The leaves are roughly puckered, conspicuously veined and supported on thick stalks about 2m/7ft tall studded with reddish bristly hairs. Rust-coloured flowers are borne on spikes to 1m/3ft long in early summer and are followed by orange–brown seed pods.
USE & CULTIVATION Locate where it will be a focal point at the edges of ponds or streams, woodland areas or large moist rockeries. Provide continual moisture for ultimate development and humus-rich soil in sun or partial shade. Shelter from very hot sun and cold drying winds. In winter give the resting crowns a protective mulch of compost or straw in particularly frosty areas. Frost hardy.

Gunnera manicata

Gunnera tinctoria
syn. *Gunnera chilensis*

ORIGIN Chile
CLIMATE M, CT

This slow-growing species forms tight clumps of kidney-shaped, palmately lobed leaves to 1.5m/5ft wide, borne on light brown prickly stalks to 1.5m/ 5ft high. Panicles of numerous rusty red flowers and fruit clusters to 60cm/24in high are formed near the base of the plant.
USE & CULTIVATION As for *G. manicata*. Moderately frost hardy.

HAKEA

Gunnera tinctoria

FAMILY PROTEACEAE

This genus of some 130 species of evergreen shrubs and small trees is endemic to Australia, with the majority occurring in Western Australia. They generally do best in areas with a dry summer and are grown mostly for their ornamental and varied leaf designs, conspicuous flowers and large woody seed cases. The Royal Hakea,

Hakea victoria

Hakonechloa macra 'Aureola'

G
H

Hakea victoria, is particularly notable for its large, variegated, scalloped leaves, which deepen in colour as they age. It is only available at some specialist nurseries, but is included here because it has probably the most spectacular foliage of all Australian plants. Propagate from seed.

Hakea victoria
Royal Hakea

ORIGIN Western Australia
CLIMATE M, SA
This is an upright shrub to 3m/10ft with large, variegated and prominently veined, scalloped leaves enclosing long sturdy stems. The floral leaves produced each season deepen in colour as they age, from yellow to orange and finally rich red. The green of the leaves at the base of the plant darkens to deeper shades with age. Small, inconspicuous,

cream and pink flowers are hidden at the base of the leaves during the winter months.
USE & CULTIVATION An outstanding feature plant best suited to warm dry areas without summer humidity. Grow in very well-drained acid soil in an open sunny position. It is best without fertiliser. Lightly prune at an early stage to encourage compact growth. Cut branches of foliage are long lasting in floral arrangements. Frost tender.

HAKONECHLOA

FAMILY GRAMINEAE/POACEAE
There is only a single species in this genus, native to Japan. It is a small deciduous grass with a few attractive variegated cultivars, used to add grace and contrast to borders and rock gardens. Propagate by division.

Hakonechloa macra 'Aureola'
Golden Variegated Hakonechloa

ORIGIN Japan
CLIMATE WT, M, CT, H
This slow-growing rhizomatous grass eventually forms dense spreading clumps to about 60cm/24in high and wide. It has bright yellow leaves to 20cm/8in long, finely striped with green and ageing to reddish bronze. Open panicles of pale green flower spikes appear in early autumn.
USE & CULTIVATION This non-invasive variegated grass adds charm to the smallest patio and rock garden. Also use in the foreground of a grass garden, for defining the edges to a path or in a shallow container. Grow in moist well-drained soil and, for best appearance, shade from the hottest sun. Fully frost hardy.

Hamamelis x *intermedia* 'Pallida'

Hamamelis virginiana

HAMAMELIS

WITCH HAZEL

FAMILY HAMAMELIDACEAE

This genus consists of 5 or 6 species of deciduous shrubs and small trees from North America and eastern Asia. The name Witch Hazel refers to the use of twigs of these plants to divine water in the same manner as hazel sticks. They are grown for their handsome autumn foliage and curious, spidery, fragrant flowers produced on bare winter wood before the spring foliage appears. The small, rather woody capsules containing 2 seeds open explosively. Usually the cutting of flowering stems is sufficient pruning, but any other necessary trimming is best done at the end of the flowering season. Propagate species from seed or selected forms from cuttings, budding or grafting.

Hamamelis x *intermedia*

ORIGIN Gardens
CLIMATE M, CT, H

This neat upright shrub to about 3.5m/12ft high and wide is a result of hybridising *H. japonica* with *H. mollis*. It has broadly oval leaves to 15cm/6in long, turning yellow in autumn. Fragrant winter flowers with 4 narrow, crimped petals appear in clusters on bare twigs. The following cultivars are vigorous and free-flowering. **'Arnold's Promise'** has a neat vase shape and soft yellow, fragrant flowers. **'Diane'** has red flowers and rich orange–red autumn foliage. **'Hiltingbury'** has coppery red flowers and gold and red autumn colouring. **'Jelena'** has good orange, red and scarlet autumn colour and large coppery red flowers in dense clusters. **'Pallida'** (syn. *H. mollis* 'Pallida') has yellow autumn colour and prolific soft pale yellow flowers. **'Ruby Glow'** has rich coppery autumn colour and coppery red flowers. **'Westerstede'** has yellow autumn foliage and primrose yellow flowers in late winter.

USE & CULTIVATION Grow these plants as a feature or in a shrub border, in sun or partial shade in humus-rich, well-drained soil that does not dry out. Avoid overcrowding with other shrubs, but shelter from strong winds. Fully frost hardy.

Hamamelis mollis
Chinese Witch Hazel

ORIGIN China
CLIMATE M, CT, H

This upright, open, spreading shrub or small tree growing to a height and spread of about 3.5m/12ft is valued for its sweetly scented, golden yellow winter blooms. The roundish oval leaves to 15cm/6in long are toothed and somewhat pleated, and downy beneath. They turn yellow in autumn. The buttercup yellow flowers of **'Brevipetala'** have shorter petals. **'Goldcrest'** is a later flowering form with larger, rich golden yellow flowers flushed red at the base of the petals, and yellow autumn foliage. The long-lasting flowering stems are cut for indoor arrangements.

USE & CULTIVATION All these plants are beautiful all year as garden or patio specimens. Avoid overcrowding in order to appreciate their winter charm. Locate in sun or semi-shade in fertile, moist well-drained soil, preferably acid. Frost hardy.

Hamamelis virginiana
Virginian Witch Hazel

ORIGIN North America
CLIMATE WT, M, CT
This erect open shrub to 5m/17ft is the commercial source of witch hazel. The dark green, broadly ovate, thick-textured leaves to 15cm/6in long turn clear yellow to orange in autumn. Golden yellow flowers with a faint sweet scent appear as the leaves begin to fall.

USE & CULTIVATION Use as a background shrub or prune to train into a small, well-shaped specimen tree. Full sun and rich, moist well-drained soil are preferred. This hardy and vigorous species is often used as an understock for grafting cultivars. Fully frost hardy.

HAWORTHIA

FAMILY ALOEACEAE/LILIACEAE
Native to southern and southwest Africa, this genus consists of over 150 species of perennial succulents. Some species are similar to the stemless aloes to which they are closely related, and form attractive cushions or rosettes of leaves, while others have longer stems. Leaves are often dotted, mottled, ridged and striped. The small tubular flowers are greenish white and inconspicuous.

Propagate from seed or leaf cuttings, or by division or offsets.

Haworthia attenuata
Zebra Plant
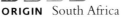

ORIGIN South Africa
CLIMATE WT, M
This clump-forming succulent forms rosettes 12cm/5in across and clusters up to 30cm/12in wide. The dark green narrow triangular leaves to 8cm/3in long bear conspicuous raised white markings arranged in rows on the lower surface. White tubular flowers are borne in racemes in summer.

USE & CULTIVATION A most attractive plant for a raised rock garden with very well-drained porous soil. In full sun the rosettes grow more tightly and take on a reddish colour. Houseplants need medium light, normal room temperatures, low humidity and good air circulation. Frost tender.

Haworthia cymbiformis
syn. *Haworthia planifolia*

ORIGIN South Africa
CLIMATE WT, M
Growing only about 8cm/3in high and 25cm/10in wide, this attractive dwarf succulent develops a tightly packed rosette of soft, pale green, rounded leaves to 4cm/1½ in long with translucent tips and pale green stripes. Slender racemes of pinkish white flowers appear in spring.

USE & CULTIVATION Ideal for a small rockery pocket, it also makes a good container and house plant. It needs partial shade to stay green and fresh and requires very well-drained soil. Indoors, provide medium light and low humidity. Keep dry in winter. Frost tender.

Haworthia attenuata

Haworthia reinwardtii

ORIGIN South Africa

CLIMATE WT, M

This clump-forming succulent has stems about 15cm/6in long densely packed with triangular dark green leaves to about 5cm/2in long and covered with tiny pearly tubercles arranged in rows. It offsets freely from the base and will develop neat clumps. The small green and white flowers are carried in clusters on long thin stems.

USE & CULTIVATION As for *H. attenuata*. Frost tender.

HEBE

FAMILY SCROPHULARIACEAE

This Southern Hemisphere genus consists of about 100 species of evergreen shrubs, most of them native to New Zealand. Some are grown for their ornamental flowers, but many have small dense leaves forming a natural compact shape and are appreciated for the structure and form they bring to the garden. Several cultivars derived from the Showy Hebe, *Hebe speciosa*, are used in mild areas of the UK for hedging. Some with scale-like leaves, known as the whipcord hebes, have a dwarf conifer-like appearance and are often grown in rock gardens for their texture and foliage colour. Propagate from seed or cuttings.

Hebe albicans

ORIGIN New Zealand

CLIMATE WT, M CT

This dense, compact, evergreen shrub has a height and spread of 60cm/24in. It has ovate-oblong glaucous leaves tightly packed along the stems and short white flower spikes in summer.

USE & CULTIVATION Good as a low groundcover, for the front of the border and for clipped formal work. Full sun, well-drained soil and plenty of moisture give best results. It rarely needs trimming and makes a good container subject. Frost hardy.

Hebe cupressoides

Hebe chathamica

ORIGIN New Zealand

CLIMATE WT, M, CT

This prostrate shrub grows to about 15cm/6in high with a spread of 1m/3ft. It has rather thick, fleshy elliptic-oblong, deep green leaves to 3cm/1¼in long carried on slender branchlets. In early summer it produces 4cm/1½in dense spikes of white flowers.

USE & CULTIVATION Useful in rock gardens or trailing from a raised garden bed. Grow in well-drained soil and full sun in colder areas. It is fairly tolerant of coastal conditions. In very cold regions grow in a pot. Frost hardy.

Hebe cupressoides

ORIGIN New Zealand

CLIMATE WT, M, CT

This whipcord hebe forms a dense rounded bush eventually reaching 1m/3ft or more. It has thin, crowded, cypress-like branches and tiny 1cm/⅓in long leaves that are bright green, often somewhat purplish in winter. Masses of tiny, pale bluish purple flowers are carried in terminal spikes in summer. **'Broughton Dome'** is a particularly attractive dome-shaped form to 30cm/ 12in; it seldom flowers.

USE & CULTIVATION Except in areas of prolonged winter cold, these hardy plants are excellent for rock and feature gardens. Grow in moist well-drained soil in sun or partial shade. Best in dry areas with low humidity. Lightly prune after flowering to maintain good form and size. Frost hardy.

Hebe pinguifolia

ORIGIN New Zealand
CLIMATE WT, M, CT

This semi-prostrate evergreen shrub grows to a height of about 60cm/24in with a spread of about 90cm/36in. It has small, fleshy, oval to round, pale blue–green leaves about 1cm/^{1}/3in long, often with reddish margins. Short white flower spikes appear in summer. **'Pagei'** is lower growing, with glaucous greyish leaves on purple stems.

USE & CULTIVATION As for *H. cupressoides*. Frost hardy.

Hebe speciosa
Showy Hebe

ORIGIN New Zealand
CLIMATE WT, M

This evergreen shrub forms a neat rounded dome with a height and spread of around 1m/3ft. Its rather fleshy oval leaves to 10cm/4in long are dark green and glossy. Large racemes of reddish purple flowers are produced over a long period, from early summer well into autumn. It is the parent of many colourful hybrids. **'Tricolor'** (syn. 'Purple Tips') has foliage heavily variegated grey–green and pale cream, flushed purple when young and in the colder months. Purple flowers appear in summer.

USE & CULTIVATION Good for low informal hedging, at the front of taller shrubs and in a large rock feature. They like sun or partial shade, well-drained soil and plenty of moisture. 'Tricolor' is less hardy and is best suited to milder climates. Excellent for defining space in small gardens; in cold regions it can be grown in a pot. Frost hardy.

Hebe cupressoides 'Broughton Dome'

Hebe speciosa 'Tricolor'

Hebe topiaria

ORIGIN New Zealand
CLIMATE WT, M, CT, H

This shrub makes a very tidy rounded shape of less than 1m/3ft in diameter. It has small, elliptic, bluish green, slightly glossy leaves to 1.5cm/½in long. White flowers are borne in short racemes between the leaves in summer.

USE & CULTIVATION A distinctive compact plant that doesn't need clipping; excellent for a formal touch to rock gardens and for edging paths and borders. It likes sun or partial shade, well-drained soil, plenty of moisture and shelter from drying winds. Frost hardy.

HEDERA

IVY

FAMILY ARALIACEAE

Although the ivies belong to a small genus of only about 10 species of evergreen woody-stemmed climbers, many ornamental varieties with immensely varied foliage have arisen . They attach themselves to any support by means of twining stems and short aerial roots, either covering trees, walls, pillars and fences or scrambling as dense groundcovers. When plants reach the top of their support they produce stiff shrubby stems which in turn produce greenish, insignificant flowers and black fruits. Regular pruning is recommended so that the attractive lobed juvenile leaves are retained and flowers do not appear. In containers they will attractively form clumps, climb, hang or spread. Small-leaved ivies are often trained on wire frames to create topiary features. The chosen frame is stuffed with damp moss and a number of rooted cuttings are trained up around it. New shoots are trained over the frame and the side-shoots are trimmed to keep the shape precise. In dry conditions ivy is susceptible to red spider mite and scale. Cuttings from mature growth produce plants with a shrub-like habit. Propagate from cuttings of juvenile growth or rooted stems.

Hedera colchica 'Sulphur Heart'

Hedera canariensis
Canary Island Ivy, Algerian Ivy

ORIGIN Algeria, Tunisia
CLIMATE ST, WT, M, CT

A fast-growing vigorous climber with triangular 3-lobed leaves to 12cm/5in long and 15cm/6in wide. The leaves are bright green with fine pale green veins, but the young stems and leaf stalks are deep wine red. The silvery green leaves of **'Gloire de Marengo'**, 8–10cm/3–4in long, have patches of creamy white markings and margins. **'Ravensholst'** has shallowly lobed dark green leaves 10–14cm/4–5½in long and with light veins.

USE & CULTIVATION Will survive mild winters and is best grown outdoors, clothing walls and fences. Also makes an effective groundcover in a sheltered spot where grass maintenance is difficult. Grow in moist well-drained soil in sun or shade. Moderately frost hardy.

Hedera colchica
Bullock's Heart Ivy, Persian Ivy

ORIGIN Caucasus
CLIMATE ST, WT, M, CT

This vigorous self-clinging ivy has heart-shaped, deep green leaves 8–12cm/3–5in long and 8cm/3in wide, finely veined and mostly with entire margins, with a resinous odour when crushed. **'Dentata'** has larger, paler green leaves to 25cm/10in long. The leaves of **'Dentata Variegata'** are heavily marked with irregular creamy white margins. **'Sulphur Heart'** (syn. 'Paddy's Pride') has elongated rich green leaves with yellow variegation.

USE & CULTIVATION All forms are suitable for covering high walls and as large-scale groundcovers. 'Dentata Variegata' and 'Sulphur Heart' will retain their variegation on the ground. Grow in moist well-drained soil in sun or shade. Fully frost hardy.

Hedera helix
Common Ivy, English Ivy

ORIGIN Europe
CLIMATE ST, WT, M, CT

This vigorous self-clinging climber or trailing plant has the familiar dark green ivy-shaped leaves with 3–5 lobes, with the lobe at the apex the longest. The species is seldom cultivated, having been superseded by its more decorative cultivars. **'Adam'**, with small 3-lobed leaves with a light green to greyish centre and irregular creamy white variegation towards the edges, is used mostly as a houseplant. **'Anne Marie'** has medium green and grey–green leaves with 5 rounded lobes and cream variegation, mostly at the margins. Its self-branching habit makes it suitable for low walls, pots and hanging baskets. **'Atropurpurea'** is an attractive wall ivy with purple stems and large 5-lobed leaves, dark green in summer and colouring to deep purple in winter. **'Buttercup'** is a climbing ivy with 5-lobed leaves that are light green in shady spots, but greenish yellow in sun, with some leaves completely bright yellow. The vigorous climbing

Hedera helix 'Anne Marie'

Hedera helix 'Glacier'

Hedera helix 'Goldheart'

Hedera helix 'Sagittifolia Variegata'

lobes and prominent veins. **'Ivalace'** is an outstanding self-branching ivy with mid-green 5-lobed leaves with light green veins and crinkled margins. Suitable for a low wall, as a groundcover in small areas or as a houseplant. **'Little Diamond'** is a slow-growing, self-branching ivy with grey–green diamond-shaped leaves, suitable for pots and small rock gardens. **'Luzii'** has light grey–green 5-lobed leaves lightly mottled with pale green and creamy yellow. It is most useful as a houseplant. **'Pedata'**, the Bird's Foot Ivy, is a fast-growing wall ivy with distinctive 5-lobed dark green leaves with an elongated central lobe. **'Pittsburgh'** (syn. 'Hahn's Self-branching') has small, closely set, 5-lobed, medium green leaves; suitable for fences, low walls, as a groundcover and houseplant. The self-branching and compact **'Sagittifolia Variegata'** has small grey–green leaves with 3 elongated lobes with irregular creamy white margins. It makes an excellent trailer for hanging baskets, window boxes, pots and rock gardens. Pinch out the tips to encourage bushy growth. **'Tricolor'** (syn. 'Silver Queen') has small, triangular, unlobed, grey–green leaves with irregular creamy white margins with a thin pink edge that becomes a darker pink in cold weather. It has rather slow growth and is best for a low wall.

USE & CULTIVATION As the above cultivars are considerably varied in their growth habit, and there is no generalisation for their landscape use, suitable uses have been included with their description. As a group, they prefer well-drained, moisture-retentive soil enriched with organic material, and light shade. Some of the variegated ivies are not recommended for groundcover, as they tend to produce all-green leaves when on the ground. Those with a compact self-branching habit make excellent pot plants for house, greenhouse or conservatory decoration. Indoors, they require bright light and moderate temperatures. Water moderately during the growth period, less in winter. Fully frost hardy.

'Cavendishii' (syn. 'Marginata Minor') has mid-green to streaky grey 3-lobed leaves with irregular creamy yellow margins. Ideal for walls. **'Chester'** is a compact self-branching variety suitable for growing on a low wall or indoors. It has small, 3-lobed, lime green to dark green leaves with creamy white variegations. **'Fluffy Ruffles'** is usually grown indoors. It has small 5-lobed or unlobed mid-green leaves with deeply waved, frilled margins. **'Glacier'** is one of the most popular indoor ivies. It has a slightly branching habit and heart-shaped grey–green leaves with 3 to 5 lobes with silvery grey and cream variegations. **'Goldchild'** has small bright green lobed leaves with broad yellow margins; usually grown as a container plant. **'Goldheart'** has dark green 3-lobed leaves, irregularly splashed in the centre with yellow. It is a beautiful wall ivy but does not do so well as a pot plant. **'Green Ripple'** is a highly decorative, branching wall ivy with bright deep green leaves with 5 forward-pointing

Helichrysum italicum

Helichrysum petiolare

Helichrysum petiolare 'Limelight'

Hedera hibernica
syn. *Hedera helix* subsp. *hibernica*
Irish Ivy

ORIGIN Western Europe
CLIMATE ST, WT, M, CT
This rampant climbing ivy has large, 5-lobed, dark green leaves to 9cm/3½ in long with light grey–green veins. **'Deltoidea'** (syn. *H. helix* 'Deltoidea'), the Sweetheart Ivy, has entire or shallowly lobed dark green leaves to 10cm/4in long with overlapping lobes at the leaf base.
USE & CULTIVATION The Irish Ivy is extensively grown as a fast-growing wall ivy or groundcover in Europe and eastern USA. It forms an excellent dark green background to other plants and in particular for other climbers. 'Deltoidea' is slower growing and used for smaller walls. Both benefit from an annual clipping in early spring to keep flush with the wall, control height

and remove any damaged growth. Fully frost hardy.

HELICHRYSUM

FAMILY ASTERACEAE/COMPOSITAE
There are hundreds of species in this large genus widely distributed in the Mediterranean region, Asia and southern Africa. There is considerable variation of form and habit within the genus and it is constantly undergoing botanical revision, with many species being reclassified under new genera. It includes annuals, perennials and shrubs, some of which bear glossy papery flowers commonly known as everlastings. A number have attractive silvery grey, felted leaves and make an appealing contrast to darker-foliaged plants. Powdery mildew may be a problem in areas with high humidity. Propagate from seed or cuttings, or by division.

Helichrysum italicum
syn. *Helichrysum angustifolium*
Curry Plant

ORIGIN Southern Europe
CLIMATE WT, M, CT
This woody-stemmed perennial grows about 30cm/12in tall and has silvery grey, very narrow, thread-like leaves that release a strong curry aroma. Small terminal clusters of deep yellow flowers are produced in summer.
USE & CULTIVATION A neat compact plant for the herb or rock garden or border, and for contrast in a mixed planting for a container. Grow in a rather poor or alkaline well-drained soil in a warm sunny position. It resents wet wintry sites and is best with dry conditions. Remove old flowerheads to encourage a flush of new silvery shoots and compact growth. Used in cooking, the dried leaves give a mild curry flavour. Moderately frost hardy.

Helichrysum petiolare

ORIGIN South Africa
CLIMATE WT, M, CT

A shrubby, spreading perennial with horizontal branching stems forming mounds to 60cm/24in high and 2m/7ft wide. It has grey–green, heart-shaped leaves to 4cm/1½in long covered with fine white hairs. Small creamy white flowerheads may appear in summer, but are not often seen on young plants. **'Limelight'** is a popular cultivar with lime green leaves. **'Variegatum'** has pretty grey leaves variegated with cream. **USE & CULTIVATION** All make excellent groundcovers, and can be used as low hedging to create boundaries within a garden, trailing from the top of a raised bed or as hanging basket subjects. In cold areas they are used as summer bedding plants, sometimes as companions to coloured-foliage plants such as the purple-leaved *Tradescantia pallida* 'Purpurea'. Grow in a sunny position in well-drained soil and rather dry conditions. Marginally frost hardy.

HEUCHERA

FAMILY SAXIFRAGACEAE

A genus of 30 to 50 species of evergreen and semi-evergreen perennials native to North America and Mexico. They form spreading tufts of long-stalked scalloped leaves from somewhat woody rhizomes, making good groundcovers and hanging basket subjects. Slender panicles of small flowers are held well above the foliage on wiry stems in early summer. A large range of hybrids and cultivars is available, many with marbled or ruffled leaves and forming attractive mounds. **'Rachel'** has lobed and crinkled dark green leaves tinged pink with pinkish purple undersides and large, pale pink flowers. **'Velvet Night'** has silvery pink-tinged leaves with a contrasting network of very dark green veins. Propagate from seed or by division.

Heuchera x brizoides

ORIGIN Garden
CLIMATE WT, M, CT, H

This is a group of clump-forming hybrid perennials between *Heuchera sanguinea*, *H. micrantha* and perhaps *H. americana*, somewhat resembling the first parent. They have rounded to kidney-shaped, shallowly lobed, hairy leaves to 8cm/3in long that are often bronzy and mottled grey and green. In summer, small bell-shaped flowers are carried on slender panicles well above the foliage. **'Coral Cloud'** has coral pink flowers with crinkled bronzy foliage. **'Pearl Drops'** has pink-tinged white flowers. **USE & CULTIVATION** Good groundcovers for the front of a border, edging a path or in a rock garden. Grow in any well-drained, humus-rich soil in full sun or light shade. Fully frost hardy.

Helichrysum petiolare 'Variegatum'

Heuchera 'Rachel'

Heuchera 'Velvet Night'

Heuchera micrantha var. *diversifolia* 'Pewter Moon'

Hosta fortunei 'Albomarginata'

Heuchera micrantha

ORIGIN Western North America
CLIMATE WT, M, CT, H

This clump-forming perennial reaches a height of 1m/3ft with a spread to 45cm/18in. It has heart-shaped, shallowly lobed leaves with grey marbling. In summer it bears numerous tiny pinkish white flowers on loose panicles to 30cm/12in or longer. **H. m. var. *diversifolia* 'Palace Purple'** is a popular cultivar with deep purple foliage and sprays of small white flowers. **'Pewter Moon'** is an attractive foliage plant with silvery green leaves with a contrasting network of deep green veins, purplish pink below. It has pale pink flowers.

USE & CULTIVATION As for *H.* x *brizoides*. Fully frost hardy.

HOSTA

PLANTAIN LILY
FAMILY HOSTACEAE/LILIACEAE

A genus of about 70 species of herbaceous perennials native to China, Korea and Japan, grown for their luxuriant and decorative foliage. They have broadly lance-shaped to almost rounded leaves, often with deeply incised veins, in colours ranging from deep, glossy green through different paler greens to waxy blue and almost yellow, some with variegations. They form large clumps; the heights given below refer to the foliage. Hostas are at their peak in summer; the leaves die down in winter. Tall spikes of purple–blue or white flowers are quite attractive in late summer and autumn, but the leaf colour and texture is the prime reason for growing them. They are valuable garden plants for shady areas and do best in cool areas. Hostas can be grown in masses to edge a garden path or to contrast with sword-shaped leaves, grasses and ferns in a waterside planting. Those with white or cream variegated leaves can enhance a white garden scheme. Both leaves and flowers are useful for indoor decoration. Guard against slugs and snails, which can very quickly disfigure the leaves. Propagate by division in early spring.

Hosta crispula
syns *Hosta* 'Crispula', *H.* 'Sazanami'

ORIGIN Japan
CLIMATE WT, M, CT, H

A slow-growing, clump-forming perennial to 50cm/20in high with large, distinctly veined, oval to heart-shaped, wavy-edged leaves, mid-green with irregular white margins, and tapering to long twisted tips. Racemes of trumpet-shaped pale lavender flowers are produced well above the foliage in summer.

USE & CULTIVATION This and the following species can be grown in bold masses as groundcover in woodland areas, as part of a border or near a water feature. They can also be used in rockeries and containers. All hostas appreciate dappled shade, moist well-drained, neutral soil and regular feeding during the growing season. Shelter from strong winds. A mulch of compost applied each spring will help conserve moisture. Fully frost hardy.

Hosta fortunei

ORIGIN Gardens
CLIMATE WT, M, CT, H

This vigorous clump-forming perennial grows to 55cm/22in tall and spreads to 1m/3ft. It has ovate to heart-shaped,

H

dark green leaves 20–30cm/8–12in long with long pointed tips. Spikes of funnel-shaped mauve flowers are produced above the foliage in summer. Popular cultivars include **'Albomarginata'**, with grey–green leaves to 30cm/12in long, outlined with a band of creamy yellow or white. **'Albopicta'** has pale green leaves with a large creamy yellow centre, fading to two shades of green later in the season. **'Aureomarginata'** has mid-green leaves to 25cm/10in long with irregular creamy yellow edges.

USE & CULTIVATION As for *H. crispula*. Fully frost hardy.

Hosta 'Frances Williams'
syns *Hosta* 'Eldorado', *H. sieboldiana* 'Frances Williams'

ORIGIN Gardens
CLIMATE WT, M, CT, H

The large puckered leaves of this hybrid are blue–green, boldly bordered with irregular yellow–green margins. Clump-forming, it reaches a height of 75cm/30in, with greyish white flowers held just above the foliage in early summer.

USE & CULTIVATION As for *H. crispula*. It is rather slow growing and should not be grown in full sun. Fully frost hardy.

Hosta 'Gold Standard'

ORIGIN Gardens
CLIMATE WT, M, CT, H

This vigorous grower forms a spreading clump to 65cm/26in high and 1m/3ft wide of oval to heart-shaped greenish yellow leaves to 18cm/7in long with narrow, dark green margins. In summer, tall flower stems bear trumpet-shaped violet flowers.

USE & CULTIVATION As for *H. crispula*. Fully frost hardy.

Hosta 'Halcyon'
syn. *Hosta* 'Holstein'

ORIGIN Gardens
CLIMATE WT, M, CT, H

This handsome species forms clumps to 30cm/12in high and 1m/3ft wide. It has striking heart-shaped, tapering, grey–blue leaves to 20cm/8in long and bears clusters of lavender grey flowers just above the foliage in summer.

USE & CULTIVATION As for *H. crispula*. Fully frost hardy.

Hosta 'Krossa Regal'

ORIGIN Gardens
CLIMATE WT, M, CT, H

This perennial forms an upright clump to 70cm/28in high of large, deeply veined, glaucous green leaves to 22cm/9in long with wavy margins. Pale lilac flowers are borne on tall stems.

USE & CULTIVATION As for *H. crispula*. Fully frost hardy.

Hosta lancifolia
syn. *Hosta lancifolia* var. *fortis*

ORIGIN Korea, Japan
CLIMATE WT, M, CT, H

This smaller-growing species forms arching clumps no more than 45cm/18in high and 75cm/30in wide. It has long, pointed, thin-textured leaves to 18cm/7in long, dark green and glossy. Deep purple flowers are produced in late summer and autumn.

USE & CULTIVATION As for *H. crispula*. Fully frost hardy.

Hosta fortunei 'Aureomarginata'

Hosta 'Krossa Regal'

Hosta sieboldiana

Hosta 'Sum and Substance'

Hosta plantaginea
August Lily, Fragrant Plantain Lily

ORIGIN China
CLIMATE WT, M, CT, H
Forming a mound to 60cm/24in high and 1m/3ft across, this species has large, wavy, heart-shaped, fresh pale green leaves to 30cm/12in long. Fragrant white flowers are borne well above the foliage in late summer. **'Grandiflora'** has larger flowers.

USE & CULTIVATION As for *H. crispula*. This species prefers some morning sun. Fully frost hardy.

Hosta sieboldiana

ORIGIN Japan
CLIMATE WT, M, CT, H
This species forms impressive clumps to 1m/3ft high and 1.2m/4ft wide of large, glaucous, bluish grey leaves to 50cm/ 20in long, broadly heart-shaped and heavily puckered. Racemes of trumpet-shaped flowers, pale mauve fading to white, appear just above the foliage in summer. **H. s. var. elegans** has thick, deeply ribbed and puckered leaves to 30cm/12in long with a silvery bloom. **USE & CULTIVATION** As for *H. crispula*. Too much sun will burn or bleach the glaucous bloom on the foliage. Fully frost hardy.

Hosta 'Sum and Substance'

ORIGIN Gardens
CLIMATE WT, M, CT, H
This outstanding foliage plant forms impressive clumps to 75cm/30in high and over 1m/3ft across of large, heart-shaped leaves to 50cm/20in long; pale green at first, they gradually turn a beautiful yellow chartreuse over summer, becoming puckered when mature. **USE & CULTIVATION** As for *H. crispula*. Fully frost hardy.

Hosta tokudama
syn. *Hosta* 'Tokudama'

ORIGIN Japan
CLIMATE WT, M, CT, H
This slow-growing species forms a clump to 50cm/20in high and 75cm/ 30in across. The heart-shaped, almost rounded leaves to 30cm/12in long are puckered and a deep bluish green. Pale lilac grey flowers protrude above the leaves from early to late summer. **'Aureonebulosa'** has irregular greenish yellow splashes on the centre of the leaves. **'Flavocircinalis'** has blue–green heart-shaped leaves with wide, irregular, creamy margins.
USE & CULTIVATION As for *H. crispula*. Fully frost hardy.

Hosta undulata var. undulata
Wavy-leaved Plantain Lily

ORIGIN Japan
CLIMATE WT, M, CT, H
The slightly pointed 18cm/7in leaves of this attractive species have strongly waved and curved margins and large central splashes of white or pale creamy

Hosta ventricosa

Houttuynia cordata 'Chameleon'

white. It forms a tall clump to 1m/3ft and bears mauve flowers in summer. **'Albomarginata'** (syn. 'Thomas Hogg') has broad oval, rather flat leaves with frilled cream edges. **H. u. var. univittata** has wavy mid-green leaves with a bold splash of white variegation in the centre. **USE & CULTIVATION** As for *H. crispula*. Fully frost hardy.

Hosta ventricosa

ORIGIN China, North Korea
CLIMATE WT, M, CT, H
This is a handsome clumping species to 50cm/20in high with rather thin-textured, strongly veined, dark green leaves to 30cm/12in long. Racemes of purple bell-shaped flowers appear above the foliage in summer.

USE & CULTIVATION As for *H. crispula*. Fully frost hardy.

HOUTTUYNIA

FAMILY SAURURACEAE
This is only one species in this genus, a spreading deciduous perennial from moist habitats of eastern Asia. It is grown mainly for its ornamental leaves. Slugs and snails can disfigure the leaves. Propagate by division or from cuttings.

Houttuynia cordata

ORIGIN China, Japan
CLIMATE ST, WT, M, CT, H
This rapidly spreading perennial to 30cm/12in high grows from under-

ground rhizomes which send up red branched stems bearing heart-shaped, aromatic green leaves to 9cm/3½in long with thin red margins. Spikes of tiny yellowish flowers with 4 white petal-like bracts at the base appear in summer. **'Chameleon'** (syn. 'Tricolor') has variegated leaves splashed yellow, pink and red.

USE & CULTIVATION This water-loving species is suitable for groundcover near streams and ponds, but can become invasive and is probably best contained. 'Chameleon' is less vigorous. Grow in rich moist soil or shallow water in dappled shade. Looks good in a shallow container, which should be kept in a saucer topped up with water. It dies back during the cooler months. Frost hardy.

Howea belmoreana

Howea forsteriana

HOWEA

FAMILY ARECACEAE/PALMAE

There are only 2 species in this palm genus, both found on Lord Howe Island, Australia and both highly successful as potted specimens for the house or conservatory. These are the classic 'Palm Court' palms. They are medium-sized and slender, with gracefully arching feathery fronds. In cultivation, the mature height is usually around 9m/30ft, though in the wild they can be much taller. Annual feeding with a balanced slow-release fertiliser is worthwhile, especially for those palms in tubs. They have a short fibrous root system and it is possible to move aged plants successfully. The long slender leaflets can be sensitive to commercial leaf-cleaning products, so it is best to hose the fronds gently with tepid water. Propagate from ripe seed.

Howea belmoreana
syn. *Kentia belmoreana*

Curly Palm

ORIGIN Australia

CLIMATE ST, WT

This species has a slender, smooth, ringed trunk 5–12m/17–40ft high, and strongly curved, dark green, pinnate fronds to 3m/10ft long forming a dense arching crown. Pendulous flowering spikes to 1m/3ft long bear glossy brownish red drupes.

USE & CULTIVATION In warm frost-free areas this is a highly decorative species for a small garden. Grow in well-drained, humus-rich soil and shade from hot sun when small. It tolerates salt-laden sea breezes, making it highly suitable for coastal gardens, where it is often most effective planted in groves, particularly as part of a swimming pool landscape. Young plants are excellent for indoor decoration, and being slow growing thrive in the same pot for many years. Lightly shade from direct sun and keep well watered during summer months. Frost tender.

Howea forsteriana
syn. *Kentia forsteriana*

Kentia Palm, Thatch Palm

ORIGIN Australia

CLIMATE ST, WT

This slender single-stemmed palm grows 5–15m/17–50ft tall. The spreading 3m/10ft long pinnate fronds are very similar to the above species, but the leaflets are gracefully drooping where those of *H. belmoreana* are held more rigidly erect. The unbranched flower spikes to 1m/3ft long bear brown or red drupes.

USE & CULTIVATION One of the most elegant and popular of plants for indoor decoration. In warmer areas it is used as a specimen, in groves or as part of a tropical garden scheme. It also grows well in seaside gardens. Shelter from harsh sun and strong drying winds when small. Moist well-drained soil with a high organic content is best. Frost tender.

HYPOESTES

FAMILY ACANTHACEAE

This is a genus of 40 species of evergreen shrub-like plants grown for their foliage and flowers. The Polka-dot Plant, *Hypoestes phyllostachya*, is a popular indoor plant grown for its colourful pink-spotted leaves. Propagate from seed or cuttings.

Hypoestes phyllostachya
syn. *Hypoestes sanguinolenta*
Polka-dot Plant, Freckle Face

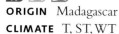

ORIGIN Madagascar
CLIMATE T, ST, WT

This small shrub-like plant to 30cm/ 12in high and wide has ovate dark green leaves to 5cm/2in long, arranged in opposite pairs and heavily spotted with pink markings. Insignificant pink flowers are produced intermittently. A range of colourful varieties is available, including **'Splash'**, which has larger and brighter pink markings.

USE & CULTIVATION In warm gardens it is grown as a pretty border plant in moist well-drained soil in partial shade. Indoors, provide bright filtered sunlight and plenty of water during the growing season, less in winter. Pinch back growing tips to encourage branching. Frost tender.

I

ILEX

HOLLY
FAMILY AQUIFOLIACEAE

Most of the 400 species in this large genus of evergreen and deciduous trees are from temperate regions of the Northern Hemisphere. They make useful ornamental shrubs with a good habit, attractive foliage and colourful berries in mid-winter. The best-known species is the English Holly, *Ilex aquifolium*, farmed in the USA to supply the florist trade during the Christmas season. Almost all plants are either male or female, which means that unless both sexes are present, berries will not be produced. Hollies respond to hard pruning in spring and make excellent hedges and clipped topiary subjects. Propagate from seed in spring or semi-ripe cuttings taken in late summer and autumn.

Ilex x *altaclerensis*
Highclere Holly

ORIGIN Gardens
CLIMATE WT, M, CT

A group of cultivars largely derived from back-crosses of this hybrid with the English Holly (*I. aquifolium*) and resembling robust forms of it, but usually with less spiny leaves. The following cultivars are all female and require pollination by a male cultivar, such as 'Silver Queen', a cultivar of *I. aquifolium*, to set berries. **'Camelliifolia'** reaches a height of 14m/45ft with glossy dark green oblong leaves to 12cm/5in long, mainly without spines. The large berries are dark red. **'Golden King'** is a large compact shrub to 6m/20ft with rich green oblong leaves that are entire or spine-tipped with a yellow margin. The large fruit is not freely produced. **'Hendersonii'** forms a compact tree to 15m/50ft with dull green foliage and bears a sparse crop of red berries. **'Lawsoniana'** forms a large shrub or small tree to 6m/20ft and has sparsely spined leaves with irregular central yellow and light green splashes. It has red berries.

USE & CULTIVATION Recommended for tall hedges, windbreaks and screens, according to their height. In cold areas they are best in an open sunny position. Grow in well-drained, fertile, moisture-retentive soil. Moderately frost hardy.

Hypoestes phyllostachya

Ilex x *altaclerensis* 'Camelliifolia'

Ilex x *altaclerensis* 'Camelliifolia'

Ilex aquifolium 'Aurea Marginata'

Ilex aquifolium 'Handsworth New Silver'

Ilex aquifolium
English Holly

ORIGIN Europe to western Asia, northern Africa

CLIMATE WT, M, CT

This well-branched evergreen tree is capable of reaching 20m/70ft or more, but in gardens usually takes on an erect pyramidal form to no more than about 12m/40ft, carrying the foliage to ground level. On young trees the shiny ovate leaves, 5–12cm/2–5in long, have spiny teeth along the wavy margins. Leaf spines are mostly absent on mature trees. The tiny white spring flowers appear in small clusters at the leaf bases and are followed by round scarlet berries on female plants in winter. **'Amber'** (female) is a tree to 6m/20ft with yellow berries and almost spineless, bright green leaves to 8cm/3in long. **'Angustifolia'** (male or female) has a slow-growing narrow habit and weakly spined, lance-shaped leaves to 4cm/1½ in long. **'Argentea Marginata'** (female) to 15m/50ft has broad spiny leaves to 7cm/2½ in long with wide, silvery white margins. **'Argentea Marginata Pendula'** (female) is a weeping tree with spiny leaves edged with creamy white. **'Aurea Marginata'** (female) is a small bushy shrub with yellow-margined spiny leaves and red berries. **'Bacciflava'** (female), a tree to 15m/50ft, has deep green spiny leaves to 8cm/3in long and waxy yellow berries. **'Ferox'** (male), the Hedgehog Holly, is a large compact tree to 15m/50ft with purplish stems and dark green spiny leaves to 7cm/2½ in long, with spines also on the upper surface. **'Ferox Argentea'** (male) is slow growing, with deep green leaves and creamy white margins. **'Flavescens'** (female), the Moonlight Holly, is a bushy shrub to 6m/20ft with red berries and spiny leaves to 8cm/3in; leaves are a clear yellow if grown in full sun. Older leaves and those in shade mature to green. **Golden Milkboy'** (male) grows to 6m/20ft with golden variegated leaves. **'Golden Queen'** (male), a dense tree to 9m/30ft, has dark green spiny leaves to 8cm/3in, marbled grey and edged with creamy white. **'Handsworth New Silver'** (male) has purple stems and spiny leaves to 8cm/3in long, mottled grey–green with broad, clear white margins. **'J.C. van Tol'** (female), to 6m/20ft, has glossy dark green, almost spineless leaves to 8cm/3in long and dark purplish stems. One of the few self-fertile forms, it produces large clusters of crimson berries. **'Madam Briot'** (female), a large bushy shrub to 9m/30ft, has attractive purple stems and strongly spiny, deep green leaves to 10cm/4in long, mottled and margined dark yellow, and bears scarlet berries. **'Pyramidalis'** (self-fertile female), to 6m/20ft, has bright red berries and almost spineless leaves to 8cm/3in long. **'Pyramidalis Fructu Luteo'** has yellow fruit and bears well. **'Silver Milkmaid'** (male or female), to 6m/20ft, has leaves with dark green margins and creamy white centres. **'Silver Queen'** (male), a non-berrying shrub to 9m/30ft, has spiny leaves to 7cm/2½in long with broad, creamy white margins. **USE & CULTIVATION** Good varieties of holly are among the most effective of small evergreen trees for winter gardens, either singly or planted in groups. They can be used as hedges and screens and clipped to shape. Berry production is best in cooler climates. Grow in moist well-drained soil enriched with organic matter, and position in full sun or light shade.

Ilex aquifolium 'Silver Queen'

Water well in summer and mulch with compost to keep roots cool in hot weather. Fully frost hardy.

Ilex cornuta
Chinese Holly, Horned Holly

ORIGIN China, Korea
CLIMATE WT, M, CT

This is a dense, rounded, evergreen shrub to 3.5m/12ft high and wide with thick, glossy, deep green leaves to 8cm/3in long, almost rectangular in shape, with 1 or 2 spines on each side and a curved terminal point. On some plants, most leaves are spineless. Large, slightly flattened red berries to 1cm/⅓in across are borne throughout summer. It is self-fertile. **'Burfordii'** is a dense, compact female form to 3.5m/

12ft tall and wide with only a single spine on the tip of the leaf.
USE & CULTIVATION As for *I. aquifolium*. In mild-winter climates, it bears berries more successfully than the English Holly; it is the best holly for use in the Southern Hemisphere as Christmas decoration. Fully frost hardy.

Ilex crenata
Box-leaved Holly, Japanese Holly

ORIGIN Japan, Korea
CLIMATE WT, M, CT, H

This compact, rigid, evergreen shrub or small tree to 5m/17ft has small, glossy green leaves to 3cm/1¼in long with rounded teeth, dull white flowers and black berries. **'Convexa'** is a bushy female shrub to 2.5m/8ft with small leaves with turned-under edges; it produces a good crop of black berries. **'Golden Gem'** is a flat-topped female shrub to 1m/3ft high and wide with yellow leaves. **'Mariesii'** is a very slow-growing female shrub to 1m/3ft with round leaves densely packed along the short stems.
USE & CULTIVATION As for *I. aquifolium*. The cultivars offer a good selection of small-leaved varieties useful for dense clipped hedges and for trimming to shapes. Fully frost hardy.

Ilex x meserveae
Blue Holly

ORIGIN Gardens
CLIMATE WT, M, CT, H

A group of hybrids derived from *I. aquifolium* and *I. rugosa*. They have a dense bushy habit, purplish stems and usually bluish green spiny leaves. Female plants bear glossy red fruit. **'Blue Angel'** (female) has a compact habit to 3.5m/12ft high and small bluish green leaves to 5cm/2in long. **'Blue Prince'** (male) has a height and spread to 3.5m/12ft and glossy bright green leaves. **'Blue Princess'** (female), to 3m/10ft high, has glossy ovate leaves to 7cm/2½ in and abundant red berries.
USE & CULTIVATION As for *I. aquifolium*. Fully frost hardy.

Iresine herbstii 'Aureoreticulata'

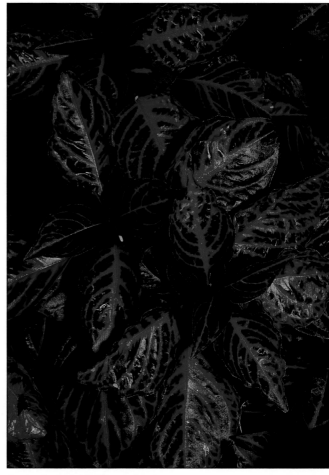

Iresine herbstii 'Brilliantissima'

IMPERATA

FAMILY GRAMINEAE/POACEAE
There are about 8 species of these perennial grasses found in tropical and subtropical regions of the world. The Japanese species *Imperata cylindrica* is widespread in the wild and is mainly grown for the ornamental appeal of its coloured-leaved cultivars. Propagate by division.

Imperata cylindrica 'Rubra'
Japanese Blood Grass

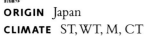

ORIGIN Japan
CLIMATE ST, WT, M, CT
This perennial grass spreads by underground rhizomes to form attractive clumps of flat linear leaves to 50cm/20in high, often a rich red from the tip to almost the base of the clump. Panicles of silky-white spikelets are produced in summer.

USE & CULTIVATION Position this dramatic plant in a rockery, courtyard or at the front of a border where the sun can highlight the red leaves. It likes full sun, good drainage, humus-rich soil, and benefits from winter mulch in cold areas. Cut back to the base before spring growth commences. Moderately frost hardy.

IRESINE

FAMILY AMARANTHACEAE
This genus consists of 70 to 80 species of perennials, climbers and shrub-like plants from tropical and warm temperate regions. A few species are grown for their brightly coloured leaves as conservatory and house plants and for bedding in warm climates. They have opposite pairs of ovate to lance-shaped leaves and tiny, insignificant, white or greenish flowers, which are usually removed to promote leaf growth. Propagate from stem cuttings in spring.

Iresine herbstii
Beefsteak Plant

ORIGIN Brazil
CLIMATE T, ST, WT
This evergreen bushy perennial to about 60cm/24in high with a similar spread has soft, succulent, red stems and purplish red rounded leaves notched at the tips, to 8cm/3in long, with veining paler red or yellowish red. **'Aureoreticulata'** has mid-green leaves and conspicuous leaf veins broadly traced in yellow. **'Brilliantissima'** has bright carmine leaves.

USE & CULTIVATION Cheerful plants for warm gardens. They make a colourful addition to a sunny border or beneath palms, mixed with other tropical-looking plants. Indoors, very good light is needed for the production of healthy, colourful leaves. Provide good drainage and plenty of moisture during the growing period; feed with a balanced liquid fertiliser at monthly intervals. Pinch out growing tips to encourage bushy plants. Frost tender.

JUNIPERUS

JUNIPER
FAMILY CUPRESSACEAE

Widely distributed throughout the Northern Hemisphere, this conifer genus consists of about 50 species of evergreen shrubs or trees. Junipers are perhaps the most commonly planted conifers for ornamental use, with a very large range of sizes, shapes and colours found among the cultivars. The juvenile leaves, always needle-like, are sometimes retained on mature plants, especially on heavily pruned branches. Adult leaves are sometimes needle-like and in 3s, more often scale-like. Male and female cones are borne mostly on separate plants. As the female cone matures, the scales become fleshy, forming a bluish black berry-like fruit. The berries of some junipers are dried and used for culinary purposes, and in the production of gin. Propagate species from fresh seed or by layering. Cuttings and grafting are mostly used for cultivars.

Juniperus chinensis
Chinese Juniper

ORIGIN Himalayas, China, Japan
CLIMATE WT, M, CT, H

When mature, this is a dense conical tree to 15m/50ft high with a spread to 3m/10ft. Needle-like juvenile leaves and scale-like adult leaves are found together on mature specimens. Female plants bear tiny, purplish brown, rounded berries. Many cultivars, in a wide variety of forms, foliage types and colours, are available. **'Aurea'**, with a tall, slender, conical habit to 9m/30ft,

has soft, bright yellow, lacy foliage and retains its colour well through winter. **'Blaauw'** is an upright shrub to 1.5m/5ft with diamond-shaped blue–grey leaves in feathery sprays; it is a popular bonsai subject. **'Blue Alps'** is a compact pyramidal shrub to 3.5m/12ft high with almost entirely very blue juvenile leaves with a silvery sheen. **'Expansa Aureospicata'** is a low-spreading plant to 50cm/20in high and 1.5m/5ft across. It has mostly dark grey–green juvenile foliage sprinkled with yellowish flecks and patches. **'Expansa Variegata'** is similar but with creamy white variegations. **'Kaizuka'** is slow-growing, eventually reaching 5m/17ft or more, with irregular spiralling branches and almost wholly adult, bright green, scale-like foliage. It is very popular in California and is sometimes known as Hollywood Juniper. The New Zealand-raised **'Kuriwao Gold'** is a slow-growing rounded shrub to 2m/7ft in diameter with pendulous tips and golden-coloured foliage. **'Obelisk'** is a slender upright shrub to 2.5m/8ft with dense, bluish, needle-like juvenile

foliage. **'Pyramidalis'** has a formal conical habit, reaching 3m/10ft at maturity and broadly spreading at the base. It has bluish needle-like foliage. **'San Jose'** is a prostrate shrub with a spread to 2m/7ft and mostly juvenile grey–green foliage. **'Spartan'** is a narrow conical tree eventually reaching 3.5m/12ft or more, with rich dark green foliage, turning slightly bronze in winter. **'Variegata'** is an erect conical bush to 3m/10ft with glaucous green foliage with creamy white variegations.
USE & CULTIVATION This ornamental species and its numerous cultivars are excellent specimen plants. Extremely effective for winter gardens, either singly or used as hedges and screens and gently clipped to shape or to restrict size. Smaller varieties are suitable for rock gardens, ornamental containers or in formal or modern courtyards. The prostrate 'San Jose' is used to soften the edges of hard landscaping or as a richly textured ground cover. Grow in any reasonable well-drained soil in full sun or light shade. Fully frost hardy.

Juniperus chinensis 'Blaauw'

Juniperus communis
Common Juniper

ORIGIN North America, northern
Europe, western Asia
CLIMATE WT, M, CT, H

This very widespread and valuable
species is most often seen as a sprawling
shrub, but sometimes attains tree-like
form to a height of 6m/20ft or more.
The leaves are all needle-like, in whorls
of 3 at a stem joint, deep green to
blue–green with a single white band
on the upper surface and mildly
aromatic when crushed. The green
male and female berry-like cones,
borne mostly on separate plants and
ripening to glossy black over 2–3 years,
are used to flavour gin. The species is
rarely cultivated as an ornamental, but
many fine cultivars are widely available.
'Compressa' is a popular, slow-
growing, spire-like dwarf form to
80cm/32in tall and 45cm/18in wide
with crowded grey–green leaves; ideal
for containers, rockery gardens and
courtyards. **'Depressa Aurea'** is a low
arching shrub with semi-erect branches,
to 60cm/24in high and 1.8m/6ft wide,
with golden yellow leaves in spring and
summer becoming coppery in cold
weather; a good colour contrast for
highlighting small spaces. **'Gold
Cone'**, to 2m/7ft tall, forms an erect
column of bright golden yellow foliage
in spring, becoming bronze in autumn
and winter; very hardy and good
colour contrast. **'Hibernica'** forms a
neat column of slender erect branches,
to 3m/10ft tall and 90cm/36in wide,
with deep blue–green foliage with a
touch of gold on young growth; use as
a formal erect pillar. **'Hornibrookii'** is
a broad, almost prostrate plant to 1.5m/
5ft across and only about 30cm/12in
high with short, mid-green, prickly
foliage; a popular rockery specimen.
'Repanda' is a ground-hugging prostrate shrub to 40cm/16in tall and 2m/
7ft across with dark green, densely
packed leaves changing to bronze green
in autumn. One of the best juniper
groundcovers, it is an excellent choice
for edging woodland gardens or spilling

over rocks. **'Suecica'** has an upright
columnar habit to 5m/17ft, and bluish
green foliage with slightly drooping
tips, making it a popular accent plant.
USE & CULTIVATION The above cultivars are considerably varied in their
growth habit and size. As there is no
generalisation for their landscape use,
suitable applications have been included
with their description. Grow in any
reasonable well-drained soil in full sun
or light shade. Fully frost hardy.

Juniperus conferta
Shore Juniper

ORIGIN Japan, Russia
CLIMATE WT, M, CT, H

This prostrate mat-forming shrub
grows to a height of 30cm/12in and a
spread of 2.5m/8ft or more. It has dense
thick branches and crowded, pale waxy
green, needle-like leaves tapering to a
soft point. The fruit, about 1cm/⅓in
wide, eventually ripens black with a

Juniperus horizontalis

waxy white bloom. **'Blue Pacific'** is a trailing variety with blue–green foliage. **'Emerald Sea'** has bright green foliage that lightens in winter.

USE & CULTIVATION It grows naturally on sandy seashores and is a first-rate groundcover for coastal planting in cooler regions, especially useful for rapidly covering and binding embankments and spilling over rocks and walls. Grow in any reasonable well-drained soil and position in full sun or light shade. The cultivars are also salt tolerant. Fully frost hardy.

Juniperus horizontalis
Creeping Juniper

ORIGIN North America
CLIMATE WT, M, CT, H

A prostrate bushy shrub with long trailing stems forming a dense mat-like habit to 50cm/20in tall and 2–3m/7–10ft across. The bluish green or grey leaves are both the prickly juvenile type and the scale-like adult form, generally to the outside of the plant. When ripe in the second year, the berry is dark blue with a whitish bloom. **'Bar Harbor'** has slender stems lying close to the ground and glaucous grey–green foliage turning mauve in early winter. **'Blue Chip'** has short branches growing slightly upwards and silvery blue foliage intensifying to rich blue in winter. **'Douglasii'** has steel blue foliage, becoming plum coloured in winter. **'Emerald Spreader'** forms a low dense mat of feathery, bright green foliage. **'Glauca'** is mat forming, with steely blue foliage. **'Grey Pearl'** is small and compact, with grey foliage. **'Hughes'** is fast growing, with distinctive silvery blue foliage. **'Plumosa'** is low and wide-spreading, with the main branches staying on the ground, others ascending, with blue–grey foliage becoming rich purple in winter. **'Wiltonii'** is carpet forming, with low stems radiating from the centre densely clothed with pale grey–blue, mostly needle-like foliage, often tinted purple in winter.

Juniperus x *pfitzeriana* 'Pfitzeriana'

USE & CULTIVATION All these are beautiful, functional and tough ground-covering plants that can be used to clothe rocks, banks and low walls. Recommended for coastal gardens. Full sun is best, but they will tolerate light shade, especially in hot areas. Grow in any well-drained soil and apply mulch to control weeds. Fully frost hardy.

Juniperus x pfitzeriana
syn. Juniperus x media

ORIGIN Gardens
CLIMATE WT, M, CT, H

This hybrid group is derived mainly from *J. chinensis* and *J. sabina*. They are flat-topped shrubs to 1.2m/4ft tall with spreading tiered branches to 2m/7ft across and drooping tips. The dull green, scale-like adult leaves give off the strong characteristic odour of *J. sabina* when crushed. The berries are pale to dark blue. **'Armstrongii'** forms a dense compact fountain to 1m/3ft tall and wide, with soft, light green, lacy foliage. **'Aurea'** is a spreading shrub to 90cm/36in tall with bold arching branches and rich golden pendulous tips in summer, becoming yellowish green in winter. **'Glauca'** has prickly, silvery blue foliage. **'Pfitzeriana'** has wide-spreading tiered branches drooping slightly at the tips. The scale-like leaves are mostly grey–green.

USE & CULTIVATION Excellent feature plants which can be grown in bold groups and used as large-scale ground-covers quite impenetrable to weeds. Also suitable for small gardens, thriving in full sun or shade. Except for trimming the odd wayward shoot, leave unpruned to develop their graceful weeping form. Fully frost hardy.

J

Juniperus procumbens
Creeping Juniper, Bonin Island
Juniper, Japanese Garden Juniper

ORIGIN Japan

CLIMATE ST, WT, M, CT

A low-spreading shrub to 75cm/30in tall with long stiff branches to 2m/7ft across. The growing tips are raised upwards and tightly packed with tufts of bluish green, needle-like foliage. The main branches are sometimes self-layering. Small mature berries are brown or black. **'Nana'** is smaller and forms a compact cushion of apple green foliage, maturing to blue–green. It is sometimes used for bonsai.

USE & CULTIVATION Naturally occurring in exposed coastal areas, this tough plant is especially suited to seaside gardens, thriving in almost any well-drained soil in full sun. Often used in rock gardens or to cover embankments to prevent soil erosion. Fully frost hardy.

Juniperus sabina
Savin

ORIGIN Europe to China

CLIMATE WT, M, CT, H

A wide-spreading shrub eventually reaching 2.5m/8ft or more high and 6m/20ft across. It has scaly, reddish brown bark and slender arching branches with a dense covering of mainly adult dark green to grey–green foliage with a distinctive, unpleasant smell when crushed. The berries are waxy blue–black, generally ripening in the first year. **'Blaue Donau'** (syn. 'Blue Danube'), a popular low-spreading form to 60cm/24in tall and 1.5m/5ft wide, has upturned branch-tips and mostly scale-like, soft greyish blue foliage. **J. s. var. *tamariscifolia*,** from mountainous regions of southern Europe, often called Spanish Juniper, has tiered branches of mostly juvenile dark green foliage and grows to about 2m/7ft tall and wide.

USE & CULTIVATION Handsome and long-lived sculptural groundcovers, useful for clothing a sloping bank or rocky outcrop. They thrive in limestone soil, but will grow in any well-drained soil in an open sunny position. Fully frost hardy.

Juniperus scopulorum
syn. *Juniperus virginiana*
var. *scopulorum*
Rocky Mountain Juniper

ORIGIN North America
(Rocky Mountains)

CLIMATE WT, M, CT, H

A small tree with a rounded crown to 15m/50ft tall, with strongly aromatic, mostly scale-like grey–green to dark green leaves and dark reddish brown bark. The berries ripen in the second year to a waxy dark blue. **'Blue Heaven'**, a slender conical form to 5m/17ft tall, has exceptionally blue foliage. **'Grey Gleam'** is slow growing, forming a neat narrow column to 2m/7ft, with silvery grey foliage becoming more silvery in winter. **'Sky Rocket'** is an extremely slender columnar tree reaching 6m/20ft, with blue–green foliage.

USE & CULTIVATION The species is rarely seen in cultivation, but the coloured-foliage forms are popular as vertical accent plants to create focal points and for formal landscaping effects. They withstand very cold conditions, thriving in dry, freely draining soil in full sun or partial shade. Fully frost hardy.

Juniperus squamata
Himalayan Juniper

ORIGIN Himalayas to western China

CLIMATE WT, M, CT, H

This variable and widely distributed species ranges from a prostrate or

Juniperus sabina

Juniperus squamata

Juniperus squamata 'Blue Carpet'

fleshy berry-like fruit is glossy black. Several cultivars are widely available. **'Blue Carpet'** is a relatively flat, prostrate form to 1m/3ft across with dense bluish foliage. **'Blue Star'** forms a dense rounded cushion to 45cm/18in tall and 1m/3ft wide with silvery blue foliage. **'Holger'** is a slow-growing, spiky bush with wide-spreading branches to 2m/7ft in diameter. Its golden yellow young tips gradually mature to steely blue. **'Meyeri'** is an informal spreading bush with pendulous outer branches, reaching a height and spread of 4.5m/15ft. The long pointed leaves are steely blue with a rich silver sheen.

USE & CULTIVATION 'Holger' and 'Meyeri' are charming small lawn specimens, especially if lightly pruned to shape and encourage the development of young leafy shoots. 'Blue Carpet' and 'Blue Star' make excellent groundcover or rockery subjects providing all-year interest. Grow in well-drained soil in full sun. Fully frost hardy.

Juniperus virginiana
Eastern Red Cedar, Pencil Cedar

ORIGIN North America
CLIMATE WT, M, CT, H
A conical or broadly bushy tree reaching 15–18m/50–60ft in cultivation, with spreading branches and reddish brown bark shredding in shaggy strips. The sharply pointed juvenile leaves and scale-like adult leaves are grey–green; both types may occur on the same plant. The pale, waxy, purplish brown berries ripen in the first year. The aromatic timber is used in making lead pencils. **'Hetzii'** is a medium-sized shrub, 3.5–5m/12–17ft tall, with layers of horizontal branches densely covered with mostly scale-like, pale waxy blue foliage. **'Sulphur Spray'** is a yellowish variant of 'Hetzii'.

USE & CULTIVATION The largest of the junipers; a popular ornamental tree for shade, shelter or as a large hedge. The shrub-like forms make attractive informal specimens. They thrive under a wide range of conditions and do well in limestone soil. Fully frost hardy.

upright and spreading shrub to occasionally a small tree of irregular form reaching 5m/17ft or more. The juvenile needle-like leaves are dark green or blue–grey and densely packed on crowded branches. The older brown leaves often persist on the reddish brown, slightly drooping branchlets. The

KALANCHOE

FAMILY CRASSULACEAE

A large proportion of this genus of perennial succulents and small shrubs hails from Africa and Madagascar. There are about 130 species, varying in size and form, but all have very fleshy cylindrical, oval or linear leaves. Some are grown for their decorative foliage; those grown for their clusters of long-lasting flowers are usually bought in bloom and discarded after flowering. The foliage types can be kept for years and thrive outside in frost-free areas; in colder areas they are ideal container plants for sheltered patios and indoors. Propagate from seed, offsets or stem cuttings.

Kalanchoe beharensis
syn. *Kalanchoe vantieghemi*
Velvet Elephant Ear

ORIGIN Madagascar
CLIMATE ST, WT

One of the most striking foliage species, this slow-growing shrub can reach more than 1m/3ft in the garden. It has olive green, triangular to spade-shaped, slightly toothed leaves to 30cm/12in long covered with fine rusty brown hairs. Insignificant, bell-shaped cream flowers appear in late winter.

USE & CULTIVATION Ideal for a rockery, succulent or desert garden in warm climates. Grow in full sun or partial shade in well-drained soil. For containers, use soil-based potting mix with added coarse sand or grit. Bright indirect light is best indoors. Allow soil to dry out between waterings. Frost tender.

Kalanchoe thyrsiflora

  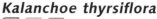

ORIGIN South Africa
CLIMATE ST, WT

This attractive species will form clumps to 60cm/24in tall and wide, although often shorter and prostrate, the stems branching from the base. The oval to rounded pale green leaves to 15cm/6in

Kalanchoe thyrsiflora

Kalanchoe beharensis

Kalanchoe thyrsiflora 'Flapjacks'

Kalanchoe tomentosa

Lamium galeobdolon

long are covered with a white bloom and often have reddish margins, particularly in late summer. Yellow urn-shaped flowers appear in spring. **'Flapjacks'** has rounded leaves tipped with bronze.

USE & CULTIVATION As for *K. beharensis*. Frost tender.

Kalanchoe tomentosa
Panda Plant, Pussy Ears

ORIGIN Madagascar
CLIMATE ST, WT
This handsome succulent has loose rosettes of densely felted, spoon-shaped leaves borne on woody stems eventually reaching 1m/3ft high with a spread of 20cm/8in. The 9cm/3½in long leaves have brownish spots along the margins. The flowers, yellow with purplish tips, are not often produced in cultivation.

USE & CULTIVATION As for *K. beharensis*. Frost tender.

LAMIUM

DEADNETTLE
FAMILY LABIATAE/LAMIACEAE
This genus of about 40 species of annuals and rhizomatous perennials is native to Europe, Asia and northern Africa. They are tufted to mat-forming, often spreading widely by surface runners, and have attractive, coarsely toothed, wrinkled leaves arranged in opposite pairs and sometimes splashed with silver markings. Some species make useful groundcovers, especially for shady places. The flowers are 2-lipped, the upper lip hooded, and are borne in short spikes from late spring to summer. Propagate from seed or by division.

Lamium galeobdolon
syns *Galeobdolon luteum, Lamiastrum galeobdolon*
Yellow Archangel

ORIGIN Europe to western Asia
CLIMATE WT, M, CT, H
This vigorous carpeting perennial grows 30–60cm/12–24in tall with an indefinite spread. It has ovate mid-green leaves to 8cm/3in long, coarsely toothed and often marked with silver. Short spikes of lemon yellow flowers are borne on erect stems in summer. The mat-forming **'Hermann's Pride'** has silver leaves netted with dark green veining. **'Silver Carpet'** is more heavily splashed with silver markings.

USE & CULTIVATION A useful and fast-growing groundcover. The species is apt to take over the garden, but the cultivars are much less invasive. Grow in any moist well-drained soil in partial or deep shade. Fully frost hardy.

Lamium maculatum
Spotted Deadnettle

ORIGIN Europe, northern Africa and western Asia

CLIMATE WT, M, CT, H

This semi-evergreen, mat-forming perennial quickly forms carpets to 1m/3ft across. The ovate, often heart-shaped leaves to 8cm/3in long are coarsely toothed with central silvery stripes. Whorled spikes of mauve–pink flowers appear in spring and summer. **'Aureum'** (syn. 'Gold Leaf') is less vigorous than the species and has bright greenish yellow leaves with silvery centres, and pink flowers. **'Beacon Silver'** has silvery green leaves edged dark green, and purplish flowers. **'White Nancy'** has silvery green leaves with narrow dark green margins, and white flowers.

USE & CULTIVATION Pretty variegated groundcovers to lighten a shaded border beneath trees. Can be used as a lawn replacement in areas of light traffic, at the woodland edge or as a rockery creeper. Grow in moist well-drained soil. Frost hardy.

Lamium maculatum

Lamium maculatum 'Beacon Silver'

LARIX

LARCH
FAMILY PINACEAE

This genus of 10 to 12 species of fast-growing deciduous conifers is native to the mountains and cooler parts of the Northern Hemisphere. They are grown for their graceful habit and foliage as well as for their strong durable timber. The soft, somewhat needle-like leaves are bright green in spring and colour to deep golden yellow in autumn before being shed. Propagate from seed.

Larix decidua

Larix decidua
European Larch

ORIGIN European Alps, Carpathian Mountains (central/eastern Europe)

CLIMATE M, CT, H

This is a slender, upright, conical tree when young, broadening as it ages, with widely spaced, horizontal branches gracefully drooping at the ends, and reaching 20–30m/70–100ft. It has greyish bark that develops an interesting pattern of cracks and ridges. The bright green, slightly flattened, needle-like

Laurus nobilis

Laurus nobilis

leaves are soft to the touch and turn bright yellow in autumn before falling. Young cones appear just before the leaves and persist after the seeds have been shed. The dwarf **'Corley'**, with a height and spread of less than 1m/3ft, can make an excellent tub specimen.

USE & CULTIVATION Both this and the following species make outstanding specimen trees for large gardens. Suited only to cool or cold areas, they thrive in full sun in rich, slightly acid, well-drained soil with plenty of moisture. Fully frost hardy.

Larix kaempferi
syn. *Larix leptolepis*
Japanese Larch

ORIGIN Japan
CLIMATE M, CT, H
This is a tall deciduous tree with a broadly conical crown to 30m/100ft. It is similar to *L. decidua* but has reddish orange new twigs that darken to almost purple by winter. The summer foliage has a distinct blue–green colouring, changing in autumn to yellowish

orange before falling. Mature female cones to 3cm/1¼in long have soft brown scales which curl back at the tips. This is an important timber tree in much of northern Europe, including the UK.

USE & CULTIVATION As for *L. decidua*. It grows more strongly and quickly than *L. decidua* and is widely used for ornamental landscaping, responds well to creative pruning and shaping, and is highly recommended for bonsai. Fully frost hardy.

LAURUS

FAMILY LAURACEAE
A genus of 2 species of evergreen trees occurring in the Mediterranean region and from the Canary Islands to the Azores. The Bay Laurel (*Laurus nobilis*) is commonly grown as a clipped foliage plant and as a pot herb for flavouring food. For many centuries its fruits and leaves have been highly valued for their medicinal properties. Propagate from seed or from cuttings in late summer.

Laurus nobilis
Bay Laurel, Sweet Bay

ORIGIN Mediterranean region
CLIMATE ST, WT, M, CT
This is a compact shrub or small tree to 12m/40ft tall with highly aromatic, glossy dark green, pointed leaves to 10cm/4in long. These are the culinary bay leaves used in the traditional *bouquet garni*. Small, star-shaped, greenish yellow flowers appear in late spring to early summer, followed by small green berries that ripen to black. **'Aurea'** is a yellow-leaved form.

USE & CULTIVATION Use as a formal specimen or screen or in a woodland garden, in a sheltered position in sun or semi-shade, in fertile well-drained soil. Often used in tubs for topiary, and trimmed during summer. In cold frosty areas the container is moved into a cool greenhouse during winter and early spring. It is tolerant of coastal conditions if protected from wind. 'Aurea' is a slightly hardier variety but is best shaded from midday sun. Moderately frost hardy.

Lepidozamia peroffskyana

LEPIDOZAMIA

FAMILY ZAMIACEAE

This genus comprises 2 species of cycads found in the moist coastal forests of eastern Australia. They are very slow-growing, palm-like plants, eventually forming a stout erect trunk with a spreading crown of shiny green pinnate fronds. The markedly different male and female cones are borne on short stalks in the centre of the crown on separate plants. They can be grown in containers for many years, and because of their tolerance of air-conditioning, they perform well indoors. Cut leaves are also used for large-scale floral arrangements. Propagate from seed, which can be slow to germinate.

Lepidozamia hopei

ORIGIN Eastern Australia
CLIMATE T, ST

This is one of the tallest cycad species in the world, known to reach 20m/70ft in its rainforest habitat. In gardens it may eventually grow to 3m/10ft, but is usually shorter. It has a widely spreading crown of large, dark green, glossy pinnate leaves 2–3m/7–10ft long, each consisting of many arching and curved strap-shaped leaflets. The slender, strongly curved male cones are up to 80cm/32in long. The massive, broadly ovoid female cones, about 80cm/32in long and 30cm/12in wide, contain numerous bright red seeds when mature. The seeds were collected and eaten by indigenous Australian peoples. Like *Macrozamia* seeds, they required lengthy preparation to remove toxins.

USE & CULTIVATION A highly attractive, long-term plant for a prominent position in the garden. Grow in a partially shady, moist position in well-drained soil. In full sun the leaves tend to bleach and fade. Fertilise annually with a balanced slow-release fertiliser, mulch and keep well watered, especially during dry summers. An excellent container plant for many outdoor uses; in frost-prone climates, suited to a conservatory or a well-lit position indoors. Frost tender.

Lepidozamia peroffskyana
Pineapple Zamia

ORIGIN Australia
CLIMATE T, ST, WT

A beautiful palm-like tree with glossy pinnate leaves radiating from a woody trunk. In the wild it may grow to 7m/22ft, but in gardens 1–2m/3–7ft is more usual, as it grows very slowly. It has dark green leaves 2–3m/7–10ft long with many curved, leathery, linear leaflets about 12mm/½in wide. The narrow male cones are twisted at maturity, to 60cm/24in long. The broad grey–green female cones, to 80cm/32in long and 30cm/12in wide, contain bright red oblong seeds when mature .

USE & CULTIVATION As for *L. hopei*. It can also be grown outdoors in warm temperate regions. Marginally frost hardy.

LEUCOPHYTA

FAMILY ASTERACEAE/COMPOSITAE

Leucophyta means 'white plant'; this genus has only one species, the horticulturally well-known *Leucophyta brownii*, which is grown for its attractive silvery white foliage and compact growth. Previously included in the genus *Calocephalus*, it is endemic in southern

Australia, where it grows on exposed coastal headlands and dunes, being highly resistant to wind and ocean spray. Propagate from seed or cuttings.

Leucophyta brownii
syn. *Calocephalus brownii*
Cushion Bush

ORIGIN Southern Australia
CLIMATE ST, WT, M

An attractive, compact shrub to around 1m/3ft in diameter, with intricate silvery grey stems and tiny grey scale-like leaves pressed tightly against them. The whole bush has a lovely silvery sheen, and in spring and summer is topped with tiny pale yellow flowerheads.

USE & CULTIVATION This charming silvery shrub makes a good foliage contrast against a background of taller dark green shrubs and is perfect for a rockery, particularly in seaside gardens. Tolerates an occasional light frost and in cold frosty climates is used as a short-term bedding plant. Grow in an open sunny position with good drainage. Pinch out growing tips and clip regularly to promote bushiness. Marginally frost hardy.

LEVISTICUM

LOVAGE
FAMILY UMBELLIFERAE

The single species in this genus is a tall herbaceous perennial from the eastern Mediterranean region. Looking like a large celery and tasting like celery with just a dash of spice, it was used as a flavouring and medicinal herb in classical times and continued to be grown in mediaeval kitchen gardens. The leaves are one of the oldest salad greens known. Propagate from fresh ripe seed or by division.

Levisticum officinale
Lovage

ORIGIN Eastern Mediterranean
CLIMATE WT, M, CT, H

This strong-growing perennial to 2m/7ft tall, forming a large clump of thick hollow stems, has deeply divided dark green leaves to 70cm/28in long. Small yellowish summer flowers are borne in umbels and followed by brown seeds which ripen in late summer or early autumn.

USE & CULTIVATION A highly decorative feature or background plant for a herb or edible garden. Grow in moist, fairly rich soil in sun or partial shade. Protect from strong winds. Fully frost hardy.

Leucophyta brownii

Levisticum officinale (centre)

LICUALA

FAMILY ARECACEAE/PALMAE

Occurring in tropical regions over a wide area, from China and Southeast Asia to the Pacific region and northern Australia, this large genus of fan-leaved palms consists of around 100 species, which may be single stemmed or clump forming. They are grown for their striking foliage, which may be almost circular and entire or variously divided by splits into wedge-shaped segments. Slender flowering spikes are produced among the leaves. Propagate from fresh seed.

Licuala grandis
Vanuatu Fan Palm, Palas Payung

ORIGIN Vanuatu, Solomon Islands
CLIMATE T, ST

This small palm has a slender erect trunk to 3m/10ft tall and large, circular, undivided, pleated leaves to 1m/3ft across with notched margins. They are borne on long erect stalks that become pendulous with age. Tiny yellowish flowers are produced on a slender hanging panicle, followed by showy clusters of glossy red fruit.

USE & CULTIVATION A highly attractive palm best suited to tropical regions and giving a dramatic focal point and distinctive shape to the landscape. Provide rich, moist well-drained soil, shaded conditions and protection from strong winds. Generally slow growing, it makes an excellent container specimen for a warm greenhouse or conservatory with high humidity. Frost tender.

Licuala ramsayi

ORIGIN Northern Australia
CLIMATE T, ST, WT

A slow-growing palm to 15m/50ft with a solitary erect trunk and a crown of bright green circular leaves to 2m/7ft across, split into wedge-shaped segments. Small creamy white flowers produced in pendulous panicles to 2m/7ft long are followed by clusters of orange–red fruit.

USE & CULTIVATION It has similar requirements to *L. grandis*, but can also be used in frost-free, warm temperate regions if given a partially shaded, sheltered position and protection from strong winds. Can be grown indoors without heating if the temperature does not drop below freezing point. Frost tender.

LIGULARIA

FAMILY ASTERACEAE/COMPOSITAE

This temperate Asian and European genus consists of about 125 species of large-leaved, clump-forming perennials grown for their foliage and large daisy-like flowerheads. They grow naturally along stream banks and in other moist situations, and are among the best of all plants for boggy soil beside ponds. Protect young growth from slugs and snails. Propagate from seed or by division.

Ligularia dentata
syns *Ligularia clivorum*, *Senecio clivorum*

ORIGIN China, Japan
CLIMATE WT, M, CT, H

This perennial forms substantial clumps to 1m/3ft high and wide of kidney-shaped to rounded, long-stalked, leathery leaves to 30cm/12in long. Orange–yellow, daisy-like flowers to 8cm/3in across are borne on long branching stems in summer and early autumn. 'Desdemona' has handsome, dark greenish bronze leaves with intensely purplish red undersides and stems.

USE & CULTIVATION Suitable for a damp herbaceous border, waterside or woodland edge. These dramatic plants are best where the soil is rich and moist. They benefit from a little shade to prevent scorching. Fully frost hardy.

Ligularia hodgsonii

ORIGIN Japan
CLIMATE WT, M, CT, H

This perennial forms large clumps to 90cm/36in high of broad heart-shaped leaves to 12cm/5in across with toothed margins, borne on long leaf stalks. In summer it bears clusters of yellow–orange, daisy-like flowers.

USE & CULTIVATION As for *L. dentata*. Fully frost hardy.

Licuala grandis

Ligularia dentata

Ligularia hodgsonii

Linospadix monostachya

Ligularia x palmatiloba

rainforest. They are grown for their attractive foliage, small elegant stature and shade tolerance, making them popular for both garden and conservatory. The long showy strands of orange, pink or scarlet berries are a further decorative feature. Propagate from fresh seed and by division of suckers.

Linospadix monostachya
Walking Stick Palm

ORIGIN Eastern Australia
CLIMATE ST, WT, M

This small palm to 3m/10ft tall has a very slender, strongly ringed trunk and a loose spreading crown of dark green fronds about 1.2m/4ft long. The leaves are divided into broad and narrow leaflets with jagged tips. Small, greenish yellow, closely packed flowers are borne in long hanging spikes to 1m/3ft long, followed by bright red edible berries in late summer. The slender stems were once used for making walking sticks.
USE & CULTIVATION An excellent palm for small sheltered gardens, where it will grow in quite heavy shade. Grow in moist well-drained soil rich in organic matter. It will live in a container indefinitely and is perfect for indoor use. Apply small quantities of liquid fertiliser regularly to indoor plants. Marginally frost hardy.

Ligularia x palmatiloba

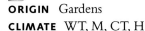

ORIGIN Gardens
CLIMATE WT, M, CT, H

This hybrid between *L. dentata* and *L. japonica* grows to 1.2m/4ft tall. The handsome broad leaves are deeply lobed with toothed margins, and held on long stalks. Yellow daisy-like flowers are borne on long branching stems in summer.

USE & CULTIVATION As for *L. dentata*. Fully frost hardy.

LINOSPADIX

FAMILY ARECACEAE/PALMAE

There are about 11 species in this genus of small slender palms native to Australia and New Guinea, where they grow naturally as understorey plants in

LIQUIDAMBAR

FAMILY HAMAMELIDACEAE

This genus comprises 4 species of deciduous trees belonging to the witch-hazel family and grown for their handsome maple-like foliage and brilliant autumn colour. Some species yield a fragrant resinous gum used in medicine and perfumery. Keep grass away from young plants if grown as lawn specimens. Prune only to shape, leaving the lower branches if possible. Propagate from seed or cuttings in summer.

Liquidambar orientalis
Oriental Sweet Gum

ORIGIN Southwestern Asia
CLIMATE WT, M, CT, H

This slow-growing, deciduous, bushy tree reaches a height of about 8m/25ft with a spread of 3.5m/12ft. The palmately lobed, mid-green leaves to 12cm/5in across turn orange in autumn. The soft inner bark is the main source of liquid storax, used in medicine and perfumery.

USE & CULTIVATION A charming lawn specimen, giving its best displays of autumn colour in cool climates. It thrives in warm conditions provided plenty of moisture is available in summer. Grow in fertile, neutral or slightly acid soil in full sun or partial shade. Frost hardy.

Liquidambar styraciflua
Sweet Gum

ORIGIN Eastern USA, Mexico
CLIMATE WT, M, CT, H

This widely grown ornamental species forms a stately, broadly conical tree to 24m/80ft tall with well-spaced branches and handsome maple-like leaves with 5–7 lobes, to 15cm/6in across. The leaves turn rich shades of orange, red and purple in autumn. The corky bark is more noticeable in winter. Small green flowers borne in late spring are followed by clusters of soft, spiky, rounded fruit. **'Burgundy'** has deep purple–red autumn foliage that remains until early winter. **'Golden Treasure'** has green and gold variegated leaves that turn to shades of burgundy, orange and pink in autumn. **'Lane Roberts'** has deep reddish purple leaves in autumn. **'Worplesdon'** takes on autumn shades of orange, apricot and purple.

USE & CULTIVATION One of the showiest deciduous trees for autumn colour, making a picturesque lawn specimen or woodland plant. Grow in deeply worked, neutral or slightly acid, well-drained soil in full sun or partial shade. Provide plenty of moisture during spring and summer and mulch during dry spells. Fully frost hardy.

Liquidamber orientalis

Liquidambar styraciflua

LIRIODENDRON

FAMILY MAGNOLIACEAE
This is a genus of 2 species of deciduous trees from China and North America, one of them commonly grown for its attractive satiny leaves, which turn bright yellow in autumn. Propagate from seed.

Liriodendron tulipifera
Tulip Tree

ORIGIN Eastern USA
CLIMATE WT, M, CT, H
A deciduous tree usually reaching 9–20m/30–70ft in gardens. It has a broad conical habit to 6m/20ft wide when mature. The 4-lobed leaves to 15cm/6in long appear to be cut off squarely at their tips. They turn yellow in autumn. Cup-shaped pale green flowers have an orange base to the petals and are very fragrant. They appear in summer, but only on mature trees. **'Aureomarginatum'** has yellow-edged leaves.

USE & CULTIVATION An excellent shade and specimen tree for large gardens in cool climates. Grow in full sun in moist, slightly acid, well-drained soil with ample summer moisture. Fully frost hardy.

LIVISTONA

FAMILY ARECACEAE/PALMAE
A genus of about 30 species of fan palms widely distributed from northern Africa to Arabia, southern Asia and Australia. Most species grow in colonies and have a thick solitary trunk and wide-spreading crown of large fan-shaped leaves on long, spiny leaf stalks. The cream or yellow flowers are produced on a large branched panicle from among the leaves and followed by glossy globular fruit. They make stately ornamental plants for the garden or decorative container specimens. Some are used as street trees. They respond to the use of slow-release fertilisers. Propagate from seed.

Livistona australis

Livistona australis
Australian Fan Palm,
Cabbage-tree Palm

ORIGIN Eastern Australia
CLIMATE T, ST, WT, M
A tall palm which may eventually reach 24m/80ft, but usually much less in cultivation. It has a dense crown of fan-shaped leaves to 2m/7ft long, deeply divided into many glossy green segments, often arching at the tips. Long sprays of creamy yellow flowers appear in early spring, followed by red to black fruit.

USE & CULTIVATION This attractive palm looks good as a single specimen or in groves in large gardens. It is excellent for avenue and driveway plantings. Grow in a moist well-drained position with some protection from strong sun and wind. Light frosts are generally tolerated. It may be grown as a tub specimen for many years and used indoors when young. Grow in a well-lit position and keep the potting mix just moist during the active growing period. Marginally frost hardy.

Livistona chinensis

Livistona decipiens

Livistona saribus

Livistona chinensis
Chinese Fan Palm

ORIGIN Japan, Taiwan
CLIMATE ST, WT, M
This slow-growing fan palm, 3.5–8m/
12–25ft tall, has a stout rough-textured
trunk and fan-shaped glossy bright
green leaves, 2m/7ft across, deeply
divided into long narrow segments
with pendulous tips. The elongated

blue–green fruits hang in dense clusters
in autumn.
USE & CULTIVATION As a specimen or
in a group as part of a tropical planting.
It withstands light frosts and can be
grown in sheltered temperate gardens.
Grow in a moist well-drained position
with some protection from strong sun
and wind. Young plants make decorative
container subjects and can be grown
indoors in a brightly lit room. Keep the

potting mix just moist during the active
growing period. Moderately frost hardy.

Livistona decipiens
Ribbon Fan Palm,
Weeping Cabbage Palm

ORIGIN Northeastern Australia
CLIMATE T, ST, WT
A stately palm to around 9m/30ft tall.
Its yellowish green, circular, fan-shaped

leaves to 2m/7ft in diameter, with long trailing ends, create a soft weeping crown in mature specimens. Large clusters of small bright yellow flowers form an attractive spray within the crown in spring and are followed by glossy black fruit.

USE & CULTIVATION As for *L. australis*. Marginally frost hardy.

Livistona saribus
syn. *Livistona cochinchinensis*

ORIGIN Southeast Asia
CLIMATE T, ST

A medium-sized to large palm, 25m/80ft tall. It has a slim rough-textured trunk and spiny leaf stalks supporting rounded, deeply segmented, rich green leaves. Creamy yellow flowers borne in clusters are followed by masses of showy blue fruit.

USE & CULTIVATION An ideal palm for group planting in tropical climates. For best appearance it needs protection from direct sun when small. Grow in moist well-drained soil and water regularly in dry periods. Frost tender.

Lobelia aberdarica

LOBELIA

FAMILY CAMPANULACEAE/ LOBELIACEAE

This is a large and variable genus of about 300 species of annuals, perennials and shrubs grown mostly as bedding plants for their brightly coloured flowers. Most species come from the Americas, but there are a few spectacular foliage plants that occur high in the mountains of Africa. A small number of these species have found their way into specialist nurseries. Propagate from seed or by division.

Lobelia aberdarica

ORIGIN Mountain areas of Kenya, Uganda
CLIMATE M, CT

This tree-like species forms large rosettes of deep green, oblong leaves with a prominent pale creamy white midrib on unbranched stems to 2.5m/8ft high.

Small blue or white flowers are carried on tall flower spikes to about 1.8m/6ft.

USE & CULTIVATION This beautiful foliage plant inhabits wet places in mountainous regions and makes an excellent feature plant for a large rockery. It does best in moist well-drained soil in full sun. Frost hardy.

Lobelia gibberoa

ORIGIN Mountains of eastern Africa
CLIMATE M, CT

This huge lobelia forms large rosettes at the top of tall slender stems that lengthen with age. The mid-green sword-shaped leaves with toothed edges have a pink midrib and a pinkish underside when young. In flower it can reach 9m/30ft.

USE & CULTIVATION A spectacular plant that needs plenty of room to be seen at its best. It does best in a mild climate with a fairly high rainfall. Grow in full sun with good drainage. Frost hardy.

Lobelia gibberoa

LOMANDRA

FAMILY LOMANDRACEAE

There are over 50 species of these decorative grass-like plants, all found in Australia, two of them extending to New Guinea and one to New Caledonia. They have slender reed-like leaves and carry creamy yellow male and female flowers on separate plants. Only a few species are in cultivation but they are tough, easily grown plants for warm climates, where they are often used massed in commercial sites and street landscaping. The flowers and fruiting stems of some species provide material for floral art, particularly dried arrangements. Propagate from seed or by division.

Lomandra hystrix

ORIGIN Eastern Australia
CLIMATE ST, WT, M
Growing over 1.2m/4ft tall and 1m/3ft wide, this species makes a dense tussock of arching, thin-textured, narrow leaves to 1.2m/4ft long and 1cm/^{1}/$_3$in wide. The creamy yellow flowers are produced in cylindrical spikes among the foliage in spring and summer.
USE & CULTIVATION An attractive, tufting species for mass planting as a tall border or for a rockery. It is a good frog-friendly plant for edging water-gardens. Well-drained soil in a sunny or semi-shaded position is best. It can also be grown in containers and makes a good foliage fountain in a tall urn. Marginally frost hardy.

Lomandra longifolia
Spiny-headed Mat Rush

ORIGIN Eastern Australia
CLIMATE ST, WT, M
This perennial forms a large dense tussock to 1m/3ft high of narrow strap-like leaves to 1m/3ft long, varying from yellowish green or blue–green to deep green. The often fragrant, creamy yellow flowers are produced in spring and summer on a dense flattened spike usually half the length of the leaves Spiny bracts to

Lomandra hystrix

2cm/^{3}/$_4$in long are present beneath the flowers.
USE & CULTIVATION A graceful foliage plant for accent near pools, in courtyards and rockeries. In Australia this species is often used in contemporary garden design and in public places for large-scale landscaping. It does well in most soils, including damp soils in full sun, but will also thrive in semi-shade beneath established trees. A good container plant. Marginally frost hardy.

LONICERA

HONEYSUCKLE

FAMILY CAPRIFOLIACEAE

This genus comprises about 180 species of deciduous and evergreen shrubs and woody-stemmed twining climbers. They are grown mostly for their ornamental, often highly scented flowers, with the shrubby Box Honeysuckle, *Lonicera nitida*, being grown for its small fine foliage and value as a low clipped hedge. Propagate from seed or from cuttings.

Lonicera nitida
Box Honeysuckle

ORIGIN China
CLIMATE WT, M, CT, H
A neat, evergreen, compact shrub to 3.5m/12ft high with short twiggy stems densely covered with dark green, glossy, oval leaves to 12mm/^{1}/$_2$in long.

Lomandra longifolia

In cold climates it bears small creamy white flowers followed by purplish blue berries. Flowers and fruit are non-existent when plants are clipped. **'Aurea'** has golden yellow leaves. The popular **'Baggesen's Gold'** has arching stems and tiny bright yellow leaves.

Lonicera nitida 'Aurea'

Lycopodium phlegmarioides

USE & CULTIVATION Often heavily clipped to produce a formal border, low hedge or tub plant. Left unclipped, they can be used informally for the same purposes. Provide good drainage in full sun or partial shade. Fully frost hardy.

LYCOPODIUM

CLUB MOSS
FAMILY LYCOPODIACEAE

There are more than 100 species in this large, widely distributed genus of ancient plants that resemble giant mosses. Most of those grown for their attractive foliage are in the group of epiphytic species known as tassel ferns. Some botanists segregate this group into the genus *Huperzia*. They form branched clumps of erect, pendent or creeping, cord-like stems, which are usually repeatedly forked, and clothed with overlapping, bright green, flat or scale-like leaves. In some species the ends of the stems branch into fine green tassels. Propagate from stem cuttings or by layering upper parts of the stems.

Lycopodium phlegmaria
Common Tassel Fern

ORIGIN Asia, Australia, Pacific islands
CLIMATE T, ST
This epiphyte forms large clumps to about 70cm/28in wide; the pendulous stems to 1m/3ft long are repeatedly forked and crowded with narrowly ovate dark green somewhat shiny leaves to 2.5cm/1in long, with prickly tips. The ends of the stems produce groups of tassels of thinner spore-bearing branchlets.

USE & CULTIVATION Most often used in hanging baskets, it thrives outdoors only in tropical climates with humid conditions. It likes a coarse, peat-based potting mix and partial shade. In cooler climates, grow in a warm greenhouse or conservatory with bright indirect light, high humidity and some air movement. Frost tender.

Lycopodium phlegmarioides
Layered Tassel Fern

ORIGIN South Pacific islands, Australia
CLIMATE T, ST
This species is very similar to the one above, but has pale yellowish green leaves arranged more or less in 4 forward-pointing rows.

USE & CULTIVATION As for *L. phlegmaria*. Frost tender.

Lysichiton americanus

Lysichiton camtschatcensis

LYSICHITON

SKUNK CABBAGE

FAMILY ARACEAE

A small genus of 2 deciduous, perennial, marginal water-plants grown for their wide arum-like flowers and attractive clusters of large, glossy green leaves. Propagate from seed when fresh or by division.

Lysichiton americanus
Yellow Skunk Cabbage

ORIGIN Western North America
CLIMATE M, CT, H
This robust herbaceous perennial forms rosettes of large, strongly veined, paddle-shaped leaves to 1.2m/4ft long. Wide, boat-shaped yellow flowers to 18cm/7in long are borne on stalks 30cm/12in or more tall in early spring, just before or with the very young leaves. The flowers have a musky scent. The leaves retain their beauty until autumn, when they die down.
USE & CULTIVATION A beautiful and dramatic plant for edging a stream or water-garden. Grow in wet or permanently moist soil in sun or light shade. Fully frost hardy.

Lysichiton camtschatcensis
White Skunk Cabbage

ORIGIN Northeastern Asia
CLIMATE WT, M, CT, H
This species has smaller proportions than *L. americanus*, with conspicuously veined, tapering pale green leaves to 1m/3ft long. The arum-like flowers to about 60cm/24in high are snowy white and slightly scented. They appear before the new foliage develops in early spring.
USE & CULTIVATION As for *L. americanus*. Fully frost hardy.

LYSIMACHIA

LOOSESTRIFE

FAMILY PRIMULACEAE

This genus of about 150 species of mainly evergreen perennials and shrubs is widespread in the temperate and subtropical regions of the world. Some make good border plants, some grow well next to water, while others, notably Creeping Jenny (*Lysimachia nummularia*), are good groundcovers. Propagate from seed or by division.

Lysimachia nummularia
Creeping Jenny, Moneywort

ORIGIN Europe, parts of Asia
CLIMATE WT, M, CT, H
A low-growing evergreen perennial which sends out long rooting stems forming a dense spreading mat. The rounded opposite leaves, less than 2.5cm/1in long, are heart-shaped at

the base. In summer the bright yellow cup-shaped flowers are fairly showy, although it is best to regard this as a foliage plant. The whole of the plant has been used for various herbal remedies. **'Aurea'** rapidly forms a spreading mat of yellowish green leaves which turn lime green in dense shade.

USE & CULTIVATION Usually found in damp woods or on shady river banks, this is an excellent groundcover for moist or even boggy soil, and will grow well in partial shade beneath mature trees. Also pretty in a hanging basket with moisture-retentive soil that does not dry out in summer. Fully frost hardy.

MACROZAMIA

FAMILY ZAMIACEAE

An Australian genus of some 25 species of slow-growing cycads from warm temperate and subtropical areas. Palm-like in appearance, they have gracefully arching glossy green fronds radiating from the top of a thick woody stem which may be underground or to 2m/7ft or more high. They are very long-lived and make beautiful accent specimens in frost-free climates or highly decorative tub plants for conservatories. Male and female cones are borne on separate plants near the centre of the crown and vaguely resemble green pineapples. The large red or orange seeds contain generous amounts of starch and were eaten by indigenous Australian peoples after elaborate preparation to remove harmful substances. Mature plants transplant readily. Propagate from seed taken from the female cone.

Macrozamia communis
Burrawang

ORIGIN Eastern Australia
CLIMATE ST, WT, M

An ornamental palm-like plant with a mostly underground or short trunk to 1m/3ft producing a crown of arching glossy green leaves to 2m/7ft long with many well-spaced narrow leaflets in 2 regular rows. The mature female plant develops up to 3 large, barrel-shaped cones about 45cm/18in long and 20cm/8in wide. The cylindrical male cones can measure 45cm/18in long and 14cm/5$\frac{1}{2}$in wide, with up to 5 being produced on a single plant.

USE & CULTIVATION A beautiful feature plant for a large sloping rockery or for a prominent position in the garden, patio or courtyard. It may take time to re-establish after transplanting. Grow in deep well-drained soil in full sun or partial shade. It tolerates light frosts when mature but needs some protection when young. Very slow growing, it makes an excellent long-lived container plant that can be taken indoors. Place in an airy well-lit position and use a free-draining, soil-based potting mix. Water during hot weather but allow to dry out completely between waterings during winter. Marginally frost hardy.

L
M

Macrozamia communis

Macrozamia miquelii

Macrozamia spiralis

Macrozamia spiralis

Macrozamia miquelii

ORIGIN Eastern Australia
CLIMATE T, ST, WT

This cycad develops an erect short trunk to 50cm/20in high and a grace-ful rounded crown of dark green leaves to 1.8m/6ft long with crowded, sharply pointed, linear leaflets, the lower few progressively reduced and rather spine-like. The barrel-shaped female cones to 35cm/14in long and 10cm/4in wide have oblong, orange to red seeds. Male cones are cylindrical, to 30cm/12in long and 6cm/2¼in wide.
USE & CULTIVATION As for *M. comm-unis*, but does best in filtered shade or partial shade. Marginally frost hardy.

Macrozamia spiralis

ORIGIN Eastern Australia
CLIMATE T, ST, WT

This smaller cycad with no visible trunk produces its arching leaves to 1m/3ft long from the crown at ground level. The flat linear leaflets are dark green to dark bluish green and slightly twisted at the main leaf stalk. Female cones are ovoid, to 35cm/14in long and 10cm/4in wide. Male cones are about the same length but cylindrical and usually curved.
USE & CULTIVATION As for *M. comm-unis*. Marginally frost hardy.

MAGNOLIA

FAMILY MAGNOLIACEAE
This genus of about 125 species of deciduous and evergreen trees and shrubs is grown mostly for its breath-takingly beautiful, often heavily fragrant flowers. The Southern Magnolia or Bull Bay, *Magnolia grandiflora*, is included here because it is among the grandest and most beautiful of shade trees, with hand-some year-round glossy foliage and magnificent fragrant flowers. Magnolias have delicate roots and do not transplant readily. It is best to buy small plants and be patient. Propagate from seed or cut-tings or by grafting in winter.

Magnolia grandiflora

Magnolia grandiflora 'Little Gem'

Magnolia grandiflora 'Exmouth'

Magnolia grandiflora
Southern Magnolia, Bull Bay

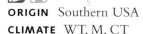

ORIGIN Southern USA

CLIMATE WT, M, CT

This dome-shaped evergreen tree can grow to 24m/80ft, given time and the right conditions, but 7–9m/22–30ft is a good average range. It has broadly ovate, glossy, dark green leaves to 20cm/8in long that are paler and felted rusty brown beneath, particularly when young. Large waxy creamy white flowers to 25cm/10in across with a lemony fragrance appear from late summer to autumn. **'Exmouth'** has a more conical habit and flowers at an early age. **'Little Gem'** is an exceptionally good semi-dwarf selection, very slow growing, to 3.5m/12ft, with smaller flowers and oval, dark green leaves to 12cm/5in long with russet brown hairs beneath. It flowers from an early age.

USE & CULTIVATION This is an excellent specimen and shade tree for medium-sized to large gardens. Grow in deep, fertile, slightly acid soil with good drainage in a position sheltered from strong winds. In cold regions it can be trained as a large shrub against a warm wall. Mulching in spring insulates the roots and helps retain moisture. 'Little Gem' is very well suited to narrow formal groups in courtyards and is a particularly good container plant. Moderately frost hardy.

MARANTA

FAMILY MARANTACEAE

From tropical America, this is a genus of about 20 species of evergreen perennials grown for their distinctively patterned foliage. The most commonly grown species is the Prayer Plant, *Maranta leuconeura* and its varieties, usually grown as greenhouse or indoor plants. They are popularly called prayer plants because they tend to stand erect and fold their leaves together at night. Propagate from stem cuttings or by division.

Maranta leuconeura
Prayer Plant, Ten Commandments

ORIGIN Brazil
CLIMATE T, ST

This leafy perennial to about 30cm/ 12in tall has a spreading habit and oval leaves to 12cm/5in long and 8cm/3in wide. The upper leaf surface is pale green, with a satiny lustre and silver or pink feathery veins; the underside is grey–green or reddish purple. New leaves appear from the sheathed leaf stalks. The flowers are white and insignificant. **'Erythroneura'**, the Herringbone Plant, bears dark green velvety leaves with jagged light green markings along the central rib and bright pinky red lateral veins. It has deep red undersides. The leaves of **'Kerchoveana'**, also known as Rabbit Tracks, have a light green upper surface with squarish, deep green or brown blotches on either side of the midrib; the undersides are pale green. **'Mass-angeana'** has oblong dark green velvety leaves to 15cm/6in long with a wide irregular silver midrib, prominent lateral veins and deep reddish purple undersides.

USE & CULTIVATION They may be grown outdoors as a decorative edging in tropical regions, but are mostly used as easy-care indoor plants. Protect from direct sunlight and keep reasonably warm. Keep moist but not totally saturated for very long periods, especially in winter. Frequent feeding with weak liquid fertiliser is best. Frost tender.

MARSILEA

FAMILY MARSILEACEAE

This is a widespread genus from tropical and warm temperate areas of 65 species of marshy and aquatic ferns, some of which have fronds resembling a 4-leaved clover which float on the surface of the water. These interesting ferns produce their spores in a specialised protective capsule about the size of a small pea, known as a sporocarp. The

Maranta leuconeura 'Erythroneura'

Maranta leuconeura 'Kerchoveana'

Marsilea mutica

Matteuccia struthiopteris

M

spores of the Common Nardoo, *Marsilea drummondii*, are rich in carbo-hydrates and were an important wild food for indigenous Australian peoples, who ground the sporocarps into a type of flour from which they made cakes. Propagate by division of rhizomes.

Marsilea drummondii
Common Nardoo

ORIGIN Australia
CLIMATE ST, WT, M

A small water or terrestrial fern with a long creeping rhizome bearing a num-ber of erect fronds with grey–green, clover-like leaflets to 4cm/1½ in across that are silky when young, borne on slender stalks 30cm/12in or more long. The Rainbow Nardoo, **M. mutica**, is similar but bears bright green glossy leaflets with an attractive brown or dark green band.

USE & CULTIVATION These ferns grow well in moist parts of the garden,

around or in water features or floating attractively in shallow ponds or streams. They can be grown in an aquarium or a wide, shallow water container. Anchor the roots in the muddy bottoms of shallow pools with sufficient water to float the leaves. They like full sun and will recover from light frosts. Margin-ally frost hardy.

MATTEUCCIA

FAMILY DRYOPTERIDACEAE/ WOODIACEAE

This is a small fern genus of about 4 species native to the temperate parts of North America, Europe and north-ern Asia. They are large deciduous ferns with long creeping rhizomes that produce a handsome vase- or shuttle-cock-shaped rosette of sterile fronds in spring. The fertile fronds are distinctly smaller and appear in summer. Propagate by division.

Matteuccia struthiopteris
Ostrich Fern, Shuttlecock Fern

ORIGIN Europe, east Asia, North America
CLIMATE M, CT, H

In spring this rhizomatous fern produces tall, erect, bright green, lance-shaped fronds to 1.5m/5ft long, arranged like a shuttlecock. The shorter fertile fronds are quite different, having dark brown leaflets with strongly inrolled margins, rather like ostrich feathers in appear-ance. They appear from the centre of the fern in late summer and persist over winter.

USE & CULTIVATION In nature this fern grows in swamps and moist wood-ed sites and is ideally suited to moist soil with shelter from direct sunlight, edging a woodland garden or beneath hardy palms. It can be rather invasive but makes a beautiful soft accent plant in difficult, damp and shady spots near water features. Fully frost hardy.

MELIANTHUS

FAMILY MELIANTHACEAE

There are 6 species in this genus native to South Africa and India, a small number of which are grown for their lush-looking ornamental foliage. Flower-heads are prominent, rusty red spikes, followed by inflated paper seed pods. In favoured climates these are tough, vigorous and often invasive plants, but in cold frost-prone areas they must be over-wintered in a cool greenhouse. They are sometimes cut back hard in early spring. Propagate from seed or cuttings.

Melianthus major
Honey Flower, Touch-me-not Plant, Honey Bush

ORIGIN South Africa
CLIMATE ST, WT, M, CT
This sprawling, sparsely branched shrub reaches a height and spread of 2–3m/7–10ft. It sends up clumps of hollow bamboo-like stems with large, bluish grey, pinnate leaves to 50cm/ 20in long, coarsely toothed and rather glaucous. Brownish red flower spikes

appear above the leaves from late spring to midsummer. The foliage has a strong unpleasant smell, hence the common name Touch-me-not Plant.
USE & CULTIVATION Suitable as a tall accent plant in a large border, it also makes a good waterside plant. Grow in well-drained fertile soil in full sun. In all but the mildest areas, place against a sheltered wall and protect with a thick mulch in winter. Also a handsome foliage plant for summer bedding or in a large tub in a cool greenhouse. Marginally frost hardy.

MELISSA

BALM

FAMILY LABIATAE/LAMIACEAE
This genus of 3 species of aromatic perennial herbs occurs naturally from Europe to central Asia. The name *Melissa*, from the Greek meaning 'bee', refers to the honey-laden flowers which attract pollinating bees. Lemon Balm (*Melissa officinalis*) was used medicinally by the Greeks some 2000 years ago and has long been praised by herbal writers for its

soothing effects on body and spirit. Propagate from seed or by root division.

Melissa officinalis
Lemon Balm, Bee Balm

ORIGIN Southern Europe
CLIMATE WT, M, CT, H
This perennial herb to about 1m/3ft high with similar spread has heavily veined, crinkly leaves to 7cm/2½in long, with scalloped margins, which emit a fresh lemony fragrance when bruised. It bears small white flowers in irregular spikes during summer. Large quantities of seed are produced. It dies down in cold weather but shoots again in spring. **'All Gold'** is a popular variety with pure yellow leaves. **'Aurea'** (syn. 'Variegata') to 30cm/ 12in high has gold-splashed dark green leaves. The fresh leaves are used for herb tea, in mixed green salads, to flavour summer drinks and sweets or as a lemon substitute in cooking.
USE & CULTIVATION Decorative foliage plants for edging paths, herb gardens or as rapid groundcovers. Grow in moist well-drained soil in full sun with

Melianthus major

Melianthus major

Melissa officinalis

Mentha x *gracilis* 'Variegata'

Mentha x *piperita* f. *citrata*

M

midday shade if summers are hot. Fully frost hardy.

MENTHA

MINT

FAMILY LABIATAE/LAMIACEAE

This widespread genus of about 25 to 30 species and many varieties of strongly scented perennial herbs occurs mainly in temperate regions. Most are rhizomatous, with erect square stems, paired, opposite, simple leaves and terminal whorled spikes of small, tubular, 2-lipped flowers appearing in late summer and autumn. They are grown for their aromatic foliage, which is both decorative and often used as a culinary herb. Peppermint is commercially grown for its essential oil, widely used in pharmaceutical products and confectionery. Most mints are invasive, spreading rapidly by runners, and are best planted away from other plants or controlled by growing in a container buried in the ground. Cut back regularly to encourage fresh growth. Propagate by division or from runners or roots.

Mentha x *gracilis* 'Variegata'
syn. *Mentha* x *gentilis* 'Variegata'
Ginger Mint

ORIGIN Gardens
CLIMATE WT, M, CT, H
This spreading perennial, a hybrid between *M. arvensis* and *M. spicata*, has upright reddish stems to 60cm/24in high. The ovate to lanceolate leaves to 7cm/2½ in long have toothed margins and yellow streaks along the veins. Lilac flowers appear in sparse clustered whorls in late summer.
USE & CULTIVATION A pretty variegated plant for adding a splash of colour and contrast to a border or herb garden. Grow in moderately rich, moist soil in a partially shaded position. Fully frost hardy.

Mentha x *piperita*
Peppermint

ORIGIN Europe, Asia
CLIMATE WT, M, CT, H
This mint has a vigorous creeping habit and upright stems to a height of 60cm/24in. It has purplish stems and smooth, dark green, oval leaves to 9cm/3½ in long with a purplish tinge. The purplish pink flowers appear in dense tapering whorls in summer. Leaves have a distinct peppermint odour and are used mostly to flavour teas, cool drinks and some desserts. *M.* x *p.* f. *citrata*, the Eau-de-cologne Mint, is widely cultivated for its attractively perfumed leaves, reminiscent of eau-de-cologne.
USE & CULTIVATION Both are excellent soil-binders and make attractive groundcovers spilling over garden edges, rocks, steps and banks or used to border a herb or vegetable garden. Grow in a sunny or partially shaded, moist position. Fully frost hardy.

Mentha spicata

Mentha x *villosa* f. *alopecuroides*

Mentha suaveolens 'Variegata'

by the Romans as *pulegium*, a word derived from *pulex*, meaning 'flea', referring to its reputed power to drive away fleas. As well as repelling fleas, Pennyroyal is known to deter lice, flies, mosquitoes and ants, and was popular as a strewing herb.

USE & CULTIVATION A charming aromatic groundcover, rockery or container plant in sun or partial shade, or for use as a herbal lawn. It prefers a moist position and needs to be able to spread its roots easily through well-composted and friable soil. Provide plenty of water, especially in hot dry weather. Fully frost hardy.

Mentha pulegium
Pennyroyal

ORIGIN Europe to western Asia
CLIMATE ST, WT, M, CT, H
Pennyroyal is a strong-smelling, downy, mat-forming herb with spreading runners that take root as they touch the ground. Stems to 40cm/16in long bear shortly stalked, oblong to oval, shallowly toothed leaves to 3cm/1¼in long. Lilac–pink flowers appear in axillary rounded clusters in late summer to late autumn. Since earliest times Pennyroyal has been used as a remedy for many complaints, including headache, nausea, upset stomachs, bronchial troubles and nervous disorders. It was known

Mentha requienii
syn. *Mentha corsica*
Corsican Mint

ORIGIN Southern Europe
CLIMATE ST, WT, M, H
This is a very low, mat-forming creeper with fine rooting stems and tiny,

rounded, bright green leaves less than 1cm/⅓in across which exude a strong peppermint-like odour when crushed. The axillary whorls of tiny pale lilac flowers appear in late spring.

USE & CULTIVATION Quickly forms a moss-like carpet around damp rocks and in shady crevices. It tolerates light foot traffic and can be used as a fragrant lawn, but in heavily trafficked areas a few paving stones will lessen possible damage. Grow in partial shade. Moderately frost hardy.

Mentha spicata
syn. *Mentha viridus*
Spearmint

ORIGIN Europe
CLIMATE ST, WT, M, CT, H

A fast-growing mint to 60cm/24in tall with hairy stems and toothed, bright green, lance-shaped or ovate-oblong, crinkly leaves to 9cm/3½ in long. Pale purple flowers are borne on spikes in late summer. **'Crispa'** has broad, dull green, wrinkled leaves to 5cm/2in long. The leaves of both forms have the strong characteristic spearmint odour and are the mints most widely used for culinary purposes.

USE & CULTIVATION An ideal border for a lightly shaded spot in a herb or vegetable garden. Grow in moist soil containing some humus. Being invasive, it should be used with caution. It does well in a pot and can be placed conveniently on the kitchen window-sill. Fully frost hardy.

Mentha suaveolens
syn. *Mentha rotundifolia* of gardens
Apple Mint

ORIGIN Europe, Mediterranean region
CLIMATE ST, WT, M, CT, H

This hairy perennial herb has a branched upright habit to 1m/3ft tall. The ovate or rounded, shortly stalked or sessile, grey–green leaves to 3cm/1¼ in long are irregularly toothed and softly hairy. The leaves have a mild apple-mint flavour. White or pink flowers appear in terminal tapering spikes in late summer.

'Variegata', an attractive variety with cream-edged leaves, is sometimes called Pineapple Mint. These are both popular culinary herbs for use in drinks, sauces, jellies and fruit dishes.

USE & CULTIVATION As for *M. spicata*. Fully frost hardy.

Mentha x villosa
f. alopecuroides
Bowles' Mint

ORIGIN Gardens
CLIMATE ST, WT, M, CT, H

This hybrid between *M. spicata* and *M. suaveolens* is a vigorous upright perennial which may reach 1m/3ft in favourable conditions. The lightly hairy, ovate to rounded leaves to 8cm/3in long are bright green with toothed margins. Pink flowers are produced in dense spikes. The leaves have a distinct spearmint-like aroma and are used to make mint sauce or jelly, fruit drinks or desserts, or mixed in potato salad or with cooked peas.

USE & CULTIVATION As for *M. spicata*. It is sometimes sold in nurseries as Winter Mint, *M. cordifolia*, and in warm temperate climates will continue to grow throughout winter. Fully frost hardy.

MICROBIOTA

FAMILY CUPRESSACEAE
This is a genus containing only one species, an attractive, low-growing, evergreen conifer from southeastern Siberia valued as a groundcover and for its ability to withstand cold winters. Propagate from seed or cuttings.

Microbiota decussata
Russian Arbor-vitae

ORIGIN Siberia
CLIMATE CT,

This low, spreading, evergreen shrub grows to less than 1m/3ft with a spread to 3m/10ft. It has branchlets in flattened sprays of bright green, scale-like leaves that become purplish brown in winter. The very small, rounded female cones have 2–4 scales and contain only 1 fertile seed.

USE & CULTIVATION An excellent groundcover for edging a path or trailing over a large sloping rock garden. Also softens the edges of hard landscaping and makes an excellent formal courtyard plant in cold climates. Grow in well-drained soil in full sun. Fully frost hardy.

M

Microbiota decussata

Microsorum punctatum 'Cristatum'

MICROSORUM

FAMILY POLYPODIACEAE

This is a genus of about 45 species of scrambling or climbing ferns mainly from tropical Asia, Polynesia and Australia. They have long creeping rhizomes that attach themselves to rocks and climb trees. The often leathery fronds are either entire or lobed and divided once, with profuse rounded clusters of spores on the upper half. The decorative and popular Australasian species Kangaroo Fern (*Microsorum diversifolium*) has been segregated into the genus *Phymatosorus*. Propagate by division of rhizomes.

Microsorum punctatum

ORIGIN Tropical Africa, Asia, Australia
CLIMATE T, ST

A scrambling fern with a thick fleshy rhizome covered with dark brown scales. The undivided sword-like fronds to 1m/3ft long and 10cm/4in wide are pale green to yellowish green. The cultivar **'Cristatum'** has large lobed fronds, often frilled at the tips.
USE & CULTIVATION These ferns form attractive spreading clumps in tropical gardens and prefer semi-shade, moist well-drained soil and high humidity, such as around a pond or near moving water. In cooler areas, grow in containers in a cool greenhouse or conservatory. Frost tender.

MISCANTHUS

FAMILY GRAMINEAE/POACEAE

Several highly desirable garden plants are included in this genus of about 20 species of robust perennial grasses occurring from Africa to eastern Asia. These are graceful billowing grasses with narrow arching leaves, and make large decorative clumps sending up silky flowering plumes which make excellent cut flowers. Propagate by division of clumps.

Miscanthus sinensis
Eulalia

ORIGIN Asia
CLIMATE WT, M, CT, H

This robust grass forms an upright arching tussock to 3m/10ft tall. Its dark green linear leaves to 1.2m/4ft long with a distinct white midrib are held on stout, reed-like stems. Creamy silky flowerheads, sometimes tinted pink, are produced in late summer and autumn, often lasting well into winter. There is a large selection of ornamental cultivars. **'Gracillimus'**, or Maiden Grass, to 1.2m/4ft tall, has very narrow curling leaves that often turn bronze in autumn. **'Graziella'** is a medium to tall form with leaves that colour well in autumn. **'Malepartus'** has broad, mid-green, arching leaves with a thin white central stripe. **'Morning Light'** has narrow curved leaves with fine silvery white edges. *M. s.* **var.** *purpurascens* has

Miscanthus sinensis 'Malepartus'

Miscanthus sinensis 'Variegatus'

Miscanthus sinensis 'Zebrinus'

Miscanthus sinensis 'Sarabande'

somewhat palm-like, pleated leaves. The short clusters of yellow flowers are borne at or near ground level. Propagate by division.

Molineria capitulata
syn. *Curculigo capitulata*
Weevil Lily

ORIGIN Southeast Asia to Australia
CLIMATE T, ST, WT
This perennial herb forms spreading clumps of erect, arching, bright green leaves to 90cm/36in long and 20cm/8in wide. The leaves are heavily pleated. In summer, bright yellow flowers appear in a dense rounded head at or near soil level. These are followed by fleshy rounded fruit.
USE & CULTIVATION In tropical and warm temperate regions it mixes well with most waterside plants but is especially attractive with groups of ferns and palms. Grow in deep, rich, moist soil in partial shade to prevent scorching of the foliage. It is fast growing and makes a good indoor specimen, looking rather like a pleated *Aspidistra*. Water well during the warmer months, less in winter. Frost tender.

Molineria capitulata

purplish green leaves that turn gradually to red and orange in autumn; the flower heads are quite orange. **'Sarabande'** has narrow arching leaves to 1.8m/6ft and profuse silky flowers in autumn. **'Silberfeder'** (syn. 'Silver Feather') grows to 2.5m/8ft and is popular for its profuse, silvery pink, silky flowers in autumn. **'Variegatus'** has pale green leaves with creamy white stripes. **'Zebrinus'**, one of the most striking cultivars, has leaves horizontally banded in creamy yellow.
USE & CULTIVATION Beautiful landscaping grasses for watersides, borders and as accents in a small garden or courtyard. The best clumps are produced in full sun in fertile, moist well-drained soil. Cut down to ground level in late winter to make way for new spring growth. Fully frost hardy.

MOLINERIA

FAMILY HYPOXIDACEAE
A small genus of 7 species of perennial herbs distributed from India to Australia. The widespread Weevil Lily (*Molineria capitulata*) is grown for its ornamental,

Molinia caerulea subsp. *caerulea* 'Variegata'

MOLINIA

FAMILY GRAMINEAE/POACEAE

This small genus consists of 2 or 3 species of small, tufted, perennial grasses extending from southern Europe to southwest Asia. They are frost tolerant. *Molinia caerulea* subsp. *caerula*, with its attractive variegated forms, is popular in cold climate gardens. Propagate from seed or by division.

Molinia caerulea subsp. *caerulea*
Purple Moor Grass

ORIGIN Europe, Asia
CLIMATE WT, M, CT, H

This grass forms large tussocks reaching 1.2m/4ft high when in flower. It has fairly broad, flat, mid-green leaves to 45cm/18in long with swollen purplish stem bases, and bears panicles of purple flowerheads in summer. **'Moorhexe'** is low growing, to 45cm/18in, with upright foliage that turns gold in autumn. The widely available **'Variegata'** is a compact form to 60cm/24in

with soft upright foliage with creamy or yellowish stripes. **M. c. subsp. arundinacea** is of medium height, to 2.5m/8ft, with attractively coloured autumn foliage. In summer it bears flowerheads ranging in colour from yellow to brown or purplish on stiff erect stems. **'Bergfreund'** has bright yellow autumn colouring. **'Transparent'**, to almost 2m/7ft when in flower, has golden flowerheads.

USE & CULTIVATION These plants like moist soil and are ideal near a water feature or pond. 'Variegata' makes a pretty contrasting border or rockery plant. Full sun or partial shade is best. Fully frost hardy.

MONSTERA

FAMILY ARECEAE

Native to tropical America and the West Indies, this is a genus of about 25 species of evergreen climbers which scramble up forest trees by means of long aerial roots. They are grown for their large perforated and indented adult leaves, which add an air of tropical luxuriance to the warm climate garden or greenhouse. The most commonly grown species, the Fruit Salad Plant (*Monstera deliciosa*) is often grown indoors, where it makes a smaller ornamental plant. Propagate from seed or cuttings or by layering.

Monstera deliciosa
Fruit Salad Plant,
Mexican Breadfruit

ORIGIN Mexico, Central America
CLIMATE T, ST, WT

In its natural jungle environment this is a large climber to 20m/70ft with thick stems and long aerial roots. The shiny leaves of a mature plant grow to 45cm/18in across, have 30cm/12in long stalks and are basically heart-shaped, but deeply cut almost to the central vein and perforated in the remaining sections. Juvenile leaves are much smaller and entire. The arum-like flower with a creamy white spathe to 30cm/12in long matures into an aromatic fruit which is edible only when fully ripe. **'Variegata'** has leaves splashed with white or cream coloured patches of irregular sizes.

USE & CULTIVATION A popular landscaping plant in frost-free climates, where it can be used to scramble over large rocky banks or be trained to climb

Monstera deliciosa

Murraya paniculata

trees or pillars. In sheltered patios and courtyards it will develop into an impressive mass of tropical-looking leaf growth. Grow in humus-rich, moist well-drained soil in partial shade. Indoor plants make dramatic specimens and need bright indirect light, moderate to high humidity and good drainage, with ample water during the growing season, less in winter. The aerial roots produced on mature plants can be trained to the support or guided back into the potting mix. A few cut leaves make a dramatic indoor arrangement. Frost tender.

MURRAYA

FAMILY RUTACEAE

A small genus of 4 species of evergreen shrubs and small trees from India and Southeast Asia. They have aromatic foliage, creamy white, often perfumed flowers and a neat overall appearance. Propagate from seed or cuttings.

Murraya paniculata
syn. *Murraya exotica*
Orange Jessamine, Mock Orange

ORIGIN Tropical Asia
CLIMATE T, ST, WT
A neat rounded shrub or small tree to 3m/10ft tall. It has pinnate leaves to 20cm/8in long with shiny rich green leaflets to 8cm/3in long. Terminal clusters of sweetly scented white waxy flowers appear in spring and summer.
USE & CULTIVATION A shapely shrub for frost-free climates that presents well throughout the year. It withstands serious clipping and is a popular hedge and screening plant. Also good for containers. Grow in full sun or partial shade and humus-rich, well-drained soil. Frost tender.

MUSA

BANANA
FAMILY MUSACEAE

This genus comprises about 25 species of very large, evergreen perennial herbs, native to many tropical and subtropical regions. They are grown for their enormous leaves, flowers and fruits, not all of which are edible, and are valuable for creating exotic effects. All bananas have soft, thick, false stems which die after fruiting. In clumping species the stem is replaced by suckers from the base. In non-clumping species the whole plant dies. Shelter from wind, which will cause the long broad leaves to become ragged. Check for red spider mite under the leaves in bananas grown indoors. Propagate from seed or by division of clumps.

Musa acuminata
syn. *Musa cavendishii*
Banana

ORIGIN Southeast Asia
CLIMATE T, ST
This is one of the parents of many popular edible bananas. It is a clumping banana with stems 3.5–6m/12–20ft tall and arching, dark green, leathery leaves 2–3m/7–10ft long. The creamy yellow tubular flowers are produced in a series of long drooping spikes with large, deep purple, leathery bracts when in bud. The flowers are followed by large bunches of elongated edible fruit which is yellow when ripe. **'Dwarf Cavendish'**, a smaller grower to about 2–3m/7–10ft with broad oblong leaves to 1.5m/5ft long, is better suited to domestic gardens.
USE & CULTIVATION In warm areas, grow as specimen plants for bold tropical effects in patios or feature gardens. They do best in full sun and fertile moist soil in a sheltered location with good drainage. 'Dwarf Cavendish', with its shorter leaves, is one of the best for indoor decoration. Use a loam-based potting mix and water freely in spring and summer. It likes full light, regular feeding and high humidity. When the main stem is no longer attractive, cut it out to give the smaller side-shoots at the base a chance to develop. Frost tender.

Musa acuminata 'Dwarf Cavendish'

Musa ornata

Musa velutina

Musa basjoo
syn. *Musa japonica*
Japanese Banana

ORIGIN Japan
CLIMATE ST, WT, CT

This clumping banana has slender cylindrical stems to 3m/10ft high topped with huge, bright green, paddle-shaped leaves to 3m/10ft long that unless sheltered from strong winds get torn to shreds. In summer it produces pendulous flower spikes surrounded by large smoky purple bracts with tiers of creamy 5cm/2in flowers and small inedible bananas forming behind. The plant is cultivated in Japan for its fibre.
USE & CULTIVATION Ideal for creating a tropical garden atmosphere, this species will survive moderately cold winters if placed in a warm sheltered position in full sun. It likes fertile moisture-retentive soil with good drainage, regular feeding and ample water. In cold climates it appreciates heavy winter mulching. If the winter is severe it can be grown in a container and moved into a brightly lit position indoors. Moderately frost hardy.

Musa ornata
Flowering Banana

ORIGIN Bangladesh, Myanmar
CLIMATE T, ST, WT

This species grows to 3m/10ft tall and has oblong to elliptic mid-green leaves to 2m/7ft long. Spikes of yellow flowers emerging from pink bracts are followed by greenish yellow fruit.
USE & CULTIVATION As for *M. acuminata*. One of the best ornamental bananas, with luxuriant foliage along at least two-thirds of the stem. Frost tender.

Musa velutina

ORIGIN Assam, India
CLIMATE T, ST, WT

This smaller growing species reaches a height of about 1.8m/6ft. It has rich green paddle-shaped leaves less than 1m/3ft long, often with pinkish shadings on the stalks and along the midribs. It bears erect spikes of yellow flowers emerging from pinkish red bracts and small, reddish, velvety fruit.
USE & CULTIVATION Good for creating a tropical accent in a small sheltered garden. Grow in a warm sunny location and water generously during dry weather. Its smaller habit makes it a preferred banana for indoors. Frost tender.

MYOSOTIDUM

FAMILY BORAGINACEAE

This is a genus of only one species, an evergreen perennial from the Chatham Islands east of New Zealand. It is a magnificent, individual-looking plant with rich green leaves and sprays of tiny blue flowers, but is not easy to cultivate. Once established, it should not be moved. Propagate from seed or by division.

Myosotidium hortensia
Chatham Island Forget-me-not

ORIGIN Chatham Islands (NZ)
CLIMATE WT, M

This clump-forming perennial forms an attractive mound to 60cm/24in high and wide of large, ribbed, glossy leaves to 30cm/12in long. It bears large clusters of blue forget-me-not-like flowers in spring and summer. **'Alba'** is a rare white-flowered form.

USE & CULTIVATION A charming plant for a humus-rich, moist rockery pocket in a well-drained position with light dappled shade. Seaweed is often recommended as mulch and a seaweed-based fertiliser is preferred. It withstands light frosts and in colder areas can be grown in a cool greenhouse or conservatory for the winter. Marginally frost hardy.

MYRTUS

FAMILY MYRTACEAE

This genus of 2 species of evergreen shrubs or small trees comes from the Mediterranean region. They are grown for their dense aromatic foliage and starry white fragrant flowers. The leaves of the Common Myrtle, *Myrtus communis*, are rich in an oil which is used medicinally and in the manufacture of cosmetics. Propagate from seed or cuttings.

Myrtus communis
Common Myrtle

ORIGIN Mediterranean region
CLIMATE WT, M, CT

This erect, densely foliaged shrub 2–3.5m/7–12ft high has dark green, glossy, oval leaves to 5cm/2in long that have a sweet spicy fragrance when crushed. Starry white fragrant flowers comprising numerous stamens appear from mid- to late summer. The fruit is a purplish black berry covered with a dusty bloom when ripe. **'Variegata'** has dark green, pointed leaves heavily bordered with creamy white. **M. c. subsp.** *tarentina* (syns 'Jenny Reitenbach', 'Microphylla', 'Nana') is more compact, to 1.5m/5ft, with smaller narrower leaves to 2.5cm/1in long and velvety stems.

USE & CULTIVATION These plants withstand any amount of clipping and pruning and are often used in topiary and for hedges. Also excellent container plants for patios or wherever a neat attractive accent plant is required. Grow in friable well-drained soil in full sun. Plants develop a more intense fragrance when grown in areas with long hot summers. In cold areas, plant against a warm sunny wall with shelter from cold drying winds. Use 'Variegata' for colour accent among darker greens. Cut foliage is useful for indoor decoration. Dried leaves and berries can be added to potpourri. Moderately frost hardy.

M

Myosotidium hortensia

Myrtus communis

Myrtus communis subsp. *tarentina*

NANDINA

FAMILY BERBERIDACEAE

The one species in this genus is *Nandina domestica*, the Sacred Bamboo, an evergreen or semi-evergreen shrub native to India, China and Japan and grown for its fine delicate foliage, neat habit and colourful berries. At first glance it bears a resemblance to bamboo, although it is a member of the berberis family. It has been cultivated for centuries in Chinese and Japanese temple gardens. The common name comes from the practice of using cut branches to decorate altars. Male and female plants are separate and both are needed for the berries to develop. In spring, prune untidy and unproductive stems at ground level to encourage fresh new growth. Propagate from seed or cuttings.

Nandina domestica
Sacred Bamboo, Heavenly Bamboo

ORIGIN India to Japan
CLIMATE WT, M, CT

This light airy shrub has short-jointed, bamboo-like stems, reaching 2.5m/8ft with age. The fine-textured, usually bipinnate leaves to 90cm/36in long are finely divided into many lance-shaped leaflets. New growth is pink; older leaves become green, turning purple and brilliant red in autumn and remaining red throughout the winter months. Small white flowers are carried in showy spikes to 30cm/12in long in summer; if planted in a group for cross-pollination, the flowers on female plants are followed by showy red berries in autumn. A number of selected dwarf forms have a smaller clumping growth habit. **'Firepower'** to 60cm/24in high has fresh lime green leaves in summer, turning bright pink and deep wine red in autumn and winter. **'Pygmaea'** (syn. 'Nana') is a dense shrub about 45cm/18in high and wide with leaves in tones of lime green, crimson and scarlet. **'Richmond'** is a popular self-pollinating New Zealand cultivar that produces clusters of abundant scarlet berries. **'Wood's Dwarf'** is a vigorous plant to 75cm/30in high and wide, with red and orange tonings in autumn and winter.

USE & CULTIVATION An elegant erect plant that is ideal as a light screen in small gardens and for oriental-style plantings. The cultivars are often used

Nandina domestica

Nandina domestica 'Pygmaea'

for mass planting as a colourful border or low hedge. Grow in fertile, moist well-drained soil in full sun or partial shade, sheltered from cold winds. Also beautiful container subjects for patios, and widely used as houseplants in Japan. Moderately frost hardy.

NEOREGELIA

FAMILY BROMELIACEAE

A genus of about 70 species of South American epiphytic or terrestrial brom-eliads, with leaves forming a flattish basal rosette, the inner ones becoming brightly coloured as flowering time approaches. The tiny purple, blue or white tubular flowers are produced in a compound head in the cup-like centre of the rosette. The flowers usually die off quickly, but the flush of colour in the foliage remains for several months. Offsets form around the flowering rosettes. Propagate from offsets, keeping as much root attached as possible.

Neoregelia carolinae
Blushing Bromeliad

ORIGIN Brazil
CLIMATE T, ST, WT
This bromeliad and its varying forms is the most widely cultivated member of the genus. It forms open rosettes to 60cm/24in across of shiny, medium green leaves about 30cm/12in long and 5cm/2in wide, the inner leaves turning red just before flowering. A compact head of bluish purple flowers surrounded by red bracts is borne in the centre of each rosette. **'Meyendorffii'** forms a small compact rosette with copper-tinged olive green leaves and a bright orange centre. **'Tricolor'** is variegated, with cream and green striped foliage; with maturity the whole plant becomes suffused with pink and the inner leaves turn a vivid crimson before producing lavender flowers.
USE & CULTIVATION In tropical gardens they make striking edging plants, particularly when mass-planted at close range in courtyards and pool

areas. Many gardeners prefer to grow them in containers tucked into the soil so that their positions can be changed and their leaves kept off the ground. Provide good drainage and dappled shade with bright light to maintain their colour. In containers, use a soil-based potting mix with pine bark, coarse sand or vermiculite added to improve drainage. Container-grown plants are suitable for well-lit situations indoors. Water moderately during the growing season and keep the centre cup filled with water at all times. Periodically change the water. Frost tender.

Neoregelia concentrica

ORIGIN Brazil
CLIMATE T, ST, WT
This bromeliad forms a dense compact rosette to 70cm/28in across of stiff broad leaves 30cm/12in long and 10cm/4in wide, edged with short black spines. The leaves are pale green, usually flecked with purple on the upper surface, with the reverse side striped with silver–grey. Prior to flowering, the centre turns a rich purple. The flowers are pale blue.
USE & CULTIVATION As for *N. carolinae*. Frost tender.

Neoregelia carolinae

Neoregelia concentrica

N

NEPHROLEPIS

SWORD FERN
FAMILY NEPHROLEPIDACEAE

There are about 30 species in this genus of fast-growing terrestrial or epiphytic ferns, with 2 species widely grown indoors. They make useful basket subjects, producing dense attractive crowns of long, often arching fronds divided into many narrow segments which grow alternately on either side of the midrib. Numerous scaly runners grow out from the rhizome and creep along the surface of the soil, putting down roots and producing new plants at their tips. Propagate by runners or division of the crowns.

Nephrolepis cordifolia
Fishbone Fern, Southern Sword Fern

ORIGIN Widespread in tropics and subtropics

CLIMATE T, ST, WT

This erect fern has short rhizomes, spreading by wiry stolons with fleshy tubers. Its light green linear fronds to 70cm/28in long are about 10cm/4in wide at the widest part, narrowing towards the tip, with oblong, finely toothed or lobed segments. **'Plumosa'** has darker green fronds; the segments are further lobed near the tips, giving a fringed feathery appearance.

USE & CULTIVATION In warm climates this fern is cultivated as a groundcover.

It looks good near a water feature set among rocks, thriving in dappled shade with plenty of moisture and some protection from harsh winds. In the right conditions it has a tendency to become invasive. It makes a trouble-free indoor plant, preferring bright filtered light, plenty of water and warm humid conditions. Remove fading fronds and divide regularly. Frost tender.

Nephrolepis exaltata
Sword Fern

ORIGIN Africa, tropical America, Polynesia

CLIMATE T, ST, WT

This tufted fern has arching, lance-shaped, pale green fronds to 2m/7ft long with shallowly toothed linear segments to 4cm/1½in long. Most of the numerous cultivars are daintier and lacier than the species. The best known is **'Bostoniensis'**, the Boston Fern, which has wide weeping fronds. **'Hillii'** has variously lobed and divided segments. **'Rooseveltii'** is a dwarf cultivar with wavy segments.

USE & CULTIVATION In warm areas these plants flourish in full shade, making attractive lush growth beneath trees or in a moist neglected area that requires little care and attention. They must be contained, as they may swamp other smaller plants. Grown in hanging baskets in a loam-based, peaty potting mix, they make highly glamorous ferns for conservatories and garden rooms. Protect from direct sunlight and water well during the growing season. Frost tender.

NOTHOFAGUS

SOUTHERN BEECH
FAMILY FAGACEAE

Found only in the Southern Hemisphere, this is a genus of about 25 species of deciduous and evergreen trees and shrubs grown for their stately habit, dainty lacy foliage and, sometimes, rich autumn colour. Although some species could be regarded as too large for the average home garden, they make outstanding specimens for larger gardens or parks. They can also be cultivated as pot plants and make interesting bonsai subjects. *Nothofagus obliqua* and *N. procera* are grown for timber. Propagate from seed or cuttings.

Nothofagus cunninghamii
Tasmanian Beech, Myrtle Beech

ORIGIN Southern Australia

CLIMATE WT, M, CT

A rather slow-growing tree to 35m/120ft in the wild, usually much less in cultivation. The deep green leaves, only about 2.5cm/1in long, are shiny, toothed and oval and produced in fan-like sprays. The young spring foliage in pink to rich bronze tones is an attractive feature. Small, insignificant, greenish flowers produced in summer are followed by very small winged nuts. The long-lasting cut foliage is highly regarded for floral work.

USE & CULTIVATION An extremely attractive tree with colourful spring foliage suitable for specimen planting or in a sheltered woodland setting. Grow in a cool moist position in sun or partial shade with some protection from wind. It requires rich deep soil with good drainage, but should not be allowed to dry out when young. It can be grown in a container for many years. Moderately frost hardy.

Nothofagus cunninghamii

Nothofagus moorei

Nothofagus cunninghamii

Nothofagus obliqua

to 50m/160ft in its cool temperate rain-forest habitat, where it develops a massive gnarled trunk. The oval, finely toothed leaves to 8cm/3in long are dark green, turning orange before falling.

USE & CULTIVATION Best as a specimen for large gardens, or in sunny woodland areas and parks where it will develop into an attractive shade tree. Unable to withstand extended dry periods, it needs cool moist conditions and deep, organically rich, well-drained soil. Mulch thoroughly and keep regularly watered. It can be grown in a container for many years and is suitable for bonsai. Moderately frost hardy.

Nothofagus obliqua
Roble

ORIGIN Chile, Argentina
CLIMATE WT, M, CT

This shapely deciduous tree, reaching 14–20m/45–70ft in gardens and much more in the wild, has a broad spread and attractive drooping habit. The ovate, dark green leaves to 7cm/2½ in long are irregularly toothed with blue–green undersides, and turn orange and red in autumn.

USE & CULTIVATION A fast-growing hardy tree suitable for large gardens, woodland settings and as a tall screen. Grow in a sunny position with some protection from wind. Organically rich, lime-free soil with good drainage is best. Fully frost hardy.

Nothofagus fusca
Red Beech

ORIGIN New Zealand
CLIMATE WT, M, CT

This species starts as a bushy shrub and as it matures forms an erect, broadly canopied evergreen tree, generally 6–12m/20–40ft in cultivation. The small, rounded oval leaves to 5cm/2in long are coarsely toothed and slightly crinkled, and assume red and copper tones in autumn and winter. The foliage is highly ornamental, both in the garden and for floral work.

USE & CULTIVATION Slow growing and manageable for smaller gardens, where it can be pruned back hard to keep it at the shrub stage. It requires deep, moist well-drained soil, protection from drying winds and plenty of room to develop. It is shade tolerant. Moderately frost hardy.

Nothofagus moorei
Niggerhead Beech
ORIGIN Eastern Australia
CLIMATE WT, M, CT

This stately evergreen tree, averaging 10–18m/30–60ft in cultivation, grows

N

Nothofagus procera
Rauli

ORIGIN Chile, Argentina
CLIMATE WT, M, CT

This fast-growing deciduous tree to 24m/80ft is distinguished by its comparatively large, prominently veined, oblong leaves to 10cm/4in or more long, with slightly scalloped margins. The leaves are bronze when young and turn a deep reddish orange in autumn.
USE & CULTIVATION As for *N. obliqua.* Fully frost hardy.

Nothofagus solandri
Black Beech

ORIGIN New Zealand
CLIMATE WT, M, CT

This evergreen species bears a mass of small, dense, shiny leaves to 1.5cm/^{1}/$_2$ in long with entire margins. Reaching a height of 15m/50ft, it forms a slender conical tree with ascending fan-like branches. The young growth is soft and downy. **N. s. var. *cliffortioides*** has closely set, deep green, oval leaves with twisted edges.
USE & CULTIVATION As for *N. fusca.* Moderately frost hardy.

NYSSA

FAMILY NYSSACEAE
A genus of about 5 deciduous trees from North America and southern Asia, grown for their picturesque habit, attractive foliage and spectacular red autumn colour. Position in their permanent site when young, as they resent root disturbance. Propagate from seed or cuttings.

Nyssa sylvatica
Tupelo

ORIGIN Eastern North America
CLIMATE WT, M, CT, H

When young, this deciduous tree has a pyramidal habit, with low, spreading, slightly drooping, horizontal branches. A mature tree becomes quite irregular in outline and wide spreading,

Nothofagus solandri

Nyssa sylvatica

ultimately reaching 20m/70ft high and 9m/30ft across. The glossy dark green, oval, pointed leaves to 15cm/6in long turn rich yellow, orange and red before falling. Greenish flowers produced in early summer are inconspicuous but abundant, and highly valued for honey production.

USE & CULTIVATION Grow as a lawn specimen, shade tree or as a background to shrubs. It likes rich, moisture-retentive, well-drained soil in a sunny position sheltered from strong winds. Apply a balanced slow-release fertiliser in summer. Fully frost hardy.

OMALANTHUS

FAMILY EUPHORBIACEAE

This is a genus of about 35 species of shrubs or small trees native to Australia and tropical Asia and Polynesia. These plants are grown for their heart-shaped leaves, which turn a brilliant red just before they are shed. Propagate from seed or cuttings.

Omalanthus populifolius

Omalanthus populifolius
syn. *Homalanthus populifolius*
Bleeding Heart Tree

ORIGIN Eastern Australia
CLIMATE T, ST, WT

A fast-growing, tall bushy shrub or small tree to 5m/17ft, with deep green, broadly ovate leaves to 15cm/6in long which turn a brilliant red as they age. The tiny yellow flowers, occurring in catkins, are insignificant.

USE & CULTIVATION An attractive background foliage plant near a water feature or at the margin of a rainforest planting imitating its natural habitat. Grow in moist well-drained soil in a partially shaded position. Prune to shape. An interesting plant for containers and can be grown indoors. Frost tender.

OPHIOPOGON

FAMILY CONVALLARIACEAE/
LILIACEAE

A genus of about 50 species of clump-forming evergreen perennials from eastern Asia. They are grown for their neat grass-like foliage, being extremely

popular where a neat border is required. Propagate from division of clumps.

Ophiopogon jaburan
White Lilyturf

ORIGIN Japan
CLIMATE ST, WT, M, CT, H

This compact tussock-forming species has lustrous, dark green, linear leaves to 60cm/24in long arising directly from the rootstock. It spreads by stolons, but is by no means invasive. Loose clusters of white or lilac-tinged tubular flowers appearing in late summer are followed by deep blue berries. **'Vittatus'** is particularly attractive, with pale green leaves striped with white, cream or yellow.

USE & CULTIVATION Excellent as groundcovers, for edging paths or as massed plantings in contemporary garden design. Grow in humus-rich, well-drained soil in full sun or partially shaded areas; they need regular water to look their best. Also highly suitable for containers, either massed in urns or as companions in a mixed potted arrangement. Indoors, place in a well-lit position. Moderately frost hardy.

N

O

Ophiopogon jaburan 'Vittatus'

Ophiopogon japonicus
syn. *Liriope japonica*
Mondo Grass

ORIGIN Japan
CLIMATE WT, M, CT, H
This tufted perennial with underground stolons forms clumps of grassy dark green leaves 10–20cm/4–8in long. Spikes of lilac to white flowers 8cm/3in tall appear in summer, followed by deep blue pea-sized fruit. **'Kyoto Dwarf'** is a compact form to 10cm/4in high.
USE & CULTIVATION As for *O. jaburan*. Fully frost hardy.

Ophiopogon planiscapus

ORIGIN Japan
CLIMATE WT, M, CT, H
This open grass-like perennial to about 20cm/8in high has curved, strap-shaped, dark green leaves to 35cm/14in long. The purplish white summer flowers are followed by fleshy blue–black fruit. It is usually represented in cultivation by **'Nigrescens'**, the Black Mondo Grass, grown for its curved purplish black leaves to 25cm/10in long.
USE & CULTIVATION As for *O. jaburan*. 'Nigrescens' should be grown in full sun to maintain good colour. Fully frost hardy.

OPLISMENUS

FAMILY GRAMINEAE/POACEAE
This is a small genus of about 6 species of trailing annual or perennial grasses from tropical and subtropical regions of both hemispheres. The highly decorative variegated form of the Basket Grass (*Osplimenus africanus*) is the only representative of the genus commonly grown, often as an indoor plant in hanging baskets. Propagate by division.

Oplismenus africanus
syn. *Oplismenus hirtellus*
Basket Grass

ORIGIN Widely distributed in tropics
CLIMATE T, ST
This evergreen branching grass has fine wiry stems that are upright when young but soon trail, taking root at the nodes and forming a clump to 90cm/36in across. The stalkless leaves are thin, lance-shaped, to 5cm/2in long and have long pointed tips. **'Variegatus'** has medium green leaves with white lengthwise stripes that are often pink-tinted when new.
USE & CULTIVATION 'Variegatus' is traditionally used in hanging baskets where the trailing stems form attractive curtains of foliage. Also looks good trailing from tall urns and as a pretty cascading contrast in a mixed potted arrangement of more upright plants. In warm gardens, use for

Ophiopogon japonicus 'Kyoto Dwarf'

Ophiopogon planiscapus 'Nigrescens'

Oplismenus africanus 'Variegatus'

Origanum vulgare 'Aureum'

The dark green oval leaves are highly aromatic and widely used in many Mediterranean cuisines. Tiny pink or white tubular flowers appear in summer. **'Aureum'** is a popular golden-leaved variety with a spread to 30cm/12in. **'Country Cream'** has a dense carpeting habit and crinkled leaves with a cream margin. **'Golden Tip'** has green leaves with yellow tips.

USE & CULTIVATION Useful for edging a herb garden or flower border, or for trailing over rocks, banks, walls and containers. Grow in full sun in well-drained, preferably alkaline soil. Fully frost hardy.

OSMUNDA

FAMILY OSMUNDACEAE
This genus of 10 to 15 species of slow-growing, deciduous, terrestrial ferns has an almost worldwide distribution. They have thin and wiry rhizomes and form clumps of erect, sterile, bipinnate fronds that are generally pinkish and downy at first. The rusty brown fertile fronds develop spike-like tips. Propagate by division.

Osmunda regalis
Royal Fern

ORIGIN Temperate and subtropical regions
CLIMATE WT, M, CT, H
This robust fern has a stout erect rootstock with abundant black roots often forming a dense clump. The bright green bipinnate fronds to 2m/7ft long are either sterile or have fertile, reddish brown, tassel-like tips. The roots provide the osmunda fibre of commerce, much used as a potting medium by orchid growers. **'Cristata'** has segments with crested tips. **'Purpurascens'** has young foliage flushed bronze–purple.

USE & CULTIVATION In nature this species grows near permanent water; it is ideal for very wet conditions such as edging a pond or water feature. Grow in rich moisture-retentive soil in light shade. Potted plants need plenty of water. Fully frost hardy.

edging paths and to soften hard landscaping. Grow in moist well-drained soil in sun or partial shade. Indoor plants need bright light and plenty of moisture. Frost tender.

ORIGANUM

MARJORAM, OREGANO
FAMILY LABIATAE/LAMIACEAE
A genus of 15 to 20 species of perennial herbs and subshrubs from the Mediterranean region and temperate Asia. They have opposite pairs of ovate leaves and small, tubular, 2-lipped flowers, often borne in leafy panicles. Some species are aromatic, others are grown as culinary herbs, still others for their showy clusters of flowers. Propagate from seed or by division.

Origanum vulgare
Oregano, Wild Marjoram

ORIGIN Europe
CLIMATE WT, M, CT, H
This mat-forming perennial herb has a height and spread of about 90cm/36in.

OXALIS

FAMILY OXALIDACEAE

This is a very large genus of about 800 species of annuals, perennials and subshrubs, some bulbous or tuberous rooted, with a wide distribution, although most species are found in South America and South Africa. They have long-stalked, mainly clover-like leaves that fold at night or during dull weather. The 5-petalled flowers are sometimes showy, but some species have become very troublesome weeds in many parts of the world and the genus is in general avoided by gardeners. The Good Luck Plant, *Oxalis tetraphylla*, is more restrained in growth than most oxalis and is cultivated for its decorative leaves. Propagate by division.

Oxalis tetraphylla
syn. *Oxalis deppei*
Good Luck Plant, Lucky Clover

ORIGIN Mexico
CLIMATE WT, M, CT
This tuft-forming tuberous perennial reaches a height of about 25cm/10in with a similar spread. It has long-stalked large leaves to 8cm/3in across that are divided into 4 notched leaflets

crossed with a purplish brown zone at the bases. Small deep pink flowers with a yellow base are borne in loose umbels in summer. **'Iron Cross'** has large purplish brown markings at the base of each leaflet.

USE & CULTIVATION Suitable for a rock garden or container, it does best in a sheltered position in sun or partial shade in moist well-drained soil. Indoors, provide bright light and plentiful water during the growing period. Pick the leaves of 'Iron Cross' for posies. Moderately frost hardy.

PANDANUS

SCREW PINE
FAMILY PANDANACEAE

This is a large genus of about 600 species of evergreen shrubs, trees or scramblers from tropical parts of Africa, Asia and Polynesia. Their erect fibrous stems, often with prop roots, are topped with crowded, spirally arranged, sword-shaped leaves. The tiny male or female flowers are produced on separate

plants. Male flowers are crowded in spikes, female flowers in short, dense, rounded heads which develop into large and often colourful fruit. Flowers and fruit appear only on mature specimens. Most species are coastal or waterside plants and make striking accent plants in tropical and subtropical gardens. They also make excellent container plants for indoors. The name is from Malay *pandang*. Propagate from ripe seed or basal offsets.

Pandanus tectorius
Coastal Screw Pine, Pandang

ORIGIN Australia, Pacific islands
CLIMATE T, ST
A branched, spreading, small tree to around 5m/17ft high with well-developed prop roots. The spiny-edged narrow leaves to 1.5m/5ft long are bluish green and spirally arranged in clusters at the ends of the branches. The white flowers are produced mainly in summer. Female trees bear pineapple-like fruit to 18cm/7in long that becomes reddish orange when ripe.

USE & CULTIVATION This beautiful sculptured plant is often used in coastal gardens as a natural protective barrier against salt spray and wind for less tolerant plants. It looks striking when planted in small stands. Grow in a sunny position with very good drainage. Water regularly in the early stages of establishment. Young plants make decorative container subjects for the house or conservatory, but need to be located where the spiny leaves will be out of harm's way. Bright light and sharply draining, gritty soil is essential. Water well during the growing season, less in winter. Frost tender.

Pandanus veitchii
Veitch Screw Pine

ORIGIN Polynesia
CLIMATE T, ST
This is a tall shrub or small branching tree to 6m/20ft with thin, well-developed prop roots. It has spirally arranged, strap-shaped, spiny leaves to 1.5m/5ft long, mid-green and striped

Oxalis tetraphylla 'Iron Cross'

Pandanus tectorius

Pandanus veitchii

Pandanus veitchii

and sometimes edged in white, cream or dull yellow. Mature female trees bear pineapple-like fruit.

USE & CULTIVATION An ornamental accent plant for tropical gardens that looks good edging a water feature or swimming pool. It is salt tolerant and grows well close to the sea. Full sun and well-drained soil are best. Makes an interesting container specimen, and thrives indoors if given very bright light and plenty of water when in active growth.

PARTHENOCISSUS

FAMILY VITACEAE

There are about 10 species in this genus native to temperate North America and Asia, all of them deciduous creepers which climb by sucker-tipped tendrils. They are often seen covering large buildings or walls. The species most

commonly grown are those with handsome lobed or palmate leaves which develop magnificent autumn colouring. Propagate from seed or cuttings.

Parthenocissus quinquefolia
syn. *Vitis quinquefolia*
Virginia Creeper

ORIGIN Eastern North America
CLIMATE WT, M, CT, H

This is a high-climbing creeper with sucker-tipped tendrils and palmate leaves divided into 5 toothed leaflets that make an attractive fresh green wallcover in summer and turn a breathtaking red in autumn. Small blue–black berries are produced in autumn.

USE & CULTIVATION Ideal for growing on buildings and high walls, it is also used as a groundcover for large banks or slopes. Grow in any well-drained soil in filtered sun. It benefits from an annual trim. Fully frost hardy.

O
P

Parthenocissus tricuspidata

Pelargonium 'Atomic Snowflake'

Parthenocissus tricuspidata
Boston Ivy, Japanese Ivy

ORIGIN China, Korea, Japan
CLIMATE WT, M, CT, H
This rapid-growing creeper clings by sucker-tipped tendrils, forming a dense covering on large masonry or brick buildings despite prevailing winds. The broadly ovate, 3-lobed leaves to 20cm/ 8in long are serrated on new growth, turning spectacular shades of red and purple in autumn. **'Lowii'** is a lower growing form with small, deeply lobed leaves to 10cm/4in long. **'Veitchii'** has spectacular reddish purple autumn colouring.
USE & CULTIVATION Excellent plants for large expanses of masonry walls and for covering wooden fences. Also train over large rocks and boulders in an oriental-style garden. Grow in humus-rich, well-drained soil in sun or partial shade. Fully frost hardy.

PELARGONIUM

FAMILY GERANIACEAE
Most of the garden plants we know as 'geraniums', including the popular free-flowering zonal, regal and ivy geraniums, are derived from the genus *Pelargonium*, which comprises more than 250 species of perennials and shrubs and a multitude

Pelargonium capitatum

of hybrids and horticultural varieties. Although there are some fancy-leaved varieties, only the scented-leaved pelargoniums, which have both attractive leaves and a distinct perfume, have been included here. While these are mostly derived from South African species, many have been grown in English cottage gardens and greenhouses for the past 300 years. Picked leaves are ideal for indoor arrangements and posies. Some are commercially cultivated for oil of geranium, often used to replace the more expensive attar of roses in perfumery. All scented-leaved pelargoniums can be dried and used in potpourri mixtures and

for scenting linen. The prettiest shapes can be floated in finger bowls. Propagate from softwood cuttings.

Pelargonium 'Atomic Snowflake'

ORIGIN Gardens
CLIMATE WT, M
This soft-wooded spreading shrub to 50cm/20in high has large lobed leaves edged with cream or yellow. When mature, they may also have darker green splotches. They have a lemon-rose fragrance. Small, single, mauve flowers appear in clusters.

USE & CULTIVATION This and the following pelargoniums form charming bushes in herb gardens, near the back door or walkways, in window boxes and containers. Most thrive in full sun, but where summers are hot and dry they do best in partial shade. Grow in light, well-drained, neutral soil. Water regularly during the growing season and keep fairly dry during winter. In areas of frost they can be treated as houseplants in winter if placed in a sunny, well-ventilated position. When young, pinch growing tips to encourage side-branching and good shape, especially those in pots. Frost tender.

Pelargonium capitatum
Rose-scented Pelargonium

ORIGIN South Africa
CLIMATE WT, M

This shrubby perennial to 1m/3ft high has hairy stems and deeply toothed, velvety leaves to 8cm/3in long and wide. The leaves have a spicy rose-like fragrance. Up to 12 small pink flowers are produced in tight umbels in early spring and summer.
USE & CULTIVATION As for P. 'Atomic Snowflake'. Frost tender.

Pelargonium crispum
Lemon-scented Pelargonium

ORIGIN South Africa
CLIMATE WT, M

This erect branched shrub to 90cm/36in high has small, crowded, shallowly lobed leaves to 3cm/1¼in wide, which are distinctly crisped or curled. When bruised, they release a pronounced lemon scent. The 2.5cm/1in wide pale mauve, purple-veined flowers are usually solitary. **'Prince Rupert'** is a more vigorous, larger-leaved form. **'Variegatum'** has ruffled green leaves outlined in cream or white.
USE & CULTIVATION As for P. 'Atomic Snowflake'. Frost tender.

Pelargonium 'Fragrans'
syn. *Pelargonium* x *fragrans*
Nutmeg-scented Pelargonium

ORIGIN Gardens
CLIMATE WT, M

This well-known variety is a small, branched, bushy plant reaching a height and spread of about 30cm/12in. It has soft, almost heart-shaped, grey–green leaves, carried on slender stalks. They are faintly 3-lobed with scalloped edges. Small white flowers with red markings on the upper petals are borne in umbels of 4–8 in late spring and summer. **'Fragrans Variegatum'** has greyish green leaves edged with creamy white.
USE & CULTIVATION As for P. 'Atomic Snowflake'. Frost tender.

Pelargonium crispum 'Variegatum'

Pelargonium 'Fragrans'

Pelargonium 'Fragrans Variegatum'

Pelargonium graveolens
Rose Geranium

ORIGIN Gardens
CLIMATE WT, M
A shrubby upright plant to 80cm/32in tall and wide, with downy mid-green leaves consisting of 5 major lobes which are deeply cut and irregularly toothed. The leaves are rose-scented, but many forms exist and the aroma varies considerably, some being quite pungent. Small mauve–pink flowers with deep red veins are borne in clusters in late spring and summer. **'Lady Plymouth'** is a smaller growing variety with finely cut leaves with pale cream edging, sometimes with a tinge of pink. They have a light rose scent with a hint of mint. The foliage is useful in floral work.
USE & CULTIVATION As for *P.* 'Atomic Snowflake'. Frost tender.

Pelargonium grossularioides
Coconut Pelargonium

ORIGIN South Africa
CLIMATE WT, M
A dainty, low-growing, trailing plant to around 20cm/8in high with straggly reddish stems and shallowly lobed, toothed leaves atop slender stalks to 12cm/5in long. The tiny deep pink flowers, in compact heads, appear intermittently throughout the year. The leaves have a strong coconut fragrance.
USE & CULTIVATION As for *P.* 'Atomic Snowflake'. Its low-growing spreading habit makes it an attractive hanging basket subject. Frost tender.

Pelargonium 'Mabel Grey'

ORIGIN Gardens
CLIMATE WT, M
An attractive upright shrub to around 80cm/32in high with rough-textured, palmately lobed leaves with pointed tips and serrated edges. It has one of the strongest perfumes of all the lemon-scented pelargoniums. Pale purple flowers with red markings appear in spring.
USE & CULTIVATION As for *P.* 'Atomic Snowflake'. Tip-prune when young to prevent it becoming leggy. Use the dried leaves in potpourri. Frost tender.

Pelargonium odoratissimum
Apple-scented Pelargonium

ORIGIN South Africa
CLIMATE WT, M
This small compact plant to 25cm/10in high has thin trailing stems to 60cm/24in long clothed with soft green leaves to 5cm/2in across that are almost round and have ruffled edges. They release a strong scent of apples when bruised. Tiny white star-shaped flowers with red markings are produced in clusters in spring and summer.
USE & CULTIVATION As for *P.* 'Atomic Snowflake'. Its cascading habit makes it a good pot or hanging basket subject. Frost tender.

Pelargonium quercifolium
Oak-leaf Pelargonium

ORIGIN South Africa
CLIMATE WT, M
This tall-growing bushy pelargonium may reach 1.5m/5ft. The leaves are triangular in outline, deeply lobed and irregularly toothed. A dark brown

Pelargonium graveolens 'Lady Plymouth'

Pelargonium quercifolium

Pelargonium tomentosum

blotch may develop on the central veins. The leaves are sticky and rough to the touch and emit a strong balsamic scent when rubbed. Showy deep pink flowers with darker veining appear in spring and summer.
USE & CULTIVATION As for *P.* 'Atomic Snowflake'. Frost tender.

Pelargonium radens
Rose-scented Pelargonium

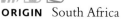

ORIGIN South Africa
CLIMATE WT, M
This is a shrubby upright plant to 80cm/32in or more. The aromatic mid-green leaves to 6cm/2¼in long are clothed with tiny white bristly hairs, deeply lobed into slender toothed segments and slightly rolled under at the margins. The teeth on the leaf margins are rounded. Small, pink, star-shaped flowers with purple veining on

the upper petals are produced in late spring and summer. This species, with one of the most pleasing rose scents of all, is the rose-scented pelargonium most used in cooking.
USE & CULTIVATION As for *P.* 'Atomic Snowflake'. Cut back regularly to prevent the plant becoming bare at the base. Frost tender.

Pelargonium 'Rober's Lemon Rose'

ORIGIN Gardens
CLIMATE WT, M
This vigorous aromatic plant may reach 1m/3ft, but is usually less. The thick felty leaves with deeply cut, rounded lobes are clothed in white bristly hairs and have a strong lemon-rose scent. Small pink flowers with darker veining on the upper petals appear in spring.

USE & CULTIVATION As for *P.* 'Atomic Snowflake'. Frost tender.

Pelargonium tomentosum
Peppermint-scented Pelargonium

ORIGIN South Africa
CLIMATE WT, M
This attractive velvety plant reaching 60cm/24in has a somewhat sprawling habit, with spreading soft stems to 1.5m/5ft long. The rich green, heart-shaped leaves are shallowly lobed and have a distinct peppermint scent. Small white flowers with deep red markings are produced in spring and summer.
USE & CULTIVATION As for *P.* 'Atomic Snowflake'. Its cascading habit makes it a good groundcover, cascading plant, pot or hanging basket subject. Keep up the water in dry weather, especially if grown in a container. Frost tender.

P

PELLAEA

FAMILY ADIANTACEAE

This genus of about 80 species of ground-dwelling ferns is found throughout tropical and temperate regions. They have branching rhizomes and furry, wiry stalks; their fronds are generally pinnate or, rarely, divided 2 or 3 times. A small number of species are popular as ornamental pot plants for indoor cultivation. Propagate by division of rhizomes.

Pellaea falcata
Sickle Fern

ORIGIN India to Australia
CLIMATE T, ST, WT

This upright fern forms large spreading clumps of clustered shiny fronds to 30cm/12in or more long. The narrow-linear dark green fronds are divided once into elongated sickle-shaped segments.

USE & CULTIVATION It spreads quite quickly and is a useful groundcover beneath trees and among rocks in moist well-drained soil containing plenty of organic matter. In cool climates grow in a fernery, greenhouse or indoors with filtered sunlight. Avoid direct sunlight and keep the potting mix moist. Frost tender.

Pellaea rotundifolia
Button Fern

ORIGIN New Zealand
CLIMATE ST, WT, M

This fern has short creeping rhizomes from which arise clusters of arching leathery fronds to 40cm/16in long. Each frond consists of many pairs of stem-clasping, roundish, dark green segments 1.5cm/½in long with finely scalloped margins.

USE & CULTIVATION A very pretty fern among rocks in a sunny position with moist well-drained soil. It is not deep rooted and can be grown in a peaty mix in shallow containers or hanging baskets for indoor use. Protect from direct sunlight, keep moist and avoid

Pellaea rotundifolia

draughts; mist-spray in hot weather. Moderately frost hardy.

PEPEROMIA

FAMILY PIPERACEAE

Widely distributed throughout the tropics and subtropics, there are about 1000 species in this large and varied genus of mostly small evergreen or succulent perennials. The foliage of many species is highly ornamental, often beautifully marked and variegated or crinkled and corrugated, making these decorative container plants for patios, indoors or greenhouses. Most types produce a long-stemmed, thin, white or cream-coloured flower spike. Propagate from stem or leaf cuttings.

Peperomia argyreia
Watermelon Peperomia

ORIGIN Tropical South America
CLIMATE T, ST

This compact perennial has a height and spread of about 30cm/12in. It has short red stems and oval fleshy leaves to 10cm/4in long, attractively striped in

Peperomia caperata

alternate bands of dark and silvery green. Tiny white flowers are borne on spikes intermittently, but particularly in summer.

USE & CULTIVATION Used as a pretty edging plant in partially shaded tropical gardens, but mostly seen as a houseplant, grown in a peat-based potting mix and requiring bright indirect light. Water when it is clearly needed; much less in winter. Established plants can be given weak liquid fertiliser once a month. Frost tender.

Peperomia caperata
Emerald Ripple

ORIGIN Tropical South America
CLIMATE T, ST

This rosette-forming perennial has a height and spread of about 20cm/8in. The heart-shaped, deeply corrugated, dark green leaves to 4cm/1½in long and the creamy white flower spikes of varying lengths are carried on red or pink stalks. **'Little Fantasy'** is a dwarf form. **'Tricolor'** has smaller variegated leaves.

USE & CULTIVATION As for *P. argyreia*. Frost tender.

Peperomia marmorata
syn. *Peperomia verschaffeltii*
Sweetheart Peperomia

ORIGIN Tropical South America
CLIMATE T, ST
This species forms a short-stemmed rosette to 25cm/10in high of fleshy heart-shaped bluish green leaves to 12cm/5in long. The ridges between the sunken veins are silvery grey. It produces long, greenish white flower spikes. **'Silver Heart'** has pale green leaves with silver markings.
USE & CULTIVATION As for *P. argyreia*. Frost tender.

Peperomia obtusifolia
syn. *Peperomia magnoliifolia*
Pepper Face

ORIGIN Tropical South America
CLIMATE T, ST
This upright perennial to about 30cm/12in tall and wide has succulent dark green oval leaves 8–15cm/3–6in long. White flower spikes 5–8cm/2–3in long appear mainly in summer. More common are the variegated cultivars, which include **'Green and Gold'**, with yellow margins, and **'Variegata'**, with patches of cream or yellow.

USE & CULTIVATION As for *P. argyreia*. The stems on mature plants may flop over and can be cut back to encourage bushiness. Frost tender.

Peperomia scandens

ORIGIN Mexico, South America
CLIMATE T, ST
This trailing species has pinkish green stems which spread to 1m/3ft across. Oval leaves to over 5cm/2in long are waxy and bright green. It produces spikes of green flowers. The more popular **'Variegata'** has light green leaves irregularly margined with creamy white.
USE & CULTIVATION As for *P. argyreia*. Also grow as a groundcover or use in a hanging basket. Frost tender.

PERSICARIA

KNOTWEEDS
FAMILY POLYGONACEAE
A cosmopolitan genus of about 150 species of mostly annual or perennial herbs. They are mostly grown for their pretty flowerheads, which last for many weeks; a few are grown for their attractively marked leaves. The aromatic leaves of the Vietnam Mint

(*Persicaria odorata*) are used as a garnish in salads and soups, and also in spring rolls. Often spreading and alarmingly invasive, some species have weedy properties and should be planted where they can be contained. Propagate from seed or by division.

Persicaria virginiana
syns *Polygonum virginianum*,
Tovara virginiana

ORIGIN Himalayas, Japan, North America
CLIMATE WT, M, CT, H
This erect perennial forms loose mounds to about 1m/3ft high and wide. It has elliptic mid-green leaves to 25cm/10in long with attractive dark green or brown markings. Wide-branching flowerheads of tiny, green, cup-shaped flowers appear from mid-summer to early autumn. **'Painter's Palette'** has mid-green leaves splashed with cream and marked with a red V-shaped pattern.
USE & CULTIVATION They like moisture-retentive soil and are suitable for naturalising near a large water feature or woodland garden. Grow in partial shade or non-scorching sun. Fully frost hardy.

P

Persicaria odorata

Persicaria virginiana

PHALARIS

FAMILY POACEAE

There are about 15 species of annual and perennial grasses in this genus, native to North and South America, Europe and northern Africa. They occur naturally in damp areas and are ideal for growing in permanently wet and boggy soils. Propagate from seed or by division.

Phalaris arundinacea var. picta
Gardeners' Garters

ORIGIN Europe, North America
CLIMATE WT, M, CT, H
This vigorous ornamental grass forms large clumps to 1.5m/5ft, but is usually less in gardens. It has flat, linear, white-striped leaves to 40cm/16in long and produces graceful pale green flowering spikes in summer. **'Feesey'** has stronger white markings and is said to be less invasive. **'Luteopicta'** is a little smaller and has gold variegation.
USE & CULTIVATION An attractive waterside plant that enjoys a damp environment in full sun or partial shade. Also provides a bright, narrow-leaved contrast to a perennial border, although it can become invasive. Fully frost hardy.

Phalaris arundinacea var. *picta*

Philodendron bipinnatifidum

PHILODENDRON

FAMILY ARACEAE

This is a large genus of about 500 species of evergreen shrubs and epiphytic climbing plants from tropical America and the West Indies. They are valued for their handsome foliage and many are popular houseplants, although they can be grown in the garden or on shady patios in favourable climates. The name is from Greek *phileo*, 'to love', and *dendron*, 'tree', referring to the tree-climbing habit of many species. There is considerable variation in form, but most of the climbing species produce aerial roots at each leaf node and can be trained up a moss-covered stake, or outdoors on any rough-textured material, such as a brick wall or rough-barked tree trunk. Small arum-like flowers are relatively insignificant. All parts of the plants are poisonous. Propagate from cuttings.

Philodendron bipinnatifidum
syn. *Philodendron selloum*
Tree Philodendron

ORIGIN Brazil
CLIMATE T, ST, WT
This shrub-like philodendron forms a rosette of leaves that radiate from an

Philodendron erubescens 'Burgundy'

erect trunk-like stem that can eventually reach 3m/10ft high. Large rich green leaves to 1m/3ft long have deeply incised wavy lobes and are carried on long arching stalks. Occasionally, greenish white spathes are produced.
USE & CULTIVATION An outstanding foliage plant in tropical garden design, and can be used to soften the edges of hard landscaping in the swimming pool area. Although non-climbing, it can be encouraged up trees or against a wall in warm areas. Grow in rich well-drained soil in a sheltered, partially shaded position. Indoors, it needs a small tub with a firm base and ample space for the spreading leaves. Keep the soil moist, not saturated, and apply a liquid fertiliser occasionally. Reduce watering during the cooler months. Hose down occasionally to keep the foliage dust-free and glossy. Frost tender.

Philodendron erubescens
Red-leaf Philodendron,
Blushing Philodendron

ORIGIN Colombia
CLIMATE T, ST, WT
This is a strong-growing climber that can reach 2m/7ft or more. It has reddish purple stems and elongated arrow-shaped leaves to 40cm/16in long that

Philodendron imbe

Philodendron 'Winterbourn'

Philodendron scandens

are shiny dark green above with coppery red undersides. **'Burgundy'** climbs much more slowly and has red-flushed leaves and red stems.

USE & CULTIVATION Although grown outdoors in warmer areas, they are usually treated as houseplants. Train up a moist, moss-covered or rough-textured stake inserted into the potting mix for support. Grow in bright filtered light, water freely, mist-spray regularly and apply a liquid fertiliser occasionally.

Reduce watering during the cooler months. Frost tender.

Philodendron imbe
syn. *Philodendron sellowianum*

ORIGIN Brazil
CLIMATE T, ST, WT

This woody-based climber will attach itself to suitable supports by means of long aerial roots, reaching a height of about 2m/7ft. Its thin-textured leaves are more than 35cm/14in long, elongated heart-shaped, glossy mid-green above and with faint tinges of red on the undersides. They are borne on 30cm/12in leaf stalks, which are held horizontally from the stems.
USE & CULTIVATION As for *P. erubescens*. Frost tender.

Philodendron scandens
syn. *Philodendron oxycardium*
Sweetheart Plant

ORIGIN Mexico, West Indies, Brazil
CLIMATE T, ST, WT

This small-leaved climbing philodendron has slender branching stems to 3m/10ft that can be encouraged to climb or trail. It has glossy, heart-shaped, rich green leaves 10cm/4in long and 8cm/3in wide with slender pointed tips, on 5–8cm/2–3in leaf stalks.
USE & CULTIVATION This fast-growing philodendron is one of the easiest of

all houseplants. It thrives in poor light and the aerial roots will attach to anything. It can also be allowed to trail over the rims of pots or hanging baskets. Keep the soil moist, but not saturated, and reduce watering during winter. Tip-prune to promote branching. Frost tender.

Philodendron 'Winterbourn'
Sold as 'Xanadu'

ORIGIN Gardens
CLIMATE T, ST, WT

This hybrid philodendron forms an attractive dome-shaped rosette to about 1m/3ft high and wide. The lustrous, mid-green, reflexed leaves to about 20cm/8in long are cut into 11–15 forward-pointed lobes and held on arching 40cm/16in stalks. There are faint tinges of pink on the midrib and veins beneath.
USE & CULTIVATION Makes an outstanding easy-care informal hedge for warm gardens. Grow in well-drained, humus-rich soil in a sheltered, partially shaded position. Also a superb weeping foliage specimen in a tall urn. Indoors, grow in bright filtered light, water freely and apply a liquid fertiliser every month during the growing season. Reduce watering during the cooler months. When potting on, use a good-quality, loam-based potting mix. Frost tender.

P

PHLEBODIUM

FAMILY POLYPODIACEAE

This is a genus of about 10 species of slow-growing terrestrial ferns native to tropical America. They generally have long creeping rhizomes densely covered with golden yellow scales and large fronds, often over 1m/3ft long, which may be entire and undivided or deeply lobed to the midrib. The spore cases are formed mostly in 1 or 2 parallel rows on each side of the midrib on the underside, often becoming bright orange. Propagate by division of rhizomes.

Phlebodium aureum
syn. *Polypodium aureum*
Hare's Foot Fern, Rabbit's Foot Fern

ORIGIN Tropical America
CLIMATE T, ST, WT

The creeping, branching rhizome of this evergreen fern is covered with furry orange–brown scales. The arching, deeply lobed, generally glaucous fronds to 1.5m/5ft long have linear, wavy-margined segments. Clusters of orange spore cases are arranged in a line on either side of the midrib on the undersides. **'Mandaianum'** is an extremely attractive variety with deeply cut, silvery blue–green fronds with wavy ruffled edges.
USE & CULTIVATION In warm sheltered gardens it will scramble short distances over rocks. It likes moist well-drained soil in partial shade. Indoors, a wide shallow container or hanging basket allows the rhizome plenty of room to branch and spread. Provide bright filtered light, water freely and apply a liquid fertiliser regularly during the growing season. Less water is required during the cooler months. When potting on, use half loam-based potting mix and half leaf mould. Frost tender.

PHOENIX

FAMILY ARECACEAE/PALMAE

Native to the tropical and subtropical regions of Asia, Africa and the Canary Islands, this is a genus of 17 species of evergreen feather-leaved palms. They include long-lived ornamentals and economically important plants, particularly the Date Palm (*Phoenix dactylifera*). They are grown largely as landscape specimens for their attractive foliage, which is sometimes enhanced by huge sprays of glossy, colourful, red, orange or yellow fruits. Male and female plants are separate, so both are needed for fertile seed production. The species listed here are relatively slow growing and will live for many years in containers, making them popular conservatory plants in cold climates. Propagate from seed.

Phoenix canariensis
Canary Island Date Palm

ORIGIN Canary Islands
CLIMATE ST, WT, M

This stately palm may reach 15m/50ft with a spread to 12m/40ft, eventually developing a stout columnar trunk patterned with the marks left by fallen leaves. The graceful arching fronds, to 6m/20ft long and spiny at the base, form a dense green crown. Bright yellow or orange fruits are produced in large clusters on female trees.

Phoenix canariensis

USE & CULTIVATION Planted in avenues or as a single specimen, this dramatic palm gives a tropical touch to any landscape. Also an excellent long-lived specimen for large lawn areas where its symmetrical shape can be appreciated. Grow in well-drained soil in full sun. Protect from frost when young and cut off dead leaves close to the stem. A popular subject for conservatories or rooms with bright light. Good drainage is essential. Thorough watering and regular applications of liquid fertiliser are needed when in growth. Reduce watering during the cooler months. Marginally frost hardy.

Phoenix dactylifera
Date Palm

ORIGIN Northern Africa, Middle East
CLIMATE T, ST, WT, SA

This species has a similar habit to *Phoenix canariensis* and produces one of the world's oldest food crops. Its leaves, 4–6m/14–20ft long, are divided into narrow grey–green prickly leaflets arching from a slender green stem. Both male and female trees are needed to set fruit, which are cylindrical, to 7cm/2½in long and yellowish brown when ripe.

Phoenix roebelenii

Phormium cookianum

Phormium cookianum 'Maori Maiden'

USE & CULTIVATION The edible fruits are produced in hot dry climates only, but this long-lived tree has high ornamental value for a spacious setting. It is extremely tolerant of salt-laden winds and coastal exposure. Also can be grown in a container for many years and used indoors in a brightly lit position. Marginally frost hardy.

Phoenix roebelenii
Pygmy Date Palm

ORIGIN Laos
CLIMATE T, ST, WT, SA

This small-scale palm grows to 3m/ 10ft tall with a similar spread. It slowly develops a slender rough-textured trunk to 2m/7ft high topped by a rounded crown of arching, dark green, feathery fronds to 1.5m/5ft long. Clusters of egg-shaped black fruits are produced in autumn.
USE & CULTIVATION An extremely elegant palm for small tropical-style gardens, patios and courtyards. Grow in a sunny or partially shaded position in moist well-drained soil. Excellent indoors and in conservatories, internal courtyards and atriums. Good drainage is essential, but regular watering and applications of liquid fertiliser promote strong, lush growth. Less water is required during the cooler months. Frost tender.

PHORMIUM

NEW ZEALAND FLAX
FAMILY AGAVACEAE/PHORMIACEAE
New Zealand is the home of the 2 species of evergreen perennials in this genus. They form clumps of stiff, ornamental, sword-like leaves. In summer, panicles of small tubular flowers are borne on long leafless stems that extend well above the leaves. Cultivars often have brightly coloured or variegated foliage. They make dramatic accent plants and are ideal for growing beside water features. The name is from the Greek *phormos*, 'basket', because the tough fibrous leaves were used extensively by Maori people in making traditional crafts. Propagate from seed or by division.

Phormium cookianum
syn. *Phormium colensoi*
Mountain Flax

ORIGIN New Zealand
CLIMATE ST, WT, M, CT

This upright perennial 1–2m/3–7ft high forms tufts of sword-shaped, dark green leaves to 1.5m/5ft long and 6cm/2¼in wide. Some forms have arching leaves. Yellowish green to reddish brown flowers are produced on stiffly erect stems to 2m/7ft long in summer. **'Maori Maiden'** (syn. 'Rainbow Maiden') has upright leaves, drooping at the tips, and striped coral pink and cream with bronze margins. The popular *P. c.* **subsp.** *hookeri* **'Cream Delight'** has arching leaves with broad bands of creamy yellow, narrowly striped green towards the edges and margined deep red. *P. c.* **subsp.** *hookeri* **'Tricolor'** has broad arching leaves striped yellow and green with red margins.
USE & CULTIVATION Outstanding accent plants, especially when grown en masse. They look good on sloping banks, as borders and besides pools. In courtyards, use for feature design or for strong foliage contrast among ornamental grasses and flowering perennials. They require well-drained soil in sun or semi-shade and will grow well by the sea. In frosty areas, apply thick dry mulch in winter. The foliage is used for indoor arrangements. Moderately frost hardy.

P

Phormium tenax 'Purpureum'

Phormium tenax 'Variegatum'

Phormium tenax
New Zealand Flax

ORIGIN New Zealand
CLIMATE ST, WT, M, CT

This is a vigorous tussock-forming perennial to 3m/10ft tall and about 2m/7ft across. The stiff strap-like leaves to 3m/10ft long are dark green above and paler beneath. In summer, panicles of dull red flowers are carried on strong erect stems to 3.5m/12ft long. Many medium height, more compact hybrids are available in a range of interesting colours. **'Bronze Baby'** is a strong-growing dwarf form to 75cm/30in with straight bronze-coloured leaves curving at the tips. **'Dazzler'**, to 1m/3ft, has rich pinky red, arching leaves with darker purplish red stripes and margins. **'Purpureum'** is a vigorous grower to 1.5m/5ft with purplish bronze leaves in many variations. **'Rainbow'** is a 30cm/12in dwarf form with red and green foliage. **'Variegatum'** has light green leaves to 2m/7ft long, striped creamy yellow and lime green.
USE & CULTIVATION As for *P. cookianum*. Moderately frost hardy.

PHOTINIA

FAMILY ROSACEAE

This is a genus of about 60 species of deciduous and evergreen trees and shrubs from Asia, grown for their colourful young foliage and, in the case of some deciduous species, for their autumn colour. The insignificant tiny white flowers are borne in clusters, followed by usually red berries. Propagate from seed or cuttings or by grafting.

Photinia x fraseri

ORIGIN Gardens
CLIMATE WT, M, CT

This is a vigorous hybrid between *P. glabra* and *P. serratifolia*. It forms an upright evergreen shrub or small tree to about 5m/17ft, and has leathery oblong leaves to 10cm/4in long with new growth in brilliant shades of salmon, bronze or bright red over a long period. Small white flowers are borne in mid- to late spring, but are often removed with repeated clipping. **'Red Robin'** is compact, to about 3m/10ft high, with shiny bright red new growth. **'Robusta'** has bright coppery red new leaves.
USE & CULTIVATION Excellent hedges as well as showy single specimens. Begin clipping at planting time to develop a thick strong frame. Frequent clipping increases the new red shoots. They thrive in a sheltered sunny position with good drainage, away from cold drying winds. Feed in spring with a balanced slow-release fertiliser. Moderately frost hardy.

Photinia x *fraseri* 'Red Robin'

Photinia glabra 'Rubens'

Photinia glabra 'Rubens'

ORIGIN Japan

CLIMATE ST, WT, M, CT

This ornamental evergreen shrub to 3m/10ft high with a similar spread can be kept lower and shapely by pruning. It has oval, pointed, shiny leaves to 9cm/3½in long that open a rich crimson red several times from early spring to autumn. If allowed to develop, dull white flowers are produced in broad clusters in late spring, followed by red berries which later turn black.

USE & CULTIVATION As for *P.* x *fraseri*. Moderately frost hardy.

PHRAGMITES

FAMILY GRAMINEAE/POACEAE

This is a small genus of 4 species of large perennial reed-grasses widely distributed throughout tropical and temperate regions. Their natural habitat is swampy ground near ponds and the margins of waterways, making them especially suited to growing in or near a water feature. Propagate by division.

Phragmites australis
syn. *Phragmites communis*
Common Reed

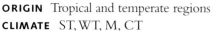

ORIGIN Tropical and temperate regions

CLIMATE ST, WT, M, CT

This handsome reed has strong erect stems to 3.5m/12ft or more tall bearing flat, pointed, mid-green leaves to about 80cm/32in long that turn golden yellow in autumn. Plumes of conspicuous, purplish brown, silky flowers are borne on stems about 40cm/16in long in late summer and autumn; they age to creamy white. **'Variegatus'** has leaves with yellow stripes that fade to white.

USE & CULTIVATION These grasses thrive in wet or moisture-retentive soil in a sunny position and can be used near a water feature. They can be planted in strong metal containers that are submerged in water to prevent unwanted spread. Can also be grown in

Phragmites australis 'Variegatus'

Phyllostachys aurea

normal garden soil and in containers that are frequently watered well. Fully frost hardy.

PHYLLOSTACHYS

FAMILY GRAMINAEA/POACEAE

This is a genus of about 80 species of medium-sized to very large bamboos from eastern Asia and the Himalayas. Although they have spreading rhizomes, some may form a clump for years before the first new shoots appear away from the parent plant. They are mainly grown for their decorative foliage, graceful habit and often attractively coloured canes, although several species are cultivated for their young edible shoots. The bamboo most commonly used in cooking in China and Japan is *Phyllostachys heterocycla* var. *pubescens*. Insignificant flowers take several years to appear. They tolerate very cold conditions and are usually grown as a grove or accent, and are useful for preventing soil erosion. Most of their growth is made in just a few weeks in spring, so thinning is recommended before the shoots have appeared. This

will keep the clumps under control and allow the sunlight to reach into the centre. They are great for growing in large tubs and are the bamboo species most widely used in bonsai. Propagate by division of rhizomes.

Phyllostachys aurea
Fishbone Bamboo, Golden Bamboo

ORIGIN China

CLIMATE ST, WT, M, CT

This clump-forming bamboo has greenish yellow canes 5–9m/17–30ft tall, with shortened internodes on the lowest part forming an asymmetrical zigzag pattern. The narrow lance-shaped leaves to 15cm/6in long are yellowish green above and bluish underneath. **'Flavescens Inversa'** is a popular ornamental form with green canes and a yellow stripe in the grooves.

USE & CULTIVATION Makes an attractive, fast-establishing hedge, ideal as a windbreak or privacy screen. Grow in fertile well-drained soil in full sun or partial shade away from strong winds. As a container specimen, use a loam-based potting mix and ensure good drainage. Fully frost hardy.

P

Phyllostachys aureosulcata var. *aureocaulis*

Phyllostachys nigra

Phyllostachys nigra var. *henonis*

Phyllostachys aureosulcata
Yellow Groove Bamboo

ORIGIN Northeastern China
CLIMATE WT, M, CT
This stately bamboo reaches 6m/20ft. It has large narrow leaves to 18cm/7in long and brownish green canes, often with crowded zigzagged nodes at the base. *P. a.* **var. *aureocaulis*** has stout golden yellow canes, often with green stripes near the base, and grows to 5m/17ft.
USE & CULTIVATION As for *P. aurea*. Thinning of the lower leaves is recommended to allow the colour to develop on the canes. Fully frost hardy.

Phyllostachys bambusoides
Madake, Giant Timber Bamboo

ORIGIN China
CLIMATE ST, WT, M
This clump-forming bamboo 3–8m/ 10–25ft or more high can grow over 20m/70ft in the wild. It has stout, erect, green stems and thick leaf sheaths covered with prominent bristles. The broad lance-shaped leaves to 20cm/8in long are glossy dark green. The flexible wood of the mature canes is of particularly high quality; this is the most important timber bamboo of the Orient. **'Allgold'** (syn. 'Holochrysa') has bright golden yellow stems which are occasionally striped with green. **'Castillonis'** is smaller growing, 3–6m/10–20ft high, with canes striped with yellow and dark green and occasionally yellow-striped leaves.
USE & CULTIVATION This rapidly growing species provides large-scale oriental effects together with effective screening or boundaries within a garden. It thrives in a sheltered sunny position with good drainage, away from cold drying winds. Fully frost hardy.

Phyllostachys nigra
Black Bamboo

ORIGIN China
CLIMATE WT, M, CT
This beautiful bamboo may spend many years as a relatively compact clump before it starts to spread moderately. It has slender canes 3.5–5m/ 12–17ft tall, green at first but turning glossy black as they mature. The prolific lance-shaped leaves to 12cm/5in long are green and pointed. *P. n.* **var. *henonis*** is taller and has stout green canes with prominent nodes.
USE & CULTIVATION Because of its striking appearance, it is frequently planted as an accent plant in oriental-style gardens and in sparse stylised gardens. It thrives in a sunny position with rich fertile soil, but needs more

Phyllostachys viridiglaucescens

Picea abies 'Maxwellii'

wind protection than most bamboos. A stunning waterside plant providing its rhizomes have very good drainage. Fully frost hardy.

Phyllostachys viridiglaucescens

ORIGIN China
CLIMATE WT, M, CT

This clump-forming, then spreading bamboo to 5m/17ft or more tall has thick, smooth, yellow canes that become dark green and glaucous. It bears narrow, lance-shaped, glossy dark green leaves to 20cm/8in long.
USE & CULTIVATION As for *P. aurea*. Fully frost hardy.

PICEA

SPRUCE
FAMILY PINACEAE

This is a genus of 30 to 40 species of evergreen coniferous trees from cool temperate Northern Hemisphere regions, where they often form extensive forests. They develop into majestic trees, often with a distinct conical outline, with whorled branches and spirally arranged needle-like leaves set on small leaf-bearing pegs. The foliage colour varies, in shades of green, blue, silver and grey, and there are many attractive dwarf and slow-growing forms available. Mature female cones are pendulous and ripen in their first year. Propagate from seed or cuttings or by grafting.

Picea abies
syn. *Picea excelsa*
Norway Spruce, Common Spruce

ORIGIN Northern Europe
CLIMATE M, CT, H

This distinctly conical evergreen tree reaches 60m/200ft in northern European forests and mountains further south, but is usually less in cultivation. The smooth reddish brown bark develops cracks with age. It has spreading branches clothed with dark green linear leaves to 2.5cm/1in long. The slender female cones to 18cm/7in long are green and erect at first, but ripen to pale brown and become pendulous. This is one of the world's most important timber trees, and the traditional Christmas tree in Europe. There are numerous attractive dwarf cultivars. **'Acrocona'** is a low, wide-spreading, pendulous form 1–3m/3–10ft high. **'Clanbrassiliana'** is rounded and spreading, to 1.5m/5ft high and 2.5m/8ft across. **'Gregoryana'** forms a dense rounded bush to 80cm/32in high. **'Little Gem'** is a very slow-growing dwarf shrub with close-set leaves, making it a very good subject for bonsai. **'Maxwellii'** is a low-growing compact form to 30cm/12in high with bright green foliage. **'Nidiformis'**, the Bird's Nest Spruce, is 50cm/20in high and spreads to 1.5m/5ft across, with a low depression in the centre of the plant. **'Reflexa'** is prostrate and mat forming, but can be trained on a stake to become a weeping standard.
USE & CULTIVATION A highly ornamental specimen tree for large gardens. It is extremely slow growing but should be given adequate space for best development. The dwarf cultivars make beautiful rock-garden subjects and are ideal for formal plantings in small courtyards. All the cultivars are suitable for containers. Grow in rich, moist well-drained soil in a sunny position. Fully frost hardy.

P

Picea breweriana
Brewer's Weeping Spruce

ORIGIN California, Oregon
CLIMATE M, CT, H

A beautiful weeping tree 10–20m/ 30–70ft high with a straight single trunk and upswept or spreading branches bearing curtains of pendulous branchlets to 2m/7ft long. The fleshy, dark bluish green leaves spread out all around the stem. Attractive slender cones to 12cm/5in long are purple at first, ripening to reddish brown.

USE & CULTIVATION An outstanding large specimen tree for cool mountain gardens. Allow adequate space so that its structural form can be fully appreciated. Plant in deep well-drained soil in full sun. Fully frost hardy.

Picea glauca
White Spruce

ORIGIN Canada, northeastern USA
CLIMATE M, CT, H

This narrow or broadly conical tree to 15m/50ft or more tall has thick bluish green leaves with bright green new growth. The cones are pale brown to 6cm/2¼in long. It is grown commercially for its timber. **P. g. var. *albertiana* 'Conica'**, the Dwarf Albert Spruce, is most often grown in gardens. It grows extremely slowly into a perfect pyramid of dense bright green foliage to 2m/7ft high, although with time it can reach 3m/10ft.

USE & CULTIVATION The species is extremely slow growing, but does need space to do it justice. Grow in a sheltered site with moist well-drained soil. The symmetrical Dwarf Albert Spruce is deservedly popular as an accent plant in formal gardens and is an outstanding container specimen. Feed annually with a balanced slow-release fertiliser. Fully frost hardy.

Picea omorika
Serbian Spruce

ORIGIN Bosnia, Serbia
CLIMATE M, CT, H

This slender conifer can grow to 30m/100ft. It has a spire-like crown and relatively short, upward-curving branches with drooping branchlets of soft, bright green foliage. Young shoots are densely hairy. The purplish cones ripen to brown and reach 6cm/2¼in long. **'Nana'** is a slow-growing dwarf form to less than 1m/3ft with glaucous, pale green leaves.

USE & CULTIVATION An outstanding specimen tree for a spacious garden or lawn. Grow in full sun in moist well-drained soil with high organic content. Protect from harsh dry winds. 'Nana' is suitable for rock or courtyard gardens and containers. Fully frost hardy.

Picea pungens
Colorado Spruce

ORIGIN Western North America
CLIMATE M, CT, H

This species forms an attractive pyramid with a conical crown to 30m/ 100ft in the wild, but is usually less in cultivation. The 4-sided needle-like leaves are usually grey–green, with young leaves slightly bluish. Mature female cones to 10cm/4in long are pendulous and broadly cylindrical. The Blue Colorado Spruce, **'Glauca'**, is a popular variety to 15m/50ft with foliage a rich blue–grey, especially when young. **'Globosa'** forms a dense rounded bush to 1.5m/5ft bearing soft

Picea glauca var. *albertiana* 'Conica'

Picea omorika

Picea pungens 'Glauca'

Picea pungens 'Montgomery'

Picea smithiana

Picea smithiana showing cones

blue–grey foliage. **'Koster'**, often considered the best blue conifer, has rich, glaucous, silvery blue foliage on spiralling finger-like branches. It grows to 12m/40ft. **'Koster Prostrate'** is a spreading dwarf form with the same colouring. **'Montgomery'** is a fine, slow-growing dwarf form to about 1.5m/5ft tall and 1m/3ft across with glaucous blue leaves.

USE & CULTIVATION These plants perform best in cool climates, free from long dry periods and drying winds. All make outstanding feature specimens and sustain interest throughout the cold winter months. The small forms are ideal for rock gardens, courtyards and containers. Provide fertile well-drained soil, ample water and occasional slow-release fertiliser, particularly when young. Fully frost hardy.

Picea smithiana
Morinda Spruce, West Himalayan Spruce

ORIGIN Nepal to Afghanistan
CLIMATE M, CT, H

This is a beautiful, symmetrical, weeping tree 15–30m/50–100ft high with upswept horizontal branches and fully pendulous side-branchlets. It has very slender, deep green leaves to 4cm/ 1½ in long. The slender, shiny brown female cones to 20cm/8in long hang gracefully in clusters at the ends of the branchlets.

USE & CULTIVATION Highly regarded as an ornamental specimen tree, this spruce thrives in cool moist regions. Give adequate space for full development. It prefers a sheltered site and fertile well-drained soil. Fully frost hardy.

P

PILEA

FAMILY UTRICACEAE

Widespread in tropical regions of the world, this genus comprises around 600 species of annuals and evergreen perennials, some of which are upright, others creeping. Some species are widely grown for their ornamental foliage and make ideal container plants indoors or in greenhouses; the trailing kinds are particularly suited to shallow containers or hanging baskets. Clusters of tiny insignificant flowers are normally produced in summer. Tip-prune overlong shoots during the growing season to avoid straggly plants. Propagate from cuttings or by division.

Pilea cadierei

Pilea involucrata

Pilea cadierei
Aluminium Plant, Watermelon Pilea

ORIGIN Vietnam
CLIMATE T, ST, WT
This bushy perennial to 30cm/12in high with a similar spread is often grown as a houseplant. The obovate pointed leaves to 8cm/3in long are marked with raised silvery patches, giving a metallic effect. **'Minima'** is similar, but with smaller leaves, and forms a compact bush to 15cm/6in high.
USE & CULTIVATION In warm climates, grow in a shady border where the patterned leaves contrast well with the foliage of other plants. Fertile, moist well-drained soil is best. Indoors, provide warm humid conditions and moderate light, away from direct sunlight. Frost tender.

Pilea involucrata
Friendship Plant

ORIGIN Central and South America
CLIMATE T, ST, WT
A creeping or neatly rounded perennial to 30cm/12in tall with a similar spread, producing fleshy, deeply quilted leaves clustered in tight rosettes. The dark green, oval to almost rounded leaves to 8cm/3in long have a reddish brown toning, and the undersides are deep purple. In summer it produces clusters of tiny pink flowers. **'Moon Valley'** is more upright and has fresh green leaves with purple colouring in the vein crevices.
USE & CULTIVATION As for *P. cadierei*. Frost tender.

Pilea microphylla
Artillery Plant

ORIGIN Florida (USA), Mexico to Brazil
CLIMATE T, ST, WT
This spreading short-lived perennial forms a mound to 30cm/12in tall with flattened fern-like sprays of tiny, soft, green leaves less than 1cm/³/₈in long. In summer it produces inconspicuous greenish yellow flowers which release a

cloud of pollen in an explosive way, giving the plant its common name.

USE & CULTIVATION As for *P. cadierei*. Frost tender.

PINUS

FAMILY PINACEAE

This genus of 120 species of evergreen coniferous trees confined to the Northern Hemisphere is widespread in temperate regions. In general, and particularly when young, they have a neat conical outline with a single erect trunk and regular whorls of horizontal or ascending smaller branches. Depending on the species, the slender needle-like leaves are carried in bundles of mostly 2, 3 or 5 on each short shoot. Male and female cones are borne on the same tree. The female cones vary in shape, reaching maturity mostly in the second year and bearing nut-like seeds usually with a pronounced wing. Apart from their ornamental value, pines are extremely important timber trees, also yielding aromatic resins, turpentine and various oils used for medicinal purposes. Some species have edible seeds. Most are fast growing and can be shaped and trained by pruning. Propagate from fresh seed; cultivars may be grafted.

Pinus aristata

Pinus aristata
Bristlecone Pine

ORIGIN North America (Rocky Mountains)
CLIMATE M, CT, H
This small, very slow-growing tree can eventually reach 9m/30ft or more. It has a short trunk with thin smooth bark becoming ridged and scaly with age. The densely crowded, stiff, pointed, needle-like leaves to 4cm/1½ in long are borne in groups of 5. They are deep green with conspicuous white dots of resin and smell of turpentine when crushed. Cylindrical brown female cones to 9cm/3½ in long ripen in the second year.

USE & CULTIVATION Reputed to be the oldest living tree, with several specimens growing in mountainous regions

of western USA dated at more than 4000 years old. It is extremely slow glowing and makes a charming feature plant for a well-drained rockery or container; also a great candidate for bonsai. Fully frost hardy.

Pinus cembra
Arolla Pine, Swiss Pine

ORIGIN Europe
CLIMATE WT, M, CT, H
This densely foliaged pine to 9m/30ft or so often retains its branches at ground level so that the trunk is almost completely hidden. It has reddish brown scaly bark and the young shoots

are covered with brownish orange hair. Stiff, shiny green leaves to 10cm/4in long are grouped in erect bundles of 5. The 8cm/3in long conical female cones ripen from bluish purple to brown. Often planted for timber in northern Europe.

USE & CULTIVATION Valued for its neat conical shape and dense foliage to ground level, this is a popular specimen for contemporary planting and for oriental-style gardens. Slower growing than most other pines, it makes an excellent container plant for many years. Grow in deep well-drained soil in full sun. Withstands low temperatures and is wind resistant. Fully frost hardy.

P

Pinus mugo

Pinus mugo var. *pumilo* 'Amber Gold'

Pinus densiflora
Japanese Red Pine

ORIGIN Russia, Korea, Japan
CLIMATE M, CT, H
This pine will reach 30m/100ft or more in height, becoming flat topped at maturity. It has reddish brown scaly bark, especially on the upper trunk. Young shoots are pinky grey at first. Slender, bright green, needle-like leaves to 10cm/4in long borne in pairs are slightly twisted. The yellowish brown conical cones are about 5cm/2in long. **'Alice Verkade'** is a multi-stemmed dwarf form to 50cm/20in high with a spread twice that size. **'Umbraculifera'** (syn. 'Tagyosho') is a slow-growing multi-stemmed tree eventually forming a flattened umbrella-like crown to 3.5m/12ft.
USE & CULTIVATION A handsome lawn specimen. The smaller cultivars are good accent plants for courtyards, terraces and Japanese gardens. Container subjects can be pruned to shape.

Grow in deep well-drained soil in full sun or light shade. Withstands low temperatures and is wind resistant. A popular bonsai subject, valued for its windswept look. Fully frost hardy.

Pinus halepensis
Aleppo Pine

ORIGIN Mediterranean region
CLIMATE WT, M, CT
This broadly domed tree to 20m/70ft or so develops an open irregular crown when mature. Young growth and branchlets are grey. The paired, shiny green leaves, 5–10cm/2–4in long, are slightly curved and spine-tipped. Smooth, glossy brown cones to 12cm/5in long are borne on thick recurved stalks and ripen in the second year.
USE & CULTIVATION A fast-growing shade and windbreak tree for particularly hot dry conditions or seaside planting. It grows naturally on dry rocky-lime sites and is good in poor soils. Moderately frost hardy.

Pinus mugo
Swiss Mountain Pine

ORIGIN Mountains of Europe
CLIMATE M, CT, H
A slow-growing, conical, resinous shrub or shrubby tree to 3.5m/12ft, often with a gnarled windswept appearance. The firm, upright, dark green needles to 6cm/2¼in long are slightly curved and develop from resinous buds. The oval cones to 6cm/2¼in long are green at first, ripening to dark brown. **'Gnom'** forms a tight rounded shape to 2m/7ft high with a similar spread. **'Mops'** is a slower-growing compact bush eventually reaching 1.5m/5ft in 10 years. **P. m. var. pumilio** grows to about 1–2m/3–7ft high and twice as wide and is the source of several interesting dwarf cultivars. **'Amber Gold'** is a very compact rounded form with bright golden yellow foliage.
USE & CULTIVATION All make decorative rock-garden subjects and look particularly good in Japanese-style

gardens. They thrive in any well-drained soil in full sun and withstand cold windy conditions. Suitable for growing in tubs. With time they become superb bonsai subjects. Fully frost hardy.

Pinus nigra
Austrian Pine, Black Pine

ORIGIN Southern Europe
CLIMATE M, CT, H
This conifer has a single straight trunk and a rounded dome, and grows to 20–40m/70–130ft tall in its natural

habitat, but usually only to 15m/50ft in cultivation. When young it forms an attractive dense pyramid of whorled branches of dark green leaves to 15cm/6in long, borne in pairs. Female cones to 8cm/3in long are paired, ripening to pale shiny brown. *P. n.* **subsp.** *laricio* (syn. *P. n.* var. *maritima*), the Corsican Pine, has fewer, shorter branches and sparser foliage. The slender grey–green leaves are longer, to 18cm/7in, and often twisted in young trees. It is widely planted for timber.
USE & CULTIVATION Both make attractive specimens and are especially valued

Pinus nigra

Pinus nigra

Pinus parviflora

for ornamental planting in coastal gardens, where they will tolerate wind-swept salty conditions. Fully frost hardy.

Pinus parviflora
Japanese White Pine

ORIGIN Japan
CLIMATE M, CT, H
This species forms an extremely elegant tree to 9m/30ft or more; conical when young, as it grows older it becomes irregular in shape, with a flat top. The bark is smooth and grey. The deep green leaves to 7cm/2½in long in bunches of 5 have white stripes. The female cones to 7cm/2½in long are reddish brown and may hang on the tree for several years. **'Adcock's Dwarf'** is dense and slow growing to 75cm/30in tall with short, bent-back, grey–green leaves. **'Glauca'** has twisted blue–grey leaves.
USE & CULTIVATION Decorative feature plants in small gardens or in Japanese-style landscapes, where they can be pruned, trimmed and trained like large bonsai. They do best in full sun and well-drained soil with additional water during dry periods. The short needles and very slow growth have made these plants highly popular for bonsai. Fully frost hardy.

Pinus patula
Mexican Weeping Pine

ORIGIN Mexico
CLIMATE WT, M
This is a fast-growing pyramidal tree to 20m/70ft, branching low to the ground with closely set horizontal branches which curve gently upwards. The slender, soft, bright green leaves to 30cm/12in long, mostly in 3s, hang straight down, giving the tree its distinctively graceful appearance. The curved oval cones to 10cm/4in long are often in clusters.
USE & CULTIVATION A good ornamental shade tree for mild climates as a lawn specimen or feature tree. It prefers good drainage, slightly acid, fertile soil, regular rainfall and full sun. Moderately frost hardy.

P

Pinus strobus
Eastern White Pine, Weymouth Pine

ORIGIN Eastern North America
CLIMATE M, CT, H

In its native forest habitat this important, straight-trunked timber tree grows to 40m/130ft or so. In cultivation it is smaller, forming a shapely conical crown to 24m/80ft. It has deeply fissured, greyish brown bark and closely whorled horizontal branches. The slender, blue–green, needle-like leaves to 10cm/4in long are carried in bundles of 5. Pendulous resinous cones are cylindrical, 8–15cm/3–6in long, slightly curved and clustered at branch ends. **'Fastigiata'** has a slender conical habit to 8m/25ft tall with closely set, upward-pointing branches. **'Radiata'** is a dwarf cultivar that develops into a spreading mound to 1m/3ft or so tall with dense, glaucous green foliage.
USE & CULTIVATION The species is a fine ornamental subject for large gardens. 'Fastigiata' is good for small gardens or in a narrow bed near a driveway. Grow in well-drained light soils in full sun. Avoid dry conditions and excessive exposure to wind. 'Radiata' is suitable for rock gardens and containers. Fully frost hardy.

Pinus sylvestris
Scots Pine

ORIGIN Europe, temperate Asia
CLIMATE M, CT, H

This is a common forest tree on high ground throughout Europe, where it may reach 30m/100ft, often with a small rounded crown. It has distinct copper red bark on the upper trunk. The paired grey or bluish green leaves to 7cm/2½in long are twisted and finely toothed. Female cones with short stalks are borne singly or in clusters. There are numerous cultivars available, most of them slow growing. One of the most popular is **'Beuvronensis'**, which eventually forms a dense rounded bush to 1.5m/5ft tall and has shorter blue–green leaves.
USE & CULTIVATION Widely planted for forestry purposes. It grows on poor sandy soil and withstands cold and seaside conditions. 'Beuvronensis' and other dwarf forms are suitable for rock gardens and containers and make fine bonsai. Fully frost hardy.

Pinus sylvestris 'Beuvronensis'

Pinus strobus 'Radiata'

Pinus sylvestris

Pinus thunbergii 'Sayonara'

Pinus wallichiana

Pinus wallichiana

Pinus thunbergii
Japanese Black Pine

ORIGIN Northeast China, Japan, Korea

CLIMATE M, CT, H

In its native habitat this pine reaches a height of 36m/120ft. The branches are often low, crooked or upswept, becoming irregular and spreading with maturity to give the tree an attractive craggy appearance. It has conspicuous white winter buds and pairs of grey–green, slightly twisted, waxy leaves to 12cm/5in long. **'Sayonara'** (syn. 'Yatsubusa') is a dwarf form with fresh green leaves.

USE & CULTIVATION In Japan this species is a popular ornamental in gardens and parks and is a good feature tree for a Japanese-style design. It can be trimmed, shaped and trained and grown in a container for many years. It is among the favourite plants of bonsai growers. Fully frost hardy.

Pinus wallichiana
Bhutan Pine, Blue Pine

ORIGIN Himalayas

CLIMATE M, CT, H

A handsome tree with a broad crown and weeping appearance, to 35m/120ft tall. It has broad-spreading lower branches and graceful grey–green leaves to 20cm/8in long, hanging in groups of 5. The pendulous cones are 25–30cm/10–12in long, pale brown and resinous when ripe.

USE & CULTIVATION An outstanding specimen tree for a large lawn in a cool moist climate. Plant in well-drained soil in full sun. It is pollution resistant and is grown for timber in Italy. Fully frost hardy.

P

Piper novae-hollandiae

Pisonia grandis

PIPER

PEPPER

FAMILY PIPERACEAE

Best known for the Black Pepper, *Piper nigrum*, this is a large tropical genus of more than 1000 species of bushy shrubs and rampant vines. In India and Southeast Asia the leaves of *Piper betel* are used as an edible wrapping for the nut of the Betel Palm, *Areca catechu*. Some species are cultivated for their handsome glossy leaves and ability to thrive in shady places. Propagate from cuttings.

Piper novae-hollandiae
Giant Pepper Vine

ORIGIN Eastern Australia
CLIMATE T, ST, WT

A moderately vigorous climber clinging by means of numerous adventitious roots. The glossy, thin-textured, heart-shaped leaves on young plants become oval and leathery, to 12cm/5in long, on mature branches. Crushed leaves are aromatic. Tiny flowers are followed by clusters of small red fruits.

USE & CULTIVATION A beautiful robust vine for training up a tree in a shady part of a spacious rainforest or tropical garden. Grow in moist humus-enriched soil with reasonable drainage. Give suitable support if grown in a container on a warm veranda, or in a conservatory in cold climates. Frost tender.

Piper ornatum
Celebes Pepper

ORIGIN Sulawesi (Indonesia)
CLIMATE T, ST, WT

A lightly climbing or trailing vine with slender wiry stems bearing pointed heart-shaped leaves to 12cm/5in long and 10cm/4in wide. The upper leaf surfaces are deep olive green with a mottled pattern of pinkish silver markings; the undersides are deep maroon.

USE & CULTIVATION An attractive climber outdoors in warm frost-free areas, although mostly grown as a conservatory or house plant. Give container-grown plants a light framework to climb on, or allow the shoots to trail down from a hanging basket. Indoors, provide good light, but avoid direct sunlight. Warmth and humidity are essential. Water moderately throughout the year, but allow some drying out between waterings. Frost tender.

PISONIA

SYN.
HEIMERLIODENDRON

FAMILY NYCTAGINACEAE

Found mainly in North and South America and Southeast Asia, this is a small tropical genus of 35 species of evergreen shrubs, trees and climbers. They are cultivated for their large ornamental leaves, some of which are variegated. The small greenish flowers are followed by masses of sticky ribbed fruit, which in some species, called bird-catcher trees, can trap small birds and in extreme cases cause their death. Propagate from fresh seed or cuttings.

Pisonia grandis
Bird Lime Tree

ORIGIN Southeast Asia, northern Australia

CLIMATE T, ST

An erect branching tree to 9m/30ft forming an open canopy of light green oval leaves to 30cm/12in long. The greenish white flowers appear in late summer and are followed by masses of small sticky fruit.

USE & CULTIVATION This tree is mostly grown in tropical gardens, where its attractive open crown provides dappled shade and protection for smaller shade-loving plants. Salt tolerant and ideal for seaside gardens and large-scale coastal plantings. Grow in fertile well-drained soil in full sun or part shade. Frost tender.

Pisonia umbellifera
syn. *Heimerliodendron brunonianum*
Bird-catcher Tree

ORIGIN Western Pacific region

CLIMATE T, ST

This erect branching shrub or small tree to 3.5m/12ft has a rounded or spreading crown and shiny, rich green, oval leaves to 35cm/14in long, closely grouped on firm upright stems. Insignificant pink or yellow scented flowers are followed by sticky-glandular fruit. **'Variegata'** has deep green leaves heavily edged with irregular patches of creamy yellow. The sticky fruits are not generally produced.

USE & CULTIVATION These small trees have a neat habit and are good foliage plants for tropical gardens and warm semi-shaded patios. 'Variegata' is a popular houseplant but good light is

necessary to retain the colourful variegation. Water freely during the active growth period and apply a balanced liquid fertiliser monthly. Water sparingly in winter, allowing some drying out between waterings. Salt tolerant. Frost tender.

PISTACIA

FAMILY ANACARDIACEAE

From warm temperate regions of the Northern Hemisphere, this genus comprises about 10 species of deciduous and evergreen shrubs and trees. They are grown chiefly for their spectacular blaze of autumn colour, and are recommended as alternatives to those species of *Rhus* which can cause serious allergies through contact with leaves or branches. The flowers are generally inconspicuous, and if pollinated are followed by peppercorn-like berries. *Pistacia vera* is cultivated extensively for

its edible pistachio nuts, but it is not grown ornamentally. Propagate from seed or cuttings or by grafting.

Pistacia chinensis
Chinese Pistachio

ORIGIN China

CLIMATE WT, M, CT

This medium-sized deciduous tree grows to 9–12m/30–40ft in cultivation. It has pinnate glossy green leaves comprised of up to 12 pairs of leaflets; they colour beautifully in autumn in shades of red, orange and yellow. Panicles of inconspicuous flowers in spring are followed by rounded red berries that turn blue in autumn.

USE & CULTIVATION Grow as a specimen tree in a lawn or spacious courtyard, as part of a woodland or in the street. Well-drained fertile soil and a sunny position give best results. It benefits from annual feeding with a balanced liquid fertiliser. Moderately frost hardy.

Pistacia chinensis

PISTIA

FAMILY ARACEAE
This genus of one species of aquatic perennial is widespread in tropical and subtropical regions. It is grown for its decorative leaves. It can be an invasive and noxious weed of tropical waterways and thus is best contained. Propagate by separating plantlets.

Pistia stratiotes
Water Lettuce

ORIGIN Tropical and subtropical regions
CLIMATE T, ST
This floating water-plant has soft green, fluted, wedge-shaped leaves to 20cm/8in long arranged in a lettuce-like rosette. Small arum-like flowers appear throughout the year.
USE & CULTIVATION A highly ornamental water-plant for warm climates, where it is often grown in water-filled containers. Also suitable for a large tropical aquarium or heated conservatory pool. Grow in sun or part shade and thin plants out from time to time. Frost tender.

PLATYCERIUM

FAMILY POLYPODIACEAE
Occurring naturally in tropical and subtropical rainforests of Asia, Africa and Australia, there are about 15 species in this genus of epiphytic ferns. They form large clumps with age and all have two kinds of fronds. The infertile nest fronds wrap around and anchor the fern to its host while the fertile upper fronds extend outwards and are usually pendent and lobed at the ends. These produce dense brown spore patches on their undersides and are shed before being replaced by new fronds. These long-lived ferns make highly dramatic specimen plants mounted on a large wooden slab. When attaching a plant to its mount initially, wrap the roots in a coarse peat mixture and keep moist until the supporting fronds have adhered to the

Pistia stratiotes

support. Scale insects and the staghorn fern beetle may be a problem. Propagate from spores or by detaching new plantlets formed from a growing point.

Platycerium bifurcatum
Elkhorn Fern

ORIGIN Eastern Australia
CLIMATE T, ST, WT
A large clumping fern with wavy or lobed nest leaves and pendulous, strap-like, fertile fronds to 1m/3ft long, forked 2–5 times. Small plants develop on the margins of the nest leaves, continually adding to the size of the clump. These can be carefully detached as new young specimens; make sure an ample layer of peat is left as a backing.
USE & CULTIVATION Allow plenty of room for this outstanding epiphytic plant. Mount it on a large hardwood slab which can be attached to walls of verandas, patios and courtyards, and to trees in a semi-shaded position with good light. Provide plenty of water in summer, and keep dry in winter. In cooler climates, protect from frosts and grow in a conservatory or indoors. Frost tender.

Platycerium superbum
Staghorn

ORIGIN Eastern Australia
CLIMATE T, ST, WT
This spectacular rainforest species has large grey–green backing leaves which eventually form an extensive collection area. The pendulous fertile fronds, to 2m/7ft long, are lobed several times. A large brown spore-bearing patch is formed on the underside around the first division and is sometimes mistaken for a problem. As this species does not produce plantlets, propagation must be from spores.
USE & CULTIVATION Attach to fences, walls or trees to create a tropical atmosphere around the home. When mounting on a hardwood slab, take care not to tie across the central crown or growing points. Place in a semi-shaded position away from harsh sun and frost. Keep the base of the plant moist and feed with diluted liquid fertiliser. It can be grown in a fernery or conservatory, but with time becomes very heavy; watering may be a problem inside the house. Frost tender.

Platycerium bifurcatum

Platycerium superbum

PLECTRANTHUS

FAMILY LABIATAE/LAMIACEAE

A few members of this mostly tropical genus of about 250 species are grown for their attractive foliage, sometimes as conservatory and house plants. They are semi-woody, somewhat succulent shrubs with fleshy, oval to heart-shaped leaves and small tubular flowers in shades of white to purple borne in loose spikes. Slugs and snails often attack young plants. Propagate from stem cuttings, which quickly produce roots.

Plectranthus argentatus
Silver Plectranthus

ORIGIN Australia
CLIMATE ST, WT

A small spreading shrub to 1m/3ft high and wide with silvery, hairy stems and ovate, silvery green, velvety leaves to 12cm/5in long with finely toothed margins. Bluish white flowers are borne in whorled spikes to about 30cm/12in long in summer.

USE & CULTIVATION A neat border plant that looks good on its own edging a narrow bed near the house where a soft colour is desired. Also suitable for a rockery feature and containers, and as a silvery highlight to green plants. Grow in a well-drained semi-shaded position. Cut back hard when plants become straggly. Frost tender.

P

Plectranthus argentatus

Plectranthus australis
Swedish Ivy

ORIGIN South Africa
CLIMATE ST, WT

This bushy plant grows to 20cm/8in tall and spreads widely, with trailing stems covered in almost circular, glossy dark green, leaves about 4cm/1½ in across with scalloped edges. Sprays of tubular lilac and white flowers are produced throughout the warmer months. **USE & CULTIVATION** A popular hanging basket subject, it is grown mostly in conservatories and as a houseplant, where it likes good filtered light. Keep moist, well fed and reasonably warm. Tip-prune regularly to encourage branching. Frost tender.

Plectranthus madagascariensis
Mintleaf

ORIGIN Southern Africa
CLIMATE ST, WT

A sprawling mound-forming plant to 30cm/12in high with self-layering succulent stems and quilted rounded leaves to 4cm/1½ in long with toothed edges and white bristles. The leaves have a strong mint-like scent when crushed. White or pale lavender blue flowers are produced in early summer. **'Variegated Mintleaf'**, with white-tipped margins, is the form most commonly seen.

USE & CULTIVATION Ideal as a ground-cover and rockery plant grown in moist well-drained soil in partial shade. Also suitable for hanging baskets; can be brought indoors during the colder months. Keep moist, well fed and reasonably warm. Frost tender.

Plectranthus oertendahlii

ORIGIN South Africa
CLIMATE ST, WT

This species grows to about 20cm/8in high and has trailing purplish stems to 1m/3ft long. Its 5cm/2in long, bronze green, almost circular leaves are strongly veined with silver; the undersides are softly felted and coloured purple. White or blue flowers are produced in short spikes throughout the year.

USE & CULTIVATION Often grown as a houseplant in hanging baskets. Provide plenty of water, full light and warmth, and feed regularly during the growing months. Trimmed plants become bushier. Frost tender.

PLEIOBLASTUS

FAMILY GRAMINEAE/POACEAE

This genus is made up of about 20 species of small to medium-sized bamboos from temperate regions. They have spreading rhizomes and some are moderately invasive, producing thickets of erect woody stems and attractive linear leaves which are sometimes brightly variegated. Propagate by division.

Pleioblastus auricomus
syn. *Arundinaria auricoma*
Kamuro-zasa

ORIGIN Japan
CLIMATE WT, M, CT

This small bamboo grows to 1.5m/5ft tall and has hollow, purplish green stems with downy nodes. The linear leaves to 20cm/8in long, edged with fine bristles, are bright yellow with green stripes.

USE & CULTIVATION It provides an attractive habit and foliage contrast in the garden and looks particularly good near a water feature. In time it can become rather invasive, and in smaller gardens is best confined to containers. Grow in moist well-drained soil in full

Plectranthus australis

Pleioblastus auricomus

Pleioblastus pygmaeus var. distichus

Pleioblastus variegatus

sun. Cut to ground level at the end of winter to produce the best new growth the following season. Fully frost hardy.

Pleioblastus pygmaeus
syn. *Arundinaria pygmaea*
Pygmy Bamboo

ORIGIN Japan
CLIMATE WT, M, CT
This erect bamboo to 40cm/16in high has a rather creeping habit to 1m/3ft across. It has flattened canes and mid-green downy leaves about 8cm/3in long. **P. g. var. distichus** is a larger plant, to 1m/3ft tall.
USE & CULTIVATION As for *P. aurico-mus*. Pygmy Bamboo can also be grown in partial shade. Fully frost hardy.

Pleioblastus variegatus
syns *Arundinaria fortunei*,
A. variegata

ORIGIN Japan
CLIMATE WT, M, CT
This upright bamboo has hollow pale green and powdery white stems to 75cm/30in high. The linear leaves to 20cm/8in long have distinct creamy

white stripes and are covered with fine white hairs, chiefly on the undersides.
USE & CULTIVATION As for *P. aurico-mus*. Fully frost hardy.

POA

FAMILY GRAMINEAE/POACEAE
This is a large cosmopolitan genus of mostly perennial grasses found in temperate regions. Some are grown for agricultural purposes or used as lawn grasses, such as the Kentucky Bluegrass, *Poa pratensis*. A few species are popular tussock grasses with landscape designers, often used in massed plantings. Propagate from seed or by division.

Poa labillardieri
Common Tussock Grass

ORIGIN Australia
CLIMATE WT, M, CT
This densely tufted perennial forms a neat mound of flat or sometimes inrolled mid-green leaves to 80cm/32in long. From late spring to late summer it produces lacy purple-tinted flowering panicles to about 25cm/10in long. There

Poa labillardieri

are a number of selected forms, some with rusty brown tints and bluish foliage.
USE & CULTIVATION It looks best massed as a grassy landscape feature. Use the blue-leaved forms for contrasting foliage in a border or in a rockery pocket. Grow in any well-drained soil in full sun or partial shade and cut back hard in early spring to rejuvenate clumps. Moderately frost hardy.

PODOCARPUS

FAMILY PODOCARPACEAE

There are about 95 species in this coniferous genus of shrubs and trees found mainly in warm temperate regions of the Southern Hemisphere, with some extending to southern Asia. Ranging from low spreading shrubs to tall timber trees, they have dense, spirally arranged, mostly flat linear leaves. Male and female flowers are usually borne on separate plants. Female flowers mature into small round fruit, often supported by a brightly coloured succulent receptacle. Propagate from seed or cuttings.

Podocarpus elatus
Brown Pine, Plum Pine

ORIGIN Eastern Australia
CLIMATE WT, M, CT

In its Australian rainforest habitat this species can reach 40m/130ft, but in gardens it is rarely more than 12–15m/40–50ft. It has a short trunk, fibrous bark and a dense conical crown of glossy dark green linear leaves 8–12cm/3–5in long with paler undersides. New growth is lime green. The fleshy bluish black receptacle is made into jellies and jam.

USE & CULTIVATION It withstands regular clipping, making it useful for hedges, screens and ornamental shade in gardens or streets. Grow in well-drained soil in full sun or partial shade. Marginally frost hardy.

Podocarpus lawrencei
Mountain Plum Pine

ORIGIN Eastern Australia
CLIMATE WT, M, CT, H

On exposed mountain slopes this species is a sprawling, densely branched bush, but in more favourable conditions it becomes a small erect tree 3.5–6m/12–20ft tall. It has oblong leathery leaves to 1.5cm/½in long densely arranged along the branches, attractive pinkish male catkins and fleshy bright red receptacles. Female cultivars such as **'Alpine Lass'**, with short, thick, glaucous leaves, and **'Blue Gem'**, with creamy young growth, are grown in the UK.

USE & CULTIVATION Slow growing when young, it makes a striking rock-garden, groundcover or container specimen. It will withstand clipping and is sometimes used for bonsai. Grow in light to medium, well-drained soil in full sun. Fully frost hardy.

Podocarpus macrophyllus
Kasamaki, Buddhist Pine

ORIGIN China, Japan
CLIMATE ST, WT, M, CT

A slow-growing dome-shaped tree 15m/50ft tall with attractive drooping outer branches and linear to lance-shaped, leathery leaves 10–15cm/4–6in long and 1cm/⅓in wide. The ovoid

Podocarpus elatus

Podocarpus macrophyllus 'Maki'

Podocarpus nivalis

Polygonatum multiflorum

fruit has a succulent purplish red receptacle. It has religious symbolism and is frequently seen in Chinese temple gardens. **'Maki'** forms a very neat erect shrub or small tree and has glossy leaves to 8cm/3in long.

USE & CULTIVATION Responds to regular pruning and is sometimes used for hedging. Also makes a highly ornamental lawn or street tree. 'Maki' is a good slow-growing container specimen that can be trimmed to shape. Grow in sun or partial shade in rich well-drained soil, preferably with plenty of moisture in summer. Frost hardy.

Podocarpus nivalis
Mountain Totara

ORIGIN New Zealand
CLIMATE WT, M, CT, H
This is a mostly prostrate shrub with wide-spreading branches that may reach 2m/7ft high and across. It has spirally arranged linear leaves 1–2cm/^{1}/$_3$–^{3}/$_4$in long, often yellow or bronze coloured. Fleshy red seed capsules appear on female plants in summer and early autumn.

USE & CULTIVATION Suitable for a large rock garden, it will gracefully trail over large boulders, slopes and raised gardens in full sun with good drainage. Fully frost hardy.

POLYGONATUM

SOLOMON'S SEAL
FAMILY CONVALLARIACEAE/ LILIACEAE
About 30 species are known in this genus of perennials. They are found only in temperate regions of the Northern Hemisphere and are usually woodland plants. Some have long been used in herbal medicine, but are grown mainly for their flowers and foliage. Propagate from seed or by division.

Polygonatum multiflorum

ORIGIN Europe, Asia
CLIMATE M, CT, H
This perennial has a thick creeping rhizome and graceful arching stems to 90cm/36in high with broad, upward-pointing, alternate leaves to 15cm/6in

long. The white bell-shaped flowers are green tipped and hang down below the leaves in late spring and early summer. **'Striatum'** has variegated leaves striped creamy white.

USE & CULTIVATION Use for edging a woodland garden or in similar shady places. Grow in humus-rich, moist well-drained soil. Fully frost hardy.

Polygonatum odoratum
syn. *Polygonatum officinale*

ORIGIN Europe, parts of Asia
CLIMATE M, CT, H
This perennial to 90cm/36in high has creeping rhizomes and arching angular stems. The ovate leaves to 15cm/6in long are carried in 2 rows. Greenish white fragrant flowers borne singly or in pairs in late spring and early summer are followed by rounded black fruit. **'Variegatum'** has white leaf margins.

USE & CULTIVATION Both will flourish in the dappled shade of a woodland garden. Grow in moisture-retentive, humus-rich soil with good drainage. Fully frost hardy.

P

POLYPODIUM

POLYPOD

FAMILY POLYPODIACEAE

A genus of 75 species of ferns with a wide distribution, but mainly from temperate areas in the Northern Hemisphere. They have scaly, reddish brown rhizomes and are found growing on trees or along the ground, forming mats or colonies. The pinnate or bipinnate fronds are on wiry stems jointed to the rhizome. Some of the frost-hardy species can be grown outside in cool areas, either in the garden or in containers. Propagate by division.

Polypodium cambricum
syn. *Polypodium australe*
Southern Polypod

ORIGIN Southern and western Europe
CLIMATE WT, M, CT, H
This terrestrial fern has creeping rhizomes with long brown scales. The mid-green pinnate fronds to 30cm/12in or more long are ovate in outline. The leaflets often have toothed margins and may become crested.
USE & CULTIVATION Grow in well-drained, humus-rich soil in dappled shade, either beneath trees or in dry walls. Established plants should not be disturbed. Fully frost hardy.

Polypodium vulgare
Common Polypod

ORIGIN Europe, Africa, eastern Asia
CLIMATE WT, M, CT, H
This fern has a thickish, brown, scaly rhizome that grows along the ground and over rocks and tree trunks. The mid-green fronds to 40cm/16in long are lance-shaped or oblong in outline and have linear pinnae. A number of attractive cultivars with crested fronds are available.
USE & CULTIVATION A good durable fern for outdoors in cool climates, where it can be planted beneath trees or in a mixed border or rock garden. Also suitable for hanging baskets. Grow in well-drained, humus-rich soil in

dappled shade. To keep the crested cultivars intact, remove any fronds that revert to the normal pinnate state. Fully frost hardy.

POLYSTICHUM

SHIELD FERN

FAMILY DRYOPTERIDACEAE

There are about 180 species in this large cosmopolitan genus of terrestrial ferns. They have mostly erect rhizomes covered with brown scales, and erect fronds forming a tufted spreading crown. Those with fancy crested or twisted leaflets were fashionable in Victorian times. Some species produce reproductive bulbils on the tips of mature fronds, which grow into young plants as the fronds wither and die. Propagate from these small plants or by division.

Polystichum acrostichoides
Christmas Fern

ORIGIN North America
CLIMATE M, CT, H
This tufted evergreen fern has lustrous deep green fronds to about 60cm/24in long, divided once and with narrow saw-toothed leaflets. Cultivars with twisted or crested leaflets are available.
USE & CULTIVATION Grow outdoors in a partly shaded rockery pocket, border or woodland garden, but it is often more satisfactory in a cool greenhouse or fernery. Provide moist well-drained soil. Fully frost hardy.

Polystichum setiferum
Soft Shield Fern

ORIGIN Europe
CLIMATE WT, M, CT
This fern forms tufts of soft, pale green, arching fronds to 1.2m/4ft long that are twice divided and borne on stalks covered with pale scales at the base. It is semi-deciduous in cool climates. Plantlets are formed along the frond midrib. Those of the **Divisilobum Group** have further finely divided leaflets, giving a soft feathery look. Several similar cultivars are available. **'Plumosum Bevis'** has fronds to 80cm/32in long with elongated leaflets.
USE & CULTIVATION This attractive fern can be grown outdoors in cool climates, where it can be planted beneath

Polystichum setiferum

Pontederia cordata

Pseudolarix amabilis

trees, or in a mixed border, fernery or rock garden. Grow in moisture-retentive, well-drained soil in semi-shade. Fully frost hardy.

PONTEDERIA

FAMILY PONTEDERIACEAE

A genus of 5 or 6 aquatic rhizomatous perennials native to North and South America, forming attractive colonies. They have distinctive lance-shaped leaves and long spikes of usually blue flowers. Propagate by division.

Pontederia cordata
Pickerel Weed

ORIGIN North America
CLIMATE ST, WT, M, CT
A marginal aquatic perennial to 75cm/30in tall with dark green, shiny,

elongated, heart-shaped leaves to 20cm/8in long. In late summer it produces dense spikes of tubular blue flowers.
USE & CULTIVATION An easy-to-grow waterside plant that thrives in a wide range of climatic conditions. It needs full sun and shallow water up to 25cm/10in deep. Remove fading flowers regularly. Fully frost hardy.

PSEUDOLARIX

FAMILY PINACEAE

This genus has only a single species, a deciduous conifer from southern and eastern China. It is closely allied to *Larix*, but differs in having longer leaves, male cones held in clusters and female cones that break up when mature. The Golden Larch is grown for its shapely habit and outstanding autumn colour. Propagate from seed or cuttings.

Pseudolarix amabilis
syn. *Pseudolarix kaempferi*
Golden Larch

ORIGIN China
CLIMATE M, CT, H
A broadly conical tree to 30m/100ft in nature, but often much less in cultivation. It has horizontal branches and fresh green linear leaves 2–5cm/$^3/_4$–2in long turning rich golden orange in autumn. The male cones are catkin-like and held in clusters of up to 25; female cones to 8cm/3in long are bright green with triangular leathery scales, rather like a small globe artichoke.
USE & CULTIVATION Slow growing at first, it makes a picturesque lawn specimen or feature without taking up too much room. Grow in rich well-drained soil in sun or partial shade. In cold areas, shelter from early spring frosts and strong winds. Fully frost hardy.

P

PSEUDOPANAX

FAMILY ARALIACEAE

A genus of about 12 to 20 species of evergreen trees and shrubs from Tasmania, New Zealand and Chile. Several species have a very pronounced juvenile phase with leaves totally unlike those on adult plants. The small yellowish green flowers borne in rounded umbels are followed by berry-like purple–black fruit. They make good architectural, feature and container plants and are ideal for modern landscaping. Some species are attractive houseplants. Propagate from ripe seed or cuttings.

Pseudopanax crassifolius
Lancewood

ORIGIN New Zealand
CLIMATE ST, WT, M, CT

This is a variable, umbrella-shaped evergreen tree which can eventually grow to 9m/30ft, its leaves progressing through several stages. The dark green juvenile leaves are slender, to 60cm/24in long and no more than 2.5cm/1in wide, with serrated edges and purplish undersides. At this stage the plant is an erect unbranched stem 3–4m/10–14ft high, and the leaves point downwards. Eventually it branches at the top of the stem and the leaves become leathery and compound, with 3–5 sword-shaped, toothed or entire leaflets to 20cm/8in long. The greenish summer flowers borne in clusters are followed on female plants by small black ornamental fruit.
USE & CULTIVATION An interesting feature plant for a large rock garden or a sparse stylised garden. Grow in well-drained soil in a sunny or partially shaded position. In very cold areas, place in a cool greenhouse, or in the house in a well-lit situation. Frost hardy.

Pseudopanax lessonii
Houpara

ORIGIN New Zealand
CLIMATE ST, WT, M, CT
This is a small, shrub-like, evergreen tree 2–6m/7–20ft high with stout

Pseudosasa japonica

branches and rich green leathery leaves, with 3–5 leaflets to 10cm/4in long. Greenish purple summer flowers are followed on female plants by small purple–black fruit. Attractive hybrids, generally with *P. crassifolius* and *P. discolor*, have largely replaced this species in cultivation. **'Gold Splash'** is a multi-branched leafy shrub with heavily marked yellow leaves. **'Purpureus'** has smaller, glossy purple–bronze leaves. **'Sabre'** has dark green juvenile leaves to 30cm/12in long with an orange midrib, becoming shorter as the bush matures.
USE & CULTIVATION Suitable for small gardens and courtyards and can be used in coastal situations. 'Gold Splash' is an outstanding variegated plant for growing among other shrubs, in containers and in the house. Grow in any reasonably well-drained soil in full sun or partial shade. In frost-prone areas they are best in a cool greenhouse or indoors away from extreme heat. Heavy pruning is tolerated if necessary. Marginally frost hardy.

PSEUDOSASA

FAMILY GRAMINEAE/POACEAE

A small genus of 3 to 6 species of running bamboos from China, Japan and Taiwan. They are easy to grow in cold climates and, as they are more wind tolerant than most bamboos, can be used for screens and hedging. Propagate by division.

Pseudosasa japonica
Arrow Bamboo

ORIGIN Japan
CLIMATE WT, M, CT, H
Reaching 6m/20ft high, this upright thicket-forming bamboo has extremely straight, narrow canes covered with white powder while young. The oblong mid-green leaves, 8–15cm/3–6in long, have yellow midribs and are blue–green on the undersides.
USE & CULTIVATION Ideal for hedging and screening, it can be invasive but is easily controlled by mowing during the

shooting season. Grow in moist well-drained soil in full sun or part shade. Fully frost hardy.

PSEUDOTSUGA

FAMILY PINACEAE

A genus of 5 or 6 evergreen conifers from North America, Mexico and eastern Asia. The stately Douglas Fir, *P. menziesii*, famous for its Oregon timber, is widely grown and cherished as a Christmas tree. Propagate from seed or by grafting.

Pseudotsuga menziesii
Douglas Fir

ORIGIN North America to Mexico
CLIMATE WT, M, CT, H

Very tall specimens of 90m/300ft have been recorded in the wild, but this fir is usually much smaller in cultivation. Forming a broadly conical tree when young, it has whorled branches, the upper ones ascending and the lower branches horizontal with pendulous tips. The aromatic, crowded, soft linear leaves to 3cm/1¼in long are dark green above and white-banded beneath. Pendent light brown female cones to 8cm/3in long with pointed papery bracts are scattered through the canopy. **P. m. var. glauca**, the Blue Douglas Fir of the Rocky Mountains, is smaller and more compact and has glaucous blue leaves.

USE & CULTIVATION A magnificent fast-growing specimen tree that requires plenty of room to develop and display its long-term charm. It is best suited to cooler climates. Grow in moist well-drained soil in full sun. Fully frost hardy.

PSEUDOWINTERA

FAMILY WINTERACEAE

This New Zealand genus consists of 3 species of aromatic evergreen trees and shrubs. They are grown mainly for their highly decorative leaves, which can be cut and used for indoor decoration. Propagate from seed or cuttings.

Pseudowintera colorata
syn. *Drimys colorata*
Pepper Tree, Horopito

ORIGIN New Zealand
CLIMATE WT, M, CT

This erect, branching, aromatic shrub to 2m/7ft tall has colourful oval, yellowish green leaves to about 7cm/2½in long, red-blotched above and with purplish margins, and silvery glaucous beneath. Tiny green fragrant flowers in spring are followed by black oval berries.

USE & CULTIVATION Ideal for shady woodland gardens. It grows best in well-drained, humus-rich soil in a sheltered site, although leaf colour is better in an open situation. In cold areas it needs a cool greenhouse. Moderately frost hardy.

Pseudotsuga menziesii

PTERIS

BRAKE
FAMILY PTERIDACEAE

This is a large genus of about 250 species of terrestrial ferns found mainly in tropical and subtropical regions. They are widely cultivated for their attractive foliage, and several species have become familiar indoor plants. Propagate from spores or by division.

Pteris cretica
Cretan Brake Fern

ORIGIN Europe, Africa, Asia
CLIMATE T, ST, WT

This evergreen fern produces an erect clump to 60cm/24in high from short underground rhizomes. The fronds, about 70cm/28in long and 20cm/8in wide, are light to medium green and carried on black stalks to 15cm/6in long. Each frond has up to 5 pairs of ribbon-like toothed segments and a single terminal leaflet. **'Albolineata'** is a popular variegated form with a broad white band on either side of the mid-rib. **'Distinction'**, to 40cm/16in high, has deeply and irregularly lobed segments with branched tips. **'Wimsettii'**, to 50cm/20in high, has segments with long lobes that are often crested.

USE & CULTIVATION In warm tropical regions they are well suited to shady borders beneath palms and tree ferns. Provide moist well-drained soil and plenty of water during the early growth period. Easily grown in containers, they are popular conservatory, fernery and house plants, responding well to warm conditions and high humidity. Keep out of direct sunlight and feed established plants regularly. Frost tender.

Pteris ensiformis
Slender Brake Fern

ORIGIN Himalayas to Polynesia and Australia
CLIMATE T, ST, WT

This small fern to 30cm/12in high has erect, leathery, dark green fronds to 40cm/16in long divided 1–3 times into 4 or 5 pairs of narrow segments. The sterile fronds are shorter with narrower segments. **'Arguta'** has segments with a silvery white central stripe. **'Victoriae'**, an especially decorative variety, has segments with white edges.

USE & CULTIVATION As for *P. cretica*. Frost tender.

Pteris umbrosa
Jungle Brake

ORIGIN Eastern Australia
CLIMATE T, ST, WT

This robust fern spreads quickly by freely branching, creeping rhizomes, forming attractive clumps of arching dark green fronds to over 1m/3ft long. The shining fronds are divided 1–2 times into spreading ribbon-like segments.

USE & CULTIVATION As for *P. cretica*. Frost tender.

PULMONARIA

LUNGWORT
FAMILY BORAGINACEAE

Native to various parts of Europe and Asia, there are about 14 species in this genus of low-growing hardy perennials with beautiful leaves often spotted with silvery markings. Both the common and botanical names refer to the former use of some species in the treatment of a range of chest complaints. In early spring, while the leaves are still inconspicuous, small, funnel-shaped, multi-coloured flowers appear. After flowering, the leaves enlarge and elongate, making these plants

Pteris umbrosa

Pulmonaria officinalis

Pulmonaria officinalis 'Sissinghurst White'

Pulmonaria saccharata 'Highdown'

excellent groundcovers for woodland gardens. Propagate from seed or cuttings or by division.

Pulmonaria officinalis
Jerusalem Cowslip, Common Lungwort

ORIGIN Europe
CLIMATE WT, M, CT, H
A clump-forming perennial to 30cm/ 12in high with alternate, mostly spotted, oval or heart-shaped leaves to 14cm/5½ in long with a slightly rough texture. From early spring it bears a succession of pinkish funnel-shaped flowers that turn violet–blue as they mature. **'Cambridge Blue'** has blue flowers. **'Sissinghurst White'** has prominently larger-spotted leaves to 25cm/ 10in long and bears pure white flowers.
USE & CULTIVATION Grow as a groundcover in cottage gardens, borders and in a wild or woodland garden in a partially shaded, moist position. Fully frost hardy.

Pulmonaria saccharata
Jerusalem Sage

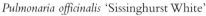

ORIGIN Europe
CLIMATE WT, M, CT, H
This clump-forming perennial to about 30cm/12in high has mid-green tapering leaves to 25cm/10in long with

bristly hairs and white spots that widen into splotches. White, pink or violet–blue flowers appear from late winter to late spring. The leaves of cultivars in the **Argentea Group** are almost entirely silvery white; their red flowers turn dark purple as they age. **'Highdown'** has silvery-spotted dark green leaves and deep blue flowers.
USE & CULTIVATION As for *P. officinalis*. Fully frost hardy.

PUYA

FAMILY BROMELIACEAE
This genus of about 170 species of evergreen, often woody-based bromeliads comes from the drier parts of South America. They form dense rosettes of hard, linear, spiny-margined leaves, some with an attractive frosted appearance. Bell-shaped flowers are carried in erect panicles well above the leaves. They can be grown in pots, tubs or borders and make fine architectural plants in modern landscape design. Propagate from seed or by division of offsets.

Puya berteroniana

ORIGIN Chile
CLIMATE ST, WT, M, SA
Forming terminal rosettes on a short, woody-based stem, this species can reach

2m/7ft high. The narrow, curled, tapering leaves to 1m/3ft long with spiny margins are greyish green above and covered with dense, silvery grey scales beneath. Mature plants produce huge panicles, over 2m/7ft long, of metallic bluish green flowers in early summer.
USE & CULTIVATION A fantastic feature plant for a large well-drained rockery, succulent garden or sparse stylised garden with pebbles or rocks. Position in full sun away from footpaths. One of the most cold tolerant of the bromeliads, it withstands brief periods below freezing. It also tolerates periods of drought. In cold climates it can be grown in a greenhouse with good air circulation. Moderately frost hardy.

P

Puya berteroniana

PYRUS

PEAR
FAMILY ROSACEAE
A genus of about 20 species of deciduous trees and shrubs from Europe and temperate Asia. They include the fruiting pears, but are also valued for their neat habit, attractive autumn foliage and pretty white spring blossoms. Propagate from seed or by grafting.

Pyrus salicifolia
Willow-leaved Pear, Silver Pear

ORIGIN Caucasus region to Iran
CLIMATE WT, M, CT, H
This deciduous tree to 9m/30ft tall has a spreading habit, with the lower branchlets more or less pendulous. The narrow willow-like leaves to 10cm/4in long are silvery grey and downy when young, later becoming smooth above. Tight clusters of pink-tinted white flowers appear in spring, followed by small, top-shaped, brownish fruit, ripening in autumn. The species is mainly represented in gardens by the smaller **'Pendula'**, to 5m/17ft, with weeping branches and brighter silvery leaves.

USE & CULTIVATION An outstanding specimen tree for cool temperate areas. Grow in full sun in fertile well-drained soil. Lightly prune in late winter or early spring to maintain shape. Fully frost hardy.

QUERCUS

OAK
FAMILY FAGACEAE
A genus of 600 species of trees and a few shrubs, mostly from the northern temperate zone. They are deciduous or evergreen, with entire to deeply lobed leaves which in some deciduous species give magnificent autumn colour. Tiny petalless male and female flowers are produced on the same plant; the males in loose pendent catkins, the females as one to several flowers in short spikes. The fruit or acorn is a solitary or paired nut. Most oaks are reasonably fast growing and long-lived, and make majestic shade trees for large gardens and parks. Propagate from fresh seed. Cultivars must be grafted.

Quercus alba
American White Oak

ORIGIN Eastern North America
CLIMATE M, CT, H
This magnificent deciduous tree to 30m/100ft high has pale grey to brown fissured bark. The deeply lobed, bright green, oblong leaves to 20cm/8in long turn purplish red in autumn. Its solitary acorns are small. It yields an important commercial wood.

USE & CULTIVATION A picturesque shade tree for specimen planting in large gardens. It is relatively slow growing and resents transplanting. Grow in deep, well-drained, slightly acid soil in full sun. Fully frost hardy.

Quercus cerris
Turkey Oak

ORIGIN Southern Europe, Middle East
CLIMATE WT, M, CT
This deciduous tree to 36m/120ft or more high has a stout trunk and deeply fissured, greyish bark. The narrow

Pyrus salicifolia 'Pendula'

Quercus alba

Quercus palustris

Quercus robur

oblong leaves to 12cm/5in long are deeply lobed or toothed. They are slightly rough and dull grey–green above, woolly below, and turn yellowish brown in autumn. The acorn to 4cm/ 1¹/₂ in long is held in a deep shaggy cup and ripens in its second year. **'Argenteovariegata'** has outstanding variegated leaves with conspicuous creamy white margins.
USE & CULTIVATION A tough and fast-growing tree developing into a magnificent broadly domed shade tree for large gardens. Plant in well-drained soil in full sun. Tolerates alkaline soil and coastal conditions. Fully frost hardy.

Quercus coccinea
Scarlet Oak

ORIGIN North America
CLIMATE M, CT, H
This is a highly ornamental tree reaching 24m/80ft in height with an open, wide-spreading, irregular crown with slightly drooping branches. Its oblong leaves to 15cm/6in long have 3 or 4 pairs of spreading spine-tipped lobes. They are bright glossy green above,

paler beneath, and turn bright scarlet in autumn. Acorns are solitary and carried in a deep cup. **'Splendens'** has larger leaves and deep red autumn colour.
USE & CULTIVATION Widely grown in parks and large gardens. Fast growing, it likes deep, well-drained, slightly acid soil in full sun. Fully frost hardy.

Quercus palustris
Pin Oak

ORIGIN Eastern North America
CLIMATE M, CT, H
This shapely deciduous tree 9–24m/ 30–80ft high has a straight trunk and broad pyramidal crown with drooping lower branches giving it a pendulous effect. Its thin, glossy, deeply cut and spine-pointed leaves to 15cm/6in long are bright green on both sides and colour beautifully from gold to deep rich red in autumn. The almost globular acorns about 1cm/³/₈in long ripen in the second year. It yields an important commercial wood.
USE & CULTIVATION A highly ornamental, reliable oak for large gardens, parks and windbreaks. It grows

moderately fast in moist, slightly acid, well-drained soil. It has a shallow, fibrous root system and transplants better than most oaks. Fully frost hardy.

Quercus robur
English Oak

ORIGIN Europe
CLIMATE M, CT, H
Attaining great age, this is a massive woodland tree with a short thick trunk and a broad, spreading crown to 36m/ 120ft. The dark green, shortly stalked leaves to 12cm/5in long are roughly oblong in outline with 3–7 pairs of irregular rounded lobes. They turn golden yellow or bronze in autumn, then brown, and hold on well into winter. Its nuts are the familiar acorns. **'Concordia'**, the Golden English Oak, to 9m/30ft, has rich golden yellow leaves in spring, turning green.
USE & CULTIVATION Definitely for large open spaces, this handsome tree is a splendid choice for rural properties where a long-lived shade tree is required. Plant in deeply worked fertile soil in a well-drained position. It is the most popular oak for bonsai. Fully frost hardy.

P

Q

Quercus rubra

Raoulia australis

Ravenala madagascariensis

Quercus rubra
Red Oak

ORIGIN Eastern North America
CLIMATE M, CT, H

The leaves of this deciduous tree turn a stunning scarlet to reddish brown in autumn. It forms a broad dome-shaped tree to 24m/80ft tall with smooth, greyish brown bark. The oblong leaves to 20cm/8in long are divided into bristle-tipped lobes, matt green above and greyish below, and hold on well into winter. Large acorns sit in shallow cups and ripen in the second year. **'Aurea'** has golden yellow new leaves.
USE & CULTIVATION A beautiful feature tree for large gardens. It is reasonably fast growing and tolerates pollution. Grow in deeply worked, slightly acid soil with good drainage. Fully frost hardy.

RAOULIA

FAMILY ASTERACEAE

A New Zealand genus of about 25 species of evergreen perennials. They form attractive green or silvery carpets or cushions of overlapping, ovate or spoon-shaped leaves and small flowerheads composed entirely of disc florets. Some species are not easy to grow and must be protected from cold winter wet or grown in pots in an alpine house. Propagate by division.

Raoulia australis
syn. *Raoulia lutescens*
Golden Scabweed

ORIGIN New Zealand
CLIMATE M, CT, H

This is a flat, ground-hugging plant to 50cm/20in or more wide. It has small spoon-shaped leaves to 1cm/$^1/_3$in long with silvery grey, downy tips. The tiny flowerheads in summer are yellow.
USE & CULTIVATION A charming carpeting rock-garden plant. Grow in

sharply drained soil in full sun and protect from heavy winter rain. In pots, use a potting mix containing coarse sand and peat. Moderately frost hardy.

RAVENALA

FAMILY STRELITZIACEAE

There is only one species in this genus, commonly known as the Traveller's Tree because fresh water collects at the expanded leaf bases and can be used as an emergency drinking supply. Propagate from seed or by division of suckers.

Ravenala madagascariensis
Traveller's Tree

ORIGIN Madagascar

CLIMATE T, ST

This dramatic evergreen plant to 9m/30ft or more has a palm-like trunk crowned with a flat fan of long, closely overlapping stalks with huge banana-like leaves to 3m/10ft long. Clusters of greenish white flowers are produced from the leaf axils in summer.

USE & CULTIVATION An outstanding accent plant suited only to tropical and warm subtropical climates. Grow in rich, moist well-drained soil in a sunny position. Shelter from strong winds, which can spoil the appearance of the

foliage. In cool climates, grow in a large, warm, humid greenhouse in bright light. Frost tender.

RESTIO

FAMILY RESTIONACEAE

A genus of about 90 species of rush-like plants from South Africa, Madagascar and Australia. Only a small number are cultivated for their attractive dense clumps of thread-like foliage, which is sometimes seen in florists' shops and used as a foliage contrast in arrangements. Propagate from seed or by division of clumps.

Restio tetraphyllus
Tassel Cord Rush

ORIGIN Australia

CLIMATE ST, WT, M

This species forms an attractive bright green tussock to over 1m/3ft high and 50cm/20in across, arising from creeping rhizomes. The soft, feathery, weeping foliage opens out from towards the tops of the smooth slender stems. Rusty brown flowers appear along the tips during spring.

USE & CULTIVATION A most decorative plant for a moist position in a rock garden or beside a water feature. Grow

in full sun or partial shade and provide adequate moisture during dry periods. Suitable for a container if ample water is supplied. Marginally frost hardy.

RHAPIS

FAMILY ARECACEAE/PALMAE

Of the 12 or so species of these small multi-stemmed palms from southern China and Southeast Asia, 2 are widely cultivated as houseplants. They form bamboo-like clumps of many slender, fibre-covered stems clad with lustrous dark green leaves. Their slow growth and attractive fan-shaped fronds make them unsurpassed as container plants, although they are also very suitable for gardens. Male and female flowers occur on separate plants. Propagate by division of clumps or from seed.

Rhapis excelsa
Lady Palm, Bamboo Palm

ORIGIN Southern China

CLIMATE T, ST, WT

This small clump-forming palm reaches about 1.5m/5ft and has long-stalked, dark green leaves divided into 5–8 widely spaced segments. The slender stems are clothed with persistent brown fibre. A number of Japanese cultivars with a dwarf habit or variegated leaves are available. These include **'Ayanishiki'**, with creamy white stripes, **'Koban'**, a dwarf compact variety to about 60cm/24in, and **'Zuikonishiki'**, to 60cm/24in, with creamy yellow or white stripes.

USE & CULTIVATION Its neat clumping habit makes a charming screen and it is well suited to swimming-pool landscapes and tropical plantings. Grow in partial shade in rich moist but well-drained soil. Very slow growing, it remains attractive for many years in the same container indoors and out, although old clumps need large tubs. Houseplants do well in normal room temperatures in bright filtered light. Cultivars are propagated by division. Frost tender.

Restio tetraphyllus

Rhapis excelsa

Q

R

Rhapis humilis

Rheum palmatum

Rhapis humilis
Slender Lady Palm

ORIGIN Southern China
CLIMATE T, ST, WT
This palm forms spreading clumps of very slender, reed-like stems 2.5m/8ft or more high, covered with fine brown fibres arising from the base of each frond. The attractive rounded leaves are divided into 10–20 dark green drooping segments.
USE & CULTIVATION As for *R. excelsa*. Frost tender.

RHEUM

FAMILY POLYGONACEAE
A genus of about 50 species of clump-forming perennials from eastern Europe and temperate to subtropical Asia. It includes the edible rhubarb, and various ornamental plants grown for their striking foliage and overall appearance. Propagate from seed or by division.

Rheum palmatum
Chinese Rhubarb

ORIGIN China, Tibet
CLIMATE WT, M, CT, H
This clump-forming perennial to 2.5m/8ft tall has thick fleshy roots and spreads to 1.8m/6ft across. The large, long-stalked, palmately lobed leaves to 90cm/36in long are dark green, prominently veined and coarsely toothed. In early summer tall plumes of small, creamy white flowers are produced on erect stems to 1.8m/6ft. **'Atrosanguineum'** has red young foliage that turns deep reddish purple as it matures, and deep pink or crimson flowers. **R. p. var.** *tanguticum* has purple-flushed leaves and ivory or sometimes pink flowers. **'Rote Auslese'** has huge, deeply cut leaves and red flowers.
USE & CULTIVATION Requiring plenty of space, these plants are very well suited to a woodland garden. Thriving in moist conditions, they are among the best foliage perennials for edging a pond or water feature. Plant in deep rich soil in full sun or partial shade. Frost tender.

Rheum officinale

ORIGIN China, Tibet
CLIMATE WT, M, CT, H
Formerly grown as a medicinal plant, this species can grow 2–3m/7–10ft tall. The rounded basal leaves are deeply

Rheum officinale

lobed and to 90cm/36in wide. Plumes of creamy white flowers are borne in early summer.

USE & CULTIVATION As for *R. palmatum*. Fully frost hardy.

RHUS

FAMILY ANACARDIACEAE

A genus of about 200 species of evergreen and deciduous trees, shrubs and climbers from temperate and subtropical regions of both hemispheres. They have simple or pinnate leaves which in many deciduous species turn brilliant shades of gold and red in autumn. The tiny inconspicuous flowers are borne in panicles or dense clusters, with some forming showy coloured fruit. Contact with the leaves of some species can cause allergic reactions. Those likely to be susceptible should consider planting the Chinese Pistachio, *Pistacia chinensis*, instead. Propagate from seed or cuttings or by division.

Rhus typhina
Stag's Horn Sumach

ORIGIN Eastern North America
CLIMATE WT, M, CT, H
A large deciduous shrub or small tree to 4.5m/15ft or more. It has pinnate leaves to 60cm/24in long with slender, pointed, toothed leaflets that become a blaze of brilliant orange–red shades in autumn. Yellowish green flowers borne in dense erect panicles in summer develop into hairy, deep crimson fruit.

USE & CULTIVATION Locate in a woodland, as a background shrub or specimen. Grow in full sun in moist well-drained soil. Fully frost hardy.

RICINUS

FAMILY EUPHORBIACEAE

A genus of only one species, a fast-growing evergreen shrub thought to be of tropical African origin and now widely naturalised throughout many

Ricinus communis

warmer parts of the world. It is grown for its dramatic foliage, particularly the bronze- or red-leaved forms. All parts of the plant are poisonous, especially the seeds, and contact with the foliage can cause severe allergic reactions. It may become a weed in warmer climates and should not be planted near natural bushland. Propagate from seed.

Ricinus communis
Castor Oil Plant

ORIGIN Northeastern Africa
CLIMATE ST, WT, M
This erect shrub to 1.5m/5ft or more is mostly grown as an annual. It has large, mid-green, palmate leaves to 45cm/18in long that are often bronze and glossy, particularly when young. Spikes of small cream and red flowers are followed by rounded prickly seed pods that explode when ripe. **'Gibsonii'** is a compact variety with metallic dark red leaves and stems. **'Impala'** has carmine red young growth and reddish purple foliage. **'Zanzibarensis'** is a tall form to 2m/7ft with bright green leaves with whitish veins.

USE & CULTIVATION Valued for their lush tropical-looking foliage, they are often grown in temperate climates as half-hardy annuals for summer borders. The seeds are sown in the greenhouse in late winter or early spring and planted out in late spring, after fear of frost has passed. Grow in rich moisture-retentive soil in a sheltered sunny position. Marginally frost hardy.

R

Ricinus communis 'Impala'

Robinia pseudoacacia

Robinia pseudoacacia 'Frisia'

ROBINIA

FAMILY LEGUMINOSAE/
PAPILIONACEAE

North America is the home of this genus of 4 species of deciduous trees and shrubs. They are widely grown as ornamentals for their attractive pinnate leaves and generous racemes of pea-shaped flowers in summer. Propagate from seed or root cuttings or by division.

Robinia hispida
Rose Acacia
ORIGIN Southeastern USA
CLIMATE WT, M, CT, H

This suckering shrub to 2.5m/8ft has a loose habit and rather brittle stems covered with reddish brown bristles. The dark green pinnate leaves are composed of up to 13 leaflets. Pendulous clusters of pink pea-like flowers open in late spring and early summer, followed by reddish brown seed pods.
USE & CULTIVATION With its spreading, suckering roots, this is a useful plant for difficult slopes and banks. Grow in moist moderately fertile, well-drained soil in a sunny position with shelter from strong winds. Fully frost hardy.

Robinia pseudoacacia
Black Locust, False Acacia
ORIGIN Eastern USA
CLIMATE WT, M, CT, H

This fast-growing, spreading, deciduous tree to 24m/80ft has spiny branches and dark green pinnate leaves to 30cm/12in long with up to 23 oval leaflets. In early summer it bears dense drooping clusters of slightly fragrant, white, pea-like flowers, followed by dark brown seed pods.

'Bessoniana' is a small oval-headed tree with spineless twigs. **'Frisia'** is a small to medium-sized tree with rich yellow foliage in summer, deepening in colour in autumn. **'Umbraculifera'** is a small mop-headed tree without spines and with only a few flowers.
USE & CULTIVATION The smaller-growing cultivars rarely exceed 9m/30ft and are quite manageable for suburban gardens, front lawns and street planting. They tolerate average garden conditions in full sun, but need protection from wind damage. Fully frost hardy.

RODGERSIA

FAMILY SAXIFRAGACEAE

A genus of 6 rhizomatous clump-forming perennials from eastern Asia. They have long-stalked palmate or pinnate leaves and large terminal panicles of small fluffy flowers in summer. All the moisture-loving species have good form and bold ornamental foliage, and are indispensable for waterside plantings. Propagate from seed or by division.

Rodgersia aesculifolia

ORIGIN China
CLIMATE M, CT, H
This robust perennial forms a clump 1–2m/3–7ft high and wide of large, 5-lobed, coarsely toothed leaves to 45cm/18in across held on long hairy stalks. In mid-summer, plumes of ivory

Rodgersia aesculifolia

Rodgersia podophylla

or pale pink flowers are borne on stout stems to 1m/3ft tall.
USE & CULTIVATION Suited to a swampy garden or poolside, this and the following species provide striking textural contrast to other waterside subjects such as grasses and ferns. They flourish in rich moisture-retentive soil in full sun or partial shade. Shelter from strong winds, which can damage the foliage. Fully frost hardy.

Rodgersia pinnata

ORIGIN China
CLIMATE M, CT, H
This rhizomatous species has strong reddish green stems and heavily veined dark green leaves that are palmate or arranged in pairs. Dense panicles of white, soft pink or red flowers appear in mid-summer. One of the best cultivars is **'Superba'**, to 1.2m/4ft in height and with bronze-tinged young leaves and fluffy spikes of bright pink flowers.
USE & CULTIVATION As for *R. aesculifolia*. Fully frost hardy.

Rodgersia podophylla

ORIGIN Korea, Japan
CLIMATE M, CT, H
This clump-forming perennial to 1.5m/5ft tall has distinct palmate leaves with jagged edges, sometimes to 60cm/24in across. They are crinkled and richly copper tinted when young, becoming smoother and shiny green with age. Branched panicles of tiny creamy white flowers appear from mid- to late summer.
USE & CULTIVATION As for *R. aesculifolia*. Fully frost hardy.

Rodgersia sambucifolia

ORIGIN Western China
CLIMATE M, CT, H
This clump-forming perennial to about 90cm/36in high and wide has dark green, occasionally bronze-tinted pinnate leaves to 75cm/30in long. Sprays of creamy white or pink flowers appear from early summer.
USE & CULTIVATION As for *R. aesculifolia*. Fully frost hardy.

Rodgersia pinnata 'Superba'

R

Rosmarinus officinalis

Rosmarinus officinalis 'Prostratus'

ROSMARINUS

ROSEMARY

FAMILY LABIATAE/LAMIACEAE

There are only 2 species in this genus of evergreen shrubs from the Mediterranean region. *Rosmarinus officinalis* is cultivated for its aromatic leaves, which are used in perfumery, medicine and cooking. Propagate from semi-ripe cuttings in summer.

Rosmarinus officinalis
Rosemary

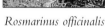

ORIGIN Mediterranean
CLIMATE ST, WT, M, CT

This upright woody shrub forms a neat bush occasionally reaching 1.5m/5ft. The dark green linear leaves to 5cm/2in long are white-felted beneath. Pale blue to white flowers are borne in small clusters in spring to summer. Improved forms offer brighter blue or pink

flowers, but are often less hardy. **'Aureus'** has gold-splashed leaves. **'Prostratus'** (syn. *R. lavandulaceus*) is a popular low-growing mat-forming variety with light blue flowers.

USE & CULTIVATION Rosemary makes a neat compact shrub or low hedge and deserves a place in every herb garden. 'Aureus' is good for parterre gardens and for foliage contrast in the mixed border. Use 'Prostratus' for covering banks, cascading over walls or rocks and alongside paths. All make excellent container plants. Grow in full sun in well-drained, not over-rich soil, and shelter in cold areas. Lightly trim after flowering. Moderately frost hardy.

RUTA

FAMILY RUTACEAE

A genus of 8 species of evergreen woody perennials, subshrubs or shrubs

Ruta graveolens

with deeply divided aromatic leaves, grown for their foliage and flowers. As well as being used medicinally, *Ruta graveolens* was once an important strewing herb and insect repellent. The leaves and sap may irritate the skin. Propagate from seed or by cuttings.

Ruta graveolens
Common Rue, Herb of Grace

ORIGIN Southern Europe
CLIMATE WT, M, CT, H
Rue is a bushy evergreen shrub reaching 60cm/24in with very pretty, aromatic, blue–green, lacy leaves to 15cm/6in long divided into small oval lobes. Small, greenish yellow, frilled flowers are borne in open clusters in late summer. **'Jackman's Blue'** has more richly glaucous blue foliage and is more compact than the type. The leaves are used in posies and small bouquets.
USE & CULTIVATION These beautiful herb-garden plants are fine foliage subjects for the mixed border and for growing in front of tall old-fashioned roses. Provide good drainage, plenty of sun and fairly poor soil for best results. Tip-prune throughout the season to encourage branching and cut back in late spring to keep shapely. Fully frost hardy.

SABAL

PALMETTO PALMS
FAMILY ARECACEAE/PALMAE
These fan palms are native to southern North America, northern South America and the Caribbean region. There are 14 species, ranging in size from dwarf stemless varieties to tall single-stemmed palms—all have unarmed leaf stalks. Although suited to mainly tropical and subtropical regions, some can be grown in sheltered temperate areas. Propagate from fresh seed.

Sabal mexicana

Sabal mexicana
Texas Palmetto

ORIGIN Mexico, southern Texas
CLIMATE T, ST, WT, SA
This relatively slow-growing, medium-sized palm to 18m/60ft has a large spreading crown of light green fan-shaped leaves to 1m/3ft long that are deeply cut into many slender, pointed lobes with conspicuous hanging threads. Cream flowers are borne between the leaves, usually in summer.
USE & CULTIVATION An impressive lawn or feature plant. It likes very good drainage and plenty of sun; once established it tolerates dry conditions. The old leaf bases persist for several years on younger plants, but on older specimens are shed cleanly. Frost tender.

Sabal minor

Salvia argentea

Salvia officinalis 'Icterina'

Sabal minor
Dwarf Palmetto

ORIGIN Southeastern USA

CLIMATE T, ST, WT

This palm usually has mainly underground stems, but can also develop a short erect trunk to 2m/7ft tall. It has long-stalked, stiff, bluish green leaves. Slender arching sprays of small, white, fragrant flowers appear in summer and are followed by shiny black pea-sized fruit.

USE & CULTIVATION Well suited to group plantings and ideal for swimming-pool garden surrounds. Grow in moist well-drained soil in full sun. It can be successfully grown in warm temperate regions. Frost tender.

SALVIA

SAGE

FAMILY LABIATAE/LAMIACEAE

This is a very large genus of about 900 species of annuals, perennials, biennials and shrubs with worldwide distribution. Many species have aromatic leaves and a number are showy flowering plants.

Some species have medicinal properties; these include the flavouring herb Sage (*Salvia officinalis*). Those species that are attractive for their foliage alone are included here. Propagate from seed, or cuttings or by division in early summer.

Salvia argentea
Silver Sage

ORIGIN Southern Europe, northern Africa

CLIMATE WT, M, CT

This biennial forms basal rosettes of pale grey–green ovate leaves to 20cm/8in long which are shallowly lobed or toothed and covered with silvery hairs, particularly when young. In the second year the leaves turn green. In summer the plant bears tall branching clusters of white or pink-tinged flowers.

USE & CULTIVATION An attractive plant for the foreground of a border or rock garden. The flower buds are often removed as soon as they appear, to maintain the handsome flat rosette of leaves and prolong the life of the plant. Grow in well-drained soil in full sun. It will survive cold winters, but resents humidity. Fully frost hardy.

Salvia elegans
Pineapple Sage

ORIGIN Mexico, Guatemala

CLIMATE ST, WT, M

This upright perennial or subshrub reaches 1.8m/6ft and has oval serrated fresh mid-green leaves to 10cm/4in long with a pineapple-like scent and flavour. Open whorls of small scarlet flowers are produced in late summer and autumn.

USE & CULTIVATION A perfect plant for the back of a border and for containers. Grow in fertile, moist well-drained soil. Trim frequently to keep bushy and cut back after flowering. It will need some winter protection in cold climates. Frost tender.

Salvia officinalis
Sage

ORIGIN Southern Europe, northern Africa

CLIMATE WT, M, CT

This small, slightly woody perennial grows 60cm/24in or more high and has oval finely wrinkled, downy grey–green leaves to 8cm/3in long. Short racemes

Salvia officinalis 'Purpurascens'

Sanchezia speciosa

'**Tricolor**' has leaves splashed creamy white with tints of pink and purple. There is also a broad-leaved form. All have a sage-like fragrance.
USE & CULTIVATION All forms deserve a place in every herb garden and make charming border plants, with leaves to tone with different colour schemes. Grow in well-drained, light-textured soil in full sun. Trim frequently to keep bushy and cut back after flowering. Fully frost hardy.

SANCHEZIA

FAMILY ACANTHACEAE

This genus consists of about 20 tropical species of shrubs, climbers and perennials native to Central and South America. Although some species are used medicinally in South America, only *Sanchezia speciosa*, a handsome foliage plant, is widely cultivated. In hot dry conditions red spider mites may be a problem. Propagate from cuttings of the side-shoots.

Sanchezia speciosa
syns *Sanchezia nobilis,* *S. glaucophylla*

ORIGIN Ecuador, Peru
CLIMATE T, ST
An erect evergreen shrub to 1.5m/5ft grown for its large, glossy, ovate leaves to 30cm/12in long and 10cm/4in wide. They are dark green with some pale yellow or white markings around the midrib and main vein areas. The yellow tubular flowers borne in terminal spikes in summer are not particularly showy.
USE & CULTIVATION Mostly grown as an indoor plant, it also makes an excellent garden foliage plant in warm humid areas. Use as contrast in tropical plantings, in moist well-drained soil in dappled shade. Indoors, provide bright filtered light, warmth and high humidity. Tip-prune young plants to encourage bushyness. Renew old plants every second year for an attractive display. Frost tender.

of light violet–blue flowers are produced in summer. '**Icterina**' has yellow and green variegated leaves. '**Kew Gold**' has golden yellow leaves and mauve flowers. '**Purpurascens**' has purple-flushed, grey–green leaves.

SANSEVIERIA

BOWSTRING HEMP

FAMILY AGAVACEAE/ DRACAENACEAE

A genus of about 60 species of evergreen rhizomatous perennials native to India, Indonesia and Africa. There are two main types: those with stiff erect leaves and those that form dwarf rosettes. They are often grown as houseplants for their ornamental succulent leaves, and some are used for their strong white leaf fibre, known as bowstring hemp. Propagate by division or from leaf cuttings.

Sansevieria trifasciata
Mother-in-law's Tongue

ORIGIN Tropical Africa
CLIMATE T, ST, WT

This succulent perennial is stemless, its stiff erect leaves arising from a central rosette. The dark green strap-shaped leaves over 1m/3ft long have darker green horizontal stripes. It infrequently bears racemes of greenish white flowers, even more rarely when grown indoors. Among its various forms is **'Golden Hahnii'**, which grows as a squat rosette to no more than 12cm/5in tall and has broad leaves with golden yellow vertical stripes. The leaves of the popular erect **'Laurentii'** have broad yellow margins. **'Silver Hahnii'** also forms a dwarf rosette, of dark green leaves flecked with silver markings.

USE & CULTIVATION Outdoors, the upright forms look best planted in masses as sculptural features in a raised bed or succulent garden, and in contemporary garden design. Large clumps also work well in pots decorating patios, window ledges and alcoves. The dwarf forms are slow growing and make neat rockery subjects. Indoors, plants are almost indestructible provided they are given bright light and warmth, not overwatered and kept on the dry side during the winter months. Frost tender.

SANTOLINA

FAMILY ASTERACEAE/COMPOSITAE

This genus of 18 species of small evergreen shrubs is native to the Mediterranean region. They are grown mainly for their finely divided and aromatic foliage. Button-like flowers, usually bright yellow, are produced in summer, but can be trimmed off to keep the plants compact. Propagate from semi-ripe cuttings in summer.

Santolina chamaecyparissus
syn. *Santolina incana*
Cotton Lavender

ORIGIN Mediterranean region
CLIMATE WT, M, CT

This species makes a dense, rounded, pale grey bush to about 50cm/20in high and 1m/3ft across. The fern-like, greyish green leaves to 4cm/1½in long are finely divided into tiny segments; new growth is silky-hairy. Bright yellow button-like flowers are

Sansevieria trifasciata

Sansevieria trifasciata 'Golden Hahnii'

Santolina chamaecyparissus

Santolina pinnata subsp. neopolitana
'Edward Bowles'

borne on slender stems just above the foliage in summer. **'Lemon Queen'** is a popular compact form with pale yellow flowerheads.

USE & CULTIVATION Good for edgings, low hedges and groundcover. Clipped plants are also used in traditional herbal knots and parterre gardens. Grow in well-drained soil in a warm, open, sunny position. They can be sheared over in spring to keep their shape neat and prevent woodiness. Moderately frost hardy.

Santolina pinnata
syn. *Santolina chamaecyparissus*
subsp. *tomentosa*

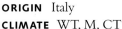

ORIGIN Italy
CLIMATE WT, M, CT
This hummock-forming shrub reaches a height of 75cm/30in with a spread of 1m/3ft. It has finely divided green leaves to 4cm/1½in long and bears creamy white flowers in summer. More commonly cultivated is **S. p. subsp. neopolitana**, which has a looser habit with feathery grey–green leaves and bright yellow flowerheads. One of its best cultivars is **'Edward Bowles'**, with dense grey–green foliage and creamy white blooms.

USE & CULTIVATION As for *S. chamaecyparissus*. Moderately frost hardy.

SAXIFRAGA

SAXIFRAGE
FAMILY SAXIFRAGACEAE
A large and varied genus of about 440 species of annuals, biennials and perennials native to mountains and rocky places in temperate, alpine and subarctic regions of the Northern Hemisphere. A number are cultivated in the alpine house, and numerous hybrids have been raised. As these are largely in the realm of alpine plant specialists, only those suited to ordinary garden conditions are included here. Propagate from seed or by division.

Saxifraga exarata subsp. moschata
syn. *Saxifraga moschata*

ORIGIN Europe
CLIMATE M, CT
This evergreen perennial grows to only 10cm/4in high, forming a moss-like cushion of entire or deeply divided bright green leaves to 2cm/³/4in long. It bears pink or yellow star-shaped flowers

on slender stems in summer. **'Cloth of Gold'** has bright golden foliage.
USE & CULTIVATION A charming groundcover for a small rockery pocket. Grow in moist, very well-drained soil in full sun or light shade. Fully frost hardy.

Saxifraga stolonifera
syn. *Saxifraga sarmentosa*
Mother of Thousands,
Strawberry Begonia

ORIGIN Eastern Asia
CLIMATE WT, M, CT
This mat-forming evergreen perennial colonises by long, red, thread-like stolons ending in little plantlets. The rounded or kidney-shaped dark green leaves to 10cm/4in across form loose rosettes. They are marked with silvery veining and are reddish beneath. Delicate racemes of little white flowers appear in summer. **'Tricolor'** has smaller leaves splashed with white and flushed pink.
USE & CULTIVATION Excellent in rock gardens, raised beds and edging paths. Grow in a sheltered shady position in moist well-drained soil. Suitable for unheated rooms and decorative in small hanging pots. Provide good light, especially for 'Tricolor', and water and feed in moderation. Marginally frost hardy.

S

Saxifraga x *urbium*

Saxifraga x *urbium* 'Miss Chambers'

Saxifraga x urbium
London Pride

ORIGIN Gardens
CLIMATE M, CT

A hybrid between *S. spathularis* and *S. umbrosa*, this is an evergreen perennial to 30cm/12in high that forms wide-spreading rosettes of spoon-shaped, toothed, leathery, green leaves to 4cm/1½in across. Tiny, star-shaped, white and pink-tinged flowers are borne on wiry stalks in summer. **'Miss Chambers'** forms a compact mat of apple green rosettes.
USE & CULTIVATION A good weed-suppressing groundcover and edging plant. It likes moist well-drained soil and thrives in shady sites. Fully frost hardy.

SCHEFFLERA

FAMILY ARALIACEAE
Native to tropical and subtropical regions, this is a large genus of over 650 species of trees, shrubs and vines. Some are grown for their handsome palmate leaves and are useful either indoors or in the garden in warm areas. Propagate from seed or cuttings.

Schefflera actinophylla
syn. *Brassaia actinophylla*
Queensland Umbrella Tree

ORIGIN Australia, New Guinea
CLIMATE T, ST, WT
This ornamental tree reaches 15m/50ft in its rainforest habitat, but usually only 9m/30ft when cultivated. It has large long-stalked glossy leaves composed of 7–16 leaflets, each to 30cm/12in long, which radiate from a central point very much like the spokes of an umbrella. Honey-rich crimson flowers are held well above the foliage in radiating spikes in spring and summer.
USE & CULTIVATION A handsome specimen tree for warm gardens, its luxurious foliage giving shade, shelter and a tropical touch. Grow in rich well-drained soil in sun or light shade with shelter from wind. Give plenty of

Schefflera actinophylla

water during early growth. In cool areas, protect from frost. It is highly suitable for indoors. Use a good potting mix and position in bright indirect light. Avoid extremes of temperature. Frost tender.

Schefflera arboricola
Hawaiian Elf Schefflera

ORIGIN Taiwan
CLIMATE T, ST, WT
This is a branching shrub of smaller habit than *S. actinophylla*. It grows to 4.5m/15ft and has glossy, dark green, compound leaves consisting of 5–10 oval leaflets each to 15cm/6in long. Greenish yellow flowers are borne in flattened clusters to 30cm/12in long in spring and summer.
USE & CULTIVATION As for *S. actinophylla*. Easily pruned, this species is good for smaller gardens and patios. Frost tender.

Schefflera elegantissima
**syns *Aralia elegantissima*,
*Dizygotheca elegantissima***
False Aralia

ORIGIN New Caledonia
CLIMATE T, ST, WT
Tree-like specimens can reach 15m/50ft in the wild, but this species usually grows about 1–2m/3–7ft tall in cultivation. It has particularly attractive juvenile foliage, graceful compound leaves consisting of 7–11 narrow, serrated, drooping leaflets radiating from stiff

upright stems. Leaves are bronze tinted at first, but change to a very deep green, almost black colouring. As the plant ages, it produces larger, coarser leaves; these can be removed and new growth will revert to the juvenile form.
USE & CULTIVATION In warm gardens the delicate foliage contrasts well with the bolder leaves of other tropical plants, and it provides a good middle storey beneath palms. Grow in dappled shade and fertile well-drained soil. Indoors, provide bright filtered light, warmth and humid conditions. Keep the soil moist over summer. Frost tender.

SEDUM

STONECROP
FAMILY CRASSULACEAE
There are about 400 species in this genus; some are fairly large subshrubs, others are low-growing creepers or trailers. They vary enormously, but most have fleshy stems and stalkless succulent leaves. Many are extremely tolerant of cold conditions and are cultivated for their bright starry flowers, attractive ornamental foliage and often neat compact habit. Propagate from seed or cuttings or by division.

Sedum ewersii

ORIGIN Central Asia, Himalayas, Mongolia, China
CLIMATE M, CT, H
This small mat-forming plant has low spreading stems to 8cm/3in high and 30cm/12in wide. The oval grey–blue leaves to 2cm/¾in long are stalkless, and heart-shaped at the base. In summer it bears small rounded clusters of pinkish red star-shaped flowers.
USE & CULTIVATION Ideal for a rock garden. Grow in moderately fertile, well-drained soil in full sun. Fully frost hardy.

Sedum 'Herbstfreude'
syn. *Sedum* 'Autumn Joy'

ORIGIN Gardens
CLIMATE WT, M, CT, H
This popular cultivar forms a neat dome to 60cm/24in tall and wide of toothed fleshy leaves to 12cm/5in long. Dome-shaped heads of rich pink flowers appear in early autumn and are long lasting, fading to coppery and rusty red shades.
USE & CULTIVATION It makes a strong herbaceous subject for open sunny beds and rockeries. Grow in light-textured, well-drained soil in full sun. Cut back to shape after flowering. Fully frost hardy.

Schefflera elegantissima

Sedum ewersii

Sedum 'Herbstfreude'

Sedum kamtschaticum

Sedum sieboldii

Sedum kamtschaticum
Kamschatka Stonecrop

ORIGIN Eastern Siberia, northern China, Japan

CLIMATE M, CT, H

This semi-evergreen perennial forms neat clumps to 10cm/4in high and 25cm/10in wide of fleshy mid-green leaves to 4cm/1½in long with toothed tips. Yellow star-shaped flowers appear in summer. **'Variegatum'** has leaves with creamy white edges.

USE & CULTIVATION As for *S. ewersii*. Fully frost hardy.

Sedum morganianum
Donkey's Tail, Burro Tail

ORIGIN Mexico

CLIMATE T, ST, WT

This species has slender trailing stems to 90cm/36in long completely covered with fleshy, overlapping, cylindrical leaves that are about 2cm/³⁄₄in long and pale greyish green with a whitish bloom. Pinkish red starry flowers may appear at the tips in summer, but it does not flower readily.

USE & CULTIVATION A charming plant for a rock garden, where its trailing stems can be easily seen. Grow in well-drained soil in full sun. In frost-prone climates use as a houseplant, ideally in a small hanging pot. For good display

Sedum spathulifolium 'Purpureum'

grow several small plants in the same container. Handle with care as the leaves break off easily. Use a well-drained potting mix and keep on the dry side in full light. Frost tender.

Sedum sieboldii

ORIGIN Japan

CLIMATE WT, M, CT, H

This spreading tuberous perennial has arching to semi-prostrate stems to 25cm/10in long. The almost rounded, slightly toothed leaves to 2cm/³⁄₄in long are arranged in groups of 3. They are a glaucous blue–green and often pink-tinged with reddish margins. Pink

flowers are borne in leafy clusters in autumn. **'Mediovariegatum'** has leaves with a central creamy yellow splash and occasionally with red margins.

USE & CULTIVATION Grow in a raised rockery pocket, hanging basket or urn where the arching stems can trail attractively. It likes fertile well-drained soil in full sun. Fully frost hardy.

Sedum spathulifolium

ORIGIN Western North America

CLIMATE WT, M, CT, H

This evergreen species forms a low mat to 10cm/4in high and 60cm/24in wide of numerous tiny rosettes of spoon-shaped, glaucous, grey leaves to 2.5cm/1in long, often tinged reddish brown. Bright yellow star-shaped flowers appear in flat sprays in early summer. The leaves of **'Cape Blanco'** are mealy white when young. **'Purpureum'** has reddish purple leaves.

USE & CULTIVATION Ideally suited to a saucer-shaped container or small rockery pocket where the offsets can happily form new colonies. Grow in fertile well-drained soil in full sun. The cultivars are sometimes used in formal bedding and colour schemes. Fully frost hardy.

Sedum spectabile
Ice Plant

ORIGIN China, Korea
CLIMATE WT, M, CT, H

This clump-forming perennial to 45cm/18in high has erect robust stems and obovate, pale glaucous green leaves to 8cm/3in long. Showy pink flowers are produced in flat-topped heads at the end of summer. **'Brilliant'** has deep rose pink flowers. **'Iceberg'** is shorter, to 30cm/12in, with white flowers. **'Stardust'** has blue–green leaves.

Sedum spectabile 'Iceberg'

Sedum spectabile 'Stardust'

USE & CULTIVATION Massed as a single-colour group, they can be used in geometric designs or to define garden beds. Also suitable for rockeries or mixed borders. Grow in light-textured, well-drained soil in full sun. Fully frost hardy.

SELAGINELLA

SELAGINELLA, LITTLE CLUB MOSS
FAMILY SELAGINELLACEAE

This is a large genus of about 700 species of perennials that resemble miniature moss-like ferns. They form low upright hummocks or have creeping stems. Several species grown for their decorative ferny foliage are sometimes used in moist positions in ferneries. Propagate from spores or by division.

Selaginella martensii

ORIGIN Central America
CLIMATE ST, WT

A low mat-forming plant to about 15cm/6in high with trailing stems bearing yellowish or pale green leaves in flattened branches which spread to 20cm/8in across.

USE & CULTIVATION A beautiful small plant for trailing over rocks in a warm fernery. It does best in shade and fertile, moist well-drained soil and humid conditions. Sometimes grown in hanging baskets or terrariums. Use a moisture-retentive, peat-based potting mix. Frost tender.

Selaginella martensii

Selaginella pallescens

Sempervivum arachnoideum

Selaginella pallescens
syn. *Selaginella emmeliana*

ORIGIN North and South America
CLIMATE ST, WT

This is a tufted plant with erect stems branching from the base to 30cm/12in tall. The tiny green leaves with a white edge are paler below and tend to curl inwards when they are dry.

USE & CULTIVATION Ideal for tucking in moist crevices in the fernery or for hanging baskets, this species has the same growing requirements as *S. martensii*. Frost tender.

SEMPERVIVUM

HOUSELEEK
FAMILY CRASSULACEAE

This genus of about 40 species of perennial succulents extends from Europe to eastern Asia and south into northern Africa. They form hummocks or cluster into large mats of dense rosettes composed of fleshy, oblong to triangular leaves often tinted or flushed red or purple. Each rosette flowers once and then dies, but is replaced by numerous offsets. Although the star-shaped flowers are attractive, flowering does not begin for several years. Propagate from offsets.

Sempervivum arachnoideum
Cobweb Houseleek

ORIGIN European Alps
CLIMATE WT, M, CT, H

This species has small rosettes about 6cm/2¼in across of fleshy green triangular leaves that readily cluster together to form low mats spreading to 30cm/12in. The red-flushed leaf tips are spun together with long white hairs to give a cobweb effect. Loose clusters of pink or crimson star-shaped flowers appear in summer.

USE & CULTIVATION Ideally suited to raised rock gardens, dry walls and containers. Grow in full sun in loose, gritty, well-drained soil. Fully frost hardy.

Sempervivum ciliosum

ORIGIN Eastern Europe
CLIMATE WT, M, CT, H

This mat-forming succulent bears very hairy rosettes to 5cm/2in across of incurved grey–green leaves to 2.5cm/1in long. It reaches a height of 8cm/3in and spreads to 30cm/12in. Greenish yellow flowers appear in summer.

USE & CULTIVATION Grow in sharply drained, gritty soil in a rockery pocket or trough in full sun. It dislikes winter wet and is best grown in an alpine

Sempervivum ciliosum

house in areas with wet winters. Fully frost hardy.

Sempervivum tectorum
Common Houseleek

ORIGIN Southern Europe
CLIMATE WT, M, CT, H

This evergreen succulent forms spreading mats to 45cm/18in wide of rosettes to 10cm/4in across of purple-tipped leaves that are sometimes suffused with deep red. Clusters of reddish purple flowers are borne on 30cm/12in high stems in summer.

Sempervivum tectorum

USE & CULTIVATION This attractive species will rapidly establish itself in a sunny well-drained rock garden. It develops its best colour in cold areas in full sun. Fully frost hardy.

SENECIO

FAMILY ASTERACEAE/COMPOSITAE

This one of the largest genera of flowering plants, containing more than 1500 species scattered through the world. It includes annuals, perennials, succulents, shrubs, climbers and trees. They are grown for their daisy-like flowers and ornamental, often succulent or silvery foliage. Propagate from seed or cuttings or by division.

Senecio articulatus
syn. *Kleinia articulata*
Candle Plant

ORIGIN South Africa
CLIMATE ST, WT

This is a most unusual perennial succulent, with tubular, weakly jointed stems to 50cm/20in high that during winter bear lobed, 5cm/2in long, fleshy leaves, mainly towards the tips. The flowerheads are yellow and appear from spring to autumn. **'Variegatus'** has pink-tinged leaves and flowers.

USE & CULTIVATION An interesting plant for a raised rockery pocket or container. Grow in gravelly, sharply drained soil in full sun. Indoors, provide full light, moderate water and plenty of air movement. Frost tender.

Senecio cineraria
syns *Cineraria maritima,*
Senecio candicans
Dusty Miller

ORIGIN Mediterranean region
CLIMATE WT, M, CT

This perennial subshrub to about 2m/7ft tall is widely grown for its stiff, silvery grey, woolly, deeply divided or lobed leaves to 15cm/6in long. Bright yellow daisy flowers appear in summer; they are often removed to encourage fresh leafy growth and preserve the plant's dominant silver colour. **'Silver Dust'** has almost white woolly leaves.

USE & CULTIVATION One of the most ornamental and reliable of the grey plants. It is equally at home in a well-drained rockery, mixed border or small garden, or in a starring role in formal bedding or colour schemes. Extremely tolerant of salt spray and air pollution, but resents summer rainfall and high humidity. Moderately frost hardy.

Senecio articulatus

Senecio cineraria

Senecio cineraria 'Silver Dust'

Senecio macroglossus
Cape Ivy, Natal Ivy

ORIGIN South Africa, Mozambique, Zimbabwe

CLIMATE ST, WT, M

This evergreen climber or trailing plant has succulent young stems that become semi-woody and up to 2m/7ft long with age. It has fleshy, ivy-like, mid-green leaves to 8cm/3in wide that are roughly triangular with 5–7 slightly pointed lobes. Small yellow flowers are borne in late autumn and winter. **'Variegatus'** has pale green leaves irregularly variegated with cream on slender purple stems.

USE & CULTIVATION Attractive trailing plants for walls, rockeries, hanging pots and urns or at the front of a border. Young plants are good for contrast in mixed container arrangements, especially with succulents. Grow in moderately fertile, well-drained soil in full sun. Frost tender.

Senecio serpens
syn. *Kleinia repens*
Blue Chalksticks

ORIGIN South Africa

CLIMATE WT, M

A low-growing perennial succulent to 30cm/12in high with cylindrical waxy blue leaves to 3cm/1¼in long branching from short stems near the base. White flowerheads appear in summer.

USE & CULTIVATION Suitable for rock gardens, borders and containers. Grow in moderately fertile, well-drained soil in full sun. Frost tender.

Senecio smithii

ORIGIN South America

CLIMATE WT, M, CT, H

This clump-forming perennial to 1.2m/4ft high has thick, dark green, oblong leaves to 30cm/12in long with a glossy finish. It bears clusters of white, yellow-eyed daisy flowers from early to the end of summer.

USE & CULTIVATION Happiest with its roots in water, this is an excellent foliage plant for a permanently wet site edging a water feature. Also suitable for a moist border in full sun or partial shade. Fully frost hardy.

Senecio viravira
syn. *Senecio leucostachys*
Dusty Miller

ORIGIN Argentina

CLIMATE WT, MT, CT

This small evergreen subshrub to 60cm/24in tall has silvery grey leaves to 8cm/3in long, dissected twice into fine linear segments. It is often confused with *S. cineraria*, but its leaves are more finely dissected and the pale yellow flowerheads at the end of summer are without ray florets.

USE & CULTIVATION A pretty silvery plant for contrast in borders, rock gardens and containers. Grow in moderately fertile, well-drained soil in full sun. Regularly tip-prune to encourage compact shape. Moderately frost hardy.

SEQUOIA

FAMILY TAXODIACEAE

Native to the Pacific coast of North America, the majestic redwood is the only species in this genus. It is well known as the tallest tree in the world, with some specimens in the wild reaching 110m/360ft; they reach more modest proportions in cultivation. They are trouble free and extremely long-lived. Their red timber is among the most valuable in the world. It is one of the few conifers that will re-shoot from mature wood when cut back. Propagate from seed or cuttings.

Sequoia sempervirens
California Redwood, Coast Redwood

ORIGIN Western North America

CLIMATE WT, M, CT

In cultivation this magnificent conifer will reach 30m/100ft or more. The

Senecio serpens

Senecio viravira

Sequoia sempervirens

Sequoia sempervirens 'Prostrata'

tapering trunk is clad with very soft, fibrous, reddish bark. It has horizontal branches, with the lower branches slightly drooping. The 2-ranked, slightly flattened, linear leaves to 2.5cm/1in long are deep green above and whitish below. Small, oval, terminal cones are green, ripening to dark brown. **'Ad-pressa'** is a slow-growing, densely branched dwarf form eventually reaching 9m/30ft. **'Pendula'** is a weeping form with arching branches and greyish green foliage. **'Prostrata'** is a dwarf form with glaucous blue foliage, spreading to 3m/10ft across.

USE & CULTIVATION An outstanding ornamental tree, ideal for large-scale gardens and parks, performing well in deep well-drained soil in full sun or part shade. It prefers a cool, moist, sheltered position and needs plenty of water through dry periods. Very cold winters will damage the foliage, but will not affect the tree itself. The cultivars make good landscaping subjects for smaller gardens. Fully frost hardy.

SERISSA

FAMILY RUBIACEAE

A genus containing only one species, a small evergreen shrub from subtropical areas of India, China and Japan, which is cultivated in warmer regions for its neat overall appearance. Propagate from cuttings.

Serissa foetida
syn. *Serissa japonica*

ORIGIN Southeast Asia
CLIMATE T, ST, WT

This small bushy shrub, growing to only 45cm/18in, has small, crowded, ovate leaves to 2cm/³/₄in long which are a dark shining green. It produces tiny white star-shaped flowers in summer and autumn. There are several cultivars, including a double-flowered form and **'Variegata'**, which has silvery margins.

USE & CULTIVATION It withstands clipping and makes a delightful low hedge,

rock-garden or container specimen. Grow in a sunny well-drained position. Trim after flowering. In cool areas, grow as an indoor plant in full light. Frost tender.

Serissa foetida 'Variegata'

S

SOLEIROLIA

FAMILY URTICACEAE

The single species in this genus is a soft-stemmed prostrate perennial that takes root at the nodes and forms an attractive dense carpet of light green foliage. Propagate by division.

Soleirolia soleirolii
syn. *Helxine soleirolii*

Baby's Tears, Mind-your-own-business

ORIGIN Western Mediterranean islands
CLIMATE WT, M, CT

This pretty carpeting plant grows no more than 5cm/2in high with an indefinite spread. It has small, rounded, fresh green leaves and tiny pink-tinged white flowers.

USE & CULTIVATION A useful plant for growing around a pond, in damp areas, or in paving or rockeries. It likes semi-shade and a moist position. Also suitable for containers, either on its own or as a dainty foreground plant spilling over the edges. Regularly trim with scissors to maintain neat shape. Although damaged by frost or drying out, it quickly recovers when conditions improve. Frost hardy.

SOLENOSTEMON

COLEUS

FAMILY LABIATAE/LAMIACEAE

There are about 60 species in this genus of perennials from tropical Africa and Asia. A small number are grown for their ornamental colourful foliage, but generally will only grow well throughout the year in warm areas. They are very easy to grow from cuttings and thus are often treated as annuals and discarded when past their best. Pinch out growing tips and developing flowers to keep them bushy. Caterpillars may be a problem outdoors. In hot dry rooms, red spider mites can cause disfiguring of leaves. Propagate from stem cuttings.

Solenostemon scutellarioides
syn. *Coleus blumei* var. *verschaffeltii*

Coleus, Flame Nettle, Painted Nettle

ORIGIN Southeast Asia
CLIMATE T, ST

A fast-growing bushy perennial to 60cm/24in high. It has weak stems and pointed, oval, serrated leaves in every shade of purple, red and pink, as well as yellow and green, often very vivid and multi-coloured. Tiny, rather insignificant 2-lipped flowers are borne in terminal spikes and are best removed. Many colourful cultivars are available.

USE & CULTIVATION Often grown as temporary bedding plants during the warmer months. They look their best when given adequate water and shelter from direct sun. All coleus prefer soil high in organic matter. Mulch to keep the roots cool. Indoors, provide a humid atmosphere and bright light at all times for fine colour. Keep the potting mix thoroughly moist and apply a liquid fertiliser about every 2 weeks. Take cuttings

Soleirolia soleirolii

Solenostemon scutellarioides 'Pineapple beauty'

Spathiphyllum 'Mauna Loa'

Spathiphyllum 'Sensation'

from those with the best colour and dispose of overgrown plants when they begin to look shabby. Frost tender.

SPATHIPHYLLUM

PEACE LILY
FAMILY ARACEAE

This genus consists of about 36 species of almost stemless evergreen perennials native to tropical America, the Philippines and Indonesia. They have beautiful, glossy, dark green foliage with prominent veins, and white lily-shaped flowers which appear for most of the year. They have become popular indoor plants and can be grown outside in humid frost-free areas. Red spider

mites might be a problem indoors if humidity is low. Propagate by division.

Spathiphyllum 'Mauna Loa'

ORIGIN Gardens
CLIMATE T, ST, WT

This robust tufted perennial to 1m/3ft high has short underground rhizomes and sends up clusters of lance-shaped, glossy dark green leaves to 30cm/12in long on sheathed leaf stalks. The white oval pointed spathe backing the green and white spadix is 15–20cm/6–8in long. It flowers intermittently throughout the year.
USE & CULTIVATION A very useful plant for tropical-style gardens, where it thrives in moist shady spots and looks good in drifts. A well-composted soil

rich in organic matter is best. Indoors, provide warm humid conditions and bright indirect light. Keep the potting mix moist, but allow it to dry out a little in winter. Mist-spray regularly and feed moderately in spring and summer. Frost tender.

Spathiphyllum 'Sensation'

ORIGIN Gardens
CLIMATE T, ST, WT

An excellent indoor foliage plant, this cultivar has very large, deep green, glossy leaves to over 1m/3ft long held on long sheathed leaf stalks. The large white flowers gradually change to light green.
USE & CULTIVATION As for S. 'Mauna Loa'. Frost tender.

Stachys byzantina

Stachys byzantina 'Silver Carpet'

Spathiphyllum wallisii

Spathiphyllum wallisii

ORIGIN Tropical America
CLIMATE T, ST, WT
This species has clusters of wavy-edged elliptic leaves to 35cm/14in long. In spring and summer fragrant white flowers are borne on long slender stalks that tower above the foliage. They turn green as they age.
USE & CULTIVATION As for *S.* 'Mauna Loa'. Frost tender.

STACHYS

FAMILY LABIATAE/LAMIACEAE
A genus of about 300 species of annuals, perennials and shrubs widely distributed in northern temperate regions. Some are popular cottage and herb garden plants. Propagate from seed or by division.

Stachys byzantina
syn. *Stachys lanata*
Lambs' Ears, Lambs' Tails, Lambs' Tongues

ORIGIN The Caucasus to Iran
CLIMATE WT, M, CT, H
This evergreen perennial makes attractive low clumps of woolly, silvery grey leaves to 10cm/4in long. Mauve–pink woolly flower spikes are borne in summer, but these are often removed to retain the neat carpet effect of the leaves. **'Big Ears'** has larger leaves and bears tall spikes of purple flowers. **'Silver Carpet'** has greyish white leaves; and as it is non-flowering, it remains more compact and is often selected for formal displays.
USE & CULTIVATION Use to add texture and colour contrast to the front of a flower border or rock garden or as a groundcover edging a path or steps.

They survive cold winters, but resent humidity and excessive wet weather. Grow in well-drained soil in an open sunny position. Fully frost hardy.

STENOTAPHRUM

FAMILY GRAMINEAE/POACEAE

A tropical and subtropical genus of about 6 species of grasses. Buffalo Grass, *Stenotaphrum secundatum*, is widely planted as a lawn grass in warmer climates while its highly ornamental variegated form is used in borders and as a houseplant. Propagate by division.

Stenotaphrum secundatum 'Variegatum'
Buffalo Grass

ORIGIN Central and South America
CLIMATE T, ST, WT
This grass has creeping flattened stems that take root at the nodes, from which arise small clusters of pale cream-coloured linear leaves 8–20cm/3–8in long which are marked with fine dark green lines.
USE & CULTIVATION Suitable for edging, but more commonly grown in hanging baskets and often as a house-plant in cool climates. Indoors, ensure a humid atmosphere and bright light at all times for fine colour. Keep the potting mix thoroughly moist. Frost tender.

STIPA

FAMILY GRAMINEAE/POACEAE

This is a large cosmopolitan grass genus of about 300 species. They form neat dense tussocks of slender leaves and in late summer bear flowers in loose open panicles towering well above the foliage. Propagate from seed or by division.

Stipa arundinacea
Pheasant's Tail Grass

ORIGIN New Zealand
CLIMATE WT, M, H
This is a tuft-forming perennial grass with slender arching leaves to 30cm/12in long that turn soft orange in late autumn. Tall purplish green flower spikes appear in autumn and gradually fade to a soft straw colour.
USE & CULTIVATION A fine ornamental grass for accent in a flower border, rock garden or in modern landscape design. Grow in well-drained soil in full sun or partial shade. Fully frost hardy.

Stipa gigantea
Giant Feather Grass

ORIGIN Spain, Portugal
CLIMATE WT, M, CT
This grass forms neat hummocks of narrow mid-green leaves to 70cm/28in long. The flowerheads are carried on erect stems to 1.5m/5ft tall in early summer. The flowers turn a deep golden brown colour as they age and persist well into winter.
USE & CULTIVATION As for *S. arundinacea*. Fully frost hardy.

Stipa tenuissima
Mexican Feather Grass

ORIGIN Texas, Mexico, Argentina
CLIMATE WT, M, CT
This neat tussock-forming grass has very narrow bright green leaves to 30cm/12in or more long. The soft, buff-coloured, silky panicles to 45cm/18in long appear in summer and stir in the slightest breeze.
USE & CULTIVATION As for *S. arundinacea*. Frost hardy.

Stenotaphrum secundatum 'Variegatum'

Stipa tenuissima

S

STRELITZIA

BIRD OF PARADISE
FAMILY STRELITZIACEAE

This is a small genus of 5 species of shrubby evergreen perennials native to South Africa. They are grown for their striking banana-like foliage and, in some species, spectacularly showy flowers that resemble the heads of exotic birds. Even when not in flower they provide year-round interest and make striking accent plants. Propagate from suckers or by division.

Strelitzia nicolai
Wild Banana, Giant Bird of Paradise

ORIGIN South Africa
CLIMATE T, ST, WT

This tree-like perennial to 6m/20ft has large oblong leaves to 1.5m/5ft long on 2m/7ft long stalks held in a fan-like arrangement. Its bird of paradise flowers in muted shades of purple, blue and creamy white appear in spring and early summer.

USE & CULTIVATION Given plenty of space and a warm climate, this lush tropical-looking species makes an excellent feature plant. It resents disturbance and only flowers well when established. Grow in humus-enriched, well-drained soil in full sun or partial shade and water regularly during spring and summer. Shelter from strong winds or the leaves will become tatty. Frost tender.

Strelitzia reginae
Crane Flower, Bird of Paradise

ORIGIN South Africa
CLIMATE T, ST, WT

A clump-forming perennial to 1.5m/5ft high with long-stalked bluish green, oblong leaves to 50cm/20in long. The bright orange and blue flowers set in pointed boat-shaped bracts appear mainly in spring and summer.

USE & CULTIVATION Grow en masse as a feature in a tropical garden setting or as part of a swimming-pool landscape with some summer shade. It likes fertile well-drained soil and regular water

Strelitzia nicolai

during the warmer months. As a container plant it grows successfully indoors when given bright direct sunlight, plenty of water during the growing season and dryish conditions in winter. Frost tender.

STROMANTHE

FAMILY MARANTACEAE

This genus consists of 13 species of perennials from tropical America. They have creeping rhizomes and bear fan-like sprays of attractively patterned or heavily veined oblong leaves, making them popular as indoor plants. They belong to the same family as the calatheas and marantas and are often confused with them. Propagate by division.

Stromanthe sanguinea

ORIGIN Brazil
CLIMATE T, ST, WT

This is a fairly slow-growing creeping perennial with a height to 1.5m/5ft

Stromanthe sanguinea

and a spread of 1m/3ft. New leaves are rolled at first and emerge from the stalks of older leaves. They are oblong to 45cm/18in long, glossy mid-green above with darker markings, and reddish underneath. Panicles of small white flower are produced intermittently throughout the warmer months. **USE & CULTIVATION** In warmer climates it looks good planted in drifts beneath trees in tropical-style gardens. Provide organically rich soil, moist well-drained conditions and a partially shaded, sheltered position to keep plants looking their best. Indoors, plants require warmth, high humidity and moderate light. Keep soil moist, with less water in winter. Frost tender.

SYNGONIUM

FAMILY ARACEAE

There are about 33 species in this genus of climbing plants native to tropical America and the West Indies. A few of them are grown for their attractive foliage as indoor plants. The lily-shaped flowers are seldom seen in cultivation. Propagate from cuttings.

Syngonium podophyllum
syn. *Nephthytis triphylla*
Arrowhead Vine, Goosefoot

ORIGIN Mexico to Brazil
CLIMATE T, ST
This weak climbing vine or trailer produces pale green arrow-shaped leaves to 15cm/6in long when young. Mature leaves to 30cm/12in long are lobed, with 7–9 leaflets. **'Emerald Gem'** is a compact variety with dark green leaves with lighter green markings along the veins. **'White Butterfly'** has pale and dark green leaves with sharply contrasting white veins.
USE & CULTIVATION They will trail or climb as required and are good for mass planting in tropical gardens. Often grown as potted or hanging basket houseplants, needing bright indirect light and plenty of moisture. Mist-spray the foliage occasionally and tip-prune to encourage compact growth. Frost tender.

TANACETUM

FAMILY ASTERACEAE/COMPOSITAE

A genus of about 50 species of annuals and perennials from the Northern Hemisphere, mainly Europe and Asia. They are grown for their often aromatic, lacy, fern-like foliage and daisy-like or tiny button flowerheads. A small number have beautiful, finely dissected, silvery foliage. Propagate from seed or by division.

Tanacetum argenteum
syn. *Achillea argentea*

ORIGIN Mediterranean region
CLIMATE WT, M, CT
This attractive evergreen perennial grows to about 20cm/8in high and creeps to form a dense mat to 30cm/12in wide. Its silvery white leaves to 7cm/2½in long are finely dissected into narrow leaflets. Masses of yellow button-like flowers appear in summer.
USE & CULTIVATION Good foliage and groundcover plants for rock gardens and for softening the edges of a border. Perfect in a silver garden planting scheme, they are also ideal for providing contrast, texture and shape to darker leaved plants or pale-coloured flowers. Grow in moderately fertile, well-drained soil in full sun. The leaves are used in small floral arrangements. Fully frost hardy.

Syngonium podophyllum 'White Butterfly'

Syngonium podophyllum

Tanacetum haradjanii
syn. *Chrysanthemum haradjanii*

ORIGIN Syria, Turkey
CLIMATE WT, M, CT

This tufted perennial has mat-forming stems to 35cm/14in tall and wide. The woolly, silvery grey, oblong leaves to 5cm/2in long are composed of many finely divided segments. Terminal clusters of yellow daisy-like flowerheads are borne in late summer.

USE & CULTIVATION As for *T. argenteum*. Fully frost hardy.

Tanacetum ptarmiciflorum
syn. *Chrysanthemum ptarmiciflorum*
Dusty Miller, Silver Lace

ORIGIN Canary Islands
CLIMATE WT, M, CT

This evergreen woody-based perennial reaches a height and spread of 50cm/20in. It has fern-like silvery grey leaves to 10cm/4in long and in summer bears clusters of white daisy-like flowerheads.

USE & CULTIVATION As for *T. argenteum*. In very cold climates use as a summer bedding plant. Moderately frost hardy.

TAXODIUM

FAMILY TAXODIACEAE

There are only 2 or 3 species in this genus of deciduous or semi-evergreen coniferous trees from North America and Mexico. They have a strong preference for swampy ground, sometimes producing woody aerial roots known as pneumatophores, used as an aid to aeration when the root system is fully

Taxodium distichum

submerged. Propagate from seed or cuttings.

Taxodium distichum
Swamp Cypress

ORIGIN Southeastern USA
CLIMATE WT, M, CT, H

Native to coastal swamp areas in south-eastern North America, this deciduous conifer forms a shapely conical form while young, becoming columnar and

Taxodium distichum var. *imbricarium* 'Nutans'

Tanacetum ptarmiciflorum

Taxodium distichum

Taxus baccata 'Dovastonii Aurea'

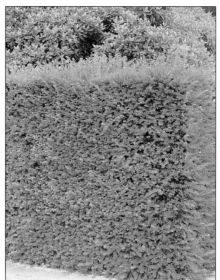

Taxus baccata 'Fastigiata'

Taxus baccata 'Fastigiata Aurea'

reaching 35m/120ft or more with age. It has dull reddish brown stringy bark and woody knee-like breathing growths around the base of its fluted trunk. The flattened, pointed, pale green, ferny leaves to 2cm/³⁄₄in long are borne spirally on the terminal shoots and take on rich rusty brown tones in autumn. Small rounded cones ripen from green to purple. **T. d. var. imbricarium 'Nutans'** is a beautiful, graceful tree with upright shoots that become pendent with age.

USE & CULTIVATION Outstanding specimen trees for growing beside streams or lakes and for taking advantage of wet problem areas, they also thrive in deep well-drained soil in full sun. Fully frost hardy.

TAXUS

YEW
FAMILY TAXACEAE

This is a small coniferous genus of about 10 species of large evergreen shrubs and small trees occurring in northern cool temperate regions. They are slow-growing, long-term plants, taking many years to reach their maximum height. In England they are much used for topiary and hedges and other formal planting. The flat dark green leaves are spirally arranged and taper to a point. When

pollinated, female trees bear berry-like fruit consisting of a single seed surrounded by a fleshy, red, cup-shaped aril. The leaves and seeds are highly poisonous to humans and animals. Propagate from seed or cuttings or by grafting.

Taxus baccata
Yew

ORIGIN Europe, northern Africa, western Asia
CLIMATE M, CT, H

This slow-growing evergreen tree, eventually reaching 9–20m/30–70ft, develops a thick dark-coloured trunk and a dense irregular crown. The flattened linear leaves to 3cm/1¼in long are spirally arranged but spread out to form 2 lateral rows. They are dark green and glossy above and yellowish beneath. Male and female flowers are borne on different trees. The red berry-like fruit encases a poisonous seed. **'Aurea'**, the Golden English Yew, forms a compact bush to 3.5m/12ft tall, densely foliaged to the ground with bright yellow young outer leaves that turn greener with age. **'Dovastonii Aurea'** is a small female tree, 3–5m/10–17ft tall, with tiers of spreading horizontal branches and green leaves edged yellow. **'Fastigiata'**, the Irish Yew, has an erect columnar habit to 6–8m/20–25ft. The closely packed branches make it a popular choice for hedging.

'Fastigiata Aurea', the Golden Irish Yew, is a smaller version of **'Fastigiata'**, to 3–4m/10–12ft tall and with golden yellow variegated leaves. **'Fastigiata Aureomarginata'**, 3–5m/10–17ft tall, has green leaves edged with yellow. **'Repandens'** is a spreading form to 90cm/36in high and 3m/10ft wide and has bright green leaves. **'Repens Aurea'** is a spreading groundcover with a height and spread of 1.5m/5ft and green leaves edged with yellow. **'Semperaurea'** has a height and spread of 2m/7ft and dense golden young foliage, maturing to bronze–yellow in winter. **'Standishii'** has an erect columnar habit to 2m/7ft tall and rich golden yellow foliage, but is very slow growing.

USE & CULTIVATION Yew has long been cultivated, and specimens in many old European gardens are known to be hundreds of years old. The slow-growing, erect columnar forms make fine long-term ornamental hedges, perfect for formal planting, carefully trained topiaries and containers. The spreading forms are often chosen as groundcovers, lawn features or for large rock gardens. Plants do best in cool regions and tolerate a wide range of soils in sun or semi-shade. They need adequate moisture when young, but withstand drought once established. Trim to shape in summer and early autumn. Fully frost hardy.

Taxus cuspidata
Japanese Yew

ORIGIN China, Japan
CLIMATE M, CT, H

This small erect tree to 5m/17ft tall is broadly spreading and shrub-like in cultivation. It has dense, dark green, linear leaves to 2.5cm/1in long, slightly curved and twisted and pale brown underneath. The bright red berry-like fruit is 1cm/^{1}/$_3$in across. **'Densa'** slowly forms a dense compact mound to 1.2m/4ft high and wide. **'Nana'** is a spreading shrub with a height and spread of about 2m/7ft and dark green leaves angled upwards.

USE & CULTIVATION Commonly used for hedging, topiary and as a tub plant. It performs well in very cold climates and tolerates dry soils, shady conditions and urban pollution. The dwarf forms are particularly useful in seaside gardens. Fully frost hardy.

TETRAPANAX

FAMILY ARALIACEAE

One species in this genus is native to southern China and Taiwan and is grown for its huge palmate leaves and woolly-white flower balls. The white pith of the stems is a source of rice paper in China. Propagate from seed and by suckers.

Tetrapanax papyriferus
Rice-paper Plant

ORIGIN China, Taiwan
CLIMATE WT, M, CT

This suckering shrub or small tree to 6m/20ft tall has large lobed leaves to 60cm/24in or more wide carried on long stout stalks. They are shiny mid-green above and downy white underneath. Sprays of fluffy, white or creamy green, globular flowers are carried above the foliage in autumn and followed by black berries.

USE & CULTIVATION A striking plant for large tropical-style settings where its spreading, suckering habit can be

Tetrapanax papyriferus

Teucrium fruticans

Teucrium marum

TEUCRIUM

FAMILY LABIATAE/LAMIACEAE

A genus of approximately 100 species of wide distribution, with many found in the Mediterranean region. They are herbaceous perennials or small evergreen or deciduous shrubs with attractive, pleasantly aromatic leaves and tubular, somewhat 2-lipped flowers in terminal whorls. They can be used for low hedges, borders and in rock gardens. Propagate from seed and cuttings or by division in spring.

Teucrium fruticans
Shrubby Germander

ORIGIN Western Mediterranean region
CLIMATE WT, M, CT
This is a dense, twiggy, evergreen shrub to about 2m/7ft tall and wide, with white woolly stems and small greyish white oval leaves to 2cm/³/₄in long

that are slightly aromatic, and felted on the underside. Pale blue tubular flowers appear in summer. **'Azureum'** has darker blue flowers.
USE & CULTIVATION This attractive herb-garden subject can be clipped to form a neat low hedge. Also a useful addition to seaside gardens, where it tolerates poor stony soil. Grow in a dry sunny position against a warm sheltered wall in cold areas. Cut back wayward shoots during the growing season. Moderately frost hardy.

used to advantage; otherwise, restrict its spread by the removal of suckers at the base. Easily grown in any well-drained soil, including sandy coastal areas. Grow in full sun or partial shade and shelter from strong winds. Container specimens need plenty of water during the growing season. Frost hardy.

Teucrium marum
Cat Thyme

ORIGIN Western Mediterranean islands
CLIMATE WT, M, CT
This small bushy shrub to no more than 30cm/12in high has twiggy white-woolly stems and tiny greyish white leaves to 1cm/¹/₃in long. Pinkish purple flowers appear in early summer.
USE & CULTIVATION Said to be attractive to cats, this is a good edging plant for the herb garden, rockery and silver planting schemes. Full sun and good drainage are best. Moderately frost hardy.

Teucrium subspinosum

ORIGIN Balearic Islands
CLIMATE WT, M, CT
This small wiry shrub reaches 15cm/6in high with a spread to 30cm/12in. It has very slender white-woolly stems and minute silvery grey leaves. Pinkish purple flowers appear in summer.
USE & CULTIVATION An attractive shrub for a small rockery pocket or for providing contrast and texture edging a border. Grow in light dry soil in full sun. Tip-prune to maintain a neat regular outline. Moderately frost hardy.

Teucrium subspinosum

THUJA

ARBOR-VITAE

FAMILY CUPRESSACEAE

This genus comprises 5 species of evergreen conifers native to China, Japan and North America. They are grown for their neat elegant form and attractive, often flat, spray-like branches of dark green leaves that are strongly aromatic when crushed. They remain compact for many years and so are ideal for average-sized home gardens; many are suitable for hedging. Several golden-foliaged cultivars are available. Propagate from seed or cuttings.

Thuja occidentalis
White Cedar

ORIGIN North America

CLIMATE WT, M, CT, H

This is a narrowly conical tree to 15m/50ft tall with a straight trunk and reddish brown bark, peeling in long vertical strips. The scale-like mid-green leaves with paler undersides carried in flattened sprays are resin-scented. Brown female cones to 1cm/^{1}/$_3$in long

have 8–10 overlapping scales. This species appears in a variety of cultivars. **'Danica'** forms a rounded bush to 1m/3ft tall and wide of closely packed vivid green leaves in flat vertical sprays. **'Filiformis'** is slightly rounded to 8m/25ft tall with trailing whip-like shoots. **'Globosa'** is a low-growing rounded form to 1.5m/5ft, with closely packed sprays of greyish green foliage. **'Golden Globe'** is a dwarf rounded bush rarely more than 1m/3ft high with golden yellow foliage. **'Hetz Midget'** is a slow-growing dark green globular bush to 80cm/32in in diameter. **'Holmstrup'** forms a dense conical bush to 3.5m/12ft high with vertical sprays of bright green scale-like leaves. **'Rheingold'** is a slow-growing neat pyramidal bush to 2m/7ft high with golden yellow foliage that takes on a coppery tinge in winter. **'Smaragd'** is a neat conical bush to 1.8m/6ft with glossy green leaves.

USE & CULTIVATION Most often seen as a specimen tree. The smaller growing forms are suitable for rock or feature gardens, parterres, as accents or tub plants. 'Smaragd' is popular for hedges

and parterres and makes a good screening plant for small courtyard gardens. Grow in fertile, moist well-drained soil in full sun or semi-shade. Shelter from harsh drying winds. Salt tolerant. Fully frost hardy.

THUJOPSIS

FAMILY CUPRESSACEAE

This is a genus of only one species, a native of moist forests in mountainous regions of Japan. It is related to *Thuja* and is grown for its distinctive large flattened sprays of tiny scale-like leaves with white bands beneath. Widely planted as an ornamental, it is also valued as a timber tree in Asia. Propagate from seed or cuttings.

Thujopsis dolabrata
Hiba Arbor-vitae

ORIGIN Japan

CLIMATE WT, M, CT, H

This attractive evergreen conifer to 18m/60ft is usually broadly conical. The trunk often divides and branches

Thuja occidentalis 'Smaragd'

Thujopsis dolabrata 'Variegata'

Thymus x *citriodorus* 'Doone Valley'

Thymus x *citriodorus* 'Aureus'

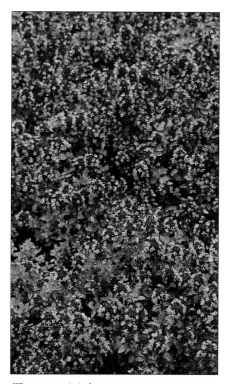

Thymus x *citriodorus*

low down and the bark is reddish brown, shredding in slender vertical strips. The aromatic foliage is carried in flattened sprays of tiny, glossy dark green leaves with silvery white undersides. Its small rounded cones to 2cm/³⁄₄in long are greyish brown with thick leathery scales. **'Nana'** is a dwarf rounded form to about 1m/3ft high, spreading to about 1.5m/5ft with age, and has rich green foliage. **'Variegata'** is a broadly conical bush to 8m/25ft tall with mid-green foliage irregularly splashed creamy white.

USE & CULTIVATION The tree and the variegated form are slow growing and make handsome specimens for large private gardens. 'Nana' can be used as a smaller feature or for edging a woodland garden. They are at their best in deep, well-drained, moist soils in full sun. Fully frost hardy.

THYMUS

THYME
FAMILY LABIATAE/LAMIACEAE
A genus of about 350 species of creeping perennial herbs and upright miniature shrubs from Europe and Asia. Most thymes have aromatic foliage. They are among the loveliest of all foliage plants for making a fragrant carpet and planting between paving stones. Upright shrubby species can be used for miniature hedges and in formal garden design, while those grown for their culinary qualities are a must for the herb garden. In summer they produce tiny flower spikes, forming a pretty carpet of colour when in full bloom. After flowering, cut back to encourage compact growth. Propagate from seed or cuttings or by division.

Thymus caespititius

ORIGIN Spain, Portugal
CLIMATE WT, M, CT
This mat-forming aromatic subshrub reaches no more than 5cm/2in high, with slender trailing stems to 20cm/8in long covered in minute dark green leaves. It bears pale lilac or white flowers in small clusters in summer.
USE & CULTIVATION Plant in border edges, between paving cracks and in rock gardens, or use as a lawn replacement or for a herb seat. It likes full sun in light well-drained soil. Frost hardy.

Thymus x citriodorus
syn. *Thymus pulegioides* x *T. vulgaris*
Lemon-scented Thyme

ORIGIN Gardens
CLIMATE WT, M, CT, H
This small spreading bush grows to 30cm/12in high and has flat, oval, lemon-scented leaves and pale lilac flowers in summer. **'Aureus'** has golden yellow leaves. **'Bertram Anderson'** has yellowish green foliage. The mat-forming **'Doone Valley'** has gold and green variegated leaves to 1cm/¹⁄₃in long. **'Silver Queen'** has silvery white variegated foliage.
USE & CULTIVATION Neat dwarf hedges good for edging a herb garden or flower border. Grow in well-drained soil in full sun. Leaves can be used in cooking. Fully frost hardy.

Thymus herba-barona
Caraway Thyme

ORIGIN Corsica, Sardinia
CLIMATE WT, M, CT

This prostrate subshrub grows to about 10cm/4in high and spreads to form a loose mat to 25cm/10in across. The tiny, lance-shaped, dark green leaves are caraway-scented when crushed. Small purple flowers are produced in summer.

USE & CULTIVATION Grow in a herb garden, alongside paths and as a groundcover. It likes well-drained, preferably alkaline soil and full sun. Fully frost hardy.

Thymus pseudolanuginosus
syn. *Thymus lanuginosus* of gardens
Woolly Thyme

ORIGIN Unknown
CLIMATE WT, M, CT, H

This mat-forming perennial herb grows no more than 5cm/2in tall and has tiny, broadly elliptic, grey–green leaves covered with long white hairs. Pink flowers appear in mid-summer.

USE & CULTIVATION An attractive carpeting species for clothing rocks, bordering edges and making thyme seats. It fills areas between paths and happily trails over the edges of raised walls and containers. Grow in any well-drained soil in full sun. Fully frost hardy.

Thymus serphyllum

ORIGIN Europe
CLIMATE WT, M, CT, H

This mat-forming subshrub reaches about 25cm/10in high and spreads to 45cm/18in. It has tiny linear to ovate leaves and purple flowers in terminal clusters in mid-summer. **'Annie Hall'** has pink flowers and rounded light green leaves. **'Elfin'** forms a miniature tight bun and occasionally bears pink flowers. **'Snowdrift'** is low growing and has white flowers.

USE & CULTIVATION Grow alongside paths, between paving stones and in rockery pockets. Forming aromatic carpets, they can also be planted as a fragrant lawn and garden seat. Well-drained soil and a sunny position are best. Fully frost hardy.

Thymus vulgaris
Garden Thyme

ORIGIN Mediterranean region
CLIMATE WT, M, CT

This dwarf woody plant grows to 30cm/12in high and has small linear to elliptic mid-green leaves covered in fine grey hairs. Whorls of white to pale purple flowers appear in late spring and early summer. **'Silver Posie'** is a popular variety with silvery white-edged leaves.

USE & CULTIVATION A must for every herb garden, and can be used to make miniature hedges, in formal garden design and in containers. These thymes are the most popular for flavouring. Grow in moist well-drained soil in a sunny position. Frost hardy.

TILIA

LIME, LINDEN
FAMILY TILIACEAE

A genus of about 45 species of handsome deciduous trees from cooler temperate regions of the Northern Hemisphere. They have toothed, usually broadly ovate, heart-shaped leaves and small fragrant flowers in long-stalked clusters in summer. The leaves briefly turn yellow in autumn. Because they tolerate heavy pruning and urban pollution, they are often planted as avenue or street trees. Lime or linden tea, made from the dried flowers of the Small-leaved Lime (*Tilia cordata*) is popular in European countries, where it is drunk

Thymus herba-barona

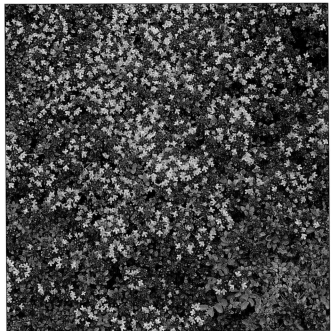

Thymus serphyllum

Thymus vulgaris

Tilia tomentosa

as a digestive and calming tonic. Propagate from ripe seed or cuttings or by layering.

Tilia cordata
Small-leaved Lime

ORIGIN Europe
CLIMATE M, CT, H
This broadly columnar tree forms a dense irregular crown of arching branches to 30m/100ft tall. The finely toothed heart-shaped leaves to 8cm/3in long are dark shiny green above and paler beneath. They turn yellow in autumn. Heavily scented white flowers are borne in pendulous clusters from the axils of pale green, wing-like bracts in summer. The thin-shelled, nut-like fruit is grey.
USE & CULTIVATION A fast-growing handsome tree for spacious gardens

and street planting. It prefers cool climates. Grow in fertile moisture-retentive soil in full sun or partial shade. Fully frost hardy.

Tilia x europaea
syns *Tilia intermedia*, *T. x vulgaris*
Common Lime

ORIGIN Europe
CLIMATE M, CT, H
This tall deciduous tree has a dense shapely crown and reaches a height of 30m/100ft. The broadly ovate, heart-shaped leaves to 10cm/4in long have toothed edges and are bright green above, paler beneath, and turn rich golden yellow in autumn. Small, fragrant lime green flowers appear during spring. It is a naturally occurring hybrid between *T. cordata* and

T. platyphyllos and has a strong tendency to sucker.
USE & CULTIVATION As for *T. cordata*. Fully frost hardy.

Tilia tomentosa
Silver Linden, Silver Lime

ORIGIN Eastern Europe
CLIMATE M, CT, H
Reaching 30m/100ft, this is a handsome compact tree with a broadly domed crown. The broadly ovate dark green leaves to 10cm/4in long have toothed margins, prominent ribs and are covered with dense silvery white hairs beneath. They turn a rich buttery yellow in autumn. Fragrant white flowers are produced in pendulous clusters in summer.
USE & CULTIVATION As for *T. cordata*. Fully frost hardy.

T

TILLANDSIA

AIR PLANT

FAMILY BROMELIACEAE

A large genus of over 380 species of epiphytic plants native to tropical and subtropical America. The spiky leaves usually form loose rosettes and the flowers often appear in spikes, sometimes with colourful bracts. Those native to hot dry regions often have greyish, green or reddish foliage covered with a silvery scale. Many have little or no root system and absorb moisture and nutrients through their leaves, making them easy to grow indoors or in greenhouses, or even outdoors in warm climates. Only one species is included here, the striking *Tillandsia usneoides*, commonly known as Spanish Moss and grown for its long tangled festoons of silvery grey leaves. Propagate from offsets or by division.

Tillandsia usneoides
Spanish Moss

ORIGIN Southern USA to northern South America

CLIMATE T, ST, WT

This is a pendent epiphytic plant with thread-like stems covered with fine, silvery grey, scaly leaves to 5cm/2in long forming a fantastic trailing mass to 1m/3ft or more long. Tiny pale greenish blue flowers are borne in the leaf axils in spring and summer.

USE & CULTIVATION Spanish Moss does not actually require a container, but is attached to a suspended piece of cork bark or hung over a branch in partial shade where the clump will increase in size and in length. Outdoors it decorates low branches and looks good on deciduous trees over a pond or water feature. Also can be draped from hanging baskets in which other more upright plants are grown. In the warm humid atmosphere of a conservatory it can be used as a feature. Ensure that the foliage is mist-sprayed regularly and grow in bright indirect light. Frost tender.

TRACHYCARPUS

FAMILY ARECACEAE/PALMAE

This is a small genus of about 6 species of highly decorative fan palms from southern China and the Himalayas. In nature they occur in cold mountainous regions and are especially useful for growing in temperate climates. Propagate from seed.

Trachycarpus fortunei
Chusan Palm,
Chinese Windmill Palm

ORIGIN China

CLIMATE ST, WT, M, CT

Growing to about 9m/30ft, this is a single-stemmed palm with a symmetrical compact crown and a brown shaggy trunk covered with persistent dark brown fibre. The fan-shaped or circular leaves to 1m/3ft across are divided more than halfway to the base into stiff pleated segments. Fragrant creamy yellow flowers are produced in branched conical clusters to 80cm/32in long and followed by blue–black fruit.

USE & CULTIVATION A popular feature plant for temperate gardens where a tropical setting is desired. Slow growing, it thrives for many years in a container, making it a good courtyard plant. Grow in well-drained soil in full sun and shelter from strong dry winds, especially when young. Indoors, it requires bright light and adequate moisture. Moderately frost hardy.

TRADESCANTIA

FAMILY COMMELINACEAE

This is a genus of about 65 species of mostly trailing perennials native to the Americas. They are grown for their showy flowers or ornamental foliage. Some make good hanging basket subjects, groundcovers or rockery plants. Pinch out the growing tips regularly to encourage bushy growth; towards the end of summer, cut back straggly stems. Propagate by division or from cuttings.

Tradescantia fluminensis
Wandering Jew

ORIGIN South America

CLIMATE T, ST, WT

This is an evergreen perennial with trailing rooting stems to 60cm/24in or more long. The fleshy, stem-clasping,

Tillandsia usneoides

Trachycarpus fortunei

pointed leaves to 5cm/2in long are light glossy green above and purplish underneath. Clusters of tiny white flowers appear intermittently. The most popular of the variegated forms are **'Albovittata'** (syn. *T. albiflora*), which has white longitudinal stripes on its green leaves, and **'Quicksilver'**, with evenly striped green and white leaves to 8cm/3in long.

USE & CULTIVATION These strong-growing trailing plants are eminently suited to hanging baskets. In cool climates, grow as showy indoor specimens, where they need bright filtered light, warm humid conditions and moist well-drained soil. Remove green shoots from the variegated forms as soon as they appear. Frost tender.

Tradescantia fluminensis 'Albovittata'

Tradescantia pallida 'Purpurea'

Tradescantia pallida 'Purpurea'
syn. *Tradescantia pallida* 'Purple Heart'

ORIGIN Mexico
CLIMATE ST, WT, M

This tradescantia forms a neat clump to about 20cm/8in high and 40cm/16in across. It has rather fleshy, stemless, rich purple oblong leaves to 15cm/6in long. Pink flowers appear at the ends of the stems in summer.

USE & CULTIVATION In warm regions it makes a richly coloured border and groundcover plant. In frost-prone areas, use for summer bedding, window boxes and sometimes in floral design work. It likes full sun and retains its colour best in well-drained soil kept on the dry side. Indoors, water moderately and provide bright light. Frost tender.

Tradescantia sillamontana
White Velvet

ORIGIN Mexico
CLIMATE ST, WT, M

This erect then trailing perennial has oval stem-clasping leaves to 6cm/ 2¼in long. Both stems and leaves are densely covered with long, white, woolly hairs. It has a height and spread of 30cm/12in and bears magenta pink flowers in spring and summer.

USE & CULTIVATION Suitable for a rock garden or border, it is often used as a houseplant in cool climates, where it must have strong direct light. Tip-prune growing tips. Frost tender.

Tradescantia sillamontana

Tradescantia spathacea

Tradescantia spathacea
syn. *Rheo discolor*
Boat Lily, Moses-in-the-cradle

ORIGIN Central America
CLIMATE T, ST, WT

This species forms a loose rosette to 45cm/18in high of mostly upright leaves to 30cm/12in long. They are lance-shaped, dark green, and have a rich purple underside. Short-lived tiny white flowers appear throughout the year. **'Vittata'** has leaves with bright yellow stripes.

USE & CULTIVATION In tropical gardens it is often planted in bold blocks, making a striking, colourful edging and ground-cover. In cooler climates it is a popular houseplant, particularly attractive in hanging baskets and trailing from urns. Indoors, water moderately and provide bright indirect light. Frost tender.

Tradescantia zanonia
syn. *Campelia zanonia*

ORIGIN Mexico, South America, West Indies
CLIMATE T, ST, WT

This clump-forming erect perennial grows to 2m/7ft tall with lance-shaped, stem-clasping, dark green leaves to 25cm/10in long. It produces clusters of small white flowers from summer to winter. The leaves of **'Mexican Flag'** have green and white longitudinal stripes.

USE & CULTIVATION 'Mexican Flag' is a particularly striking cultivar for partial shade among shrubs, palms and ferns. As a container plant, its dracaena-like appearance is best suited to an upright pot. Pinch growing tips to encourage bushy growth. Indoors, water moderately and provide bright light. Frost tender.

Tradescantia zanonia 'Mexican Flag'

Tradescantia zebrina

Tradescantia zebrina
syn. *Zebrina pendula*
Silver Inch Plant

ORIGIN Mexico
CLIMATE T, ST, WT
This trailing plant has oval leaves to 5cm/2in long with 2 broad silver bands, an iridescent upper surface and a rich purple underside. In spring and summer, clusters of small pink or violet–blue flowers appear at branch ends. **'Purpusii'** has larger, rich bronze–purple leaves and pink flowers. **'Quadcolor'** has irregular pink, green, cream and silver stripes on the leaves.
USE & CULTIVATION In warm climates it makes an attractive groundcover, thriving in moist well-drained soil in quite dense shade. It is one of the easiest plants to care for indoors and a few young plants together in a single hanging basket make a good display. Place in a well-lit position and water well while in active growth. Regularly pinch out growing tips to encourage side-branching. Frost tender.

TSUGA

HEMLOCK
FAMILY PINACEAE
This genus comprises about 14 species of evergreen coniferous trees and shrubs native to North America and temperate Asia and widely grown as ornamentals in cool climates. They are mostly conical in habit with a central trunk and irregular whorls of horizontal branches clothing the trunk almost to the ground. The flattened linear leaves have 2 broad white bands below. Both male and female cones are small and are borne on the same tree. All species are suitable for bonsai. Propagate from seed or cuttings.

Tsuga canadensis
Eastern Hemlock,
Canadian Hemlock

ORIGIN Eastern North America
CLIMATE CT, H
This broadly crowned coniferous tree reaches 30m/100ft or more in the wild, less in cultivation. The trunk is often forked near the base and the pale brown scaly bark becomes ridged in older trees. It has drooping tips and dark green linear leaves to 2cm/³/₄in long arranged in 2 rows. They release a lemon scent when crushed. Ripe female cones to 2cm/³/₄in long hang from short slender stalks. Popular cultivars include **'Bennett'**, a low-spreading dwarf form to about 1.5m/5ft tall and 2m/7ft wide, with short bright green foliage giving a fan effect. **'Jeddeloh'** forms a flattened mound to about 1.5m/5ft tall and wide, arching outward from the hollow centre, and with bright green leaves. **'Pendula'** forms a pendulous dome-shaped bush to 2m/7ft tall and wide with vivid green young foliage in spring.
USE & CULTIVATION A fine ornamental tree for specimen planting in spacious gardens. It is a tree for cool moist climates with clean air, thriving in slightly acid, humus-rich, well-drained soil. Protect from strong drying winds. The low-growing forms are perfect for rock or feature gardens. All forms are good bonsai subjects. Fully frost hardy.

Tsuga heterophylla
Western Hemlock

ORIGIN Western North America
CLIMATE M, CT, H
This tall graceful conifer reaches 60m/200ft or more in the wild, but in cultivation about 30–50m/100–160ft. The grey bark becomes reddish brown and fissured with age. It forms a symmetrical conical outline with weeping horizontal branches clothing the trunk almost to the ground. The soft flattened leaves to 2.5cm/1in long are a lovely light green when young, maturing to dark green with 2 broad white bands below. The drooping ovoid female cones to 2.5cm/1in long are purple at first, ripening to reddish brown.
USE & CULTIVATION As for *T. canadensis*. Its strong pale yellow timber is used commercially. It is very shade tolerant, withstands clipping well and is useful for hedging. Fully frost hardy.

T

ULMUS

ELM

FAMILY ULMACEAE

This genus comprises about 45 species of mostly large deciduous trees found in northern temperate regions. They are among the loveliest of all trees, and with their high domed crowns make excellent shade and specimen trees. The alternate, asymmetrical, toothed leaves have prominent veins and take on attractive rich yellow tones in autumn. Tiny petalless flowers appear in bud-like clusters mainly before the leaves in early spring; the small papery-winged fruits (samaras) ripen in summer. Populations of elm trees in Europe and North America have been devastated by the bark beetle-transmitted fungus *Ceratocystus ulmi*, better known as Dutch elm disease. In areas where the disease is known to be present, it is best to grow disease-resistant species. Propagate from seed, cuttings or suckers.

Ulmus americana
American Elm, White Elm

ORIGIN North America
CLIMATE WT, M, CT, H

This wide-spreading tree reaches 40m/130ft in the wild, less in cultivation. It has coarsely ridged bark and slightly pendulous branches. The large, oval, dark green leaves to 15cm/6in long turn bright yellow in autumn. It bears clusters of winged green fruits. **'Delaware'** is reputedly disease resistant.

USE & CULTIVATION A stately long-lived specimen tree, best suited to large gardens and parks. It is susceptible to Dutch elm disease and it is not recommended in areas where the disease is a threat. Otherwise it is worthy of extensive planting, being quite indifferent to soil conditions provided the drainage is good. Fully frost hardy.

Ulmus x hollandica
Dutch Elm

ORIGIN Europe
CLIMATE M, CT, H

This spreading, somewhat open tree to 35m/14in tall is believed to be a hybrid between *U. glabra* and *U. minor*. It has a short trunk and pendulous branches and toothed, glossy, dark green leaves to 12cm/5in long that turn yellow in autumn. **'Jacqueline Hillier'** is a small rounded shrub to 2.5m/8ft tall with small rough leaves to 3.5cm/1½ in long.

USE & CULTIVATION The Dutch Elm produces prolific root suckers, useful for combating gully erosion. Grow in any well-drained soil in full sun or partial shade. 'Jacqueline Hillier' is partially resistant to Dutch elm disease and suitable for hedging. Fully frost hardy.

Ulmus minor
syn. *Ulmus carpinifolia*
European Field Elm

ORIGIN Southern Europe
CLIMATE WT, N, CT, H

This deciduous tree to 30m/100ft has arching branches and a fairly narrow habit. The oval, bright green, toothed leaves to 8cm/3in long are glossy above and turn golden yellow in autumn. There are several varieties, most of which are fast growing and disease resistant. **'Variegata'** has deep green leaves densely mottled or speckled white. It is less inclined to sucker.

USE & CULTIVATION Use as a lawn specimen or street tree. It produces prolific root suckers, so plant only where they can be tolerated or controlled. Grow in any well-drained soil in full sun or partial shade. Fully frost hardy.

Ulmus parvifolia
Chinese Elm

ORIGIN China, Japan
CLIMATE WT, M, CT, H

This very attractive tree reaching 6–9m/20–30ft tall has a fine, weeping, rounded crown. Mature trees have attractive grey peeling bark. Small leathery oval leaves to 8cm/3in long, evenly toothed and glossy green, turn yellow or brownish red in cold areas. It is semi-evergreen in warm climates. The winged green fruit mature in late autumn. **'Frosty'** is a shrubby form with smaller, neatly

Ulmus parvifolia

Veratrum viride

arranged leaves less than 2.5cm/1in long with white toothed margins. **'Hokkaido'** (syn. *U. pygmaea*) is a slow-growing dwarf form with corky bark. **USE & CULTIVATION** The most popular elm for small gardens. It is tolerant of most climates and conditions and will grow in any well-drained soil. It withstands wind and is relatively resistant to Dutch elm disease. Fully frost hardy.

V

VERATRUM

FAMILY LILIACEAE/MELIANTHIACEAE
A genus of 45 species of robust clump-forming perennial herbs found in Europe, Siberia and North America. These remarkable foliage plants have large leaves, folded and

pleated like a fan, encircling strong erect stems that push through the soil in early spring. Established plants produce tall leafless panicles of small star-like flowers in summer. Slugs and snails can damage the leaves. Propagate from seed or by division in autumn.

Veratrum nigrum
Black False Hellebore
ORIGIN Europe to Siberia, China
CLIMATE M, CT, H
This erect perennial to 1.2m/4ft tall is rare in the wild, but well established and popular in cultivation. It forms clumps of boldly ribbed and pleated leaves, to 30cm/12in long at the base, becoming smaller and fewer along the stems. Tall erect flowering spikes to 45cm/18in long bear tiny maroon star-shaped flowers in late summer.
USE & CULTIVATION A native of the woodland edge, it does best grown in a semi-shaded protected position to prevent its attractive foliage from scorching. Grow in deep, rich, moisture-retentive soil. Fully frost hardy.

Veratrum viride
Indian Poke
ORIGIN Eastern North America
CLIMATE M, CT, H
This perennial herb reaches 1.2m/4ft high and has whorled, boldly ribbed leaves to 30cm/12in long and a few smaller stem leaves. The yellowish green flowers are borne in panicles 30–60cm/12–24in long.
USE & CULTIVATION As for *V. nigrum*. Fully frost hardy.

VERBASCUM

MULLEIN
FAMILY SCROPHULARIACEAE
This is a large genus of over 350 species of mostly biennials or short-lived perennials from Europe, the Mediterranean region and Asia. They are rosette forming, often developing large clumps of soft-textured hairy leaves, and generally bearing tall

flowering spikes or racemes of saucer-shaped flowers. The huge rosettes of woolly white leaves are of sufficient beauty in themselves, and the plants are often grown as much for these during the first year as for their flowers. Some species self-seed freely. Propagate from seed or by division of perennials.

Verbascum bombyciferum
syn. *Verbascum broussa*

ORIGIN Turkey
CLIMATE M, CT
This biennial growing to almost 2m/7ft tall has ovate, grey, felted basal leaves to 40cm/16in long. The summer flower spikes are also densely woolly. The yellow flowers are carried on branching stems to 1.2m/4ft or more above the leaves, giving a showy candelabra-like effect.
USE & CULTIVATION Especially valuable for accent and foliage contrast in a herbaceous border or woodland garden. It resents wet winters and likes well-drained soil in a sunny position. Fully frost hardy.

Verbascum bombyciferum

VICTORIA

FAMILY NYMPHAEACEAE

This is a small genus of only 2 species of water lilies from tropical South America. They have fabulous huge floating leaves and produce nocturnal water lily-like flowers. Propagate from seed.

Victoria amazonica
Amazon Water Lily

ORIGIN South America (Amazon region)

CLIMATE T, ST

This aquatic annual or perennial has strong stout rhizomes supporting huge flat rounded leaves reaching 1.8m/6ft across. They have upturned margins with soft prickles and a reddish purple colouring on the underside. White flowers to 30cm/12in across with pink tints are borne in summer.

USE & CULTIVATION This extremely glamorous water lily needs a large deep pond in full sun to look its best. Grow in containers with rich organic soil and submerge in water at least 1m/3ft deep. It can be grown in a deep heated pool at a water temperature of 26°C/80°F in a large conservatory, but needs full light. Frost tender.

Victoria amazonica

VITIS

GRAPE VINE
FAMILY VITACEAE

This genus of about 65 deciduous woody tendril-climbers from the northern temperate regions is well known for its edible fruit (grapes) which provide us with food and wine. In addition to the valuable fruiting species with their long history of cultivation, there are several with ornamental foliage and superb autumn colour. Vines need heavy pruning in winter to confine their spread and encourage density of foliage and successful fruiting. Grape vines are subject to a number of pests and diseases. Powdery mildew is most troublesome in climates with a humid summer. Propagate from cuttings.

Vitis coignetiae

Vitis coignetiae
Crimson Glory Vine

ORIGIN Japan, Korea

CLIMATE WT, M, CT, H

This vigorous woody climber has large heart-shaped leaves to 30cm/12in long with 3–5 shallow lobes. They are dark green with deeply impressed veins above, and rusty-downy beneath. The leaves turn shades of crimson and scarlet in autumn. The small blue–black unpalatable grapes are borne in late summer and autumn.

Vitis vinifera 'Purpurea'

Vriesea hieroglyphica

USE & CULTIVATION Excellent for training over a sturdy pergola, trellis, veranda or anywhere that summer shade and winter sun are required. It can also be trained against a wall or fence. Grow in deep well-drained soil in full sun. Ample water is necessary during periods of rapid growth. Leaf colour is best where winters are cold. Fully frost hardy.

Vitis vinifera
Grape Vine

ORIGIN Europe, Mediterranean region
CLIMATE WT, M, CT
This robust deciduous tendril-climber has large palmate leaves and bears edible grapes. In addition to a multitude of fruiting varieties, several are grown for their ornamental foliage, including the popular **'Alicante'**, with large, deeply divided palmate leaves and rich red

autumn colour, and **'Purpurea'**, with deep claret red leaves turning dark purple in autumn.
USE & CULTIVATION As for *V. coignetiae*. Fully frost hardy.

VRIESEA

FAMILY BROMELIACEAE
Most of the 250 species in this large bromeliad genus are epiphytic. They are native to Central and South America with their main concentration in Brazil. The smooth-edged, sword-shaped leaves are arranged in large decorative rosettes and are often attractively marked with cross-banding or variegation. The long-lasting flower spikes often have brilliantly coloured shiny bracts which are usually more attractive than the short-lived flowers. Propagate from seed or offsets.

Vriesea hieroglyphica
King of Bromeliads

ORIGIN Brazil
CLIMATE T, ST, WT
This outstanding species forms a large rosette over 1m/3ft high and 1.5m/5ft across. The arching strap-shaped leaves are bright green and prominently marked with cross-banding of dark green to blackish purple. The flower spike, to 80cm/32in long, has yellowish green bracts and yellow petals.
USE & CULTIVATION In warm climates it can be grown beneath trees in part shade. A very well-drained soil is essential for container-grown specimens; a standard bromeliad compost is recommended. Indoors, provide moderate light and good air circulation. Water moderately during the growing period, ensuring that the central rosette cup is filled with water. Frost tender.

V

Vriesea splendens

Xanthorrhoea australis

Vriesea splendens
Flaming Sword

ORIGIN Northern South America
CLIMATE T, ST, WT
This species forms a loose rosette to 1m/3ft high composed of pale bluish green, arching, sword-shaped leaves with broad purple–black bands. In summer it bears prominent flower spikes to 60cm/24in tall with brilliant red or orange bracts and yellow flowers.
USE & CULTIVATION As for *V. hieroglyphica*. Frost tender.

XANTHORRHOEA

GRASS TREE

FAMILY XANTHORRHOEACEAE
There are about 30 species in this distinctive Australian genus of evergreen woody perennials. They are extremely slow growing, with the trunk above or below the ground. The very long narrow leaves are crowded at the top of the stem, from which also arises the long cylindrical flower spike. They make striking feature plants or can be grown in a large tub. Grass trees do not happily transplant, but are readily grown from seed. Propagate from seed.

Xanthorrhoea australis
Austral Grass Tree

ORIGIN Australia
CLIMATE WT, M
This species may have a short or tall trunk, depending on its age. An old plant can reach 3m/10ft in height with a single or forked trunk. It has a crown of narrow grass-like leaves to 1m/3ft long. The small creamy white flowers are densely packed on a thick flower spike to 1.5m/5ft long arising from the centre of the crown. They are produced spasmodically on mature plants, with outstanding displays following bushfires in the wild.
USE & CULTIVATION A mature plant with a well-developed trunk makes a spectacular architectural plant for modern landscape design. It also makes a handsome rock-garden feature or container plant. Grow in a well-drained, open, sunny position in light-textured soil. Marginally frost hardy.

XANTHOSOMA

FAMILY ARACEAE
This tropical American genus comprises about 40 species of tuberous perennial plants. They are related to and somewhat similar to taro (*Calocasia* species) and some are grown for their yam-like edible tubers. They have large, ornamental, heart-shaped or arrow-shaped leaves on long thin stalks and make striking foliage plants for tropical gardens. Green or cream spathes surround the oblong flower spike. Propagate by division.

Xanthosoma violaceum
Blue Taro

ORIGIN Tropical America
CLIMATE T, ST, WT
This tuberous perennial has large arrow-shaped leaves to 70cm/28in long held on dark purple leaf stalks to

1m/3ft long. Leaves are deep green above with purplish veins and margins and light purple undersides when young. Pale yellow arum-like flowers appear occasionally.

USE & CULTIVATION In warm climates this is a dramatic foliage plant for growing beneath palms in the swimming-pool landscape. Grow in humus-rich fertile soil with good drainage. In a large fernery it blends well with ferns and other shade-loving plants. It also makes a handsome container plant. Indoors, it likes bright indirect light, warm humid conditions and plenty of moisture. In winter, watering should only be enough to keep the soil barely moist. Frost tender.

YUCCA

FAMILY AGAVACEAE
A genus of about 40 species of evergreen perennials, shrubs and trees native to southern USA, Mexico and the West Indies. They may be stemless or have erect woody stems, with sword-shaped leaves arranged in a loose terminal rosette. In addition to their year-round value as striking foliage plants, yuccas have tall showy spikes of waxy, night-scented flowers, usually creamy white, but occasionally violet-tinged. Propagate from seed, root cuttings or suckers.

Yucca aloifolia
Spanish Bayonet

ORIGIN Southern USA, Mexico, West Indies
CLIMATE WT, M, SA
This slow-growing species forms an evergreen shrub or small tree with a single or branched stem to about 3m/10ft high in cultivation. The trunk terminates in tufts of densely arranged, narrow, sharply pointed leaves to 60cm/24in long and 5cm/2in wide. Large spikes to 70cm/28in tall of purple-tinted, creamy white flowers, bell-shaped and pendent, appear in summer and autumn. **'Marginata'** has dark green leaves bordered in yellow. **'Tricolor'** has white or yellow stripes, tinged with red when young, running along the centre of the green leaves. **'Variegata'** has leaves with creamy white margins.

USE & CULTIVATION Ideal for complementing architectural features, this and the following species make dramatic accent plants for large or small gardens, courtyards or modern interiors. The variegated forms can be grouped with broader foliaged plants to create interesting texture and colour contrast. They are best in poor, well-drained soil in full sun. Locate those with spine-tipped leaves away from paths and gates, where they are unlikely to cause harm. Indoor plants need bright light, normal room temperatures and regular watering during the growing period. Less water is required in winter. If possible, spell the plants outdoors during the warm summer months. They will withstand a dry atmosphere. Marginally frost hardy.

Xanthosoma violaceum

Yucca aloifolia 'Marginata'

V X Y Z

Yucca elephantipes

Yucca elephantipes 'Variegata'

Yucca elephantipes
Giant Yucca, Spineless Yucca

ORIGIN Southern Mexico, Central America

CLIMATE ST, WT, SA

This species produces a thickened, branched trunk often with a swollen base. It can reach a height of 9m/30ft in the wild, usually less in cultivation. The stems are topped with rosettes of narrow mid-green leaves to 1m/3ft or more long and 8cm/3in wide. They are roughly toothed, but the leaf tips are soft. Creamy white flowers are produced in large erect panicles to 2m/7ft long from summer to autumn. **'Variegata'** has leaves edged with creamy white.

USE & CULTIVATION As for *Y. aloifolia*. Frost tender.

Yucca filamentosa 'Bright Edge'

Yucca glauca

Yucca filamentosa
Adam's Needle

ORIGIN Southern USA

CLIMATE WT, M, CT

This frost-hardy evergreen is usually stemless, forming a large rosette of sharply pointed leaves to 1m/3ft long with coarse curly threads forming along the margins. The flower spikes to 2m/7ft or more long carry a mass of fragrant, white, bell-shaped flowers in summer. **'Bright Edge'** has variegated cream and blue–green leaves.

USE & CULTIVATION As for *Y. aloifolia*, but this species will withstand colder conditions. Frost hardy.

Yucca glauca
syn. *Yucca angustifolia*
Dwarf Yucca, Soapweed

ORIGIN Central USA

CLIMATE M, CT, SA

This low-growing short-stemmed species forms a rounded clump of narrow, glaucous, greyish leaves to 45cm/18in long edged with white and a few

thread-like hairs. Erect spikes to 1m/3ft tall of greenish white flowers are produced during summer.

USE & CULTIVATION As for *Y. aloifolia*. Frost hardy.

Yucca gloriosa
Spanish Dagger

ORIGIN Southern USA

CLIMATE WT, M, SA

The species is usually stemless, but with age can develop branched or stout trunks. The whole plant reaches a height of 2m/7ft, and has sharply pointed blue–green leaves to 75cm/30in long that become a deeper green with age. The flower stem, often 2.5m/8ft high, bears large, drooping bell-shaped white flowers in summer. **'Variegata'** has yellow leaf margins.

USE & CULTIVATION As for *Y. aloifolia*. Marginally frost hardy.

ZAMIA

FAMILY ZAMIACEAE

This American genus of over 60 species of cycads has a wide distribution, from Florida in North America to Bolivia in South America. They are grown for their highly decorative, arching, pinnate leaves held in a spiral arrangement on a thick woody stem, which is usually underground, but can be above-ground to 2m/7ft tall on some large specimens. Male and female cones are produced on separate plants. Propagate from fresh seed.

Zamia furfuracea

Zamia furfuracea
Cardboard Palm

ORIGIN Eastern Mexico
CLIMATE T, ST, WT

This small cycad grows from branching underground stems and has semi-erect to spreading pinnate leaves to 1m/3ft long, each with up to 40 oblong, olive green, leathery leaflets. The male cones are cylindrical, the female cones are ovoid; both are grey–green to brown and shortly hairy.

USE & CULTIVATION An attractive addition to the tropical border, especially when grown in association with palms, ferns and other cycads. It is slow growing, becoming increasingly handsome as it develops, either in a container or in the soil. Grow in fertile, moist well-drained soil in a sunny position. Indoor plants need bright indirect light, well-drained fibrous soil and plenty of water during the growing period. Frost tender.

ZANTEDESCHIA

ARUM LILY
FAMILY ARACEAE

The familiar arum lily with its pure white flowers and handsome arrow-shaped leaves belongs to this genus of 6 species of perennials. They all have tuberous rhizomes and bear large clumps of arrow-shaped leaves. The typical arum flower has a central erect spadix surrounded by a showy spathe. In the wild these plants grow in swampy marshlands and watercourses, and are perfect for waterside plantings. Propagate from seed or by division.

Zantedeschia aethiopica
Arum Lily

ORIGIN South Africa
CLIMATE WT, M, CT

This tuberous perennial reaches 90cm/36in high and wide, with large clumps of lustrous arrow-shaped deep green leaves. The pure white flowers to 25cm/10in long with a yellow spadix are produced generously from late

Zantedeschia elliottiana

spring to mid-summer. The shorter **'Apple Court Babe'** grows to only 60cm/24in high. **'Crowborough'** is more compact and reputedly hardier than the type. **'Green Goddess'** has a green-splashed white spathe and dull green leaves.

USE & CULTIVATION Ideal as drifts by streams or ponds, they can also be grown in 30cm/12in of water as marginal water-plants. Grow in rich moist soil in full sun or partial shade. Frost hardy.

Zantedeschia elliottiana
Golden Arum Lily

ORIGIN Unknown
CLIMATE ST, WT, M

This tuberous perennial forms attractive clumps to about 1m/3ft high of heart-shaped, semi-erect, dark green leaves with transparent white spots or streaks. The yellow summer flowers are about 15cm/6in long.

USE & CULTIVATION This outstanding waterside plant likes rich, moisture-retentive but well-drained soil in full sun or part-shade. Container-grown plants need constant moisture and a fortnightly liquid feed when in active growth. Marginally frost hardy.

GLOSSARY

ACID (OF SOILS) With a pH value below 7 and containing relatively little lime.

ACUTE Having a short sharp point.

AERIAL ROOT A root that arises from a stem above ground level and grows in the air.

AIR-LAYERING A method of propagation that involves wounding the stem of a plant and wrapping the wound with damp sphagnum moss. This is sealed in airtight plastic wrap to induce rooting.

ALKALINE (OF SOILS) With a pH value above 7. Alkaline soils usually contain lime and are sometimes referred to as limy or calcareous soils.

ALPINE Strictly, a plant native to high mountain regions and occurring above the tree-line. Generally, any small-growing plant suitable for a rockery.

ALPINE HOUSE A type of unheated greenhouse used to grow alpines.

ALTERNATE (OF LEAVES) Arranged at different levels along a stem; not opposite.

ANNUAL A plant which completes its life cycle from germination to fruiting and dying within a single year.

ANTHER The top part of the stamen, which produces the pollen.

AQUATIC A plant growing wholly or partially submerged in water.

APEX The tip or growing point of an organ.

ARIL The fleshy outer covering of some seeds, often brightly coloured.

AROID A member of the Araceae family characterised by an inflorescence composed of a spadix and spathe. Includes *Arum, Caladium, Monstera* and *Philodendron*, also grown for their ornamental foliage.

ASCENDING Growing at an angle at first, then upwards.

AXIL The upper angle between a stem and leaf.

AXILLARY In, or arising from, an axil.

BAMBOO Member of the grass family Poaceae, often with hollow woody stems (culms) and grass-like leaves.

BARBED Bearing sharp, spine-like hooks which are bent backwards.

BARK The outermost protective layer of the stems, branches and trunk of a tree or shrub.

BASAL At the base of a plant or organ.

BEARDED With tufts or zones of stiff hairs.

BEDDING PLANT Any plant used for temporary display in the garden.

BERRY A fleshy, many-seeded fruit with a soft outer portion which does not open when ripe.

BIENNIAL A plant that requires two years to complete its life cycle.

BIPINNATE (OF LEAVES) When the first divisions of a leaf are further divided and similarly arranged.

BISEXUAL Having both sexes, as in a flower bearing both male (stamens) and female (pistil) reproductive organs.

BLADE The flat part of a leaf.

BLOOM A thin layer of white waxy powder on some stems, leaves and fruit, primarily to prevent moisture loss.

BOLE The lowest part of the trunk of a tree, from the ground to the lowest branches.

BONSAI A tree or shrub that has been trained through pruning and root restriction to resemble a mature plant in miniature.

BRACT A small leaf-like structure which surrounds or encloses a flower or group of small individual flowers. Bracts are occasionally highly coloured, resembling petals.

BRACTEOLE Small bract-like structure on the stalk or calyx of a flower.

BRISTLE A short stiff hair.

BULB A swollen underground organ comprising a short stem surrounded by tightly overlapping leaf bases.

BULBIL A small immature bulb.

BURR A prickly fruit.

BUSH A low, thick shrub, usually without a distinct trunk.

BUTTRESS (OF ROOTS) A flattened extension of the lower part of the trunk of trees thought to strengthen and support trees growing in shallow rooting conditions.

CALYX The outer series of floral leaves, each one a sepal.

CAMPANULATE Bell-shaped.

CANE A slender reed-like jointed stem.

CANOPY The topmost layer of branches and foliage of a tree or community of trees.

CAPSULE A dry fruit which when mature dries and splits open to release the seeds.

CARPEL Female reproductive organ, comprising the stigma, style and ovary.

CATKIN A flexible, usually pendulous, spike-like inflorescence of tiny unisexual flowers without petals.

CAUDEX (PL. CAUDICES) The thickened trunk-like stem of plants such as tree ferns, palms, cycads or some succulents.

CHLOROPHYLL The green pigment of leaves and other organs that is the light-absorbing agent in photosynthesis.

CILIATE With a fringe of hairs.

CLIMBER A plant that has adapted some means of attaching itself to objects or other plants in order to grow further and higher to reach the light.

COMPOUND LEAF A leaf divided into two or more separate leaflets.

CONE A woody fruit of a conifer or cycad made up of overlapping scales.

CONSERVATORY A glassed-in structure, usually attached to the house, in which cold-tender plants can be grown.

CORDATE (OF LEAVES) Heart-shaped, usually referring to the base of the leaves.

CORM An underground bulb-like storage organ. Most corms are replaced annually.

COROLLA All the petals of a flower.

CORYMB A type of inflorescence where the flower stalks arise at different points, but flowers are at the same level, giving a flat-topped arrangement.

CRENATE (OF LEAF MARGINS) Scalloped into shallow rounded teeth or lobes.

CROWN All the branches of a tree.

CROWNSHAFT Upper part of some feathery palms made up of tightly packed frond bases and forming a smooth cylinder shape.

CROZIER Coiled juvenile frond of a fern.

CULM Jointed flowering stem of a grass or sedge; usually used to describe the canes of bamboos.

CULTIVAR Short for cultivated variety. A selected form of a species or hybrid that is grown in cultivation. Cultivar names are given in roman type and indicated by single quotes, for example, *Acer palmatum* 'Butterfly'.

CUTTING A piece of stem or root taken from a plant and used for propagation.

CYCADS A group of cone-bearing plants related to conifers but more palm-like in their appearance.

DEAD-HEAD To remove spent flowers to tidy the plant, induce further flowering or prevent self-seeding.

DECIDUOUS Falling or shedding annually; refers to any part of the plant at the end of the growth period.

DECUMBENT Spreading horizontally, but with the tips growing upward.

DECURRENT Extending down along a stem after joining with it, as in leaf bases.

DECUSSATE (OF LEAVES) Arranged in opposite pairs, each pair at right angles to the next pair below it.

DEHISCENT (OF FRUITS) Opening at maturity to release the seeds.

DELTOID (OF LEAVES) Triangular in shape, often with rounded corners.

DENTATE (OF LEAF MARGINS) Having tooth-like triangular indentations.

DIFFUSE Open and loosely spreading in habit.

DIGITATE (OF COMPOUND LEAVES) Leaflets spreading like the fingers of a hand from one point.

DISC FLORET One of the inner tubular flowers of the flowerheads of some Asteraceae, as distinct from the outer ray florets.

DIVISION A method of propagation whereby a clump of plants is dug up and divided into several pieces which are then replanted.

DORMANT A period of temporary inactive growth or germination.

DRUPE A succulent fruit with a stone enclosing one or more seeds.

ELLIPTIC (OF LEAVES) Oval and flat, broadest across the middle and tapered equally at both ends.

ENDEMIC Confined to a specific country, region or location.

ENTIRE (OF LEAVES) Having smooth margins without teeth or division.

EPIPHYTE (ADJ. EPIPHYTIC) A plant that grows well above the ground on another plant but is not parasitic.

ESPALIER A tree or shrub with branches trained flat against a wall or trellis.

EVERGREEN A plant that retains its leaves all year round.

EXOTIC A species introduced from a foreign country

FALCATE (OF LEAVES) Curved and tapered to a point like a sickle; for example, many eucalypt leaves.

FAMILY A group of genera which are considered to be closely related.

FAN PALM A palm with palmate or palmately lobed leaves, roughly rounded in outline.

FEATHER PALM A palm with elongated pinnate leaves.

FERN A group of spore-bearing plants, often with feathery fronds.

FILAMENT The thread-like stalk of a stamen bearing the anther.

FLOWER The part of the plant that contains the reproductive organs; some flowers are single-sexed (unisexual) but most contain organs of both sexes (bisexual).

FLOWERHEAD A dense cluster of small, crowded and often stalkless flowers at the end of a common stalk.

FOLLICLE A dry fruit which splits open along one side only and contains more than one seed.

FROND The (often divided) leaf of a fern, cycad or palm.

FROST HARDY A plant able to withstand exposure to frost without damage to any part of it.

FROST TENDER A plant damaged or killed by even the lightest frosts; usually at temperatures below 5°C/40°F.

FRUIT The seed-containing structure formed from the ripened ovary after the flower is pollinated.

GENUS (PL. GENERA) A subdivision of a family; a group of species that are closely related to each other because they share a number of similar characteristics.

GLABROUS Smooth and hairless.

GLAND (OF A PLANT) A liquid-secreting organ, usually on leaves, stems and flowers.

GLAND-DOTTED With translucent or coloured dots when viewed against the light.

GLAUCOUS Covered with bloom, often giving a greyish or powdery appearance; usually refers to stems and leaves.

GRAFTING A propagation technique involving the satisfactory uniting of the stem of a desirable plant to a compatible rootstock of another so that they eventually function as one plant.

GRASS Any member of the large grass family Poaceae/Gramineae, including bamboos.

GROUNDCOVER A low-growing plant with a spread greater than its height and able to cover the soil surface.

GROWING SEASON The time of year when a particular plant is in active growth.

HABIT The general appearance of a plant, including shape, size, type of growth and the arrangement of various parts.

HABITAT The place or environment in which a particular plant occurs in the wild.

HARDINESS The ability of a cultivated plant to withstand adverse conditions. In cold climates, usually applied to its tolerance of low temperatures.

HEATH A plant community dominated by small, usually small-leaved shrubs.

HERB A flowering plant which does not produce a woody stem.

HERBACEOUS BORDER A section of a garden used for the planting of perennial plants which die back each winter and resume growth in spring.

HIRSUTE Covered with long, coarse, spreading hairs.

HOARY Covered with short hairs giving the surface a greyish appearance.

HOUSEPLANT Any plant that can be grown for a long period inside the house.

HUMUS Topsoil containing organic matter formed from the decomposing remains of wastes of plants and animals. In gardens it can be added in the form of compost, manure, leaf mould and peat to improve texture, fertility and water-holding capacity.

HYBRID A plant originating from the cross-fertilisation of two different species, either in the wild or as a result of cultivation.

INCISED (OF LEAVES) With deep and narrow finely pointed teeth or lobes.

INCURVED (OF LEAVES) Curved or bent inwards or upwards.

INDEHISCENT Not opening at maturity.

INDIGENOUS Naturally occurring in an area.

INFLORESCENCE The arrangement of one or more flowers in a group, such as a corymb, panicle, raceme or umbel.

INTERNODE The part of a stem between two successive nodes.

INTRODUCED Not native (indigenous) to the area.

INVASIVE A tendency to spread freely and vigorously, often overwhelming other plants in the area.

INVOLUCRE A ring of leaf-like bracts surrounding the base of a flower or group of flowers.

KINO A dark-coloured resin-like substance developed in the veins of bark or wood, especially common in eucalypts.

LANCEOLATE (OF LEAVES) Shaped like the blade of a lance, usually broadest at the lowest half.

LATERAL A shoot or leaf arising from, or located at, the side of a plant part.

LATEX A white milky fluid exuded from the cut surfaces of the leaves or stems of some plants.

LEACHING The process by which chemicals and nutrients are removed from a soil, usually by the passage of water.

LEADER The main, usually central growing shoot of a plant.

LEAF The primary photosynthetic organ of plants. It is usually green and typically consists of a leaf stalk (petiole) and flattened blade (lamina).

LEAFLET One of the several segments into which a compound leaf is divided. A leaf has a bud in its axil; a leaflet does not.

LEGUME A dry fruit that splits open along two sides to form two halves, sometimes called a pod. In general, any member of the family Leguminosae/Fabaceae, including peas and beans.

LIGNOTUBER A woody swelling developed partly or wholly underground. It acts as a storage organ and enables the plant to re-sprout after it has been destroyed above ground level, usually by fire.

LINEAR (OF LEAVES) Long and narrow with more or less parallel sides.

LITHOPHYTE A plant adapted to growing on rocks.

LITTORAL Growing near the shoreline.

LOAM Good fertile, well-drained soil containing evenly balanced parts of clay, sand and silt and considerable organic matter.

LOBE (OF LEAF MARGINS) Having deeply curved indentations.

MALLEE A shrubby eucalypt with multiple stems arising from an underground rootstock known as a lignotuber.

MARGIN The edge or boundary line of any flat organ, such as a leaf or petal.

MARGINAL PLANT One that thrives in permanently moist conditions such as the swampy margins of ponds or lakes.

MIDRIB The main central vein that runs the full length of a leaf.

MONOECIOUS Having separate male and female flowers on the same plant.

MONOTYPIC A genus with only one species.

MULCH A layer of material spread over the bare surface of soil to act as an insulation against cold and heat, or to prevent loss of moisture.

NATIVE A species that naturally grows in a particular area.

NATURALISED A plant introduced from a foreign area which has become established and is reproducing successfully in the new area.

NECTAR A sweet, sugary liquid secreted from a gland known as a nectary.

NUTRIENT The water-soluble minerals taken up by the roots of a plant and necessary for healthy metabolism and growth.

NEUTRAL (OF SOILS) With a pH value of 7; that is, neither acid or alkaline.

NODE The point on a stem from which shoots and leaves arise.

NUT A dry one-seeded fruit with a hard or leathery shell that does not split open when mature.

OBLANCEOLATE (OF LEAVES) Lance-shaped, with the broadest part towards the tip.

OBOVATE (OF LEAVES) Egg-shaped, with the broadest part towards the tip.

OFFSET A shoot arising from the side or base of a plant which can be detached and used for propagation.

OPPOSITE (OF LEAVES) Arising in pairs at the same level, but on either side, of the stem.

ORBICULAR (OF LEAVES) Circular, or almost so.

OVARY Female flower organ which produces the fruit after fertilisation takes place.

OVATE (OF LEAVES) Egg-shaped, with the broadest closer to the stalk.

OVOID Egg-shaped; applied to a solid form.

PALMATE (OF COMPOUND LEAVES) Divided into leaflets that radiate from the leaf stalk like the fingers on a hand.

PALMATELY LOBED (OF LEAVES) Deeply divided into three or more lobes, but not divided into leaflets as are palmate leaves.

PANICLE A compound inflorescence with many branches, each of which bears two or more flowers.

PEAT/PEAT MOSS Partially decomposed plant remains that collect in bogs. It is acidic by nature and adds organic matter to the soil.

PEDICLE The stalk supporting an individual flower or fruit.

PEDUNCLE The common stalk that supports a group of flowers or fruits.

PELTATE (OF LEAVES) With the stalk attached at the middle of the underside instead of at the edge of the leaf.

PENDENT Hanging downwards.

PERENNIAL A plant with a life span of more than two years. Usually applied to non-woody plants.

PERIANTH The calyx and corolla of a flower.

PERSISTENT A structure that remains on the plant after it has reached full maturity.

PETAL The often brightly coloured segment of a flower; collectively, the petals are called the corolla.

PETIOLE The stalk of a leaf.

PH (OF SOILS) Measurement used to indicate the level of acidity or alkalinity. The scale of pH units ranges from 1–14. A value of 7 is neutral; all figures below 7 become progressively more acidic and those with a pH over 7 become more alkaline.

PHOTOSYNTHESIS The process by which plants draw upon the energy of sunlight through the agency of chlorophyll to make their food and substance from water and carbon dioxide.

PINNA (PL. PINNAE) One of the leaflets of a pinnate leaf.

PINNATE (OF COMPOUND LEAVES) Divided once, with leaflets arranged on both sides of a common stalk.

PISTIL Female reproductive organ of a flower, composed of the stigma, style and ovary.

POD A general term applied to any dry fruit that splits when ripe to release its seeds.

POLLEN Grains formed in the anthers, containing the male element necessary for fertilisation.

POLLINATION Fertilisation of a flower by the transfer of ripe pollen from anthers to a receptive stigma. In the case of conifers and cycads, the transfer is from male to female cones.

PROPAGATE To increase new plants by sowing seeds or by vegetative means such as taking cuttings, grafting, layering or by division.

PROSTRATE With stems lying flat on the ground.

PRUNE To remove branches, stems or roots (or parts thereof) in order to rejuvenate, control size or reshape the plant.

PSEUDOBULB The thickened, bulb-like stem found on many orchids.

PUBESCENT Covered with short soft downy hairs.

PUNGENT Ending in a sharp point.

RACEME A type of inflorescence where a series of lateral flowers are arranged along a single stem. Each flower has a stalk and the youngest is at the tip.

RECEPTACLE The enlarged uppermost part of the flower stem on which all the floral parts are attached.

RECURVED (OF LEAVES) Curved downwards or backwards.

REFLEXED Bent downwards or backwards at a sharp angle.

RESINOUS Covered with a hardened sticky substance.

RETICULATE Marked with a network of veins.

REVOLUTE (OF LEAF MARGINS) Tightly rolled backwards to the undersurface.

RHIZOME A creeping horizontal stem that grows along or below the soil surface.

RHOMBOID/RHOMBOIDAL (OF LEAVES) Roughly diamond-shaped.

ROSETTE A cluster of leaves radiating from a central point on a stem, or near ground level.

RUNNER A slender, horizontal-growing stem that trails across the soil and may form roots at the nodes.

SCALLOPED (OF LEAF MARGINS) Notched with shallow, rounded teeth.

SCLEROPHYLL Term describing a plant with hard, stiff leaves.

SCLEROPHYLL FOREST A forested area dominated by trees with sclerophyll leaves, such as the eucalypts.

SEPAL One of the separate parts of the calyx, usually green and leaf-like.

SERRATE (OF LEAF MARGINS) Having sharp forward-pointing teeth, like a saw.

SESSILE Without a stalk.

SHEATH Expanded base of a leaf that wraps around the stem, as in many palms. A large bract that encloses a group of flowers in bud.

SHRUB A deciduous or evergreen woody plant with usually two or more stems arising from or near its base.

SILKY Having a flattish covering of soft, fine hairs.

SIMPLE (OF LEAVES) Having a single blade and not divided into leaflets.

SOLITARY (OF FLOWERS) Occurring singly in each axil.

SPADIX A fleshy, spike-like inflorescence, embedded with tiny sessile flowers and usually enclosed in a spathe, as in members of the Arum family.

SPATHE A large hood-like bract surrounding a spadix.

SPATHULATE (OF LEAVES) Spoon-shaped, being larger and rounded at the top and tapered towards the base.

SPECIES A unit of classification ranked below the level of genus and used to designate groups of similar individuals that are capable of breeding true in the wild. Abbreviated 'sp.' when used in the singular and to 'spp.' when used in the plural.

SPHAGNUM A type of very porous moss found in bogs. When dried, it is used in potting mixes and for lining hanging baskets.

SPIKE An unbranched, elongated inflorescence with stalkless flowers.

SPINE A hard, pointed structure.

SPORES Minute reproductive structures of non-flowering plants. Examples are ferns, mosses and fungi.

STAMEN The male portion of a flower, comprised of a pollen-bearing anther and the supporting stalk (filament).

STANDARD 1. A tree or shrub trained to form a single bare trunk and topped by a neat rounded head of foliage. 2. In botanical terms, the large upper petal that stands at the back of a pea-flower.

STELLATE Star-shaped.

STIGMA The female part of a flower that receives the pollen, usually at the tip of the style.

STIPULE A leaf-like appendage at the base of the leaf stalk in some plants; usually paired; sometimes modified as spines.

STOLON A horizontal stem which grows just above the ground and takes root at its tip.

STRIATE Marked with fine parallel lines or grooves.

STYLE The stalk of the female organ connecting the stigma and the ovary.

SUBSPECIES A plant within a species that is slightly different from the others, but not sufficiently to rank it as a species.

SUCCULENT A plant with thick, fleshy stems or leaves that store water.

SUCKER A new shoot growing from the roots or base of a tree or shrub.

SYNONYM (SYN.) The scientific name under which a particular plant was previously known.

TAPROOT A stout central root that grows directly downwards and bears smaller side roots.

TENDRIL A slender, usually coiling part of some climbers that serves to support the stem.

TERETE (OF LEAVES) Slender and cylindrical in cross-section.

TERMINAL Located at the extreme end.

TERRESTRIAL Growing in the soil on the ground.

THORN A sharply pointed branch or twig.

THROAT (OF FLOWERS) The inside part of a tubular or funnel-shaped flower.

TOOTHED (OF LEAVES) A generalised term referring to margins which are toothed in various ways, including crenate, dentate and serrate.

TOMENTOSE Covered with short, closely matted hairs.

TOPIARY The art of clipping suitable trees or shrubs into artificial shapes, such as domes, pyramids, birds, etc.

TREE A woody plant, usually with a single main stem (trunk) and a distinct upper crown.

TREE FERN A terrestrial fern that develops a single upright trunk topped by a single crown of long spreading fronds.

TRIFOLIATE (OF COMPOUND LEAVES) Having three leaflets.

TUBERCLE small wart-like projection.

UMBEL A cluster of individual flowers where several flower stalks arise from the same point; a compound umbel is when the umbels themselves are arranged in an umbel.

UNDULATE (OF LEAF MARGINS) Wavy.

UNISEXUAL (OF FLOWERS) Of one sex only; having either functional stamens or pistils, but not both.

VARIEGATED Where a leaf or petal has irregular patterns of another colour.

VARIETY (VAR.) A variant of a species that originally occurred in nature. In plant classification, variety is below the level of a subspecies.

VENATION (OF LEAVES) The arrangement or pattern of veins.

WHORL Ring of leaves or floral parts encircling a stem at the same level.

WINDBREAK A row of trees or shrubs planted to provide shelter from strong or persistent winds; some windbreaks are planted to protect the soil and prevent erosion.

WOOLLY With long, soft, rather matted hairs.

XEROPHYTE A plant adapted to surviving in dry areas and displaying drought-resistant features.

BIBLIOGRAPHY

Anderson, M. *The Ultimate Book of Cacti and Succulents*, Lorenze Books, 1998.

Bailey, L.H. Hortorium Cornell University, *Hortus Third*, Macmillan, 1976.

Bell, M. *The Gardener's Guide to Growing Temperate Bamboos*, David & Charles, 2000.

Brickell, C. (ed.) *The RHS A–Z Encyclopaedia of Garden Plants*, Dorling Kindersley, 1996.

Clarke, E. *Leaf, Bark and Berry*, David & Charles, 1999.

Elliot, W.R. and Jones, D.L. *Encyclopaedia of Australian Plants Suitable for Cultivation*, Vols 1–8, Lothian, 1980–2002.

Greig, D. *Scented Geraniums and Pelargoniums*, Kangaroo Press, 1991.

Grenfell, D. *Hosta*, Batsford, 1990.

Jones, D.L. *Cycads of the World*, Reed New Holland, 2000.

Jones, D.L. *Palms Throughout the World*, Reed New Holland, 2002.

Lennox-Boyd, A. *Designing Gardens*, Francis Lincoln, 2002.

Mabberley, D.J. *The Plant Book*, 2nd edn, Cambridge University Press, 1997.

Nash, H. and Stroupe, S. *Plants for Water Gardens*, Sterling Publishing, 1999.

Palmer, S.J. *Palmer's Manual of Trees, Shrubs and Climbers*, Lancewood Publishing, 1990.

Phillips, R. *Trees in Britain, Europe and North America*, Pan Books, 1978.

Philips, R. and Rix, E.M. *Shrubs*, Pan Books, 1989.

Reader's Digest *Complete Guide to Indoor Plants*, Reader's Digest, 1980.

Recht, C. and Wellerwald, M. *Bamboos*, Batsford, 2001.

Romanowski, N. *Grasses, Bamboos and Related Plants in Australia*, Lothian, 1993.

Rose, P.Q. *Ivies*, Blandford Press, 1980.

Royal Horticultural Society *The RHS Plant Finder*, Dorling Kindersley, published annually.

Schofield, L. *The Garden at Bronte*, Penguin Books, 2002.

Spencer, R. *Ferns, Conifers and Their Allies*, UNSW Press, 1995.

Taylor, J. *Weather in the Garden*, John Murray, 1966.

Valder, P. *The Garden Plants of China*, Florilegium, 1999.

Vertrees, J.D. *Japanese Maples*, Timber Press, 1978.

Warren, W. *Balinese Gardens*, Periplus Editions, 1995.

Warren, W. *The Tropical Garden*, Thames & Hudson, 1991.

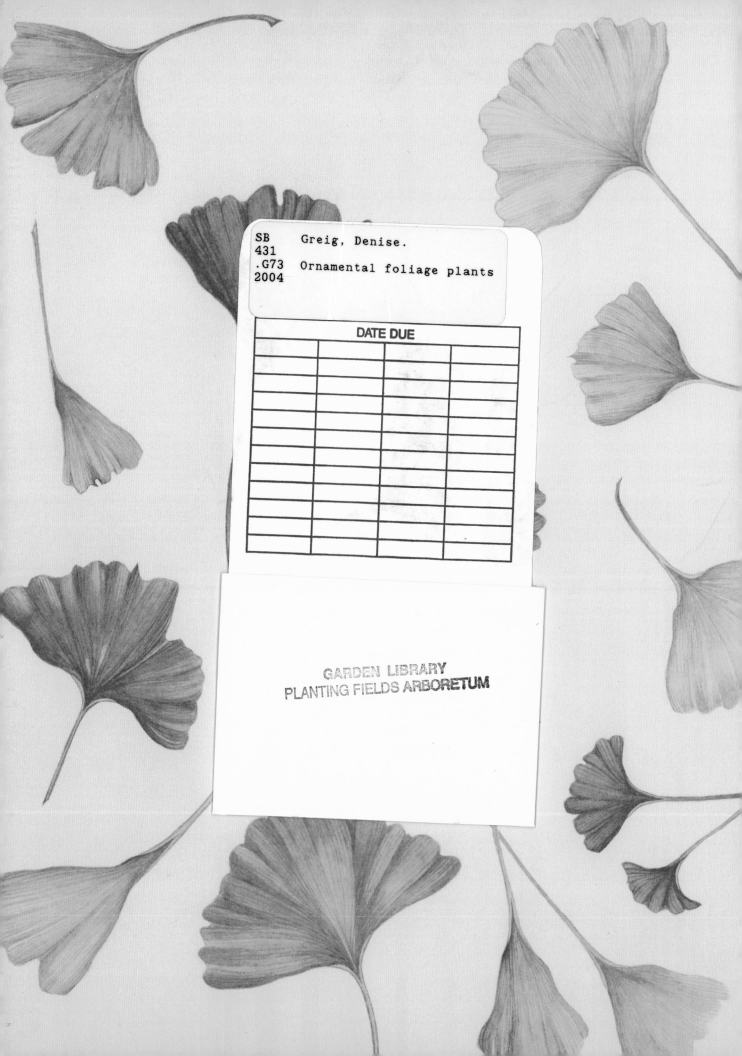